Thousands of luscious tidbits of useless information are crammed into the pages of this intriguing volume.

Here, in kaleidoscopic array, are hundreds of facts to marvel about which you never knew before. Each one of these morsels will provide great entertainment.

Profusely larded with humorous cartoons.

The Great
Big Book of
ASTOUNDING
FACTS

A COMPENDIUM
OF EVERYTHING
YOU NEVER KNEW
YOU NEEDED
TO KNOW

Bruce D. Witherspoon

Published in 1993 by

Bristol Park Books
A division of Budget Book Service, Inc.
386 Park Avenue South
New York, NY 10016

Published by arrangement with Hart Associates.

Library of Congress Catalog Card Number: 90-86019

ISBN: 0-88486-084-1

Printed in the United States of America.

The Great
Big Book of
ASTOUNDING
FACTS

The Long and the Sport of It

Athletic competition may be one of the healthiest forms of human combat It certainlv has a long history.

The first Olympiad is said to have taken place in ancient Greece in 776 B.C. Every four years from then on athletes gathered at Olympia in the summer to honor Zeus with their displays of skill and prowess.

The first games were confined to running. In 776 B.C the official winner of the first foot race was Coroebus Gradually other events were added—the pentathlon, boxing, chariot racing, etc. However, the competition which was essentially nationalistic for the Greeks, became more and more professionalized, and at the end of the 4th century A.D., Emperor Theodosius I of Rome discontinued the games.

Pierre, Baron de Coubertin, of France revived the Olympic games and in 1896 the first modern contests took place in Greece. Since then, the Olympics have been held more or less regularly (a few wars interceded) in different cities throughout the world. The number of individuals and nations participating, as well as the number and variety of events, have steadily increased. Winter Olympics were originated in 1924.

Up until 1912, women were barred from participating in Olympic events. The women of ancient Greece held games of their own, called Heraea. After 1912, women's Olympic games became increasingly popular and important.

Sheep have three times as many red corpuscles as humans.

In your day, when you lost a baby tooth you found a quarter under your pillow, right? Rosemary Wells, of the Northwestern University School of Dentistry in Evanston, Illinois, wanted to see if the Tooth Fairy was keeping up with inflation. According to a survey she made, the money left under the pillow nowadays averages out to 66 cents.

The most malleable or ductile of all metals is gold. One ounce of gold can be drawn into a continuous wire thread to a length of 43 miles. A cubic inch of gold can be beaten into a leaf so as to cover nearly 1,400 square feet. It has been estimated that all the gold mined since A.D. 1500, if beaten into a leaf, could be stored in a vault 55 x 55 x 55 feet.

The youngest man who ever sat as a member of the U.S Senate so far as is known was Henry Clay He took office in 1806 when he was less than 29 years old. Although the U.S. Constitution stipulates that a Senator be at least 36 years old, apparently the question of Clay's age was not raised at the time he took his seat

Vocal Power

A woman can talk with less effort than a man because her vocal cords are shorter than those of the male. Not only does this cause her voice to be higher pitched, it also requires less air to agitate the cords, making it possible for her to talk more, yet expend less energy.

If you've ever wondered why adolescent boys go through such dramatic voice change, it's because their vocal cords double in length during those crucial years.

Beauty and the Beast

If you've ever had the misfortune to find that your favorite sweaters have provided tasty meals for moths, you might be very curious about how to distinguish a moth from a butterfly. Well, it's not so easy. There are many differences, but try these three for starters

One of the things you'd have to look at would be the insect's feelers If the feelers are thin and end in small elongated knobs, that's the sign of a butterfly. A moth's feelers are usually broad and feathery, or hairy and tapering.

Next, try observing the insect when it's resting. A butterfly will fold its wings in an upright position, with the undersides facing you. A moth sits holding its wings horizontally, with the upper sides only showing.

The easiest difference to note is that butterflies fly during daylight, while moths fly at dusk or at night.

If all this doesn't help, better put in a supply of mothballs.

Chew Chew Training

A fad that had a vogue in the early 1900s was dubbed "Fletcherism." It was started by one Horace Fletcher, who composed the catch phrase "Nature will castigate those who don't masticate." Fletcher had the notion that digestion was linked to prolonged chewing of food. He promulgated the idea that every morsel that went into your mouth should be chewed at least 32 times.

Fletcher himself was a phenomenon. When he was 50 years old, he bicycled 200 miles a day. He once lived on only potatoes for 58 days.

But the most notable thing about him was how persuasive he was. Thousands followed his tenets, and would chew and chew and chew everything they ate for breakfast, dinner, and supper. Meals became long and boring, and restaurateurs were frantic. Yet the vogue held on for quite a while in the early 1900s. In fact, many people today believe this is a necessary step to good health.

The world's biggest garbage dump is the Fresh Kills landfill in Staten Island, New York

In 1980, a burglary was reported every three minutes in New York City.

Out of Sight!

The longest subway tunnel in the world is the Northern Line Underground in London, which runs for a span of better than 17 miles.

The boy was delighted when, after months of prodding, his father agreed to let him keep a dog. When a fox terrier down the block had a litter, the father brought home one of the pups, but insisted that the new pet be kept in the basement at night.

The first night, not surprisingly, the puppy howled until dawn, keeping the entire neighborhood awake. The second night, he again disturbed the neighbors with his mournful cries.

The next morning, the boy's mother heard a pawing at the front door. She opened it to find the pup's mother standing on the porch. The terrier walked in, picked up her puppy by the scruff of the neck and, leaving the woman aghast, walked back out the door and returned home.

Fish Can Drown!

Of all the perils that beset fish, one of the most unbelievable is that—fish can drown! Fish do not drown because they cannot swim, of course, but because they may be prevented from getting oxygen and breathing normally.

Fish breathe, fundamentally, the same way that people breathe. That is, they take oxygen into their blood stream which circulates it to the body tissues. We accomplish this by breathing air into our lungs. Fish breathe by filtering water through their gills and getting the oxygen they need out of the water.

When this oxygen supply is interfered with, the fish drowns. Sometimes this can happen when an object gets entangled in a fish's mouth or gills and interferes with its normal breathing rhythm. Occasionally, microscopic plants or animals will multiply so fast in a pond or a lagoon that they will use up the entire oxygen supply in the water.

Fish can die by the thousands if rivers or streams become polluted by city or factory waste materials. Bacteria feed greedily on these wastes, and in doing so they use up all the oxygen in the water.

So, when we say fish can drown, what we are really saying is that they can die of suffocation.

The longest competitive span of any Olympic Games participant was achieved by Dr. Ivan Osiier, of Denmark, who competed as a fencer in games spanning a forty year period from 1908 to 1948.

The largest opera house in the world is the Metropolitan Opera House, in New York City. It has a capacity of 3,800 seats in an auditorium 451 feet deep. The stage is 243 feet in width and 146 feet deep.

Henry Wadsworth Longfellow is the only American whose bust is in the Westminster Abbey.

Roads Royce

Of all the world's ancient civilizations, only two ever produced a complete network of roads. The first such system was organized by the Romans. Their roads covered 56,000 miles, linking countries in Europe, the Near East, and parts of Africa.

Second only to the Romans were the Incas. Like the Romans, the Incas themselves did not create anything new. Thus, a road network begun by the Chimus was improved and extended. At its peak, the Inca empire could boast 10,000 miles of highway extending from present-day Argentina to Colombia.

Roads were vital to the unity of the Inca empire. They provided the links between the provinces and Cuzco, the capital and hub of the Inca territories. All roads in the empire led to Cuzco.

As each fresh Inca conquest enlarged the empire, a new village or tribe would be added to the service of the Lord-Inca, and the network of roadways extended. Some roads were paved, others carved from living rocks, and still others, more modest, were just paths with markers to show the way.

Since the wheel was not known by the Indians, they had no vehicles that could roll along the roads. Llamas and vicunas were used only as beasts of burden, and the Indians had no animals to ride on. Thus, the highways were used exclusively by travelers on foot. To serve the transient population, inns were maintained at intervals of 12 to 18 miles along the road where one could stop to eat or pass the night.

Something to Crow About

The sheep has a life expectancy of about 15 years, the lion about 25 years, the horse about 30, the ostrich 50, the elephant 60, and the crow 70.

While it is young, a blue whale puts on weight at the rate of two to three hundred pounds a day.

There is no recorded instance of a golfer's scoring three consecutive holes-in-one, but there are more than a dozen cases of "aces" being achieved on two consecutive holes. Probably the greatest of these was achieved by Norman Manley, at Saugus, California, in September of 1964, when he recorded consecutive aces on two par-4 holes, 330 yards and 290 yards.

Natural Dentures

A snake's teeth are very delicate and break off easily. They are not meant to be used either for chewing or tearing food. The sole purpose of a snake's teeth is to hold its struggling prey until its swallowing process begins. A snake's teeth slant backward toward its throat. This makes it easier for the victim to be slid in but almost impossible for it to escape. When the victim tries to snuggle out, the snake's teeth penetrate deeper.

In struggles with larger animals, the snake's teeth are often broken. This presents no serious problem for the snake. It possesses a full set of spares, an extra tooth for every one in its mouth. These spare teeth are carried in a fold of the mouth lining, tucked out of the way until they are needed. When a tooth is accidentally broken off, the extra tooth behind it simply moves down and takes the old one's place. In a short time, the new tooth has fused into the jawbone, every bit as solid as the tooth it replaced.

Temporary Tenant

Shells serve as homes for mollusks and crustaceans. The shells also provide protection in the form of a sturdy shield against enemies.

Pity, then, the poor hermit crab! For although he has a shell over the front part of his body, the hermit crab has no shell at all to protect the soft and vulnerable hind part of his body. So the hermit crab is constantly house-hunting for the discarded shells of other sea animals in the hopes that he will find one he can use for himself.

When the hermit crab is young, he rummages through the litter of cast-off or empty snail shells that can be found on many ocean beaches. The hermit crab uses his claws to turn these shells over and over, sifting through them to examine their color and shape. When the hermit crab finally finds a shell that he likes, he hooks his tail in it, pulls it over his back, and carries it about with him wherever he goes.

But just as any youngster outgrows his clothes and shoes, the hermit crab quickly outgrows his borrowed rear shell. Soon he must look for another, larger shell to replace it.

It took Leonardo da Vinci about five years to complete his famous *Mona Lisa.*

Ambergris is a grayish, evil-smelling lump of material secreted inside a whale's body when something is wrong in the whale's digestive tract. Ambergris is found floating in great lumps in the ocean after the whale has cast it off.

Oddly enough, this morbid material is highly valued in the manufacture of perfume. For ambergris fixes the aroma of a perfume. That is, it keeps the fragrance of the perfume from evaporating and disappearing after a woman applies a dab of it to her skin.

So it is an amazing fact that a woman smells sweetly because a sperm whale had an upset stomach!

Youthful Heroes

The World Almanac conducted a poll among 13 and 14 year-olds in junior high schools asking them to name the famous or important living person they admired most. Heading up the list was actor Burt Reynolds. Following behind in succession to complete the top five were comedian Steve Martin, speed skater Eric Heiden, TV star Erik Estrada, and actor Alan Alda.

Today's youth evidently admirer the light of heart. The list of the top 32 heroes chosen is heavily weighted with TV and movie entertainers (18 out of the 32) and sports figures (10 in the top 32.) The remaining four top heroes were cartoonist Charles Schulz of *Peanuts* fame, astronaut Neil Armstrong, writer Judy Blume, and author Alex Haley, whose *Roots* broke records as a TV series. Not one politician, statesman or government official made the top list; nor did any educators, philosophers, Nobel Prize winners.

Only six of the top 32 were women. Nine on the list of tops are under thirty years of age. The heroes chosen tend, in fact, to be young, none being over 60, only four over 50, only nine over 40, and ten over 30.

Marc Antony had a goblet molded in the shape of Cleopatra's breast. This was his golden drinking cup.

The lobster automatically acquires a new, perfect-fitting shell every year. He sort of just steps out of one shell and lets another grow over him.

A lobster's body is of a rubbery texture. As a result, the lobster can simply stretch and squeeze and pull until he has worked himself out of his shell. The hollow shell is left in perfect shape, down to the feet and feelers. Then the lobster's body grows a new shell around itself. Each year, without benefit of seamstress or tailor, the lobster has a brand new outfit.

Presidential Material

On April 5, 1978, triplets were born to an Israeli Arab at the Assaf Harofeh Hospital. Their parents named them *Carter, Begin,* and *Sadat.*

Catch On?

The largest fish that have ever been caught on a rod were white sharks caught in Australia. One, caught in 1959 weighed 2,664 pounds, and one caught in 1976 weighed 3,388 pounds.

Which state in the US has the largest farm acreage? Texas, naturally, where everything is BIG. Texas has the largest number of farms in the US, but not the largest farms. That distinction goes to Arizona where the average farm size is 6,539 acres. The average farm size in Texas is a mere 771 acres.

The state that ranks second in total farm acreage is Montana, where the size of an average farm is 2,665 acres.

The state with the least number of farms is— you guessed it — Alaska, which has a mere 291 farms. Although not many people may farm in Alaska, when they do, they do it on a grand scale. The average farm size in Alaska is 5,612 acres, the second highest in the country.

The state with the largest average farm size is Arizona, where there are only 5,803 farms, but they average 6,539 acres each.

The state with the smallest total farm acreage is little old Rhode Island.

A Great Team

In their underwater dance of life, the clown fish and the sea anemone are excellent partners. The sea anemone usually fastens itself to rock or shells. It moves so slowly—perhaps three or four inches an hour—that it cannot readily go after food. It protects itself by means of long tentacles which have a deadly sting.

The clown fish is also slow moving. Its bright orange color makes it an easy target for other, faster fish.

Thus, separately, the clown fish and the sea anemone each has problems. But, together, the clown fish and the sea anemone are an almost unbeatable team. The clown fish can live right in among the deadly tentacles of his partner because he is immune to them. The clown fish's bright color and clumsy movements lure other fish within stinging distance of the anemone's tentacles. The victim quivers and dies, and the clown fish and the anemone share the meal.

Thus the little clown fish gets food and protection, and the dangerous but almost immobile sea anemone is able to get his food supply to swim to him.

The world's longest bridge has a span of 23.8 miles. It is the causeway over Lake Pontchartrain in Louisiana.

To describe the sound erupting from a noisy crowd, the expression "hue and cry" is often used. The term has its origin in an old English law. Anybody who saw or discovered a crime was required by law to cry out to call attention to the offense, and then to pursue the offender. Likewise, all those within hearing were obliged by law to join in the chase.

This law was abolished in the early 19th century. Today, unfortunately, people who witness a wrongdoing are afraid to get involved. Not only do they not give chase, they often pretend not to see.

He or She, as the Case May Be

Dr. James Barry was born in London in 1795; achieved an M.D. degree from Edinburgh Medical School in 1815; served as a surgeon with the British armed forces for many years in many different areas.

On July 25, 1865, John, the valet who had tended Dr. Barry for 40 years found his master dead in bed. A charlady who was called in to lay out the body made the startling discovery that Dr. Barry was a woman.

Very little is known about Dr. Barry's life, or about why she chose to hide her real identity. But she was the first woman doctor of the British Isles, albeit under disguise.

The thick walls of the Castle of St. Suzanne in Le Mans, France, were built as sturdy defenses against enemy attack. Today, however, they look as if they could be shattered by a single blow. Over the years, the surfaces of the stone walls have become vitrified—or changed into a glasslike substance When the walls are struck they give off a musical sound similar to what is heard when fine crystal is rapped. Indeed, in years gone by, the castle's defenders struck the walls to give the alarm when an enemy threatened to attack.

Mrs. Dolly Madison, wife of President James Madison, was an habitual user of snuff.

Hunger Pangs

A hungry shrimp will steal food right out of an anemone's mouth. And if the anemone has already swallowed the food, the undaunted shrimp will literally hijack it.

The shrimp sits on its victim, slowly forces its claw into the anemone's mouth and down into the digestive cavity, seizes whatever food may be there, and takes it out. With the stolen food still clutched in its claw, the shrimp swims calmly away, leaving the outraged anemone sitting on his rock — angry and hungry.

The shrimp can usually outmaneuver the anemone and avoid the anemone's deadly tentacles. But if the shrimp fails to do this, then the anemone eats the shrimp!

Belfast, Ireland, is the largest linen manufacturing center in the world.

Playing for Time

Daylight saving time was established in the United States on March 31, 1918. This law was subsequently repealed, and various versions have been in existence ever since. In 1967, the Uniform Time Act decreed that Daylight Saving Time be observed beginning at 2:00 A.M. on the last Sunday in October. Any state can exempt itself.

To conserve energy during World War II, most of the nation was put on year-round Daylight Saving Time from 1974 through 1975, but Standard Time was restored after that, and still prevails except from April through October.

Oklahoma, Arizona, and New Mexico contain nearly half the entire Indian population of the United States.

A man's beard grows an inch in about eight weeks.

Slow Burn

Cigarettes were first manufactured in France in 1843, but the French were slow in becoming addicted. Not until 1972 did French consumption reach the 100-million mark.

Nature's Neons

Bigness isn't everything. Small is beautiful. For instance, a little animal called a salp glows like an electric bulb if it is touched or disturbed. The salp is luminescent. It shines when stimulated. This is a chemical reaction scientists do not understand exactly.

Salps often live together in colonies. These colonies are shaped like dunce caps, and sometimes grow to be four feet tall.

If you run your finger over a colony of salps, you can write your name on it in lights!

Hogs eat any and all kinds of snakes.

The largest litter ever thrown was 23, by a foxhound called Lena, on February 11, 1945.

A Toothache That's a Headache

The man who took care of George Washington's teeth was John Greenwood. It was he who made the famous set of dentures (on view at the Smithsonian Institution) carved from hippopotamus ivory (not wood), embedded with eight human teeth, and retained with gold pins.

Poor George Washington had lots of trouble with his teeth and amassed sizeable dental bills. The story goes that he was so ashamed of this that he tried to cover it up by a special arrangement. Instead of paying for the dental work, he offered to pay his dentist's hat bills.

Alcoholism has been a terrible scourge throughout all generations. Yet there are some individuals who, despite their fearful addictions, have been able to surmount their curse and achieve greatness. Among the famous achievers who were also stalwart alcoholics one must mention Sinclair Lewis, Edgar Allan Poe, John Barrymore, Eugene O'Neill, Ulysses S. Grant, Jack London, O. Henry, Dylan Thomas, and F. Scott Fitzgerald.

Others who hit the bottle with regularity, but who nevertheless rose to the top were: Walter Hagen, Theodore Dreiser, Douglas Fairbanks, Sr., Jim Thorpe, Sherwood Anderson, Eugene V. Debs, Isadora Duncan, Edna St. Vincent Millay, Rube Waddell, Grover Cleveland Alexander, John L. Sullivan, Mickey Walker, and Tony Galento.

Praying With a Grain of Salt

In Zipaquira, Colombia, there is a salt mine which was built 400 feet deep into the mountainside. This is the largest salt mine in the world.

Within its confines you will find the Great Salt Cathedral. The ceilings are 73 feet high, and are supported by columns of solid salt. It took six years to excavate this cathedral, but the sanctuary is now able to seat five thousand people.

Wide Open Spaces

The Dallas-Forth Worth Airport in Texas is the largest commercial air terminal in the world, occupying 17,500 acres of land.

The Jeddah airport in Saudi Arabia, which is still being constructed, will be even larger.

150 a Minute

The Environmental Fund, in Washington, D.C., has a population clock that keeps tabs on the population throughout the world. At 2:42 P.M., on March 14, 1981 the clock reached the 4.5 billionth mark.

The rate at which the population is growing world-wide is still accelerating; obviously, the more people there are in the world, the more they will breed, even with efforts at population control. It took more than a million years for the world's population to reach the first billion. It took only 120 years more to add the second billion. In the next 32 years, the third billion was added; and it took only 15 years to reach the fourth billion mark.

It is estimated that today about five people are born every two seconds — a quarter of a million people a day!

Six presidents of the United States were married twice: Millard Fillmore, Benjamin Harrison, Ronald Reagan, Theodore Roosevelt, John Tyler and Woodrow Wilson.

What was the best rock group of all time? Kudos for this almost unanimously go to the Beatles. The first album that they released, *Sergeant Pepper's Lonely Hearts Club Band*, took the world of modern music by storm. One critic even went so far as to compare the songs to those of Schubert and Mahler.

More than half the fresh water area of the world is contained in the rivers and lakes of Canada.

Lope de Vega Wrote More Than 1,500 Plays

Félix Lope de Vega Carpio, the renowned Spanish dramatic poet born in 1562, wrote an estimated 1,500 plays—not to speak of countless poems, epics, and prose works. Of these 1,500 plays about 500 survive.

De Vega penned his first drama at the age of 11 while a student at a Jesuit school. From that moment on, he poured out a torrent of theatrical works the like of which has never been equaled.

Father Knows Best

The greatest racing dog in history was Mick the Miller, a greyhound owned by an Irish priest named Father Brophy. Mick flashed sensational speed on the English tracks, and the Father was offered $4,000 for the beast. He accepted on the condition that he receive the Derby purse if the dog won the classic. The Miller came through, winning $50,000. In his three-year career on English soil, Mick never lost a race.

Amplification Unnecessary

You can hear sounds many miles away in the cold, dry air of the Arctic. For sound travels farther and easier in air made dense by the chilling cold.

At 60 degrees below zero, you could sit on the New York side of the George Washington Bridge and eavesdrop across the Hudson River on two men talking together on the New Jersey side.

John Firth, a trader at Fort McPherson, Canada, has reported hearing the cracking of a whiplash ten miles away.

The famed Arctic explorer, Vilhjalmur Stefansson, has reported that a man stamping his feet could be heard for two miles, and that the bark of dogs and the sound of wood-chopping could be heard twelve miles away.

If you should happen to drink a large amount of salty sea water, it would probably be fatal. But, as scientists have discovered, ice formed from the salty sea provides perfectly fresh drinking water after it is about a year old. The salt gradually disappears as the ice freezes, melts, freezes, and melts again.

Forty to fifty tons of ore must be refined to obtain one ton of uranium.

Not The Least Bit Bored

When it comes to board games, Monopoly tops the list. Invented in 1930 by Charles Darrow, its streets are named after those in Atlantic City, New Jersey where he used to vacation. Parker Brothers, the largest game manufacturer, acquired the game in 1935 and it is the company's top-selling item. The company prints more paper money for these games per year than all the real paper money printed throughout the entire world.

In 1790, the first United States census showed a population of 3,929,214 persons in the thirteen states.

The first airplane ever purchased by any government in the world was in 1908, when the U.S. Army, at a cost of $30,000, bought a plane from the Wright Brothers. It was tested before large crowds at Fort Meyer, Virginia. This craft could carry two persons at a speed of 42 miles an hour.

The Northeastern School of Taxidermy in Omaha, Nebraska, has graduated during the last 70 years over 450,000 bird and animal stuffers.

Dote on This Antidote

If you happen by mischance to ingest opium, prussic acid, strychnine, or some other poison, the thing to do is to act quickly: throw a teaspoonful of common salt and ground mustard into a glass of warm water. Swallow this immediately.

This will cause you to vomit instantly, and so get rid of the poison. After your retching stops, swallow the whites of two eggs and drink plenty of strong coffee.

This may not be all that pleasant, but it will keep you alive and determined not to swallow poison again

The three Brontë sisters were all noted novelists. Charlotte (1816-1855) wrote *Jane Eyre*; Emily (1818-1848) wrote *Wuthering Heights*; and Anne (1820-1849) wrote *Agnes Grey*. Their mother having died when they were very little, they and their two other sisters and brother were raised by their aunt. The three girls created an imaginary world in their writing as an escape from the reality of their harsh lives. They first published their works under pseudonyms and the identity of the sisters as authors was unknown even to their publishers at first.

Living It Up

Life span is the maximum number of years an individual may live. This varies with different species, so that, for example, the life span for humans is about 115 years, while the span for a mouse is only between one and two years, you may be happy to know. Efforts to discover the secret of eternal life through medicine, or through magic, religion, or force of will notwithstanding, very little or nothing has been discovered to extend the life span, which seems to be a genetic factor.

Life expectancy is the number of years an individual within a given species can hope to live, given the particular circumstances of his birth. Life expectancy is subject to environmental control to a degree, and the average life expectancy has been rising sharply for humans.

With longer life expectancy, the focus is on how to improve the quality of health and well-being in old-age. So the quest for the secret of eternal youth wages. Anyone care to follow in the footsteps of Ponce de Leon, Dorian Gray, or depart for Shangri-la?

The greatest distance a baseball has ever been thrown was 445 feet, 10 inches. Glen Gorbous set this record on August 1, 1957.

The world's tallest tree is a 308-foot redwood in Humboldt County, California, which is taller than a football field is long.

In 1969, Mario Procaccino, the candidate for mayor of New York, addressed a group of black voters and delivered himself of the following blooper, "My heart is as black as yours."

The famous artist of birds and wild life, John James Audubon, was born in Haiti, the son of a French sea captain and a black Creole servant girl.

Let's Face It

The cosmetic industry notwithstanding, and plastic surgery notwithstanding, the ancient philosophers said it all a long time ago. Aristotle called beauty "the gift of God;" Socrates called it "a short-lived tyranny;" Theophrastus "a silent deceit;" and Theocritus "an ivory mischief."

Any way you look at it, if you weren't blessed with a beautiful face like the one that made Christopher Marlowe proclaim about Helen of Troy: "Was this the face that launch'd a thousand ships," then you had better develop your character. If you happen to have the kind of face that made Shakespeare's King Lear exclaim,

> I have seen better faces in my time
> Than stands on any shoulder that I see
> Before me at this instant

then perhaps you'd go along with Anthony Eden who wrote:

> As a beauty I am not a star;
> There others more handsome by far;
>   But my face—I don't mind it
>   Because I'm behind it—

It's the people in front that I jar!

It's remarkable what an artist can do with a few strokes of his pen or pencil, how he can capture expressions and personalities with a mere line. The faces on these pages are the works of gifted artists who have been able to portray a character in inimitable style.

Works of Rabelais

Early Advertising Art

Quaint Cuts

16

Fifty Years of Soviet Art

That Sister-in-Law of Mine

Punch

Quaint Cuts

Drawing by Ashley Havinden

Punch

Judge

Rabelais

Drawing by Grandville. *La Caricature*

Designs and Borders

Do You Know Your Onions?

The onion is a species of lily known as *Allum. cepa*. *Cepa* and the Italian word for onion, *cipolla*, com from *caepa*, one of a number of Latin words for the vegetable. Onions contain volatile oils heavy with sulphur compounds that account for the pungent fumes so familar to onion peelers. These oils disturb the eyes, which tear in order to wash away the offending fumes.

The Good Old Days

In 1753, Benjamin Franklin, who had served as Postmaster General of Philadelphia since 1737, became Co-Postmaster General of the American Colonies. At the time, riders traveled between New York and Philadelphia three times each week, making the journey in an average of 33 hours. The following decade brought the introduction of night riders. But still mail service was generally slow, undependable, and expensive, with couriers often carrying goods, driving horses, and performing other jobs while on their rounds. Consequently, private postal companies began to flourish, though outlawed by the British crown. Reliance on the offical postal system continued to dwindle until 1775, when all colonial mails were taken over by the Continental Congress.

The word "parchment" comes from the name of the ancient city of Pergamum, in which it is thought that parchment was invented and manufactured in the 2nd century B.C.

The Assyrians Had Umbrellas

Assyrian tablets dating from 1350 B.C. depict a king leading his retinue while servants shade the royal head with a long-handled parasol. In India, a religious group known as the Jains called their ultimate heaven of perfected souls by a name that translates as "The Slightly Tilted Umbrella."

There are three types of animal horns. Some are hollow, like the permanent horns of cattle; some are solid, like the annual horns of deer; some are made up of both living and non-living material, like the nasal horn of the rhinoceros.

The Gordian Knot was tied by Gordius, king of Phrygia. Rather than struggle to untie it, Alexander the Great cut it in two with his sword.

The oldest alcohol beverage known is mead, a wine made from honey. It is stored in wooden casks and left for five years to mature. Mead is the national drink of Poland.

Those Infernal Machines

Officer William C. Potts of the Detroit Police Department became tired of the constant traffic tangles experienced in that city and reasoned that if the intersection could be controlled by lights it would give police officers a chance to do more important duties. Traffic lights were introduced in Detroit in 1920. However, the first electric traffic lights in America had been installed in Cleveland, Ohio on August 5, 1914.

Funny Bunny

What distinguishes a rabbit from a hare?

They both have large front teeth, short tails, long ears, and large hind legs. But the rabbit is smaller and shorter legged, even though it is capable of running long distances. Newborn rabbits are blind and naked.

The hare is a larger beast, with longer legs and ears. It runs very fast, and its young are born with fur and with their eyes open.

Besides, who ever heard of keeping a hare as a pet? And nobody welcomes a harelip, while a rabbit's foot is quite a nice thing to have!

Amish men shave until they marry; then they grow a beard.

Two Hearts in ¾ Time

When anything pleased Giuseppe de Mai, a resident of Naples, he was doubly excited, for not one, but two, hearts pounded away inside his chest.

This condition occurs so rarely that scientists throughout Europe became interested in Signor de Mai. In 1894, the London Academy of Medicine offered de Mai $15,000 to leave them his body upon his death.

A Horse Of A Different Color

The seahorse is aptly named. It has a head that looks like a miniature horse's head, and it has a ribbed tail somewhat like a monkey's tail. The seahorse swims in an upright position. When it wants to rest, it curls its tail around seaweed.

The male seahorse is both father and mother to his children. For seahorses are a most unusual kind of fish, and males have a most unusual broodpouch.

Seahorses make musical sounds while they mate. The female expels her eggs into the pouch attached to the stomach of the male seahorse. This pouch is very much like the pouch on the kangaroo's stomach.

Then for the next 45 days, the father seahorse takes over the entire job of nourishing and protecting the eggs as they grow. At the end of 45 days the eggs are fully developed; the stomach pouch opens, and the father seahorse "gives birth" to his young. There can be as many as 600 baby seahorses born in one litter.

Human blood is six times thicker than water.

Gravid fish generally lay eggs in large quantities. This assures that at least some will survive and the species will not die out. There are a few species of fish that build "nests" to protect their young and give them a better chance for life.

The female argonaut, or paper nautilus, builds a "nest" for her young out of her own bodily secretions. She exudes a white, chalky substance that forms a sort of papery shell. The argonaut places her eggs in this floating egg case and then pulls it around herself with her octopus-like arms and her head protruding.

Perhaps the most unusual "nests" of all are created by the exotic Asian paradise fish. The paradise fish makes her nest out of bubbles. She blows a group of strong bubbles which mass together. After she lays her eggs, the male paradise fish pushes them into the bubbles, which float gently on the surface of the water until the eggs hatch.

Home of the Free

The face of America keeps changing as different ethnic groups join the melting pot. In the decade from 1961 to 1970, more than half the immigrants to America came from the other countries in North America, the largest percentage coming from Mexico (13.7%) and Canada (12.4%). About a third of all immigrants during this decade came from Europe, primarily from Italy (6.4%), Great Britain (6.3%) and Germany (5.7%). About 13% came from Asia.

In the eight-year period from 1971 to 1978, immigration from Asia more than doubled; immigration from the Americas declined somewhat, (to about 45%) and from Europe sharply (to under 20%). Immigration from Mexico continued strongly and, in fact, increased somewhat (to 15.1%). The greatest increases were in immigration from India, Korea, and the Philippines. The greatest declines were in immigration from Canada, Germany, Great Britain and Italy.

Of course, these statistics are based on figures from the U.S. Immigration and Naturalization Service, and do not take into consideratin illegal immigration.

The private chapel of the popes, the Sistine Chapel in the Vatican, houses some of the world's most outstanding 15th century art. Tourists come from all over the world to gape at the ceiling of this chapel where Michelangelo painted scenes from the Bible. Michelangelo's famous *Last Judgment* is on the altar wall.

The marvelous statue of Abraham Lincoln in the Lincoln Memorial building in Washington, D.C. is the work of Daniel Chester French. The statue was fashioned out of 28 blocks of Georgia white marble. The seated figure of Lincoln measures 19 feet from his head to his foot. The armchair is 12½ feet high. The cost of the statue was $88,400.

The beaver has large lungs which enable it to carry enough air and oxygenated blood to stay under water for about fifteen minutes. The beaver also has glands near the root of its tail which secrete oil that waterproofs the animal's fur. Its ears and nose are equipped with valves that close automatically when it submerges and open again when it returns to the surface of the water.

Strike Me Pink!

In bowling, knocking down all the pins with one ball is called a *strike*. To bowl a perfect game, a player must throw 12 strikes in a row, earning a perfect score of 300. Such a perfect performance is not impossible, but is a rarity. It is estimated that a perfect game may be bowled just about once in every 450,000 tries.

During an exhibition at Price Hall in Cincinnatti, Ohio, in 1937, Ned Day of West Allis, Wisconsin, bowled 33 strikes in a row! This was equivalent to bowling almost three perfect games in succession.

John Pezzin of Toledo, Ohio made a record 33 consecutive strikes in 1976.

A perfect score of 300 yards was achieved by Les Schissler of Denver in the classic team event of the American Bowling Congress tournament in 1967. Ray Williams of Detroit got a perfect score in regular team play in 1974. A total of only 34 perfect games have been bowled in ABC tournaments.

Swimming in Sand

An amazing inhabitant of our deserts is the fringe-footed lizard. Its toes are fringed with scales, useful in "swimming" through loose sand.

When attacked, the fringe-footed lizard drives headfirst into the sand and literally swims out of sight. It undulates its body and uses its feet and tail as paddles in the same way that other lizards swim in water. Although it is only a tiny five-inch lizard, it can swim at a speed of fifteen miles an hour.

During the heat of the day, the fringe-footed lizard swims down into the cool sand below the surface of the desert. Its eyes are protected by fringed eyelids. Its ears and nostrils are protected by valves to keep out the sand. This lizard is quite at home and comfortable underground

Camel hair brushes are not made of camels' hair. They are made of squirrels' hair.

More than 150 different flavors of ice cream are now manufactured.

The opossum can give birth to 13 young in one litter. The elephant gives birth to only one offspring. The giant toad lays 35,000 eggs at one time; a queen termite can lay 8,000 eggs per day for years; and *over a lifetime, one Russian mother gave birth to 69 children.*

Fine Distinctions

If you wanted to say someone is stolid like a cow, you might call that person *bovine.*

If, on the contrary, you thought a person sly, you might call him *vulpine*, like a fox.

And if he somehow reminded you of your Doberman, you might use the word *canine*; or of your tabby, you could say *feline.*

A sheep-like individual is *ovine*; and if he's like porky, he's *porcine.*

If he's as big as a bear, he's *ursine*; and if he swims like a fish, he could be *piscine.*

And if he strikes you as being as wise as an owl, he'll understand if you call him *strigine.*

If he's the horsy kind, he's *equine*; but if he's more like a wolf, he'd be *lupine.*

If the dear seems more like Bambi, why he's *cervine*; but if he's more like the king of the jungle, then he's *leonine.*

If something about him makes you think of a snake, he could be *serpentine*, or *anguine*, or even *colubrine.*

And if contemplating it all gives you goose flesh, why that's *anserine.*

If he's the kind of bird that perches and has well-developed vocal cords, that makes him *oscine.*

But whatever you do, don't call him *asinine.*

In Amsterdam, Holland, more than one-third of the population owns bicycles.

Batman

No reptile can really fly, but there is an Oriental lizard called the flying gecko that has wings. These consist of a broad flap of skin along each side of its body, flaps along the rear edges of its legs, along the sides of its flat tail, and even on the sides of its head.

If a flying gecko is dropped or forced to leap from a height of 20 feet or more, it will spread its legs and all its flaps wide, hold its legs and tail stiff, and glide quite nicely to the ground.

The Sperm Whale Eats the 50-foot-long Giant Squid

While the biggest whales, like the blue whale, belong to the *baleen*, or toothless, kind, there is one large whale that not only has plenty of teeth, but uses them too. This is the sperm whale, which grows up to 60 feet long, and was respected by the old whalers for its fighting spirit.

The sperm whale has powerful jaws with long teeth, which it would not hesitate to use against a whale boat when too closely pursued. Mostly, however, these weapons are used to secure its favorite food, the giant squid—up to 50 feet long. Countless battles between these two giant creatures are doubtlessly fought in the gloomy depths of the ocean, with the squid usually, judging from the squid remains found in whales' stomachs, winding up the loser.

The octopus can protect itself with an undersea version of the mythical cloak of invisibility. Like the chameleon, the octopus can change the color of its body at will. But even more remarkable than this, the octopus can turn different parts of its body into different colors—and all at the same time!

By taking on the colors of the sea around it, the octopus blends with its background and escapes detection.

Nature put a special spoon in the mouth of the paddlefish, also called the spoonbill or duckbill.

Although the paddlefish may weigh well over 100 pounds, it does not eat big fish. Instead, it prefers to feed on the tiny shellfish that live in the mud at the bottom of streams and rivers.

When the paddlefish is ready to eat, the paddle-shaped spoon in the front of its mouth moves about and acts as a feeler to locate the shellfish. Then, as the water flows over the paddlefish's gills, the shellfish are strained out in a sieve-like action.

The famed London auction gallery, Sotheby's, once auctioned off a stuffed great auk for $21,000.

The higher up the scale of evolution that a species is, the longer it takes for the young of that species to mature. The more complex the organism, the more its adaptation depends on learned behavior; the simpler the organism the more instinctive its behavior.

Human beings—who live in a most complex environment requiring most complex skills and abilities—generally do not go out into the world to make their own way untiul they are in their late teens or early twenties.

Chimpanzee babies are considered to be adult when they are four years old. Elephant youngsters are on their own at from 2 to 4 years. Smaller mammals such as mice and rabbits mature in three weeks. Even small birds are cared for by their parents for two weeks before they fly away from their nests.

Fish are far down on Nature's schedule of maturity. One of her earlier creations, they have relatively simple structures and live relatively short and simple lives. So, in general, their young must fend for themselves as best they can almost as soon as they are born.

Through Rose-colored Glasses

The Arctic explorer may see pink snow. This is no illusion.

The strange coloring comes from tiny microscopic plants growing in the snowbanks. Sometimes their coloring throws a pink glow across the sky.

Seal of Approval

Eskimos usually hunt two types of seals—the 200-pound hair seal and the 600-pound bearded seal—for these animals remain in the Arctic all year round.

Another member of the seal family is famous as a champion long-distance swimmer and navigator. It is called the fur seal.

Each spring fur seals leave their winter home off the California coast to swim for 3,000 miles to the Pribilof Islands in the Bering Sea. No one knows how they navigate, although some scientists believe they are guided by ocean currents.

The male fur seals reach the islands in May. Then the females arrive and take over tiny private plots of land. Within a few hours they give birth to the pups they have been carrying since the previous year.

The newborn pups get their parents' full attention. In six weeks, the pups have learned to swim. Pups and mother start the long swim south in November. Soon after they arrive at their home in California waters, they are joined by the male seals.

A violin contains about 70 separate pieces of wood.

The highest numbered street in the United States is 326th Street in Toledo, Ohio. Numbered streets in New York City only run up to 264th Street, in Chicago to 146th Street, and in Los Angeles to 142nd Street.

Mistaken Identity

One of the greatest miscarriages of justice on record is the case of Leonard Hankins. In 1933, in Minneapolis, Minnesota, Hankins was accused of robbing a bank and murdering two policemen and a passerby. He was convicted and sent to jail.

In 1936, the F.B.I. arrested Jess Doyle. Doyle confessed to the bank robbery for which Hankins was serving a term. Later, the F.B.I. advised the Minneapolis police that Hankins was clearly innocent, but the local authorities refused to release Hankins because the F.B.I. did not release their files on Doyle.

Even though it was known by all concerned that Hankins was guiltless and had already served many years in jail for no wrongdoing, it was a full 15 years before Hankins was pardoned in 1951.

Handsewn Nest

The Indian tailorbird builds a most peculiar nest. She first finds two leaves close together near the end of a branch. Then, using her bill as a punch and a needle, she puts holes along the edges of the leaves and sews them together with thin vegetable fibers. The swinging, pocketlike nest is finished as soon as she lines it with cottony down.

Saves Electricity

The sun, which doesn't rise during the Arctic winter, does just the opposite in the summer. Then it never sets, shining right on through the days and nights. But at the poles winter darkness and summer sunshine last for months. If a man stayed at the North Pole all year long, he would see daylight from the first day of spring until the last day of fall. There is more daylight at the poles than anywhere else on earth—eight months of it each year. Then the long polar winter night begins, and continues for four months.

Winter night in the polar regions is not the pitch black darkness many visitors to the Arctic expect to see. For the reflection of the moon and stars on the glinting snow lights up the landscape. Some airplane pilots have even said that it is just as easy to land an airplane by Arctic moonlight as it is by the light of day.

United States Air Force pilots also discovered another strange fact about the North Pole during the season of long nights. Flying at 3,000 feet, they found the clear air was sometimes 90 degrees warmer than on the ground. And it was actually warmer over the top of the world than at their home base in Fairbanks, Alaska.

One of the most notorious of the Nazis, Dr. Josef Mengele, is alive today and lives in Paraguay, safe from extradition because of the protection of the government of that country. It is estimated that he was responsible for the deaths of 400,000 people.

Ethelred the Unready, king of England from 978 to 1016 earned this epithet because he was unable to repel the continuous invasions of England by the Danes during his reign. He was a weak king and suffered, too, from a lack of good counsel, whence came his famous name *unroed* meaning *without counsel* in Old English.

Mean, but Beautiful

Ounce for ounce, the slender ermine is one of the most savage animals in the world. Weighing less than a quarter of a pound and measuring less than a foot in length, this bloodthirsty creature will ferociously attack anything that moves. Unlike the polar bear and most other meat-eating creatures, the ermine kills even when it is not hungry.

A member of the weasel family, the ermine changes its soft fur from brown to snow white during the Arctic winter. Beautiful white ermine fur pelts have been fashioned into robes for kings and queens for many centuries.

The most popular street name in the United States is Park, and the next five, in order, are Washington, Maple, Oak, and Lincoln.

Main Street lags behind in 32nd place.

Summertime and the Livin' is Easy

Very welcome are the lovely flowers, berries, vegetables, and grains that spring up during the Arctic summer.

The long sunny days help the growth of wheat, barley, oats, and rye. Lettuce, corn, potatoes thrive in the sun. Alaskan cabbages grow to the size of watermelons. Even strawberries and raspberries have sprung from the thawed soil within the Arctic Circle.

Canadian government officials have found beautiful blue lupines, yellow Arctic poppies, white and red saxifrages, blue forget-me-nots, Arctic daisies, rhododendron, and even some kinds of orchids dotting the Arctic plains.

Some investigators who traveled to the northern tip of Ellesmere Island, one of the last islands before reaching the North Pole only some five hundred miles away, found hundreds of different kinds of mosses, lichens, and brilliant flowers.

The Playful Crow

No one is going to wipe out the crow. It is just too smart for foxes or hawks. In fact, it is too smart for most human hunters.

A flock of crows, feeding in a cornfield, always watches for danger. If one crow caws "danger," the whole flock will take off instantly.

A team of three crows will work a fast "snatch game" on a not-so-intelligent animal. Two crows alight on the ground, one on either side of the animal. Each pretends it is going to steal the animal's food. At just the right moment, a third crow swoops down, snatches up the befuddled animal's food, and the three thieves fly off to enjoy their feast together.

These smart and mischievous birds like to play games and pull pranks. One of them may silently glide down on a sleeping animal, peck him on the head, and fly off cawing with delight when the animal leaps up.

Crows are fascinated by bright objects. They steal jewelry, silverware, little toys, coins, and all kinds of odds and ends which they hide in secret places.

Antisocial

Snakes do not seem to care for one another's company except during the brief mating season or when snakes congregate to hibernate. Outside of these two seasons snakes do not seem ever to communicate with one another or to show any interest in one another.

A snake may use one particular hole or den for a time. If it moves a short distance away from its den, the snake seems to have no urge to find its way back. It simply searches for the nearest hole and uses that instead.

The revolving door was patented on August 7, 1888, by its inventor, Theophilus Van Kannel, of Philadelphia, Pennsylvania.

Lofty Perch

Simeon Stylites was a Syrian shepherd who became a monk. He chained himself to the top of a column sixty feet high, and he remained there for the rest of his life. Through thirty summers and thirty winters, he sat in that one spot. To while away the decades, Simeon prayed a great deal, and did sit-ups.

The Proctor & Gamble Manufacturing Company in St. Louis, Missouri had eight job openings on the production line at $10.25 an hour. A notice to that effect was posted on the bulletin board, and the Missouri Division of Employment Security was notified. The word spread fast. By 8:30 on the morning of June 16, 1981 the line stretched for five blocks, with some 3,000 to 4,000 applicants patiently waiting. There had to be a lot of disappointed people there!

The Cold, Cold Ground

In Arctic Siberia, parts of Alaska, and northern Canada the cold has frozen the ground for millions of square miles. Summer warmth thaws only a thin top layer of soil. Beneath this layer, the ground remains eternally frozen, summer and winter, year after year and century after century. Scientists found the Siberian subsoil at Kozhevnikov Bay in northern Yakutia to be frozen as far down as 1,700 feet.

Iron that has been coated by a thin layer of zinc is called galvanized iron. This process offers protection against oxidation and moisture.

All Men Are Brothers

To save their children from the Nazi Holocaust many Jewish families gave their youngsters into the hands of sympathetic Catholics and Protestants. Some of these children were baptized and raised as non-Jews. One such Jewish child, hidden from the Nazis by a French Roman Catholic family, was Jean-Marie Lustiger, recently appointed Archbishop of Paris.

A year on the planet Jupiter is twelve times the length of one year on earth.

Chinese typewriters are so complex that even a skilled operator cannot type at a rate of more than three or four words per minute.

There is no such thing as a living sardine.

Baseball was invented in 1839 at Cooperstown, New York by Abner Doubleday.

Winners

There are nine actresses who have won more than one Academy Award. They are: Ingrid Bergman: *Gaslight, Anastasia, Murder on the Orient Express*; Betty Davis: *Dangerous, Jezebel*; Olivia De Havilland: *To Each His Own, The Heiress*; Jane Fonda: *Klute, Coming Home*; Katharine Hepburn: *Morning Glory, Guess Who's Coming to Dinner, The Lion in Winter*; Glenda Jackson: *Women in Love, A Touch of Class*; Vivien Leigh: *Gone with the Wind, A Streetcar Named Desire*; Luise Rainer: *The Great Ziegfeld, The Good Earth*; Elizabeth Taylor: *Butterfield 8, Who's Afraid of Virginia Woolf?*

How many actors have earned a similar distinction? Only five: Marlon Brando: *On the Waterfront, The Godfather* (which he refused); Gary Cooper: *Sergeant York, High Noon*; Frederic March: *Dr. Jekyll and Mr. Hyde, The Best Years of Our Lives*; Laurence Olivier: *Henry V, Hamlet*; Spencer Tracy: *Captains Courageous, Boys Town.*

That's Using Your Bean!

Baked beans are an extremely popular food in Great Britain. The British, according to existing records, consume twice as much baked beans per capita as do the Americans. Apparently 84% of English housewives buy the beans regularly.

Sales in Great Britain exceed a million cans a day, and a great many of them come from the H. J. Heinz plant in England.

No Telephone Charge

In the Arctic and Antarctic regions it is possible to carry on an ordinary conversation with someone at a distance of more than a mile. The cold, dense air and smooth ice surface favor the transmission of sound waves.

Mistery

With only one pail of water it is possible to produce enough fog to cover 105 square miles to a depth of 50 feet.

How Wrong Can You Be!

A German painter by the name of Berlin rendered a *Madonna and Child* being serenaded by a violinist! This blunder was probably outdone by a French artist who painted *The Last Supper,* showing a table completely set—including cigar lighters.

Just Gave Up

After flourishing for 140 million years, the dinosaur suddenly died out some 65 million years ago.

Fad Diet

Most lizards live on insects, spiders, and other small creatures. A few lizards will eat smaller lizards and other small animals.

The biggest lizard of all is the *Komodo* dragon lizard. It can grow to a length of ten feet and a weight of three hundred pounds. This giant lizard is a meat eater and can put away a small deer.

On the other hand, the big iguanas, four to seven feet long, are exclusively vegetarian, and never eat meat. Some smaller lizards are also vegetarian or partly so.

Perhaps the most amazing diet is that of the four-foot crested iguana, the land iguana of the Galapagos Islands. This iguana includes cactus, among many other plants, in its diet. It does not seem in the least to mind the sharp spines, which it consumes right along with the rest of the plant.

You Can Recognize It by Its Jumpsuit

The klipspringer, or "African chamois," a pygmy antelope, is only three feet long and weighs 20 pounds. It can get a foothold on a rock which is only a few inches in diameter and can scale heights of 25 feet in a single leap. It is the "high-jumping" champion of animals.

Get The Point?

The ball point pen is the most common writing instrument today. It was devised in 1919 by a Hungarian by the name of Lasalo Birow, who patented his pen in 1943. The first commercial pens made under the patent were manufactured in 1945 in Buenos Aires.

Birow had failed to have his pen protected under U.S.A. patent law. An American, taking advantage of the oversight, turned out pens which sold at Gimbels for $12.50.

Jaws

If an American alligator is fifteen feet long it is considered a giant. But the crocodiles of Malaya often grow much larger. Twenty feet is not an unusual length for these monsters. And they are as savage as they are huge.

The Malayan crocodile fears no other creature on earth. Unlike its smaller relatives in other countries, it shows absolutely no wariness of man. When hungry, this crocodile will go after a human being as readily as after any other prey. Its method of killing is the same as with crocodilians elsewhere; it drags the prey, however big or hard to handle, underwater until the captive drowns.

Many Malayan crocodiles become deliberate man-eaters. Apparently they develop a taste for human flesh and will go out of their way to get it. However, not to worry—such a man-eater quickly becomes known and is savagely hunted down until it is found and destroyed. Unfortunately, some may take a frightful toll of human lives before they themselves are finally cornered and slain.

There are 3,070 counties in the United States.

Don't Hold Your Breath

It has been calculated that in a five-card game of poker, only once in 4,165 times will four cards of one kind be dealt.

If It Winks, It's a Lizard

The amazing world of lizards includes some startling pretenders. The so-called glass snake looks like a snake and lives like a snake, but it is actually a lizard.

At another extreme, the worm lizard looks very much like a common earthworm. It has rings like the earthworm and has no legs or ears. It even burrows into the ground like a worm.

What's the difference between a lizard and a snake? The major differences are usually internal, but the most obvious difference to the casual observer is that most lizards have movable eyelids, the lower ones, and can wink. Most lizards also have ears, while snakes generally do not. But this characteristic does not always hold true—the worm lizard, like several others of the species, has no ears and no ear openings. Thus, the presence of movable eyelids is the only true test.

Genius on Paper

The Egyptians used papyrus as their writing material. So did the ancient Greeks and the Romans. In the West parchment on vellum made of sheep or calf skin was used. In China bamboo was used.

All these materials were scarce, expensive to prepare, inconvenient to use. About the year 105, an official at the Chinese imperial court presented the Emperor with samples of paper. His name was Ts'ai Lun. Ts'ai Lun had invented a way of converting bamboo into pulp and then into paper. In this seemingly simple way he succeeded in transforming the way of the world.

The Chinese kept their technique of papermaking a secret until 751 when the Arabs wrested the secret from some Chinese they had captured. Around the 12th century, the Europeans learned the art from the Arabs. After Gutenberg invented a printing press in the mid-fifteenth century, paper became a universally important commodity.

Can you imagine what life would be like without paper?

Shall We Dance?

Dancing is an art form that, according to anthropologists, preceded speech. It is believed that prehistoric man started to dance before he had music of any kind.

Primitive dancing was ritualistic and ceremonial. Dancers expressed the hopes, fears, prayers of man. Man danced to ask the gods for help, or to thank the gods for helping. Man danced to mark important events. To this day, man dances to express feelings and ideas.

Social dancing is a relatively recent phenomenon, starting in some of the more enlightened courts during the Middle Ages. Of course, each place and each epoch contributes its special dance form to the history of human movement. Thus we have—to name just a token few—waltz, minuet, mazurka, bolero, tarantella, highland fling, Virginia reel, Charleston, tango, rumba, cha cha, twist, hustle.

Depicted here are dancers both ridiculous and sublime, as seen primarily by artists of the 19th century.

Punch

Samantha at the World's Fair

Wudu Feuer

Wilhelm Butch Album

Harper's

Nana

31

Quaint Cuts

Leslie's

For Whom the Cloche Tolls

Wudu Feuer

32

She-Shanties

Drawing by anonymous artist. Jerusalem, Israel, circa 1925

Drawing by Grandville.
Un Autre Monde

Quaint Cuts

Decorative Silhouettes

33

A Red Tide off Florida Killed a Thousand Million Fish

A red tide can bring death to marine life in the areas it colors. These foul-smelling, discolored waters are often caused by tiny animals called *dinoflagellates*. From a thousand in a quart of sea water they may suddenly multiply to a staggering sixty million or more.

When dinoflagellates burst into this sort of bloom, they may color the surface waters of the ocean for miles around. Poisonous substances are released into the water by the tiny organisms. And the death-causing blooms may give off a terrible stench, especially when they have killed other sea life.

Sometimes the waters become so crowded with dinoflagellates that fish and other kinds of sea life are killed in great numbers. During the red tide of 1946 and 1947 off the west coast of Florida, an estimated thousand million fish perished. This so-called "red tide," however, actually turned the water yellow!

In 1874, Philadelphia became the first American city to have a zoo.

Among some species of fish, father does a lot of the work of caring for the young. The male lumpfish, for instance, is a devoted and watchful parent. His unattractive appearance alone is almost enough to scare off any small fish that draw near. If larger fish approach to threaten the young, the father lumpfish swims to attack them.

In addition to guard duty, the father lumpfish makes sure that his children stay clean. He continually fans his babies with his fins and his tail. This prevents them from getting covered with the infinitesimal particles of dirt and dust and debris that constantly fall down through the waters.

By the Hairs of my Chin

When Hans N. Langseth died, in 1927, his beard measured 17½ feet, the longest on record.

The beard of Janice Deveree, the bearded lady, measured 14 inches in 1884.

Green Thumbs

In a world that takes for granted strawberries and corn and tomatoes, it is hard to conceive that before Columbus discovered America none of these fruits and vegetables were known in Europe. Yet the South American Indian had for generations planted a great variety of crops, including 20 varieties of corn. They also had 240 varieties of potatoes—one of which grew at 15,000 feet of altitude and yet resisted the heavy frosts of the mountain climate. Other Indian crops were sweet potatoes, yams, squash, beans, manioc—from which we get our farina and tapioca—peanuts, cashews, pineapples, chocolate, avocados, tomatoes, peppers, papaya, strawberries, blackberries and many other plants.

Around 500 A.D., the only plant that existed in Eurasia and America at the same time was cotton. And no expert has been able to account for this!

Open the Door, Richard

Alligators and crocodiles lay their eggs, thirty-five or forty at a time, in the warm sand. The eggs are about the size of tennis balls, but lopsided in shape.

The mother heaps a mound of sand over her nest and then goes on about her business. When the eggs are ready to hatch—in nine or ten weeks' time, depending upon how warm the weather has been—a most amazing scene takes place.

At the proper moment, the mother alligator comes back and listens at the mound. If her babies are ready to hatch, they announce this fact with little grunting noises that sound like hiccups. Sometimes the mother will grunt like a pig and then listen for an answer. If she hears nothing, she returns and tries again, day after day, until she gets a response.

The moment she hears the babies, she quickly sweeps away the covering of sand. This exposes the eggs so that the young, each about eight inches in length, can break out into the open, grunting loudly. The baby alligators then start looking about for something to eat.

They grow about a foot a year until they reach maturity.

The expression, "blind as a bat," is unscientific. Bats can see fairly well. However, bats are nocturnal and rely heavily on their well-developed sense of hearing.

The ancient Egyptians first began to make glass in 3500 B.C.

The Magic Year

On the average, men are taller than women at just about every age—except one. The average height of a girl of twelve is higher than the average height of a boy of twelve.

The tallest basketball player of all time was Vassiliy Akhtayev of Russia, who played in 1956. He measured 7 feet 7.3 inches tall.

The largest land mammal that ever lived, and which still survives in a smaller form, was a long-necked hornless rhinoceros, which lived in Europe between 20 million and 40 million years ago. It stood up to 17 feet 9 inches to the top of its shoulder hump, measured 28 feet in length, and weighed at least 22 tons.

Paraguay, in South America, is probably the only county in the world today which doesn't use coins—it uses paper money only.

Back Pack

In 1915, the world's record for the mile run was four minutes 14.4 seconds. On April 12th of that year, Noah Young, an Australian, ran around a Melbourne track for the length of a mile in eight minutes, 30 seconds, and established a world's record. How come?

Well, Young was carrying a man on his back. The runner weighed 198 pounds. The lad he was lugging along weighed 150. It was quite a performance.

It's About Time

We all complain that time passes too fast, but we take the telling of time for granted. After all, we learned to do that in grade two, and now with our magical digital clocks we don't even have to know how to count; one glance keeps us up to the second. But the measurement of time is actually a fairly complicated process.

If you want to telephone someone in another country, or in a city quite a distance away, unless you're willing to risk disturbing them at some startling hour, you'd make it your business to find out what time difference is involved.

We measure time by means of the mean solar day; that is, by the rotation of the earth in relation to the sun. We divide the period between two successive high noons into 24 hour intervals. We tell what time of day it is according to our position in relation to the sun at that particular point. If the sun is directly overhead, it is high noon. Before that, the sun will be seen to our east, and after that to our west.

But people in different locations on earth are also computing time in this way. When it is noon and the sun is directly overhead where we happen to be, its position will be quite different in some distant place. So now we have to take longitude into consideration. The earth has been divided into 24 time zones, each 15° of longitude corresponding to one hour of time. Most countries in the world have agreed to use coordinated Universal Time which replaced Greenwich mean time as the basis for standard time.

As the earth revolves, noon reaches each longitudinal area in successive stages. If you were to start traveling westward when it was noon at your starting point, it would not yet be noon at the point of your final destination. By figuring the longitudinal zone of your ultimate destination, you could figure the time.

Tears for the Crocodile

Practically all the giant reptiles of the United States are alligators. There are only a very few crocodiles, and these may be found in one section of the Florida Everglades. Wild life experts warned that the crocodile was becoming extinct, and estimated that there were fewer than fifty crocodiles in the whole country. Since then, due to government protection and the breeding of crocodiles on private wildlife preserves, the number has been increasing.

In 1981, for the first time in its history, a victory at the Indianapolis 500 was voided when Bobby Usher, who came in first, was subjected to a one-lap penalty for reentering the field from the pit area under a yellow caution flag, advancing his position in the race. The winner then became Mario Andretti.

Dying or Dyeing?

To preserve a corpse, Egyptians embalmed it in a substance called asphaltum. This preservative, especially if it has been aged, happens to make an excellent base for paint.

In recent centuries, Egyptians have exhumed bodies in order to recover the value of the asphaltum, which they grind to dust to produce a paint highly prized by discriminating artists.

Carrot-tops

Did you know that three presidents of the United States were redheaded? There was George Washington, Martin Van Buren, and Thomas Jefferson.

Among other notables so endowed, the following can be mentioned:

Rod Laver, tennis champion

Sinclair Lewis, author, who was nick-named "Red"

Walter Reuther, famous labor leader

Margaret Sanger, pioneer in birth control

George Bernard Shaw, iconoclastic playwright

Emily Dickinson, poet

Mark Twain, great American author

Oh For the Good Old Days

The income tax may be one of the two dreaded inevitabilities in life, but it is of relatively recent vintage. England first imposed an income tax to raise money for the Napoleonic Wars from 1799 to 1816. A permanent income tax was adopted by the British in 1874.

In the United States the income tax was also first imposed to finance a war, in 1864 during the Civil War. But it was not until 1913, when the 16th Amendment to the Constitution was adopted, that the income tax became a fact of life in America.

Some Islands are Undersea Mountain Tops

Although most of the underwater mountain tops lie out of sight beneath the ocean, some of the highest peaks stick up above the water as islands. The beautiful Hawaiian Islands in the Pacific, for example, are actually the tops of a 16,000-mile-long range of underwater mountains.

The Azores Islands, which lie west of Portugal, consist of Mid-Atlantic Ridge mountain crests. Mount Pico, highest peak in the Azores, rises 20,000 feet from the ocean floor to sea level. Then it towers another 7,600 feet above the surface of the sea!

Bleak and isolated Ascension Island, which lies midway between South America and Africa, is also part of the Mid-Atlantic Ridge. St. Helena, where Napoleon was banished in 1815 after his defeat at the battle of Waterloo, is the top of another great undersea mountain.

In 1921, the Bolsheviks established a prison camp at Archangel, Russia.

All historians agree that no fewer than 10 million people died in Russian prison camps between 1921 and 1953.

The fastest dog in the world is either the saluki or the greyhound, depending on whom you talk to. The greyhound has been clocked at 41.7 miles per hour.

You Should Live So Long

Among the longest lived men in history were George Bernard Shaw, who lived to 94; Pablo Picasso, who attained 91; Michelangelo 88; Giuseppe Verdi 87; Francois Voltaire 83; Bernard Baruch 95; and Goethe 82.

Handy Feet

Chameleons, which often walk along twigs, conveniently have two toes pointing directly to one side, and three toes pointing in the opposite direction. On their front feet, the three toes point inward and the two outward. On their hind feet, the two toes point inward and the three outward. The toes on each side are bound together up to the tips, so that each foot becomes a most efficient pair of claspers.

To capture an insect apparently beyond its reach, a chameleon can stretch a good way forward into empty air, holding on to its perch with only its hind feet and its tail.

When a chameleon moves, whether it is stalking or merely strolling, it is so extremely slow it must be seen to be believed. With each step, the chameleon pauses and its body rocks. Some scientists think that this pattern aids the chameleon in estimating the exact distance to a prospective prey, and that it helps the lizard to fool its prey into believing the chameleon is nothing but a fluttering leaf.

Fishing in Air

As soon as the snow begins to disappear in the spring, North Greenland Eskimos prepare special nets hooked on the ends of long poles. When the last snow melts, millions of large sea birds arrive to blacken the sky. The Eskimos scoop their nets through the air much like fishermen working in the sea. They often catch more than a hundred birds in an hour.

The Naughty Haughty

Pope Boniface VIII (1235-1303) may have been the most impious churchman who ever lived. He did not believe in the immortality of the soul and is reported to have said that a man has about as much chance of enjoying life after death as a roast fowl on a dining table.

Nothing Sacred

The worst Pope ever was John XII (937-964). In order to maintain his power, he recruited armed gangs who terrorized the citizens. He gambled incessantly, and according to a biographer, his sexual hunger was insatiable. He depleted the wealth of the Papacy by disposing of church lands and holy relics to his favorite mistresses. According to some, he turned the papal apartments into a brothel. And to cap it all, in his political dealings, he was both stupid and untrustworthy.

Figuero Street in Los Angeles, California, is the longest street in the world. It runs north and south through the city for a distance of 30 miles.

You'd Swear They're Alive

Carl Akeley is responsible for the magnificent Akeley Hall of African Mammals in the American Museum of Natural History in New York. Akeley's unique and original method of taxidermy makes it possible to mount the animals in lifelike poses in environments that accurately represent their native habitats.

Instead of stuffing the animals, Akeley devised a painstaking process in which a mannikin is created over which the tanned skin is pasted. This enables Akeley to retain for his animals their own individualities, and to pose them in natural positions in relation to each other.

All About Fiddles

String instruments in general, including the ancient lyre and lute, originated in Asia. The bow, from Persia, was applied to early string instruments by the Arabs to produce the forebears of the modern violin family. In Europe, medieval bowed instruments included the *veille*, with four fingered strings and a drone string, and the *rebec*, which probably had two or three strings. Of these, not a single specimen survives. Both instruments were small, and rested on the shoulder when played.

The *viol*, which developed from these medieval fiddles, was the principal bowed instrument that was played from the 15th century until the 17th century. Normally, the viol had six strings, and a fingerboard with frets, like the guitar. The body sloped down obliquely from the neck, and bore sound holes in the shape of the letter *c*. The instrument was held downward on, or between, the legs when played.

In its earliest use, the viol doubled vocal parts, for through the Middle Ages vocal music had been more important than instrumental music. The viol family included three instruments, one for each of the three voice parts: a treble viol, a tenor, and a bass—and later, a double bass. Eventually, composers began to write instrumental pieces for the viol trio and the solo viol.

But the viol had a weak, delicate tone. Gradually, it was altered to increase its resonance, becoming lighter, with more lightly strung strings. The treble viol evolved into the violin, while the tenor viol became the viola. The new instruments featured fretless fingerboards, and four strings like the medieval fiddles, with sound holes in the shape of an *f* rather than a *c*. But the bass viol, or *vola da gamba*, survived into the 18th century, until supplanted by the cello. The double bass viol, or *violone*, is the ancestor of the modern double bass.

The most easterly point in the United States is West Quaddy Head, Maine.

Aphrodisiac

Over the centuries, truffles have become an integral part of many French dishes. The French satirist Rabelais's favorite snack was oysters with hot truffle-flavored sausages. Gastronomist Brillat-Savarin—born, appropriately enough, in the town of Belley—was convinced that the truffle is an effective aphrodisiac, proclaiming that "whoever says *truffle* utters a grand word, which awakens erotic and gastronomic ideas."

Today, American cattle are raised for beef in the sparsely populated rangeland states of the West, while dairy farming predominates in Midwestern and Eastern states close to urban centers. Texas leads all states in the number of cattle, and most of these are beef cattle. The American "dairy belt" stretches from New England through New York and Pennsylvania to Michigan, Minnesota, and Wisconsin. Southern Wisconsin can claim the heaviest concentration of cows per square mile in the United States.

Acetic Acid

Vinegar is simply a dilute solution of acetic acid. The strength of the solution is usually between four and 12 percent, depending on the type of vinegar and its intended use. Household vinegar is low in acetic acid; vinegar used for pickling is usually of higher grain. *Grain* is the term used to measure the strength of vinegars: 10 grains are equal to one percent acid; thus "40 grain" vinegar is a four percent solution of acetic acid.

Telly Savalas, who has been cast as Theo Kojak, a New York City detective, has become a hero for thousands of television viewers all over the world. To stop himself from smoking, he sucks Tootsie Roll pops. Savalas has made bald heads romantic and popular.

George I, king of Great Britain and Ireland from 1714-1727, was born in Germany. He spent much of his time in Hanover, and was unable to speak English.

La Paz, Bolivia, has the highest altitude of any capital city in the world. It is nested in the Andes at 11,916 feet above sea level. No wonder visitors pant at its beauty.

Lhasa, in Tibet, has an elevation of 11,800 feet.

Benjamin Franklin was the first postmaster general under the Continental Congress, serving from 1775 to 1776. He had served the crown as deputy postmaster general for the colonies from 1753 to 1774.

In 1789 President George Washington appointed Samuel Osgood as first postmaster general of the United States.

To Cap it Off

In 1958, two U.S. Navy atomic submarines, the *Nautilus* and the *Skate*, made history by being the first ships to sail *under* the North Pole. This event was hailed as heralding a new—*underwater*—route between continents.

But perhaps even more exciting are the predictions some scientists are making of what may happen to the North Polar ice within the next three quarters of a century. They say that surface ships will be able to steam *over* the North Pole, for, they report, the polar ice is melting away rapidly. Already, during the past fifty years or so, more than a third of the thick ice has been thinned out of the frozen-over parts of the Arctic Ocean. Within the next seventy-five years, scientists estimate, the ice may have shrunk to such a degree that a ship will be able to head straight across the top of the world en route to other continents!

Hedy Lamarr lost an opportunity of a lifetime when she turned down the role of Ilsa for the film *Casablanca* in 1942. Ingrid Bergman took the part, and with Bogart as the male star, made film history. Presumably, the reason for Lamarr's refusal was that the script had not been completely finished.

The hummingbird of Cuba is the smallest bird in the world. An average male adult weighs about seven one hundredths of an ounce!

Seaworthless

In 1628, the Swedes built a battleship which they called the *Vasa*. It was a beautiful boat, but it was very poorly designed and did not have adequate ballast.

It started on its maiden voyage from the harbor in Stockholm, and in a little while the ship heeled. It took some time for the Vasa to right itself, but then it listed again. Water washed over the ship, and then it sank, to the utter consternation of the people on shore who watched it go down, suffering a loss of 50 lives.

Talk about ego, the great French painter, Paul Cezanne, acquired a parrot, and spent endless hours teaching the parrot to proclaim "Cezanne is a great painter."

The International Airport in Los Angeles is considered to be the most dangerous airport in the world, according to the International Federation of Airline Pilots. The runner-up for this dubious honor goes to the Kaitak Airport of Hong Kong.

Franz Joseph Haydn, who flourished in the latter part of the 18th century, lived to age 77. During his productive span of some 54 years of musical composition, he composed music that would take 340 hours to play. His works include over 100 symphonies, more than 80 string quartets, over 50 piano sonatas, as well as many operas, songs, masses, and chamber music pieces. He wrote *The Seasons* when he was 69 years old.

Of all the films that have ever played in the United States, *Gone With the Wind*, filmed in 1939, achieved the highest box office response ever. Produced over 40 years ago, this epic film has played continuously ever since, to gross 382 million rental dollars.

Two current films, *Star Wars* and *Superman II* show promise of making box office history.

If a woman who is color-blind marries a man with normal vision, their sons will be color-blind, and their daughters will have normal vision. Color-blindness is a sex-linked genetic characteristic which is transmitted by females, but which is recessive in females.

Ike Eisenhower, 34th President of the United States, was known as an inveterate cat hater. He ordered that any cat found on his grounds in Gettysburg, Pennsylvania, should be shot on sight.

Burma Shave achieved its fame through billboards placed on the highways. These were famous for many years. Here are some of the slogans that amused motorists:

Don't take a curve
At 60 per
We hate to lose
A customer

A peach looks good
With lots of fuzz
But man's no peach
And never was

Henry the Eighth
Prince of Friskers
Lost five wives
But kept his whiskers

Past schoolhouses
Take it slow
Let the little
Shavers grow

Penny Ante

If you start with a penny and you double it, and then you keep doubling the amount each successive day for 30 days, you will wind up with $5,368,709.12.

The first day you'll have one penny, the second day 2¢, the third day 4¢, the fourth day 8¢, the fifth day 16¢, the sixth day 32¢, the seventh day 64¢, and the eighth day $1.28. If you keep this up, you'll wind up at the end of 30 days with the unbelievable sum of 5 million dollars plus.

Strange as it seems, in not one of the 46 detective movies featuring the Chinese detective, Charlie Chan, created by Earl Derr Biggers, was the role ever portrayed by a Chinese.

The Long and The Short of It

The longevity in the Scandinavian countries is amazing. In Sweden, the average life span is better than 74 years. In Iceland, Norway, and Denmark, it is bette than 73 years. Also in this group are The Netherlands, where life expectation is almost 74 years.

People of Africa live the shortest lives. In Mali, for example, the average life expectancy is about 40 years. In Upper Volta, it's around 31, and in Chad it's 32. Life expectancy in underdeveloped Africa is less than half what it is in highly developed industrial countries.

Tell It on the Mountain

Few pre-Columbian Indian tribes have had a more mysterious past than that of the Tiahuanacos, a people who left behind neither history nor legend to explain their civilization. That they were great builders becomes evident to anyone visiting the remnants of their ancient ceremonial edifices, erected many centuries ago, high up in the Andes mountains of Peru.

Ruins of colossal Tiahuanaco fortresses and temples still stand at an altitude of more than two miles. These buildings were constructed painstakingly from huge stones, each one weighing many tons. Working without iron tools or steel tools, the Tiahuanacos fitted the stones together — some measuring as much as 30 feet long and five feet thick — so perfectly that not even a knife blade can be inserted between them.

This Indian civilization's technical know-how was later emulated by the Incas, who used it in building Cuzco, their capital city. Just how these ancient Indian tribes managed to accomplish such engineering marvels remains an unsolved archeological puzzle.

Thomas A. Edison held over 1,300 U.S. and foreign patents for his inventions.

A grown circus lion consumes about 30 pounds of horse meat each day.

Washed-up

The first bathtub installed in the United States was installed in a Cincinnati, Ohio, home in 1842. It was made of mahogany and was lined with sheet metal. Water was poured in by hand.

The first public bath in America was opened in 1852. Since very few people had bathtubs, to promote public health legislation made it mandatory for large cities to provide free public baths in 1895.

Tusk, Tusk

One variety of whale called a narwhal inhabits Arctic waters. The male narwhal's claim to fame is that he has one tooth that can be as much as nine feet long!

If the narwhal sleeps with this long spiral tooth protruding through a hole in the ice, he makes it simple for the Eskimos to catch him.

The bagpipe, the national instrument of Scotland, did not originate in Scotland.

Bagpipes were known in Persia in ancient times, and actually their antiquity has been traced back to ancient Mesopotamia.

Possibly the most unusual airline ever was Freelandia, which Newsweek described as "America's newest and freakiest." Passengers would be served organic peanut butter and honey sandwiches and carrot juice.

The line was operated by an air travel club, and the fares were unbelievably modest. For example, you could ride from New York to Geneva for $100. P.S.: The line went out of operation.

Rare Delicacy

It was incredible; it was shocking; it was tragic; but it happened. It was in 1971 when a Swiss couple visiting Hong Kong stopped in to eat at a Chinese restaurant. They had their poodle with them and asked the headwaiter to take care of their Rosa, to take her to the kitchen and find her something to eat.

The waiter, who spoke Chinese, and didn't understand Swiss, evidently misunderstood and a half hour later waltzed into the dining room with Rosa lying on a frying pan, marinated in sweet and sour sauce surrounded by Chinese vegetables.

The couple were treated for shock.

Louis Glass, General Manager of the Pacific Phone Company, installed the first juke box at the Palais Royal Saloon in San Francisco. It was an electrically operated Edison phonograph with four listening tubes. Each of the tubes was controlled by a separate nickel-in-the-slot device, and that's how the juke box was born.

In 1934 in Fort Worth, Texas, a washeteria was opened by J. F. Cantrell. It contained four electrical washing contrivances, and Cantrell charged for the use of them by the hour. This operation constituted the first self-service launderette in the United States.

Of all the animals tested so far, only monkeys and apes seem capable of color perception.

The earth is traveling through space at the rate of 72,600 miles an hour. It moves 1,100 miles every minute.

Technology to the Rescue

The thirteen original volumes of the Oxford English Dictionary have been compacted into two. Each page of the condensed version constitutes four pages of the original edition.

Of course, the small type is now all but illegible. The publisher judiciously includes a magnifier with each two-voume set.

The original 13-volume set cost over $300. The new edition costs less than $100.

Have you ever wondered why the horseshoe serves as an emblem of good luck? Well, it comes from its fancied resemblance to the nimbus or halo found above the heads of saints or angels in pictures.

Finland is smaller than the state of California.

The legislative assembly with the oldest continuous history in the world is the Tynwald Court, of the Isle of Man, in the Irish Channel, which is believed to have originated more than 1,000 years ago.

The large town located at the greatest distance in the world from the sea is Urumchi, in Skinkiang, China, at a distance of about 1,400 miles from the nearest coastline.

Enough Snuff

The popularity of snuff during the 17th and 18th centuries made the handkerchief indispensable to men or women of breeding. The hanky functioned as both a wipe for the itchy nose and a shield to cover the sneeze. European aristocrats developed great skill at elegantly hiding their snuff-induced sneezes. Most hankies of the era were quite large—about 30 inches square on the average—and darkly colored, to hide the brown tobacco stains.

The pocket handkerchief made its appearance during the 18th century, when middle-class Europeans adopted the hanky to emulate the aristocracy. The invention of the power loom and other advances in textile production in the 1780s ushered in the mass-produced handkerchief, and its artistic design has suffered ever since.

The use of the handkerchief as an ornamental accessory died out in Europe for a time, and in France, any reference to the item was considered the height of vulgarity. But the Empress Josephine reintroduced the lace-bordered *mouchoir* among polite society, reputedly so that she could raise the hanky to her lips when she smiled and hide her imperfect teeth.

Mass-produced hankies of the late 18th and 19th centuries frequently bore illustrations, with satirical cartoons and commemorative tableaus the most popular. Other hankies were imprinted with calendars, almanacs, or railroad timetables.

Today, the handkerchief has to a great extent been superseded by the throwaway tissue. Oddly enough, at their inception, facial tissues had nothing to do with handkerchiefs and were originally manufactured as gas mask filters during World War I. Then, Kleenex was used primarily by women to remove their makeup and cold cream. Finally, it came into general use as a convenient, dispensable substitute for the handkerchief. The familiar Kleenex dispenser was invented in 1959.

In the age of the Kleenex, the handkerchief has almost disappeared from use, but as a piece of costume ornamentation, it periodically falls in and out of fashion. Most recently, it found its place neatly folded and protruding from a man's jacket pocket. Who knows? Tomorrow we may see the perfumed, fringed, and embroidered lace handkerchiefs back among the accoutrements of high fashion.

In August, 1981, Flossie, a Holstein dairy cow, gave birth at the Bronx Zoo to Manhar, a gaur, or wild ox native of India. This remarkable event marked the second successful use of a domestic animal as a surrogate mother for a completely different and endangered wild species. This was achieved by transferring a gour embryo into the cow's uterus. After a gestation period of 300 days, Flossie gave birth to her 73-pound baby gaur.

The other successful interspecies transfer occurred when a domestic sheep gave birth to a mouflon, or wild Sardinian sheep, at Utah State University in 1977.

The famous Orient Express ran from Paris, France to Istanbul, Turkey.

Among the many great players in the history of tennis there were only four, Don Budge, Rod Laver, Maureen Connolly, and Margaret Court, who have won the *Grand Slam* in any one year. By popular consent, the Grand Slam in tennis consists of winning the national championships of the United States, Great Britain, Australia, and France.

Ever wonder how much a trillion dollars *really* is? Well, a stack of a trillion new one-dollar bills would reach 69,000 miles high. High indeed.

In a year, your eyes move up and down and sideways some 36,000,000 times; you blink them some 84,000,000 times!

The largest snowflake on record measured eight inches in width.

During the Prohibition era, most intoxicating liquor was a home-made product. A good many alcoholic beverages were produced by folks who went to a store and bought mixtures and bottles which contained the following legend: "Do not mix this with two quarts of pure alcohol, or else you will get the most delicious plum brandy you ever drank, and this would result in your breaking the federal law of Prohibition."

One of the most popular drinks of the Prohibition era was a concoction called *bathtub gin*. Since there was generally no pot or vat big enough to hold the liquid, it was generally made in a bath tub. Folks would buy essence of juniper berries, mix it with pure alcohol, and come up with something that resembled gin.

No less than 13 movies have been made about the story of *Dr. Jekyll and Mr. Hyde*. The first one was created in 1908, and since then, the most famous have starred King Baggot in 1913, John Barrymore in 1920, Frederic March in 1932, Spencer Tracy in 1941, and Paul Massie in 1961.

In 1844, in Lajore, India, the death of Raja Suchet Singh led to one of the greatest mass suicides of all time. When the Raja died, age-old Hindu custom decreed that his widows be cremated with their husbands. The Raja had 10 wives and 300 concubines, and all of them sacrificed themselves on funeral pyres to be burnt along with their deceased husband.

It seems that we're all looking to get more fun out of life. Yet there are some individuals who psychiatrists claim are *cherophobiacs*—people who fear having fun. It reminds one of the statement made about the Puritans who were opposed to bear-baiting, not because it gave pain to the bear, but because it gave pleasure to the spectators.

Nero Wolfe, the corpulent detective created by Rex Stout, raised orchids as a hobby. In the movies, Nero Wolfe owned over 10,000 orchids, weighed about 278 lbs., stood 5 feet, 8 inches tall, and declared that his favorite color was yellow. He was played by Edward Arnold, and also by Walter Connolly.

Money Is Simply Lovely

The inflation rate in Chile, between 1950 and 1973, was an outlandish 423,100 percent—meaning, in American currency, that what could once be bought for one dollar eventually cost $4,231!

NATO stands for the North Atlantic Treaty Organization, which was established in 1949. The countries who are members of NATO are:

Belgium
Canada
Denmark
France
Greece
Iceland
Italy

Luxembourg
Netherlands
Norway
Portugal
United Kingdom
United States
Turkey

West Germany

Long John Silver was a peg-legged pirate in *Treasure Island*, a book written by Robert Louis Stevenson. It turned out to be one of the most popular of all books ever written for boys.

So It Shouldn't Be A Total Loss

During the 1890s, Emperor Menelek II, monarch of Ethiopia, had heard that electric chairs were being used in the United States to execute criminals. It seemed like a good idea to the king, so he ordered three of these electric chairs. But electricity had not yet been introduced into Ethiopia, and the chairs were useless. So Menelek decided to use one of the chairs for his royal throne, and the hot seat was actually employed in this way for many years.

When Prince Charles visited New York for 24 hours in 1981, it cost the city $300,000. Most of the expense was due to police overtime.

Some American Indians once printed paper money. The Chocktaws issued a 75-cent note in 1862. The Arapahoes issued a $5 bill in 1850, and the Cherokees issued a $1 bill in 1862. Both of these bills are on view in New York City in the collection of Moneys of the World, owned by the Chase National Bank.

Scotch Entrepreneur

One enterprising Scot may have invented the world's first pay toilet when he carried around a bucket and shielding cloth for any fastidious pedestrian who would not condescend to relieve himself in the nearest alleyway. Temporary rental of the bucket and cloth would set you back a mere half-penny.

Automobiles

If the price is more important to you than speed, you might want to test-drive a Mercedes 600 Pullman, the most expensive standard car now on the market. One of these six-door beauties will set you back $90,000—less your trade-in, of course. And if used cars are your preference, you might be interested in a Rolls-Royce Phantom, once owned by the Queen of the Netherlands, that sold in 1974 for a record $280,000!

Cities have monikers. Some of the most famous are:

Boston	Beantown
New York City	The Big Apple
Philadelphia	The City of Brotherly Love
Paris, France	The City of Light
Rome, Italy	The Eternal City
Hartford, CT	The Insurance City
Chicago	The Windy City
Denver	The Mile-High City

A hump back whale often covers more than 4,000 miles in a single year.

My *Fair Lady* is a musical adaptation of George Bernard Shaw's play, *Pygmalion*, which was written in 1912. The role of Eliza Doolittle in *My Fair Lady* was played by Julie Andrews. The play was a great hit, and has been revived in 1981.

Pinball is International

Along with Bally, D. Gottlieb and Company, Williams Electronics, and Chicago Coin are the major pinball manufacturers in the nation. To suggest the size of the pinball industry: the Gottlieb Company was recently sold to Columbia Pictures for the sum of $47 million!

Each of the four major manufacturers now brings out from six to 12 new games every year. It's a long road that takes a new machine from the designer's head to the arcade floor. After a new design is presented by one of the company's staff, a mock-up of the new playfield is constructed and tested. Care must be taken that the game is neither too easy nor too difficult—and most important, that an average game will be completed in about two-and-a-half minutes, considered the ideal time for a pinball game. Designers aim for a game that demands about 75 percent skill but allows for 25 percent luck, so that unskilled players can enjoy playing, too.

After all features are in place in the final mock-up, from 50 to 200 complete test samples are constructed and shipped around the world for on-the-floor testing. If the game meets with the approval of its most demanding critics— pinball players—the game is placed in full production. The success of the test models in various countries will determine where most new models will be shipped.

Basketball Miracle

Like all sports, basketball has produced its moments of greatness. One of the high points of college basketball was reached in the 1949-50 season, when the underdog City College of New York became the first—and only—team to win both the NCAA and NIT championships in the same year. The Beavers had finished their schedule that year without ranking among the top 20 teams, and had been the last squad to be invited to both tournaments. Yet they went on to victory in both competitions, in the process of defeating the teams ranked one, two, three, five, and six.

Do You Know Your Onions?

If you were asked to guess the most widely used vegetable in the world, you might think first of corn or potatoes, or perhaps lettuce or tomatoes. Because it is most often used in the United States as a flavoring to other foods, the plant that rightly deserves the award for culinary prevalence might not even come to mind as a vegetable at all. We're talking, of course, about the odorous, oft-derided vegetable that is so essential to any chef, and so unessential to any chef's eye—the onion.

In total production, both the potato and tomato surpass the onion, but neither is used in such a wide variety of cuisines as the onion. The list of recipes, Western and Oriental, that require the services of the onion or its cousins would probably fill a small library. And since it appears both as a flavoring in much *haute cuisine*, and as a staple in much peasant cookery, the onion has traditionally been one of the few vegetables popular with both commoners and kings.

Oratory is defined as the art of swaying an audience by eloquent speech. Oratory first appeared in the law courts of Athens, and soon became important in all areas of life. Classic Rome's great orators were Cato the Elder, Marc Antony, and Cicero, and their followers and disciples have assailed the innocent ever since.

Nest Egg

The tegu is a large yellow-spotted lizard, measuring about three feet overall, native to tropical South America. The tegu is notorious as a poultry thief. This lizard runs off with eggs and young chickens. It also eats tiny creatures such as insects, not to speak of other lizards, frogs, and plant food such as fruit and leaves.

Many termites in tropical America build bulky nests up in trees. These nests are further protected from enemies by being extremely hard. A man has to use a saw or a hatchet to break into one. The female tegu's eggs have been found repeatedly inside tough termite nests. Imagine what strength is in her muscles and claws!

Even more surprising is the fact that the tegu is a terrestrial, not a tree-dwelling lizard, and that termites' nests may be nine to twelve feet high up in trees. Imagine how determinedly the tegu protects its eggs. She can count on the industrious termites to mend any break in their castle wall, and so the tegu's eggs are as secure as if locked in a virtual safe.

Perhaps the most amazing thing of all is that the baby tegus are tough enough to break out of this strong-walled nest.

Oddities

The shortest odds ever quoted on any racehorse were the 1 to 10,000 on" Dragon Blood" in the Premio Naviglio Milan, Italy, 1967.

Odds of 1 to 100 were quoted on the American horse, "Man O' War," in three separate races in 1920.

Blessing or Curse?

Nescafe, introduced by Nestle's of Switzerland, was the first instant coffee. The public was introduced to it in 1938.

American consumers spend a billion dollars a year for cold relief preparations.

It was in New Orleans that the first movie house was opened back in 1896. Admission was 10¢ to see the projection room, and one could view the Edison Vitascope Projector for another 10¢. The doors of the New Orleans theater were open from 10:00 a.m. to 3:00 p.m., and then again from 6:00 p.m. to 10:00 p.m.

One of the first English films to be shown in America was *Waves Off Dover*.

The largest cinema house ever built was the Roxy Theater in New York, which contains 6,200 seats.

Geese can fly more than five and one-half miles above the earth, higher than Mount Everest.

In May of 1980, one Edwin Budding of Gloucestershire, England, made an agreement with the Phoenix Iron Works to manufacture machinery "for the purpose of cropping and shearing the vegetable surface of lawns." Thus the first lawn mower came into existence.

Previous to this invention, lawns were cut with scythes, but this operation was ineffective unless the lawn was wet.

The sale of lawn mowers got a great boost when lawn tennis came into vogue in 1870.

Fly Me

Back in 1930, Miss Ellen Church, who came from Iowa and was trained as a Registered Nurse, was hired by United Airlines to be an air hostess. She got the job because she herself had proposed such a job to the company. She was the first woman in the world to hold such a job. She worked the United Airlines flight from Oakland, California to Cheyenne, Wyoming.

She was later commissioned by United to train others to be airline hostesses. To qualify for this job, a young lady had to be twenty-five or under, be a Registered Nurse, weigh less than 115 pounds and be under 5′4″. The munificent salary was $125 a month. For that great emolument, each girl had the privilege of spending about 100 hours every month flying around in planes which were neither heated nor pressurized. In those days, a flight of 950 miles took 18 hours.

The duties of the early airline hostesses included carrying the baggage of the passengers, helping the pilot and the mechanics push the machine in and out of the hangar, and collecting tickets. And if all this were not enough, the girls had to endure harassment by the wives of the pilots, who resented their presence. As far as the wives were concerned, the proximity during 18 hours in the air with no place to go was much too dangerous a threat to domestic tranquillity.

Reno, Nevada, is located farther west than Los Angeles, California.

The crossword puzzle, which has millions of addicts throughout the world, made its first appearance in the New York World on Sunday, December 21, 1913.

The author of that puzzle was Arthur Wynne, who was born in Liverpool, England.

What Fools these Mortals Be

Hans van Meegern was probably the best art forger who ever lived. He was actually a very good artist in his own right, but he soon discovered that painting out-and-out fakes paid off better. Van Meegern painted *Christ at Emmaus* in the style of Vermeer, and earned himself a neat $250,000.

His imitations were so good that art experts refused to believe they weren't original. When he was brought to trial on the criminal charge of *stealing* the paintings, the only way van Meegern could demonstrate his innocence was to assert to the court that he would sit down and paint a new Vermeer right before their very eyes.

The critics scoffed; no one believed van Meegern but that is exactly what he did. He executed a masterpiece in court. Then he was sentenced to a year in jail *for forgery!*

There are at least 1,500 varieties of mosquitoes.

Artistic incompetence is nowhere made more manifest than in the painting of *The Sacrificing of Isaac by Abraham*, rendered by a Dutch artist. Abraham, instead of holding a knife to Isaac's throat, is depicted as holding a loaded blunderbuss to his son's head—possibly the worst anachronism ever set down on canvas.

Naming Time

This kid was taken to the Planetarium and was utterly fascinated. He loved looking through the huge telescope. But what he couldn't get over was how the astronomers could know the names of the planets and stars!

You might be interested in knowing the origin of the names of the our days and months. Our days were adapted from the Saxon, which, in turn, were based on the Roman. The Romans named the days after the planets, the sun and the moon being considered planets. Thus:

Sunday comes from the Saxon's Sun's Day, from the Latin Dies Solis

Monday comes from Moon's Day, from the Latin Dies Lunae

Tuesday comes from Tiw's Day, Tiw being substituted for Mars, from the Latin Dies Martis

Wednesday from Woden's (or Wotan) Day, corresponding to the Roman god Mercury, or Dies Mercurii

Thursday from Thor's Day, Thor being the Saxon equivalent of Jupiter or Jove, Dies Jovis

Friday from Frigg's Day, the Saxon counterpart of the Roman goddess Venus, Dies Veneris

Saturday from Seterne's Day, equivalent to the Latin Dies Saturni

So far as our months are concerned, their names were adapted from the Latin. The early Latin calendar was a ten month calendar, beginning with March.

January after the two-faced Roman god Janus who looks simultaneously at the past and at the future

February after Februa, a Roman feast of purification

March after Mars, the god of war, to mark the reopening of the campaigns in the spring

April from the Latin aperire, to open, referring to the buds

May after Maia, the goddess for the growth of plants

June's origin is not clear; perhaps from the Latin family name Junius, perhaps from juvenis, Latin for youth, perhaps from the goddess Juno

July named after Julius Caesar for the month when he was born

August after Augustus, the first Roman emperor

September from septem, Latin for seven, from the month's original position in the Latin calendar

October from octo, Latin for eight

November from novem, Latin for nine

December from decem, Latin for ten

A football is made from cowhide, not from pigskin.

The temperature in Alaska often goes up to 85 degrees. The U.S. Weather Bureau Station at Fort Yukon, Alaska, once recorded 100 degrees in the shade—nearly a 200-degree difference from the Arctic's coldest winter spot.

It's a love story for the books. Liza Alekseyeva and Aleksei Semyonov fell in love and hoped to marry. They also hoped to emigrate from Russia. In 1978, Mr. Semyonov, who is a stepson of the Soviet dissident Andrei D. Sakharov, emigrated to America. But Liza was unsuccessful and was left behind.

Undaunted, with Liza in Russia and Aleksei in America, the lovers were married. Montana is one of the states that permits proxy marriages. So in a ceremony performed in Butte in June, 1981, the marriage took place. The couple hope that Russia will now allow Mrs. Semyonov to emigrate to join her husband.

The Sahara Desert is over three times as large as the Mediterranean Sea.

The United States government paid Russia $7,200,000 for Alaska—which comes to slightly less than two cents an acre.

An average adult has about six quarts of blood. Certain structures on the surface of red blood cells vary from one individual to another. On the basis of these differences, people have been categorized into blood groups. Your blood group is inherited.

The chances are your blood group is O. The most common blood group in the world is Group O; 46% of the world's population belongs to this group. However, if you happen to be Norwegian, the chances are good that your blood type is A because in this area this is the most common blood type.

The importance of knowing your blood type relates especially to transfusions. The donor's blood must be compatible with the recipient's blood. If they are not, antibodies in the recipient's blood will clump with the red blood cells of the donor's blood. Persons in the AB group are considered universal recipients because they can generally safely accept blood from A, B, AB, or O donors. Persons with O blood are considered universal donors because they can generally safely give blood to the other three groups.

The holiest city of Islam is Mecca, in Saudi Arabia, where the Prophet Muhammad was born. This city, which is banned to unbelievers, is visited by Muslims making the pilgrimage. Every Muslim tries to make the pilgrimage to Mecca once in his life.

The Great Mosque in the center of Mecca encloses the Kaaba, a small building which houses the Black Stone, the most venerated object in Islam. It is this stone that pilgrims journey many miles to kiss. And, wherever they are, Muslims all over the world face the Kaaba when they stop for prayers.

Henry Ford first introduced his famous Model T Ford October 1, 1908. By 1928, when this model was discontinued to be replaced by the Model A, some 15 million model T's had been sold.

Sharpshooter

In the late 1800s, American shooting contests drew crowds of 100,000 people. Captain A. H. Bogardus, New York born, moved to the Midwest in 1856. The lad found his new home to be great bird country, and he soon learned that a youngster could make a name for himself if he was considered to be the best shot around. Within the next dozen years, Bogardus became the finest trapshooter the Midwest had ever known.

As the nation's bird supply diminished, shooters turned to clay pigeons, and to glass balls. In the early 1890s, when Bogardus was at his peak, the marksman put on a memorable performance before a record crowd in New York's Gilmore Garden. While timers kept the score, Bogardus started shooting away at glass balls which were catapulted about 30 feet or so into the air. He shoved shells quickly into his breechloader, and ping! ping! ping! he banged down the balls one after another at record speed. He missed very few.

As Bogardus popped his 1,000th target, the official timer stopped his watch. The man had been shooting but one hour and 42 minutes, and had hit his targets on the average of 10 a minute. For almost two hours steady, Bogardus hit a glass ball every six seconds.

Without Benefit of Clergy

Some of the most renowned men and women in history and art were born bastards. Among this very imposing list are the following:

Alexander Hamilton, U.S. Secretary of the Treasury

Sarah Bernhardt, world-famous actress

William the Conqueror, the first Norman ruler of England

Jenny Lind, renowned singer

Marilyn Monroe, world-famous actress and movie star

Giovanni Boccaccio, the Italian author of X-rated stories

Frederick Douglass, famous abolitionist

Alexandre Dumas, French novelist and playwright

Leonardo da Vinci, great inventor and artist

Bernardo O'Higgins, one of the liberators of South America

Richard Wagner, famous German composer

Josephine, wife of Napoleon

Juan Peron, Argentine president

For the past 17 years the winner of the National Basketball Association's most valuable player award has been a center. This pattern was broken in 1981, when Julius Erving a forward for the Philadelphia team was chosen. In 1964 the winner was Oscar Robertson, a guard for the Cincinnati Royals.

Calling all Swimmers

What would happen if all the glaciers in the world were to melt?

Were this to occur, the level of the sea would rise 100 feet, and half of all land on earth would be under water.

Uncanny!

It was one Nicolas Appert, a Parisian confectioner, who found a viable way to can foods. This was back in 1810, when Appert won a 12,000 franc prize offered by the French government for an improved method of preserving foods.

Appert did his canning not in cans but in bottles. The French government stored his bottles for three months, and then tested them. The food was appraised as tasty and safe, and his method of heating foods for varying periods to preserve them was approved. Some time later, the same methods were applied to metal enclosure, and the canning industry was on its way.

Pictorial labels on cans were introduced in New York around 1860.

Pet a Toad and He'll Love it

The horned toad is not a toad at all, but a lizard. The horned toad gets its name from the horn-like spines that bristle out from its head and body.

Curiously, for all its hard, spiny hide, the horned toad likes to be stroked. It will lie quiet and happy as long as its head is being scratched or its chin tickled.

To escape an enemy, the horned toad burrows into the sand with the edges of its body and sometimes with its head. When attacked and in grave danger, the horned toad's blood pressure increases tremendously. Sometimes the pressure becomes so great that a few drops of blood are squirted from its eyeballs.

By Hook or by Crook

Living on the parched coastal plain of Peru, the ancient Chimus depended on water from mountain streams for their very existence. To protect their irrigation system, this tribe built an enormous wall, studded with fortifications and linked by roads to their capital city. Some historians believe that the Incas conquered the Chimus by diverting the streams, thus cutting off their water supply.

Inca conquests were very carefully planned. Usually a kind of "advertising campaign" preceded military aggression. First, the Inca rulers dispatched messengers who pointed out how pleasant it was to live under Inca rule. These "publicity men" also hailed the superiority of the Inca religion. Only if such peaceful measures failed to win over the population, did Inca soldiers invade a foreign territory.

Built Like a Submarine

The beaver has large lungs which enable it to carry enough air and oxygenated blood to stay under water for about 15 minutes. It also has glands near the root of its tail which secrete oil that waterproofs the animal's fur. Its ears and nose are equipped with valves that close automatically when it submerges and which open again when it returns to the surface.

For Auto Buffs

James Bond used a low-slung racer in the movie *Goldfinger*. The front was mounted with machine guns and an ejection seat. The rear vents spewed a smokescreen or an oil slick. The car was called the Espionage Special DB-5. It was built by Aston Martin Lagonda Ltd. in 1963.

In 1979, the British company introduced this car, minus the 007 features, to the American market for $80,000, and in two years sold as many as 120. The price has gone up since, and now hovers around $100,000.

Not Every Frenchman Is a Lover

Chaqu' on à son gout! "Each to his own taste" was never more appropriately applied than in the appraisal of *Remembrance of Things Past*, the voluminous novel written by Marcel Proust. Speaking of this work, Clifton Fadiman, one of America's foremost critics, said "For some, this is the greatest novel in the world. For others, it is unreadable." The book was published piecemeal in sixteen volumes between 1913 and 1978.

Proust himself was something of an eccentric. Born in Paris in 1871, his work is semi-autobiographical. Sickly, asthmatic, and neurotic, he spent most of his hours in bed, where he lay swaddled in gloves, blankets, and scarves. He had his room lined with cork to shut out noise, and even during the most terribly sweltering of Parisian summer days, his windows were kept tightly shut. Visitors could hardly bear the awful smell of his miserable room which reeked of inhalants.

That's Life!

Scientists are of the opinion that the first primitive organisms that appeared on earth came into being some 3,500 million years ago. This was roughly over 1,000 million years after the formation of the earth.

Some Tides Are Fifty Feet High

Coast lines can affect the size of the tides. One of the largest tides in the world is in the Bay of Fundy on the east coast of Canada between New Brunswick and Nova Scotia. During the spring tides the water may rise fifty feet. The great size of the tides in the Bay of Fundy is the result of the bay's geographic location and its funnel shape.

Twice each day as the tide sweeps in from the open Gulf of Maine, it is forced into the ever narrowing bay. Its waters pile up with mounting strength to produce the great tide at the head of the bay.

Because of the Bay of Fundy's huge tides it has one of the strangest fisheries in the world. There, the fishermen string their nets at low tide from large wooden frames set right in the bottom of the bay. The fishermen drive out across the wet sands with their horses and wagons to collect the fish caught when the nets were covered by the flooding high tide.

Hidden Treasure

Kit Williams, an English artist with a pixie imagination, is the originator of a most unique buried treasure mystery. He did the story and art work for a presumably simple fairy tale published by Schocken Books under the title *Masquerade*. And, as the title suggests, there is an intriguing deception afoot here.

It seems that, along with the book, the artist-author created a gold hare embedded with jewels. This he buried somewhere in England. But where? OK, the hiding place is buried somewhere in the book. All you have to do is figure out the clues, which according to the author are obvious in the pictures and the text.

So far nobody has succeeded in unlocking the secret, but the author has an unexpected treasure in the prodigious sale of the book.

An Inca Courier System Could Send a Message 1,250 Miles in Five Days

The fastest means of communication before the invention of the telegraph was the highly-organized messenger system conceived by the Incas.

Because the Incas had no horses, men had to carry messages on foot. Inca messengers, called *chasquis* station, about a mile and a half away. ground between Quito and Cuzco—a distance of 1,250 miles—in five days, or at an average speed of more than ten miles per hour.

Even more astounding, the mountain route was at altitudes of one to three miles above sea level where the air is thin and it is difficult to breathe. Thanks to the *chasquis*, the Lord-Inca could eat fresh fish brought to him from the distant sea every day, if he cared to.

A *chasquis* would start the journey having memorized a message for the Lord-Inca. The messenger was armed with a mace and a slingshot to defend himself from any attack. Slung over his shoulder was a sack containing a conch shell to be blown when he arrived at the next *chasqui* station, about a mile and a half away. Other *chasquis* would be waiting to carry the message to the next station, and so on and on until the last messenger would breathlessly deliver the news to the Lord-Inca himself, in Cuzco.

The Glass Snake—a Lizard—Escapes by Coming Apart

Anyone who grabs a fleeing glass snake by the tail is likely to get a big surprise.

When a glass snake tries to get away, the part of the snake in greatest danger of being caught is its wriggling tail. For that reason nature apparently has given it an amazing way of escape, shared by most other lizards. Its tail simply breaks off! The enemy is left holding a little squirming fragment of bone and muscle while the glass snake itself wriggles safely away.

This sounds unpleasant, but the glass snake doesn't seem to be bothered in the slightest. In a short time a whole new tail grows out to replace the lost one. If the snake gets into the same trouble again, the new tail breaks off just as readily as the old one did.

Despite its name, the glass snake isn't a snake at all but a lizard. It has no legs and it crawls exactly like a snake, but it differs in two important ways from a true snake.

The glass snake's eyes can close and it has tiny ear openings on each side of its head. True snakes have neither movable eyelids nor ears. Since all lizards have movable eyelids, and most lizards have ears, this shows that the glass snake is really a legless lizard that merely looks like a snake.

But, snake or not, it is beautiful. Its body seems to be so highly polished that it looks as if it had just been shellacked or coated with glass. This is one of the reasons why it was named glass snake. The other reason, of course, is the way its tail snaps off, like brittle glass.

Lacrimose

Someone's in the kitchen crying. Why is he sad? He's not—he's peeling onions. Why does peeling onions make us cry?

When you slice into an onion, a chemical called propanethiol S-oxide is released. When this gas mixes with the water in your eyes, it forms sulfuric acid, which induces lacrimation, or crying.

The question is how can you avoid this unpleasant effect? Well, there's no sure-fire way, but you might try holding the onion under running water while you slice it. This might weaken the power of the propanethiol S-oxide.

The Scots once refused to cultivate potatoes because the Bible did not mention the plant.

Always True To You in My Fashion

Scripture tells us that King Solomon of the Old Testament took unto himself 700 wives. No one knows whether this is exactly true, but it seems likely that the approximation can't be far off.

Yet this was child's play compared to the exploits of King Mongut of Siam, the famous monarch of *The King and I*. It is reliably reported that his wives and concubines numbered no fewer than 9,000. No polyandrous female has been a match for this polygamist. The best record was posted by Queen Kahena of the Berbers, who is said to have amassed 400 husbands.

Although paled by these gargantuan exploits, worthy of mention are the following: The Mormon founder, Brigham Young of Salt Lake City, had 27 wives. Tommy Manville, a 20th century playboy, married 11 times. Artie Shaw, the bandleader, married 8 times. It is also recounted that the famous, or infamous, Calamity Jane acquired 12 husbands.

Tightwad

Hetty Green, who died in 1916, was known as the "Witch of Wall Street." She was generally considered to be the greatest woman financier in the world. Her father had been very rich and she inherited six million dollars from him, which she managed so well that she accumulated an enormous fortune from her investments on the stock market.

Her investments were indeed canny, but she herself was nothing less than mad. She wore the same black dress for years, even though it turned green with age, and then brown. Her lingerie consisted of old newspapers which she collected from trash baskets in Central Park.

She lived in the Chelsea section of Manhattan in an unheated apartment, and the diet of this tycoon consisted of onions, eggs and dry oatmeal.

Hetty Green was incredibly stingy. When her son, Edward, was run over by a wagon when he was nine years old, Hervy Green refused to call a doctor. Although his leg was seriously injured, she took the boy to a number of free clinics. This rich woman enjoyed being a miser more than anything else. She left an estate valued at 100 million dollars.

Big Ben is actually the name of the bell in the Westminster Parliament tower in London, but most people associate the name with the big clock in the tower. The bell was named after Sir Benjamin Hall, the commissioner of works in 1856.

The fastest animal of all is the cheetah, which can attain a speed of 70 miles per hour. The slowest of all animals is—you guessed it—the snail, which moves at .03 miles per hour.

Malaria is the most prevalent infectious disease in the world today.

Stork on the Roof, Forsooth

Storks repair the same nest year after year. But they don't build delicately.

A white stork throws together a large pile of sticks, usually near some human dwelling. For the white stork is one of the few species of birds that seems to be happiest when near human beings. Throughout Holland, this bird nests on unused chimneys or on roof peaks. Dutch householders believe the big, handsome birds bring good luck; they wouldn't think of removing the nests. In fact, many a homeowner puts a cartwheel on his roof or chimney as an invitation to a young pair of the friendly birds to make their first nest there.

In the fall, the storks leave Europe for their long flight to their winter home in Africa. But when the snow melts during the following year, the Dutch people once again hear the familiar clattering noise on their roofs—an unmistakable sign that the big birds have returned.

The skin of a hippopotamus is two inches thick in some places.

The orchid has always had a very special reputation. Orchids are hard to seed, and they grow slowly. But their value is not altogether related to their exquisite decorativeness, or to their relative scarcity. Throughout the centuries, the orchid has had symbolic meanings to different peoples.

In Mexico, orchids are used symbolically in various religious ceremonies. In the Orient, the orchid was associated with virtue, while in ancient Greece it had sexual connotations and was used in witchcraft. Today, many varieties of orchids are used in folk medicine to effect cures for various diseases. Vanilla comes from a plant that belongs to the orchid family.

A Whale of a Difference

Most whales are even-tempered. Most whales do not, for example, kill other creatures wantonly. They kill for food, or to protect their mate or babies, or in self-defense.

Except for one kind of whale. He has a vicious temper and often slays with no other reason except a lust for killing. Naturally this whale has been named the killer whale. And he is the fiercest and most dangerous of all sea creatures!

The accordion was invented in 1829, by Damian of Vienna. The first U.S. patent was issued to Anthony Faas of Philadelphia in 1854.

Some icebergs are vast—weighing as much as two billion pounds. But, as they float into warmer waters, they begin to decay. Ice on the outside may melt on a warm day. The water seeps into crevasses and freezes, expanding and building up tensions.

The crack of a rifle, or some other noise, may trigger a sharp explosion causing the iceberg to blow up, cascading chunks of ice into the sea.

Something to Be Thankful about

The Puritan Lord Protector of England, Oliver Cromwell, recited grace before dinner as follows: "Some people have food, but no appetite. Some people have an appetite but no food. I have both. The Lord be praised."

The reputation of Sir Francis Page as a severe jurist earned him the moniker of "The Hanging Judge." When he was nearly 80 and quite feeble, an acquaintance asked him how his health was holding up.

"My dear sir," Judge Page replied, "you see I keep hanging on."

Some Submarine Canyons Are as Vast as Arizona's Grand Canyon

All over the world, canyons have been found under the sea. These canyons extend out from the edge of the land and plunge down to the depths of the oceans. They have been found in the Mediterranean, off the mouth of the Congo River in Africa, along the coasts of India, and around the Philippine Islands. There is even one great submarine canyon which extends from the deep ocean right into the heart of Japan's Tokyo Bay.

The famous Hudson Canyon, which lies off New York City, starts near the mouth of the Hudson River. It extends about 60 miles south-eastward across the underwater edge of the continent down to the floor of the Atlantic Ocean. The main part of the canyon is five to six miles wide, and the deepest part extends some 3,000 feet from top to bottom.

Along the California coast, the Monterey Submarine Canyon is as enormous as the immense Grand Canyon in Arizona.

Money is So Confusing!

In the early days of our nation, English, French, and Spanish monies all circulated through the American colonies, with a concomitant confusion of trade. In 1785, the dollar was adopted by Congress as the unit of exchange, and the decimal system as the method of reckoning. The U.S. monetary system was established in 1792; the first mint began operation in Philadelphia the following year.

Tomatoes are Red/ Violets are Blue!

Spanish explorers in the New World found the Mayans cultivating a plant they called *tomatl*, and brought back some seeds to Europe for experimentation. Tomatoes, it was found, would grow well in Iberia. At first, the Spanish didn't know what to do with them—the tomato was considered too tart to be enjoyed as a fruit. But an adventurous chef at the Spanish court combined tomatoes with olive oil and onions for Europe's first tomato sauce, creating a culinary sensation at the royal dinner table.

Traffic Lights

The first modern traffic light, in fact, did not appear until 1914, on Euclid Avenue, Cleveland, Ohio. And in England driving tests were not required for would-be drivers until 1935!

Post Haste

The French, incidentally, were the first to depend upon "airmail" delivery for any length of time. During the siege of Paris in the Franco-Prussian War of the 1870s, mail was sent out of the capital by balloon, as well as by hundreds of homing pigeons. Return letters were photoreduced to one four-thousandth of their original size, then delivered to the capital by pigeon. Thirty-five pigeons carried the identical 30,000-message mail cannisters so that at least one was certain to survive the Prussian pigeon snipers. In Paris, the messages were enlarged on a projection screen, copied by clerks, and delivered to addresses within the city.

It's a Cold, Cold World!

A prominent encyclopedia has suggested that the invention with the greatest impact on worldwide economic life since the railroad is—no, you'd never guess—the refrigerator! Isn't the refrigerator more of a convenience item? Hardly. Refrigeration technology has completely revolutionized farming and has led to the rapid development of a world-wide food trade. It would be difficult, indeed, to find a person in the world today who has not benefited in some way from the introduction of refrigerated food preservation.

The growth of cities and suburbs in the last century has steadily moved most of us further and further away from our food source, the farm. Without food preservation techniques, especially refrigeration, it's doubtful that this urban growth could have moved ahead so rapidly. And since the advent of refrigeration, a nation no longer has to feed itself—the abundant supply of one nation can balance the scarcity in another, allowing many nations to industrialize more quickly. Improved food preservation has also helped increase the world's food supply by eliminating much waste. Foods that would otherwise perish can remain in storage until needed.

Peace-Nik

The great green iguana, largest lizard in the New World, is one of the most ferocious appearing creatures imaginable. It grows to six feet or more in length and looks very much like a miniature dinosaur.

In spite of its looks, however, the iguana is actually the most timid of creatures. Its threatening appearance is all bluff. It looks fierce enough to eat a human being, but what it actually eats are fruits and flowers. Its favorite food is the tropical orchid that grows in the trees nearby.

Without being either savage or aggressive, the green iguana can still be dangerous. When cornered and forced to defend itself from an enemy, its sharp claws can inflict terrible damage. Its jaws are powerful enough to snap off a man's finger, or even his whole hand.

But an iguana will go to almost any extreme to avoid a fight, and will seize the first opportunity to run away. It would seem from the iguana's huge, thick body as if the reptile would be slow and clumsy. But when the iguana scampers off, it moves at a good clip, and few of its enemies are fast enough to overtake it.

It is quite apparent when the iguana is afraid. When the iguana stands up to an enemy and fights, its skin stays its normal green color. But when the iguana "turns yellow" and tries to get away, it literally *does* turn yellow! The moment it tries to flee from danger, its skin changes from green to a muddy, mottled yellow color.

The first motion picture "drive-in" theater was opened in 1933 in Camden, New Jersey.

Frigid—But Good!

Eric the Red named the land of cold, ice and snow he discovered in 985 A.D. Greenland in order to entice colonists from Iceland to settle in the new country.

If it were not for the water vapor of the atmosphere and for the clouds, the temperature of the earth would be at least 50 degrees higher than it is.

During the winter more snow falls on the southern state of Virginia than on the average Arctic land.

Nuclear Dilemma

At this point in history, nuclear power is regarded both as the scourge of mankind, or as the hope of mankind. The ranks of supporters on each side are equally numerous and equally illustrious.

In addition to technical problems, such as waste disposal, there are overwhelming political and ethical problems, involving human contamination, and the risk of nuclear war. How to develop the peaceful uses for nuclear power without blowing mankind off the map, that is the question.

Senator John Glenn of Ohio feels that the Nuclear Non-Proliferation Act of 1978 which he sponsored helps the United States to provide nuclear power reactors to those nations who agree to limit their use to peaceful purposes. Senator Glenn points out that it does not take a high level of technical sophistication to make atom bombs once you have nuclear power reactors and plutonium.

It takes only 10, or even five in the case of technical sophistication, kilograms of plutonium to make a bomb. There are now 247 nuclear power reactors in the world. Each of these develops about 146 gigawatts (or 146 billion watts) of power. Each gigawatt develops about 250 kilograms of plutonium a year. Between 25 and 50 bombs could be made from the leftover fuel of each gigawatt a year. If each of the possessors of the 247 reactors used the plutonium this way, they could produce some 4,000 to 8,000 bombs per year!

Husky Like a Horse

Eskimos have been able to harness the strength, endurance, and intelligence of the Arctic wolf. Occasionally they cross-breed a female husky dog with a wild wolf. Some authorities say that through the years this practice has helped develop a tremendously strong and hardy dog. The husky may weigh only 60 to 80 pounds, but it is able to pull 100 pounds for 10 to 12 hours a day.

The husky is jealous and proud. Each dog will fight to defend its place on the sled line. And if this place is changed, the dog may sulk and refuse to move.

Admire the Murre

There are but few birds that can swim under water. The Arctic murre is one of them. Diving into the water and moving its stubby, powerful wings to propel itself, it usually can catch the fish it wants for its dinner.

The murre will go back to the same breeding ground year after year to lay just one egg per season. Either the male or the female will incubate the egg.

The murre is an Eskimo favorite, both as food and as a provider of soft skin for comfortable slippers. Murre eggs, when fried, are highly colorful. Unlike hens' eggs, they have blood red yokes and azure blue "whites."

Come Back, Little Swallow

Traditionally, each year on March 19, the Feast of St. Joseph, the swallows come back from their winter home in Argentina, some 6,000 miles away, to San Juan Capistrano, California, to nest in the old church. The original church, built by Spanish Franciscan missionaries, was largely destroyed by an earthquake in 1812. Although tourists continue to come to Capistrano, albeit in reduced numbers, the swallows have been abandoning the adobe ruins for more attractive sites. Plans are now in the making to rebuild the church, replicating the old one, to lure the swallows — and, incidentally, the tourists — back in large numbers.

The Packard was the first automobile to cross the American continent under its own power. The trip, in 1903, required fifty-two days.

Xylophone's Grandpa

The glockenspiel is a percussion musical instrument dating from medieval times. It was originally a kind of small carillon or set of bells played mechanically. In the 16th century the instrument was given a keyboard, and in the 19th century the keyboard disappeared and hammers were used to strike the bars. Mozart was the first composer to use the glockenspiel, in his opera *The Magic Flute*.

The California Board of Equalization has ruled that bartenders cannot be held culpable for misjudging the age of midgets.

The mightiest creature of the seas — the whale — has legs. But don't expect to see a whale walking — for the whale's legs are vestigial.

Nearly one million women in the United States go hunting.

In the United States a baby is born every eight and one half seconds.

Steadfast

Bobby Sands, a leader in the Irish Republican Army, was serving a 14-year sentence in Maze Prison, outside Belfast, for firearms possession. Without leaving his prison cell, Mr. Sands managed to be elected to the British Parliament!

Mr. Sands achieved still another, unfortunately fatal, distinction. Demanding that I.R.A. prison inmates be treated as political prisoners instead of as ordinary criminals (which, if granted, would allow them to wear their own clothing and be exempt from prison labor), Mrs. Sands launched upon a fast. After some 56 days of fasting, he was given last rites. He died on the 66th day of his fast. Prime Minister Thatcher refused to concede to Mr. Sand's demands. Other Maze prisoners took over the battle, fasting unto death.

About four hours are required to boil an ostrich egg.

Easy to Miss

If the whale is the biggest creature in the sea, the goby is the smallest. The freshwater dwarf goby lives in streams and lakes in the Philippine Islands, and grows to be one-third of an inch long! The marine goby lives in the Marshall Islands in the Pacific Ocean, and although it is somewhat larger than the freshwater goby, it generally weighs less. In fact, it may weigh only two milligrams, which means 17,750 of them to an ounce!

The goby is almost transparent, and, as you see, easy to overlook.

The standard fee for stuffing a lion is $800, a deer's head $90, and if you find a taxidermist who wants to undertake stuffing an elephant, he will probably charge around $14,000.

Many Eskimos live on the ice-covered sea in igloos above the sea. They have found it is often warmer on snow and frozen water than on the frozen earth.

In the northern forests of North America temperatures drop to 60 degrees below zero. It is so cold that the breath and perspiration of animals turn into a smoky vapor called *biofog*. Reindeer or musk-ox herds are quickly hidden in this fog of their own making.

Flies but no Fleas

Swarms of mosquitoes and flies come with the Arctic summer. The Arctic lowlands during the early summer have more mosquitoes to the square mile than any other region in the world. And the flies—so small they slip through screens and netting—bite just as painfully as their southern relatives.

However, the Arctic *is* free of one pest. There isn't a single flea to bother the foxes, wolves, or Eskimo dogs.

The ostrich can cover 25 feet in one stride.

Pastime Repasts

The noted polltaker, Louis Harris, reported that when he asked Americans what their most important leisure activity was, 54% of the men said eating, and 41% said watching television.

The women weren't very different from the men in their responses. The same proportion, 54%, said eating, but 47% said reading books.

CONSTABULARY

In 1963, the Common Council of New York ordered the mayor to provide the police with shoes and stockings, a coat of livery, and a badge, at the city's expense. And ever since we have dressed our cops in diverse ways throughout generations.

Whether you find cops hateful or lovable may depend less on their personalities than on which side of the bars you see them through, so to speak.

On these pages, you will find a few examples, both American and European, that have been captured by the pen of the artist.

Police Gazette

Punch, 1876

Punch, 1870

Munsey's Magazine

Wilhelm Butch Album

Century Magazine

Strand Magazine

Quaint Cuts

63

Snake Courtship

During the mating season, several male snakes may be attracted to one female. Each tries to win her. Male vipers, rattlesnakes, and other serpents attempt to become the successful Lothario by rearing from the ground and shoving each other around. They will place their bodies, one against the other, and push. During this struggle, these snakes will never bite each other. The strongest male will remain to mate with the female.

The Aesculapian snake puts on a very spectacular performance during courtship. A male will begin by slowly following a female and flicking his tongue against her scales. As she moves away, he follows. On and on they rush through grass, over boulders, and up and over shrubs. After a long chase, the male catches up with the female and twines his neck about her. She now contentedly goes along with him.

The only American serpent that will rush at a human being is the black racer. This serpent can frighten the wits out of someone who doesn't know that the snake is only bluffing. Like most snakes, the black racer is completely harmless.

This snake is normally timid; but once a year, during mating season, the black racer acts as if he is ferocious. If someone walks too close to where his mate is hiding or is sunning herself, he rushes out to protect her. Weaving and hissing noisily, the black racer will charge straight at the intruder as if it intended to strike him down. However, if a man stands his ground,

the black racer quickly drops his hostile pose and slips away. But if the person becomes frightened and starts to run, the black racer may give chase. However, he never carries his bluff very far. As soon as he has demonstrated his courage, he glides back to his nest.

Worms Don't Turn

Young Christopher Hudson of Brighton, England has an unusual hobby. He trains worms for racing. He has five, but is counting on the best of the lot, a 12-inch earthworm he calls Willie. Christopher feeds Willie chocolate and cabbage, a diet he claims increases the worm's speed.

Christopher used to train racing snails but gave them up for worms. He claims that worms are less trouble because they need less training; they instinctively go in a straight line and do not turn.

A Tree Is a Friend

Some of us may hate to see a forest cut down because "Only God can make a tree," but there's sound scientific as well as esthetic ground for concern.

The problem is that the amount of carbon in the earth's atmosphere has been increasing. The increased use of fossil fuels releases tremendous quantities of carbon dioxide. Plants store carbon within their tissue, which they do not release back into the atmosphere until they decompose. When forests are cut down, the trees no longer absorb carbon. Moreover, the vegetation on the cleared land actually contributes to the carbon released into the air.

Scientists anticipate that if the atmospheric carbon continues to increase at the present accelerated rate, it may ultimately lead to a rise in global temperature. This, in turn, might lead to such changes as melting polar icecaps and shifts in climate that could affect crops.

It's an Ill Wind

Everybody knows that if you want to know how to dress on any given winter day, you need to know not just what the temperature will be, but also how windy it will be. Given the same temperature, a calm day will feel much warmer than a windy day.

Arctic explorers and military experts have worked out tables to show the "wind-chill factor," or the combined effects of wind and temperature. Thus, for example, when the temperature is 20°F and there is little or no wind, that's exactly how it will feel to the skin—20°F. But should the windspeed rise to five miles per hour, the same temperature (20°F) will feel like 16°F; and if the windspeed goes up to ten miles per hour, the same 20°F temperature will fell like 2°F to you; should the wind begin to rage at 15 miles per hour, you will feel the temperature as 6°F below zero!

The Reason for Seasons

As both the sun and the earth rotate, their positions in relation to each other give us light and dark, hot and cold. The equinox marks the time at which the sun seems to cross the celestial equator. This happens twice a year. The vernal equinox, which marks the beginning of spring in the Northern Hemisphere, occurs on March 21st. The autumnal equinox takes place around September 21, and marks the beginning of fall in the Northern Hemisphere.

On the two days of the equinox, night and day are each 12 hours long in all parts of the world.

When the sun is directly overhead at the Tropic of Cancer at noon, this marks the summer solstice. This occurs around June 21, which is the first day of summer in the Northern Hemisphere, and the day in which the daylight lingers longest and the nighttime is shortest.

When the sun is overhead at the Tropic of Capricorn at noon, it marks the winter solstice. This, the beginning of winter in the Northern Hemisphere, occurs around December 22.

Hot Stuff

The sun is the star that is closest to the earth—a mere 93 million miles away. Without heat and light from the sun, there would be no life on earth. Fortunately, sunlight (traveling at the speed of light—186,000 miles per second) traverses the distance from sun to earth in about eight-and-a-half minutes.

Compared to the earth's diameter (right through the middle) of about 8,000 miles, the sun's diameter is 864,000 miles, or more than 100 times as much. This gigantic orb is essentially a huge ball of hydrogen, with a surface temperature of about 11,000° F, and interior temperatures that can be as high as 25,000,000° F.

The sun moves in much the same way as does the earth; that is, in terms of direction, not rate. The sun rotates on its own axis clockwise as does the earth. But, while it takes the earth 24 hours to complete this rotation, it takes the sun about 30 days to complete its rotation.

And, just as the earth revolves around the sun, so the sun revolves around the Milky Way galaxy. It takes the earth one year to revolve around the sun (moving at about 18.5 miles per second). The sun travels at about 150 miles per second, but it takes about 225 million years for the sun to make one complete orbit.

The proportion of American adults with at least a high-school diploma has increased within the last ten years from about 33 per cent to more than 60 per cent at latest estimate.

The famous cherry trees that encircle the Tidal Basin in Washington, D.C. generally burst into bloom at the beginning of April, and like many other things of beauty, are highly ephemeral, lasting but one week.

The trees were a gift from the mayor of Tokyo to the city of Washington. They were first planted on March 27, 1912, by President Taft's wife and the wife of the Japanese ambassador.

Hotel Chic

In 1829, the Tremont House which opened in Boston wanted to make a splash, so to speak, and was the first hotel to install bathrooms and toilets. It had eight water closets and eight bathing rooms.

It was the year 1844 when Irving House, a hotel in New York City, announced a bridal suite, the very first nuptial quarters.

And, in 1859, wanting to rise above it all, the then six-story Fifth Avenue Hotel opened in New York City, with the first elevator ever in a hotel.

Susan and Tim Frommelt of Dubuque, Iowa spent a June vacation in Wausau, Wisconsin. It was fine, except that their cat, Tiger, got lost and couldn't be found. So the Frommelts had to go home minus a pet.

But suddenly in February guess who showed up? Yup, Tiger the cat. He had journeyed 250 miles by himself. Nobody but Tiger knows how he managed to cross the Mississippi.

In 1966, England almost lost the World Soccer Cup. It came about this way: The famous cup was on display in a shop window in Westminster. Suddenly, it disappeared.

Some time later, the famous cup was unearthed in a garbage pail by a dog named Pickles.

Fetch a Wave for a Getaway

Weathermen and oceanographers using instruments and complicated calculations can often tell how strong a storm is, how big it will grow, and how long it will probably last. From these predictions—and knowing the *fetch*, or distance over which the storm-built waves can travel without meeting any obstacles, such as islands or continents—the scientists can tell approximately how high the largest waves will be.

They know that to raise the giant forty-foot waves of the worst storms takes winds of sixty miles an hour, blowing steadily for two whole days over a nine-hundred-mile *fetch* of open ocean.

When a storm prediction has been made, this information is radioed to ships at sea. A ship's captain can then alter his course to avoid being delayed too much by the storm, a procedure that has come into practice only with the advent of modern communication.

Perrier, Anyone?

Water dissolves almost everything with which it comes in contact, so that it is virtually impossible to have strictly pure water. Rain water is traditionally water in its purest form, but even that has absorbed air and ammonia.

In 1980 Exxon's sales exceeded $100 billion.

How Dry I Am

A "drought" is distinguished from any other dry spell of weather when the rainfall over a period of three weeks is but 30 per cent of the average for that period and place.

007 Lives Again

James Bond aficionados can heave a sigh of relief. After 14 years of quiescence, 007 is resuming his activities as the world's most famous spy.

Gildrose Publications, a subsidiary of Booker and McConnell, which owns the Ian Fleming copyright, has chosen the English writer, John Gardner to take up the Fleming mantle. The new, somewhat changed, but still charming and urbane Bond is the hero of *License Renewed*. This should mark the renewal of a lively career for Mr. Bond, for Mr. Gardner (who is not to be confused with the American writer of the same name) is quite a prolific author. He already has 23 novels to his credit and intends to continue doing both the Bond series and his other tales.

How far away is the moon? About 240,000 miles. If you traveled around the earth going either around the poles or around the equator, you would traverse a little under 25,000 miles.

A song in *South Pacific* explains that "You've Got to Be Taught to Hate"—it's not instinctive. Experimental psychologists are proving that this is true.

Probing the origin of likes and dislikes, Terry F. Pettijohn of Ohio State University in Marion injected a Mongolian gerbil with lithium chloride after it had spent five minutes with another Mongolian gerbil. This chemical induces stomach-ache, which the injected animal apparently associated with his playmate.

The gerbils were released in an open field. Gerbils that had not been injected displayed normal behavior—they approached other gerbils and sniffed them. However, gerbils that had been injected displayed fearful behavior, avoiding the other gerbils and retreating to a corner.

It's Disheartening

In summer, the Eskimos eagerly await the return of the whales. For whale blubber is a staple of Eskimo diets, and whale skin is used for making water-tight skins for Eskimo kayaks. And whale meat is, say the Eskimos, delicious.

The Eskimo whale hunt is a simple one. The men wait until a whale surfaces to spout and refill its lungs with fresh air. Then they all fire their weapons at its heart.

Hitting the heart of a whale is not so difficult as it might seem. In line with all of the whale's other gigantic proportions, the whale's heart is as big as a barrel!

Eggsactly!

Why are some eggs white and some eggs brown? Actually, the mystery is not why there are two colors, but why aren't there more? In the old days, when chickens ran wild, the differences in eggs were a matter of protective coloration. The differences in color were related to variations in breeds. The hens of a brown breed produced eggs with a brown shell, while the white breeds created white shells.

Why there are differences in prices for white and brown eggs is probably related only to their availability, since the shell color has absolutely no effect on the taste or nutritional value of the egg.

The first successful operation separating Siamese twins who had been joined at the skull took place on May 29 and 30, 1979 at the University of Utah Medical Center in Salt Lake City. It was executed by a team of 20 surgeons and nurses and took 16½ hours. Now, Lisa and Elisa Hansen, who spent their first 19 months of life head-to-head, are happily leading separate lives.

High Jinks

The flea, believe it or not, cannot fly. It's a jumper. It jumps from one animal to another.

The flea has no wings, but compensates for this by being able to jump 100 times its own height. That's equivalent to a person jumping as high as a 40-story building.

The novel *Les Miserables* by Victor Hugo contains one of the longest sentences in the French language. It consists of 823 words without a period.

Louder, Please

The first patent for a hearing aid was registered in April, 1880 by Francis D. Clarke and M.G. Foster. It made its own electricity and used bone conduction.

The first electrical hearing aid to be produced was invented by Miller Reese Hutchinson. It was marketed by Acousticon in 1901.

Around 1935, Edwin Stevens of London put the first battery-operated hearing aid on the market. He called it the amplivox, and it weighed 2½ pounds.

The Sonotone Corporation began to manufacture and sell transistor hearing aids in 1952. They were quite tiny, weighing just 3½ ounces.

Don't Scratch, Stir

If you are plagued by mosquito bites and you can't stand the itching any longer, hie thee to a drug store and get 50 grams of powdered alum, 10 grams of aromatic vinegar, and 10 grams of glycerine. Mix these together and apply them to your skin, and the itching will be soothed.

There are over 20 college "Bowl Games." The most famous are the Rose Bowl Game in Pasadena, the Sugar Bowl Game in New Orleans, and the Cotton Bowl in Dallas. Others that you may not have heard of are: The Boardwalk Bowl Game in Atlantic City, the Gator Bowl Game in Jacksonville, Florida, the Ohio Shrine Bowl Game in Columbus, the Peach Bowl Game in Atlanta, the Sun Bowl Game in El Paso, and the Tangerine Bowl Game in Orlando, Florida.

Bette Davis committed one of the greatest boo-boos of her career when she turned down the role of Scarlett O'Hara for the film *Gone With the Wind*. Davis was under the impression that the male lead would be played by Errol Flynn, and she just refused to work with him. The role of Scarlett was finally awarded to Vivien Leigh, playing opposite Clark Gable in what turned out to be one of the masterpieces of the cinema.

Destructive Construction

In 1883, the Brooklyn Bridge spanning Brooklyn and Manhattan was constructed, and during the construction 20 lives were lost. Compare this to the building of the Madeira-Mamore Railway which was completed in western Brazil in 1912. During the construction, more than 6,000 people lost their lives due to malaria, poison arrows from Indian attacks, snake bites, etc.

President John Tyler was the father of 15 children.

Some of the great men of history have grown marihuana. As a source of fiber, marihuana was actually a major crop in colonial America. George Washington imported seeds, and planted them in his vineyard at Mount Vernon, because he was interested in establishing an American industry in hemp. Thomas Jefferson planted an acre of marihuana at Monticello in 1811, because he wanted to research hemp.

Theodore Roosevelt planted fields of mari-huana and other drugs on his "prison farm" in Washington, D.C. in 1904, so he wouldn't have to import these drugs into the United States.

The great Swedish scientist, Carolus Linnaeus, who is recognized as the father of modern botany, planted marihuana on his windowsill in 1760.

Shiver my Timbers

There was a lady in Chicago by the name of Annetta Del Mar who thought of a unique way to achieve fame. She would freeze her body, all but her head, in ice. For the New York World's Fair, held in 1939, she would have herself frozen as often as 30 or 40 times a day. When asked how she did it and managed to survive, she answered "Will power."

It is generally considered that the best TV and radio newscaster was Edward R. Murrow, who flourished during the 1950s. He was greatly admired for his courage in confronting Joseph McCarthy, the rabble rouser of the Senate, when all the rest of the broadcasting professionals withdrew for fear that McCarthy might chew them up.

When Murrow died, Eric Severeid said "He was a shooting star, and we will live in his afterglow a very long time."

A male kangaroo is called a boomer; a female is a flyer; and the young are called joeys.

Maine is the only state in the United States that adjoins only one other state.

The game of volleyball was invented in 1895, by William G. Morgan, physical director of the Young Men's Christian Association in Holyoke, Massachusetts.

There are some 850 active volcanoes in the world. Over 75 percent of these are to be found within the so-called Ring of Fire, an area stretching along the west coast of the Americas from Chile to Alaska, and along the east coast of Asia from Siberia to New Zealand. The greatest concentration is in Indonesia.

The plow was first patented in 1797 by Charles Newbold, a New Jersey farmer. It was made of cast-iron and did not find favor with farmers.

In 1837 the first steel plow was made by John Deere, a blacksmith in Grand Detour, Illinois, who produced them in association with Leonard Andrus.

More than 90 percent of flowers have an unpleasant odor, or no odor at all.

The age of a mountain sheep is determined by the number of rings on its horns.

The Greek philosopher, Thales, in 585 B.C. accurately predicted an eclipse of the sun.

Windfall

Steve Jakubowski, operator of the HyLo Gas Station in Milwaukee, Wisconsin, wanted to deposit his cash in the bank. He put the $500 in an envelope, took one of his deposit slips and put it in the envelope, and went out to his car. But then he remembered he had forgotten something. He put the envelope on the roof of his car and went back into the station office to get what he wanted. He got it, and finally drove off.

David E. Sellnow and his wife were driving on the far south side in Milwaukee when dollars started raining down on them. They got out of the car and scooped up as many bills as they could find. They took the money, which added up to $246, and the deposit slip which they also found, but which had no name on it, to the Greendale Police Station. The police chief called the Southgate National Bank, which had issued the deposit slip, and they traced the account number on the slip to the HyLo Gas Station.

So Steve got back almost half his money. He had, of course, returned to his car and driven off, forgetting that he had left the envelope on the roof. What happend to the other $254? Gone with the wind.

Normal adults and growing children require one gram of protein daily for every 2.2 pounds of body weight.

To qualify for burial in Arlington National Cemetery, the 420 acres of land in Virginia across the Potomac from Washington, D.C., one must have been a member of the armed forces, a Medal of Honor winner, or a high-ranking Federal government official (or a dependent of one). Presidents William H. Taft and John F. Kennedy are buried there. So are General Pershing and Admiral Peary. The Tomb of the Unknown Soldier is also to be found at Arlington National Cemetery.

Taking It In Stride

In a stunning upset, Summing won the 1981 Belmont Stakes, carrying off the $170,580 purse. The favorite (4-5), Pleasant Colony, came in third behind Summing (7-1) and Highland Blade (13-1).

Pleasant Colony had won the Kentucky Derby and Preakness. Had he won at Belmont he would have been the 12th horse in 62 years to sweep the classic Triple Crown. The 11 who won the trinity are:

Sir Barton	1919
Gallant Fox	1930
Omaha	1935
War Admiral	1937
Whirlaway	1941
Count Fleet	1943
Assault	1946
Citation	1948
Secretariat	1973
Seattle Slew	1977
Affirmed	1978

As it was, Pleasant Colony joins another eminent group of racers, becoming the 10th horse to have won the Kentucky Derby and Preakness but not the Belmont Stakes. The other nine are:

Pensive lost to Bounding Home	1944
Tim Tam lost to Cavan	1958
Carry Back came in 7th, Sherluck won	1961
Northern Dancer came in 3rd, Quadrangle won	1964
Kauai King came in 4th, Amberoid won	1966
Forward Pass lost to Stage Door Johnny	1968
Majestic Prince lost to Arts and Letters	1969
Canonero II came in 4th, Pass Catcher won	1971
Spectacular Bid came in 3rd, Coastal won	1979

The five most populous cities in the world, according to latest figures, are Shanghai, Tokyo, New York, Peking and London.

It *is* as you suspected—there *are* more divorces today than ever before. The National Center for Health Statistics reports that the number of divorces granted in the United States tripled between 1959 and 1979, and the rate more than doubled. In 1959 there were 395,000 divorces; in 1979 1.18 million.

The median length of the marriages that ended in divorce was 6.8 years in 1979.

The highest divorce rate was in the West, the lowest in the Northeast.

With political corruption making daily headlines, and with elected officials serving jail terms, one can't help but marvel at the fact that the word CANDIDATE derives from the Latin root *candare* which means *to be shining white*, White, of course, symbolizes purity.

The meaning of the root originated with an old Roman custom. When a man ran for public office in ancient Rome, he bought himself a toga—a long, shining, white cloak. With this garb, the candidate stood out in the crowd. The people took notice of him and, because of his white garment, associated the candidate with purity and goodness.

Life expectancy at birth 100 years ago was only 38.3 years for males and 40.5 years for females. At latest estimate, life expectancy at birth is 68.3 years for males and 75.6 years for females.

The largest palace in the world is the Imperial Palace in the center of Peking, China. It covers an area of 177.9 acres.

The single record that has the highest sales record to date is an old favorite, *White Christmas* by Irving Berlin. The Bing Crosby recording of this number, made May 29, 1942, has sold 25 million copies, and other recordings have sold over 100 million.

Leading Normal Lives

"Siamese twins" are two separate, identical organisms, each a complete or nearly complete individual. While such births occur with some frequency, only rarely do the twins survive.

Siamese twins may be joined at either the chest, the abdomen, the back, or the top of the head. In cases where the twins share a vital organ, surgical division is not possible, and the twins must go through life together, just as Chang and Eng did in the last century.

Chang and Eng were born on May 11, 1811 of Chinese parents in Maklong Siam (whence the name for the condition). They were joined at the breastbone, but were otherwise fully developed, independent beings. They toured with P.T. Barnum's circus for years before settling down as farmers in North Carolina. They adopted the last name of Bunker—why, no one knows—and simultaneously married two daughters of a farmer named Yates.

Chang and Eng each ran his own farm one mile from the other's. How, you ask? Chang and Eng would spend three days of each week with one wife and three days with the other wife. What they did on the seventh day, the Lord only knows.

They lived very happily in North Carolina, and between them produced 22 offspring. When one twin died on January 17, 1874, the other survived for only two more hours.

A Shift in Ocean Currents Killed Almost a Thousand Million Fish

In the spring of 1882, New England fishing boats returning from the fishing grounds about a hundred miles off the coast, reported finding millions of dead and dying tilefish floating on the surface of the sea.

The beautiful yellow-spotted tilefish abounded on the fishing banks—or shallow waters—off the New England coast because of the warmth brought to these waters by the Gulf Stream. These fish did not actually live in the Gulf Stream itself, but the warmth of the stream tempered the water they did live in.

It has been estimated that dead fish covered an area of 15,000 square miles. Altogether, a thousand million fish had probably perished!

What caused all these fish to die? Heavy spring gales evidently had forced the course of the Gulf Stream farther off shore than ordinarily. As a result, cold water flowed in over the banks to kill the tilefish, which were accustomed to warmer water.

Uninvited Guest

How would you like to have your breakfast interrupted by a visit from a deer? One January morning in 1979 people who were dining in the Sears, Roebuck cafeteria in a suburban Indianapolis, Indiana shopping mall had just that experience.

The deer had evidently wandered into the parking lot in search of food after a heavy snowstorm. American civilization apparently overwhelmed the poor deer and it panicked, crashing through the window and into the dining room. (Or maybe it was just in a hurry to be seated!) The deer was finally captured and turned over to the Indianapolis Humane Society, where it was treated for cuts (and a broken antler.)

In case you wondered, the Statue of Liberty which stands in New York Harbor is approximately 20 times life size.

Breakfast Champion

Shredded wheat was the very first breakfast cereal put on the market. It was created by one Henry D. Perkey of Denver, Colorado in 1893. Breakfasting in a Nebraska hotel one day, he met somebody who was eating wheat boiled with milk. Since Perkey happened to have very poor digestion, he was immediately impressed by this idea, and worked at it to develop what has now become a favorite breakfast for millions of Americans.

One Big Gulp

As you would expect, everything about whales is on a gigantic scale. The sperm whale, for instance, has such an immense gullet that it could easily swallow a man in one gulp without hardly noticing it.

It might have been a sperm whale that swallowed Jonah, in the Bible story. But how he could get out of the whale alive is not so easy to explain.

Man's first flight into the stratosphere was achieved in May of 1931, when the famous physicist, Professor August Picard, ascended in a balloon from Augsburg, Germany, and reached a height of 51,790 feet in a 17 hour flight.

Stainless steel, a valuable alloy of iron, is noted for its ability to resist rust and tarnish, and the effects of heat and water. It contains about 74 per cent steel, 18 per cent chromium, and 8 per cent nickel.

In Triplicate

If you happen to be a tour guide, it's very easy to memorize the facts about the Church of the Trinity in Waldassen, Germany. The secret for remembering the details is the number three. For this unusual house of worship has:

Three towers and three turrets. And each turret has three dormer windows.
Three roofs and three openings in each roof.
Three windows and three doors in each part of the structure.
Three large crosses and three small crosses.
Three altars and three staircases.
Three doorways and three columns.
Three lights and three niches.
Three bays and three windows in each bay.
Three statues of the Virgin Mary.

What's more, the designer of the church was Georg Dientzhofer, himself the third architect in his family. The building of the church took exactly 33 months, and 333 weeks, and 33 days. The cost? 33,333 florins and 33 kreuzer!

Britain's Salisbury Cathedral has been hailed by many experts as England's most beautiful house of worship. It has been described as a "great chiseled diamond in a setting of emeralds."

Another unique aspect of the Cathedral is that it is a kind of calendar hewed from stone. It has as many doors as there are months in the year, as many windows as there are days, as many pillars as there are hours in a day, as many pieces of sculpture as there are minutes in an hour, and as many crosses for consecration as there are seconds in a minute.

The average American housewife opens 788 cans each year.

Snakes Alive!

One of the most unusual Buddhist temples of worship in the Far East is the Snake Pagoda at Arakan, Burma. Carved from stone, the outside of this 45-foot-high structure resembles a monstrous snake, coiled and ready to strike. Inside, however, the giant monument takes on the appearance of a Buddhist temple. The Snake Pagoda is widely believed to have miraculous curative powers. Indeed, persons bitten by venomous serpents are sometimes rushed to the shrine to pray for deliverance from death.

Have House, Will Marry

In East Java, instead of carrying the bride over the threshold, many a young man carries his house to the threshold of his hoped-for bride-to-be. The customary way for a young man to propose marriage in this Indonesian island is to carry a simple shelter on his shoulders to the home of his prospective bride and leave it there for a day or so. If the girl finds him acceptable, she makes two holes in the portable structure. These will serve as windows in the house once she occupies it as the young man's wife. Should the young fellow come back and find the house without holes the following day, he knows his proposal has been declined and he can try his luck elsewhere.

An Inca Rope Bridge Was Used For 500 Years

Bridges were sacred to the Incas, who called them "little brothers of the roads." Anyone caught tampering with a bridge was condemned to death.

Most famous of the Inca bridges was the *Apurimac-chaca*, which got its name because it spanned the Apurimac River. Later, during the Spanish rule, it became known as the Bridge of San Luis Rey. Built around 1350 A.D., the bridge was in use for more than five hundred years.

The Bridge of San Luis Rey was a suspension bridge supported by cables almost 150 feet long and as thick as a man's body. These cables, twisted and intertwined to give them strength, were made of the same raw material as modern rope, the *agave* plant.

Borne down by its own considerable weight, the bridge sagged in the middle. The wide span also swayed dangerously during high winds. No wonder then that the first Spaniards to cross the bridge were frightened. But the surefooted Incas crossed the bridge with a confidence rarely achieved by the white man.

In the 1870's, engineers constructing New York City's Brooklyn Bridge employed some of the same techniques devised hundreds of years before by the Incas. In other, less technical, respects, the Inca bridges were also like many bridges of today. On both sides of each bridge stood a toll station, and travellers had to pay to cross.

Plankton Makes the Red Sea Red

Plankton often colors the surface waters of the ocean. When conditions are favorable, plankton suddenly becomes very abundant. It may color the water brown, red, white, green, or yellow, depending on the kind of plankton involved.

These plankton blooms, or *red tides* as they are sometimes called, are particularly common in certain warm seas. The Red Sea, east of Africa, was so named by the ancients because its waters are often tinged red by plankton blooms. The Gulf of California, lying between Lower California and Mexico, is also called the Vermilion Sea because of the frequent red tides there.

In 1958, along the coast of Southern California, a vast tide colored the waters a tomato red for miles. At night, the water glowed with a mysterious green light—a light produced by the millions of small organisms that caused the red tide. Unlike some other red tides, this one did not kill large numbers of sea creatures.

Stick 'Em Up

We all learned in history class that in seeking a short route to India, Columbus not only discovered America, but demonstrated that the world was round, not flat. How did he do this? Simply by not falling off the face of the earth.

But long before 1492, in fact, in the third century B.C., an Egyptian named Eratosthenes performed an experiment that showed that the earth was round. He planted one stick vertically at Syene, and another vertical stick at Alexandria, 500 miles to the north. At Syene, the sun was overhead and cast no shadow, while at Alexandria the sun threw a long shadow. Not only did this show the roundness of the earth, but it made it possible to estimate that the earth's circumference was about 25,000 miles.

The Marianas Ocean Trench is Over Six and a Half Miles Deep

Many deep, narrow trenches, or chasms, are found in the floor of the Pacific Ocean. These trenches are the deepest parts of the ocean. Although you might expect to find the deepest parts close to the center of the ocean, these trenches are actually located near the continents and island chains.

The six-and-a-half-mile-deep Mindanao Trench, near the Philippine Islands, was thought until recently to be the deepest in the world. As a result, it is probably the best-known. The Marianas Trench in the West Pacific, however, has the greatest measured depth. This tremendous chasm at its deepest reaches down to somewhere between 35,290 and 35,640 feet—almost seven miles—below the surface of the sea

The Dominion of Canada has a greater land area than the continental United States.

A Coat of Many Colors

Few Indians have had a better understanding of color than the ancient Peruvians. This may be seen in their weaving, for centuries an important art form in Indian culture. Studies of the ruins of the Tombs of Paracas disclosed that as many as 190 different hues were used in the making of cloth.

The Chimus, who preceded the Incas in Peru were famous for their long tunics made of feathers. Sometimes they cemented the feathers together, but usually they attached the feathers to a cord and stitched this cord to a fabric.

The feathers commonly used were those from domesticated macaws and parrots. But the richest of their garments were covered with the feathers of rare birds from the tropical forests.

Crocodile Soup

In Malaya, the crocodile sometimes finds man to be a delectable dish. In the wilds of Africa, it is the other way around. Of course, the crocodiles eaten are much smaller than the Malayan monsters.

African pygmies enjoy eating crocodile meat so much that they will hunt these reptiles in preference to other game. These people have become very adept at capturing and killing the awesome giants with their primitive weapons, so much so that the crocodile is almost extinct in parts of pygmy territory. Only a few years ago, streams and rivers in pygmy country swarmed with the monsters. Now, in many places in Africa, it is possible to travel for days without seeing a single crocodile.

At one time, pioneer settlers in the southern United States ate alligator meat, particularly the flesh of the tail. However, this was usually a matter of necessity when no other meat was available. Few people ever developed a taste for alligator meat. Today, only the most venturesome try it out of curiosity.

Ulderico Longobardi left his truck parked on the street in Naples, Italy. Next thing he knew, his truck was gone. Mr. Longobardi just wished he could have been there when the thief looked inside the truck. Mr. Longobardi is an undertaker, and had 100 empty coffins in his truck.

Venus, the planet nearest Earth and the brightest in the sky, rotates around the sun at a much faster rate than it spins around on its own axis. It completes one revolution around the sun in about 225 days, while it completes one rotation on its axis in about 243 days. Thus, Venus' "day" can be said to be longer than its "year" (by Earth's measures.)

As Grandpa used to say, "People are dying every day who never died before." If it seemed to you that a great many notable people died during 1979-1980, you're right. Here are some of them:

Joy Adamson, author of *Born Free*, "mother" of Elsa
Cecil Beaton, English designer
Al Capp, cartoonist, author of *Lil Abner*
Gomer Champion, choreographer
Harold Clurman, stage director and critic
Jacqueline Cochran, aviator
John Collier, English author
Oliva Dionne, father of the famous quintuplets
Helen Gahagan Douglas, U.S. representative
William O. Douglas, Supreme Court justice
Jessica Dragonette, soprano
Jimmy Durante, comedian
Ann Dvorak, actress
Mamie Eisenhower, Ike's First Lady
Jame Froman, singer
Erich Fromm, psychoanalyst and author
Alfred Hitchcock, filmmaker
Jose Iturbi, pianist and conductor
Oskar Kokoschka, Austrian expressionist painter
Andre Kostelanetz, conductor
Sam Levenson, humorist
George Meany, labor leader, head of AFL-CIO
Elliott Nugent, actor, writer, director
Merle Oberon, actress
Jesse Owens, track and field star
Mohammad Riza Pahlevi, Shah of Iran
Jean Piaget, Swiss psychologist
Katherine Anne Porter, writer
Stanley F. Reed, Supreme Court justice
Richard Rodgers, composer of hit musicals
Lillian Roth, singer and actress
Muriel Rukeyser, poet
Jean-Paul Sartre, French existentialist philosopher
Dore Schary, film producer
Peter Sellers, English actor
Archbishop Fulton J. Sheen, Catholic author and preacher
C. P. Snow, English scientist and writer
Josipi Broz Tito, president of Yugoslavia
Darryl E. Zanuck, film producer

Winning Is Losing

When August Gary Muhrcke of Huntington, New York won a race he made a big mistake. Mr. Muhrcke raced up the 85 flights of stairs of the Empire State Building in 12 minutes, 32 seconds, coming in (or up) first out of 14 contestants.

The problem is that after 11 years of service in the Fire Department, Mr. Muhrcke was retired with a back injury. The 37-year-old retired fireman was receiving a sizeable tax-free disability pension. When the news of Mr. Muhrcke's feat got out, the deputy fire commissioner felt that the pension board should review the case.

On August 29, 1778, during the American Revolution, black soldiers fought alongside white soldiers against the British and Hessians in the Battle of Rhode Island. The blacks were slaves who had been freed for the emergency.

Stairways to the Stars

The tallest building in the world is the Sears Tower in Chicago. It stands 1,450 feet high, and was completed in 1974.

The runner-up is the World Trade Center in New York City, which consists of two buildings, each 1,350 feet high. Third place is held by the Empire State Building of New York City, which was completed in 1931 and towers 1,250 feet into the sky.

Spring Tides at Mont-Saint-Michel Travel Forty-four Miles a Day

Off the coast of Brittany in France rises a small rocky island known as Mont-Saint-Michel. On the island stands a beautiful abbey which was built over twelve hundred years ago. Tourists come from all over the world to visit the abbey. So that people can reach this famous landmark at high tide, a causeway, or raised road, has been built across the tidal flats from the coast.

At low tide, however, Mont-Saint-Michel becomes part of the mainland of France. At that time as much as eleven miles of land lie exposed above the retreating waters. This means that every twenty-four hours the tide travels back and forth a distance of about forty-four miles. The tide advances as a shallow flood at the speed of a fast walk.

What's New?

The gnu has the feet of an antelope, the mane and body of an ass, the head and humped shoulders of a buffalo, and the beard of the goat.

The earliest pendulum clock was manufactured in 1656 by the Dutch scientist, Huygens.

Chinese Americans represent less than one percent of the United States population. Despite the fact that they have been an almost constant object of discrimination and violence, the Chinese Americans today earn, on the average, higher incomes than white Americans, have longer and better educations, and have a greater proportionate representation in the professions.

Boo!

Remember the scarecrows farmers made to keep crows out of their crops? The same idea is used in some areas of Africa's Sudan by native farmers to keep rats and mice out of their rice.

The farmers construct special granaries in the form of scary masks. After harvesting their crop, the farmers store the rice in these masklike granaries, hoping they will frighten the hungry rodents to death.

Have you ever envied royalty their privilege and power? Don't. In the days before the French Revolution, court protocol and procedure were very rigidly defined. If a queen wanted a glass of water, she didn't just get up and take it. The request had to go through channels while the thirsty queen waited. The footman would bring in a silver plate on which there were a covered gold cup and a small carafe. This he handed to the *dame d'honneur*, who in turn handed it to the comtesse, who could then give it to the queen.

Felix Mendelssohn, the famous German composer and musician, made his debut as a pianist at the age of 10, began to compose while only 12, had written an opera, several symphonies, and the *Midsummer's Night's Dream* overture before he was 17.

A Fish of Extinction

About 300 million years ago, in the Devonian period, the first amphibians began to appear on earth. These were thought to have emerged from the lobefins, a group of lunged fish, with paired stumpy fins that may have been the precursors of limbs.

The lobefins were thought to be extinct, but in 1938 a live coelacanth (a branch of the lobefins) was caught. Since then other coelacanths have been caught. These five-foot long fish with vestigial lungs are "living fossils."

Fishing is a sport to some, a business to others, but there is no doubt that man finds the fish a very useful animal. Just look at the cookbook section in any bookstore to get an idea of the variety of ways a variety of fish grace man's dinner table.

But man uses fish for other purposes as well. Glue is made from fish bones. The shark's skin provides elegant leather for shoes, bags, wallets. It is also used to make a high grade sandpaper called shagreen, used by cabinet makers for sanding expensive woods. And how many of us have grown up without encountering cod liver oil? The oil of the whale used to be used in lamps in olden days, and is still used commercially today in some products, such as soap.

Shaky Foundation

The Miss U.S.A. Pageant, initiated 30 years ago, was sullied with the first taint of scandal in 1981. It seems that Miss New York, a young lady by the name of Deborah Ann Fountain, had padded her bathing suit! So, for the very first time, a contestant was disqualified.

Incidentally, the contestant ultimately chosen winner of the Miss U.S.A. title was Kim Seelbreede, a 20-year-old modeling instructor from Germantown, Ohio.

If you've ever tried to make saffron rice, you know that saffron is one of the most expensive spices in the world. How come?

Saffron comes from the crocus flower. Specifically, it comes from the stigma of the plant. The stigma is the female pistil which receives the pollen produced by the stamen, or male organ. Over 12,000 stigmas are needed to produce one ounce of saffron.

Practically the only memory of Sylvester Graham that remains is the graham cracker, but in his day (1794-1851) Graham made quite a stir. This Presbyterian minister advocated a vegetable diet as a cure for intemperance. In 1847, his pitch for whole wheat bread was so powerful that the bakers of Boston rioted, intent on lynching the mad enthusiast. He espoused taking cold showers, sleeping on hard mattresses with the windows open, and eating coarsely ground whole-wheat cereals. Graham flour was named for him. Apparently, he was just ahead of his time—he would have been delighted to see the current proliferation of health food stores.

The Studebaker was a good car, but it stopped being made in 1964. Mr. Tom Hazzard of Idaho thinks they're so good that he collected 60 of them.

Friday, the 13th of January, 1967 is a date Miss Alice Prior of Sunnyside, Queens, New York is not likely to forget. The evening before, when Miss Prior was getting ready for bed, she had run some water in her bathtub and was sitting on the side of the tub. She happened to slip and fell backward into the tub, where she became wedged in. Try as she might, she could not extricate herself. She cried out for help, but nobody heard her.

She spent the rest of that night, as well as all of the next day, Friday, the 13th, crammed into her bathtub. About 6:00 A.M. on Saturday morning, a next-door neighbor thought she heard some moans. She went and got the superintendent and they went into Miss Prior's apartment, where they thought the sounds were coming from. Sure enough, they found the poor woman trapped in the tub. They called a police emergency squad to get her out and get her medical attention.

Isn't it time someone designed a bathtub that's easier to get in and out of?

The most common hand in Bridge has a suit distribution of 4-4-3-2. You're likely to be dealt a hand like this one out of four times.

The least likely distribution in Bridge is all 13 cards in one suit. The odds are you'll be dealt a hand like this once out of 158,753,389,899 times.

There are 132 rooms in the White House.

What do you do if your dog becomes deaf? Buy him a hearing aid, of course. Ray Berwick noticed that his dog, Jake, was not hearing his commands so well. Jake, who has been in the movies and on TV, performs at Universal Studio's guided tour for visitors. Mr. Berwick had Jake fitted with an ear mold, but the dog kept shaking it out. So now he's equipped with a bone conduction type hearing aid.

Is the penny obsolete? The United States Mint, anticipating the nation's future coinage needs, is asking this question.

With inflation, the purchasing power of the penny is mighty slight. No coin has a face value equal to the material of which it is made, but in the current economy it is foreseeable that the value of the copper in the penny will exceed the coin's face value. Of course, the penny could be made of a different metal, as was done with the other coins. Still, 10 billion pennies are minted each year, so even using an alloy the cost would be high.

It is conceivable that the U.S. could go back to coining a two-cent piece, which went out of circulation in 1873. However, the Treasury Department's attempt to revive the two-dollar bill was not a roaring success. Nevertheless, the banks, the vending machine operators, and numismatists are watching carefully to see what will happen.

A black woman who had been an orphan and had supported herself as a scrubwoman and laundress became the first self-made millionairess. Madame Charles Joseph Walker, born in 1867, became a successful cosmetician and amassed a fortune selling a hair straightener.

John Patterson and his younger brother, Fred, worked together at the Brewster Aircraft Company in Pennsylvania until Fred enlisted in the Army in 1939. John joined the Air Force in 1943. After that the brothers lost track of each other.

One morning in January, 1967, a cook at a Holiday Inn in Atlantic City, New Jersey noticed a waiter make a facial expression and decided that he had to be his brother. He was. John Patterson had been working as a cook, and Fred Patterson as a waiter in that restaurant for three weeks without recognizing each other. No wonder—it had been 28 years since they had last seen each other.

Where There's No Will

The ranks of the despairing have included many an admired and noted personality, such as Ernest Hemingway, Virginia Woolf, Freddie Prinze, James Forrestal.

Jack London, born in 1876, committed suicide at age 40. His books, *The Call of the Wild*, *The Sea Wolf*, and *White Fang* had won wide acclaim. During a highly checkered career, he worked as a sailor, an oyster pirate, a hobo, a gold prospector, a war correspondent, and a factory hand. He wrote 51 books, and most of them were translated into a dozen different languages. Why would he take his own life? Because his alcoholism and his poor diet resulted in severe illness. He simply didn't want to live to endure the pain of uremia, rheumatism, and assorted digestive ailments.

First published when she was only eight years old, Sylvia Plath committed suicide when she was but 31. During her short span of life, her poems and short stories were published in leading magazines. She continuously wrote about death, and attempted suicide many times. She is considered by many to be a superior poet.

Want to gain weight fast? A body on the surface of the sun would weigh about 28 times as much as it weighs on earth.

Want to lose weight fast? A body on the surface of the moon would weigh about one-sixth of what it weighs on earth.

It's all a matter of gravitational pull.

Better Late Than Never?

One day in 1976 Mr. Lorne Gascho of Elkton, Michigan opened his mailbox and found in it a penny postcard addressed to J.G. Gallman, who was his grandfather. Examining the card, Mr. Gascho found that it had been postmarked January 8, 1908!

Did you hear about the man who lived through his own funeral? Joseph Cormier of Toronto, Canada had gone to Hamilton, Canada in search of a job. When he returned home, he found his house empty, and sensed that something was wrong. He picked up the phone and called his wife's father. Then he knew something was wrong. As soon as his father-in-law recognized his voice he dropped the phone, apparently in a dead faint.

It seems that while Joseph was away his family received news that he had died. His wife was out making arrangements to fly the body home, ordering a coffin, and flowers. The relatives had been informed of his death.

Joseph got home just before the body arrived. Apparently it belonged to another Cormier.

The world's first novel is said to be *The Tale of Genji*, created by Lady Murasaki Shikibu about the year 1015. This long romance provides an excellent portrait of medieval Japanese court life.

To Top It Off

Sir Edmund Percival Hillary climbs mountains because they're there. He and Tenzing Norkay of Nepal were the first to reach the top of Mt. Everest, the highest mountain in the world.

If you're a climber, the highest tree, the highest mountain, the highest building presents a challenge. In May, 1977 George Willig scaled the World Trade Center tower in New York City.

But the Sears Tower in Chicago topped the World Trade Center, making it an inevitable target. So, on May 25, 1981, Daniel Goodwin, a 25-year old stunt man from Las Vegas, Nevada hitched a rope and suction cups and, dressed in a bright blue and orange Spiderman outfit climbed the Sears Tower, the tallest building in the world. It took him seven and a half hours to scale the 110-story, 1454 foot high building.

He was arrested when he reached the roof.

Stamped with Talent

Like a lot of other kids, Donald Evans was a stamp collector. But Donald Evans' fascination with stamps was somewhat unusual. By the time he was 15, he had a collection of about 100,000 stamps. But he also had a collection of imaginary stamps—that is stamps that he had drawn to represent imaginary countries that he had invented.

Evans studied art and architecture at college, and in 1972 he sold his stamp collection to his father, and went to live and pursue his unique interest in Holland. Here he created myriads of imaginary stamps for imaginary places. His mind was fertile and his artistic skill was dexterous. His motifs included all sorts of objects and animals—dominoes, apples, whales, beer, shells, mushrooms.

Unfortunately, Evans died before he was 32 years of age.

In 1978 41,216 books were published in the United States. The category with the greatest number of titles was Sociology/Economics, with 6,465. Second was fiction, with 3,693 titles.

Using Your Noodle

In 1971, when Pat Nixon, the wife of the President, was voted "Macaroni Woman of the Year" by the American Macaroni Institute, her likeness was sculptured in macaroni.

Unearthly

The Earth which we inhabit so briefly is itself about five billion years old. Its total area is about 197,000,000 square miles, of which 70% is land and 30% water. The weight of the Earth is over six and a half sextillion tons. (A sextillion is one followed by 21 zeros.)

If you dug down through the Earth's surface, you would not get to China because what you would have to go through is: 20 miles of rocky crust; then about 1,800 miles of solid rock with temperatures of 1600°-to 4400°F; another 1400 miles of molten iron and nickel with temperatures of 4000°F to 9000°. This would bring you to the Earth's center or Inner Core, a ball of solid iron and nickel with a temperature of about 9,000°F. After you penetrate this, you'd have to work your way through the second half.

This massive, ponderous ball of Earth moves around the sun at the rate of 18½ miles per second and takes but a year to complete this orbit.

Sarah, in the Bible, gave birth to Isaac at a ripe old age, but she had some special help from the angels. The oldest mother on record, with certain proof, is Mrs. Ruth Alice Kistler. She gave birth to a daughter in Glendale, California in 1956, when she was over 57 years old.

London, England, was the first city in the world to attain a population of 1,000,000 persons. Today its populatioon is about 7,000,000.

Sing Sing, the famous prison in New York where Lewis Edward Lawes was warden for many years, actually took its name from the village in which it is located. The town of Sing Sing was incorporated in 1813, but was renamed Ossining in 1901. So if you thought it had anything to do with special talents of the inmates, be disabused.

Locked in a Trunk

For 30 years, the Greek town of Vostitza on the island of Zante maintained its local jailhouse in the trunk of a tree. From 1791 to 1821, the hollow trunk of a giant platan, or plane tree served as the local lockup. The prisoners' quarters were quite roomy since the tree had a circumference of more than 50 feet

Volcano ash has been known to remain hot for a period of nearly one hundred years.

The Pentagon is equipped with some 25,000 telephones—is there some kind of communication problem?

Kharkov Prison in Russia is the largest prison in the world, and has, at times, accommodated 40,000 inmates.

Goldbrick

Sea water contains large amounts of gold. But before you equip yourself with skindiving equipment to go panning, keep in mind that the average amount is about one grain (or five cents worth) of gold to one ton of sea water. That means the cost of recovering it would exceed its value. Sorry.

The largest English-speaking city south of Miami, Florida, is Kingston, Jamaica.

As Fat as a Crocodile

The saltwater crocodile will generally weigh more than a horse. The average horse will tip the scales at around 950 pounds, and the crocodile will be 150 pounds more than that.

Approximately 16,000 conventions of various kinds are held in the United States each year.

Copy Cat

Photocopiers, these days, seem to be all over the place. Most of us think of the copier as a very recent invention.

The fact, however, is that the first photocopier was marketed back in 1907 by the Rectigraph Company of Rochester, New York. It had occurred to George C. Beidler, the inventor, that there was a constant need for duplication of legal documents, and this realization led him to search for a better means than laboriously typing copies by hand. Beidler patented his invention in 1906.

But Does It Wear a Jumpsuit?

Although a small snake—rarely reaching a length of three feet—the stout, large-headed jumping viper has a most savage disposition. It attacks in a most remarkable manner.

Most snakes, when striking, keep the greater part of their bodies firmly on the ground while shooting their heads forward to bite. By contrast, the jumping viper flings itself at its enemy in a spectacular jump that lifts it completely off the ground and propels it upward in the air as high as two feet.

Sick as a Fish

Fish can get sick just as you and I can. They can catch cold (although nobody has seen a fish sneeze), and they can get upset stomachs. Fish can also suffer from more serious diseases such as tuberculosis and dropsy. Dropsy is an accumulation of surplus water in the body tissues—an odd disease for a fish to get!

Heart Attack

If you have ever seen a fisherman land a fish, you saw the fish flop and wriggle about with terrific energy before it finally quivered and died. We have always thought that the fish out of water died because of lack of oxygen. But scientists tell us that the fish died not because of a lack of oxygen, but because the violent struggle to get free of the hook literally exhausted the fish to death.

A pig always sleeps on its right side.

The Aging of America

What is called the median age is the age that would divide a country into two equal halves; that is, half the people in that country would be younger than that age, and half the people would be older. Because of improved living conditions, and advances in medical science, the number of older people has been rising steadily. In the past decade, the median age in the U.S. rose to 30 years from 28.

The Census Bureau reported that from 1970 to 1980 there was a 28 percent increase in the number of people over 65. The number of children under the age of 15 dropped by over 12 percent.

If you've suspected that women live longer than men, you're right. There were six million more females than males in the U.S. in 1980.

Money From Heaven

The John D. and Catherine T. MacArthur Foundation of Chicago has hit upon a unique way of distributing its money. After months of secret search, 21 "exceptionally talented individuals who have given evidence of originality, dedication to creative pursuits and capacity for self-direction" were chosen as recipients of awards ranging from $24,000 to $60,000 annually for five years.

The awards are outright gifts, with no strings attached—no projects, no reports, no requirements whatsoever. The intention is to give these geniuses creative freedom in the hope that their own talents will impel them to come up with "discoveries or other significant contributions to society."

The recipients range widely in age and in area of specialization. The oldest winner, Robert Penn Warren, is 76 and will receive the maximum award of $60,000 per year. Robert Penn Warren is a distinguished novelist, poet and critic who concerns himself deeply with the moral dilemmas faced by man and society. He won his first Pulitzer in 1947 for his famous novel *All the King's Men*, a second in 1958 for his collection of poems, *Promises*, and a third in 1979 for his poetry collection, *Now and Then*.

The youngest award winner, Dr. Stephen Wolfram, 21, will receive $24,000 a year. Dr. Wolfram is a research associate in physics at the California Institute of Technology. His field of specialization is quantum chromodynamics, which involves him with things like quarks and gluons.

A man whose normal weight is 150 pounds would weigh about 50 pounds if all the water in his system were extracted.

The fish in Mammoth Cave, Kentucky have lived for generations in the dark. Their optic nerves have become atrophied and they are quite blind.

PEDAGOGUES

The earliest schools were affiliated with religious organizations. Then, little by little, governments began to support existing schools through tax money. Then public schools were started, completely supported by government tax money. And ultimately compulsory education laws saw to it that every child had some schooling. The laws varied considerably as to the span of years that was subject to compulsory education, but for most children there was no way to avoid the school experience.

One study indicated that when people were asked to recall early school experience, it was the unpleasant experience that was most often remembered, Freud notwithstanding. Whether your school experiences were happy or miserable, you probably had some teachers you loved and some you could have done without. Perhaps you'll find them in this gallery of teachers from the past.

Bundle of Sunshine

Lustige Blätter

Punch, Vol. 25

Rabelais

Harper's, Vol. 58

Life

Birds Can Hear Worms Under the Grass

Coverings of special feathers protect the bird's sensitive ear openings located just below and behind the eyes. The feathers are like bristles and do not interfere with the faintest sound waves.

Some birds can hear the sound of a tiny insect crawling across a leaf, or the far-distant warbling love song of a mate, or even the crawling of an earthworm under the grass.

In one experiment, owls were blindfolded and placed on a perch near the ceiling of a room. Mice were released in the room and ran around the floor. The owls, relying solely upon their hearing, were able to swoop down to catch the mice. They did not go after *dead* mice, so that it was clear they were hearing, not smelling, them.

Underwater Earthquakes Produce Gigantic Waves

One important reason why underwater trenches greatly interest oceanographers is that many earthquakes occur in their vicinity. The island nation of Japan, which lies near one of the great trenches, has suffered many times from earthquakes and the gigantic waves caused by them. Often these huge waves are mistakenly called *tidal waves*, but they have nothing to do with the tides.

The U.S. record for a single snowstorm is 175.4 inches at Thompson Pass, Alaska, on December 26-31, 1955.

O

n March 8, 1976, the largest meteor in history fell near the Chinese city of Kirin. It weighed 3,902 pounds.

The bluejay has a life span of four years, the robin 12, the sparrow 20. And if you give your canary TLC, it may be able to fulfill a life span of 24 years. But the raven tops them all with a possible span of 69. Is that why he kept protesting Nevermore?

The Conquering Heroes

The greatest conqueror in human history was Genghis Khan, who was born around 1167. Between 1206 and 1227, this Mongol chieftain conquered nation after nation and swept through and annexed to himself 4,860,000 square miles—practically everything from the Pacific Ocean to the Black Sea.

Although more famous than Genghis Khan, Alexander the Great, 356-323 B.C., the Macedonian king, conquered approximately 2,180,000 square miles, less than half the land span that fell under the sway of the Mongol. Alexander held all of the Balkan Peninsula, Egypt, all of Asia Minor. His domain extended as far as the Indus River of India.

Tamerlane, who was born around 1336 and claimed to be a descendant of Genghis Khan, conquered almost as much land as Alexander the Great. And Cyrus the Great, who flourished around 550 B.C., also conquered approximately 2,090,000 square miles.

These four conquerors make Attila the Hun seem like a second-rate runnerup. Of course, Attila, in roughly 440 A.D., controlled most of Europe.

Richard Bach's *Jonathan Livingston Seagull*, published in 1970 by Macmillan, was turned down by 18 publishers before Macmillan took a chance. By 1975, over seven million copies of the book had been sold in the United States.

Perhaps the very first list that appeared was The Seven Wonders of the World, compiled by Philon in ancient times. This included: the Pyramids of Egypt, the Hanging Gardens of Babylon, the Colossus of Rhodes, the Mausoleum at Halicarnassus, the statue of Zeus by Phidias at Olympia, the Temple of Pharos, Artemis at Ephesus and Sostratus' Lighthouse, at Alexandria.

Oh! Calcutta!

World travelers might not agree on much else, but most of them would accord Calcutta, India the honor, or dishonor, of being the poorest and most overcrowded city in the world. With a population of over three million, Calcutta is the second largest city in India. Thousands of people sleep in the streets every night, where they lay claim to a little portion of pavement as their "home." The amount of begging that goes on in Calcutta dwarfs the imagination; the poverty in this city is utterly disheartening.

Many people think the expression "the black hole of Calcutta" describes the blighted city today, but in reality, the term refers to the small room in which the nawab of Bengal imprisoned the Calcutta garrison when he captured the city in 1756.

Name Your Home State

There is a spot in the United States where a house could conceivably be built with each of its four corners in a different state. That spot is at the common meeting point of Utah, Colorado, Arizona, and New Mexico.

Canada is composed of 12 provinces, and the capitals of some of them are rather well known. For example, the capital of Manitoba is Winnipeg, the capital of British Columbia is Victoria, and the capital of Ontario is Toronto. But did you know that the capital of the Northwest Territories is Yellow Knife, or that the capital of Yukon is White Horse?

Now You See It, Now You Don't

Exceptionally strong winds in central Asia's Gobi Desert have been known to cause sand dunes to move as much as 65 feet in a day.

The deepest part of the ocean yet discovered is in the Marianas Trench, in the Pacific Ocean, near the Philippine Islands. A metal object, for instance a pound ball of steel, dropped into the water above this trench would take nearly 63 minutes to fall to the sea bed 6.85 miles below.

Beating a Hasty Retreat

Flying has reached a new stage of development today in the jet plane. But Nature gave the evil-appearing octopus a jet propulsion engine ages ago.

The eight-tentacled devilfish, an American species of octopus, can squirt a powerful stream of water through a tube that is part of its body. The octopus moves in reaction to the pressure of this stream of water, just as a jet plane is powered by its reaction to the thrust of powerful rockets against the air.

The octopus has one handicap, however. His "jet tube" points in only one direction—forward. This means the octopus can jet-propel himself in only one direction—backwards.

This is the reason why the octopus can move backward with amazing speed, but can move forward only in a slow and clumsy crawl.

It's a Matter of Degree

Temperature, obviously, measures warmth or coolness in degrees. The trouble is, the size of a degree is not fixed but depends on the particular temperature scale. Temperature scales use the boiling point of water and the melting point of ice as their two reference points, and then divide the difference between these two points into a dozen number of degrees. The Celsius (or centigrade) scale takes 0° as the melting point and 100° as the boiling point and divides this up into 100 degrees. The Fahrenheit scale (used mostly in the United States) takes 32° as the melting point and 212° as the boiling point, and divides this up into 180 degrees.

If you hear the temperature given in Celsius degrees and you're used to Fahrenheit, don't be alarmed. Just remember that a Fahrenheit degree is smaller than a Celsius degree. One Fahrenheit degree, in fact is 5/9 of a Celsius degree.

Should you want to convert from Celsius into Fahrenheit, multiply by 9, divide by 5, and add 32. To go the other way, from Fahrenheit to Celsius, you more or less reverse the process; subtract 32, then multiply by 5, and divide by 9.

Simple, no?

Please Don't Smoke Me Out

The original Smokey Bear was rescued by forest rangers in 1950. An orphan, he was found clinging to a charred tree in the Lincoln National Forest in New Mexico. After his burned paws were treated and he was nursed back to health, he went to live in the National Zoo in Washington, where he became one of the most popular animals among visitors. Clad in his forest ranger's hat, Smokey won international fame as a symbol of the campaign against forest fires.

Smokey died at the age of 26 and was buried back home in Capitan, New Mexico, near where he was first found. The new Smokey is another orphaned cub from New Mexico.

Live Toothpick

The Egyptian plover dines in one of the strangest way. It has worked out a mutually satisfactory arrangement with the crocodile. The bird gets food. The crocodile gets service.

The plover rides on the crocodile's back and serves as a lookout, giving shrill cries to warn the crocodile of any approaching danger. It digs out parasites as it rides on the tough hide back of the reptile.

And when the crocodile finishes its dinner, it opens its mouth so that the small bird can hop inside and pick its teeth clean of uneaten food. The crocodile seems to understand the services performed by the plover, for the reptile never tries to kill and eat the little bird.

Teacher, What's A Million?

A very ingenious math teacher is Mrs. Debby Tvriek of the Algona Middle School in Iowa. In order to give her pupils some idea of just how much a million is she dreamed up a special project. She had the children collect the pull tabs from beverage containers. They stored them in huge cartons, keeping tabs on the number collected by individuals, as well as on the cumulative total.

Just 15 months later, they reached their quota and made their dramatic presentation. They dumped all the tabs on the stage so everyone could see what a million looks like.

Divide And Conquer

As anyone who has ever thrown dice knows, a number can be broken up in different ways. The larger the number, the greater the possible ways to compose it. For example, the number 5 may be composed of any of the following combinations:

$$5 + 0$$
$$4 + 1$$
$$3 + 2$$
$$3 + 1 + 1$$
$$2 + 2 + 1$$
$$2 + 1 + 1 + 1$$
$$1 + 1 + 1 + 1 + 1$$

The number 200 can be divided up in almost four trillion ways—3,972,999,029,389 to be exact.

Stone Walls Do A Prison Make

It happened in Killingworth, Connecticut. The police arrested Dale J. Pauk for stealing a stone wall. Mr. Pauk was loading fieldstones from the wall into his truck. He was charged with criminal trespass and third-degree larceny.

Robert J. Netto, a 19-year-old gas station attendant won the grand prize in New York State's lottery. Mr. Netto, who is a newly-wed, is looking forward to the $1,000 a week he will receive for life. He's young, with a good life expectancy, but the guaranteed minimum payment of one million dollars sure makes a feller feel comfortable.

The Pacific Ocean is the largest body of water in the world—measuring about 64 square miles in area. The shortest straight navigable line across this ocean would be between Bangkok in Thailand and Guayaquil in Ecuador, a distance of almost 11,000 miles.

Take It To Heart

What's the difference between measuring your pulse and measuring your blood pressure? Well, they both have to do with the pumping action of the heart. The pulse indicates the rate of the heartbeat, and the pressure indicates the force of the blood coursing through the arteries.

When the heart contracts (during systole) it spurts blood into the aorta, the major artery leaving the heart. The aorta becomes distended to receive this increased blood volume. Then the heart relaxes (during diastole); the blood volume in the aorta decreases and its walls contract. This propels the blood out of the aorta and through the other smaller blood vessels throughout the body (the arteries, capillaries and veins). It takes about a quarter of a second for a wave of blood to go from the aorta to the arteries in the soles of the feet. The pressure of the blood diminishes as it runs through the smaller blood vessels, and is at its lowest in the veins.

When the doctor takes your pulse rate, what is usually being counted is the pulsations per minute in the radial artery in your wrist. The normal rate for adults is 70 to 90 pulsations per minute. For children the normal rate is 90 to 120. The doctor observes the force of the pulse as well as the rate and rhythm.

When the doctor takes your blood pressure, an instrument known as sphygmomanometer is attached to your arm and the pressure in the brachial artery is measured. Normal pressure for young people is 120 over 80 (or 120 mm. for systolic pressure and 80 mm. for diastolic pressure). As you grow older, there is a constriction or hardening of the arteries and the blood has to work harder to get through. Blood pressure at age 50 normally increases to about 140 to 150 over 90. Physical activity, nervous or emotional strain may cause increases in blood pressure.

The commonest non-contagious disease is tooth decay. Almost nobody is able to escape this.

The commonest contagious illness is the common cold. Almost nobody is able to escape this.

Adam vs. Pithecanthropus

In 1925 John T. Scopes was tried for violating a Tennessee law that prohibited teaching theories that contradicted the Bible's account of creation. Scopes had been teaching Darwinism in his biology classes in a Dayton, Tennessee public school. In the famous trial, marked by memorable rhetoric, Scopes was defended by Clarence Darrow, among others, and prosecuted by William Jennings Bryan, among others.

Darrow argued that the law was unconstitutional because it violated academic freedom as well as the separation of church and state. Bryan proclaimed, "You believe in the age of rocks; I believe in the Rock of Ages," and preached, "I would rather begin with God and reason down than begin with a piece of dirt and reason up."

Scopes was convicted, but later released by the State Supreme Court on a technicality. The law was repealed in 1967.

In 1981 there seems to be a return to an anti-evolution movement, in a new movement called scientific creationism. The Creation Research Society, organized in 1963, is finding increased support in the Moral Majority movement.

The founders of the Creation Research Society claim to be strongly committed both to science and to a literal interpretation of the Bible. They are opposed to evolutionary theory and claim that the Bible's account of creation can be validated by scientific evidence.

Today, in many states, there is a movement to enact legislation that would require public schools to present the Biblical creation as a scientific model along with the theory of evolution.

You're playing a board game and when it's your turn you get just one chance to roll two dice. What are you most likely to get? The chances are you'll throw a seven; the odds are you will get this one out of five times. The next most likely throw would be a six or an eight. The odds of throwing a two or a 12 are 35 to 1.

How long is a day? 24 hours, of course. Well, not exactly. Subjectively, of course, some days fly by, and some days drag out endlessly. Objectively, there are slight differences depending on the measuring scale.

One day is the time it takes for the earth to make one complete rotation of its axis. The 24-hour day is actually the mean solar day, or the time on the average that it takes the sun to be directly overhead on two successive days.

The sidereal day is about four minutes shorter than the mean solar day. Sidereal time is measured relative to the stars rather than the sun. The sidereal day is the time, on the average, it takes for some chosen star to be overhead on two successive days.

There's a lovely mnemonic device in common use for those who know the names but can't seem to remember the order of the planets. The ditty "My very educated mother just served us nine pizza pies" will help remind you that starting from the sun, the planets are: Mercury, Venus, Earth, Mars, Jupiter, Saturn, Uranus, Neptune and Pluto.

It's Never Too Late

A 53-year-old grandmother from London, England made a solo voyage across the Atlantic Ocean in a 26-foot yacht. Her name is Shirley Ravenscroft. She sailed from Tenerife in the Canary Islands on January 4, 1979 and arrived in Barbados in the West Indies on February 11, taking 37 days.

Think about that when you're making your next New Year's Resolutions.

Ronald Spicer told the judge that his wife cut the buttons off his shirt to prevent him from going out. The 49-year-old machinist won the divorce decree.

Getting Hitched

A woman in London found an easy way of making a living. She marries. The marriage is arranged through a broker, who charges the groom over $600, of which the "bride" gets about $180.

The bridegrooms are Turks, Moroccans, Cypriots, Indians and Egyptians, who are illegal immigrants and are under the impression that marrying would give them legal status. The broker arranges for the bride and groom to meet; they sign a book, shake hands, and part, presumably to wait for the application to the Home Office for their residence rights to be approved.

The only hitch is that the woman has done this about 50 times using aliases and false addresses. The "grooms" remain illegal immigrants subject to deportation.

Edith Wharton, who was born to money, married it, and made a good deal of it from her novels, would sometimes take Henry James for rides through the countryside. Once, when she mentioned that the car in which they were riding had been paid for from the royalties of her last novel, James told her that with the proceeds of his last novel he had bought a cart which he would use to haul his guests' luggage from the railroad station to his house. He added that he expected that with the royalties from his next novel he might get enough money to have the cart painted.

An oxymoron is not some kind of bovine retardate, as you might think, but a figure of speech which combines contradictory elements. For example: *thunderous silence* greeted his speech; it was full of *solemn jest* which had the effect of imbuing everyone with *sweet sorrow*; all agreed that although the delivery was *awfully good*, the content was *mighty slight*.

Tooth Power

Eskimos have always been hearty eaters. Their diet consists almost entirely of meat and fish. They are excellent chewers. In fact, they are perhaps the best all-around chewers in the world, chewing for both pleasure and profit.

The Eskimo hunter, returning to his family after a long day's hunting, may have ripped the seams of his boots. He gives the untanned sealskin boots to his wife, who chews the stiff leather until it is supple enough to sew easily.

Chewing on tough dry meat and eating food containing sand has worn the teeth of many primitive Eskimos down to stumps. But the Eskimos' teeth and jaws are still stronger than most Americans', and can be used for tasks where hands are too weak.

Professor Leuman Waugh, of Columbia University's Dental School, analyzed measurements of Eskimos' biting power. A group of fifty-six Alaskan Eskimos, including men, women, and children, were tested. Their average height was only five feet four inches and their average weight was 126 pounds. Yet these Eskimos registered bite strengths of about 345 pounds. That was nearly twice as powerful as the bites registered by University of Minnesota football players. And the Americans averaged six feet in height and 178 pounds!

Vikings Accidentally Discovered America 500 Years Before Columbus

A great seafaring people were the Vikings, hardy Scandinavian warriors whose communities flourished from the eighth to the tenth centuries. The Vikings took to the sea because their rugged homeland, on Europe's glacier-carved northern shores, failed to supply all the food they needed.

These men of the North built large, open boats, fitted with both oars and a large square sail. The high prows of the Viking ships were often decorated with dragons and other monsters. In their hardy "dragon" ships, the war-like Vikings ranged far and wide. They sailed deep into Russia along the great rivers which flow from that land. They raided French and English coastal towns and terrorized other peoples living in northern Europe.

In time, the Vikings colonized some of the more fertile lands of their neighbors. Normandy in northern France received its name from Vikings, or *Norsemen*, who settled there. Normandy literally means "place of the North Men."

Other countries, however, stubbornly resisted Viking attempts to settle in their lands. So these mighty seafarers began exploring the North Atlantic in search of new regions to colonize. Sailing westwards, they discovered Iceland with its volcanoes and hot springs lying amid glaciers and snowfields. Still further to the west they found Greenland.

It was on a journey to Greenland in the year 986, that a Viking named Bjarni accidentally discovered America. His ship was blown off course by a severe storm. When the storm cleared, he saw a low-lying coast covered with trees—part of the continent of North America.

Bjarni did not touch shore. But upon reaching Greenland, he told his story to a young Viking named Leif Ericcson. In the year 1000, Leif as the brave captain of his own ship led an expedition to the coast of America. He called the new land Vinland for the wild grapes he found growing on vines there. We are not sure where Vinland was, but most historians now believe that it lay somewhere along the shores of southern New England, probably Cape Cod.

The Mouth of the Amazon River is 150 Miles Wide

High in the lofty snow-covered Andes Mountains rises the Amazon River. It runs eastward across the continent of South America flowing through the jungles of Brazil. Finally it empties through its enormous mouth into the Atlantic Ocean.

The mighty Amazon has more water flowing through it than America's Mississippi, Egypt's Nile, and China's Yangtze River put together. This is because the drainage basin of the giant South American river lies in one of the rainiest regions in the world.

In many places the Amazon is so broad that a man standing on one bank cannot see across to the other side. The mouth of this huge river measures 150 miles across.

Superlative

Asia, the largest continent in the world, with more than half the world's population, has the highest mountains, the deepest valleys, the greatest peninsulas, the hottest and the coldest regions in the world, some of the driest and wettest places on earth, and some of the most densely as well as the most sparsely populated areas in the world.

Without Benefit of Tintex or Clairol

If someone called you a chameleon, would it be a compliment? A chameleon is a pretty, friendly, little lizard belonging to a family made up of over eighty species of lizards.

The chameleon is justly famous for its amazing ability to change its color. For a time many people believed that the lizard did this in order to match its background. But this has been found to be untrue. Actually, the chameleon alters its coloring in response to changes in light, temperature, and its own emotions.

Have Water Gun. . .

The Siamese archer fish kills like an archer of old—or like a gunman of today. The archer fish shoots its insect victims down with "bullets" of water.

This fish likes to eat insects that live in plants and shrubs overhanging shallow streams. The archer hides just beneath the surface of the water and waits for an insect to land on a bush about four or five feet away.

Then the archer fish strikes swiftly. Taking aim with its beaked snout, the fish shoots a pellet of water at the insect. If the bullet strikes home—as it almost always does—the insect is knocked from its perch by the impact and tumbles into the water. Then the archer fish snaps and gobbles up his prey.

Slow Motion

Scientists have discovered an astounding fact about the Louisiana swamp alligator. Its body processes and mechanisms are very much like those in a human being—with one important difference. In the alligator, all these functions take place *eight times slower than in man*. Thus, watching an alligator's body processes is like watching those of a human being in slow motion. This is extremely helpful since it enables scientists to study the exact operation of certain organs which had baffled them, since in man these body processes were too swift to be easily studied.

Water Skiing

Ordinarily, the frilled lizard of Australia scurries around on all four legs like any other lizard. But if hotly pursued, it rears up on its hind legs and runs like a man. It tucks its front legs out of the way and takes off at great speed.

Even more surprising, however, are the large East Indian water lizard and the tropical American *basilisk*. They run on their hind legs across water—*not*, as you might imagine on floating vegetation but across plain open water!

These two lizard species are not web-footed, but have long toes equipped with fringes of scales along the sides. When they swim, they do not use their feet to propel themselves along, but, like the other swimming lizards, employ their long, flattened tails. Interestingly, lizards belonging to these two species also climb trees.

After John Lennon was assassinated in late 1980, letters of sympathy poured in to his widow from all over the world.

Unable to cope with the stacks of mail which inundated her, Yoko Ono wrote a full-page letter of thanks and placed it in newspapers all over the world. The cost of the ad was $200,000, making this the most expensive thank-you note in history.

Gold Storage

Near Poona, India, stands the Fortress of Purandhar, erected by the Rajah of Bedar in the year 1290. It is an imposing edifice, with a huge stone gate. This gate, alone among all the structures of the world, is built on a foundation of solid gold!

Before the fortress was erected, the Rajah's master builders informed him that the site chosen for the structure was swampy, and that the planned fortification could not survive for long on such terrain. Soon afterward the Rajah had a dream which advised him to first lay down a foundation of gold, then build the gate to his fortress atop the gleaming metal.

The Rajah ordered that two great holes be dug in the soft ground, each 35 feet square by 12 feet deep. Then he had 50,000 gold bricks removed from his treasury and thrown into the giant excavations. The weight of this gold totaled 37,500 pounds. At $600 an ounce, as gold was recently, that would be over $350 million worth of the precious metal!

The stone gates were then erected on this costly foundation. To make sure that his deed would not be forgotten, the Rajah had the story of the gate inscribed on two metal plates. The gate and the gold remain where they have been for more than six-and-a-half centuries.

Who are the most prolific people on earth? Without question, the Africans. In Kenya, Malawi, Botswana, Niger, Nigeria, Rwanda, Dahomey, and Togo the birth rate is better than 50 per 1,000 inhabitants.

There are three countries which do not have a standing army of any sort. They are Costa Rica, Iceland, and Malta. At the other extreme is Taiwan, where just about one of every thirty people is a member of the active armed forces.

Ever Hug a Whale?

For all its size and power and awesome appearance, a whale is a gentle, playful animal. A whale likes to bang its huge tail on the water and hear the noise that it makes and see the splash that it creates.

Whales also show affection. They do it by slapping each other with their fins, just as you show affection for a friend by slapping him on the back.

Whales play with one another and they play games with their little baby whales.

In fact, whales have a whale of a time!

Through Thick and Thin

Whales are pretty hard to wound. In the early whaling days, harpooners used to wonder why even their direct hits would often have little or no effect at all upon a whale.

The reason is that whales have a protective coat of fat, or blubber, under their skin. This layer of blubber is as much as eight inches thick. The blubber layer serves a dual purpose. It acts as a coat of armor, and it keeps the whale warm.

A whale will not even bleed when stabbed unless the weapon goes deep enough into its body to penetrate the blubber and reach the flesh beneath it.

But the whale lost this advantage over his enemy, the whaler, when the whaler put an explosive warhead on the tip of his harpoon. When the harpoon strikes the whale the impact detonates the explosive. The result is a giant wound in the whale's body.

Noah started it, and ever since pigeons have been used to carry messages. It is claimed that a carrier pigeon can see for 150 miles in clear weather, and that one of these grown birds is able to fly for 400 miles at a speed of 50 or 60 miles an hour.

Beware of Small Dog!

What dog is most likely to take a nip at your trousers, or to be otherwise uncivil?

According to a study made by the United States Public Health Service, the dog to be most feared for uncordial behavior is the German shepherd. Following close behind are these canine malefactors:

Chow chow
Poodle
Italian bull dog
Fox terrier
Airedale
Pekingese

Please note that the very largest of breeds, such as the St. Bernard, the Irish wolfhound, and the Great Dane, are relatively placid and cordial.

Nincompoop

The most amazing thing about the gecko is its empty head. The formation of its skull is such that there is nothing at all between the two tiny ears. You could actually look in one ear and see right through and out the other! Next time you want to tell someone he's got nothing between the ears, just call him a gecko.

Sediment Two Miles Thick Covers Parts of the Ocean Bottom

The sediment carried down to the sea by the rivers is made up of sand, mud, and silt. These substances have been produced from the weathering of rock that has been gradually worn away by the action of wind, water and climate acting upon it. This disintegrating process is called erosion. The land-derived sediments are usually found in greatest abundance close to the edges of the continents.

Although in some parts of the Atlantic sediment reaches a depth of two miles, it averages about half a mile thick over most of the sea floor.

In parts of the Pacific Ocean, the sediment measures only 1,000 feet, or about a fifth of a mile in depth. We see, then, that the amount of sediment covering the sea floor varies from place to place in the oceans.

The White Cliffs of Dover were Formed by Tiny Plants and Animals

The famous white cliffs of Dover—a landmark familiar to travellers approaching the south coast of England—are actually the skeletal remains of tiny organisms. At one time, millions of years ago, the sea covered what is now the southern coast of England. Over the many, many thousands of centuries, countless tiny skeletons were deposited on the ocean floor. Then the sea withdrew, and sections of the ancient sea bottom were raised up leaving the high white cliffs behind as a great tombstone to life that lived long ago.

Voltaire drank seventy cups of coffee every day.

Making a Living

It will come as no surprise that the nations with the highest per capita income today are not the Western nations, but the oil-rich countries. First on the list is Kuwait, with a per capita income of almost $16,000! Kuwait, incidentally, also has the highest average annual population growth rate, of 6.2%—at least they can afford it!

Qatar and the United Arab Emirates rank second and third respectively, with a little over $15,000 per capita income for each country. Switzerland ranks fourth, with a per capita income of close to $13,000; West Germany is only eighth; and the United States, with a per capita income of under $10,000, is in ninth place.

Obviously, per capita income depends on two factors: gross national product and population. Thus, in 1978, half the world's population was concentrated in 36 countries that had per capita incomes of $300 or less. These included such countries as Uganda, Guinea, Madagascar, Pakistan, China, Sri Lanka, India, Afghanistan, Bangladesh. How does that saying go—God must love poor people, He made so many of them!

In 1929 a seat (or "chair") on the New York Stock Exchange sold for $625,000!

The best recorded win-loss record for a racehorse was earned by "Kincsem," a Hungarian mare who, during 1876-1879 was unbeaten in 54 races.

The Riddle of the Sphinx

Legend has it that the famed Sphinx of Egypt would not let a traveler pass by safely unless he could answer this riddle:

What is it that walks on four legs in the morning, two legs at noon, and three legs in the evening?"

The answer was, of course, Man.

For in the morning of his life Man is a baby and crawls on arms and legs. In the high noon of his life, as a strong upright adult, Man walks erect on his two feet. And in the evening of his life, in his old age, Man hobbles about with the aid of a "third leg," a stick or cane.

The greatest money-winning racehorse of all time was "Kelso," who retired in 1966. In 63 races, he won 39 of them, placed second in 12 of them, and third in two, winning a total of $1,977,896.

Break a Leg!

Starfish like to feed on baby oysters. The oyster breeders would net the starfish, cut off their arms, and toss them helter-skelter into the sea, thinking that in this way they were ridding the oyster beds of a pest. Actually, instead of killing the starfish, the breeders were unwittingly creating five times as many new enemies for their baby oysters. Each of the parts of the original starfish will have grown a complete new set of arms.

The oldest European settlement in the New World is Santo Domingo, on the island of Haiti. It was founded in 1496 by Christopher Columbus.

The first U.S. President to ride in an automobile was Theodore Roosevelt, who rode in a purple-lined Columbia Electric Victoria, in 1902.

The Fish Are Jumpin'

The flying fish has greatly enlarged side fins, big enough to get a purchase on air almost the way the wings of an airplane do.

To escape its many enemies, the flying fish leaps out of the water and glides through the air on its side fins. In a single glide the flying fish can cover as much as 500 feet. And a flying fish's muscles are so powerful in relation to its size, it can jump completely over the deck of a small ship.

A Fish Out of Water

The Australian walking fish is an extraordinary creature. Its two strong fins are bent into such a position that it can stand and walk upon them. When the tide is out, the walking fish squirms playfully in the mud. Then it often takes a walk—right out of the water!

The crawling fish of Asia will never break any track-meet records, but it is the only fish that can leave the water and crawl for a mile or more over dry land.

When drought or some other calamity dries up the stream where the crawling fish lives, it climbs up the river bank and moves on its fins across the country. Instinctively it knows in which direction to head to find water.

The crawling fish can live out of water for as long as a week, living on a reserve water supply it stores in its body. Ashore, the walking fish spends its time hunting for insects to eat; then it climbs the lower branches of trees that grow along the water's edge, and roosts there for hours.

At least three other kinds of fish are also almost as much at home on land as they are in the water. One of these fish is the anaba, which can also climb trees to search for insects. The ugly frogfish can walk on its fins, too. And the hassar often makes long night marches on land to find a new pool when drought dries up one of its watery homes.

The Arctic musk ox, or *ovibos*, is an invaluable animal. It gives milk which is as rich or richer than a cow's and from which excellent butter and cheese can be made. Its wool is as good as the sheep's wool we use for our clothes, and in one way even better—for it will never shrink. But that is not all. An *ovibos* steak tastes just like the juicy grade-A-beefsteak sold at the butcher shop.

Life Begins at Forty

The Bible, it would seem, has a fixation on the number 40. During the flood, it rained for 40 days and 40 nights. Moses went up on Mount Sinai and remained there for 40 days and 40 nights. The Israelites, when they left Israel, spent 40 years in the wilderness. The Prophet Elijah spent 40 days and 40 nights in the wilderness. Jesus sojourned in the wilderness for 40 days.

The umiak—or woman's boat—is just as necessary to the Eskimo family as is the hunter's kayak. It serves as a means of transporting family, possessions, or cargo. Like the kayak, the umiak is covered with skins, but it is larger, open on top, and rowed by oars.

Sometimes as many as 13 persons—mother, father, children, and relatives—may crowd into a boat only 15 feet long. The tiny boat looks as if it is sure to sink. But it doesn't. The secret of what keeps it afloat lies in a lot of air-filled balloons, made from seal bladders or seal skins called *seal* pokes. Before the family gets into the umiak, the Eskimo blows up the balloons and ties them around the boat. Even with a heavy load, the umiak will stay above the waves.

When the Empire State Building opened in 1930, it quickly acquired the nickname "Empire State Building." It was only 25% rented. Today it is more than 99% rented!

Beware the Hungry Bear

The most dangerous animal in the Far North is the famous polar bear. This Arctic killer has the power in one lightning-like swipe of its paw to stun a ninety-pound seal and hoist it out of the water and onto the ice.

A hungry polar bear is far different from a polar bear with a full belly. When it needs food, the bear is absolutely without fear, a relentless killer. But once its hunger is satisfied, the polar bear becomes a good-natured, harmless cuss. Often it will poke a curious black nose out from behind ice or snow to sniff at man-scented air and watch the stranger.

The highest inhabited point in the United States is Point Barrow, Alaska.

The most southerly inhabited point in the U.S. is South Cape, Hawaii; the most easterly point is West Quoddy Head, Maine; and the most westerly point is Cape Wrangell in Alaska.

The highest uninhabited point in the U.S. is Mount McKinley in Alaska, and the lowest is Death Valley in California.

Don't Mess with the Wolverine

The wolverine, a cousin of the ermine, is the largest member of the weasel family. Like the ermine, it is a savage killer—striking with swiftness at any animal, even a large caribou. Although it weighs only forty pounds or so, and is a solitary hunter, this flesh-hungry creature's sharp teeth are feared throughout the Arctic.

The wolverine—rather than the Arctic fox—is the real sly animal of the Arctic. It can, in the words of one trapper, dig like a badger, climb like a squirrel, and jump the height of a man.

The wolverine will rob the most cleverly constructed traps. The French-Canadian trappers call it *carcajou*—glutton—because it will gorge itself whenever it can.

He Should Have Baked a Cake

Visitors to Salzburg in Austria often admire the huge Castle of Monatsschloss which overlooks the city. Built during the early 17th century, the immense edifice was a gift from Salzburg's ruler of the time, the Count of Hohenems, to his sweetheart, Barbara Mabon.

It seems that the Count had promised a castle to his lady love and then had forgotten about it until a month before her birthday. Determined to keep his word, he ordered thousands of masons, bricklayers, carpenters and other master builders to begin work instantly to keep his pledge. On the face of it, the task seemed insurmountable. To build a castle usually took years.

With the count's determination, and his subjects' hard work, they managed to achieve the impossible. Working in relays, day and night, and without pay, the count's subjects finished the job just in time for Barbara's birthday celebration. Monatsschloss still stands as a symbol of a romantic impulse—and is an unchallenged record for speed in castle-building.

The goldenrod has been falsely accused of causing hay fever. In fact, so lovely is this flower considered that both Nebraska and Kentucky have named it their state flower. There is even a movement afoot to make the national flower of the United States the goldenrod.

A temperature of about 125 degrees below zero is required to freeze alcohol.

There are millions of adherents of Buddhism, and all the world has heard of Buddha, but not too many know that his given name was Siddhartha and his family name Gautama.

The greatest depth of the ocean has been found to be something over six-and-a-half miles. A steel ball dropped into the Pacific Ocean at this depth would take over an hour to reach bottom.

The average depth of the Pacific Ocean is 14,000 feet.

Bathing Beauty

While porpoises like to frolic, the ocean sunfish likes to take a sunbath. Since he cannot stretch out on a beach like people, the ocean sunfish floats comfortably on the surface of the sea when the sun is shining brightly.

The Republican Party is represented by an elephant, and the Democratic Party is represented by a donkey. Where did these symbols come from?

Thomas Nast was a brilliant cartoonist whose cartoons were greatly instrumental in busting New York's Tweed ring. Nast created drawings of a donkey to symbolize the Democrats, an elephant to symbolize the Republicans, and a tiger to represent the voracious, wicked Tammany Hall.

Nast's influence was so strong that these symbols came to be permanently attached to the parties.

The first piano ever built was built in Florence, Italy, about 1720. It is now housed in the Metropolitan Museum of Art in New York.

Food for Thought

It took almost 30 chefs about four hours to put together the world's longest sandwich, at the second annual Culinary Arts Festival in Peekskill, New York. Masterminded by Franz Fichenauer, of General Foods in Tarrytown, the sandwich reached a length of 1,058 feet, 10 inches — about one-fifth of a mile.

No make-believe sandwich this, it was stuffed with goodies consisting of: 100 pounds of ham, 80 pounds of liverwurst, 60 pounds of cheese, 40 pounds of bologna, 40 pounds of chicken, 40 pounds of salami, 30 pounds of peanut butter, about 2,000 heads of lettuce, and some 5,000 slices of tomato!

Slices to a total of about 6,000 were sold for $1 each. The proceeds went to a local health center.

The first professional football game was played on September 3, 1895, in Latrobe, Pennsylvania. The Latrobe Young Men's Christian Association team beat the Jeannette Athletic Club team 12-0.

A clever bit of sea camouflage has been worked out by the decorator crab.

This crab collects bits of seaweed and sponge which become anchored to the hairs of his legs and his shell. Thusly attired, the decorator crab hopes that his enemies will mistake him for a clump of slowly-moving seaweed, and leave him in peace.

The largest iceberg on record covered 12,000 square miles; it was 208 miles long and 60 miles broad. It was first sighted November 12, 1956.

Motel Inn, in San Luis Obispo, California, was opened on the 12th day of December 1925 under the management of Hamilton Hotels. This motel is notable only because it was the first motel in the United States.

Lucky Strike

John Walker of Stockton-on-Tees in Durham, England, was a chemist. In 1826, Walker invented the match. The invention came about by accident.

Walker had been stirring a mixture of potash and antimony with a stick when he accidentally scraped the stick on his stone floor. The stick burst into flame, and Mr. Walker sold his first box of matches on April 7, 1827.

The wood splints of the early matches were cut by hand.

Joshua Pusey invented the book match in 1892. In 1896 it was manufactured by the Diamond Match Company.

A man-carrying glider was designed by Sir George Cayley in Yorkshire, England, as far back as 1852. The contraption was a kite-shaped wing with adjustable fin. The wing area is estimated to have been 500 square feet. This glider weighed 300 pounds.

Fluorescent lighting was developed by the General Electric Company at Neala Park, Ohio, in 1936. Commercial production of fluorescent lamps was begun by both General Electric and Westinghouse in 1938.

Augsburg, Germany, seems to be the first city in the world that had a fire engine. In 1518, a contraption for this purpose was constructed by Anthony Blatner. It appears that Blatner constructed a large lever-operated squirt mounted on a wheeled carriage.

Ulysses S. Grant was arrested for exceeding the speed limit while driving a team of spirited horses through the streets of Washington.

Fingernails grow faster than toenails.

No Warmongering, Please

The army of The Netherlands might not be out of place in a comic opera. Most of these soldiers are long-haired men, and they wear sneakers. A possible explanation for these anti-martial shenanigans is that the army is unionized. The union eschews protocol and discipline, and has put its disapproval on saluting. The union has close affiliations with pacifist organizations, and is not very eager to turn the Dutch army into fighting men.

The most expensive motion picture film ever produced was "War and Peace," the Russian adaptation of Tolstoy's novel. The total cost of this film has been stated to be more than $95 million.

Gurgle, Gurgle

You might think that since whales spout, they are well equipped to communicate by smoke signals. But whales don't need this old Indian device. They have excellent hearing and use sonar for underwater navigation and to communicate with one another.

During World War II, U.S. Navy technicians were puzzled when submarines picked up mysterious sound impulses on their sonar sets that they could not account for. Scientists investigated and found that these sound impulses were being sent by the natural sonar system of whales.

Imagine how puzzled the whales must have been by the sonar signals from the submarines!

Why do people like to sing in the bathtub? Because they can hear themselves easily in such a small, highly reverberant room. To say nothing of the uninhibiting effect of being clad in nothing but soap bubbles.

Good Reads

It is estimated that between 1815 and 1975, one and a half billion copies of the Bible were distributed by Bible Societies, making the Holy Scripture by far the best circulated book of all time. In the year 1979 alone, over 9 million copies were distributed.

The runner-up spot is held by *Quotations from the Works of Mao Tse-tung*, which has fallen into the hands of 800 million people.

Neither of these facts may be startling, but how about this one? In third place stands *The Truth That Leads to Eternal Life*, a publication of Jehovah's Witnesses, who have distributed 97 million copies since 1968.

Another surprise is *A Message to Garcia* by Elbert Hubbard, an inspirational book which, in 1899, took the United States by storm. Some 50 million copies of this tract have been printed and distributed.

It will come as no surprise at all that the *Guinness Book of World Records* has, since 1955, sold over 40 million copies in 23 languages.

In 1946, the famous pediatrician, Dr. Benjamin Spock, wrote *Baby and Child Care*. It would seem that from the way this book has been swallowed up, nobody is relying on grandma anymore for child rearing information. Spock's work has sold some 24 million copies.

Horatio Alger was a most prolific author. He wrote, and had published, 119 full-length novels in thirty years.

A watermelon is 92 percent water.

A Little Goes a Long Way

The average world rainfall is about 16 million tons of water per second. One inch of rainfall over one acre represents 113 tons of water.

One jelly bean contains seven calories.

The well-known military bugle call, *Retreat*, is of ancient origin. It is one of the few calls known to have been used by the medieval Crusaders.

There are about 10,000 geysers in Yellowstone National Park — more than in all the rest of the world together.

The Emperor's Clothes

Henri Matisse was and is accounted to be a great artist. In 1961, his painting *Le Batteau* was exhibited for 47 days. During that period, 100,000 people passed in front of the painting and admired it, but not a single one of them reported that the painting had been hung upside down.

ANIMALS IN DRESS

Some people may simply call it anthropomorphism, but as anyone who has ever cherished a pet will avow, some animals are more human than some people. Many illustrators have shared this conviction and have limned animals in human dress, to the great delight of children of all ages.

In these few pages we show some of the best illustrations of this type. The original source is noted below the picture.

Punch

Punch

Mark Twain's Library of Humor

Drawing by Grandville. *La Vie des Animaux*

Police Gazette

Strand, 1898

Punch

Bashful Earthquake

St. Nicholas, 1908

Mark Twain's Library of Humor

Life

Punch

Punch

Drawing by Grandville.
La Vie des Animaux

Fifty Years of Soviet Art

An Empire of An Emporium

The biggest department store in the world, R. H. Macy & Co. in New York City, sells more than 400,000 different items.

Rowland Hussey Macy opened the forerunner of this huge store in 1858. His small shop specialized in fancy dry goods—gloves, laces, linens, ribbons, hosiery, feathers, and the like. Macy's store was an almost immediate success. He employed 15 sales people and the store took in a total of $90,000 during the very first year.

By 1860, R. H. Macy's had become a department store. From dry goods it branched out to include chinaware, luggage, sporting goods and other wares. Indeed, by the time the year 1874 rolled around, the Macy enterprise had come to occupy the ground floor areas of 11 different stores. In that same year L. Straus & Sons, who sold wholesale crockery, began to provide the merchandise for two of Macy's departments. So successful was this joint venture, that Straus and Macy formed a full-fledged partnership. When, in 1896, Straus & Sons took over complete ownership of the business, they kept the name R. H. Macy & Company, Inc.

Eight Lives Left

Buddy, the pet kitten belonging to the Davidson family of Clarkston, Washington, was hurt in an accident. There was no pulse so the cat was thought to be dead, and the sorrowful family buried Buddy in a box in their back yard.

Five days later, eight-year-old Barbette Davidson was picking apples in the back yard. She heard what she thought was a cat's meow and called her sister Kelly. They dug up Buddy's box, to find the kitten very weak, but alive! Apparently, Buddy had gone into a coma after the accident, but managed to remain alive much in the way that animals hibernate. Anyway you look at it, it was a miraculous recovery.

The Halt Leading the Blind

It happened in Jackson, Mississippi in 1972. A car was zigzagging through the streets, and the police stopped it. To their amazement, they found that the driver was blind. The man sitting next to him was drunk, and admitted that he knew he was simply too drunk to drive himself, so he had entrusted the job to the blind man and was giving him directions.

Smart Psychologist

It was a Parisian psychologist by the name of Alfred Binet who pioneered the I.Q. test. He began his work in 1896 when he examined eighty children using the material he devised. In 1904, with Theodore Simon, Binet created a scale with 54 tests.

In 1906, the Binet Scale was used by the Paris Educational Authority. In 1908, Oxford University used the Binet Scale to conduct I.Q. tests.

The 10th president of the United States, John Tyler, served from 1841 to 1845. His wife had been paralyzed by a stroke in 1839, and died in 1842. The role of official hostess was performed by Tyler's daughter-in-law until 1844, when the 54-year old president married a 24-year old, Julia Gardiner. This lively First Lady carried out her social duties enthusiastically and lavishly.

Lefthanded people may not be so common, but it seems that masny of the famous have been southpaws.

Consider the following: Harpo Marx, Charlie Chaplin, Leonardo da Vinci, Judy Garland, Paul McCartney, Babe Ruth, Harry S. Truman, Betty Grable, Cole Porter, Gerald Ford, Rex Harrison, and Kim Novak.

Clam Lovers, Beware

Did you ever get an almost completely closed clam that turned out to be empty when opened? Here's what might have happened.

Starfish are carnivorous. They love clams and oysters and can destroy an oyster bed. Many starfish have a protrusible stomach, which gives them a unique eating style. This kind of starfish will wrap its arms around a clam or oyster, and grip the shell with its feet. Through suction, the starfish will open the shell just slightly. Then the starfish can extrude its stomach through its mouth and insert it inside the shell of its prey, and suck out the inner tissue.

The dogs who are reputed to have lived the longest were a black Labrador named Adjutant, who died on November 30, 1963 at the age of 27 years and three months, and Bluey, an Australian sheep-herding dog who was over 29.

If anyone tries to sell you an antique cash register and tells you it's over 150 years old, don't believe it. The cash register was patented in 1879 by James J. Ritty of Dayton, Ohio. In 1884, the National Cash Register Company took over the production and marketing of his invention — and you know how successful they've been!

Sesquipedalianism

We all know people like that, who would never use a one-syllable word if they can use a word of three or more syllables — officer instead of cop, attorney instead of lawyer, apprehend instead of catch, etc. etc. These people are guilty of sesquipedalianism, an addiction to the use of long words.

Governmental bureaucrats often suffer from this disease, being fond of attaching prefixes and suffixes to perfectly useful words, turning them into verbal monsters. One such worthy example is the word reprioritization, seven syllables and 16 letters, which when broken down, yields up a simple: assigning new priorities. And how about this one: deinstitutionalization — nine syllables and 22 letters, all adding up to: releasing patients from (mental) hospitals.

You may remember the word that everybody thinks is the longest one in the dictionary: antidisestablishmentarianism, 11 syllables and 28 letters. Well, it is outdone by: floccinaucinihilipilification, 12 syllables and 29 letters. Spring that on your friends the next time you have occasion to use a word that means evaluating something as worthless.

To supply its cars, factories, buildings with the energy needed, America consumes about 19 million barrels of oil each day, 8 million barrels of which are imported. If you want a graphic picture of how much this is, it's enough to fill the Empire State Building three times over each day.

Ring Out, Wild Bells

Do you have a kid who doesn't ever seem to remember to zip up his fly? Your problem is solved—the forget-me-not zipper, patented in 1964, attaches to a little boy's zipper and causes an alarm bell to ring if the kid's fly is open.

The first pure food and drug legislation was enacted in the United States on June 26, 1848, to prevent the importation of adulterated drugs and medicines.

A bean stalk will climb the bean pole from right to left, but hops will climb the pole from left to right.

Santa Claws

A certain crab will snap a claw on the finger of a fisherman who catches it. Then the crab will escape by dropping that claw from its body, leaving it hanging on the fisherman's finger. The crab scuttles away while the startled fisherman is still trying to figure out what happened.

These crabs will also drop a claw or a leg if they are alarmed by a thunderclap or some other sudden loud noise. Then they will scuttle away from the sound. A new limb always grows back.

About one person out of a million is injured or killed by lightning throughout the world each year.

Man Bites Man

There seems to be a lot of biting going on in New York, not all of it being done by four-legged animals.

Some 22,000 New Yorkers were bitten by dogs in one year, and about 1,150 by cats. But only 229 rat bites were reported. Compare this last figure with the astonishing statistic that 892 people were bitten by *other people*!

Human bites seem to follow seasonal and geographical lines. Spring and early summer seem to bring out the beast in man, and Saturdays are the worst days. The Fort Greene section of Brooklyn had a rate that was five times greater than the citywide rate.

A hummingbird lays only two eggs during its entire lifetime.

Tower of Babel?

There are between 3,000 and 4,000 languages in the world. Some languages have millions of speakers, and some 25 speakers or even less. The language with the greatest number of speakers is Mandarin. English is second.

When the sight of one eye is lost, one's vision is reduced by about one-fifth.

Piggish Appetite

Alligators are meat-eaters, and any kind of meat will do. Their appetites are enormous. A deer, a large calf, or a 300-pound hog provides only a snack to an alligator. On occasion, alligators have been known to attack children and even adults.

Alligators are also fond of eating dogs. Even today in Florida if a number of pet dogs disappear about the same time, people suspect that a hungry alligator has probably invaded the neighborhood. An alligator hunt is immediately organized.

But if the 'gator is found, the law forbids killing it. Instead, the giant reptile is tied securely and turned over to a game warden or a wildlife expert. Then the alligator is taken to the Everglades and set free. In that vast animal refuge, the alligator is free to fend for itself.

Perfect Refrigeration

Scientists who study animals and plants of the past have found the Arctic to be a vast storage house of fascinating creatures. The permanently frozen regions of the Far North have perfectly preserved animals that abounded there tens of thousands of years ago.

Camels and elephants—who are generally associated with the desert and jungle—have been dug up in snowy Alaska. And giant mammoths—ancestors of today's elephants—have been dug out of their icy resting places in Soviet Siberia. Complete with huge tusks and hairy skins, these huge beasts have been thawed and, on several occasions, their flesh has been found good enough to eat!

The average seven-inch lead pencil is capable of drawing a line 35 miles long.

Married people live longer than those who remain single.

Stainless steel can be rolled into strips thinner than a human hair. A stack of 1,000 pieces is only about one inch thick.

In skywriting, the average letter is nearly two miles high.

There are five counties in Texas each of which is larger than the state of Rhode Island.

Abraham Lincoln was the tallest president of the United States. He was six feet, four inches tall.

Extraordinary Beachball

No summer vacation at the beach would be complete without a beachball. And if you took your vacation at a tropical sea shore, you would have no trouble at all finding one. For a puffer fish will happily turn itself into a beachball for you.

A puffer fish has a valve in its throat. When the fish is taken out of the water, it opens its valve and swallows air. It is then inflated to the size and shape of a ball. The puffer fish can stay out of water a little while.

You can bounce or throw an inflated puffer fish across the beaches like a great big beachball! And when the game is over and you throw the puffer fish back in the sea, the fish closes its throat valve, deflates itself to its normal size and shape, and swims away.

The push-key adding machine was patented on February 5, 1850 by Du Bois Parmelee of New Paltz, New York. But this impractical machine was not generally used.

On August 21, 1888, William Seward Burroughs of St. Louis, Missouri patented an adding machine which was successfully marketed.

Queen Anne, who ruled over England from 1702 to 1714, gave birth to seventeen children, not one of whom survived her.

Thomas Jefferson was 33 years old when he drafted the Declaration of Independence.

Amen means "so be it."

There are more than one hundred different breeds of domesticated dogs.

Charles S. Wilson 3rd, an attorney in Waukegan, Illinois, asked an appellate court to free his client on the grounds that he or she had committed no crime and was in jail illegally. His client was a five-month fetus. The mother, Carole Hubbard of Chicago, had been charged with shoplifting.

Real Live Dragon

The only spot in the world where the marine iguana can be found is in the Galapagos Island group in the Pacific Ocean. This fearsome-looking lizard, often more than four feet in length, resembles in miniature the savage dragon of legend. This illusion is reinforced by the fact that when attacked, the marine iguana actually spouts clouds of vapor from its nostrils. This vapor resembles smoke and gives the iguana the frightening appearance of a genuine, fire-breathing dragon.

Like its land relative, the marine iguana is actually timid and harmless. When attacked or threatened, it puts up a fierce bluff, with the hope that its frightening appearance will scare off the enemy. If it sees that the bluff has failed and there is no way of escape, it surrenders without even attempting to bite its attacker.

The marine iguana is the only lizard in existence that depends entirely upon the ocean for its food. It feeds exclusively on seaweed found in the salt water. To get this food, the marine iguana often swims many miles out into the ocean. Nature has given it a broad, powerful tail which it uses as an oar to drive itself through the water at a good rate of speed.

Easy Comes, Easy Goes

If one spent at the rate of one dollar per minute, it would require approximately two thousand years to spend a billion dollars.

Eggspertise

You were getting ready for Easter. You took a batch of eggs out of the refrigerator and started boiling them, six at a time. But you were interrupted by a phone call in the middle of the job, and when you got back to it, you had a problem. Which eggs were boiled, and which were still raw? Don't panic.

A very good way to find out whether or not an egg has been cooked is to attempt to spin it. A raw egg will not spin.

The life span of the trout is four years. The goldfish has a life span of 25 years, and the sturgeon can live to a ripe old 50.

The first toothbrushes were invented in China in 1498. They had bristles and from the description did not differ too much from the modern counterpart.

Oh Say Can You See

America's national anthem, *The Star Spangled Banner,* is actually based on a popular British drinking song. On September 14, 1814, Francis Scott Key, an American lawyer detained aboard a British vessel at Baltimore's Fort McHenry, awoke at dawn and saw that the American flag was still flying after a night of bombing by the British. He was inspired to write the poem which, on March 4, 1931 was decreed the national anthem.

Sweet Tooth

Birds must eat—and eat a lot—to live. Because of their great activity and high body temperature, birds burn up energy much more rapidly than do most animals. Some baby birds may eat food equal to their own weight every twenty-four hours.

When birds eat insects, their ravenous appetites are a big help to farmers. For these birds destroy enormous numbers of harmful insects by just doing what comes naturally—that is, eating.

Unfortunately, the bird's eating habits are not all helpful. As many gardeners know to their sorrow, many birds have a strong liking for fruit. In fact, birds pick and choose carefully when dining on fruit. Birds like the best, the ripest, the sweetest fruits—and they have an uncanny knack for selecting them. While half-ripe cherries, strawberries, or grapes will be left alone, sweet, juicy fruits are favorite targets of hungry birds.

Immemorial

The longest role that Shakespeare ever wrote was that of Hamlet. Anyone who essays this trying part will have to grapple with 1,422 lines.

Only four other roles in the Shakespeare repertoire require the actor to memorize more than 1,000 lines. These parts are: Henry V, 1,025 lines; Iago in *Othello*, 1,097 lines; Richard in *Richard III*, 1,124 lines; and Falstaff in *Henry IV Parts 1 and 2*, 1,178 lines.

The largest ship afloat is a French tanker by the name of *Pierre Guillaumat*, which is 1,359 feet long.

The diamond is ninety times as hard as the next hardest mineral, corundum.

The smallest breed of dog going is the Chihuahua. At maturity, this Mexican wonder generally weighs somewhere between two and four pounds, but some Chihuahuas tip the scales at no more than a pound.

There are only 12 letters in the Hawaiian alphabet.

Unwitting Wit

The Reverend William A. Spooner, who died in 1930, served for many years as Dean of New College, Oxford. His gaffes with the language became so notorious that a neologism was created based on his blunders. Bloopers of inverted speech came to be called "Spoonerisms."

Spooner once asked if it was "kisstomary to cuss the bride." One day Spooner rebuked one of his students with this barrage: "You hissed my mystery lectures."

Spooner once referred to dear old Queen Victoria as the "queer old dean."

There's Gold In Them There Pants

Jeans, enormously popular these days, were first made in 1850 by a Bavarian immigrant whose name was Levi Strauss. Strauss had headed for San Francisco during the gold rush. He had a number of bales of cloth which he had intended to convert into tents, but there were too many people ahead of him in this trade, so he thought he'd try using the material to make hard-wearing work trousers. He got the idea from a miner who complained that ordinary trousers wore out too fast and became tattered while digging.

In 1874, Strauss added rivets to his trousers. In those good old days, his jeans sold for $13.50 a dozen.

Porpoiseful Play

The porpoise is among the sea's most playful and charming creatures. Porpoises love to sport among the waves, and sailors often see them doing their sea-going acrobatics for hours as they follow a boat.

The porpoise is not a cold-blooded fish but a mammal, which may account for its human-like cavorting.

One of the porpoise's fascinating accomplishments is its ability to make all sorts of amusing noises while underwater. The porpoise can whistle, chirp, squeak, and make a sound that has been described as the "grating of a rusty hinge."

The porpoise is one of the most intelligent of sea animals, as anyone who has been to a water show can attest. One six-foot, 200-pound porpoise in an aquarium is famous for his repertoire of tricks. This porpoise can ring for his dinner, chase and retrieve sticks, sound a horn, leap through hoops, and even tow a surfboard with a girl riding on it.

All the blood in the human body passes through the thyroid gland every seventeen minutes.

Oysters Grow on Trees

Oysters on trees are a common sight on many islands in the Caribbean Sea — for instance, Cuba, Trinidad, and Barbados. There you can see mangrove trees whose lower trunks and branches are festooned with living oysters.

The tree-climbing oyster lives in swamps and lagoons along the coasts of these islands. As incoming tides raise the water level in the swamps and lagoons, the oysters manage to attach themselves to the lower parts of the mangrove trees (which themselves grow in water). The oysters go as far up the tree as the tide will lift them.

When the tide goes out, the trees bearing their oyster "fruit" make a strange picture.

A baseball can be made to curve six and a half inches from its original course.

The mammoth clams off the Malaysian coasts often measure as much as four feet across, and weigh as much as 500 pounds.

The giant clam lies on the bottom of the coastal waters, its two great shells slightly open. If a careless swimmer or pearl diver inserts a hand between the opened shells, the giant clam slowly closes.

There are stories about men who have had an arm or a leg clamped between the shells of a giant clam, and who were trapped that way under the water until they drowned.

Hidebound

Until man came along with his traps and his powerful guns, the alligator was king of the swamps. With its armor-plated hide for defense, terrible jaws and tail for attack, and heavy weight, it was a living tank, almost impossible to halt.

No animal is capable of clawing or biting through an alligator's hide. Consequently, once it reached a respectable size, the wild alligator of the past had a good chance of living out its allotted forty to sixty years of life.

An alligator's thick, scaly hide will turn aside bullets from most guns. Until the invention of high-powered hunting rifles, most alligators were killed by being shot through the eye. Even then, the reptile's brain is so small and so heavily armored with bone that only a direct hit proved fatal.

There is no scientific distinction between pigeons and doves.

William Harvey, an English physician, was the first to demonstrate the circulation of blood and the function of the heart in the early 1600's.

Able Swordsman

The swordfish has a powerful ling snout shaped like a sword.

Occasionally fishermen have been attacked by swordfish they have hooked. If an angry swordfish lunges straight at a fisherman's small boat, it can pierce a hole right through. A boat with a copper-plated hull was reported to have been pierced by a swordfish's snout.

William Howard Taft was the largest president of the United States. He weighed over 300 pounds. A special bathtub had to be built for him in the White House.

Andrew Jackson was the only president of the United States to fight a duel, although this occurred before he became president. On May 30, 1806 Jackson shot and killed Charles Dickinson in a duel in Kentucky. Jackson served as president from 1829 to 1837.

The sea hare, a marine snail the size of a man's fist, inhabits the seaweed off the coasts of California and Florida. At the top of a sea hare's jelly-like body are two long, tentacle-like antennae which look something like a rabbit's long ears. The sea hare smells with these antennae.

The only remarkable thing a sea hare does is to produce 500,000,000 eggs during its lifetime.

A newborn kangaroo is about one inch in length.

Socrates, the Greek philosopher, left no writings of his own. His philosophy is known only through writings of his pupil, Plato, and from Xenophon.

Eighty-four percent of a raw apple is water.

Switchblade

Although he appears harmless and would seem to be ready prey for any hungry enemy, the doctor fish carries a surprise weapon concealed in a pocket of flesh in front of its tail.

When the doctor fish is menaced, this pocket of flesh opens and a sharp object like a knifeblade, snaps out. The combination of pain and surprise that the hidden weapon can inflict is usually enough to discourage most attackers.

Harriet Beecher Stowe's famous book, *Uncle Tom's Cabin*, was published March 20, 1852. It was the first American novel to sell one million copies.

The largest bullfighting ring in the world, located in Mexico City, had a seating capacity of 48,000. It was closed in 1976. Today, the largest ring is in Madrid, Spain. It has a seating capacity of 24,000.

Venus, the planet nearest to Earth, is only about 26 million miles away.

Towards the end of 1903, an Italian immigrant by the name of Italo Marcioni patented a mold for the making of an ice cream cone.

For Spouting Out Loud!

When a lookout on a whaling ship shouts "Thar she blows!" he is announcing that he has seen a whale spouting in the distance.

Most of us think that a whale spouts water. This is not so. Most whales have to surface every 15 or 20 minutes to breathe. When a whale rises to the surface of the water after being submerged for many minutes, his huge lungs are filled with stale air. The whale exhales this stale air through the nose openings in his head.

What happens then is the same thing that happens to you when you exhale on a cold day and you can see a puff of your breath coming out of your mouth. The warm air that has been inside the whale turns to vapor as it strikes the cold air.

Different whales have different kinds of spouts. Some whales, for instance, have one nose opening and thus make only one spout. Other whales have two nose openings and so they send up two spouts.

Some whales spout straight up in the air, and some whales spout at an angle, depending on the location of their nose openings.

Whales also spout to various heights. The blue whale spouts higher than any other. Its spout can go 10 to 15 feet into the air.

Veteran whalers pride themselves on being able to identify what kind of a whale they have sighted just by the spout.

The largest assembly of musicians in the world, so far as is known, were those assembled on Band Day at the University of Michigan in Ann Arbor. In some of the years between 1958 and 1965, the total number of instrumentalists reached 13,500.

The whale is not really a fish, but a mammal that lives in the water. The whale is warm-blooded, gives birth to baby whales instead of whale eggs, and suckles its young.

A Better Mouse Trap?

An army of mice and rats once overran some of the islands off the northeast coast of Donegal, Ireland. The rodents, ravenous for food, prowled the waterside at low tide. Some of them pushed their noses inside the partly-opened shells of the oysters in an effort to get at the tasty flesh of the mollusks.

But oysters are extremely sensitive to the slightest touch. Instantly, the oysters snapped their shells shut on the rodents. And the vise-like grip of the oyster shells was as effective as any mouse trap. The rodents were held fast, and were drowned when the rising tide covered them.

The fastest domestic passenger elevators in the world are the express elevators to the 103rd floor of the 109-floor, 1,452 foot tall Sears Tower in Chicago. They operate at a speed of 1,800 feet per minute, or about 20.45 mph.

Up in Smoke

According to the National Institute of Education, in 1979 10.7 percent of boys between the ages of 12 to 18 were regular cigarette smokers. A surprising 12.7 percent of 12-to-18-year-old girls were regular cigarette smokers. Although this represents a drop for both sexes as compared with the prevalence of the smoking habit among teenagers during the previous five to seven years, it is the first time the female ratio outdid the male.

Bagging The Lady

Maximillian II of Germany had an extremely attractive daughter who was named Helene. This beauty was wooed by two gentlemen of equally high rank, one German and one Spanish. So great was their desire for the girl that they were willing to risk their lives to get her; so they proposed a duel. However, the prospective father-in-law, the king, intervened and said he would not allow them to risk their noble blood. Instead, he proposed a different and strange contest. He presented a gunny sack, and told the two suitors to fight it out—whoever could put the other gentleman into the bag would become his son-in-law.

The rivals wrestled for more than an hour, and then the German, Baron Von Talbert, succeeded in bagging his opponent. The Baron lifted the bag, carried it across the room, and placed it at the maiden's feet, making his proposal of marriage, which was immediately accepted.

After being in orbit for nearly four years, the Soviet Union's Salyut 6 space station probably reached the end of its life. In May, 1981 the Soyuz T 4 spacecraft returned to earth, concluding the final manned mission to the space station.

The census indicates that some 37,780 New Yorkers ride to work by taxi every day.

It takes but one-fortieth of a second for the human eye to wink.

Nobody can explain why it is that humans have a distinct preference with respect to handedness, but the fact is that about two-thirds of mankind is right-handed.

Time And Tide

Scientists have learned not only how to predict the ebb and flow of future tides, but they are also able to work out the tides of the past. Machines have been specially built to analyze the height and the time of the tides. These tide computing machines can draw diagrams that show the ebb and flow of tides of the past as well as those of the future. The machine can tell about tides years in the future. For example, it can tell you how low the tide will be in Miami, Florida, on the Fourth of July three years from now.

This information about tides is of great interest to naval historians. For example, suppose someone were writing about a great naval battle that took place many years ago off the coast of England. It could be that the shifting tides played an important part in the victory of one side or the other.

According to United Nations' statistics Hungary has the highest recorded suicide rate, and Mexico the lowest.

Arms But No Armor

To defend themselves against armed marauders, Buddhist monks, who did not believe in bearing arms, developed a weaponless system of self-defense, called jujitsu, over 2,000 years ago. In the 19th century, a Japanese jujitsu expert named Jigoro Kano made some changes in the jujitsu holds and created judo. Judo is a sport as well as a system of self-defense. To know how expert a player is just look at the color of his belt. If it's white, he's a beginner; if it's black, he's an expert. Then there's a whole range of colors in between.

Karate has been developed as a separate self-defense art. It involves using the side of the hand to deliver blows to sensitive parts of an opponent's body.

Smart as a Pig

Scientists have been continuously engaged in measuring the intelligence of animals. Most people would be surprised to learn that the pig is considered one of the most intelligent of animals, occupying place 10 on a list which puts the chimpanzee first, the gorilla second, the orangutan third, the dolphin eighth, and the elephant ninth.

Mighty Mites

Although we customarily think of noted warriors as being large of frame, big-boned, tall, and visibly athletic, the fact is there have been a few outstanding generals and warriors who were extremely short. For example, the British soldier and writer, T. E. Lawrence of Arabia, was only 5'5½" tall. Napoleon Bonaparte was only 5'6". Horatio Nelson, British naval hero, stood 5'5½".

The Naming Game

You probably know, or at least would guess, that the most common name in the English speaking world is Smith. But could you guess what other names follow in popularity?

Here they are: Jones, Johnson, Williams, Brown, Miller, David, Anderson, Wilson, Thompson.

Really no surprises here. But anyone who bears one of these cognomens had better acquire an uncommon middle name.

Still, this doesn't hold a candle to the name of Chang, the most common name in the world. It is estimated that there are some 75 million Chinese who bear this surname.

Normally healthy persons can lose as much as one-third of their blood without fatal results.

John Davidson, noted singer and entertainer, has appeared over 57 times on the Tonight Show.

John F. Kennedy, President of the United States, was reputed to be a noted libertine. Senator Smathers once said, "There's no question about the fact that Jack had the most active libido of any man I've ever known." His female companions cut across all social lines. Movie stars, socialites, hatcheck girls, secretaries, and maids—when it came to women, Mr. Kennedy was no snob.

Comedian Dave Brenner has appeared more than 32 times on the Mike Douglas television show.

Not So Kindly Light

Thomas Edison, a genius in invention and in the practical application of science, was of not much account in human relations. He had his employees work for long hours in poor conditions, and paid them the lowest possible salary. Edison paid little heed to his family. Both of his wives suffered from acute depression, and his eldest son became an alcoholic and committed suicide.

Fortnight is a contraction of "fourteen nights." Although it is a common term in England, it has been supplanted by "two weeks" in the United States.

Forty-one percent of the moon is not visible from the earth at any time.

Asia is four times the area of Europe.

Population Explosion?

Remember when Pharoah decided to get rid of the Jews for fear they would multiply and outnumber the Egyptians? No need to fear today—the most populous nation in the Middle East today is Egypt, with 39 million people; second is Iran, with 35 million; followed by Iraq, with 12 million, and Saudi Arabia and Syria, with 8 million each. Israel, with a population of less than 4 million, is not even in the running.

But none of this compares with the real winners—China, with 952 million, is the world's most populous nation; India is second, with 643 million; and in third place is the Soviet Union, with 261 million people. The United States comes next, with a population of 218 million; and in fifth place is Indonesia, with 135 million people.

George Raft was offered leading parts in *High Sierra* (1941), *The Maltese Falcon* (1941), and *Casablanca* (1942), but didn't like the idea of being directed by John Huston, who was unknown at that time. Humphrey Bogart played all three of these roles to great acclaim.

On Staten Island in New York City, the census discovered that 479 households shared a bathtub with a neighbor.

You Can Go Home Again, If You're an Eel

Everyone knows about the salmon's habitual migration to its breeding ground, but did you know that the great fresh-water eel takes part in an equally startling journey. The unerring homing instinct of the fresh-water eel operates like a built-in radar or sonar set, and it takes the eel as far as 4,000 miles to its spawning ground.

The fresh-water eel is born beneath the weeds of the Sargasso Sea. As a larva, the eel floats on the ocean currents, being borne to the shores of Europe and of America. There the eel chooses a fresh-watr stream and settles down.

When the eel reaches maturity, instinct takes command. The eel is suddenly filled with an all-consuming desire to return to the place of his birth.

And so down the streams and rivers of Europe and America, the eels slither their way in a great migration back to the Sargasso Sea. As soon as the eels reach their home waters, the female lays eggs, and the male fertilizes them. The purpose of their journey is now fulfilled.

Young salmon swim downstream tail first.

The geographic center of North America is in Pierce County, North Dakota, six miles west of Balta and about 50 miles west of Devil's Lake.

The two longest rivers on this earth are the Nile, which flows a distance of 4,160 miles, and the Amazon, which with its tributaries runs about 4,000 miles. Compare this to the combined Missouri-Mississippi, which has a length of 3,740 miles.

The Empire State Building has 6,400 windows.

Just Call Me Baby

Everybody knows that a baby cat is a kitten and a baby dog is a puppy. And most people know that a calf is the young not just of the cow, but also of the antelope, rhino, hippo, whale, elephant, among others. But how many of the names for the young of the animals below could you have given?

bird–fledgling, nestling	kangaroo—joey
eel—elver	rooster—cockerel
fish—fry, fingerling	salmon—parr
grouse—cheeper	swan—cygnet
hare—leveret	turkey—poult
hawk—eyas	zebra—foal

Saving Souls

The Salvation Army was originated by a Methodist minister, William Booth, and his wife, Catherine, whose goal it was to declare war on evil. There are now branches all over the world. The first branch in the United States was established in Pennsylvania in 1880.

Although the organization is modeled along military lines, its functions are religious and humanitarian. It provides physical and spiritual assistance to the needy through its hospitals, community centers, soup kitchens, rehabilitation programs, and emergency services.

There are 206 bones in the human body. The femur, or thigh bone, is the longest. The stapes, one of the three bones in the middle ear, is the smallest.

When we are very young, our bones are composed mostly of cartilage, which makes them pliable and less prone to breaks. As we grow older, the mineral content of our bones increases. Elderly people's bones become very brittle and break easily.

Music plays no part in the religious services of orthodox Mohammedans.

Big and Small, We Love Them All

Did you think that Texas was the largest state of the Union? Well, it was until Alaska was admitted to statehood, and now Texas is only second. In fact, Alaska has more than twice as many square miles of area than Texas. Third in size is California, and not much smaller is Montana. In fifth place is New Mexico.

How about the smallest members of the Union? Well, everyone knows the smallest is Rhode Island, with a total area of 1,214 square miles. That's smaller than one average-sized farm would be in Arizona, Alaska, Nevada, New Mexico, Wyoming, Montana or Colorado! The second smallest state is Delaware; the third, Connecticut; the fourth, Hawaii; and the fifth, New Jersey.

It didn't take long for Lyndon Johnson to make important decisions. The day after he met Lady Bird he proposed to her, and two months later they were married.

In 1869, Ives McGaffey of Chicago, Illinois, invented the suction-type vacuum cleaner.

Magic Carpet

The notorious Cardinal Richelieu, who was Louis XIII's most powerful minister, occupied an extraordinary bed. The Cardinal was afflicted with headaches, hemorrhoids, boils, and a disease of the bladder. Since he couldn't get around, he had a vast litter built, and he was carried around town by 24 bodyguards. On this litter there was a chair, a table, and a private secretary. It is reported that when the traveling bed proved too large to enter through the doors of any building Richelieu wished to enter, he commanded his bodyguards to batter down the walls.

The letters RX on a doctor's prescription mean "take," from the Latin *recipe*.

Landing a jet plane on the deck of an aircraft carrier is said to be one of the most difficult maneuvers in aviation. These landings take place at 100 miles an hour.

Don't Mess with the Cobra

The great King Cobra of southeast Asia is one of the most dangerous serpents in the world. It is the largest poisonous snake on earth. An adult may be as long as 18 feet. Its poison sacs are enormous, and the venom they secrete is one of the deadliest known.

Moreover, the King Cobra is one of the very few snakes that will attack with little or no provocation. These snakes are especially aggressive during mating and breeding time, for they are among the few snakes which make a nest for their eggs and then guard it. Anyone venturing near a King Cobra's nest may be in for a nasty surprise. The male keeps close to the nest where the female is guarding her eggs, and stands ready to attack anything appearing on the scene. To be confronted by a King Cobra with four or five feet of its length reared upward is a most nerve-shattering experience.

In Siam, even a huge elephant may fall victim to the attack of a King Cobra. The snake strikes either at the tender tip of the elephant's trunk or at the one thin-skinned spot where the elephant's toenail joins its foot. An elephant, so bitten, usually dies within three hours.

I Won't Fight, Don't Ask Me

During the Civil War, it was a common practice among people who could afford it to hire substitutes to take their place in the fighting forces. One such draft dodger was Grover Cleveland, who later became President of the United States. If Cleveland's supporters were worried that if this information were made public it might have an adverse effect on his chances of being elected, they were relieved to discover that his opponent, James Blaine, was in the same boat, and that he, too, had used this means of evading military service.

On May 18, 1980 residents of the state of Washington in the United States suffered a shock. Mount Saint Helens in the Cascade Range erupted. The thud was felt over a 100 mile area. Volcanic ash spread across large areas, endangering crops and water supplies and creating a health hazard.

Anomalous Creature

The aweto, an insect that flourishes in New Zealand, is something like a cross between a caterpillar and a vegetable. The aweto buries itself among the roots of the myrtle tree a few inches below the ground, and lives in that locus until it is full grown. At this time, it undergoes a strange metamorphosis. The spore of a vegetable fungus fastens itself to the neck of the aweto, and from this spore there grows a stalk that might be as much as eight inches high. Gradually the vegetable takes over the aweto, filling up all the space within the skin of the aweto, but leaving the body of the insect unchanged. Then, when the vegetable has completely replaced the caterpillar, both the vegetable and the insect grow hard and dry, and then die.

The curious life of this insect-vegetable is not fully understood, for scientists have not been able to determine how the aweto reproduces itself.

A Bell Untolled

The largest bell in the world is to be found not in a belfry, but on exhibition square in Moscow, Russia. Cast in the year 1733, the huge bell weighs 440,000 pounds. The bell stands 19'6" high, and its base measures 22'8" across.

Formerly known as the Tsar Bell, the gigantic bell was never rung. When efforts were made to hang it, the bell fell down and a piece of it broke loose. The Tsar ordered that the bell be placed in a public square and used as a small chapel or church. The piece that broke off was placed in front of the entrance.

The ear is the most intricate, complicated organ in the human body.

Trouble in Paradise

The Frenchman who painted *Adam and Eve in Eden* must have lost his mind. Both characters were appropriately dressed in fig leaves, but sitting next to them was a fully dressed hunter, pursuing ducks with a shotgun.

Only three percent of Norway is under cultivation.

Elephants can swim, and they like water.

Weighty Matter

We all know about the gigantic monsters of prehistoric ages — ferocious creatures like *Tyrannosaurus rex* and woolly mammoths. Yet the truth is that many of today's whales are the biggest animals that ever lived.

The blue whale, for example, is larger than any land or sea animal of the past or present. The largest blue whales on record reached 100 feet in length. And their weight was calculated as 180 to 195 tons — that's well over a quarter of a million pounds!

The average blue whale is not quite so monstrous. It grows to be about 80 feet long.

Rattlesnakes do not lay eggs. They give birth to living young.

All That Glitters

Your pet goldfish, swimming around in his tank in the living room, is a creature with an interesting history. Hundreds of years ago, goldfish were green-colored fish swimming in silvery-clear streams in China.

The patient Chinese bred these fish carefully and slowly, over many generations, and gradually developed many new kinds of goldfish — gold goldfish, silver goldfish, blue goldfish, black goldfish, gray goldfish.

While the run-of-the-mill gold goldfish live only a few years, some of these Oriental varieties may live to be 70 years old!

The capacity of the human stomach is about one quart.

Right to Life

A large female cod can lay more than 9,000,000 eggs. Most of these baby fish die. They are either eaten by other fish, or fall victim to such other perils of their surroundings as storms and starvation.

But this very helplessness is why Nature has made the codfish so fertile. Without this tremendous birth rate to make up the losses to other fish and to man, the cod would long ago have vanished from the oceans.

There are a few fish that go to unusual lengths to care for their young as well and as long as possible. These fish do not go about their parental duties consciously. Their actions are instinctive—a sort of built-in assist from Nature to help protect the existence of the species.

Wholly Holy

St. Peter's, in the Vatican City State area of Rome, is not only the largest church in the world, it is also one of the world's most renowned works of architecture. The Italian architect Bramante is generally given credit for the original plan, but the great Renaissance architect and artist Michelangelo made some important changes. He designed St. Peter's great dome and painted the famous ceiling of the Sistine Chapel. This work of great beauty took the artist two full years to complete.

St. Peter's is also one of the world's treasuries of fine art, for Michelangelo's great painting, *The Last Judgment*, as well as many other masterpieces are on exhibit there.

So vast is St. Peter's that on some occasions more than 80,000 worshippers have crowded into it at one time. The church measures 1,151 feet—almost two city blocks—in length, and is 767 feet wide. Eight large staircases and 11,000 rooms are included in its huge expanse. One of its most imposing features are the great promenades of pillars and columns with 162 giant statues atop their heights.

Serpentine

In early Christian times, there were many divergent sects. One of these were Ophites who maintained that the temptation of Eve brought knowledge into the world and revolt into the world, and that Eve's tempting Adam with the apple was not so much a sinful event as a positive event.

The Ophites therefore revered serpents, and they gave high credit marks to the devil for opening Eve's eyes. An important ritual in their services required that the bread of the Eucharist be licked by snakes before being served to communicants.

One of the greatest chess players the world has ever seen was Wilhelm Steinitz, who held the world championship from 1886 to 1894. But as he grew older, he grew quite insane, and is reputed to have challenged God to a game of chess. To cap it off, he offered God a handicap of one pawn.

In 1928, Dr. Alexander Fleming of St. Mary's Hospital in Paddington, London, described the effect of penicillin in combatting bacteria. Strangely enough, when Fleming read his paper to the Medical Research Club in 1929, the reaction was practically nil. But, in 1945 the Nobel Prize in Physiology and Medicine was awarded to Fleming and Ernst Chain and Howard Florey for their work on penicillin.

In 1944, Fleming was knighted.

A French physicist, Georges Claude, first demonstrated Neon lighting at the Paris Motor Show of 1910. In 1915, Mr. Claude secured a U.S. patent on his neon tube.

In July, 1923 a neon tube advertising sign appeared at the Cosmopolitan Theater in New York City for the show *Little Old New York*, starring Marion Davies.

Pearls are the Only Gems Produced in the Sea

Among all the precious jewels man values, only the pearl is produced in the sea, and that by a living process.

The pearl oyster, a small mollusc, rarely measuring over three inches across, is found in all tropical seas of the world. When the soft shell-producing tissue is attacked by a parasite, the pearl oyster encloses the small intruder in a hard, pearly substance called *nacre* and eventually forms a pearl. Sand grains inside its shell may also occasionally cause the oyster to produce pearls.

Not every pearl oyster produces a pearl, however. And of those oysters that do, only a few produce a pearl of value. Only translucent spherical or pear-shaped pearls are considered gems. About one precious pearl usually is found, on the average, for every thousand pearl oysters opened!

Ducks and Geese Waterproof Their Feathers

Ducks and geese would drown as quickly as non-water birds if their feathers got wet. But they keep dry with a waterproofing oil from the preen gland located at the base of their tails.

Each water bird must spend many hours preening, combing, and spreading the oil waterproofing on its feathers with its beak.

Practically everyone knows that the largest island in the world is Greenland.

But what is the second largest island in the world? Not many people would be able to identify it as New Guinea.

The largest lake in the world is lake Superior, which has an area of more than 31 square miles.

Giant Seaweeds May Grow to 200 Feet in Length

Ocean beds of giant seaweed, called *kelp*, come as close to being a forest as anything that can be found in the sea. Many fish make their homes in the jungle of long seaweed stalks, while lobsters and crabs find refuge in the rocky caves or under the small plants at the bottom of these ocean forests.

Kelp plants have no roots, but are anchored to the ocean bottom by *holdfasts*. Holdfasts are rightly named, for they are the tough tendrils which *hold* the sea plants *fast* to the rocks.

Each kelp plant has fronds—something like the leaves of a land plant—with little gas-filled floats at their base. This enables the giant seaweed to float just below the surface of the water, even though it is attached by its holdfast at a depth as much as ninety feet. A giant kelp plant if stretched out against the face of a tall building with its holdfast on the pavement, would reach to about the twentieth story.

Audie Murphy, the most decorated American World War II hero, received the Congressional Medal of Honor and 23 other U.S. medals for his bravery in combat. He died in an airplane crash on May 31, 1971, at the age of 46.

If your clock goes on the fritz and loses 30 minutes of time a day, don't give up—it will show the correct time again in 24 days!

Looking for a really smashing wedding gift? How about stationery from Cartier, New York, at a mere $10,000 per 100 sheets—that includes envelopes, too. The paper is handmade in Finland, and has a personalized portrait watermark. What every newlywed couple yearns for!

John Gully Boxed His Way from Prison to Parliament

One day in 1805, Henry Pierce, heavyweight boxing champion of England, came to a debtors' prison to entertain the inmates. For Pierce's victim, the warden chose John Gully. To the warden's surprise, and the howling cheers of his fellow convicts, Gully battered Pierce all around the ring.

The taverns soon were bubbling with the story of Gully's victory. A group of gamblers determined to pay off Gully's debts, and get him out of prison. To repay the gamblers, Gully agreed to fight exhibition bouts for them.

And Gully really fought. He fought so well that he soon amassed sufficient winnings to buy himself out of the clutches of the gamblers.

From 1806 on, Gully managed himself. He signed for an official championship bout with Henry Pierce, and lost the fight in the 59th round. But after that single defeat, he never was beaten again. When Pierce retired in 1807, John Gully was acclaimed heavyweight champion of England.

Unlike many prize fighters, Gully saved his money and knew when it was time to quit. He left the boxing ring, and invested his savings in horse racing. Two of his horses won the famous English Derby.

And then John Gully took a real jump—all the way from the race track to politics. In 1832, he was elected to the House of Commons.

Thereafter, he served several terms in Parliament.

When he died in 1863 at the great age of 90, Gully left a substantial fortune and a fine country estate.

And it all began with a roundhouse right. . .

Superman

They may be laughing at Paul MacCready, but they laughed at the Wright Brothers and look what happened. Dr. MacCready is an aeronautical scientist who has designed a 210-pound plane called *Solar Challenger*. It uses no fuel except for sunlight. Dr. MacCready isn't too serious about its possibilities and is just doing it as a personal challenge, but on July 7, 1981 the small plane succeeded in making the 165-mile journey across the English Channel.

MacCready, by the way, is the same guy who designed the *Gossamer Condor*, a completely man-powered aircraft. Who knows, there may be some ingenious solutions to the traffic problem in the offing.

Ship-Shape

The longest warship ever built is the *U.S.S. Enterprise*, constructed in 1960 as a nuclear powered aircraft carrier. The *Enterprise* is 1,123 feet long. Compare this to Nelson's flagship at Trafalgar (1805), *H.M.S. Victory*, which was 226 feet long.

Some bits of Americana die hard. No American has ever gone through elementary school without learning how Betsy Ross made the first Stars and Stripes for George Washington in 1776. Well, Betsy Ross was a seamstress who made flags during the American Revolution, but there is no evidence to prove that she did indeed make the first American national flag.

The Social Scene

You have but to attend an opening night at the opera, or see the envious glances cast at a vintage Rolls Royce, to realize that even in the egalitarian American society, the foibles of the rich are a source of great interest.

If you haven't yet successfully climbed the ladder of success, you can comfort yourself with these words from Oliver Herford:

> Ermined and minked and Persian-lambed,
> Be-puffed, (be-painted, too, alas!)
> Be-decked, be-diamonded—be-damned!
> The woman of the better class.

Or with this, from Edgar Smith:

> You may tempt the upper classes
> With your villainous demi-tasses,
> But Heaven will protect the Working Girl.

But, however you identify yourself socially, you should be entertained by these witty portraits of the upper classes at play, executed by classic graphic illustrators.

Judge

Art of the Silhouette

Judge

Punch, 1879

Judge □

Drawing by Grandville. *Autre Monde*

Samantha at the World's Fair

That Sister-in-Law of Mine

Harper's

La Vie Parisienne

Bab Ballads

Deutsches Lachen

127

Phonomenal!

Which city in the U.S. has the most telephones? Why, New York, of course, with close to six million. Los Angeles does not lag very far behind, and Chicago is third with better than two-and-a-half million. Other cities with over a million phones are: Philadelphia, Detroit, Minneapolis, St. Paul, Baltimore, Houston, Denver, San Diego, Washington D.C., and Miami.

About 35 percent of the earth's surface never receives any snowfall.

What's the difference between a contagious disease and an infectious disease? A contagious disease is spread from one person to another by direct or indirect contact. An infectious disease is caused by the invasion of the body by disease-producing matter, such as bacteria, viruses, or other parasites. If they got there by way of another person, then the disease was contagious. In other words, an infectious disease may or may not be contagious, depending on how it is transmitted.

As amazing as the speed of the Concorde is—it can race along at 1,450 miles per hour—it's not nearly as impressive as the air speed record of a military plane—2,193 miles per hour.

The Rafflesia Is the World's Largest Flower

The mammoth *Amorphophallus titanum* (krubi or giant arum) is commonly referred to as the world's largest flower, but in fact this plant is a collection of flowers simulating one huge flower. The real giant among flowers is the rafflesia, a parasitic plant found in the same Sumatran rain forests as the *Amorphophallus titanum*.

Designed for Speed

For man or beast, two of the most fundamental methods of defense are running away, and going into hiding. Running away is not practicable for most fish. The marauders of the deep are generally speedy themselves, and few fish can generate the necessary speed to escape enemies simply by fleeing.

The fastest fish is the Wahoo. The wahoo can swim at 60 miles an hour—faster than anyone ought to drive! The wahoo can reach this speed despite the fact that it often weighs as much as 130 pounds. But it has a pointed snout and a long, low body. This structure gives it a sort of streamlining that lowers the water resistance, just as long, low lines on an automobile cut down air resistance.

The ubiquitous banana split is surely one of this country's most popular dishes. A classic recipe calls for a banana sliced lengthwise and topped with vanilla, chocolate, and strawberry ice cream, whipped cream, nuts, and marshmallow, chocolate, and pineapple or strawberry sauce. A special dieter's banana split substitutes cottage cheese for ice cream—and, of course, omits the whipped cream and sauce. Presumably, few dieters could be found in the vicinity of the largest banana split in history, a mile-long feast concocted by the Alpha Phi Omega of Texas A & M University in 1980. That record breaker included 11,400 bananas, 1,500 gallons of cream, 380 galllons of topping, 170 pounds of nuts. It was over a mile long.

A Bootless Task

If a jogger ran steadily at a pace of six miles per hour, he could run around the equator in 173 days. But if he were trying to run around Jupiter, the largest planet, it would take him more than five years to complete the task.

Ferdinand Waldo Demera Was the Greatest Imposter of the 20th Century

Ferdinand Waldo Demera saw no reason why his lack of a high-school diploma should stand between him and a professional career. So, through ingenious deceptions and a lot of *chutzpah*, Demera opened the doors that society had closed in his face.

Knowing he would need an impressive resume and references, Demera compiled a fanciful history of previous jobs, and wrote his own references under fictitious or forged signatures.

During the Korean War, Demera somehow found his way onto a Royal Canadian ship as Surgeon Lieutenant. He had had no previous training in medicine. Nevertheless, when he was called upon to operate—and he operated on 19 soldiers during his stay—he acquitted himself well, as Canadian military records indicate.

Another highlight of Demera's career was the time he spent as a professor of applied psychology at several colleges. Passing himself off as a Ph.D., he was academically respected and well-liked by students, faculty, and administration at each school he fooled.

When Demera's academic con game was exposed, he dipped out of sight for a few years before turning up as a guidance counselor for inmates at a Texas prison. Once again, he performed admirably while thumbing his nose at the professional requirements for training.

No institution ever brought criminal proceedings against Demera, knowing that its own reputation would suffer more than Demera's. A Hollywood movie was made of Demera's life more than a decade ago, and since then he has dropped out of sight. But no one knows for sure that he will not strike again—or that he is not out there at this moment, poking fun at some pillar of the Establishment.

The highest sand dunes in the world are those in the Sahara, in east Algeria. They attain a height of 1,410 feet.

Plt hbwt lz I ueenb

In 1925, a large crowd filled a hall in New York's Hotel Roosevelt to watch Yale defeat Harvard in the first intercollegiate crossword puzzle tournament.

Ten inches of snow equals one inch of rain in water content.

Chamberlain Scored 100 Points in a Professional Basketball Game

It figured to be a no account game in a no account place. Neither the New York Knickerbockers nor the Philadelphia Warriors were going anywhere in the National Basketball Association standings in 1962, and the neutral site where they played, the little Hershey Arena in Hershey, Pennsylvania, was well off the major league road map.

But on the night of March 2 Wilt Chamberlain made basketball history. Standing 7-feet, 1-inch, Wilt the Stilt heaved 100 points into the basket! In compiling his score, the perfectly coordinated giant scored on 36 field goals in 63 tries, and sank 28 out of 32 free throws. Since that day, no one has come close to Chamberlain's record—not even Wilt himself.

Needless to say, his team won, 169 to 147.

Oh, Have You Got The Wrong Number

Mrs. Louis Nakielski applied at a Milwaukee government office for a job as a switchboard operator. Sometime later, she received a letter notifying her that she had been placed on the waiting list for a job as a state trooper.

Kapok, that stuffing that you often find in your sofa or bedding, is not a synthetic fabric. It is a fiber that is extracted from the seeds in the pods of the kapok tree. The floss, which is freed from seeds and dried, is extremely useful since it is light and resistant to water and decay. The seeds are not discarded. The oil in the seeds is used for soap, as well as for salad and cooking oil.

Anything For a Laugh

Chris Burton had himself crucified on the roof of his Volkswagen. Real nails were driven through the Californian's palms.

Recovering from this, he then had himself filmed crawling on his naked stomach across a Los Angeles parking lot which was littered with broken glass.

The Hebrew language, which lay as dormant as Latin for many centuries, experienced a rebirth and vitalization in modern times. Hebrew, the language of the Old Testament, was the everyday language of the Jews in Biblical times. But it began to fade out after the Babylonian exile in 586 B.C. Aramaic more or less replaced Hebrew as the spoken language of the Jews, while Hebrew remained the language of learning and religion.

After 70 A.D., the Jews were widely dispersed and they began adopting and adapting the languages wherever they settled. Around 1100 Yiddish emerged as the language of the Jews in the ghettos of Central Europe. Many people confuse Yiddish with Hebrew because they make use of the same alphabet. However, the vocabulary and grammar are different. Yiddish, which started out basically as a corruption of German, spread to Eastern Europe, and from there to all the corners of the earth to which Jews migrated. As the Jews spread out, the Yiddish language grew, acquiring, in addition to its German and Hebrew words, adoptions from Spanish, Russian, French, Rumanian, and many other languages.

In the 19th century, with the emergence of the Zionist Movement, the Hebrew language was revived in its spoken form. (It had always continued to serve as the language for scholars of religion.) In 1948, with the establishment of Israel as the homeland of the Jews, Hebrew was proclaimed the official language. The scholarly language was brought up to date, and with many additions and revisions, now serves as the spoken and written language for both scholars and lay people. Today Hebrew is taught in 470 universities around the world, including colleges in Nigeria, Hong Kong, Poland, New Zealand, and Japan.

Yiddish continues to coexist with Hebrew, in both spoken and written form, and, in fact, periodic efforts are made to revive Yiddish through its literature and theater. In 1978 Isaac Bashevis Singer, a Polish born Yiddish writer won the Nobel Prize for Literature, giving this movement a healthy boost.

No Dime For Comedy

It could have been a scene from a movie comedy. But it wasn't—it was for real.

A Wells Fargo armored truck loaded with bags of coins was heading down South Street to the Federal Reserve Bank at Liberty Street in New York City. Coming the opposite way along the cobblestone street was a cement truck. The street was a little too narrow for the trucks to pass each other easily, so, to avoid a collision, the armored truck swerved to the right. It hit a bump hard.

Yes, you get the picture. The rear doors of the armored truck flew open; eight bags tumbled into the street; three of them split open; and 15,000 dimes spilled out.

The armored truck screeched to a halt, and four guards with drawn pistols jumped out. Borrowing shovels, some old fish boxes and an old broom from the A and J parking lot at Peck Slip, they scooped up all the coins. In 15 minutes they had them all back in the truck.

On second thought if it *had* been a movie, it might have been a bill day instead of a coin day. Imagine what a good wind could have done!

The busiest telephone number in New York City may be 911, the Police Department's emergency number. About 18,000 calls pour in a day at a rate as high as 800 an hour. Calls for help vary from complaints about noisy neighbors and broken traffic lights, to burglary in process and heart attacks.

Senator William Proxmire's Golden Fleece Award goes to a federal agency that he has selected as using poor judgment in spending public funds. For example, the Agriculture once won this dubious award for funding a research project which aimed to find ways of reducing psychological stress and boredom in pregnant pigs.

Hey! That Ain't Hay!

Mrs. Lucy Casswell took her son to the zoo in San Diego, California. They stopped at the elephants' cage and the boy held out a peanut. Sure enough, an elephant stuck her trunk under the railing—but she wasn't after peanuts! The elephant devoured Mrs. Casswell's purse! What was in it? Only a passport, checkbook, photographs, two gold, emerald and turquoise rings, and a wallet with $140 cash.

It's Just Justice

Somehow, it never worked when the teacher tried it in class, but out there in that big bad world things are taken more seriously.

It seems that when Swedish Ambassador Rune Nystroem and his wife, June, were staying at the Intercontinental Hotel in Lahore, Pakistan, the lady's ring disappeared. The ring was worth $10,000. The Lahore police came up with a plan for recovering the ring.

All the room attendants were called together. They were each given an unmarked envelope which they were to drop in a sealed box in an isolated part of the hotel within 24 hours. They were told that unless one of the envelopes contained the missing ring, they would all be arrested.

It worked. The ambassador's wife has her ring back. Now the only thing that's missing is the identity of the thief.

Much to everybody's surprise, in a survey conducted among Japanese university youth 77 per cent said they would prefer to work for an easygoing employer for lower pay rather than for a strict employer for higher wages. When British youths were given the same choice, 80 per cent favored the higher pay with a tough boss, and 60 per cent of West German youths also chose the higher paying job.

In Many Tongues

Mandarin, the tongue of 605 million Chinese, tops the list of the ten most widely spoken languages.

English comes second, and is spoken by 333 million people.

Then follows Russian with 206 million speakers, outdistancing Spanish, which is spoken by most nations of South America, as well as by the people of Spain, making 192 million people who speak Spanish. Approximately the same number of people, 192 million, speak Hindi.

The next five most spoken languages are: German, 129 million; Arabic, 109 million; Bengali, 108 million; Portuguese, 108 million; and Japanese, 105 million.

A Noble Deed

Catherine de Medici was known for many things, but possibly one of the weirdest details of her weird life was the tale of how she happened to send a pilgrim to Jerusalem.

She had asked the Lord for a great favor. In return she vowed to endorse a unique pilgrimage. Her representative was to take one step backward for every three steps he took forward. The man she hired to fulfill her vow was trustworthy, and he walked from France to the Holy Land in the manner she had designated. When he returned to France, she made him a noble.

Well Builders

Today instead of wanting the alligator wiped out, some people are working to increase its numbers. They have discovered that this reptile actually saves far more creatures than it destroys. The reason has to do with water, so essential to animal life.

An alligator must have plenty of mud and water in order to be comfortable. To make sure of a constant supply, it hunts out places where underground water comes close to the surface. Then the alligator digs great muddy wallows in which to soak its body. In times of severe drought, these wallows sometimes hold the only water to be found for many miles. Thirsty animals of many kinds come here to drink.

Naturally, the alligator, whenever hungry, takes advantage of their presence to grab a meal of fresh meat. But the number of animals it kills adds up to only a fraction of the number whose lives are saved by the precious water.

Some ranchers even claim that their cattle herds have survived during a bad drought through the availability of alligator wallows.

Oh! The Lonely People!

In 1976, census statistics indicated that more than one out of every five households in the United States consisted of only one person.

Sticky Story

Chewing gum was commercially produced by John Curtis of Bangor, Maine in 1848. The first chewing gum manufactured from chicle is the work of Thomas Adams, who was a photographer in Staten Island, New York. Adams started his factory in 1872 and built his enterprise into a big business. In 1888, his vending machines were installed on the platforms of the New York Elevated Railway Company, and then his business started to boom.

Keeping a Cool Head

There are some 150 different species in the *lacertid*, or lizard, family. Some of these are viviparous, bearing their young alive, and some are oviparous, laying eggs. It all depends on the climate where they live. Those that live in cooler climates generally bear their young alive. Where the weather is not hot long enough for the eggs to hatch, the baby lizards are safer within the mother's body.

About half of the skink family of lizards bear their young alive. One particular species of lizard is viviparous when found north of the Arctic Circle. But this same lizard lays eggs when found in northern Spain, the southern limit of its range. Here, the weather is warm enough for the eggs to hatch.

Multi-Talented Men

Sidney Poitier trained as a physiotherapist at a mental hospital. He bought a cheap radio and repeated everything to lose his Bahamian accent, then tried acting while keeping himself alive by washing dishes. Sidney directs as well as acts—and his book "This Life," won praise.

Are You My Mother?

For many years no one succeeded in hatching baby alligators or crocodiles in captivity. For some reason, the expectant mothers buried their eggs and then just seemed to forget about their young. As a result, the babies smothered under the mound of sand.

Then somebody in Florida tried approaching an alligator's nest and imitating the mother's grunts. When the alligator babies within the eggs heard this noise, they answered. The eggs were then uncovered and the young came tumbling out, safe and healthy. Since then, by using this method, alligator eggs have been hatched and young alligators raised by the hundreds.

String Abacus

Thanks to a piece of cord with knots of different colors, the king of the Incas could keep track of his empire. This cord was called the *quipu* (pronounced "khipo") which means *knot*. It consisted of a main cord from which dangled smaller strings with knots tied in them. They used strings of different colors, and no one today knows for sure what the different colors meant.

These strings served to record numbers in a decimal system and were a great aid to the king's accountant. If, for instance, the king wanted to know how many subjects he had in a particular province, the governor of that province would tie knots in the quipu to indicate the number, and a quipu reader in Cuzco would translate these numbers to the king.

That's Endurance

Possibly the most amazing knockout bout waged under the Queensbury rules of boxing took place on February 2, 1892, between Harry Sharpe and Frank Crosby, at Nemeoki, Illinois. Sharpe KO'd Crosby in the 77th round.

In 1825, Jack Jones beat Patsy Tunney in Cheshire, England after going 276 rounds in 4½ hours.

Immense Waves Under the Sea Measure 260 Feet High

On an ocean exploration trip over fifty years ago, scientists were taking the temperature of the deep water between Iceland and Scotland. They accidentally discovered that there were gigantic waves under the surface of the sea, for their rise and fall took place deep down in the ocean depths.

The scientists found out about these unseen waves by noting that the colder water from the deeper levels rose and fell just as a surface wave rises and falls as it passes a rock.

These waves, called *internal waves*, sometimes reach the enormous size of two hundred and sixty feet from top, or *crest*, to bottom, or *trough*. Such an invisible wave is about as tall as a giant redwood tree in the majestic forests of California.

What causes these mysterious undersea waves is still not known for certain. Some of them appear to have about the same rhythm as the tides and might be produced by tidal forces.

Jump-Off Point

The iguana may be timid by nature, but it has one of the most rugged bodies of any living creature. In southern Mexico, iguanas love to sun themselves on the towering cliffs along the ocean. When something startles them, they do not hesitate to hurl themselves right off into space. This apparently suicidal act is less harmful to the iguana than falling out of bed would be for a human.

Iguanas have been known to drop as much as sixty feet onto jagged rocks at the foot of a cliff. Such a fall would smash most creatures to bits, or at least stun them for a time. But the iguana does not even seem to be bothered by the impact. It lands and immediately goes racing away without any apparent injury.

A Nameless City Lies Beneath the Bay of Naples

Earthquakes and volcanoes have even caused cities to sink beneath the sea. One such city, long forgotten, was recently discovered in fairly shallow water along the north shore of the Bay of Naples in Italy. This city sank during an eruption of Mount Vesuvius, a volcano a few miles away.

The ancient Roman city of Pompeii, not far from the Bay of Naples, was also destroyed by an eruption of Mount Vesuvius. The ruins of this famous city have been excavated and are visited by thousands of tourists every year.

But the streets of the nameless sunken city in the bay are empty of tourists. Only fish swim around the ruins of the city's ancient buildings. Divers have visited this city under the sea, however, and recovered statues and other interesting relics of the distant past.

The Anableps, a fish that inhabits the waters of the Amazon, has four eyes. That is, the fish has two pupils in each projecting eye. With its "air eyes" the Anableps is able to see food that is floating on the surface of the water, and with its "water eyes" it can search for food below the surface of the water. And it can do both at the same time!

Niceland

The average winter temperature along the southern section of Iceland is higher than the average winter temperature in Milan, Italy.

Non-Nonagenarian

Through the ages, people have had all kinds of queer notions about the age of alligators. Some people actually believed that these reptiles lived forever. Only a few generations ago, scientists thought the life span of an alligator was several hundred years.

Now we know better. Scientists have raised and studied alligators on alligator farms. They have turned newly hatched baby alligators loose in the wild with their birth dates marked on their hides. Then the scientists go back each year and find these alligators.

Out of this careful study has come the realization that alligators are not so long-lived at all. Fifty years seems to be a ripe old age for the average alligator. The oldest alligator of which we have any record reached a doddering sixty-two.

The hottest city in the world is Timbuktu in Mali, where the average temperature throughout the year is better than 84.7 degrees. This average temperature is just slightly more than at Khartoum in the Sudan, or Aden in Yemen, or Madras in India.

Let's All Sing Like The Geckos Do

Reptiles are for the most part a curiously silent class of animals. They contribute nothing to the wonderful dawn chorus of bird song or evening chorus of such amphibians as frogs and toads. Some snakes hiss, and male alligators bellow, but mum's the word for most reptile species. However, a conspicuous exception among the most quiet reptiles is the gecko family.

Imagine making your first visit to the land of the geckos. Suddenly your sleep may be interrupted by a loud, hard voice shouting "Geck-oh" from behind the table or from the ceiling. You are likely to be startled, to say the least.

If you happen to be in Southeast Asia, the voice you hear is likely to be coming from a small lizard. This, one of the biggest of the geckos, is only about a foot long, and has a call that sounds something like "to- kay;" and so it is called the tokay.

On the other hand, if you're visiting Southwest Africa, you might find some smaller species of this lizard—most geckos are under six inches in length—with a chirp that sounds like "chee-chak." Toward the end of the afternoon, each one of a large colony of those garrulous geckos thrusts its head out of its foot-deep burrow and shouts at its neighbors. The chorus is said to be deafening—and almost unbelievable since these tiny lizards are only three inches long.

Hidden Sting

Jellyfish belie their helpless, blob-like appearance by concealing a powerful weapon. The jellyfish has stinging cells in its tentacles, which is how it renders its prey helpless. The famous and feared Portuguese Man-o-War jellyfish can have tentacles as long as 60 feet, and creates more terror among pearl divers in tropical seas than do better known menaces such as sharks.

At its least harmful, the sting of the jellyfish can be extremely painful.

Inca Doctors Were Highly Skilled

Like all primitive peoples, the Indians thought that disease was the result of evil spirits. Nevertheless, their medical practice seems to have been rather sophisticated. Some of the mummies that have been discovered in the ancient cemeteries disclose operations on their skulls. These were very delicate operations on the brain that many times saved the lives of wounded soldiers. Even though we don't know exactly what kind of anesthetics they used, historians are sure that they had ways to dull the pain. It is probable that they used cocaine and other plants that influence the nervous system to produce at least a numbness.

Two modern Peruvian doctors, not long ago, decided to test the techniques of the Inca surgeons. They performed an operation on the brain using the old instruments. The results were very successful and the instruments proved to be quite practical.

Baron Dominic Jean Larrey was the surgeon-in-chief of Napoleon's army. He is notable for one good reason. Many a soldier owed his life to Larrey.

In 1792, he devised a field ambulance. The conveyance was drawn by one horse, and the contraption was mounted on springs so that the injured might not sustain further damage in the journey from the field back to the camp.

Smarter Than a Fox

The fisher, a foxlike marten of North America, is one of the few animals that can attack and kill a porcupine without being affected by the quills. It strikes at the unprotected underbelly.

Despite its name, the fisher does not catch fish and will only eat them if found dead.

Tons of Headaches

Aspirin, invented in Germany in 1853 but not marketed commercially until 1899, is probably the most widespread pain relief drug in use today. In the one year of 1964, twenty-seven million pounds of aspirin were manufactured in the United States. This quantity is enough to fill a 100-car freight train.

A Built-in Fishing Line

If you want to catch a fish for supper, you have to have a net, or a fishing rod and special kinds of bait. But when a frogfish wants to catch a fish for supper, he uses a fishing line that is literally part of his own body.

The frogfish's built-in hook-and-line consists of long, movable strands attached at the top of his head. The frogfish lives on the bottom of the ocean, where he cannot be easily seen by other fish. But the frogfish has two eyes on the top of his head, so *he* can see *them!*

The strands from the frogfish's head float in the water, just like a fisherman's line. Other fish see the strands moving in the current like live worms or other bait, and draw near to eat them. Then the frogfish's enormous, gaping jaws grab the fish. The frogfish does not "hook" his prey; he lures it close enough to be gobbled.

Little Macy's

In 1823, one Alexander Turney Stewart opened up a department store in New York. It was called the Marble Dry Goods Palace, and at that time was the largest shop in the world.

The Statue of Liberty in New York Harbor is without doubt the most famous statue in the world. Lady Liberty measures 152 feet from her base to the tip of her torch. If measured from the base of the pedestal to the tip, the figure more than doubles—at 305 feet 6 inches. The base houses the American Museum of Immigration.

Originally a symbol of friendship from the people of France to the people of the United States, it has become over the years a symbol of the freedom to be found in America. New immigrants arriving by boat never fail to thrill at the sight of the Lady in the harbor.

The statue was designed by the French sculptor Frederick Augustus Bartholdi. He used his mother, Charlotte Beysser Bartholdi, as his model. Bartholdi's original statue was only 9 feet high. This statue was then recreated 32 feet in height. From this statue Gustave Eiffel, designer of Paris's famed Eiffel tower, drew the proportions for the final gigantic statue which we know today. The statue was begun in 1874 and completed in 1883, almost a decade later, at a cost of $600,000. Shipped across the Atlantic in pieces, the statue was assembled on Bedloe's Island in New York Harbor on Independence Day, July 4, 1884.

The following statistics give some idea of just how big the Statue of Liberty is: The statue's right hand alone measures 16 feet 5 inches in length. The length of the index finger is 8 feet. The right arm is 42 feet long. And the statue's total weight adds up to 450,000 pounds.

An elevator will take you to the top of the pedestal, but if you want to venture further you'll have to wend your way up winding stairs to the crown.

Built to Last

What are the oldest cities of the world? Tops on the list is Jericho in Israel, which archaelogists believe was inhabited almost 8,000 years ago, but was destroyed during periods of its history. Runner-up is Jerusalem, which began its career in 3000 B.C. Two other cities are thought to have begun around the same era. They are Zurich in Switzerland, and Kirkuk in Iraq. Damascus, the capital of Syria, has been continuously inhabited since about 2500 B.C. And here is a surprise: Lisbon, Portugal is said to have been started around 2000 B.C., long before many Asian cities.

According to the 1980 census, there are 202 families in New York City who use wood as their cooking fuel.

A Fine Legacy

In the popular imagination, the centipede has 100 legs. There are some centipedes that have an even 100 legs, but there are also centipedes which have 28 legs. And there are other centipedes that have as many as 354 legs. The number of legs, of course, varies with the species.

A Venezuelan Waterfall is Over 19 Times Higher Than Niagara

The rugged, mountainous back country of south-eastern Venezuela still remains largely unexplored. Only small bands of wild Indians live in this wilderness. This wild area is so difficult to reach overland that the little exploration to date has practically all been done by aeroplane.

One of these flights, in 1937, led to the discovery of beautiful Angel Falls. This magnificent ribbon of water plunges 3,212 feet over an enormous cliff deep in the jungle-covered mountains of Venezuela. The falls are named after the American aviator, Jimmy Angel, who first discovered them.

One-tenth of the Earth's Surface is Covered by Ice

Today, great icecaps and glaciers cover one-tenth of the earth's surface. The largest icecaps are in Antarctica and Greenland. Around the edges of these huge ice sheets lie countless glaciers.

Apart from these giant masses of ice, tens of thousands of glaciers exist in Canada, Iceland, Norway, Sweden, New Zealand, and high in the Himalaya Mountains of Asia.

Elementary

When the Russian scientist, Mendeleev, drew up the first Periodic Table classifying the elements in 1869, only 65 elements were known. He predicted the properties of elements still unknown at that time, and today there are 104 known elements. The discovery of still more elements has been predicted, and names have already been prepared for the elements we expect to find.

Icebergs are Sometimes Blue, Green, or Black Instead of White

Instead of the usual white, some icebergs appear blue or green or even black in the sun. These colors are caused by the presence of frozen vegetable matter or earth and dust which was swept from the land on to the ice when the iceberg was still part of a glacier.

At night, icebergs sometimes gleam with a mysterious beauty. The feeble light rays of the moon are reflected by the surface of the ice, making the whole iceberg glow with a strange light.

The Tortoise and the Hare

A camel cannot, of course, outrun a fast horse. But, after the first four miles, a camel has the durability to outrun a horse over almost any extended route.

Sandy Allen is the tallest living woman in the world. At seven feet, seven and one-quarter inches, she towers over most people. She is only 26. She is a resident of Niagara Falls, Canada. The strange part is that the parents of Miss Allen are of normal height. Her weight hovers around 400.

Cold Fish

The fish that live in the Arctic Ocean pose a mystery for science. These fish include the sea char, the cusk, and the Arctic grayling.

These fish defy study because although they have normal blood circulation in the icy Arctic waters, the blood of these fish freezes when it is tested in a laboratory under Arctic temperatures.

Sponges are Skeletons

When you use a natural sponge to take a bath or to scrub the dishes, you are actually using the skeleton of an ocean animal. The sponge is not a plant, but an animal covered with soft flesh. Various hard materials become imbedded in the body wall forming a skeleton.

Since the sponge has no legs or fins or other means of moving about, and attaches itself firmly to a submerged rock or other object, Nature devised an ingenious plan. She created tiny holes in the sponge skeleton so that the water, flowing in and out of these holes, would carry food and oxygen to the sponge, and carry waste materials away.

Commercial sponges are found mostly in the Mediterranean Sea, and in waters of Florida, Cuba and the Bahama Islands. Commercial sponge fishermen take advantage of the fact that some sponges can regenerate themselves—that is, grow whole sponges from small fragments. The fishermen will plant the fragments and harvest them two or three years later when they have grown to marketable size.

Well, Shut My Mouth!

After a female catfish lays her eggs, they are incubated inside the father catfish's mouth. As many as 50 eggs at one time have been found inside a male catfish's mouth. Daddy catfish holds his offspring in his mouth for 30 days.

Ante Up

In the game of poker, a flush ranks higher than a straight. And rightly so, because the chances are one in 255 that you will hold a straight, but only one in 509 that you will hold a flush.

The odds of holding a royal flush in poker—that is, the Ace, King, Queen, Jack, 10 all in one suit—are just one out of 649,740.

In other words, holding a royal flush is something to dream about, but the likelihood that it will ever happen in your lifetime is very, very remote.

Over 20 percent of the people in the United States play some kind of musical instrument.

Seasonal Business

The FBI has determined that most burglaries in the United States are committed during the months of December, January, and February; and during these cold months, burglaries are highest on Saturday night. Nothing else to do?

On the other hand, most assaults, rapes, and murders take place during the hot months of July and August; and most murders happen on a weekend. Too much to do?

One Submarine-Mountain Is Over Five and One-Half Miles High

Mauna Kea, a volcanic peak in the Hawaiian Islands—and not the famed Mount Everest in the Himalaya Mountains to the north of India—is the tallest mountain in the world. From its base on the ocean floor to its summit high above the Pacific, Mauna Kea towers to a height of 31,800 feet—or six miles high. Mount Everest, the highest mountain on land, reaches over 29,000 feet into the sky.

John Spilsbury put out a jigsaw puzzle made up of a hand-colored map of England and Wales as far back as 1767.

When you were a kid, every time you went through a tunnel did you give a shout and listen for the echo? Well, here's a place to go to recapture your youthful caper. Perhaps the structure with the record for echo-making is Villa Simonetta, near Milan, Italy. An echo there can be heard 60 times.

When a Little Goes a Long Way

You sit down to relax after a hard day and you munch a little; let's say you pick up a one-ounce shot of whiskey and down it with two ounces of peanuts—not an awful lot, right? Would you believe that you have actually consumed the same number of calories as you would have had you eaten a meal consisting of four ounces of chicken, four ounces of baked potato, four ounces of cabbage, and four ounces of grapes!

Gourmet, Beware

The fruit with the highest number of calories is the avocado. An average avocado will run 370 calories. This compares with a slice of apple pie, which will run 350.

Look, Ma, No Arms

Losing one of its five arms is no tragedy for a starfish. For, within ten days or so, the starfish can grow a new arm with the greatest of ease.

One variety of starfish uses its ability to grow new arms to outwit his enemies. This starfish is called the *Luidia*. When it is disturbed or attacked, it breaks its arms into small pieces. If the *Luidia* is caught in a net, for example, it confounds the fisherman by breaking into bits and slipping between the strands. Then each piece of the *Luidia* swims away to grow into a whole new starfish!

Even complete dismemberment holds no terrors for a starfish. If a starfish is cut into five parts, and each part is thrown back into the sea, there will soon be five starfish where there was just one to begin with. Each of the parts of the original starfish will have grown a complete new set of arms.

The Mighty Pen

Books have been censored and banned since the earliest times. The list is long and impressive. Many illustrious writers and their writings have been banned and censored at one time or another. Homer, Socrates, Confucius, the Bible, the Talmud, Roger Bacon, Dante, Boccaccio, Erasmus, Virgil, Martin Luther, Michelangelo, Calvin, Francis Bacon, Cervantes, and William Shakespeare, among others, shared the honor of having been heavily disapproved.

Coming up to modern times, we find that Anatole France, the great French writer, was interdicted by the Pope in 1922; that George Bernard Shaw was taken off the shelves of the New York Public Library in 1905; that Theodore Dreiser's *An American Tragedy* was banned by the Superior Court of Boston in 1930—at the same time that it was required reading for an English course in Harvard College across the Charles River.

Bertrand Russell's writings were banned in Boston in 1927. Sherwood Anderson's *Dark Laughter* was banned in Boston in 1930. Upton Sinclair's *Oil* was banned in the same city in 1927. And James Joyce's *Ulysses* was banned by the United States Post Office Department in 1918. In more recent times, we find that Norman Mailer's *The Naked and the Dead* was refused entry into Canada in 1949; that New Zealand, in 1964, declared James Baldwin's *Another Country* obscene; and that in 1954 James Jones's *From Here to Eternity* was declared unmailable by the United States Post Office.

A drama as mild and non-controversial as *A View From the Bridge* by Arthur Miller could not obtain a license to be performed in London in 1956, even though the play had been awarded the New York Drama Critics Circle Award and the Pulitzer Prize.

As recently as 1968, a group in Minnesota attacked a local high school administration for permitting J.D. Salinger's *A Catcher in the Rye* to occupy a place in the local library.

Early, But Not Primitive

Around 1300, when the Incas were still a primitive tribe fighting for survival in the highlands of the Andes, the Chimu Empire was in full glory in northern Peru.

Around 1200, the Chimus succeeded in conquering their enemies. One hundred years later, they built their capital, a city called Chan-Chan. Their rule was to last 250 years. Today, one can see the remnants of Chan-Chan.

Chan-Chan was built in the dry coastal plains and it stretched over 12 square miles. The whole city was surrounded by adobe walls—in some places three of them—that were as high as 27 feet. Inside the enclosed space, they built streets, long rows of houses with gabled roofs, temples, great pyramids with imposing steps on the sides, granaries, cemeteries, irrigated gardens, orchards, and stone-lined reservoirs.

Some archaelogists think that around 1350, Chan-Chan was as big as Paris or London.

Cleanliness and Godliness

King Chulalongkorn of Siam is familiar to theater and movie goers as the young prince who grew up to become King in the play, *The King and I.*

In 1887, the king built a gleaming Golden Temple on the Menam River—a pagoda that cost $500,000 to erect. This beautiful temple was not ever intended to be occupied; it was built solely to house a marble and gold swimming pool in which the 10-year-old Crown Prince Vajikanahit was given a ritual bath. After the hour-long ceremony was completed, the building was never again used.

The Temple still stands, surrounded by four other pagodas, each of which is studded with plates of gold and precious stones. As for the Crown Prince, the subject of perhaps the costliest bath in all history, he died in 1895 before he could succeed to the throne.

Phi Beta Kappa was the first college fraternity in America. It was founded at William and Mary College in Williamsburg, Virginia in 1776. In 1779 branches were established at Yale and Harvard. Later, Phi Beta Kappa became a scholarship honor society and other fraternities were formed as social clubs.

If someone referred to you as a drone it might mean you're being compared to a stingless male bee that gathers no honey; or, if you prefer, it could be you have something in common with a pilotless reconnaissance plane.

The late President John F. Kennedy established the world's record for being the fastest talker in public life. In a speech he made in December, 1961, he spoke at the rate of 327 words per minute.

"Stars and Bars" was the name given the first Confederate flag. It had one white bar between two red bars, and in the upper left-hand corner a blue field with a circle of white stars, one for each state that had seceded.

In 1873, E. Remington & Sons manufactured the first practical typewriter. This machine had been patented in 1868 by Christopher Latham Sholes, who made up the word type-writer.

The first submerged circumnavigation of the earth was accomplished in 1960 by the nuclear powered submarine, the "U.S.S. Triton," which traveled under water around the world, 41,500 miles, in 84 days. The hull of this submarine was submerged during the entire trip, but the upper portion broached the surface twice.

A Chip On His Shoulder

Like potato chips? Of course! How old are potato chips? Well, it seems potato chips were prepared in 1853 at the Moon Lake House Hotel, Saratoga Springs, New York, by Red Indian chef George Crum. Someone had sent back a dish of the usual French fries complaining they were too thick. The chef answered the challenge by creating potato slivers. These were so well received that Sarotoga Chips became a featured item on the restaurant's menu.

The town of Stuttgart, Germany, can claim at least one first. It was in this city that the first taxicabs plied their trade. In the spring of 1896, one Herr Dutz operated cabs in that city. In May of 1897, a Herr Greiner started a rival company. Greiner's cabs were fitted with taxi meters.

Fish do not have a keen sense of hearing, but they do have a keen sense of smell.

Fleet Feet

A cheetah can run about 70 miles per hour, a jack rabbit 35, an ostrich 30.

Compare these to man's speed of 27 miles an hour, the top speed reached by a man during a 100-yard race.

Prophet Without Honor

The book, *SUMMERHILL: A Radical Approach to Child Rearing*, by A. S. Neill, has sold more than a million copies in the United States, and has been translated into 14 languages. Educators consider it a landmark work, and it has had lasting influence in the theory and methodology of education. Yet, despite the eminence that this book has achieved in professional circles, and despite its widespread dissemination in the United States, Australia, Germany and many other countries, few people in Great Britain even recognize the name of A.S. Neill.

One of the strangest cities in the world is Brasilia, the new capital of Brazil. This artificial city which rises above a treeless plain, now has a population of half a million. The city was laid out by architect Lucio Costa in the shape of an airplane.

The architecture of this newfangled urban development is disturbingly surrealistic. Its public buildings are ultramodern. Its streets are the widest in the world. The main avenue sprawls for a width of 370 yards; it is five times as wide as the famed Champs Elysees in Paris.

Living here gives one the sense of being on another planet.

A grasshopper is capable of jumping a distance of about two feet.

The first system of shorthand was published by Dr. Timothy Bright in London in 1588. It was a very difficult system, but it started this very useful idea out.

In 1681, John Llywellin made the first shorthand report of a trial held in the Provincial Court in St. Johns, Maryland.

Pregnant Imprecations

The Jewish people have always had a penchant for colorful cursing. Instead of ventilating their feelings by smiting with a fist or attacking with a weapon, Jews from time immemorial have displayed their wrath by uttering imprecations. Here are some of the most famous of such curses:

"May God call the tune, and may your enemies play the music."

"May you lose your faith and marry a pious woman."

"May your wife eat matzohs in bed, and may you roll in the crumbs."

"May all your teeth fall out except one, which should remain for a toothache."

"May you grow like an onion, with your head in the ground and your feet in the air."

"May you have a good long sleep, and may your dreams be only of your troubles."

"May you be the proof that man can endure anything."

"Go hang yourself on a sugar vine, and may you so achieve sweet death."

"May you inherit a fortune, but be too ill to enjoy it."

"May you lose all your money and be compelled to go from house to house to borrow or beg food for the day; and may you eventually come to my house, and I shouldn't have enough to give you either."

President Andrew Johnson offered a reward of $100,000 for the capture of Jefferson Davis, president of the Confederacy.

Horsing Around

The saying "He eats like a horse" could use some examination. A horse will eat about 15 pounds of hay and nine pounds of fodder each day, which makes about 24 pounds of food. The average horse weighs about 1,000 pounds. This means that a horse consumes about 1/50 of its own weight each day.

Compare this to birds, who consume more than 90 times their own weight in food each day.

The Bible Tells Me So

Of the 200 or so "Guttenberg Bibles" printed, only 48 survive, and one of these recently fetched $2.5 million at auction—making it the most expensive book ever purchased!

William Henry Harrison served the shortest term of any American president—one month. He was elected president at the age of 68, but caught pneumonia during his inauguration and died on April 4, 1841.

On February 13, 1741, Andrew Bradford of Philadelphia, Pennsylvania, published *The American Magazine,* the first magazine in America. Three days later, Benjamin Franklin's *The General Magazine and Historical Chronicle* appeared.

Tongue-Tie

The periwinkle is a mollusk that grows to be only one inch long. Yet, the periwinkle has a tongue that is several times longer than its body. And on this tongue the periwinkle grows an astounding 4,000 tiny teeth!

And what does the periwinkle eat, with this gigantic tongue and all these teeth?

The periwinkle eats nothing but seaweed!

Bicarb Anyone?

Ronald Sloan, in 1976, established a hamburger-eating record by devouring 17 burgers, with buns, in a mere 30 minutes—appropriately enough in Cincinnati.

A Shell with Ells

One of the most complex of mollusks is the chambered nautilus, a distant cousin of the squid. Most Crustaceans shed their shells to grow bigger ones, or scavenge for shells that will fit them as they grow. The chambered nautilus simply builds on more and bigger "rooms" to its original shell.

The shell of the nautilus is one of the most beautiful that nature has contrived. When the nautilus is quite young, it has a single shell, or a one-room house. As the mollusk grows and gets too big for its original shell, it builds a new, larger shell as an *addition* to its original shell. This process continues as the nautilus grows larger until its shell is literally a house of many rooms or chambers. That is where the name "chambered nautilus" comes from.

But in these days of housing shortage, the nautilus is an extravagant mollusk. For it lives always in only one room at a time — the last room that it has built. And the other chambers built earlier remain empty.

Hydrogen is the most common or abundant element in the universe, the first element in the Periodic Table. It is the least dense gas known, and is thought to compose about 90 percent of the molecules in the universe.

At birth, the hippopotamus weighs about one hundred pounds. Not so astonishing, considering that its parents weigh between four and five tons each.

Any plum which has sufficient sugar in its substance to dry without souring is called a prune.

The longest navigable inland waterway in the world is the Amazon River. Seagoing vessels can ascend it for a distance of over 2,200 miles.

Ducks and geese can fly at a speed of 70 miles per hour in level flight.

The world-wide production of cigarettes is about three trillion or about 1500 for each person on the earth!

I've Got Spurs

Most of us are familiar with the spurs a cock has on its legs. But not many birds can claim spurs on their wings! One such well-armed bird is the screamer of South America.

Each of the wings of this bird is equipped with two sharp spurs—one large and one small. Yet, despite these excellent weapons, the screamer is not a fierce combatant.

A Fish Out of Water

While the starfish plays tricks with its arms, there is another group of fishes that play tricks with their legs. That's right, legs. For there are some fish that have turned their fins into leg-like structures and can use them to walk, to hunt for food, and even to climb trees.

The walking perch is one of these extraordinary creatures. Its two strong fins are bent into such a position that it can stand and walk upon them. It often takes a walk — right out of the water!

The walking perch can live out of water for considerable periods of time. The fish has a labyrinthine chamber over its gills in which oxygen is stored. Ashore, the walking perch spends its time hunting for insects to eat; then it climbs the lower branches of trees that grow along the water's edge, and roosts there for hours.

At least three other kinds of fishes are also almost as much at home on land as they are in the water. The mudskipper and the ugly frogfish can walk on their fins, too. And the hassar often makes night marches on land to find a new pool when drought dries up one of his watery homes.

The rapid-firing machine gun was invented by Richard Jordan Gatling, an American schoolteacher and physician. He demonstrated it for use during the Civil War, but the Ordnance Department did not get around to accepting it until 1866, when the war was over. However, it remained in use for a long time until it was replaced by improved models.

The first daily newspaper in the United States made its appearance on September 21, 1784. The *Pennsylvania Packet and Daily Advertiser* was published in Philadelphia, Pennsylvania by David C. Claypoole and John Dunlap.

Fickle Female

The male fox will mate for life, and if the female dies, he remains single for the rest of his life. However, if the male dies, the female will get a new mate.

The largest, most complicated musical instrument is the organ. It has been the chief church instrument since the 4th century.

No Umbrellas Needed

Australia is the world's driest continent. It gets an average yearly rainfall of 16 inches. Compare this with the world annual average of 26 inches of rain.

Good, Clean, Long Life

There are three areas in the world where it is not uncommon for people to live exceptionally long lives: in Hunza, Kashmir, in the Caucasus mountain region of South Russia, and in Vilcabamba in Ecuador.

Miguel Carpio, Vilcabamba's oldest citizen, was 129 years old in 1976. The town, an isolated village in the Andes, with a population of 1,819 persons in 1972, numbered among its residents two women and seven men who were over 100 years old. No one knows exactly why certain people live so long, but some researchers have ascribed the longevity of the Hunzakats to strenuous exercise and a vegetarian diet. This factor gains credibility considering that all three of these communities are situated high in the mountains where life is hard and physical activity is essential.

Of course, long-lived individuals are occasionally to be found elsewhere as well. Javier Pererira, an Indian in Bogota, Columbia, is said to be 167 years old.

Fat Chance

Guru Maharaj Ji claims to be a living incarnation of God. He is known by his detractors as "That Fat Boy." But such pejoratives do nothing to diminish the absolutely frenzied adoration of his followers.

The Guru is rich. He owns a town house in London, Telex machines, private jets, and private yachts. He is married to a beautiful airline stewardess.

Accounted by some as an out-and-out fraud, and by others as a man of great piety, he bestrides his world like a young colossus, for Maharaj Ji, just turned 23 on December 10, 1980.

The only threat to the Guru's immortality is a report that he suffers from a duodenal ulcer.

An Antelope Like a Canteloupe

The smallest antelopes in the world are in Africa. The dik-dik of East Africa is the size of a full-grown rabbit and weighs about five pounds.

The royal antelope of West Africa is even less tall, but weighs about seven pounds.

The largest antelope in the world is the African eland. It is equal to a full-grown horse in size and weighs over a ton.

Clever Tykes

The chuckwalla, a denizen of the American desert, is a highly unusual lizard. It is an extremely playful little fellow. A group of chuckwallas will get together and seem to organize a game of hide-and-seek. They run and hide, then peep around rocks to see if they can spy their companions. Sometimes a chuckwalla will jump out of hiding and grab another's tail just for the fun of it.

When a snake or a bird attacks a chuckwalla, this lizard saves itself in an amazing way. It squirms in between rocks and blows up its body like a balloon. By doing this, the lizard wedges itself in so tightly that the enemy cannot pull it loose. When the attacker finally gets tired of the futile tugging and goes off to hunt an easier meal, the chuckwalla lets the air out and scurries off.

A Deep-water Squid Glows Red, White, and Blue

The ocean's black abyss is so dark that the faint flickerings of light there come from only one source—the creatures of the deep themselves.

Many deep-sea creatures do indeed produce their own light. Luminescent spots on their bodies usually shine blue-green or yellowish green, but sometimes red, blue, white, or violet.

Some of these amazing creatures can turn their lights on and off, while others glow continuously. One fish has a light-emitting organ on the roof of its mouth with which it is thought to attract food. Thus, a seemingly "patriotic" deep-water squid glows red, white, and blue.

Fish living in the profound depths of the sea often have greatly enlarged eyes which concentrate what little light there is. Other creatures are equipped with highly sensitive feelers or other organs which help them find food and escape enemies.

The 100-foot Blue Whale Is the Largest Animal Known

Long ago fish-like sea creatures developed into land animals. They in turn gave rise to the mammals, which are animals that give birth to live young and nourish them with milk.

After millions of years, some forms of mammals, finding abundant food in the sea, returned to the watery world. But these animals, as mammals, still give birth to live young, still nurse their babies, and still breathe air. Among them are the huge whales, larger than the largest of the dinosaurs, the tusked walruses, the playful seals, and sea lions.

The blue, or sulphur-bottom, whale is the largest animal ever known to have lived on the earth. This leviathan of the oceans sometimes measures over a hundred feet long. The extinct *Brontosaurus*, giant of the dinosaurs, was only seventy-five feet long. A newborn blue whale is twenty-three feet long, and much bigger than a full-grown elephant.

These great whales feed on tiny plankton animals, called *krill*. Krill consists mostly of shrimp-like crustaceans about two inches long. They abound in polar waters and the whales graze through these floating pastures much as cattle browse in a grassy meadow. A blue whale may eat two or three tons of krill at a single meal.

Word Over All

The British Museum is considered to house one of the best libraries in the world. It contains over six million printed volumes, and 60,000 unpublished manuscripts, as well as the world's most extensive collection of ancient Egyptian papyri. It houses the original manuscripts of such precious works as the *Magna Carta* and *Beowulf*.

Abertondo Swam The English Channel Round Trip

The English Channel has been licked by such a legion of athletes that today the feat of swimming its treacherous 22 miles is old hat. But the particular Channel feat of Antonio Abertondo, though dreamed of for decades by swimmers, had never been achieved before.

When on September 21, 1961, Abertondo waded into the chilly sea off Dover, he had set himself an unprecedented challenge; he would swim not only from Dover to Calais, France, but—without a break—from Calais back to Dover—a round trip, without rest, of 44 miles!

The Argentine, then 42 years old and a hefty man with a trace of middle-age spread, and greased from head to toe to protect himself against the cold, entered the water in the morning. Abertondo negotiated the first half of the trip in 18 hours and 50 minutes. Ashore in France, he paused for two minutes—only long enough to sip a hot drink. Then he plunged once again into the tide-tossed waters.

After a few miles, weariness set in—extreme weariness. On the return trip, the waves hit harder, belting his face until it swelled. Even under the goggles his eyes grew sore. Hallucinations followed, the swimmer imagining that huge sharks were in his path.

But Abertondo pumped on, arm over arm and kick after kick, and yard by yard he put the miles behind him.

It was more than a day since he had last touched land—a full 24 hours and 25 minutes after he had left Calais—and 43 hours and 15 minutes after he entered the water at Dover—that Antonio Abertondo writhed out of the surf onto the English shore. The last mile had taken a full two hours. Then, like an agonized shipwreck, he collapsed in the arms of his astounded observers.

Ever Heard of Wu?

There are over 40 million people in this world who speak the language called *Wu*. *Wu* is a language spoken in the remote parts of China.

The Portuguese province of Macao is the most densely populated land on earth. It has an area of 6.2 square miles, with 44,500 people to each square mile.

No Doing Your Own Thing

Nothing in the life of the Inca was left to his own wishes. He had to live according to a strict code of behavior that shaped all his actions.

By the time a young Inca reached the age of 20, he had to get married. If by that time a youth hadn't been able to find himself a wife, the chieftain of his tribe chose one for him. The realm had no use for bachelors. What the Lord-Inca needed were soldiers and farmers, and the whole Inca economy and civilization was based on a strict concept of family relationships.

Men and women did not marry for love, but to fulfill economic and social obligations. For a man, a woman was not only the mother of his children but a beast of burden who helped with the farming and other tasks.

The world's largest religious organization is the Roman Catholic Church, with more than 585 million members, 425,000 priests, and 900,000 nuns, according to latest count. There are about 420,000 churches.

The country with the most frontiers in the world is Russia, with 13—Norway, Finland, Poland, Czechoslovakia, Hungary, Rumania, Turkey, Iran, Afghanistan, Mongolia, People's Republic of China, North Korea, and Japan.

The highest regularly performed dive into water is that of the professional divers at Acapulco, Mexico, from a height of 118 feet. The base rocks are 21 feet out from the kickoff, necessitating a leap of 27 feet outward. The water is only 12 feet deep.

The wettest state in the U.S. is Louisiana, with a 65-year annual average of 57.34 inches. The driest state is Nevada, with a 60-year annual average of only 8.60 inches. The average annual precipitation for the United States is about 29 inches.

One pound of nickel, because of its exceptional ductility, can be stretched into a fine wire 80 miles long.

The Pacific Ocean Covers Nearly One-half the Earth's Surface

The vast Pacific is the largest ocean. Its volume is so great that it could hold all the water of the Atlantic, Indian, and Arctic Oceans and still not be completely filled. The Pacific Ocean is also the deepest. Its average depth of 14,000 feet is greater than that of any other ocean.

Peter Sellers was not a car racer but was a compulsive car-buyer! He owned more than 100 autos in his lifetime and kept them an average of three months! Sellers once bought a car which he drove around the block and sold within 5 minutes.

Paul Newman the real "cowboy" of the celebrity-racers is Newman, who keeps winning important meets in great style.

The largest solar telescope in the world is one of 480 feet at Kitt Peak National Observatory near Tucson, Arizona. It has a focal length of 300 feet and an 80-inch heliostat mirror. It was completed in 1962 and produces an image measuring 33 inches in diameter.

Jose Ferrer, the noted Puerto Rican actor/director of TV, stage and screen excels in nearly all forms of athletics and hobbies. He also was a student of architecture (Princeton).

Of all the presidents of the United States, James Madison was the smallest in stature. He weighed less than a hundred pounds, and was five feet, four inches in height.

The mushroom, considered a delicacy for the elite in early Roman times, is actually a type of fungus. In Europe there are more than 50 kinds of edible mushrooms on the market. Most of the mushrooms grown in the United States come from Pennsylvania. Mushrooms have very little nutritive value, but they serve as a source of inspiration to imaginative chefs who use them to enhance many a dish.

The eating of wild mushrooms is not to be encouraged since it is not so easy for a non-expert to recognize the poisonous kind. The amanita mushroom is poisonous and can be deadly.

Signs of Spring

Some people call it superstition; some people think it is folk wisdom; any way you look at it, all peoples have such quaint beliefs.

In America, February 2nd is Groundhog Day. Tradition has it that on this day the groundhog comes up out of his burrow. If it is a sunny day and he sees his shadow, he scoots back down to remain holed up for six more weeks; which means we will have six more weeks of winter. If he doesn't see his shadow, we will have an early spring.

In Russia, March 14th is St. Evdokia's Day. Tradition has it that if chickens can drink from thawing puddles that day, spring will be early. If the puddles are still frozen over, look for more wintry weather.

The president of the ecclesiastic court that convicted Joan of Arc at Rouen in 1431 was Pierre Cauchon, bishop of Beauvais, France. He was extremely partisan to the English, who ruled France in the Hundred Years War, and totally unsympathetic to Joan's attempts to put the dauphin Charles on the throne. In fact, so clear was it that he did not give Joan a fair trial that a rehabilitation trial was held in 1456.

We all know the expression "as scarce as hens' teeth." It's hard to know why hens were singled out for this distinction, for the fact is that no birds have teeth.

Birds swallow their food whole. The process of breaking food up into little particles, which humans accomplish by chewing, takes place in the birds' gizzards.

Another expression that comes from birdland is "It sticks in my craw." This, too, is something of a misnomer. The bird's craw is just in front of its gizzard and is used for storing food. A bird can gobble up a large quantity of food and store it in the craw, where it can be safely held for a time until it is ready to be passed into the gizzard.

It's a Miracle, Naturally

According to the Bible, it was divine intervention that made it possible for the Jews to escape from Egypt. You remember that when they fled across the desert, the Egyptian soldiers were hard on their heels in pursuit. When the Jews reached the Red Sea, they thought they were goners. But the waters parted miraculously allowing them to cross, and closed just as miraculously, drowning their enemies.

Well, Dr. Hans Goedicke, chairman of the department of Near Eastern studies at Johns Hopkins University, has another explanation for this auspicious event. Dr. Godicke says that a volcanic eruption at Thera, an island 70 miles north of Crete, caused the towering tidal waves that parted the sea when the Jews reached it. He claims his studies show that the Exodus from Egypt took place in 1477 B.C. (200 years earlier than normally assumed), and that the Pharoah at the time was Hatshepsut, a woman.

Four states in the Unites States are called commonwealths: Kentucky, Massachusetts, Pennsylvania, and Virginia.

The linen bandages that were used to wrap Egyptian mummies averaged one thousand yards in length.

Adult king cobra snakes commonly measure 15 feet or more.

You've always known that you have to be sure to cook pork a long time, but do you know why? It seems that thorough cooking is advisable in order to kill any trichinae that may be present. Trichinae are parisitic worms that cause trichinosis disease. This disease is pretty rare in the United States. When hogs feed on uncooked garbage, they become hosts to trichinae.

Versatile Horns

The Goliath beetle of West Africa is the world's heaviest insect, weighing about three ounces. This awesome creature is magnificently colored, with a deep red, velvety body and a black-and-white striped head and neck. But the giant's most impressive characteristic is a pair of black horns, each close to a quarter of an inch long—larger than the bodies of many insects!

Ordinarily, the beetle uses these horns to dig into the bark of a tree for its favorite meal of juicy sap. But when one of these Goliath beetles was placed in a museum and fed a diet of bananas, it used its horns to slowly peel the fruit!

On November 28, 1977 an English Court of Appeal ruled that a mistress must get the same protection as a wife against the use of violence in the home.

At birth, 270 opossums weigh only one ounce.

Thomas Jefferson was never a member of any church.

A Falling Stone Might Take Ten Hours to Reach the Bottom of a Trench

Suppose you were to drop a stone into the ocean over one of its deep trenches. How long would it take to reach the bottom? Well, if the stone fell through the water at the rate of a foot a second, it would take about ten hours to reach the bottom of the trench.

All the major ocean trenches seem to have about the same maximum depth of 35,000 feet, which is over six and a half miles. If the world's tallest land mountain, Mount Everest, were placed in any of the major ocean trenches, its summit would lie over one mile *below* the surface of the sea.

Next time someone stops you on the street and asks you to name the letters of the alphabet in order of their relative frequency of use, just say: "ETAISONHRDLUCMFWYPGVBKJQXZ!"

If anyone has ever accused you of sowing the apple of discord, you might be interested in the history of that term.

It goes back to Greek mythology. It seems that it all started with a troublemaker named Eris. She had not been invited to the wedding of Peleus and Thetis and thought up a neat way of getting revenge. It was she who threw the golden fruit which was inscribed "to the fairest" out to the goddesses attending the wedding. Naturally, Hera, Athena and Aphrodite each claimed possession of the fruit.

Paris was chosen to settle this dispute among the goddesses, each of whom tried to bribe him to choose her. Hera promised Paris fame and riches; Athena promised success in war; but it was to Aphrodite that Paris awarded the apple because she promised him the beautiful Helen.

Aphrodite kept her promise. She helped Paris kidnap Helen from King Menelaus of Sparta. And that's how the Trojan War started.

Dental Detective

Very often the police will call upon a special dentist to help them establish the identity of a dead body. How come? Well, a person's tooth structure is as unique to him and as unlike anyone else's as are his fingerprints. There are times when fingerprints cannot be used and a forensic dentist, trained to do specialized identification, is called in to analyze the subject's dental characteristics. This can be especially effective in identifying the victims in mass disasters, identifying badly damaged victims in cases of murder or accident, and in identifying persons who are unconscious or suffer from amnesia.

The dentist photographs and X-rays the victim's teeth and then records the number, position, sizes, shapes, dental work done, on a dental record form. The antemortem and the postmortem records may then be compared.

In the summer of 1794, on a very hot afternoon, in the village of Lalain, France, a rain fell which lasted for 30 minutes. What was unusual about this rainfall was that tiny toads in great numbers dropped from the sky.

The Bible student will remember this phenomenon as one of the plagues visited on Pharoah's Egypt just before the Jewish exodus.

Quick of Tongue

Flies and other small insects are the preferred food of most chameleons. To help stalk and capture these swift creatures, the chameleon has some unique talents. It can stay completely motionless for hours at a time, if necessary, waiting for its prey to wander within reach. Meanwhile, it can keep a look-out in all directions.

The chameleon's sharp little eyes work independently. One eye can be watching a fly in front, while the other eye follows the movements of a bug behind. Whichever is the first within the lizard's reach becomes the first to be eaten.

The chameleon's tongue is an amazing organ. It is actually longer than its body, and is equipped with a sticky tip. A seven-inch-long chameleon looking sluggish and half asleep can suddenly pick off a fly more than a foot away. Its slender tongue flashes out and back so swiftly that the human eye cannot follow its movement. The chameleon is such a superb marksman that it almost never misses a target.

Chameleons make splendid pets. In addition to being interesting to watch, and completely harmless, they will keep a home free from flies and mosquitos. Sometimes their owners feed them little bits of raw hamburger, which the lizards enjoy. But you need sharp eyes to actually see the chameleons eat, since the morsels of meat disappear as if by magic.

The phrase "bedtime sports" may have illicit connotations, but there are indeed a number of athletic contests involving the bed. The Australian Bedmaking Championships are one example. The record time for bedmaking under stringent rules of the tournament is 35.7 seconds, but we're not sure what kind of bed, or bedding, was used in that monumental performance. Since 1966, the annual Knaresborough Bed Race has thrilled participants in Yorkshire, England, with the record time for the two-and-a-half-mile course now standing at just over 14 minutes.

Banner Headline

The world's largest flag is a U.S. stars and stripes measuring 411 feet by 211 feet made of nylon taffeta. The stars are 13 feet wide. Spread out for display on a softball field in Central Park, New York City, the flag covered two acres. The Great American Flag Fund is trying to raise $650,000 to build special rigging that would make it possible for the flag to be raised and lowered on the Verrazano-Narrows Bridge spanning Brooklyn, Manhattan, New Jersey. With a weight of seven tons that's not so simple! But what a sight it would make for ships and planes arriving in New York!

There are 35 known species of coconuts.

And Not Even in his Cups

Robert Mayer had an attack of hiccups which lasted eight days. To most of us, hiccups are a source of amusement or at worst, minor embarrassment, but an attack of hiccups may actually be very dangerous. Where the tempo is fast, the victim can become totally exhausted. When hiccups are prolonged, radical measures, such as stomach lavage or even nerve surgery, may be needed.

For mild attacks of hiccups, some doctors recommend a teaspoon of granulated sugar taken with water. Other common remedies are deep breathing and holding the breath.

In 1975, a furniture company and a chemical engineer combined to bring out a new kind of water bed that might eliminate most critics' objections. Called a Gel-bed, the bed is filled with a plastic substance called Flo-lok that can't leak in quantity from the bed, doesn't make waves and remains warm enough to eliminate the need for the heater found on other water beds. A Gel-bed mattress can presently be purchased for under $200—and a frame is not required!

Novelties

The great French literary figures, François Mauriac and André Maurois, chose Charles Dickens' *Great Expectations* as the greatest English novel of all time. The work is singularly free of improbable coincidences, and the poignant story is told with superb grace.

The critics regard *Moby Dick* as the most eminent American novel, and William Rose Benet has called it one of the greatest novels in the literature of the world. Written in 1851 by Herman Melville, the novel took years and years to really catch on. Melville had achieved some fame in his earlier years by living among cannibals in the South Seas, but his masterpiece became famous only after his death.

The best American novel written about World War II is considered to be *The Naked and the Dead* by Norman Mailer. The New York Times's David Dempsey wrote that "It is undoubtedly the most ambitious novel to be written about the recent conflict," and the Atlantic Magazine said it was "By far the most impressive piece of fiction about Americans in the Second World War."

A group of 21 bridge players made an agreement. Each week five members of this group meet to play bridge. The group has agreed to continue this practice only as long as it takes to exhaust every possible combination of five players. How long can they continue before they have to repeat a fivesome? Only 20,349 weeks!

Tableaux

A tableau is a conventional form of art depicting a scene in which individuals are captured in a contrived pose. It is as if the camera stopped, so to speak, at a set instant and time, and the result is a scene of arrested action. Artists have been intrigued by this form for centuries. Here on these pages you will find some amusing examples of their efforts.

Baseball Lore

Cautionary Catches

For Whom the Cloche Tolls

Harper's

Punch

Punch, 1870

Punch

Harper's

Graphics of Lvov

Harper's

Drawing by Jessica Sporn

Harper's

Punch

Triviata

Baseball Lore

Punch, Vol. 12

There are four states in the United States in which more than 10 percent of the population use French as their mother tongue. Of these states, the largest French-speaking population is in the state of Louisiana. Some of these are Creoles, or descendants of early French and Spanish settlers, and some are Cajuns. The Cajuns are descendants of the Acadians, French settlers in Nova Scotia whom the British forcibly shipped to Louisiana in 1755. The other states are New Hampshire, Maine, and Rhode Island, and obviously these French-speaking people have come down from Canada to make the United States their home.

There are five states in the United States in which more than five percent of the native population uses Italian as their mother tongue. Of these states, seven percent of the people in Rhode Island speak Italian as their native tongue. Then, in order, come Connecticut, New Jersey, and New York.

Skate Board

Penguins are excellent swimmers. But sometimes they prefer to ride. Often, they'll climb onto a floating mass of ice, bob along for a while, then dive off into the cold sea and swim for home.

Pro Basketball

Basketball has become a big-money professional sport only in the past few decades, but professional basketball teams have existed almost from the beginning of the game. A team from Trenton, New Jersey became the nation's first professional five in 1898, when the squad rented a Masonic Hall for a game and charged admission to pay for the $25 rental.

The first widely-known professional basketball team was the Original Celtics, begun in 1915 by a group of New York City youngsters. During the 1920s, older, more skilled players were gradually added to the team, and by 1928, when the squad disbanded, they were considered invincible. The team was regrouped in the 30s, as the New York Celtics, before permanently disbanding in 1936. At the height of their popularity, the Celtics played a game every night, and two on Sunday, and were almost continually on the road—yet during the 1922-23 season the Celtics amassed a whopping 204 wins against just 11 defeats!

The first professional basketball association, the National Basketball League, was formed in 1898 to protect players from unscrupulous promoters. The league was disbanded and reorganized many times over the years, with the last NBL established in 1938. A rival organization, the Basketball Association of America, was founded in 1946, and after two years of "war" the leagues combined to form the National Basketball Association, with 17 member teams. A rival league, the American Basketball Association was founded in 1967, but disbanded after the 1975-76 season, with four teams joining the NBA. The NBA now includes 22 teams in four divisions.

The professional basketball player of today probably logs more travel miles than the politician or business executive. Unlike baseball teams, who usually play three or four games on each trip to another city, basketball teams play single-game series, with more than 40 road games each season. Cities with basketball franchises now range from Boston in the East all the way to Portland and Seattle in the West, and to New Orleans and San Antonio in the South.

The north Midwest was the haven of German immigrants from Europe. As an average, better than two percent of the population of the United States speak German as their mother tongue; but the concentration of German-speaking Americans is in North Dakota, Wisconsin, and South Dakota. In each of these states, better than 10 percent of the native population speak German as their mother tongue.

The saltiness of the world's ocean water staggers the imagination! Statisticians estimate that the ocean may contain as much as 50 million billion tons of dissolved solid, which spread over the earth's land area would form a layer more than 500 feet thick—nearly the height of the Washington Monument.

The longest hole-in-one in golf, according to the existing records, was one of 440 yards recorded on October 7, 1965, by Robert Mitra, at a club in Omaha, Nebraska. His normal drive was 245 yards, but a 50-mph gust of wind aided his shot on this particular hole.

Largely Innocuous

The largest member of the python family—the reticulated python of southeastern Asia—grows to a length of 25 feet. Some specimens of this nonvenomous snake have been measured at 28 feet, with a weight of over 220 pounds! So strong is this gargantuan serpent that, in captivity, the efforts of a dozen zookeepers are sometimes required to hold the snake for forced-feeding.

To determine what the snakes eat, the stomachs of dead pythons have been examined. Incredibly enough, the belly of one medium-sized python contained a full-grown leopard! The claws and teeth of this animal had proved insufficient against the terrible strength of the giant serpent.

A Board for the Bored

The 17th century saw the first wide use of the word *backgammon* in place of *tables*, along with a number of other innovations. For the first time, doubles entitled the roller to play the roll twice, as in the modern game. The concept of the *backgammon* victory was also introduced, although as used at the time a *backgammon* was actually the modern *gammon*—a victory in which the winner succeeds in bearing off all his men from the board before his opponent can remove any of his men.

The word *backgammon* itself has been traced to a number of sources. Some etymologists point to the Welsh *bach cammaun*, "small battle." But most favor the Middle English *baec gamen*, or "back game," traced by some to the medieval custom of constructing a backgammon board on the back of a chessboard, as is often done today. Thus, tables became known as the "game on the back" of the chessboard, and later, "back game."

On the Continent, the game was known as *tavole reale* in Italy, *tablas reales* in Spain, and *trictrac* in France. The French term is thought to owe its origin to the sound made by tumbling dice on a wooden board. A number of *trictrac* boards were used by the French court at Versailles. One elaborately decorated board belonging to Marie Antoinette was reputed to have cost over a quarter-million francs.

For some reason, backgammon became very popular among 18th-century clergymen. During the same era, physicians also seem to have favored the pastime. One doctor wrote that backgammon was an "anodyne to the gout, the rheumatism, the azure devils, or the yellow spleen." Even Thomas Jefferson was a backgammon fancier, playing the game in his off hours, while drafting the Declaration of Independence.

The lowest temperature ever recorded in the United States was at Prospect Creek Camp in Alaska. Here the temperature once dropped to 80° below zero—a pale cry from the world record low of 126.9° at Vostok, a Soviet weather station in the Antarctic.

Eyeglasses

In the 19th century, European men could wear glasses anywhere, but spectacles remained taboo for fashionable women. The spyglass was now more diplomatically called an *opera glass*, due to its nearly universal use at the theater. After the invention of binoculars, in 1823, single and double-lens opera glasses became so popular that a contemporary writer advised: "A bunch of violets, an embroidered handkerchief, a large opera glass, and a bottle of smelling salts—these are four things a lady of fashion must have at the theater."

The *pince-nez*—literally, "pinch-nose"—first appeared around 1840, and gradually began to supersede temple glasses. By the end of the century, the pince-nez was in almost universal use among European and American men, though it was almost never worn by women. The *monocle*, long associated with aristocratic snobbery, first appeared in England around the beginning of the century, and became all the rage among the European elite—despite warnings from physicians against their use.

Americans drink almost twice as much of spirituous liquors than do the citizens of Great Britain, Australia, Austria, or Belgium.

The city in the United States that experiences the most snow is Buffalo, New York, whose annual inches of snowfall come to more than 88.

Gold

Gold has been an alluring object since civilization began. It has been valued for its unparalleled beauty, the ease with which it can be shaped, resistance to rust, and most of all for its rareness.

Gold became a symbol of achievement. It made an ideal medium of exchange and became the embodiment of money and the epitome of wealth.

Gold madness drove the early explorers, the pioneers who crossed the Rockies and those who braved the Klondike gold and it is gold that sends people down 2.2 miles to the bottom of the deepest mine in the world.

If all the gold that has been mined in 5,000 years were assembled in one place, it would make a cube only 65 feet on each side, or it would cover a football field of 360 X 160 feet to a depth of only 4¾ feet.

Dining in Style

It's been estimated that a New Yorker can dine out every night of his life until age 65 without visiting any establishment twice!

Among New York's restaurants, *Lutèce* and *La Grenouille* have been given high marks by Michelin, and certainly rank among the finest restaurants on this side of the Atlantic. *Windows on the World*, located atop one of the 110-story World Trade Center towers, has been lauded for its view more than its food. Reservations for dinner at the sky-high restaurant must sometimes be made weeks in advance. And any list of Gotham's posh restaurants must include *The Palace* where dinner prices are, at this writing, $75 per person—without drinks!

Hip to Roses

Quick, name a flower. Well, you may not have said *rose*, but if you were to experiment with the question you'd probably find that, of the estimated 300,000 species of plants on earth, the rose is the first flower to pop into most minds.

Why? It's difficult to say. Many other flowers are larger, more colorful, more fragrant, or more valued. But no single flower is so universally known, so closely connected with the culture of many civilizations, so rich in poetic and mythologic significance as the rose. Symbol of beauty, romance, love, secrecy, perfection, elegance, and life itself, the rose has figured in legend, heraldry, and religion, and has served as the favorite of poets and artists from time immemorial.

Immortalized in songs, such as *The Last Rose of Summer*, *Sweet Rosie O'Grady*, and *My Wild Irish Rose*, the rose has been, and will likely forever remain, the queen of flowers.

The botanical family Rosaceae, which includes close to 200 species and thousands of hybrids, has flourished for millions of years. Indeed, roses have been cultivated for so long that it's impossible to determine where or when the flower was first domesticated. The Egyptians were familiar with cultivated roses by 3000 B.C., building rose gardens in their palaces and often burying roses in their tombs. By the time of Cleopatra's reign, the rose had replaced the lotus as Egypt's ceremonial flower.

The mythologies of various ancient cultures touched on the rose. Most agreed that the flower was created when the gods were still on earth. The Greeks called the rose, "the king of flowers" until the poet Sappho, in her *Ode to the Rose*, dubbed it as the "queen of flowers" forevermore. According to the Greeks, the rose first appeared with the birth of Aphrodite, the goddess of love and beauty. When Aphrodite (in Roman mythology, Venus) first emerged from the sea, the earth produced the rose to show that it could match the gods in the creation of perfect beauty. The well-known painting by Botticelli, *Birth of Venus*, depicts dozens of roses in a scene of the goddess emerging from the sea.

Another myth tells of a beautiful maiden named Rhodanthe (*rhodon* in Greek means "rose") who was tirelessly pursued by three suitors. To escape her pursuers, Rhodanthe fled to the temple of Artemis, where her attendants, convinced that Rhodanthe was even more beautiful than Artemis, flung a statue of the goddess from its pedestal and demanded that Rhodanthe be represented there instead. The god Apollo, angered by the insult to his twin sister, Artemis, turned Rhodanthe into a rose and her attendants into thorns. The three suitors were changed into the three courtiers of the rose: the bee, the worm, and the butterfly.

Christmas Warmth

Icelandic custom has the populace lighting huge bon-fires to burn on Christmas Eve. Cemeteries are festively decorated with lights.

It shouldn't be surprising that Kansas tops all other states in the use of motorcycles. Kansas is flat and widespread, and the motorcycle is ideal for transportation on such terrain. Better than one out of every 20 persons in Kansas owns a motorcycle.

In the early days of basketball, some courts were irregularly shaped, twisting around pillars or other impediments. In some courts, balls going out of bounds were considered in play, forcing players to dash into the stands and fight with the spectators for the ball, while in other courts ropes were strung around the playing area as boundary lines, with players rebounding from the ropes like boxers in a ring. It wasn't until 1903, that straight, marked boundaries became part of the standard court.

Yess, We Have Some Bananas

Many Americans caught their first glimpse of the banana at the 1876 Centennial Exposition in Philadelphia. Bananas were still so unfamiliar to most Americans that the fruit and the telephone became the two most popular exhibits at the Exposition. The fruits sold for 10¢ apiece, a high price at the time. Each banana was wrapped in tin foil, although the fruit was naturally protected by its thick skin.

The high price of the fruit was perhaps due to the fact that up to half of each banana cargo was lost to spoilage en route. Then, in 1899, the plantations of Minor Keith, the ships of Lorenzo Baker, and the sales network of Andrew Preston were combined to form the United Fruit Company, which soon became the largest importer of bananas to America. Using modern farming techniques and refrigerated ships, the firm set up a network that brought fresh bananas to market within a month of harvest. This process eliminated the large-scale spoilage that had plagued earlier importers.

It was the United Fruit Company (now the United Brands Company) that devised the advertising campaign featuring the now familiar Chiquita banana. Beginning in the early 1940s, the lively banana with high-heeled shoes, ruffled dress, and fruit-bowl hat served as spokeswoman for the firm's principal product. Chiquita sang clever calypso jingles on radio, and later appeared in animated form on television. Chiquita is the official logo and trademark for bananas sold by United Brands.

The greatest concentration of Catholics in the United States is in the state of Rhode Island, where better than 63 percent of the population acknowledge this persuasion.

It is recorded that there are 6½ million persons in the United States who play tennis at least twice a week. Of this number, almost 20 percent live on the Pacific Coast.

In the District of Columbia, statistics say that there are more abortions per capita than in any state in the Union—in fact, almost four times as many per capita as there are in New York State.

The largest state in the Union is not Texas. Alaska is almost three times the size of Texas.

Only one person out of 100 in the United States is a Mormon, but if you go to Utah you'll find that three out of four people belong to this church.

To Sleep, Perchance to Dream

Roughly a quarter of a million people in the United States suffer from narcolepsy, a disorder in which there is a frequent uncontrollable desire for sleep. The precise cause of this disease is unknown, and there is no cure presently available.

This disease can have unforeseen tragic consequences. The victim may experience sleep paralysis and, being unable to move just as he is about to fall asleep, may end up in a dangerous spot. A victim of a sleep attack may, for example, fall asleep against a radiator, and be awakened by a very painful burn.

Backgammon in Earnest

The most recent backgammon rage had its beginnings in 1964, when Russian Prince Alexis Obolensky of Palm Beach, Florida, founded an international tournament in the Bahamas for jet-set backgammon buffs. The tournament has been held there every year since then. The maiden 1964 tourney included just 32 players; by 1968, the number had swelled to 128, with additional tournaments for beginners and "consolation fights" for first-round drop-outs. The number of backgammon players in the United States, meanwhile, soared from about 200,000 in 1969 to over two million today. In 1973, game board producers sold more backgammon sets than they had sold in the previous 20 years combined!

Prince Obolensky went on to found similar tournaments in Las Vegas and other places. Since 1966, an annual international backgammon tournament has been held in the London Clermont Club. The 1978 tourney included 100 players competing for $100,000 in prizes. And private gambling matches, played for up to $25 a point, have been known to cost unlucky participants as much as $100,000!

The greatest crime rate in the United States is not in New York City nor in Chicago, but of all places, in Nevada, where for every 100,000 population there are 8,306 crimes committed.

The state where infections of a sexual nature are greatest is Alaska. Here for every 100,000 people, over 1,215 have gonorrhea.

Where do actors live? Well, predictably, most actors live in New York. The runner-up state in this respect is California. Although there are seven actors who said that they lived in Mississippi, there are none who claimed that their place of residence was Wyoming, Idaho, Delaware or Maine.

Hoop-La

Baseball may be our "national pastime," and football may draw the largest crowds per game, but surprisingly enough, it's basketball that claims the honor as the largest sport in America. A 1950s survey showed that basketball attendance at all games was, at least at the time, larger than the combined annual attendance totals of baseball, football, hockey, and other major sports.

More teams are organized each year to play basketball than any other sport, and no American playground or gymnasium is complete without at least two basketball hoops. And basketball, now the third largest sport worldwide, is the only widely played game with an exclusively American origin.

Write, Don't Talk

Leo Tolstoy, the great Russian novelist, was nicknamed by his friends "Crybaby Leo." His was a troubled life, and his complaints advertised his plight.

He fought continually with his wife. When he was eighty-two, he finally left her. She had objected to his decision to divide up all the property they owned among his servants.

By all accounts, Count Tolstoy was a miserable man—and a genius.

Campus Basketball

Basketball is the number-one college sport in the United States. Football is bigger at some of the larger universities, but most smaller schools that can't afford a football team still field a basketball squad. Where did it all begin? It depends upon whom you ask.

Some sports historians say that the first college basketball team to be organized represented Geneva College of Beaver Falls, Pennsylvania, while others claim it was the University of Iowa or Mount Union College of Alliance, Ohio that first fielded a basketball squad. In any case, all three schools formed teams in 1892. The first intercollegiate basketball game was played in 1896, with a seven-man Wesleyan University team defeating Yale, 4-3. According to whom you believe, the first intercollegiate game with five-man teams was played between either the University of Pennsylvania and Yale in 1897, or one year earlier between the University of Chicago and the University of Iowa.

The first University of Chicago team was organized by Amos Alonzo Stagg, the school's athletic director, who'd learned the game from a student from Springfield, Massachusetts. The squad won its first five-man game against the University of Iowa, 15-12, with the coach of the Iowa five acting as referee. Although the majority of the spectators at the game hadn't the foggiest notion of basketball rules, it's recorded that many vociferously expressed their disapproval of the referee's calls.

National basketball tournaments have been held since 1897, when the 23rd Street YMCA of New York won an AAU competition, but the first national college tourney took place in 1937 in Kansas City, Missouri. The National Invitational Tournament (NIT) was organized by a group of New York sports writers in 1938, and the following year the NCAA organized its first national championship tournament. College basketball became front-page news in the early 1950s, when two investigations uncovered widespread game-fixing by gamblers. Ultimately, 49 games in 17 states were declared fixed, and 30 persons were arrested in all.

Precious Little

Gold is very dense and a half-inch layer covering the Pentagon floor area, 6,500,000 square feet, would weigh 100,000 tons.

The world supply of gold is being increased by 1,420 tons each year. About one half of this is being produced in South Africa, one quarter comes from the Soviet Union. It will take only 70 more years to produce as much gold as was produced in the previous 5,000 years.

Each ton of sea water contains about 1/5,000,000 of an ounce of gold. It is estimated that about 10 million tons of gold is in all the tons of sea water in the oceans.

Never a Wink or Blink

The snake is unable to close its eyes or even to blink them. Even during its long hibernation, a snake's eyes remain wide open and staring.

A snake's eyes, like those of a fish, have no movable eyelids that can be pulled down. The absence of eyelids is one sure way to distinguish a snake from a legless lizard, which can blink and close its eyes.

The main purpose of the eyelid is to protect the delicate pupil of the eye from dirt and damage. To make up for this lack, the snake has a kind of window over each eye. This window consists of a hard, transparent scale, like a tiny pane of glass that covers the whole eyeball and guards it against being scraped by grass and twigs.

A Hands-down Winner

The most prolific of all food plants, the banana "tree" is actually not a tree at all, but a giant herb—the largest plant on earth without a woody stem. The "trunk" of the banana plant is not a trunk at all, but is made up of thick leaves furled one upon another in overlapping layers, combining to form a shoot that can reach heights of up to 30 feet. And the palmlike leaves themselves often grow up to 10 feet long!

A banana plant will bear fruit only once, but each rootstock of the plant can, in turn, produce an unending series of plants, assuring a continuous crop. Cultivators allow one plant from each rootstock, or rhizome, to mature and bear fruit. Then, they cut down the plant and nurture another shoot from the rhizome.

Each plant bears about 10 bunches of fruit, called *hands*, and each hand contains from 10 to 20 bananas, or *fingers*. Thus, one banana plant will produce an average of 150 bananas, weighing about 85 pounds altogether.

A new banana plant sprouts quickly, producing leaves in as little as three weeks. Some old-time banana plantation workers claim they can "hear" the plants growing in the dark. After about eight months, a single bud pushes through the center of a leaf cluster. Small flower clusters then appear, which eventually bend outward and upward as they turn into the hands. Thus the fruits actually grow upside-down. As soon as the fruits begin to form, plantation workers place plastic bags over each hand to protect the bananas from insects, birds, and scarring by wind-battered leaves.

Within a year, the bananas are ready for harvest. Unlike most other fruits, bananas are picked green and ripen later. If the fruits were allowed to ripen on the plant, they would split open and lose much of their sweet flavor.

At harvest time, the fruits are cut from the plants in their plastic bags, then sent by overland cable or truck to nearby boxing stations. At the boxing station, the bananas are washed, cut into clusters, labeled, boxed, and sent by rail to port.

The boxed bananas are loaded quickly aboard refrigerated ships—banana boats are often in and out of port within 12 hours—and delivered to ports in the United States. Before being shipped to markets, the fruit is stored in ripening rooms for a few days until the green color changes to a golden yellow. The entire trip from plantation to consumer's shopping cart can take as little as 10 days.

More murders per capita population are committed in Alabama than in any other state in the Union.

Welcome Light

In Ireland a candle is placed in the window on Christmas Eve as a welcome light to all who, like Mary and Joseph, may be in search of shelter.

A Hole Is to Nest In

Unlike most other birds, the house wren will build her nest in any sort of a hole in trees or buildings. Her nests have been found in—among other places—old shoes, hats, tin cans, and mailboxes. One surprised housewife found a newly-built nest tucked neatly into the pocket of a pair of trousers she had hung on the clothesline.

The Road To Riches

Next time you buy an 18 cent U.S. stamp, see if you recognize the man in the picture. The United States Postal Service has issued a new commemorative stamp honoring Joseph Wharton. You don't know who Joseph Wharton is? That's not strange, not many people do know.

Joseph Wharton founded the first school of business in the world. In 1881 he granted the University of Pennsylvania a fund of money to establish a school to train young men who intended to engage in business, property management, or civil government. Thus was the Wharton School of Finance and Political Economy founded, and a new educational discipline established.

There were only 13 students in Wharton's first class. Philadelphia's outstanding businessmen were delighted to send their scions there for training. These young men usually went on to management positions in their fathers' firms. But some chose careers in academia and government.

The education that Joseph Wharton outlined as essential for potential business and government leaders was heavily weighted in classic languages and in moral and ethical precepts. There were also courses in bookkeeping, contracts, banking, and trust management. The idea of such course of study must have had appeal; in 1898 the University of California and the University of Chicago set up the second and third business schools in the world, and in 1901 the University of Wisconsin, Dartmouth, and New York University followed suit; and in 1908 Harvard set up its Business School.

Joseph Wharton, by the way, was something of a business genius himself, and a philanthropist. He was interested in metallurgy and initiated some important commercial innovations in this field, and founded some companies that later became giants in their field, such as the Bethlehem Steel Company. You might call Joseph Wharton an overachiever.

More Methodists per capita live in Iowa than in any other state in the Union.

Queen Elizabeth was the daughter of Henry VIII and Anne Boleyn. Anne Boleyn, Henry VIII's second wife was beheaded in 1536, when Elizabeth was three years old.

The Old Testament of the Bible consists of 39 Books, 929 Chapters, 33,214 verses, and 593,493 words. The New Testament contains 27 Books, 260 Chapters, 7,959 verses, and 181,253 words.

Twirl That Wand

On August 2, 1934, working out in a gymnasium in Newcastle, Australia, William Franks picked up a heavy club and began swinging it around his head at an amazing speed. It was the typical Indian club, shaped like a bowling pin, popularly used by gymnasts until the early 1950's.

But Franks wasn't just out for exercise. Twirling the club at a rate of about 300 times a minute, Franks kept up his performance for a full hour. When he was done, the scorekeepers and timekeepers had recorded 17,280 twirls of the wooden pin—a record for sure!

Not Checkproof

Next time you check your mink in a restaurant checkroom in New York you had better have second thoughts. If you go to collect it after you've dined and discover that it's missing you may be out of luck.

The New York Court of Appeals has defined the conditions under which a patron can collect under such circumstances. To begin with, if the restaurant left the tip up to your discretion and did not exact a formal fee for the checking service, the restaurateur is not liable for more than $75.

And even if there had been a checking charge, to recover full value for a lost coat, you would have had to present a written statement of the value of your coat and receive a receipt for that amount before leaving your coat. And that's not all. To recover the full amount stated on the declaration and receipt, you would have to prove negligence. If you can't do this, the most you can collect is $100.

You may have wondered why so many ladies choose to drape their coats over their chairs instead of checking them. Now you know.

When Louis Pasteur was a college student in Paris one of his professors ranked him as mediocre in chemistry.

When My Hare Has Turned to Silver...

The largest of all American hares is the husky Arctic hare. Its average length is two feet, and it may reach a weight of 12 pounds. In summer, the Arctic hare is brownish-gray, but in the winter it is all white, except for black-tipped ears.

The "snowshoe hare" of North America grows large pads of coarse hair on the soles of its hind feet. These snowshoes are nearly six inches long and enable the hare to run easily on the surface of snowdrifts.

More people per capita get married in the state of Nevada than in any other state of the Union. In South Carolina, which ranks second, the marriage is almost 18 per thousand of the population. Compare this with Nevada where the rate per thousand is over 171. It should come as no surprise that the divorce rate in Nevada is higher than in any other state in the Union.

You Could Bowl Me Over

No matter how crippling a physical handicap seems to be, there are always people who manage to overcome it. Indeed, some of these courageous, determined individuals succeed in performing feats that would be considered outstanding even with a normal physical condition.

Take the inspiring case of Lyman Dickinson, of Watervliet, New York. Both his legs were amputated, and were replaced with artificial limbs. Dickinson had to learn to walk all over again. Thanks to plenty of guts and hard work, Dickinson trained himself to use his new legs so well that he was once again able to engage actively in fishing, hunting, golf, and bowling.

Though hunting and golf involve a considerable amount of walking, bowling presents an even more difficult obstacle; for to roll a bowling ball properly, one has to start by taking a series of quick steps, and then come to a complete stop just short of the foul line.

On July 2, 1970, at a bowling alley in Albany, New York, Lyman Dickinson rolled a 299 game. As all bowling fans know, this is just one pin short of a perfect score, a feat very, very few bowlers ever attain.

Cubidity

Some think it is fascinating; some find it frustrating; from six to sixty, everybody's buying it. What is it? Rubik's Cube. The Ideal Toy Corporation alone has sold more than nine millin of these.

Erno Rubik, a Hungarian teacher of architecture, invented this ingenious instrument of torture. It became very popular in Europe, and is now afflicting the American population.

When you first buy this cube you will have an attractive $2^1/_8$″ × $2^1/_8$″ cube with each of its sides showing one of these colors: blue, yellow, green, red, white, orange. But once you start moving one of the 26 small boxes that compose the cube, not only do you disturb this simple color scheme, but you are launched on a journey through puzzledom that may last for days or weeks. The small blocks rotate on spindles inside the cube, and you can move them about in more than 43 quintillion arrangements. That part is fun. The trick, though, is to restore the cube to its pristine state with solid colors flanking each side.

No matter what the birth certificate may say, in England it is customary for royal birthday celebrations to be held in June.

The first person to swim the English Channel under water was the American frogman, Fred Baldasare. He accomplished this feat on July 11, 1962, using self-contained underwater breathing apparatus.

Scince today is making such rapid strides that one almost needs an electronic brain to keep abreast with developments. For example, in the field of biology, there are more than 5,200 learned journals published and in chemistry more than 4,800 publications circulated to keep chemists up on all the latest developments.

Light Up The Sky

The Arctic has its own strange climate. It can be so cold one day that your breath will freeze, while at the same time your skin becomes severely burned from the brilliant reflected sunshine.

During the long winter night, however, the sun never shines. The day disappears. But sometimes the sky displays one of the most spectacular sights in the world, the *aurora borealis* or northern lights. Brilliant bands of red, yellow, blue, and green stream across the sky from 50 to 190 miles up in the outer atmosphere. Some bands have been traced as high as 600 miles.

The lights, more colorful than fireworks, are believed linked somehow to electrical storms, called *solar flares*, on the sun. Then, sometimes slowly, sometimes suddenly, the bands disappear from the sky. The winter night goes on, dark and sunless and cold.

Bottled Up

The weaver bird of Asia lives in large nest colonies—with as many as 70 birds populating a single tree. Their nests look a great deal like large bottles or flasks hanging down from the tree branches.

Holding On For Dear Life

When you see them, you can hardly believe they are alive, but the fact is that as sedentary as they may be, barnacles are nevertheless crustacean animals.

Barnacles have a cement gland and produce a limestone shell around themselves which enables them to adhere to boats and piers. Barnacles feed by sticking their legs, or urri, out of their shells and sweeping minute plankton into their mouths deep in the shell.

Barnacles are the bane of the ship owner. When they settle on a ship's hull they cause increased friction, decreased speed and increased fuel consumption.

What Price Alligator Shoes?

When the early colonists first began to settle America, the swamps and rivers of the South literally teemed with millions of alligators. From Florida and the Gulf Coast and north as far as the Carolinas, their booming bellow was heard each night.

Then men discovered that the alligator's tough hide could be tanned into beautiful and extremely durable leather. At once a terrible slaughter began. Hunters went out and killed alligators in droves. In a very few years the great creatures were almost extinct. The sight of a single 'gator in Georgia or the Carolinas was a rarity. The only survivors were scattered colonies that had retreated into the depths of impenetrable swamps where the ruthless hunters could not reach them.

People who wanted to conserve our vanishing wildlife became worried. In time, they persuaded most of the states where the alligator lived to pass laws protecting this vanishing reptile. These laws either entirely forbade the killing of alligators or limited killing to a very short hunting season.

Under the protection of the law, the alligator population began to increase again. Now it is quite large, although it will probably never reach enormous numbers as in the past.

The Regal Eagle

The American, or bald eagle, became the national emblem of the United States by a 1782 Congressional act. The eagle is a solitary bird and chooses only one mate for its whole lifetime. It builds a single nest high up in a great tall tree. Each year the eagle adds more material to repair this big nest. After a few years, the nest may weigh as much as 2,000 pounds. Sometimes, a tree dies and the nest comes crashing to the ground. The eagle must then construct a new nest in another tree.

Have you ever been stuck in a situation where just two courses of action were open to you, both perilous? This is the situation classically described as "between Scylla and Charybdis."

Scylla, according to Greek mythology, was transformed into an ugly monster and lived on the rocks on the Italian side of the Strait of Messina, where she wrecked passing ships and seized their sailors.

On the other side of the narrow strait was Charybdis, another monster, who spewed out water creating whirlpools in which vessels foundered.

Odysseus and Jason both managed to pass through these straits without falling prey to Scylla or Charybdis, so don't you despair.

The Written Symbol

There are three fundamental kinds of writing systems: logographic, syllabic, and alphabetic. They differ from one another in the kinds of units their symbols represent. Basically, the three systems evolved one from the other in that order, but all three are still in use.

In a *logographic* writing system, each symbol represents a word. Logographic writing systems developed directly from the oldest form of written communication: pictures representing objects or actions. Unlike a letter of the alphabet, a logographic symbol has no phonetic value, though the word it represents has a pronounciation. Our symbol 3, for instance, has no phonetic value, in itself, but does stand for a word prounced *three*.

Chinese is the most familiar example of a contemporary logographic writing system. For the most part, each Chinese character stands for a single word rather than a sound. Learning to write Chinese requires memorizing many thousands of characters, a skill well beyond any first-grader. And the number of characters makes Chinese a difficult language to reproduce with a printing press.

But Chinese does have one advantage: the written language can be understood by people all over China, even though they speak dialects that are not mutually intelligible. The sign for "house," for instance, is understood by all Chinese to mean a dwelling, no matter how the word for "house" is pronounced in the speaker's dialect.

In a *syllabic* writing system, each symbol stands for a single syllable. A syllabic transcription of our word *alphabet* would require three signs: one for *al*, one for *pha*, and one for *bet*. Since the number of different syllabic sounds in any language is often less than a hundred, a syllabic written language is much easier to learn than a logographic system with its thousands of characters.

Japanese is an example of a written language that is basically syllabic. In the fifth century, the Japanese adopted Chinese script and selected 47 Chinese characters to represent 47 syllabic sounds of the Japanese language.

In one corner of the world, the neighboring countries of China, Japan, and Korea, we find all three kinds of writing systems in current use: the Chinese logographic, the Japanese syllabic, and the Korean alphabetic—the Koreans adopted an alphabet from Sanskrit forms.

By far the most common form of writing system around the world is the *alphabetic*, in which each symbol represents a single sound element. The number of single sound elements in a language is lower than the number of syllabic sounds, and so an alphabetic system can be learned easily at a young age. Our own alphabet makes do with just 26 letters; other alphabets have fewer.

Hats Off

The longest National Anthem is that of Greece, containing one hundred fifty eight verses.

The shortest National Anthems are those of Japan, Jordan, and San Marino, containing but four lines.

The National Anthems of Bahrain and Qatar have no words.

Zanesville, Ohio has the distinction of having the only bridge in the world shaped like the letter Y. You can actually cross the bridge without crossing the river.

Keeping One's Head

The age-old custom of laying a deceased relative to rest in his or her bed through the mourning period prompted the families of many beheaded aristocrats to have their dear ones' heads sewn back on, so that the body could be more decorously displayed. A nobleman fortunate enough to keep his head, and perhaps a bit wary of losing it, often ordered servants to remain in his bedroom for as long as he might nap. One English duke insisted that his two daughters stand beside his bed during his afternoon nap. When he awoke one day to discover that one of the young woman had had the audacity to sit down, he promptly sliced 20,000 pounds off her legacy.

All About Coffee

Coffee is the major export crop of many of the countries between the two tropics. A price drop in coffee can throw the economy of many nations into complete turmoil, as happened in Brazil in the decade between 1925 and 1935.

After Brazil, Colombia is the world's second largest coffee exporter. In 1973, the Ivory Coast ranked third.

Brazil once accounted for 66 percent of all coffee exports, but as Africa production has continued to rise, that figure has dropped to 40 percent. Today about 30 percent of all coffee comes from Africa.

To make one pound of butter, about 21 pounds of milk are required.

The insect known as *daddy long legs* has 50 joints in each leg.

Fashion in Bathing

Among the medieval landed classes, the lack of a need to bathe was considered a sign of wealth and leisure. Many an aristocrat bragged of never having taken a bath. Consequently, the demand for perfume and aromatic oils was very high, and the need for spices helped spur the explorations of the 15th century which led to the discovery of America. By the way, Queen Elizabeth of England reportedly bathed once a month, "whether she needed it or not."

After the institution of bathing was revived by the Crusaders' contact with Eastern bathhouses, the common people took frequent public baths. Public baths were common in France as early as the 12th century, and were reputedly as notorious for their promiscuous activities as had been their Roman precursors. By the 17th century, no decent citizen would consider entering a public bath, and the Church frequently decried the excesses of the institution.

Lightening Power

A lightening bolt does not move at the speed of light. Most downward bolts do not reach speeds of over 1,000 miles a second. The upward return stroke that follows most downward bolts can reach speeds of 87,000 miles a second, nearly half the speed of light. Common length of a lightening bolt is about half a mile. Bolts may be as short as 300 feet or as long as five miles.

A single flash of lightning can carry as much as 100 million volts of electricity. Over 100 lightning flashes occur each second.

Lightning takes its biggest toll on trees. Over 7,000 forest fires a year are caused by lightening, resulting in the destruction of millions of trees. Chances of being struck by lightening are more than a million to one. Lightening may strike as many as ten times in a single spot. Lightening produces intense heat, strong enough to weld all the links in a chain one yard long.

The Original Cardigan

This garment was a knitted woollen jacket worn over a waistcoat and was popularized by the Seventh Earl of Cardigan who led the famous charge of the Light Brigade at Balaclava in 1854. It was noticed that the Earl was seldom without this jacket so the fashion-conscious folk of the time decided it should bear his name.

Belladonna

Also known as *Deadly Nightshade*, this plant was originally used by Roman women for darkening around the eyes in times of mourning. The early form of eye shadow enhanced the eyes of the women of early Rome so much that the plant was named *bella donna*, which is Italian for "fine lady."

You don't know who the Marquis of Salbrena is? Well, perhaps you will more readily recognize him as Andres Segovia. The 87-year old classical guitarist was awarded this title by King Juan Carlos of Spain.

An elephant smells through its mouth—not its snout.

Teng Hsiao-P'ing is Vice-Premier of China (population 800,000,000) ... yet Teng stands only 4 foot 11 inches tall!

The giant panda of western China resembles a bear. However it is more closely related to the raccoon!

The panda can attain a weight of 350 pounds. This black-and-white fellow usually eats plants, but occasionally will feed on fish or rodents.

The renowned Sir Walter Raleigh remained in jail under sentence of death for 13 years.

Eavesdropper

Before the advent of guttering and down-pipes, rainwater would simply drop over the eaves. A person spying at a window while it was raining, would be spattered with drops. He was known as an eavesdropper and the word gradually came to describe any person generally doing a bit of snooping for himself.

Curfew

In the Europe of about 900 A.D. people in villages and hamlets all doused their lights at a given signal which was usually a bell or a blast from a horn. This signal was known as couvre-feu (pronounced curfew) and really meant *cover the fire.*

Lower Case

Our alphabet has 26 letters, of course, but if you examine modern script you'll find that we really have two different alphabets: the lower case and the capitals. Look, for instance, at the upper and lower case forms of A and a, or G and g, D and d, or R and r. You'd have little reason to guess that these symbols are different forms of the same letters!

The Roman alphabet consisted solely of capitals for many centuries. But the large, angular Latin letters that were suitable for carving in stone were less suitable for quick everyday writing. By the fourth century, scribes had adopted a set of letters, called *uncials*, that were developed from the capital forms, but were more rounded and easier to write quickly. These uncials later contributed to the formation of the *miniscule* alphabet, forerunner of our lower case letters. Minuscules were far easier and quicker to write with a pen than the older majuscules, or capital forms.

The country with the lowest average ages for marriages is India, whose brides average 14.5 years of age and whose bridegrooms average 20 years. At the other extreme is Ireland, with 26.5 years of age for brides, and 31.4 years for grooms.

In England coins are baked into the Christmas pudding. The person who receives them in their portion is to have good luck for the next year. "Crackers", a party favor with small trinkets inside, are used at each place setting at the table. A tradition of pulling the "crackers" and having the trinkets spill out was set many years ago.

Admire, Don't Acquire

A Roman myth blames the god Eros, or Cupid, for the rose's thorny stem. According to the tale, the god of love was enjoying the aroma of the thornless rose when he was stung by a bee lurking in the petals. To punish the flower, Cupid shot the stem full of his arrows, and the rose forever after was cursed with arrowhead-shaped thorns. Yet, according to a Chinese proverb, "The rose has thorns only for those who gather it."

The word *rosary* comes to us from the Latin *rosarium*, meaning a "rose garden," and later the word came to mean "a garland of roses." Christian legend tells of a monk who made a garland of 150 roses each day as an offering to the Virgin Mary. Later, the monk substituted 150 prayers for the flowers.

Decked with Roses

Almost all ancient cultures valued the rose for its beauty and fragrance. Roman aristocrats strewed roses around their banquet halls and served a wine made from roses. Moslem monarchs in India bathed in pools with rose petals floating on top of the water. According to *The Thousand and One Arabian Nights*, the Caliph of Baghdad served a jam made from roses that held captive anyone who ate it.

The more clean and tidy ladies of the 1780s are responsible for originating the pinafore. A pinafore was any cloth with which you covered your best clothes. It was something you would "pin afore it."

The Ice Age

Modern American refrigeration techniques and ice cream infatuation notwithstanding, the frozen dessert is neither a recent concoction nor a product of Yankee ingenuity. Most historians would trace the first bowl of ice cream to 15th- or 16th-century Italy, or perhaps England, but the story of ice cream's rise to gustatory prominence is a good deal more interesting than a simple date.

In ancient Rome, the Emperor Nero had snow transported from nearby mountains to cool his wine cellar, and reportedly concocted some of the first water-ice desserts by mixing the snow with honey, juices, and fruit. But the first forzen dessert made from milk didn't reach Europe until the 13th century, when Marco Polo returned from the Orient with a recipe for a milk-ice, presumably similar to sherbet.

Improvements in ice and sherbet-making probably led to the invention of ice cream some time in the 16th century. We know that early in that century Italian noblemen were enjoying a frozen milk product called "flower of milk." Yet Anglophiles may proudly point to a 15th-century manuscript, reporting on the coronation of Henry V, that mentions a dessert called *creme fréz.*. If creme frez was indeed ice cream, then the manuscript proves that the reputedly Italian invention was actually being made in England before the 16th century.

Italian ice cream arrived in France in 1533, along with Catherine de Medici and her retinue of chefs, when the 14-year-old Florentine moved to Paris to marry King Henry II. For many years, the chefs of various French noblemen tried to keep their recipes for ice cream a secret from other chefs—and from their masters, who were frequently astounded by their cooks' talent for serving a cold dessert even in the warmest weather.

Ice cream remained a treat for the rich and regal until 1670, when Paris's first cafe, the *Procope*, opened its doors and made the frigid dessert available to the masses for the first time. Other cafes quickly followed—including *Cafe Napolitain*, whose proprietor, a Monsieur Tortoni, concocted the creamy delight that still bears his name.

The first mention of ice cream in America occurs in 1700, but the dessert was not made here in any quantity until much later in the century. Both George Washington and Thomas Jefferson were known to be ice cream fanciers. Jefferson, who had learned how to make French ice cream during a visit to France, was one of the first officials to serve the confection at a state dinner. Jefferson once served a dessert of crisp, hot pastry with ice cream in the middle, perhaps the first ice cream sandwich in America.

The two hottest cities in the United States—and remarkably they have the same average temperature throughout the year—are Houston, Texas and Honolulu, Hawaii. Each of these cities averages 76.1° Fahrenheit, according to the records of the National Oceanic and Atmospheric Administration.

Where do most American travelers go? According to the State Department, almost 34,000 United States citizens traveled to Africa, and 187,000 traveled to the Far East in 1977. In that year, almost 2,300,000 Americans traveled to Europe.

In proportion to its small size, the common ant has the largest brain of any other creature on earth.

Talk about crazy laws. In Centralia, Washington, it is illegal for any man to shave between July 26th and August 12th.

The most risky state in which to own a car is Massachusetts. In this state, in 1976, 76, 257 cars were stolen. This adds up to a rate of 1,312.7 per 100,000 population. Though seemingly incredible, these figures emanate from the Federal Bureau of Investigation.

To make sugar white, the sugar is passed through black bone char.

With Social Security records showing his date of birth as June 28, 1860, Arthur Reed, of Oakland, California, is the world's oldest man whose age is authenticated.

In the United States as a whole, less than two percent of the population is Baptist. The state with the largest concentration of Baptists is Mississippi, where almost a third claims this persuasion. In North Dakota, too, better than one out of every three people is a Baptist.

There are more lawyers in Washington, D.C. than in any other community in the United States. In the District of Columbia, for every 100,000 people you will find close to 1,500 lawyers.

Merrily We Roll Along

In the United States, surprisingly enough, more bicycles are manufactured each year than automobiles. During the five years ending in 1977, over 68 million bikes were sold in the United States, compared to 60 million automobiles during the same period. In 1973, bicycle sales in America reached a peak of over 15 million, but the year 1977 still showed a healthy total of about nine-and-a-half million new bikes. Some 100 million Americans—almost half the population—now ride bikes.

What kinds of bicycles are Americans buying these days? Increasingly, they're turning to lightweight 10-speed models. In 1970, lightweight, narrow-wheeled bikes accounted for only 20 percent of the market; they now account for more than half. A decade ago, the sale of 10-speed bikes stood at just five percent of total bike sales, with an overwhelming 73 percent single-speed, coaster-brake models in use. By 1977, 10-speeds accounted for 36 percent of the market and three-speeds for 11 percent, while single-speeds had dipped to 52 percent.

Men's bikes continue to outsell women's models by almost two-to-one. Bicycles imported from more than 20 foreign nations continue to account for about 20 percent of all American sales.

A Different Drummer

The "Gay Movement" is of quite recent origin. Nowadays, it is not considered a disgrace to be gay. Because of the change in public attitude, many homosexuals have "come out of the closet." But history records that there were many homosexuals, both male and female, who achieved greatness despite being denigrated by a callous public.

Among the great women who were acknowledged gays are Sappho, the Greek poet; Emily Dickinson, a great American poet; and the noted British authors, Virginia Woolf and Vita Sackville West. Among familiar American authors, one must mention Gertrude Stein and Willa Cather.

The list of male gays is much longer. Among outstanding personalities were: Zeno, Greek philosopher; Sophocles, Greek philosopher; Alexander the Great, Macedonian ruler; Richard the Lion-Hearted, King of England; Leonardo da Vinci, artist and inventor; Benvenuto Cellini, Italian sculptor and goldsmith; John Milton, British poet; Frederick the Great, Prussian ruler; Lord Byron, British poet, Hans Christian Andersen, Danish author; Walt Whitman, American poet; Samuel Butler, British author; Algernon Swinburne, British poet; Peter Ilyich Tchaikovsky, Russian composer; Oscar Wilde, Irish playwright; T.E. Lawrence, British soldier-author; Dag Hammarskjold, Swedish secretary-general of the United Nations; Tennessee Williams, American playwright; and Brendan Behan, Irish author.

Esperanto Needed

There are 140 languages on this earth that are each spoken by a million or more people.

Five million people speak Afrikaans, and four million people speak Zulu. But in between this A and Z, there are 138 other languages, each spoken by at least one million people.

Lizards Can Tell their Own Eggs by the Taste

Once a female lizard has dug a hole and laid eggs, she can always find her way back to it. To test this mysterious capacity, scientists have sometimes played tricks on a mother lizard.

The mother lizard is never fooled. By some uncanny means she finds her way back to her own nest, no matter how many obstacles are put in her path. Once there, she has only to flick the tip of her tongue over the eggs to know whether or not they are her own. If they are not, she rushes away and will have nothing at all to do with the strange eggs.

The Fish Are Jumpin'

Suppose someone told you that a fish can travel the way vertical take-off planes do—that is, leaping straight up into the air? Would you believe him? You should.

For salmon do just that. When salmon are fighting their way upstream to find a place to lay their eggs, they will jump straight up in the air to hurdle obstacles such as dams and waterfalls.

A salmon heading upstream can swim as fast as 30 miles an hour against the current.

And a 25-pound salmon can leap as high as 10 feet into the air!

The highest waterfalls in the United States are the Yosemite Falls, in California, with a total drop of 2,425 feet.

Lake Michigan is the only one of the five Great Lakes which lies entirely within the United States. The border between the United States and Canada passes through the other Great Lakes.

The bridge with the widest roadway in the world is the Crawford Street Bridge in Providence, Rhode Island, with a width of 1,147 feet.

The smallest antelope in the world is the dik-dik of Africa, which is about the size of a full-grown rabbit. The largest antelope, such as the eland, attains a height of six feet and a weight up to 1500 pounds.

The lightest of all metals is lithium, which weighs about 33.29 pounds per cubic foot. The densest of all metals and therefore the world's most effective paperweight is osmium, which weighs about 1,410 pounds per cubic foot.

Using Your Bean

The magnificent Cathedral of Cologne, Germany, one of the gems of Gothic Architecture, took more than 600 years to build. Construction was begun in the early 13th century and was continued in on-and-off fashion for more than six centuries.

For 400 of these years a token rent was paid to the Lords of Doyme, noblemen owning the property on which the church stands. This rent consisted of a dish of baked beans, to be paid once annually. It was paid each and every year from the 13th century well into the 1600's.

Heard of any Good Books Lately?

The Library of Congress, located in Washington, D.C., ranks first among the libraries of the world—ahead of both the famous Bibliotheque Nationale de Paris and London's British Museum.

The United States Congress established the library for its own use in the year 1800. For almost a century the library was maintained in the Capitol building itself. But as the services were extended to other agencies and libraries and to the public at large, it outgrew its premises. In 1897 it was transferred to far more spacious quarters—a specially-built $7,000,000 Italian Renaissance building, the largest and most expensive library building in the world.

And, in 1939, the modern Thomas Jefferson Building was built on the library's 15-acre site. These two buildings cover six acres and provide 35 acres of floor space. But the library continues to burst its seams and a third building, The James Madison Memorial Library, is under construction and almost completed.

Today, the Library of Congress employs over 5,000 people, and its 50 miles of book shelves accommodate over 74 million items, including over 18½ million books and pamphlets. Its collection of rare books and literally hundreds of thousands of priceless original letters and historic documents make it a researcher's paradise. The original copies of the Declaration of Independence and the Constitution of the United States are possibly the most popular exhibit. Both are locked in an airtight case and are under constant guard by a sentry.

Moreover, the Library of Congress is sure to continue to grow by leaps and bounds, for the United States Copyright Office is a department of the Congressional Library and receives tons of new material annually.

A normal person has twelve pairs of ribs.

Unstoppable

Although in his later years, George Handel, the famous German composer, suffered from paralysis of the left hand and was totally blind, he continued to conduct and compose music.

Something Owls Crow About

Even at a very early age, screech owls have an innate dislike for crows. The feeling is mutual. They both prey on each other's eggs—the owls prey by night, and the crows during the day.

A Glacier in Glacier Park Traps Grasshoppers

Glacier Park in northwestern Montana is said to have "more geography to the square mile" than any other place in the world. In this beautiful national park are more than sixty small glaciers. They vary in size from only a few acres to the three-mile-long Blackfoot Glacier. Among the glaciers are over two hundred beautiful lakes—some with icebergs floating on them—cascading streams, and deep canyons.

In this park is found one of the strangest glaciers in the world—Grasshopper Glacier. For hundreds of years grasshoppers and other insects, for some still undiscovered reason, have been leaping on to this glacier. And swarms of grasshoppers still continue to take the fatal plunge.

The grasshoppers soon become frozen into the glacial ice and may remain there for years. When the ice melts a little, it frees the frozen insects. The "deep freeze" grasshoppers thaw and then become tasty meals for birds and other wild creatures.

Built-in Sun Glasses

Two species of Cuban lizards, called anoles, are cave dwellers, but they do at times venture out into the sun. Apparently, to shield their eyes from the glare on such occasions, these lizards close them and look through the transparent "windows" in the lower lids.

Many other lizards possess similar windows, especially some of the *skinks*. The skinks, numbering over six hundred species throughout the world, are among our most common lizards. Members of the skink family are to be found in almost every state of the Union.

The lower eyelid of the desert skink has a little round window covered by a hard, transparent pane. When storms set the desert sand to swirling and scratching, the desert skink has the amazing ability to shut its eyes and still see where it is going.

Some species of the skink even have wholly transparent lower lids permanently covering their eyes. These skinks, in effect, look out through protective sun glasses all their lives.

Word of Mouth

No ancient South American Indian knew how to write. They had no alphabet and everything was handed down by mouth through memory.

Every little scrap of Inca literature that has come to us was the result of the labors of the Spanish priests who set down the old stories and traditions, told to them by the Indians afer the Conquest.

Although it had no written form, their language called Quechua had rules of grammar and there was an extensive body of oral literature, including poetry and drama. They had plays that were staged in the palaces of the rulers and in the villages. Their dramatic literature was probably sung by professional bards who attended all the important religious festivals.

Cut It Out!

It was Dr. George Thomas Morton who performed the first known appendectomy on April 27, 1887. George Thomas was the son of William Thomas Morton who pioneered the use of anesthesia in operations.

The first patient ever to undergo the appendectomy was a twenty-six year old, and was suffering from acute appendicitis. The operation was performed as a last resort. It was believed the patient was going to die anyhow, so there was nothing to lose by Morton's cutting him open. Morton's patient lived to tell the tale.

Trade Your Car in for a Camel

Some dromedary camels have been known to cover as much as 115 miles in 11 hours.

Wake Me in the Spring

We all know that bears hibernate during the winter when it's cold and food is scarce. But did you think that alligators hibernate? Actually, cold-blooded animals, whose temperature varies with the climate, must hibernate if they live in environments where the temperature falls below freezing.

The alligator prefers to hibernate through a good part of the colder winter months. To do this, it builds a winter home where its sleep is not likely to be disturbed.

This home consists of a deep cave beside a stream or a river, or at the edge of a self-made wallow. The entrance is always beneath the surface of the water. The alligator pushes and claws its way into the soft earth, thrashing its powerful body around to enlarge the tunnel and pack the loose dirt. When it feels it has gone in far enough, it hollows out a sizeable space for itself and settles down to sleep.

In Florida, alligator caves have been found extending thirty feet back from the water.

In 1970, Louis Sherry, head of the ice cream firm, hired sculptor John Bertolini to do a bust of President Richard Nixon in ice cream. But apparently no one was tempted by this artistic morsel, and ultimately Sherry was obliged to store the masterpiece in a freezer vault in Brooklyn, New York. What has happened to it since, deponent sayeth not.

Rabbits and hares differ from other rodents, such as beavers, gophers, squirrels, etc. Rabbits and hares have four incisor teeth in the upper jaw. All other rodents have two.

Leapin' Lizards

Lizards, with the conspicuous exception of the chameleons, are usually speedy. Some lizards can run on their hind legs, leaning more or less forward, with their long tail acting as a counterbalance. The American zebra-tailed lizard is credited with doing 15 to 18 miles an hour in this fashion.

In Malaya lives the flying lizard, a curious creature that can spread the skin along the erected ribs on the sides of its body and form a sort of glider so that it may soar from tree to tree.

Up In Smoke

Despite the Surgeon General's warning that appears on every pack of cigarettes sold in the United States that smoking is injurious to one's health, millions of people continue this dangerous habit.

The American Indians were probably the first to indulge in this pastime, possibly for religious or medicinal purposes. But the use of tobacco must answer some human need for it has become a widespread, persistent practice. The drawing of tobacco into one's lungs somehow suggests sublime levels of sophistication, relaxation and creature comfort. So millions are willing to risk the consequences.

Depicted here are portraits by artists of people indulging in this deadly sin through the ages.

Catchpenny Prints

Drawing by Grandville. Petites Misères □

Bab Ballads

Art of the Book

Punch

Harper's

Caruso

Art of the Book

Wilhelm Butch Album

Wilhelm Butch Album

Mark Twain's Library of Humor

Peck's Compendium of Fun

Police Gazette

The Nose Knows

Rip was one of several dogs employed at major airports around the country to sniff out drugs that might be concealed in incoming cargo or luggage. Rip was the star of Miami International Airport's customs inspections team, but officials began to doubt Rip's sense of smell when he commenced to bark at some crates containing massive concrete pedestals for lawn statues.

But Rip's past record induced the officials to check out the cargo. Each pedestal was five feet tall and weighed 400 pounds. After drilling through 1½" of steel-reinforced concrete on the first pedestal, the customs men discovered a sealed, galvanized steel container which held 80 pounds of marijuana! The other nine pedestals yielded the same trove. The street value of this haul was $160,000.

It will be a long time before anyone questions the super schnozzola of Canine Agent Rip.

The female giraffe gives birth to a single calf, which is about six feet tall at birth.

The most successful major league baseball club in the World Series play has been the New York Yankees, with 20 victories in 29 appearances. The most successful National League club has been the St. Louis Cardinals, with seven victories in 11 appearances.

Two Heads Are Better Than One?

There have been instances of different kinds of animals being born with two heads, but such freaks are rare. But for some strange reason, an unusually large number of snakes are born with two complete heads growing out of the front of one body. As a rule, both heads are fully developed. Many of these snakes also have two tails.

Well-trained

A female mongrel was stretched out before the living-room fireplace as the woman of the house sat knitting nearby. The bored animal woke up, yawned, and looked around absently. Her eyes fell on a plate of chocolates in a dish on a low table.

The pet was very fond of sweets, but she had been taught never to help herself. Furtively, she sauntered over to the low table, picked up a piece of chocolate, and dropped down before the hearth with the candy between her paws.

There she nuzzled her prize for a while, avoiding the woman's eyes, then gave a long, sad sigh of resignation. As the woman watched, the dog took the chocolate in her mouth again, returned to the table, and dropped the candy back into the dish.

Pueblo, Colorado, is justly proud of its own version of "The Odd Couple." Charlie the Cat and Daisy the Dog set up joint residence in a doghouse owned by Jeff Anderson. Each critter has its own entrance to the house and, according to Mr. Anderson, both eat, sleep, and play in perfect harmony. What makes this story doubly amazing is that Charlie and Daisy did not grow up together; they are both strays.

Mrs. Arlene Higuera's pooch had had that hangdog look for a couple of days, and just wasn't the playful pet it had always been. So, naturally, Mrs. Higuera rushed her darling to the vet. After a simple operation to extract the 267 marbles in the dog's stomach, Fido was soon romping around the house with his accustomed panache.

A camel can drink 25 gallons of water in half an hour.

The heart of a normal man will beat 38 million times each year.

Bonehead

For a month, a mongrel pup maintained a lonely vigil above an old well near Rockford, Illinois. The townspeople, fearing that the dog's master had fallen down the 100-foot well, insisted that the water in it be drained. Thousands of curious onlookers watched as the 10-day, $1,000 pumping job was completed. At the bottom of the pit, the rescuers found only an ancient, five-inch bone.

Pard playing is of ancient origin. It has been recorded that cards were played in Egypt during the days of Joseph, and that they were used as far east as Hindustan and China at a period long before their introduction into Europe.

Kexas is the only state that was an independent republic, recognized by the United States before annexation. Over Texas have flown the flags of Spain, France, Mexico, the Lone Star Flag of the Republic of Texas, the Confederate States, and the United States.

Khe only currently ruling monarch in the world, so far as is known, who was born in the United States is the present king of Thailand, Bhumibol Abulyadj, born in 1927 in the U.S.

Vital Core

The average employee of A.T.&T. remains beings is about five inches.

Persistence

The average employee of A.T. & T. remains with the telephone company for about 32 years.

The first medical school in the United States was established in 1765, in Philadelphia, Pennsylvania, at what is now the University of Pennsylvania School of Medicine. Ten graduates were issued the first medical diplomas in 1768.

Roadblocked by Blockhead

When the Mobile and Southern Railroad explained to Deacon Smedly that a proposed cut-off would run right through the spot where his barn stood, and offered him ten times the worth of the property for his consent, Smedley turned a deaf ear to the proposal. He defended his stand to his outraged wife by shouting, "Do ye think I'm goin' to keep running out to that barn day and night to open and shut the door every time they want to run a train through?"

A snail may take as long as 12 hours to consummate the mating act. No wonder this event occurs only once in the snail's life.

Approximately 75 percent of all ulcer patients are men.

The average woman in the United States walks a distance of 10 miles each day—one more than the average man.

Twenty-four percent of the state of California is classified as desert.

The federal government forbids the portrait of any living person to appear on a U.S. postage stamp.

Safe in Bed

Among his other idiosyncracies, English monarch Richard III carried along his heavy wooden bedstead when touring his domain. After King Richard's death, the bedstead remained in the inn where he'd last slept. A century later, the landlord of the inn took apart the bedstead and found a double bottom filled with Richard's stash of gold coins.

Golf

Golfing records are difficult to compare, since golf courses vary in difficulty. But the lowest golf score ever recorded for an 18-hour golf course of at least 5,000 yards was a 55, achieved by E.F. Stauggard in California in 1935, and matched in 1962 by Homero Blancas in Texas.

The longest golf drive on record is 515 yards, by Michael Hoke Austin in Las Vegas, Nevada, in 1974. Prior to that, the record belonged to Englishman E.C. Bliss, who walloped a ball 445 yards during a 1913 match.

The microscopic amoeba never dies of old age when conditions are favorabe, instead it simply divides into two new individuals, in effect, being truly immortal!

Believe it or not, it snows less in the Arctic than it does in most parts of the United States. In fact, New York State has about three times the precipitation of snow as does the Arctic zone.

On June 29, 1921, one Dan O'Leary celebrated his 92nd birthday by walking 102 miles from Jersey City, New Jersey to Chester, Pennsylvania.

The word *honeymoon* derives from an old custom of drinking wine that was made from honey for 30 days after the marriage.

Catgut comes from sheep.

Some fish can remain frozen in a block of ice for as long as six months, then emerge quite alive, and swim around as usual.

Mordecai Brown, one of the greatest pitchers in the history of baseball, had only three fingers on his pitching hand.

In 1870, U.S. Patent 109644, was issued for the invention of an automobile that would run on the power supplied by two dogs. These dogs were to be placed in the wheel of an automobile between the spokes. By running, they would turn the spokes and thus power the automobile.

Vanilla

Unripe vanilla is green; it turns yellow when ripe. Harvested vanilla beans are cured by immersion in hot water, and stored for several months to develop the full bouquet. The beans are then shipped to factories for the production of vanilla extract. At the factory, the beans are first chopped, then steeped in a solvent to extract the vanilla essence. At some factories, the vanilla extract is aged for six months to a year before being shipped to confectioners and retail stores.

Though a native of Mexico and Central America, and a favorite flavoring in Europe and the United States, vanilla is today almost entirely a product of various Indian Ocean islands, where it was brought for plantation cultivation by French colonists. The Malagasy Republic (formerly Madagascar), Reunion, and the Comoro Islands now account for about 75 percent of the world's vanilla supply. Quantities are also produced in Tahiti, Indonesia, Mexico, and the Seychelles Islands.

Artificial vanilla flavoring can be produced from the sapwood or fir trees; and vanilla flavoring, synthesized from chemicals, is becoming increasingly popular as the cost of the raw vanilla bean rises.

Now chocolate, too, is being synthetically produced; it's possible that the dish of vanilla and chocolate ice cream you just enjoyed owed nothing to either bean. The next time you buy a vanilla or chocolate product, check the list of ingredients to find out if you were given the real McCoy—you'll find it all printed there in black and white.

The emu is a strange bird. In this species, it is the male that mothers the young.

So When Did He Sleep?

Mozart played the harpsichord at age three, composed his first minuet at five, wrote his first sonata at seven, and his first complete symphony at eight.

Mozart wrote at least one symphony each year, produced over 600 symphonies, opera, operettas, concertos, string quartets, sonatas, masses, and other classical pieces. He died at 35.

All Wet

The bathtub was introduced in England in 1828. The first tub in America was used by a Cincinnati resident named Thompson in 1842. After an argument among medical authorities concerning the benefits and hazards of bathing, the bathtub was banned in Boston in 1845. Six years later, the first bathtub was installed in the White House for Millard Fillmore.

Believe it? Well, this capsulized history of the bathtub appeared in the *New York Evening Mail* in 1917, and was immediately accepted as fact by many readers. But the article was actually the devious work of humorist H.L. Mencken, and was—as Mencken readily admitted—a "tissue of absurdities, all of them deliberate and most of them obvious." Yet, much to Mencken's amazement, more than one lazy writer subsequently published this information as the gospel truth.

High Spirits

Rum is obtained from fermented sugarcane or fermented molasses. It is produced primarily in the Caribbean. Different varieties derive from Puerto Rico, Cuba, Jamaica, and Mexico.

Flavored spirits, including gin, aquavit, absinthe, and zubrovka, are produced by redistilling alcohol with a flavoring agent. Juniper is used to flavor gin, caraway seeds to flavor aquavit.

Vodka is obtained from potatoes or grain. It is filtered through vegetable charcoal. In the United States, this process produces a liquid at over 190 proof.

Always on Sunday

The ice cream sundae emerged during the 1890s, and there are many claims for its invention. Contemporary laws forbade the sale of soda on Sunday, and this, undoubtedly, had a hand in popularizing the dessert. The first sundaes were sold in ice cream parlors only on Sunday, and thus were called "Sundays" or "soda-less sodas." The spelling change to "sundae" was made later by ice cream parlor proprietors eager to see the dish shed its Sunday-only connotation.

The best-known explanation for the invention of the ice cream cone traces its origin to the 1904 Louisiana Purchase Exposition in St. Louis. According to the tale, an ice cream salesman by the name of Charles E. Menches gave an ice cream sandwich and a bouquet of flowers to the young lady he was escorting. She rolled one of the sandwich wafers into a cone to hold the flowers, then rolled the other wafer into a cone for the ice cream.

Ice cream parlors were an integral part of American life early in the 20th century. In these emporia, busy soda jerks developed a lingo all their own. *Adam's ale*, for instance, was water, while *belch water* meant seltzer. A *pair of drawers* could mean only two cups of coffee.

Fortunes were made in the ice cream trade during the heyday of the soda fountain. Louis Sherry, a Frenchman from Vermont, began his career as a famed restaurateur when he was granted the ice cream concession at the Metropolitan Opera House in New York.

In 1925, Howard Johnson—father of American franchisers—opened his first ice cream store in Wollaston, Massachusetts. Johnson, incidentally, once sold 14,000 ice cream cones in a single day at his Wollaston Beach stand.

What They Were Reading

In 1938, Daphne Du Maurier's *Rebecca* became the first best-selling Gothic novel in America. The next year, John Steinbeck's *The Grapes of Wrath* was the top seller, and in 1940, Ernest Hemmingway first reached the list with *For Whom the Bell Tolls*—though number one that year was *How Green Was My Valley*, by Richard Llewellyn.

Although TNT is notorious for its explosive power, it is absolutely harmless when lighted with a match.

Next to Godliness

Although the porcelain tub is now indispensable in every home, it is a rather recent innovation. The fact is, regular bathing has periodically gone in and out of fashions over the centuries.

From time immemorial, the act of bathing has been regarded as a sacred rite in many cultures. The ancient Egyptians bathed before worship, in the belief that both the body and soul should be pure in the presence of the gods. Christian baptism is a bathing rite, symbolizing the washing away of original sin. To the devout Hindu, a bath is a once-yearly rite, taken only in the sacred waters of the Ganges.

The ancient Greeks are thought to have introduced the bathtub, or at least the wash basin. The Greek vessels were used to hold water for rinsing, but were too small to accommodate a bather. The ruins of the palace at Knossos, Crete, reveal a number of bathrooms that were apparently supplied by a relatively advanced plumbing system. Vase paintings suggest that the Greeks used some form of shower as well. Most early Greeks, by the way, washed only with cold water—hot water was considered effeminate.

In later periods, the Greeks built public baths; but it was the Romans who made the bathhouse the center of their social lives. In the early days of the Roman Republic, wealthy citizens often installed private baths in their homes, similar to the modern Turkish bath.

Later, the public bath came into vogue in almost all cities and towns of the Empire. Huge baths, or *thermae*, became the recreation centers of the Imperial City itself, providing not only bathing facilities but gyms, libraries, theaters, gardens, and assembly halls.

In Iceland many residents heat their homes with hot water radiators. Where do they get the hot water? Answer: Directly from natural hot springs.

Prolific

Two dogs share the honor of having thrown the largest recorded litter of puppies. Lena, a foxhound threw 23 on June 9, 1944, and Careless Ann, a St. Bernard, produced the same number on February 7, 1975.

In eight years, a male greyhound in London managed to sire 2,414 registered puppies, as well as over 600 others that were unregistered.

Babe Ruth, the renowned slugger, led the American League in pitching in 1915.

When in Rome

The Roman baths were masterpieces of architecture and engineering, and the epitome of imperial luxury. The walls were usually covered with marble; the high, vaulted ceilings were decorated with colorful mosaics. The water taps were made of silver. Statues were everywhere, with small cubical lockers set in the niches between them. Hot water, provided by furnaces, was piped into the bath. The rooms were kept warm by smoke and by hot air circulating under the floors and in the hollow walls.

The first large Roman public bath was built by Agrippa in 27 B.C. Others were constructed by Nero (65 A.D.), Titus (81 A.D.), Domitian (95 A.D.), Trajan (100 A.D.), and Commodus (185 A.D.). Diocletian built baths in the year 302 that were large enough to accommodate 3,200 bathers at one time!

The Roman's bathing ritual consisted of a series of baths, each taken in a different room. The bather began in the undressing room, then moved to another room where he was anointed with oil, then to the gym for exercise. After the gym came the *calidarium*, or hot bath; then the steam room, the *tepidarium*, or lukewarm bath; and finally, the *frigidarium*, or cold bath which was usually a sort of swimming pool. Sounds much like our modern health spa, doesn't it?

According to the dictionary, a *village* is a small rural population unit held together by common economic and political ties. A village is smaller than a town, and has been the normal unit of community living in most areas of the world throughout history.

The typical village used to be small, consisting of perhaps five to 30 families. Homes were situated together for sociability and defense, and the land surrounding the living quarters was farmed. This land was parceled out to each family.

The village also contained woods and meadows used for pasturage. Most villages in ancient times were largely self-sufficient. Now, most villages secure a great many of their necessities from the nearby town.

Truffles Are Expensive!

The scene: winter in a wooded area of southern France. A group of farmers moves among the trees, following the meanderings of a half-dozen pigs. Suddenly, one of the pigs noses into the dirt, grunting and snorting in hungry anticipation, and begins to dig into the ground with its hooves. The farmers rush over and chase the animal, then complete the excavation job. Yes, they're searching for buried treasure —but what kind? They're hunting for the most expensive natural food in the world: truffles.

The heaviest sportsman in history, according to record, was the wrestler, William J. Cobb, of Macon, Georgia, who about fifteen years ago weighed in at 802 pounds and was billed as "Happy Humphrey."

The tallest columns in the world are the 16 pillars in the Palace of Labor in Turin, Italy. These columns are 82 feet tall and are built of concrete and steel.

Brandy Is Dandy

Brandy is distilled from wine or the fermented mash of fruit—grapes, cherries, apples, plums, apricots, peaches, blackberries, or whatever.

That Model "T"

Henry Ford began his motor company in 1903 with capital of only $28,000, twelve workers, and a plant only 50 feet wide. Additional funds were supplied by the Dodge brothers, themselves auto manufacturers. The Dodges' initial $20,000 investment was eventually worth $25 million.

Soon afterward, Ford improved on Olds' mass-production ideas and introduced the conveyor-belt assembly line. Ford's first successful mass-produced car was the Model N, brought out in 1906 for $500. (From the very beginning, Ford used letters of the alphabet to identify his models.) But the car that made Henry famous was the Model T.

Contact lenses—small optical lenses worn directly against the eye—were suggested as early as 1845, by Sir John Herschel, an Englishman. But the first pair of contacts was the work of a German, who constructed a pair of protective lenses for a patient who had lost his eyelids due to cancer. The term *contact lenses* was first used in 1887, by a Swiss doctor named A.E. Fick, but the first pair of contacts did not reach the shores of America for almost 40 years.

Washed Out

The earliest bathtubs in America were simple wooden tubs, lined with metal and the water was poured in by hand. The first public bath was opened here in 1852. An 1895 law ordered all municipalities in New York State to provide free public baths for their citizens, many of whom had no other means of washing.

In the early decades of this century, many apartments in American cities were equipped with a bathtub in the kitchjen. When European immigrants arrived here, many considered the bathtub an unnecessary luxury, and used the tub as a planter for flowers and vegetables.

America easily leads the world today in bathtubs per capita. Many American homes are equipped with two or three or even four tubs. The shower has recently replaced the bath as the preferred washing ritual. A shower, by the way, uss up only about half as much water as a tub bath.

Golf

In addition to a hall of fame of great players, golf has certainly produced some marvelous additions to our vocabulary. The word *golf* itself is probably derived from the Dutch *kolf* or *kolven*, or the German *Kolbe*. Some authorities claim that the source is the Scoth *gowf*, "blow of the hand."

The word *caddie* (the youth who carries the golfer's bag and often chooses the club for each shot), comes from the French *cadet*, "young lad." The term *putt*, like the verb "put," is rooted in the Middle English *putten*, which means "push" or "thrust."

The hedgehog cactus of Mexico can live five years without getting any water.

At times snow falls in the center of the Sahara Desert.

In November 1929 at Hayback Park of England, the longest of long shots came in first. Coole paid 3410 to 1.

Vanilla

The vast legions of American ice cream-lovers fall basically into two camps: those who favor chocolate, and those who champion its chromatic antithesis, vanilla. Although vanilla and chocolate—long the most popular ice cream flavors in the United States—may be diametrically opposed on the color scale, they share more in common than you might imagine. Both cocoa and vanilla come from a bean. Both are natives of Mexico and Central America. Both are used primarily as a confectionary flavoring. In fact, for many years *chocolate* and *vanilla* were not thought of as opposites at all—they were almost always used *together*!

Now here's a surprise. The wettest city in the United States is, believe it or not, Miami, Florida. This town has an average rainfall of 59.2 inches.

The next three cities in order of being wet towns are all in the Sunbelt. They are New Orleans, Birmingham, and Jacksonville, and they are followed by Seattle, Washington.

Sound Symbols

The development of our alphabet—the Roman—follows an evolution from logographic to syllabic to alphabetic writing systems. Writing systems developed independently in the Far East and the Americas, but writing as we know it took shape in the Near East, beginning with the cuneiform writing of the Sumerians and the hieroglyphics of the ancient Egyptians—which may themselves have evolved from Sumerian writing.

The cuneiform writing of the Sumerians and Babylonians was in use by 3,000 B.C. Originally, Mesopotamian tongues were represented by pictures carved in stone. But the picture forms evolved into a syllabic shorthand of some 150 symbols, consisting of lines ending in the wedge-shaped marks that gave cuneiform its name. (The word comes from *cuneus*, Latin for "wedge.") The change may have been due in part to a move from the stone tablet to the clay tablet as a writing surface. Carving intricate pictures with a stylus is difficult with clay; pressing in wedge-shaped marks is far easier.

The hieroglyphic writing system of ancient Egypt originally consisted of word signs alone. Gradually, some of these symbols came to represent word sounds instead. A symbol standing for the word *ray*, for instance, could come to stand for the sound "ray," and thus could be joined with the sign for the word *sing* to produce *racing.*.

With only word sounds to represent rather than the individual words, the Egyptian written language was reduced to a system of about 80 characters. Since each symbol no longer had to look something like the object or action it represented, and was less likely to be confused with another sign, writing could be executed much more quickly and carelessly. These hieroglyphic symbols, as written hastily by ordinary Egyptians, became the hieratic and demotic scripts of Egypt, and perhaps the syllabic symbols of other Near Eastern languages, such as Aramaic, Phoenician, and Early Hebrew.

Some Tomato!

The largest tomato on record, a proud 1974 product of the British Isles, tipped the scales at a whopping four-and-a-half pounds—that's a lot of catsup!

The word *bonfire* has a very, very strange origin. Originally, the word was *bonefires* because the fire was made by burning human corpses. In the Middle Ages, the victims of war or plague were too numerous to be buried individually. Their bones were burned in a huge fire.

If you stand on the Tri-States Rock in the Delaware River, you will be standing at one and the same instant on the soil of New Jersey, New York and Pennsylvania.

In 1929, Al Trout and Billy Long fought for the seventh time. They had been in the ring six times before, and each fight was declared a draw. But in this bout in Tampa, Florida, somewhere along the line they swung at each other and connected. Each fighter knocked out the other.

The Versatile Bed

Although the bedrooms in most large Roman homes were arranged around an open central court, the average bedroom, or *cubiculum* was as small and dark as the Greek *thalamos*, with glassless windows shuttered during sleeping hours to keep in heat and shut off light. A *cubiculum*, customarily contained a bed, or *lectus*, along with a chair, chest, floor mat, and chamber pot. Although the Romans used both single and double beds, only in the poorest homes would you find two beds in the same room. In larger homes, curtains divided the bedroom into a space for attendants, a dressing room, and the sleeping area proper. Some of the homes found in the ruins of Pompeii contained sleeping alcoves set in wall niches behind curtains or sliding partitions.

Roman bedsteads were often mounted on a platform, and many were fitted with a canopy from which curtains or mosquito netting was hung.

The Romans, like the Greeks, customarily went to their tomb on their bed. Many *lecti* also doubled as couches for dining, and some could hold as many as six people. Wealthy Romans were evidently quite proud of their elegant bedding. The author Martial wrote of a rich man who feigned illness so that he could show off his bed coverings to visiting wellwishers. The poor, on the other hand, usually slept on masonry shelves along the walls of their *insulae* or tenements. Others had to make do with a simple wood plank covered with a bug-ridden pallet.

No matter what their social class, Romans rarely owned special sleepwear. Men removed their toga and climbed into bed in their undergarments, while women went to bed laden with their *capitium, mamillare,* and *strophium*—corset, bra, and panties. Bedtime was usually between seven and nine o'clock, and the dawn crowing of the rooster provided the only alarm clock. A breakfast of more than plain water was rare, as was a morning wash-up, since most Romans included a trip to the public baths as part of their daily routine.

Like many other luxuries, the comforts of the Roman boudoir, vanished with the end of the Empire. The Germanic tribes that overran Europe were accustomed to sleeping on the ground, atop piles of leaves or skins. During the early Middle Ages, many peasants slept in the barn along with the animals, or on the earth floor, or on a wooden bench in the hall, the only room in the house with a fireplace. Some enjoyed the luxury of mattresses stuffed with feathers, wool, hair, or straw. The Old English expression for "make a bed" literally meant "prepare straw."

A male seal will go without food, drink or sleep for three months at a stretch.

In 1897, in Belleville, Illinois, Jacob Wainwright rode his bicycle backwards for 440 yards. But what is more remarkable is that he did this in 39 seconds.

The oldest house in America stands in Santa Fe, New Mexico. It is built of mud.

The biggest log cabin in the world stands in Portland, Oregon. It is a museum which is built of 2 million feet of lumber, and covers a square block.

Although the capital of Iceland, Reykjavik, lies within the Arctic Circle, its weather is nevertheless warmer than Salt Lake City, Boston, Albany or Detroit during the month of January, which is the coldest month in Iceland. In July, the temperature of Reykjavik is just about the same as that of Buenos Aires, Argentina or Sydney, Australia.

Nothing New Under the Sun

Historians have traced the origins of backgammon to many sources. The fact is, the game was never "invented." Instead, backgammon evolved from a number of old games, including the earliest known board games enjoyed by man.

In the 1920s, during British archaeologist Sir Leonard Woolley's excavation of the ancient Sumerian city of Ur, he found five game boards in the royal cemetery that bore a resemblance to early backgammon boards. The 5,000-year-old Sumerian game was played on a board of 20 squares, with six dice and seven pieces for each player.

A game board similar to those unearthed at Ur was found among the treasures in the tomb of the Egyptian king Tutankhamen, dating from 1500 B.C. Egyptian wall paintings show that the board game, called *senet*, was popular among the common people as well as among royalty. The Egyptians even had a sort of mechanical dice cup, a machine that shook and threw the dice to protect against dice cheats, who seem to be as ancient as dice themselves.

Oddly enough, the Spanish explorer Ferdinand Pizarro found the Aztecs in Mexico playing a game, *patolli*, that bore a remarkable similarity to the games enjoyed by the ancient Egyptians. Nobles in the court of Montezuma played *patolli* for high stakes, using semiprecious stones as game pieces. Some anthropologists view the similarity between the Aztec and Egyptian games as proof that the people of the Americas migrated to the Western Hemisphere from Africa or Asia.

Bonanza

This is a Spanish word meaning fair weather at sea and general prosperity. Miners on the Pacific Coast of North America first began to use it whenever a rich body of ore was mined. The word began to catch on and now is regarded as a synonym for any type of rich prize.

The Colt .45 Peacemaker has been called "the gun that won the West!" The most famous firearm ever made, it was the first cartridge revolver to be officially adopted by the United States Cavalry.

Dame Sybil Leek is the world's busiest witch. In addition to practicing her "craft," she has authored numerous books; acts as a spirit medium; directs a chain of astrology schools; gives stock market advice, and travels the lecture circuit.

Confucius (551-479 BC) was not always a famous Chinese philosopher. At age 17, he was an inspector of corn markets!

In the animal kingdom the goat is notorious for eating almost anything imaginable. Among reptiles, the alligator has the same dubious distinction.

No one knows exactly why alligators swallow all the things they do. The stomachs of alligators have been found to contain rocks, cinders, shotgun shells, uncracked hickory nuts, and chunks of wood.

Alligators penned in zoos and parks have been known to kill themselves by gulping such indigestible items as pop bottles, rubber balls, and inner tubes.

With Respect to the Banana

The banana has been called the most ancient fruit on earth. Most botanists believe bananas first grew in southeast Asia, perhaps on the Malay Peninsula. Primitive people there considered the fruit so important that they took banana rootstocks with them wherever they migrated.

The fruit undoubtedly reached India and China at a very early date. The Chinese scholar Yang Fu, in a second-century work called *Record of Strange Things*, extolled the banana as having "a very sweet-tasting pulp, like honey or sugar. Four or five of these fruits are enough for a meal," he noted, "and after eating, the flavor lingers on among the teeth." The neighboring Koreans, however, considered the banana, rather than the apple, the forbidden fruit of the Garden of Eden.

Alexander the Great and his conquering Macedonians were probably the first Europeans to savor bananas in India during the fourth century B.C. We are told by the Roman historian Pliny that the Macedonians found wise men in India sitting in the shade of a banana tree, eating the fruit and discussing philosophy. Many centuries later, when the Swedish botanist Linnaeus classified the plant kingdom, he called the banana *Musa sapientum*, "fruit of the wise men."

Scholarly Game

College basketball teams now play coast-to-coast schedules. The 1968-69 UCLA team logged some 22,500 travel miles and played before almost 400,000 fans. In 1970, more than 30 college fives were traveling over 10,000 miles and playing to more than 200,000 fans in an average season.

There are now about 20,000 high school basketball teams from coast to coast, and attendance at these games is said to approach 125 million in a season! In areas such as Indiana, where basketball has become a way of life, many small communities have built high school gymnasiums with a seating capacity larger than the population of the town.

A Fine Kettle of Fish

Ever queried the logic of this phrase? Why put fish in a kettle? Mispronunciation is responsible for this odd expression. The common Teutonic saying was a pretty kittle of fish—a kittle of those days being a dam with nets positioned for catching fish.

The Egyptians are shrinking. The average 20-25 year old is 5'4½" today compared with 5'6" for that age group prior to the study.

The Bactrian camel carries 400-600 pounds and can travel 30 miles a day ... and all the food it requires are some tough desert plants!

Raining Fish

Near Killarney Station in Australia's northern territory, about 150 silverfish fell from the sky during a rainfall in February 1974. Scientists explained that the phenomenon was probably caused by a whirlwind. Whirlwinds create a waterspout effect. A whirlwind can suck up a huge amount of water, and of course all the fish that are swimming in that water.

Mad as a Hatter

Mental disorders were common in the hat trade of the 14th century. This was due to the effects of mercurial nitrate which was used in treating felt. For example, Robert Crab of Chesham became eccentric and gave all he owned to the poor. Lewis Carroll popularized this phenomenon by featuring a *Mad Hatter* in his *Alice in Wonderland,* which was written in 1865.

But How Did It Smell?

A chemist who lived in Cologne in 1709, Jean Marie Farina, first introduced eau de cologne. The original recipe consisted of equal amounts of bergamot, citron, neroli, organe, and rosemary mixed with one dram of malabar cardamom and one gallon of rectified spirits.

The soy bean is probably the most versatile vegetable on earth. Four hundred different products can be made from the soy bean.

Hock

Originally known as hochheimer this white wine first appeared in England well before the Norman Conquest. It was mainly produced along the Rhine River in Germany, the chief wine producing town of which was Hochheim. Taking the first four letters of this name and substituting a K for the H gives us hock.

Louis XIV owned an estimated 413 beds in his various palaces. Louis's favorite bed at Versailles was fitted with crimson velvet curtains so heavily embroidered with gold that the crimson was scarcely visible. A ribald painting called "The Triumph of Venus" originally adorned the king's bed, but his second wife, a woman of a more religious bent, had it replaced with "The Sacrifice of Abraham."

Delectable

Imagine a dish by the name of "The Priest Has Fainted." Yet, possibly the most famous of all eggplant dishes is that *tour de force* known as *Iman Bayeldi,* whch owes its name to the Ottoman Turks of the 16th century.

According to legend, a holy man was making a routine call at the home of a particularly beautiful lady. Out of a spirit of hospitality, she insisted that he partake of an eggplant dish she had been preparing. When she bent over to present the dish, her veil slipped off, and for a brief moment, the priest caught a glimpse of her two delectable eggplants. Overpowered by the sight and the aroma of the succulent food, the holy man passed out. From that time on, the dish was christened *Iman Bayeldi* (The Priest Has Fainted).

A Place to Sleep

Beds are virtually unknown in much of India, though one Indian maharaja of recent times boasted a one-ton bed complete with four life-sized nudes that automatically began fanning and playing music the moment the monarch put his weight on the mattress. Wealthy Arabs sometimes sleep on elaborate tentlike beds, but most people in the Mideast still slumber on simple piles of rugs.

The Japanese customarily catch their shuteye on a mat, called a *tatami,* spread over the floor. Many Japanese do not even have a bedroom— in the morning, they roll up their *tatami* and their *futon* or quilt, and use the sleeping quarters as a dining room.

The Chinese, on the other hand, have a long tradition of bed slumber. Wooden beds similar to those made in ancient Egypt were in use in China as early as 2,000 years ago. Even the four-poster bed is not unknown in China. But, by our standards, old Chinese beds would not be very comfortable, with matting substituting for a mattress, and pillows made of wood or stone, carved to fit the head or neck.

In the West, the history of the bed begins in ancient Egypt. To our eyes, Egyptian beds look more like couches. And well they should, for Egyptians made no distinction between a day bed, or couch, and a night bed; they used the same item for both lounging and sleeping. The earliest known models were made of palm sticks or palm leaf wicker, lashed together with pieces of cord or rawhide. Later, Egyptian bed-makers introduced mortise-and-tenon construction and wood bed frames veneered with ivory or ebony. In the royal household, beds made from timbers were sometimes sheathed in gold. Most mattresses were made of woven cord, interlaced like the modern chaise longue or beach chair.

The Egyptian bed was equipped with a footboard, but not with a headboard. Egyptian pillows would seem appallingly uncomfortable by modern standards: most were raised headrests, curved to fit the head or neck, made of wood, ivory, or alabaster, and sometimes inlaid with ivory or colored stones. Many beds, especially those in poorer quarters, were fitted with a canopy of some kind from which mosquito netting could be hung. The Greek historian Herodotus claimed that contemporary Egyptians used the nets by day to catch fish.

Even in wealthier households, the Egyptian bedroom was starkly furnished, with just a bed and perhaps a chair and a small table. In many houses, there was but one bedroom for the master of the house; the servants slept in the hall. The ruins of one aristocratic Egyptian home suggest that younger children sometimes slept in their parents' bedroom.

Chris Pepple of Vermont (U.S.A.) at 17 became an expert skier and was instructed by Jim Gardner. Chris is blind and Jim is an amputee.

Visionary

For many Europeans, the Dark Ages must have been quite literally dark—or, at least, fuzzy. With no eyeglasses of any kind, medieval man had to rely on medicinal remedies of dubious value. One Anglo-Saxon remedy counseled persons with poor vision to comb their heads, eat little meat, and drink wormwood before meals, and perhaps apply salve made from pepper, nuts, salt, and wine. Fourth-century Italians believed that a person seeing a falling star should quickly begin counting— the viewer would be free from eye inflammations for as many years as he could count before the star disappeared.

For those too slow to catch a falling star, another medieval antidote to eye inflammation required that the sufferer tie a piece of linen around his neck with as many knots as there were letters in his name. White spots before the eyes? Simply catch a fox, cut out his tongue, tie it in a red rag, and hang it from your neck. As for casting out motes, just touch your eyelid, say "I buss the Gorgon's mouth," and spit three times.

Through Rose-Colored Glasses

Sunglasses are nothing new in optometry. Tinted lenses were already in common use during the 16th century. By the mid-17th century, amber or mica lenses in several colors were available. Samuel Pepys bought a pair of green spectacles in London during the 1660s, and reported their popularity. It wasn't until around 1885, however, that tinted glass spectacles began to be widespread.

As the use of spectacles became common among all social groups, class distinctions began to arise in eyeglass design. In England, the upper classes preferred the single-lens eyeglass, or *perspective glass*, which was usually left dangling from the neck by a ribbon. The poor opted for double-lens eyeglasses, most often sold by itinerant peddlers. Some peddlers touted their wares with a claim that viewing the sun or moon through colored spectacles would bring both improved vision and good luck.

In Spain, meanwhile spectacles of any kind were considered so chic that no fashionable man or woman would be seen without them—whether they were needed or not!

The early 18th century saw the first appearance of spectacles with the now familiar rigid sidepieces, or *bows*. The English called the bows *temples*, since they pressed against the temple of the wearer, and dubbed the spectacles *temple glasses*. In France, advertisers promoted "English style" spectacles, by promising that wearers would "breathe more easily" than they would with the older, nose-pinching styles.

Scissors glasses were also popular for a time, serving as a compromise for fashion-conscious Europeans who dared not wear double-lens eyeglasses, yet could not see well enough with the more fashionable single eyeglass. Scissor glasses consisted of two lenses joined by a forked handle. When the glasses were held before the eyes, the handle appeared poised to "scissor off" the nose.

The *spyglass*, an earlier invention, also became fashionable—although, for discretion's sake, the spyglass was often hidden in a cane, fan, perfume bottle, or other accessory.

Bifocal lenses were suggested as early as 1716, and may have been first made in London around 1760. However, Benjamin Franklin has generally been credited with their invention. A bifocal lens consists of two semi-circular lenses joined together in a frame; the upper portion of the lens corrects for distance viewing, while the bottom half is used for reading. Franklin assembled his first bifocals around 1784, when he tired of carrying around two pairs of spectacles. Bifocal lenses made of fused glass segments did not appear until the 1900s.

Franklin's invention was not without a precedent in nature. The eyes of a tiny tropical fish called the *anableps* function just like a pair of bifocals. The upper half of each eye is focused for water-surface vision; the lower half for underwater sight.

It's All in the Bag

The haversack is a carry-all used by hikers and army personnel. But it didn't start out that way. The haversack really was a bag for carrying oats or *hafer*.

Paradise Cream

Ice cream was an expensive dish until the early 19th century, which saw the invention of the insulated icehouse and the hand-crank ice cream freezer. By the 1820s, the dessert was being sold by street vendors in New York City, who beckoned passersby with shouts of "I scream ice cream."

By the middle of the century, ice cream was so popular that a magazine editor was moved to write: "A party without ice cream would be like a breakfast without bread or a dinner without a roast."

The father of the American ice cream industry was Jacob Fussell. Beginning in 1851 with a small ice cream store in Baltimore, Fussell was soon selling his wares in shops from Boston to Washington. During the Civil War, Fussell sold huge quantities of ice cream to the Union army. By the end of the century, ice cream could be bought almost anywhere in the nation. New inventions such as steam power, mechanical refrigeration, electricity, and the homogenizer made the ice cream plant virtually as modern as it is today.

In the early decades of this century, the popularity of the soda fountain made ice cream an American institution. Temperance preachers urged listeners to give up the grape in favor of the cool confection. Baseball star Walter Johnson—no relation to Howard—boasted that all he ever ate on the day he was to pitch was a quart of ice cream.

Beginning in 1921, officials at the Ellis Island immigration station in New York, intent on serving newcomers a "truly American dish," included ice cream in all meals served at the station.

By that time, the three mainstays of the ice cream parlor—the soda, the sundae, and the cone—were already popular from coast to coast. The first to appear was the ice cream soda. In 1874, a soda-fountain manufacturer by the name of Robert M. Green was busily vending a cool drink made of sweet cream, syrup, and carbonated water (now known as the egg cream) at the semicentennial celebration of Philadelphia's Franklin Institute. One day, Green ran out of cream and substituted vanilla ice cream. The new treat quickly became a sensation. Green went on to make a fortune selling ice cream sodas. His will dictated that "Originator of the Ice Cream Soda" be engraved on his tombstone.

An infant cannot shed tears when he cries until he is 3 months old.

Portable Beds

Camp beds were in use as early as the 15th century for traveling gentry. The camp beds of the era were hardly cots, though, and some of the heavier four-posters must surely have required a wagon all their own for transport. The trundle bed also appeared during this era, originally for servants who slept in their master's room. (Queen Elizabeth herself had a bedroom guard of 18 persons.) By day, the beds were rolled under the master's four-poster.

The familiar lullabye "Rock-a-bye Baby" is at least as old as the Elizabethan period. The lyrics may harken back to an earlier epoch when a mother might place baby's cradle in the branches of a tree to be rocked gently by the wind.

Creatures of Fancy

For his own survival, man had to gain control over at least some of the species of the animal kingdom. It is likely that the first animal to have been domesticated was the sheep, in Iraq around 9000 B.C. Goats, pigs, cattle and horses followed successively.

But there are certan species that retain their autonomy in the wild. And perhaps it is because man still retains primordial fear of these animals that we delight in "taming" them in our art and literature.

Life

Early Advertising Art

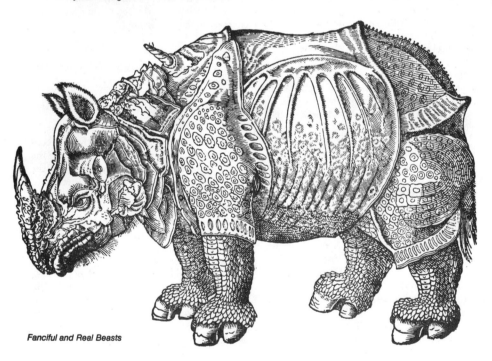

Fanciful and Real Beasts

The Land that Waited

Harper's Roundtable

Cautionary Catches

Art of the Silhouette

French Advertising Art

Gebrauchgraphik, No. 6

Drawing by Harold Montiel

Calligraphy

Fanciful and Real Beasts

Early Advertising Art

203

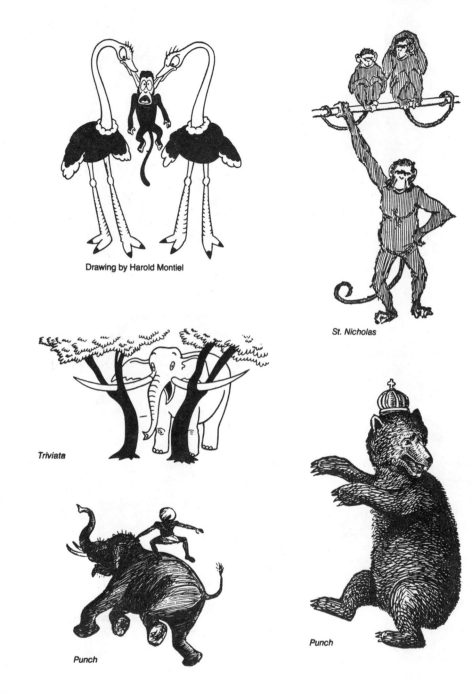

Drawing by Harold Montiel

St. Nicholas

Triviata

Punch

Punch

Punch

Triviata

Fliegende Blätter

Art of the Book

Calligraphy

Apple Hero

One of the men we might thank for spreading the apple tree in America was Jonathan Chapman, better known as Johnny Appleseed. Many people think Johnny was merely a legendary figure, but he lived, indeed. Born in Massachusetts around 1775, Chapman set out alone into the unexplored wilderness that is now Ohio, Indiana, and western Pennsylvania, with a sack of apple seeds he'd collected from cider mills. Wherever he went, he planted apple seeds, and retraced his paths to prune the trees he'd planted. Before he died in 1846, he covered more than 100,000 square miles with apple trees!

The fruit that gave Jonathan Chapman his nickname is known in botanical circles as *Malus pumila*. The apple is a pome, or fleshy fruit, like the pear and quince. The *Malus* genus, which includes about 25 species, owes its name to the Latin word for "evil," due to its Biblical reputation.

To Catch a Thief

Formed from two words, *burg* and *lar*, this word actually means a city thief. Old English for town was burgh which became burg and *lar* was used from the Latin word larron which meant a thief.

From Pillow to Post

Most ancient peoples of the Mideast slept on beds similar to those in Egypt. Phoenician beds often sported foot panels with erotic ivory carvings—the Bible, you'll recall, equated "beds of ivory" with sinful luxury. Sardanapalus, the last great king of Assyria, evidently had quite a thing for beds, right to the end. According to an apocryphal Greek fable, the Assyrian king committed suicide, along with his wives and concubines, on a pyre fueled by his 150 beds.

Since almost all the beds of ancient Greece were made of wood, none survive today. But artwork from the period shows that the Greeks slept on beds very similar to those of Egypt. The earliest models consisted of a wood frame and a mattress of lashed rawhide bands. Later, the wood frames were veneered with ivory, bronze, or silver. For some reason, the Greeks dropped the footboard in favor of the headboard.

As described in *The Odyssey*, Penelope's couch was fitted with a stuffed mattress, a purple linen sheet, and blankets made from fleeces and rugs. Considerably less fortunate, and less comfortable, were the men of Sparta, who were required to sleep in a tent along with 15 other compatriots, while their wives remained at home. Even married men were not permitted to sleep away from their tents until the age of 30!

The Greek sleeping chamber, called a *thalamos* was small and windowless, with light reaching the room only through the large doorway. The master bedroom, which was often in the women's quarters, usually contained a bed and perhaps a few coffers and chairs. The Greek's idea of bedroom luxury was a bed of roses with "no rooster within earshot."

Leonid Brezhnev, General Secretary and Marshall of the Soviet Union, is a master politician and able executive. Unknown to most people, is the fact that Brezhnev is also one of Russia's best dressed men.

Studies show that as status rises so does the production of sex hormones. The Yerkes Research Center says, "If you depose a leader, his testosterone level sinks; if you create a leader, it rises."

Grin and Bear Them

In the 16th century, when lenses for myopic persons first appeared, eyeglasses were still selected by trial and error. A person seeking eyeglasses stepped into a spectacles maker's shop, and sampled the wares until he found a pair of specs that seemed appropriate. Spectacles makers scratched a number on each lens they made, to indicate the age of the person they thought the lens would suit. It wasn't until the 18th century that lenses were identified by the radius of curvature.

Toward the latter part of that century, spectacles makers began to turn their attention to devising a means of holding the lenses in front of the eye for longer periods of time. First to appear were spectacles held in place by a strap tied behind the head. Next came glasses with two straps, one to loop around each ear, or spectacles with two weighted cords that were tucked behind the ears and hung almost to the wearer's waist. These latter styles were particularly popular in Spain. The Chinese preferred similar glasses right up to the 20th century, though until recently, Oriental lenses were made from crystal, rather than ordinary glass.

To Go Berserk

In Norse mythology, there was a warrior who refused to wear mail or anything but a bearskin. Because of this, he was known as Berserker or "bear shirt." This fighter would tear at his enemies unencumbered and would win his battles by sheer ferocity. He had twelve sons who all fought like him and this legendary family gave us the modern expression "to go berserk" a phrase that describes the act of going into a furious rage.

Fromage, Ooh La La

France, third after the United States and Italy in total cheese production, can boast the most varieties of cheese—some 240 in all. Among the most popular is *Camembert*, produced by inoculating ripening cheese with the *Penicillum candidum* mold. Legend has it that Camembert was first produced around 1780, and made famous by Napoleon, who was so pleased with his first taste of the cheese that he kissed the waitress who served it.

Another French cheese of ancient vintage is the butterlike *Brie*, which may have been developed as long ago as the 12th century. Brie is sometimes known as the "cheese of kings," since it has earned the praise of so many monarchs.

Grog

Admiral Edward Vernon, during his command of the Royal Navy, decreed that rum issued to British seamen be diluted with water. This rendered it useless to keep and so prevented topers from storing it and then drinking themselves incapable for duty.

The admiral was known as "old grog" because of his liking for grogram (or grosgrain), a weather proof material made from silk, mohair and gum. Seamen of that day applied the admiral's nickname to the diluted rum issue. The word grog is now widely used for any intoxicating drink.

Feats with Hands

Perhaps the most breathtaking shot in college basketball history occurred during the 1946 NIT games in New York. An underdog Rhode Island State team was trailing the Bowling Green Five, 74-72, with only three seconds left to play. Taking possession of the ball under their own basket, the Rhode Island team managed to get the ball to five-foot, 10-inch Ernie Calverley, who lofted a desperation shot from well behind the midcourt line. As the buzzer sounded, the Madison Square Garden crowd of 18,548 rose in astonishment—Calverley's shot had whisked through the mesh without even touching the rim! Rhode Island had tied the score, and went on to win in overtime, 82-79. Observers have estimated that the distance Calverley's shot traveled was somewhere between 55 and 65 feet!

Then there's the incredible streak of the UCLA teams, who won seven straight national championships during the late 1960s and 70s, and 10 championships in 12 years. And let's not forget the fantastic professional career of Wilt "The Stilt" Chamberlain, regarded by most aficionados as the best basketball player of all time. As a pro, Chamberlain became the career leader in almost all offensive departments, finishing his 13-year career with a lifetime average of 30.1 points per game! Chamberlain is still the only professional player ever to score 100 points in a game, accomplishing the feat on March 2, 1962, during a 169-147 rout of the New York Knickerbockers.

Another enviable scoring record was set on February 28, 1975, when an amateur player named Ted St. Martin sank 1,704 consecutive free throws without a miss.

John T. Sebastian of Illinois accomplished a similar feat in 1972 when he sank 63 consecutive free throws—blindfolded!

The water strider, or water skipper, is a bug that moves lightly across a pond, never breaking the water-film on the surface. Therefore, the water strider never gets its feet wet!

Free-wheeling

All bicycle records seem to pale when compared to the feats of a number of individuals who have taken it upon themselves to pedal around the world. As early as 1897, Mr. and Mrs. H. Darwin McIlrath accomplished the feat on a pair of safety bikes. In 1971, Englishman Ray Reece set the record for round-the-world cycling by circling the globe in just 143 days. Itinerant lecturer Walter Stolle has pedaled an estimated 270,000 miles in his lifetime, traveling through 140 nations—and suffering 26 robberies en route.

But surely the most incredible feat of bicycle daring in history was the round-the-world journey of American Thomas Stevens. Beginning in San Francisco, Stevens pedaled across America, sailed across the Atlantic, cycled through Europe, the Middle East, India, and the Orient, then boarded a ship for San Francisco, completing the round-the-world journey in under three years. What makes Stevens' feat so remarkable was its date: 1884 to 1887, *before* the development of the safety bike. Stevens actually circled the globe on a highwheeler with a 50-inch-diameter front wheel! Since John Dunlop was not to invent the pneumatic tire until 1894, Stevens' "vicious cycle" was equipped with rough-riding solid tires. Ouch!

Shocking Business

The queer-looking, circular-shaped fish called the electric ray has a most unusual method of catching its dinner. This soft-skinned creature is equipped with two muscular organs, one on each side of its head, which are capable of giving off strong electrical impulses. The ray captures its prey by "butting" the victim with these organs and thereby stunning or killing it with an electrical shock.

The ray also uses its electric organs to fight off enemies. Any creature that tangles with one of these deepwater fish is in for a rude shock, for the current produced by a large electric ray is powerful enough to kill a man!

Rulers Without Kingdoms

For a measuring device, early man probably first used his arm or his foot—but even during the Egyptian era, when the cubit was the unit of length measurement, a ruler of some kind was more often used. There are two basic kinds of length-measuring devices: the end standard, and the line standard. With an end standard, the unit is defined from one calibration on the device to another. Most modern rulers are end standards; that is, a foot ruler is one foot long from end to end, and a yardstick is one yard long.

How accurate is a modern ruler? Suppose you want to draw a two-inch line on a piece of paper. First of all, the calibrations on the ruler are a fraction of an inch thick. Thus, a dot that looks correctly placed to you, may appear off-center to another eye. The calibrations themselves are never absolutely precise, and the edges of most rulers are slightly warped. The chance of your line measuring precisely two inches, then, is slim, indeed.

Rulers come n many shapes and sizes, among them the three-edged or triangular ruler so often used by students—both for measuring and for launching rubber bands across the classroom.

The yak is a beast of burden of central Asia. The yak, when over-loaded, grunts and is often called the "grunting oxen."

On April 10, 1849, a New Yorker by the name of Walter Hunt was granted a patent Number 6,281 for a device he called the safety pin. Never heard of Walter Hunt, you say? Well, Hunt was not destined to be pinned with the tag "inventor of the safety pin" for one simple reason: the safety pin, or devices virtually identical to it, had been in use for more than 2,500 years—since the days of ancient Greece!

Playing By the Rules

Edmond Hoyle has been credited with formulating the rules to many popular games, but actually Hoyle never heard of most of the games for which he is supposed to have codified the rules. In the case of backgammon, however, Hoyle rightly deserves recognition. In 1743, Hoyle wrote a treatise on the game laying down many of the rules we follow today.

Backgammon waned in popularity during the 19th century, although Mississippi riverboat gamblers frequently included a backgammon board in their bag of tricks. Then, in the 1920s, interest in the game was suddenly revived when an unknown American player devised the concept of "doubling"—a rule by which a player can double the stakes in an attempt to force his opponent to concede the game. Doubling did away with long games that had to be played to a finish even after the eventual winner was already fairly obvious.

The concept of redoubling was added shortly thereafter, by another unknown genius. After a few thousand years of evolution, backgammon became the game we know today. But the modern rules weren't completely cofified until 1931, when Wheaton Vaughan of the New York Racquet and Tennis Club prepared the first universally recognized rulebook for the modern game. Backgammon has undergone few changes since then.

A piece of pie eaten just once each week can add more than three pounds of body weight in a year.

Bicycle Lore

The popularity of the bicycle is well deserved. An extremely efficient machine, the bicycle is light but strong, capable of supporting a load over 10 times its weight. Bicycles are inexpensive to purchase, simple to maintain and repair, easy to store both at home and away, and relatively safe to drive. In 1979, the number of pedacycles in use in the U.S. was a hefty 98.5 million. The bike does not pollute the environment, and is an excellent instrument for promoting physical fitness. Over short distances, in fact, the bicycle is actually more efficient—and convenient—than the automobile.

The bicycle commonly used in most of the world is a far cry from the elaborate 10-speed models that now fill American bikeways. As late as the 1960s, three-speed "racers" were considered the epitome of biking pleasure. Today, 10-speeds make uphill pedaling a breeze. But even the crudest of today's bikes would look like streamlined speedsters compared to the heavy iron-wheeled contraptions that began the curious history of the bicycle.

Suggestions of wheeled vehicles propelled by the muscle power of their riders are found among the artifacts of various ancient cultures, including the bas-reliefs of Egypt and Babylonia and the frescoes of Pompeii. A design for a wheeled machine propelled by cranks and pedals was found among the writings of Leonard da Vinci, dating to about 1493.

The so-called "cycle window," made in Italy in 1580 for a church in Stoke Poges, England, shows an angel astride what appears to be a wheeled vehicle made of wood. A trumpet attached to the front handlebars suggests a horn used to warn pedestrians of the vehicle's approach. But we find no reference to such a vehicle in the writings of the period.

The earliest prototypes of the bicycle appeared in France and England late in the 18th century. These simple vehicles consisted of two wheels linked by a wooden "backbone" upon which the rider sat, propelling the machine by pushing with his feet against the ground. The backbones often took the shape of snakes, lions, horses, and other animals, leading to the name of "hobby horse." But these vehicles were virtually useless until 1816, when Baron von Drais of Karlsruhe, Germany, introduced a pivoted front wheel that could be turned by a handle, enabling the rider to steer his hobby horse for the first time.

Linoleum

In 1863, one Frederick Walton created a material from burlap and linseed oil. It was called linoleum, from the two Latin words *linum*, meaning flax, and *oleum*, meaning oil. When the durability of this product was established, it was patterned and coated.

The koala bear, a marsupial of Australia, can eat only Eucalyptus leaves. It will die of starvation if these leaves are not available.

Pravda, the official Soviet newspaper, is read by over nine million persons each day!

Although the FBI says that only about 30% of all rapes are reported, in one recent year in the US there were 51,000 rapes.

Schistosomiasis, the world's greatest killer, afflicts some 250,000,000 people. It is spread by a parasite found in rice paddies.

Knuckle Down

Knee joints and elbow joints were all called knuckles in medieval days. *To knuckle down* to something literally meant to get on one's knees so as to do a better job.

The meaning is still in the phrase used today although it is more loosely applied.

Watch It

When the English developed a watchmaking industry in the 17th century, they concentrated on the mechanism of the watch rather than its aesthetic design—the inside rather than the outside—and thus English watches soon surpassed their fancier French counterparts in accuracy. By 1800, England reigned supreme as the watchmaker for the world, with over 70,000 people involved in an industry centered around London's Clerkenwell district.

The English reign lasted only until the middle of the 19th century, when Swiss watchmaking began its ascendancy. According to legend, an Englishman passing through the Swiss town of Le Locle in the late 17th century brought a broken watch to a Monsieur Jean-Richard for repairs. The device so intrigued Jean-Richard's son, Daniel, that the boy decided to make one for himself—and did so in 18 months. Later, Daniel's five sons followed their father into the trade to help establish the Swiss watchmaking industry. A statue of a boy in blacksmith's robe stands today in a square in Le Locle, a tribute to Daniel Jean-Richard, the "father of Swiss watchmaking."

Umpire

The Old English word *noumper* was the equivalent of the Old French words *non per,* which meant not equal. The noumper was always called in where parties could not agree in matters of sport. Over the centuries, the noumper, through mispronunciation, became umpire.

Only ten inches long, the Pirania (Serrasalmus nattereri) of South American streams has probably killed more humans than any other fish! They have been known to completely strip the flesh from a 100-pound capybara in less than sixty seconds!

The Germans completely dominated the art of watchmaking until the early 17th century, when Germany was ravaged and the industry was destroyed by the Thirty Years War. The French then took over the watchmaking leadership, with their industry centered around Blois.

Most French watches were oval, not circular, their faces covered either by glass or a metal lid that had to be opened for a peek at the time. French watch cases were often elaborately decorated with engravings of figures, foliage, and domestic or religious scenes, and rank among the most finely crafted objects of their time.

"Don't kiss anyone with warts," we are advised by a dermatologist because warts are caused by a contagious virus and can be caught by kissing.

There are over twice as many chickens in the United States as there are people! The chicken population is about 450 million!

Children of different racial backgrounds grow at different rates. The average American boy grows to a height of 30 inches by his first birthday; by his second, he has reached half his adult height.

One out of every seven school-age children suffers a respiratory condition, with asthma being the most common. Swimming is the best exercise for asthmatics.

At one time the highest number of known cases of leprosy in the U.S. was in Hawaii. New York City alone had some 200 residents suffering from leprosy.

Cold Banana

Bananas undergo their final ripening in the home. For best results, the fruits should be stored at room temperature until fully ripe, then placed in the refrigerator. Many Americans are reluctant to store bananas in the refrigerator, lessoned by an earlier Chiquita Banana song that warned:

> Bananas like the climate of the very,
> very tropical equator,
> So you should never put bananas in
> the refrigerator.

Actually, however, refrigeration will cause the skin to turn brown, but the fruit itself will remain unspoiled for a few days inside its natural shell. The browner the banana's skin, the sweeter the fruit. As Chiquita banana sang:

> Where they are flecked with brown and
> of a golden hue
> That's when bananas are the best for you.

Are You Jaded

The supposedly medicinal value of this stone is the reason for its name. Jade is from the Spanish *piedre de ijada* which means stone-of-the-side. The belief was, if it was worn on the side it would guard against colic and other organic stomach troubles. Jade is also known as nephrite which is from the Greek *nephros* meaning kidney.

Robber Baron

The tropical man-of-war, or frigate, bird likes a fish dinner. But it doesn't fish like most other birds. Instead, it has a method of stealing food.

It waits until another bird has done the work. Then it swoops down and beats the bird with its wings. The unlucky bird, trying to defend itself, lets go of the fish. The swift man-of-war dives, snatches the fish, and zooms away.

Occasionally this robber does its own fishing in mid-air above the ocean. It dives down and grabs flying fish when they sail above the water.

Old Wine in New Bottles

Just 20 years ago, most Americans probably regarded backgammon—if they knew the game at all—as an exotic, unfamiliar game whose board often turned up, quite uselessly, on the back of checkerboards. Times have changed, and the games played have changed as well. While checkers has lost a good deal of its popularity, "exotic" backgammon is now the fastest-growing game in America, with millions of dedicated players, hundreds of backgammon clubs, and an international circuit of major tournaments. Today, backgammon experts command lesson fees of up to $150 an hour!

But the current backgammon craze is hardly a phenomenon unique to our age. The popularity of backgammon has not risen steadily to its present peak, but rather has surged and ebbed through the ages. After a priod of obscurity, backgammon is now riding the crest of a new wave of interest. Who knows? If backgammon continues to grow at the present rate, it might even become as popular as it was 2,000 years ago!

When the dial appeared on old timekeeping devices, there was only one hand, with the perimeter of the dial calibrated for the hour and the quarter-hour. In some early clocks, the hand revolved; in others, the hand remained stationary and the dial itself revolved. An Italian, Jacopo Dondi, has been credited with designing the first clock dial in 1344. A reconstruction of one of Dondi's clocks is now on display at the Smithsonian Institution in Washington.

Bistro

Hungry troops of the Russian Army entering Paris in 1815 wanted a quick meal at a low price. They would shout *bistro, bistro*, which was Russian for quick. The French adopted the word and applied it to cafes where a quick cheap meal was served.

Blenk — $4,000,000

Bible doesn't menton Potatoes

Zactar? fingernails or Toenails

Calories in a Jelly Bean? -?

Like all sports, basketball has produced its moments of greatness. One of the high points of college basketball was reached in the 1949-50 season, when the underdog City College of New York became the first—and only—team to win both the NCAA and NIT championships in the same year. The Beavers had finished their schedule that year without ranking among the top 20 teams, and had been the last squad to be invited to both tournaments. Yet they went on to victory in both competitions, in the process defeating the teams ranked one, two, three, five, and six.

In humans, the right lung weighs more than the left! The average for adult males is 625g (right) and 600g (left).

Just Hold Your Nose

The durian is a most unusual food. Speaking plainly, it stinks. The nasal assault of the durian when in season is overwhelming. You might think that you were walking behind a garbage truck. But, somehow, the fruit itself is delicious and appeals to many people who manage to get past the smell. One English writer has described it as "eating a vanilla custard in a latrine."

When not in season, this delicacy is extremely expensive, costing $5 or more apiece.

That's Endurance

In 1891, the first of the legendary six-day bicycle races was held in Madison Square Garden, New York. The maiden race included 40 entries, of which only six finished, with Bill Martin winning on a highwheeler. The event became an immediate spectator sensation, attracting close to 100,000 persons over the course of a week. The race remained a one-man event until 1899, when two-man teams first appeared. The record for six-day marathon racing is an impressive 2,093 miles.

Today, the most important bicycle race in the world is the annual Tour de France. Begun in 1903, by a publisher as a circulation stunt, the race is now one of Europe's major sporting events. Originally 3,560 miles long, the present course stretches about 2,780 miles through France, Spain, Switzerland, Italy, and Belgium. Sometimes bikers average 200 miles per day although they stop riding at sunset. An estimated 1 million people in France alone turn out to watch the bikers as they wend their way over hill and dale, and climb over mountain passes as high as 8,000 feet. In some towns, petty criminals are released from jail for the day so that they can take in the spectacle. One observer has calculated that if one-third of all the Frenchmen lose one-third of a day's work due to the race, the Tour de France takes a toll of close to two billion dollars on the French economy!

There is no comparable event in the United States, but American cyclists have proved quite adept at cross-country biking—literally cross-country, that is. In 1940, Raymond Bryan rode from New York to San Francisco in 27 days, 11 hours. By 1973, Paul Cornish had lowered the coast-to-coast time to a mere 13 days, five hours, averaging 225 miles per day. The year 1973 also saw a pair of young Americans pedal around the country on a tandem bike, covering 4,837 miles in four months.

The Russians have 13 times the number of centenarians that we have in the United States.

Look Ma, No Hands!

Like the clocks of their time, early watches struck the hour and were equipped with only one hand. The word *watch* in the sense of timepiece is derived from *watchman*, since in England the town watchman, the caller of the hours or town crier, was among the first to carry a portable timepiece. The minute hand was not to appear on the watch until 1670 in England—and much later in Europe! The Roman numbers I through XII marked the hours, and some watch faces also showed the numbers 13 through 24 beneath the lower numbers for Italians and Bohemians who favored the 24-hour system. But early watches were predominantly jewelry pieces, and few of their owners actually expected them to tell the correct time.

Nice Paddling

The New York census disclosed that 42,426 New Yorkers work in New Jersey, that 2,282 have jobs in Connecticut. But believe it or not, 652 New Yorkers claim that they work in California, and 128 claim that they work in England. Among those who say that they work in England, 54 insist that they travel to work by car.

The Whole World's Doing It

Canada was the first country outside the United States to adopt basketball, with a men's college team from Toronto playing in open competition as early as 1893. The game reached France the same year, and England, Australia, China, India, and Japan soon after. The sport grew rapidly on an international scale after World War II, and today basketball ranks as the third most popular sport worldwide after soccer and cycling. Since 1936, basketball has been a part of the Olympic competition, with the United States dominating the sport.

Rodeos came into being in the early days of the American cattle industry, in about 1847. The largest rodeo in the world today is the one held annually in Calgary, Alberta, Canada. The record attendance has been 993,777 in 1973.

Bicycle Corps

The armed forces took advantage of improved bicycle technology by constructing special vehicles for their "bicycle corps." Troops were equipped with lightweight folding bikes that could be carried on the back when the roads were muddled. The frames were fitted with special attachments to hold a rifle. During World War I, bicycles were used extensively to lay telegraph wire. There was even a tricycle fitted with a mounted gun!

The smallest unit of length measurement in the world is the *atto-meter*, equivalent to a mere quintillionth of a centimeter. Your pinky is probalby about 7,000,000,000,000,000,000 atto-meters long!

Dash It All

When Jesse Owens graduated from East Technical High School in Cleveland, Ohio, he had established three national high school records in track. At Ohio State University, Jesse ran like the wind and broke a few more world marks. And in the 1936 Olympic games at Berlin, the lithe Negro racer—who had by now acquired the nickname of *The Ebony Express*—built imperishable fame by winning four gold medals!

But Jesse Owens' performance on May 25, 1935, at the Big Ten conference championships held at Ann Arbor, Michigan was truly spectacular. Getting up from a sickbed, Jesse, in his first event, ran the 100-yard dash in 9.4 seconds, to tie the world's record.

Ten minutes later in the broad jump, Jesse leaped 26 feet eight and one quarter inches *on his first try* to best the world's record.

Then, running the 220-yard dash, Jesse sped down the course in 20.3 seconds to smash another world's record.

And just about 45 minutes after he had participated in the first event, Jesse negotiated the 220-yard hurdles in 22.6 seconds, shattering still another world's record.

In one single afternoon—within the space of three quarters of an hour—Jesse Owens established world records in four events.

Game Book

At the time of the Crusades, the Saracens enjoyed a game called *nard* that they'd learned from the Persians. The Persians, in turn, may have developed *nard* from earlier Mesopotamian or Indian games, or from parcheesi, or from the board games of Greece and Rome. *Nard* employed black and white pieces on a checkered game board with 12 divisions, and unlike *tabulae*, was played with two dice. By the time of the Third Crusade in the 12th century, backgammon-like games were so popular among the Crusaders that Kings Richard I of England and Philip II of France issued a joint edict prohibiting all gambling games among their troops.

A number of games similar to backgammon have been enjoyed for centuries in the Orient. The Chinese play *shwan-liu*, the Japanese enjoy *sunoroku*, the Koreans *ssang-ryouk*, and the Thais, *len sake*. But most historians believe that these oriental equivalents of backgammon were imported from the West, and therefore played no part in the development of backgammon itself.

Tables, which included elements from both *tabulae* and *nard*, was widely played by the aristocracy through the Middle Ages, and the game eventually found its way to the lower classes as well. Medieval innkeepers customarily kept boards and dice on hand for their patrons. The Church opposed the game, as it did all gambling pastimes. In 1254, Louis IX outlawed it in France. Suppression of the game continued right up into the 16th century, forcing diehard players to disguise their boards as books, the hinged game board masquarading as the book cover, with the dice and pieces hidden inside.

Foolscap

In the period between the thirteenth and seventeenth centuries, fine paper bore a water mark depicting a jester with a cap and bell. In Italian this mime was known as *foglio-capo*. Foolscap is a corruption of this term.

Golf

The Dutch played a game called *kolven* on frozen rivers and canals. The players used a wooden club to putt a ball toward a stake pressed into the ice. Sixteenth-century illustrations from Bruges, in Belgium, show players putting a ball at a hole in the ground.

Norbert Weiner, prodigy and Massachusetts Institute of Technology mathematician, read at 3½ years; was a college freshman at 12; got his BA degree at 14; earned a Ph D at 18. He was also a vegetarian.

Reading does not weaken the eyes and old people should be encouraged to read as much as they like even if they have to use magnifying lenses.

The *fathom* was originally thought to be the length to which a man can extend his arms—if you can fathom that. Today, the fathom is equivalent to six feet, and is used most often in reference to water depth and cable length.

The *knot* is not a measurement of length, so if you ever hear a sailor say "knots per hour" you'll know he's a landlubber in disguise. The knot is actually a measurement of speed, equivalent to one nautical mile per hour.

Punctured Romantic

Lord Byron, the passionate poet and darling of the drawing rooms of London, was 5'8" tall and weighed well over 200 pounds, being forced to go on strict diets and rigorous exercise programs.

Swiss Ascendancy

How did the Swiss become the superb watchmakers they are? The historic causes were many, but one explanation attributes the development of the craft to religious reformer John Calvin's decree to end the manufacture of all jewelry and other "vanities" in Geneva. Swiss jewelers then turned to watchmaking, which Calvin did not condemn.

In any case, watchmaking fit in perfectly with the Swiss way of life. Since most Swiss were farmers, watchmaking at home provided an excellent source of income during the otherwise unproductive Alpine winter. By 1800, entire families in French-speaking Switzerland were engaged in making watch parts. The components were usually assembled in factories.

The Swiss invested heavily in watchmaking machinery during the mid-19th century, but the English continued to rely on hand craftsmanship. While simple English watches frequently sold for as much as 10 pounds—a great deal of money at the time—a Swiss named Roskopf brought out the world's first cheap, reliable watch in 1865. By 1900, the Swiss takeover was complete, and English watchmaking has never since recovered.

In 1626, Francis Bacon, the English Philosopher and statesman wrote the story, "The New Atlantis," in which the people concerned had airplanes, submarines and sound-carrying devices. Bacon also predicted the telephone 250 years before Alexander Graham Bell's patent.

Chair time for the average patient in the US orthodontist's office is 20 to 25 hours; in Europe it is 2 hours.

We shiver when cold because shivering increases muscular action thereby heightening the heat of the body.

Ludwig II, known for his Byronic beauty, among other things, in his later years hated eyes and forbade anyone to look at him. Servants who entered his room at Neuschwanstein in Germany had to bend double to approach the king.

Pasteur believed wine the most healthful beverage. Recent studies have shown that wine with meals may reduce the incidence of arteriosclerosis in people by as much as 50%.

Everyone is born farsighted. Most develop 20-20 vision at about the age of 5. However, 20-20 vision in the US is the exception, not the rule. Half the US population wears glasses.

"Men wanted for a hazardous journey. Small wages, bitter cold, long months of complete darkness, constant danger, safe return doubtful. Honor and recognition in case of success. Ernest Shackleton."

This ad appeared in London papers in 1900. Shackleton, the famed explorer, was swamped with overwhelming response!

At least 1,000 people every day commit suicide throughout the world. In the U.S., every 20 minutes someone commits suicide.

Terrier

This word evolved from the French *terre* and the Latin *terra* meaning earth. The English called this dog a terrier because its initial use was to hunt the hare and the badger. Both these animals lived underground and the terrier had to dig for them.

Riding in Tandem

Tandem bicycles enjoyed a vogue during the Gay Nineties. Successful tandem bikes had been built as early as 1869, but the vehicle remained a curiosity even during its heyday, and never achieved the widespread popularity legend might suggest. The words of a well-known 1890s song were probably invented to be more humorous at the time than the modern master might realize:

Daisy, Daisy, give me your answer, do.
I'm half crazy, all for the love of you!
It won't be a stylish marriage,
I can't afford a carriage.
But you'll look sweet, upon the seat
Of a bicycle built for two!

Like the single-passenger vehicles of their time, tandem bikes took many shapes. Some placed the riders side by side, others positioned the rear rider higher than the front rider so that both could enjoy the view. Three-seaters began to appear, then four-seaters, culminating in the monstrous 10-seat *decemtuple*, a 23-foot-long curiosity that toured Europe and America late in the decade. But even the *decemtuple* would seem a mere child's trike compared to the 72-foot-long, 34-seater built in 1876 by a Danish manufacturer.

People of India have always greeted one another with a prayer-like gesture (Namaskar), avoiding direct contact with the hands. Now we learn that the most common way to catch a cold is via the hands. Infections often take the route, "hands to nose."

The duck-billed Trachodon, an extinct dinosaur of about 260 million years ago, had around 2000 teeth, which formed a pavement over the entire roof of its mouth, enabling it to crush the reeds which formed its diet.

The Main Reason to Go to Maine

In America, we are apt to apply the word *lobster* to a number of different crustaceans. The French are more prcise in their terminology, as they usually are in most matters gustatorial. If you discover *langouste* on the menu of a French restaurant, then find the word translated as "lobster" in your pocket dictionary, you're in for a surprise when the dish arrives. *Langouste* is the French word for the sea crawfish, or rock lobster, and not the crustacean we commonly enjoy in America. But the sea crawfish, which is smaller than the lobster and lacks claws, is preferred by most Frenchmen to the true lobster.

Langoustine, meanwhile, is the French word for the large prawn often used in the Italian dish *Scampi. Ecrevisse* refers to the crayfish, or freshwater lobster, which is often referred to simply as a lobster in this country. Actually, the crayfish is a small shellfish found in the muddy banks of rivers in many parts of the world. Then how do you say "lobster" in French? Only the word *homard* refers to the creature we commonly know as the lobster.

"Rock lobster tails" found in the frozen foods compartment of any supermarkets are actually the tails of sea crawfish. Rock lobster has become popular in the United States only within the past 40 years. In 1936, a South African firm could not sell a 1,000-pound shipment of sea crawfish here. Ten years later, South African fishermen could barely satisfy the American demand. About 100 million pounds of South African rock lobster tails are now imported here each year.

Lobsters have been eaten for thousands of years by people on both sides of the Atlantic, including the Mayans of Central America. Lobsters were once so plentiful near Plymouth, Massachusetts, and other parts of New England that they were gathered for use as fertilizer when washed ashore during a storm.

Massachusetts provided the bulk of the lobster catch in this eountry until 1840, when lobstermen began fishing the waters off Maine in great numbers. By 1880, over two million pounds of Maine lobster was being canned each year. The state of Maine now accounts for about 25 million pounds of lobster yearly, although the term "Maine lobster" is also applied to much of the shellfish caught off the Maritime Provinces of Canada. Much of the Canadian catch ends up in the United States, which imports over 20 million pounds each year.

Speaking of motorized beds, the late billionaire Howard Hughes designed a bed for himself that employed 30 electric motors, to move himself and various parts of the bed. The bed was also equipped with piped-in music and hot and cold running water!

Paradoxically, the U.S. state with the largest number of Indians has no Indian reservation—Oklahoma.

The U.S. Postal Service has an annual volume of business equal to almost half the world's total mail volume. On a typical day, the U.S. Postal Service processes almost as much mail as the rest of the world combined.

The State of Ohio has long been a very fountain of educators, from McGuffey of the famous "McGuffey's Readers," to Horace Mann and his experimental college, Antioch. Oberlin College was the nation's first co-educational university, and one of the first co-racial colleges. So many colleges—97 in all—now dot this state that most Ohioans live within a few miles of one.

The largest underground chamber in the world is the Big Room of the Carlsbad Cavern, in New Mexico. This room is 4,270 feet long, and reaches 328 feet in height and 656 feet in width.

One a Day—But Which One?

Over 7,000 varieties of apple have been recorded in the United States, only a handful of which have become commercially important. Apple trees do not grow true to type by seed, and therefore are propagated by budding and grafting. Most varieties arose from chance seedlings that produced trees with good qualities, including resistance and high yield. A good tree can produce over 30 bushels of fruit each harvest. That means that when Geoffrey Cash set the current world's record for apple picking—341 bushels in eight hours—he must have stripped the fruit from 11 trees!

The *Delicious*, grown largely in the Northwest, is the most common variety of apple in the United States, accounting for about 20 percent of the annual production. The *McIntosh*, widely grown in the Northeast and in western Canada, accounts for about 10 percent. Other popular varieties are the *Winesap*, grown largely in the Northwest; the *Jonathan*, popular in the Midwest; the *Rome Beauty*, another Midwestern favorite; the *Baldwin*, grown in the Northeast and especially suited for apple juice; the *Northern Spy, York Imperial, Stayman Winesap,* and *Grimes Golden*.

More than half of the apples grown in the United States are eaten fresh, while about one-fifth are used for vinegar, juice, jelly, and apple butter, and one-fifth for canned pie stock and applesauce. In Europe, a far higher percentage of the apple production is used for cider. The average American consumes from 20 to 25 pounds of apples a year, in one form or another.

The longest animal in the world, so far as is known, is the giant jellyfish, which is found in the northern Atlantic Ocean. one of these, which was washed up on the coast of Massachusetts in about 1865, had a bell seven and one-half feet in diameter and tentacles measuring 120 feet, thus giving a theoretical tentacular span of some 245 feet.

The country which had the highest percentage of its people killed during World War II was Poland, with 6,028,000, or 22.2 per cent of her population of 27,700,000 killed.

Probably the marathon record for bowling was achieved by Bob W. Petersen in Sacramento, California, in June of 1973. He bowled 1,242 games, walked 192 miles, and lifted 12 and a half tons in 82 hours, 20 minutes of consecutive bowling.

A newly-hatched crocodile is three times as large as the egg from which it has just emerged.

The world's biggest candy-eaters are the people of Britain, with 7.8 ounces of confectionary per person per week during a recent year. The figure for Scotland alone was more than 9 ounces.

Only two U.S. cities rank among the first twenty in the world in population. These are New York City in third place and Chicago, in twentieth place.

As Old as the Hills

The still popular Persian game of *parcheesi* may have been a remote ancestor of backgammon. In parcheesi, as in backgammon, the object of the game is to remove all of one's pieces from the board. Single pieces left on the parcheesi board may be "hit" by an opponent and sent back to the beginning of the board. Two or more of a player's pieces on a single square, or point, capture the point in parcheesi as well as in backgammon. Parcheesi also includes bonus provisions for a player rolling doubles.

Games far closer to modern backgammon were widely enjoyed by the ancient Greeks and Romans. Plato commented on the popularity of these games, and Homer mentions them in the *Odyssey*. The Greeks, by the way, had names for various dice throws reminiscent of our *snake eyes*. A six was known as *Aphrodite;* a one was called a *dog*.

In ancient Rome, we find the first game board featuring 12 points on each side, like the backgammon board. The Romans' *ludus duodecim scriptorum,* or "12-line game," is thought to have been adapted from earlier board games similar to the one found in Tutankhamen's tomb. But the Roman game board included *three* rows of 12 points. A later Roman game, called *tabulae,* reduced the number of points to 24, with 12 on each side, as in the modern game. The Romans played both games with three dice rather than two.

Tabulae was very popular among the Roman aristocracy. In the ruins of Pompeii, we find a *tabulae*-board table top in the courtyard of almost every villa. Nero was known to play the "sport of emperors" for as much as $15,000 a point, and the Emperor Commodus sometimes dipped into the royal treasury to pay off his *tabulae* gambling debts. But Roman paintings tell us that the game was popular among plebians as well. One painting depicts a fight in an inn arising from a game of *tabulae.* Another suggests that the Romans used *tabulae* to play a form of classical "strip poker."

The beginning of the Christian era did little to stamp out *tabulae* in Europe. A marble slab game board dating from the early days of Christian Rome bears a cross and the inscription: "Christ grants aid and victory to dicers if they write His Name when they roll, Amen." Modern backgammon gamblers have been known to utter the name of the deity in a slightly different vein.

Roman legionnaires spread *tabulae* throughout the Empire. In England, the game became known as *tables,* a term which persisted well into the 17th century. But *tabulae* and similar games gradually waned in popularity in France until revived by Crusaders returning from the Mideast.

Cleopatra, the famous Egyptian queen noted for her beauty and wisdom, was a direct descendant of four generations of brother-and-sister marriages. Not only was Cleopatra the daughter of brother and sister, but her parents were born of brother and sister, who were likewise inbred. Cleopatra herself married two of her own brothers, and afterwards killed them.

The bird of paradise has long breast feathers which, when spread out, look like a ballet dancer's skirt.

An Apeeling Fruit

The first banana recipe in history appears in the writings of the 10th-century Arab poet Masudi. He described a dish of bananas, almonds, honey, and nut oil that was all the rage in Damascus, Cairo, Constantinople, and other eastern cities. By the year 1000, the banana plant was a familiar sight throughout much of the Mideast.

During the 15th century, the Portuguese brought bananas from the Guinea Coast of Africa to the Canary Islands. It was the Portuguese who coined the word we use today to identify the fruit. The Indians of Alexander's time called the fruit *pala*; while in Africa, it was termed in various languages *banna, abana, gbana,* and *funana.* The Portuguese combined a number of these African words into the easily pronounceable *banana.*

Bananas first arrived in the New World in 1516, just 24 years after Columbus' first journey. A Spanish priest named Fra Tomas de Berlanga brought dry rootstocks from the Canary Islands to Santo Domingo, the first colonial city in the Americas. Bananas were found to grow well in the American tropics, and were soon placed under cultivation in South and Central America, Cuba, Jamaica, and "all other islands peopled by Christians."

One story has it that Puritan settlers in North America sampled bananas in the 1690s, and found them unpalatable—probably because they boiled them, skin and all. But the first recorded appearance of the banana in the U.S. dates from 1804, when a ship brought 30 bunches of the slender fruits from Cuba. Bananas remained rare and expensive items here through most of the 19th century.

The tallest and heaviest boxer ever to fight professionally was Gogea Mitu, of Rumania, in 1935. He was 7 feet four inches tall and weighed 327 pounds.

In England nearly ¾ of early syphilis is homosexually acquired.

Originally, acupuncture was thought to have been a semi-magical rite to drive demons from the body! Gradually over hundreds of years, acupuncture developed into a part of Chinese medical treatment.

The Union Army lost more men by disease than by battle during the Civil War.

On the Rebound

On January 6, 1918, Captain J. H. Hedley, an American, was flying 15,000 feet over German territory in a plane piloted by a Canadian named Makepeace. Suddenly, their craft was attacked by German fighters. Trying to evade the enemy, Makepeace took his plane into a nearly vertical dive. The suddenness of this maneuver jolted Hedley out of his seat and off into the ozone.

Makepeace gave his comrade up for lost and continued his rapid descent for several hundred feet more before leveling off. Then, incredibly, Hedley alighted on the tail of the airplane! Evidently, the steep dive created a powerful suction in which the American captain had been caught.

Hedley hung on to the tail of the plane for dear life. Later, he managed to climb back into his seat. The plane touched down safely behind Allied lines, and Hedley celebrated his reprieve from death.

The Bigger They Come...

The tallest of all dog breeds are the Irish wolfhound and the Great Dane. The male wolfhound averages from 31 to 34 inches at the shoulder and weighs about 120 pounds. The female averages 28 inches and weighs about 90 pounds.

The tallest dog on record is a Great Dane named Shamgret Danzal that lives in Buckinghamshire, England. It's 40½ tall and weighs 224 pounds.

The Irish Wolfhound, Broadbridge Michael, owned by a woman in Kent, England, measured 39½ inches at the age of two.

The heaviest dogs are the St. Bernards; the record breaker, Benedictine, weighed in at 305 pounds.

New Zealand has a most strange cave known as Glowworm Grotto. This cavern is illuminated by the fluorescence of millions of tiny glowworms. It is located in Waitomo Caves in New Zealand.

How big are the Pyramids of Egypt? Well, if all the material of one pyramid were extracted, that material would make a wall four feet high and one foot wide and that wall would stretch from New York to San Francisco.

In France, the king's bed—known as the "Bed of State"—was treated with a reverence that sometimes surpassed that accorded the throne. Persons entering the king's chamber were expected to genuflect in front of the bed, even if the king was not in the room. A railing separating the sleeping area from the rest of the room was originally intended to keep dogs from the bed. The king's bed was also known as the "Bed of Justice," where from the period of Louis XI on, *le roi* customarily reclined while parliament was in session.

The spider spins his web of a substance so thin and ductile that one ounce of this substance could be stretched across the Atlantic Ocean from New York to Paris.

Room Without Bath

Because of the aristocracy's aversion to bathing, many of the more famous palaces surviving today are completely without sanitation facilities. Although many people dispute it—and others refuse to believe it—there were evidently no toilets of any kind in either the Louvre or in the palace at Versailles. Members of the court were expected to relieve themselves before they entered the palace; the rows of statues that lined the garden provided convenient niches for an undisturbed tinkle.

Hoop Hipsters

Despite the popularity of school, professional and international basketball, the honor of playing before the largest crowd in basketball history belongs to the Harlem Globetrotters, who drew 75,000 people to a Berlin stadium in 1951. The zany club, combining real basketball talent with comic relief, was formed by Abe Saperstein in 1927, and played its first game in Hinckley, Illinois. Over the years, the Globetrotters have become virtually an international institution, and now play before two or three million fans each year. At one time, three separate Globetrotter teams barnstormed at the same time to satisfy the demand for the club. By 1970, the Globetrotters had played in 57 nations on all five continents, amassing 6,569 wins against only 303 defeats during the first 33 years of their existence!

Many meteorites fall to earth every day of the year. Yet despite this constant bombardment, only one person in the world has been known to have been killed by a stone falling from the sky. This calamity happened in 1887 when a man in India was struck by a falling rock.

It has been estimated that if all the descendants of just one pair of flies lived, and their progeny lived, by the end of a single summer there would be 335,923,200,000,000 flies.

The fairy fly is probably the smallest fly in the world. It is so small that if five of them walked abreast they could pass through the eye of a needle.

Universal Education

In July, 1948, the New York Legislature created a State University to provide free education to returning veterans. During the 50's the State University started to grow—and grow—and grow. Today, after 33 years of growing, the State University of New York is the largest university system in the world.

Although the State University does not enjoy the prestigious reputation of some of the better known private universities, it serves the unique purpose in a democracy of providing a good low-cost education to every qualified state resident.

The University is enormous. There are 237,000 full-time students, 137,000 part-time students, and 21,000 faculty members. There are 2,200 buildings spread out on locations throughout New York State. Courses and degrees ranging to Ph.D. are offered in 3,700 academic fields.

Odoriferous

As the city of Paris grew during the Middle Ages, most people disposed of their waste directly into a nearby stream, or into the Seine. When open ditches were constructed solely to carry off rainwater, many citizens began dumping their waste and garbage into the nearest ditch. Flushed only by an occasional downpour, the ditches quickly became noxious cesspits. During the 13th century, the stench moved Philip Augustus to order that all citizens transport their refuse outside the city walls. However, few citizens heeded the royal decree.

The sewer system of Paris was gradually improved. By 1663, there were only one-and-a-half miles of underground drainage mains and five miles of open canals serving the city, most of them emptying directly into the Seine. By 1800, Paris could boast 16 miles of underground drains, but much of the effluent was delivered to nearby swamps and ponds. An outbreak of cholera around the middle of the 19th century convinced city officials that, at last, something had to be done to improve the sanitation system. Parisians called on Georges Haussman, who was to oversee the construction of vast public works in 19th-century Paris.

High Blood Pressure persists in one out of 10 adults and is considered the most common disease in the US today. Medical men do not know what causes it; nor does it present symptoms. Some 60,000 deaths a year occur from it; many are avoidable.

Someone choking on a piece of meat will die in four minutes. What to do? Stand behind the victim; place your arms around him above the waist; allow the victim's head and torso to lean forward; tightly grasp your own wrist; press your fist into the victim's abdomen forcefully, rapidly; repeat. (Developed by Dr. H.J. Heimlich.)

Eve's Apple Could Have Been a Banana

Nothing may be as American as apple pie, but there's really nothing American about the apple at all. This familiar fruit is now grown in every state, and eaten in some form by almost all of us. Yet when Columbus set foot in the New World, there wasn't a single apple tree on this side of the Atlantic!

The apple is actually native to parts of Europe and western Asia, and may have originated in the area of present-day Iran. The fruit has been eaten by man since earliest times. How early? No, it wasn't necessarily the apple that Adam and Eve tasted in the Garden of Eden.

The Bible tells us only that Adam and Eve sinned by eating the fruit of the "tree of knowledge of good and evil." The word *fruit* came into our language as *apple*, which was formerly used to mean any fruit. Nowhere does the Bible claim that the forbidden fruit was actually what we now call the apple. In similar legends from the East, the forbidden fruit was the *banana!*

The word *apple* was also used in past centuries for the pupil of the eye, a translation of the Latin *pupillam*. The Latin phrase "apple of the eye" thus meant simply the pupil of the eye. But the phrase has been used to refer to something precious.

Mt. McKinley, Alaska, the tallest mountain peak on the North American continent at 20,320 feet, ranks only 74th among mountain peaks of the world. Of the 25 tallest peaks in the world, 19 are in the Himalayan range in Asia.

What Started It All

The first practical gasoline-powered car with a modern-type chassis and gears was the work of a Frenchman named Krebs, who designed the Panhard in 1894. In the early years of the industry, France led the world in automobile production. The still-flourishing Renault company was founded before 1900. But around the turn of the century, Americans began to take the lead in automotive innovation.

The first successful internal-combustion car in the United States was the work of the Duryea brothers, Charles and J. Frank, bike manufacturers from Springfield, Massachusetts. The Duryeas had read of Karl Benz's work in Germany, and they built their first car in 1893. Two years later, the brothers formed the Duryea Motor Wagon Company, the first automobile manufacturing firm in the nation. They later went on to win one of the most important races in automobile history.

Each quill of the porcupine has about 1,000 tiny sharp barbs.

The Great American Yen

If the popularity of the frankfurter has tapered off somewhat in recent years, the hamburger is certainly on the rise. Chopped meat now accounts for about 30 percent of all consumer meat sales. As late as the 1920s, many American dictionaries still did not contain the word *hamburger* though most did mention the *Hamburg steak*. Today, it would be hard, indeed, to find a restaurant, a diner, a coffee shop, or a roadside stand that did not serve the burger in some shape or form.

In Many Tongues

The Semitic scripts that evolved into our Roman alphabet also produced many of the world's other alphabets. Semitic traders brought an alphabet to India that was to become the Brahmi script, the parent of all Indian alphabets. The Aramaic alphabet became Persian script. The Aramaic alphabet as used by peoples in Arabia also evolved into the modern Arabic script, now the second most common in the world, after the Roman. Looking at a page of modern Arabic, it's hard to believe these symbols evolved from the same source that produced our own alphabet!

The Runic alphabet, used by Teutonic peoples in Northern Europe during the Roman Empire, was probably derived from either the Greek alphabet employed in the area close to the Black Sea, or the Latin alphabet of the Romans who colonized the area. The Slavic alphabets used today by many people in Eastern Europe were invented by the ninth-century missionary Cyril to transcribe the Slavic tongues; the forms were adopted from a Greek alphabet of the time. Two scripts developed, the Glagolithic and the Cyrillic, but since the 17th century only the Cyrillic has been used.

Traditionally, Americans are a nation of carnivores, consuming some 15 pounds of meat per person per month. The Japanese, by contrast, eat only about a half pound of meat per person per month.

The four major blood groups of persons are A, B, AB, and O. About 41 per cent of people fall into the A group; 45 per cent into the O group; ten per cent into the B group; and four per cent into the AB group. The blood type of a person is inherited and remains the same throughout his life.

The first U.S. coin to bear the portrait of an actual person was the famous Lincoln one-cent coin in 1909. Up to that time, there had been a prejudice against the use of portraits of individuals on U.S. coins, but the centennial of Lincoln's birth, 1909, produced the famous Lincoln penny.

The largest national park in the world is the Wood Buffalo National Park in Alberta, Canada, established in 1922. It has an area of 11,172,000 acres, 17,560 square miles.

Statistics keep proving every month that gasoline and alcohol don't mix. A recent investigation on one of the nation's expressways showed that 12 out of 16 traffic deaths were directly due to drunken driving.

The leading untreated illness in the United States, according to certain medical authorities, is not cancer, heart diesease, or diabetes —it's mental depression. It is estimated that at least 20 million adults suffer serious depressive symptoms each year—lethargy, sadness and a total absence of any feeling of pleasure or enjoyment.

Flavorful

The quality of ice cream products differs greatly from brand to brand, due to such factors as the amount of fresh milk, cream, or eggs used, the naturalness of the flavoring ingredients, and the presence of preservatives and synthetic flavor and texture enhancers.

Americans presently consume over a billion gallons of ice cream, ices, and sherbet each year—enough to completely fill the Grand Canyon. Americans are by far the world's largest consumers of ice cream. The average person in the United States puts away about 23 quarts each year—that's roughly equivalent to a cone per person every other day. Only Australians, Canadians, and New Zealanders eat even half that much. Compare that figure with the average yearly consumption of 100 years ago—about one teaspoon per person!

Only in America, then, could you expect to find the largest ice cream sundae of all time. The 3,956-pound monster, concocted in McLean, Virginia in 1975, contained 777 gallons of ice cream, six gallons of chocolate syrup, over a gallon of whipped cream, and a case of chocolate sprinkles. The world's largest popsicle, meanwhile, was a paltry 2,800 pounds.

Most ice cream stores today point with pride, not to the size of their wars, but to the sheer length of their flavor list. The Baskin Robbins company lists over 300 flavors in its repertoire, and the number is still climbing—though you'll have a tough time finding half that many in any one store. The winner of the Baskin Robbins America's Favorite Flavor Contest, by the way, was Chocolate Mint ice cream.

The modern ice cream maker will go to any length to outdoo the competition with bizarre new taste treats, and novelty flavors such as *iced tea, bubblegum root beer,* and *mango* ice cream. The newcomers occasionally outsell the old standbys—*vanilla* and *chocolate.*

But don't think that exotic flavors belong solely to the modern ice cream maker. A recipe book dating from 1700 shows that even at that date, French confectioners were turning out such tempting ice cream flavors as *apricot, violet,* and *rose.*

Robert Redford, noted screen actor, had a baseball scholarship at the University of Colorado, studied art at Pratt Institute, wrote "The Outlaw Trail," designed his own solar home, is an ardent champion of environmental causes, served as sewer commissioner (of Provo, Utah). He recently directed a film called "Ordinary People" with Mary Tyler Moore

Humble Pie

In Early Europe, when a nobleman returned from a deer hunt, his servants took from the slain animals the inferior parts such as the heart, kidney and entrails These sections of a stag were known as the umbles and a pie made from them was known as umble pie. While the lord and his household dined from the venison, umble pie was served to the lower classes. Umble pie became humble pie over the years and meant much the same then as it does now—to suffer the humiliation of having to come down a peg or two.

A Rose Is a Rose . . .

Roses are grown extensively in many parts of the world, especially in France, India, and the Balkans, and attar of roses is used in perfumes, cosmetics, and flavoring syrups. Rose hips, the fruits of the rose plant, are used to make tea, or as a source of Vitamin C.

The Empress Josephine of France, the wife of Napoleon, put the rose to a more singular use. Josephine built a huge rose garden at her estate at Malmaison, with over 250 varieties of the flower flourishing—every variety known at the time. The Empress often carried in hand a Malmaison rose that she could raise to her lips when smiling, since she was particularly sensitive about her imperfect teeth.

The rose has been cultivated and hybridized for so long that there are, strictly speaking, no species of purely wild rose left on earth. The flowers extant today range in size from just half an inch in diameter to varieties that spread to more than seven inches. Colors range from white through yellow, pink, red, and maroon.

Some roses smell like—well, roses, while others suggest green tea, hay, or various spices. Biologically, the rose's fragrance is quite important, since roses normally do not secrete nectar and depend mostly on aroma and color to attract pollinating insects.

The largest blossoming plant in the world is the giant Chinese wisteria at Sierra Madre, California. It was planted in 1892 and now has branches 500 feet long. It covers nearly an acre, weighs 253 tons, and has an estimated 1,500,000 blossoms during its blossoming period of five weeks.

Gold Standard

Gold is one element that has no practical uses.

Only about 20 percent of the gold in the world is in the open, mostly in jewelry and the arts. Almost all the metal is in vaults serving as a financial hedge against the economy.

Bedecked with

By the 1870s, the United States was the world's largest manufacturer of eyeglasses. The trained vision specialist had taken over from the itinerant peddler—though as late as 1960, some Americans still bought' their glasses by mail-order. In 1935, the country could boast 10,000 oculists and 22,000 optometrists, with a total annual outlay for glasses topping the $100-million mark. By now, those figures have more than doubled. One of America's largest eyeglass firms, Bausch & Lomb, had its humble beginnings late in the 19th century, when Mr. Bausch sold Mr. Lomb half interest in a supply of miscellaneous optometry equipment for the sum of $66. By 1961, the Bausch & Lomb company alone was selling glasses to the tune of $68 million a year!

The terms oculist and optometrist are not interchangeable. An *oculist* is a medical doctor who treats the eyes, while an *optometrist* is an eye-care professional without a medical school degree. An *optician*, meanwhile, is a technician who grinds and sells optical lenses, while an *ophthalmologist* is a medical doctor with several years of specialized training in eye care.

The 20th century marks the first time in history that eyeglasses are fashionably acceptable for any man or woman who needs them. In fact, a 1929 poll found that 53 percent of all spectacles wearers considered their glasses "more or less becoming." Beyond mere social considerations, the most important developments of our century are plastic eyeglasses frames and contact lenses.

Fooling Around

It seems that the world has always had its quota of simpletons. The Good Book (Proverbs XXVI, 5) says "Answer a man according to his folly." And in the same volume, the injunction reads, "Do not answer a man according to his folly." Are you bright enough to make sense of that?

Artists have often depicted fools, usually in a kindly way. Here are some classic pictures.

Droll Stories

Punch

Rabelais

Punch

Harper's

Harper's

Punch

Punch

Punch

Harper's

On a Mexican Mustang

Punch

An Old-Fashioned Christmas

230

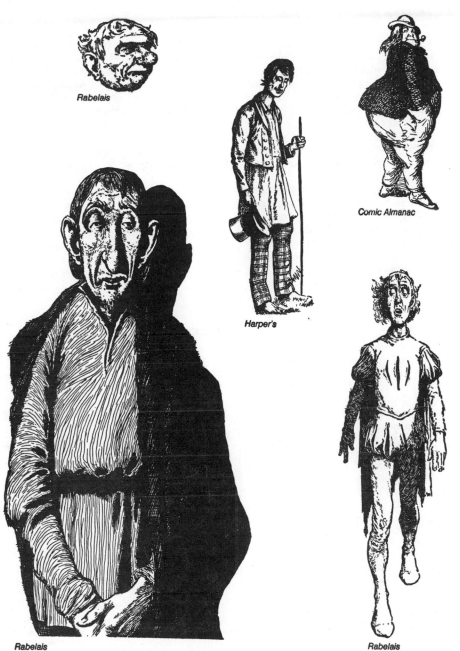

Rabelais

Comic Almanac

Harper's

Rabelais

Rabelais

Sock it to Me

In 1823, a student plahing football at the Rugby School by the name of William Webb Ellis, frustrated after failing to kick a bouncing ball, picked it up and dashed downfield. Ellis was severely criticized for his infraction, but word of his deed spread throughout England, and other players began to experiment with new rules. In 1838, players at Cambridge decided to try "the game at Rugby," and within 10 years the new game was being played at almost all English schools.

Gradually, the games of football and rugby began to diverge, with some clubs and schools adopting the new game and others staying with the older "feet-only" sport. In 1863, a group of football enthusiasts met in London and adopted a set of rules that forbade using the hands, publishing them under the title of *Rules of the London Football Association*. From the term *association football* came the modern word *soccer*. But many other players continued to enjoy "rugger."

During the 19th century, both rugby and soccer were played in the United States, especially at Eastern colleges. Football of any kind was banned for a time at Harvard and Yale, but in 1867, a set of rules was drawn up at Princeton. Two years later, a team from that school took on a squad from Rutgers University at New Brunswick, New Jersey, in a match often called the first intercollegiate football game in America. But the fact is, the game that day was soccer and not football: each team consisted of 25 men; a round ball was used; and running with the ball was not permitted.

For more than 40 years, *Uncle Tom's Cabin* played all over the United States. When the small towns grew tired of seeing the original play, the traveling actors put in a new gimmick. They promised to give twice as much of *Uncle Tom* for the same price. And they did. They came on strong with two Uncle Toms, two Simon Legrees, two Little Evas, and two sets of bloodhounds. For the same entrance fee, they doubled the attraction.

Skipper

An early form of water transport of early Anglo-Saxon times was a boat known as a scif or skip. It wasn't much more than a hollowed log and the word sciffer or skipper was applied to anyone in command of one. Today's word, skipper, is from those times and is generally applied to the captain of any sort of craft.

Nuts in May

Gathering nuts in May would be quite impossible as there are no nuts in May. "Nuts" in this case comes from knots and according to the Oxford English Dictionary a knot is a bud. Gathering knots in May was an old English custom always performed on May Day when clusters of spring flowers were gathered from the fields.

Magnolia

Pierre Magnol (1638-1715) is responsible for the name of this tree. He was a foremost professor of botany at Montpellier, France.

Calendula

This flower is a member of the Marigold family and gets its name according to John Gerard in his "Herball" of 1597, from the fact that "as it is to be seene to flower in the calends (first) of almost everie moneth." Originally it was a native of Central America.

In the No Theater in Japan, the stage has no curtain, but a special exit is supplied which is called the *Hurry Door*. This door accommodates all persons who must leave the stage in a hurry, such as those who have been killed.

Coconut

The exciting world of Spanish galleons and buccaneers gave us this word. Coco was a word used by Spanish seamen and explorers of the sixteenth century to describe the black-dotted end of the nut. It meant ugly-face or bogey man and was used mainly when talking to children.

Lavender

The dainty lavender flower for centuries was used by laundresses to lay on freshly washed clothing. The perfume of the flower enhanced the cleaned linen and countered the strong smell of soap. This practice was the reason for its name which is from the latin *lavare* meaning to wash.

Pucker Up

Hockey, by far the most popular team sport on ice, was enjoyed in some form by the Dutch as long ago as 1670, for a Dutch painting from that year shows a number of players with sticks in their hand batting a small object across the ice. The first record of an organized hockey game dates from 1855, and took place in Kingston, Ontario, with players using bent branches as sticks. The rules of the game were formalized 20 years later at McGill University, Montreal.

The first electric watch was brought out in 1957 by the Hamilton Watch Company, an American firm. In most electric watches, an electrically driven tuning fork provides the motive power, with each oscillation of the fork advancing a wheel and in turn moving the hands. The electricity is provided by a small energy cell. The watch has no mainspring, and 35 percent fewer parts than a mechanical device.

Some female snakes can store sperm for several years to insure future fertilization.

Fancy Seeing

In a person suffering from *hyperopia*, or far-sightedness, light rays are focused behind the retina; a convex lens focuses the rays on the retina. *Astigmatism*, caused by an irregularity in the curvature of the cornea, can be corrected with the use of a cylindrical lens—which was not invented until 1827!

The earliest optical lenses were made from beryl or quartz, and set in frames of brass or iron—and later, in bone, horn, gold, or even leather. Single glasses were held in the hand; double glasses were balanced precariously on the nose. Obviously, neither style was suited for continual use, but rather for short periods of reading. Some early spectacles were held on the nose by a hook affixed to the cap. Eyeglass cases, made of decorated wood, metal, or ivory, were usually hung from the belt. One odd eyeglass case from around 1400 was a receptacle built into a book cover, so the reader could leave his specs behind without fear of breakage.

What's Good for General Motors...

What is the most popular car in America? For years it's been the Chevrolet. In 1975, 1.6 million new Chevys left the assembly line, while the Ford ranked second with 1.3 million cars, followed in order by the Oldsmobile, Buick, Pontiac, Plymouth, Mercury, Dodge, and Cadillac. Among American auto manufacturers, General Motors was far and away the leader, with 3.6 million cars produced; Ford was second with 1.8 million, Chrysler third with 900,000 and American Motors fourth with 320,000.

Undoubtedly the most famous carpet in all history was the Ardebil carpet which was completed in Ardebil, Persia in 1540. The famous carpet hung there in the local mosque until it was purchased in 1893 by the English to exhibit in the Victoria and Albert Museum in London. The carpet itself was roughly 34 feet by 17 feet, and contained no less than 29 million knots, some 340 per square inch. At the time of its purchase it was valued at half a million dollars.

In early 19th-century America, laws restricted the importation of clocks and watches. The real beginning of the American watch industry didn't come until 1849, when the American Horologe Company was founded in Roxbury, Massachusetts. Until then, watches in the United States were handmade, and each could be repaired only by the craftsman who made it. Aaron Dennison, the founder of the Roxbury firm, introduced mass-produced parts to the American watchmaking industry—an innovation that earned him the nickname "The Boston Lunatic" from some doubting Thomases. The first American watch to be entirely mass produced was the Waterbury, in 1880. By 1890, the Waterbury Company was producing over a half-million watches per year.

You'd Never Know It from the Taste

The kind of milk used—cow or goat, whole or skimmed—plays a large part in determining the taste and texture of a cheese. But elements, such as the types of grasses and herbs common in an area, and the mineral content of the soil, will also influence the cheese produced there. The milk-producing animal's diet will determine the amounts of acidity and butterfat in the milk. The types of bacteria or molds used in ripening the cheese also play a part in determining the final product, as do the amount of salt and other seasonings added and the methods used in coagulating and curing the cheese.

The story of Liederkranz cheese illustrates the delicacy of cheese production. In 1892, a cheese maker named Emil Frey set out to duplicate a certain German cheese at a plant in Monroe, New York. Instead, he produced an entirely new cheese. Frey named his cheese after a choral group he belonged to in New York City: *Liederkranz*, or "wreath of songs."

Rolling Along

If roller skates have proved less than ideal for high speed skating, they have certainly fared better in endurance trials. In 1975, a Canadian named Clinton Shaw set the nonstop roller skating record when he remained atop his wheels for over 183 hours at a California rink. Before that, Shaw had already made his mark as a marathon skater, having covered 4,900 miles roller skating across Canada, and later, logging up to 106 miles per day from New York to California in just 78 days.

Roller hockey exists, but the game is far less popular than ice hockey. A more familiar roller skating sport is roller derby. Roller derby originated as a marathon relay race, when in 1935, 25 two-person teams met at the Chicago Coliseum to race a distance of 3,000 miles. Today, roller derby is predominantly an all-woman rough-and-tumble entertainment spectacle.

Gumdrops

Gumdrops are made from gum arabic, a substance obtained from exudations of certain types of acacia tree. Gum arabic products were used as medicaments for many years, since the slow solution of gum in the mouth allowed a steady release of the active ingredients.

France, the largest country in western Europe, measures only one-sixth the area of Canada's Northwest Territories.

If you don't mind smelling like a peanut for two or three days, "peanut butter is a darned good shaving cream." So says the Republican from Arizona, Senator Barry Goldwater.

In 1976 Greenland's population of 50,000 people consumed 30 million cans of beer. That would come to some 230 quarts per person.

If you're going to have a champagne celebration, might as well do it on the grand scale. Get yourself a complete set of champagne bottles. Here's what you'd have:

$1/4$ bottle - a split	about 6.4 oz.
$1/2$ bottle	about 12.8 oz.
bottle - a fifth (of a gallon)	about 25.6 oz.
magnum - 1.5 liters (two fifths)	about 51.2 oz.
Jeroboam - four fifths	about 102.4 oz.
Rehoboam - six fifths (5 quarts)	about 153.6 oz.
Methusaleh - 8 fifths ($6^1/2$ qts.)	about 208 oz.
Salmanazar - 12 fifths (10 qts.)	about 320 oz.
Balthazar - 16 fifths (13 qts.)	about 416 oz.
Nebuchadnezzar - 20 fifths (16 qts.)	about 512 oz.

There are approximately 430 volcanoes in the world with recorded eruptions in historical times. Of the 2,500 recorded eruptions, more than 2,000 have taken place in the Pacific area.

It is generally conceded that the most difficult tongue-twister in the English language is: "The sixth sick sheik's sixth sheep's sick."

One of the longest sermons on record was delivered by Clinton Locy, of West Richland, Washington, in February of 1955. He spoke for 48 hours and 15 minutes, ranging through texts from every book in the Bible. A congregation of eight was on hand at the close.

The record, however, was set by the Reverend Donald Thomas of Brooklyn, New York, who sermonized for 93 hours from September 18 to 22, 1978.

The ant family contains 2,500 different species.

The 555-foot Washington Monument, in Washington, D.C., completed in 1884, was for five years the tallest structure in the world. It was superseded by the famous Eiffel Tower, in Paris, France, 986 feet high.

As Old as the Hills

Cheese-making was an extensive industry among the ancient Romans, who also imported cheeses from various parts of the Empire. The historian Pliny the Elder tells us that Roman legions in Britain favored a sharp, *Cheshire*-like cheese, while Roman gourmets were particularly fond of *caseus helveticus*, a Swiss cheese much like the modern *Sbrinz*. The homes of Roman aristocrats often included special kitchens for cheese-making, while plebeians visited public smokehouses to cure their farm cheese.

"Tabby" Cat

In old Baghdad a part of the city named Attab (from Prince Umyyad Attab) produced a cloth named Attabi which was marked much in the same way as a cat. The word *attabi* was applied to cats marked like the cloth. General usage of the word *attabi* has caused it to change to Tabby.

Rough Stuff

Henry II banned football for fear that Englishmen were spending too much time playing it, to the neglect of the more militarily useful sport of archery. King Edward II banned the game due to "great noise in the city caused by hustling over large balls from which many evils might arise which God forbid." Other monarchs, including Richard II, Henry VIII, and Elizabeth I, also tried to eradicate the sport, with little success.

During an Anglo-Scottish war late in the 12th century, English soldiers reportedly sought to settle the dispute on the football field instead of the battlefield—which suggests not only the popularity of the sport, but its violence. At the end of the 16th century, the game remained so violent that an English writer claimed it seemed more like "a bloody and murdering practise than a felowly sporte or pastime..." often involving "fighting, brawling, contention, quarrel picking, murther, homicide, and great effusion of blood."

In the 17th century, when archery was no longer important in warfare, James I lifted the official ban on football and the game quickly found its way into almost every town in the British Isles. Matches were still held between adjacent towns, with the "goal lines" as far as three or four miles apart. And the sport was still quite violent, with tripping, shin-kicking, and rough tackling an integral part of the game.

The game as played from the 11th century to the middle of the 19th century was basically a kicking game, much closer to modern soccer than to football or rugby. Rules varied from place to place and from school to school, but there was one universally observed rule: the ball could not be picked up with the hands. It was the flagrant violation of that rule that was to spawn the game of rugby, and in turn, American football.

Natural Setting

Talk about realism! The dramatization of *The Count of Monte Cristo* probably takes the cake on that score. The action of the play in the novel took place for a good part of the story on the island of If, off Marseilles, where Dantes, the hero, spent 20 years in a dungeon. Now when the play is staged in that area, the performances are given in a prison courtyard. The curtain is drawn aside, and the convicted hero, Dantes, appears on the scene. The audience sees him led through the actual door which Dumas writes about in the novel.

And when Dantes escapes by occupying a sack to take the place of the dead abbot who was to be thrown into the sea, the leading actor is actually sewn into a sack and hurled from a turret on the top of the Chateau d'If, and cast into the sea, from whence he soon escapes and emerges on the surface of the water.

The long journeys undertaken by European Crusaders made stronger, longer-lasting shoes a necessity, but medieval aristocrats still took their cue from fancy. The wearing of elaborate, unwieldy footwear was an indication of lordly rank, demonstrating that the wearer did not—and could not—perform manual labor. Such shoes were genuine "loafers."

Porpoise

Because of its resemblance to a pig this mammal gets its name from the Old French word *porcpeis* which meant pig fish.

Alphabets

The Roman alphabet was derived directly from the Greek. It may have reached Italy with the Etruscans who settled there in the ninth century B.C., bringing with them a Greek alphabet from Asia Minor, or with Greeks who settled in southern Italy a century later. A number of languages and alphabets were used in Italy for a time. But as the Romans gained predominance, their alphabet and language, called Latin, replaced all others. The oldest surviving example of Latin writing dates from the sixth century B.C., and was written right-to-left.

The Romans borrowed 16 of the 24 letters of the Greek alphabet, discarded other Greek letters that stood for sounds absent in Latin, and invented or adapted other letters for Latin sounds that did not exist in Greek. For instance, the Romans developed both the *c* and the *g* from the Greek letter *gamma*, and changed the Greek symbol for a long *a* to our *h*.

The Romans had no use for the sixth letter of the Greek alphabet, the *z*, since that sound did not exist in their language. It was reinstated in the first century B.C., along with the *y*, to transcribe Greek words, and placed at the end of the alphabet. The Romans introduced the letter *f*, taking the form from an old Greek symbol for a *w* sound. Initially, the *f* sound was represented in Latin by the letter combination *fh*.

The Romans also used the letter *v* to stand for three sounds: the *u*, the *v*, and the *w*.

Three Greek symbols that the Romans did not incorporate into their alphabet were adopted for use as numerals. The Greek *theta* became the C, standing for 100; the Greek *phi* became the M, standing for mille, or 1,000; the Greek *chi* became the L, standing for 50.

Thus Latin was written with an alphabet of 23 letters. Around the 10th century, the *v* split into two letters, *u* and *v*. Soon after, the letter *w* entered the alphabet. The last of our 26 letters, the *j*, didn't appear until the 15th century; previously the *i* had stood for both the *i* and the *j* sound. The oldest letter in our alphabet is the *o*, which has remained unchanged since its use in the Semitic alphabets.

Cobweb

Ever wondered why we sometimes say cobweb and not spiderweb? Simply because cob or cop is an old Anglo Saxon word meaning *spider*. Attorcoppa was at that time a common word for poisonous spider.

The most popular play in American history was a melodramatic thriller which went on the boards by the name of *Ten Nights in a Barroom*. It premiered in Boston in 1854, and it is still being presented over the country. Between 1909 and 1931, four films were made of this classic, and as late as 1932 *Ten Nights in a Barroom* was staged on Broadway.

The English King Edward II decreed in 1324 that an inch was equal to three average-sized barleycorns laid end to end. The normal shoe was declared to measure 39 barleycorns, and this size, for some reason or other, was designated by the number 13. Other sizes were graded from this standard, with one barleycorn difference between each successive size.

Cutting a Fine Figure

In the United States, figure skating is a far more popular pastime than speed-skating for participant and viewer alike. Figure skating was first mentioned in London in 1772, but it's likely that skaters began to twist and twirl—or at least, attempted to—from the moment they first put on cow-rib skates. In 1876, with the construction of the first indoor rink with artificial ice, figure skating received a major boost. The London rink, called the *Glaciarium*, measured but 24 feet by 40 feet. Ice was mechanically produced from water and glycerine refrigerated with ether. Three years later, Americans had an indoor rink of their own, a 6,000 square-foot surface in New York's Madison Square Garden.

An even bigger spur was provided by Jackson Haines, an American ballet teacher who raised figure skating to the level of a fine art. Haines combined music with skating to transform the sport from an aimless series of random movements into a precise, rhythmic exercise. Haines's innovations were largely ignored in America, but the skating master captivated Europe during the middle of the 19th century, and was instrumental in evolving the international style of figure skating that now predominates the world over.

Freewheeling It

You've seen little kids jump on the rear bumper of a public bus in order to cop a free ride. Well, that kind of sport is for the birds.

The cowbird often lands on a cow's back. The little oxpecker, or tick bird, of Africa is equally unafraid of its frequent host—the rhinoceros. It alights on the rhino's back and hops about in search of blood-sucking ticks, thus performing a service for the large animal.

The lovely cattle egret often rides like a thin but well-plumed maharajah on the back of an elephant or a water buffalo.

Gym Dandy

The game of basketball, as played today, is actually less than a hundred years old, the brainchild of Canadian-born James A. Naismith. In 1891, while working as a physical education instructor at the International YMCA training school in Springfield, Massachusetts, Naismith sought to invent a new indoor game to relieve the boredom of contemporary gym classes, which were usually limited to less-than-thrilling calisthenics, marching, and apparatus work. After much trial and error, Naismith borrowed and modified elements from football, soccer, hockey, and other sports to produce his new ball game.

Naismith's original plan was to set up square boxes as targets at opposite ends of the gym, nailing them to the overhead board track. When the square boxes were unavailable, Naismith substituted two half-bushel peach baskets, and the new game immediately became known as basketball.

Naismith first tested his game with a gym class of 18 boys, dividing the class into two teams of nine. The first basket in the sport's history was scored by young William R. Chase, who led his team to a 1-0 victory. The game was an immediate sensation among the boys at the school, and the word spread among their friends at other schools and YMCAs. Soon, gym instructors from around the nation were writing to Naismith for the rules of the game.

Naismith first published his rules in a local paper, *Triangle Magazine*, in 1892, and later that year brought out the rules in booklet form. Naismith's booklet contained only 13 simple rules including four principles that are still the basis of the game: (1) The goal is to be elevated and horizontal; (2) No running with the ball is permitted; (3) All players may handle the ball at any time; (4) No personal contact is allowed.

While the peak in frequency of sexual activity is usually in the 20's and 30's it can remain at a high level even in old age.

Sewers

Films such as *Phantom of the Opera* may have contributed to the popular misconception that the city of Paris is built over a vast maze of ancient sewers and catacombs. While it is true that a network of caverns lies under Paris, these caverns are neither ancient nor catacombs. Most of the present sewer system was constructed during the mid-19th century by Georges Haussman. The sewers Haussman constructed were large underground channels roofed by a masonry vault. Porcelain plaques along the walls indicated the street directly above.

By 1878, the Paris sewer network stretched for 385 miles, and the Seine was at last freed from sewer duties. By the middle of the 20th century, the system contained over 800 miles of underground mains. Visitors to Paris can still tour the city's sewer system, entering at the Place de la Concorde, where several lesser mains converge to carry sewage to treatment plants.

Tutankhamen, Egyptian king of the 18th Dynasty, died and was buried in 1355 B.C. It was 3000 years later—in 1922—before his tomb was discovered.

Can you believe it? In 1965, an American advertising code declared that the following four words were not to be used in advertising: *Cutie, Girlie, Immorality, Naked.*

Upward Mobility

Tiny hummingbirds are master craftsmen of the art of flight. They are the only birds that can fly backwards.

Hummingbirds are neither swift nor large, but they can move straight up, straight down, forward or backward, or even hover motionless in one spot, like a tiny, whirring helicopter.

The largest publisher in the world is the U.S. Government Printing Office in Washington, D.C. More than 150 million items are dispatched every year, and the annual list of new titles and annuals is about 6,000.

The largest antique ever sold has been the London Bridge, of England, in March of 1968. The bridge was bought by a corporation of Los Angeles, California, for $2,460,000. The bridge was reassembled at Lake Havasu City, Arizona, and rededicated in October of 1971.

Salt of the Earth

Rock salt deposits are almost entirely the result of sea water evaporation in areas once covered by the oceans. In Utah, salt can literally be scooped up off the ground, but in other places salt domes may be found more than 1,000 feet below ground. The Wieliczka mine near Cracow, Poland, is one of the world's most famous, with almost 70 miles of multi-level tunnels, a restaurant and two chapels with rock-salt walls and statues hewn from salt, and an underground salt lake that tourists can row across.

Women's basketball has been around since the 1890s, when Clara Baer introduced the game at a New Orleans college using Naismith's published rules (although another claim traces the first women's basketball to Smith College in 1892). But Clara misinterpreted some of Naismith's diagrams, assuming that certain dotted lines Naismith had drawn to indicate the best area for team play were actually restraining lines to be drawn on the court. Thus, for many years, women's basketball was played under different rules than the men's game, with each player limited to movement only within certain parts of the court. Today, women's games are played under men's rules and the old game is now called "rover" or "netball."

Automobiles of Old

In 1885, Gottlieb Daimler of Germany became the first to patent a high-speed four-stroke engine.

Around the same time, Karl Benz, another German, was building an internal-combustion tricycle that could reach a speed of 10 miles per hour. The general public remained largely unimpressed. A German newspaper, reporting on Benz's work, asked the question: "Who is interested in such a contrivance so long as there are horses on sale?"

Pomme-Pomme

The apple was flourishing in Europe by the third century B.C., when Roman censor Cato described seven varieties. The Romans did a great deal to spread the apple through the Empire, although certain species were probably already growing in Europe. The Druids of Britain, for instance, venerated the apple prior to the arrival of the Romans. Perhaps they knew that, centuries later, one of the fruits was to fall on the head of Isaac Newton and help man gain his first insight into gravity.

Salty Language

Salt was used to seal covenants among ancient men, for its preservative qualities made it a fitting symbol for an enduring agreement. The Arab expression "there is salt between us" means a binding agreement has been reached, while the Persian "untrue to salt" refers to a broken covenant. The Biblical phrase "salt of the earth" still implies "elite."

Homer called salt divine, and mentioned its use at feasts. The ancient Greeks ate salted fish, and sometimes used salt in bartering for slaves and other items. The expression "worth his salt" may have first been uttered by a satisfied slave buyer who'd made his purchase with a quantity of salt.

Salt was a major commodity in ancient Rome. The *Via Salaria*, or salt route, was one of the oldest roads in Italy, the route by which salt was transported from salt pans near Ostia to other parts of the peninsula. By Imperial times, the salt oases of Northern Africa were linked by caravan routes, and other trade routes brought salt to Italy from salt pans around the Black Sea. Roman soldiers were given a ration of salt, called a *salarium*, which later became an allowance of money with which to buy salt—thus the origin of our word "salary."

The phrase "with a grain of salt" also dates back to Roman times. The Triumvir Pompey was known to add a grain of salt to his drinks as a supposed antidote to poison. Therefore to take something *cum grano salis* is to regard it with suspicion, or accept it with reservations.

Cut Up

Modern scissors usually have steel blades, while the handle section may be made from aluminum or other light metals. The pivot screw is made of hard steel, and firmly riveted to one blade; the other blade turns on the pivot screw. The blades are slightly bent toward each other to produce a close contact along the cutting edge.

George Washington wore dentures made of lead and looked so stern in his portraits because if he relaxed his teeth would fall out.

It's Greek to Us

The earliest surviving Greek writing dates from the eighth century B.C., and was written right-to-left, as are Semitic tongues, or with alternating rows of right-to-left and left-to-right. All Greek writing wasn't left-to-right until the fifth century B.C. The Greeks directly borrowed some signs of the Semitic alphabet and adopted some of the unused symbols for use as vowels, since the Semitic scripts did not have vowel forms.

It was the Greeks, then, who first employed a truly alphabetic writing system like the one we use today. Originally, the Greek letters, like the Semitic, stood for syllable sounds: the letter *t*, for example, stood for either *te*, *ti*, or *ta*. To distinguish between the syllable sounds, the Greeks added vowel symbols after the *t*, and these vowel signs came to represent the vowel sound itself; the *t* then came to represent the consonant alone.

Mother Goose Nursery Rhymes

Thomas Fleet, a printer of Boston in the year 1719 published a book of nursery rhymes he had heard his mother-in-law sing to his infant son. His wife's maiden name was Goose so he entitled his book Mother Goose Nursery Rhymes.

Boycott

An Irish landlord of 1881, Captain Boycott, was accused of taking a farm from which a tenant had been evicted. He was branded a grabber and in a speech to the Land League by J. Dillon, M.P., of February 26, 1881, it was suggested that such people be ostracized by society. "Do him no violence" he said, "Just act as though he didn't exist."

In the Bodmin Register of 1525 reference was made to inhabitants carrying away a burden of lop, crop, hook, crook and bagwood. The saying by hook or by crook comes from those days when peasants were not allowed to use axes to collect firewood but could take as much as they were able to carry by hook or by crook (a billhook and a shepherds crook). This ensured that the best and thickest trees were left for the lord's fireplace.

Kindergarten, which in German means a children's garden, is a term applied to schools in which very young children are taught. The system was begun by Friedrich Froebel in the Germany of 1840.

In 1975, 700 men developed breast cancer. 300 of them died. Cancer of the breast behaves the same way in men as in women. Radical mastectomy is the treatment.

The loftiest high-heeled and platform shoes you can find today are flat pumps compared with some of the shoes in fashion during earlier European eras. No, our ancestors didn't don stiltlike monsters to raise themselves above muddy streets, or for any other utilitarian reason. In former times, as today, shoe style was dictated by fashion—among the upper classes, at least. Class distinction via footwear? Yes—differentiation of shoe styles to indicate social rank is as old as Western civilization.

Underground Movement

Concrete proof that what goes on beneath the surface is of vital consequence may be more certainly demonstrated by sanitation engineers than by psychiatrists. We may not find looking at sewers any more agreeable than we find examining our own subconscious terrains, but their salutary effects cannot be denied. It's been a long time since mankind was assailed by such killers as cholera and plague, and the hero in the tale of horror is the sewage system.

In 1842, a British Royal Commission was appointed to suggest various means of improving the sanitation system of London. For their model, the commissioners looked to neither the contemporary systems of other European cities, nor to the facilities then in use in large American cities. Rather, they chose to emulate a sanitary system employed nearly 2,000 years earlier—the sewers of Imperial Rome.

The Roman system was simply superior to anything London could boast at the time, better in fact than anything that had been seen in Europe since the decline of the Roman Empire. Although the Romans generally shunned the construction of grandiose temples and tombs, they were justly proud of their magnificent achievements in civil engineering: bridges, roads, baths, aqueducts, and sewers. Frontinus, the water commissioner of the Imperial City for part of the first century A.D., went so far as to boast: "With such an array of indispensable structures...compare, if you will, the idle Pyramids or the useless, though famous, works of the Greeks."

In fact, the Romans were not the first people to devise a means to carry off waste materials from an urban area. Street drains have been found in an ancient Mesopotamian ruin near Nimrud, Iraq. In the Assyrian palace at Dur Sharrukin, water for flushing was provided by a jar and dipper beside each latrine, and drains carried waste away. Some ancient cities of the Indus Valley could boast brick-lined ditches that carried waste off from the home to larger masonry drains.

But, for the most part, the sewers of ancient pre-Roman cities were not waste drains, but storm drains intended to get rid of water from the streets after a heavy rain. The derivation of our word *sewer* suggests the original function of most early drains. The Latin words *ex*, "out," and *aqua*, "water," were combined to form the Vulgar Latin *exaquare*, which developed into the Middle French *essever*, "to drain off." The Middle French *esseweur*, and our word *sewer*, were derived from this term.

The famous insurance organization of Lloyds of London started in 1688 as a sideline to a coffee shop. Edward Lloyd, who ran the shop, began to help some of his customers who were seamen with their records and soon he was in the business of insuring their ships and cargoes.

Salting It Away

Salt was used as currency in Tibet, Ethiopia, and other parts of Africa, in some cases until relatively recent times. During an invasion of Ethiopia in the late 19th century, Italian soldiers found blocks of salt stored in bank vaults along with more familiar forms of currency. Tribal Africans have been known to prefer salt to cash payments for their wares, explaining "you can't eat dollars." And when salt has not been used by governments as official currency, it's often been used to *raise* money. European monarchs at various times taxed salt so heavily that it became affordable only on the black market.

The first American colonists had their salt shipped across the ocean from England. But a salt factory was established in Virginia as early as 1630, just a few years after the arrival of the colonists at Jamestown, and was probably one of the first factories of any kind on this side of the Atlantic. Americans continued to rely largely on imported salt until the War of 1812 cut off English shipments, at which time an American salt industry began to flourish in the area around Syracuse, New York.

In 1900, a popular song was titled, "Well, That Explains Everything." The following verse from that song was banned by the Lord Chamberlain of England:

Suppose you spend a week or two at a gay
* watering place,*
You tell your wife that business has detained
* you with His Grace;*
But when she finds within your bag a garment
* trimmed with lace*
Well, that explains everything!

In 1930, a 52-foot lizard was found at Glacier Island, Alaska. Citizens estimated that it had been preserved in ice for just about a million years.

Swift Pedalling

Bicycle racing had begun in the days of the highwheeler, but with the advent of the safety bike, racing reached unprecedented heights in Europe and America. In 1896, bike racing was included in the reinstituted Olympic games. For a time, bicycle racing outdrew even baseball in this country. During the 1950s, bicycle racing as a gambling sport was the rage in Japan, topping all other forms of entertainment, including the movies. In a typical year, Japanese gamblers bet over $150 million on bicycle races—and that figure accounts only for legal wagers.

Bicycle racers of the 1890s achieved speed records that would startle the modern cyclist. In 1889, Charles "Mile-a-Minute" Murphy earned his nickname by covering a mile in just under 60 seconds on a board track laid over the tracks of the Long Island Railroad. Murphy had help in his feat—he pedaled behind a train fitted with an enormous windshield so that the cyclist was riding in a near vacuum.

In 1941, Alf Letourner also had the benefit of a windscreen when he achieved a mark of 108.92 miles per hour on a California highway. Alf followed a midget auto racer. In 1973, Dr. Allan Abbott pedaled in a near vacuum when he set the modern record for bicycle velocity, 140.5 miles per hour, racing behind a car over the Bonneville Salt Flats in Utah. One old record that remains unbroken is the mark set in 1926 by Leon Vanderstuyft. Racing behind a motorcycle, but without a windscreen, the Belgian cyclist covered 76 miles, 604 yards in one hour on a bike track in Montlhery, France. Modern cyclists might find it difficult to achieve such a speed even on a downhill incline.

Even the earth itself is not an entirely accurate timekeeper. The length of time required by our planet to complete one orbit of the sun is, on the average, 31,556,925.9747 seconds. But the earth can take as much as three seconds more or less to complete an orbit—one year is not always the same length as the next!

Seeing is Believing

The earliest surviving portrait of a man wearing glasses was a fresco painting of Hugh of Provence, Cardinal Ugone, painted by Tommaso da Modena in 1352—though the Cardinal died around 1250 without ever knowing about eyeglasses.

Spectacles were not immediately popular in Europe. Early lenses were always convex, and therefore could not be used by nearsighted persons. Concave lenses for myopia were not to appear for several centuries after the invention of convex optical lenses. The earliest surviving painting depicting concave eyeglasses was a 1516 Raphael portrait of Pope Leo X.

The delay in the development of concave lenses was due more to the practical applications of early eyeglasses than to a lack of technical sophistication. Glasses were at first perceived as reading tools only, and no one immediately saw the need to turn a convex lens around for use as a corrective to *myopia*, or nearsightedness. In a myopic person, the eyeball is elongated in such a way that parallel light rays are focused in front of the retina. Concave lenses cause rays to diverge and meet at the retina.

Two-thirds of the human race does not get enough to eat.

The two coldest cities in the United States—and in this respect they run neck and neck—are St. Paul, Minnesota and Minneapolis, Minnesota. The average temperature in these cities throughout the year is 44.9° Fahrenheit.

By Any Other Name

There are about 35 species of roses thought to be native hybrids of North America. Various roses are the state flowers of Iowa, North Dakota, and New York. While the Greeks and Romans named their roses after gods, and the English after court figures, in America the preference is for descriptive or geographic names, such as the *pasture*, the *prairie*, the *smooth*, the *prickly*, or the *California rose*. The Chinese, meanwhile, have long used metaphoric names for the flower. The names of some Chinese rose varieties translate as *After Rain, Clear Shining, Tiny Jade Shoulders,* and *Three Rays of Dawn*.

Speaking of poetic descriptions, the prominent metaphoric use of the rose through the ages has left us with a considerable body of "rosy" verse. Robert Herrick wrote *Gather ye rosebuds while ye may*, William Blake gave us *The Sick Rose*, and W.B. Yeats, *The Rose of the World*. But surely the simplest observation concerning the queen of flowers came from the pen of Gertrude Stein, whose poem, *Sacred Emily* includes the line, "*A rose is a rose is a rose is a rose.*"

Plumb the Pudding

In England coins are baked into the Christmas pudding. The person who receives them in his portion is to have good luck for the next year. "Crackers", a party favor with small trinkets inside, are used at each place setting at the table. A tradition of pulling the "crackers" and having the trinkets spill out was set many years ago.

Dining with Stars

Today, the last word in gastronomic excellence is the guide published by the Michelin Corporation, a French tire firm. Michelin annually rates restaurants in thousands of towns and cities, awarding each from zero to three stars according to culinary quality. One star indicates good quality in its class; a rating of two stars suggests the restaurant is well worth a detour; and three ranks the establishment among the best in the world.

In a recent typical year, Michelin rated a total of 3,036 restaurants in Fance: 2,382 were rated as unstarred; 581 received one star; 62 received two stars; and only 11 restaurants earned the highest Michelin compliment of three stars. Five of these gastronomic palaces were in Paris, among them *Grand Vefour* and *La Tour D'Argent*, the oldest surviving restaurant in Paris.

Many culinary connoisseurs, however, maintain that for the best in *haute cuisine* you'll have to travel to Vienne, near Lyons, where you'll find the renowned *Pyramide*. Other gourmets would name Paul Bocuse's *Auberge Pont de Collonges*, near Lyons, as the world's premier restaurant, or perhaps the *Auberge de l'Ill* in Illhausen, Alsace, or the *Hotel Côte D'Or* in Saulieu, near Dijon.

France, of course, has no monopoly of fine food. (Modern French cuisine, by the way, is Italian in origin.) Many gourmets avow that Chinese cuisine is actually the world's finest, and excellent Oriental restaurants can be found in most cities of the world.

The Koala bear, a marsupial of Australia, can eat only eucalyptus leaves. It will die of starvation if these leaves are not available.

Each year, the world produces one automobile for every person on the earth! Recent production ran about 26.5 million cars!

The Rose Knows

The use of the rose as a symbol of beauty, frailty, and love is quite understandable, but the flower has also symbolized creation, secrecy, the Church, and the risen Christ. The rose windows featured in most Gothic cathedrals are thought by some to represent life and creation, or hope radiating from faith and the Church.

As a symbol of love and romance, the rose needs little introduction. As some are fond of noting, *rose* is an anagram of "Eros."

Robert Burns compared his "love" to a "red, red rose, that's newly sprung in June." And a German custom dictated that a groom send a silver rose to his bride before the marriage ceremony—a custom that forms the basis of the plot of Richard Strauss's opera *Der Rosenkavalier*.

Since classical times, the rose has been a symbol of secrecy. In 16th century England, a rose was sometimes worn behind the ear by servants, tavern workers, and others to indicate that the wearer heard all and told nothing. In Germany, roses in a dining room suggested that diners could speak freely without fear that their secrets would travel beyond the room. The expression *sub rosa*, which literally means "under the rose," actually means "secretly," and is thought to have originated in the custom of carving a rose over the door of the confessional in a Catholic church.

The largest planet in our solar system is Jupiter; the smallest Pluto.

Jupiter has a diameter of about 88,700 miles. Its mass is about 2½ times the mass of all the other planets combined.

Estimates of Pluto's size are difficult to make since it is so very far away. Scientists guess that its diameter is about 3,600 miles.

People in predominantly Mormon Utah hardly drink alcoholic beverages. Citizens of Washington, D.C. consume five times as much liquor as the citizens of Utah.

The Clergy

These illustrations of the clergy were done by famous illustrators of the 19th century, each in his style portraying his own viewpoint. The source of each drawing is identified.

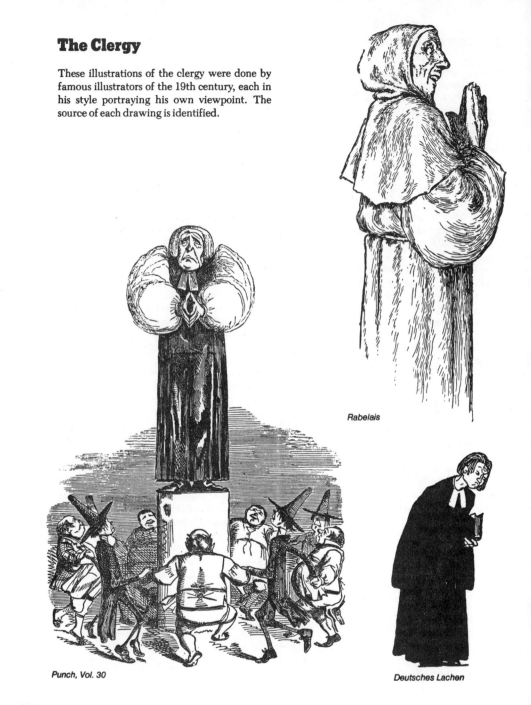

Rabelais

Punch, Vol. 30

Deutsches Lachen

Bab Ballads

Froissart's Modern Chronicles

Art of the Book ▫

Punch

247

The highest large lake above sea level is Lake Titicaca in South America. About 3,200 miles in area, Lake Titicaca is 900 feet deep and 12,500 feet above sea level.

Riding High

Early velocipedes were very heavy. Their wooden wheels fitted with iron tires vibrated so furiously over the rough roads of the time that the vehicle quickly earned the nickname "boneshaker." Nevertheless, during the 1860s, a velocipede craze swept both England and America. Within three months in 1869, 50 velocipede riding schools were opened in New York City alone—bearing names such as *Amphcyclotheatrus* and *Gymnocyclidium*. Newspapers derided the craze by dubbing the heavy vehicles "wood locomotives." Like the earlier hobby horse craze, velocipede mania vanished as quickly as it had appeared.

But bicycle innovators had not given up. The year 1868 saw the introduction of rubber tires. In 1869, the word *bicycle* itself was patented in England by one J. Stassen. Meanwhile, the size of the vehicle's front wheel grew to outlandish proportions. Since one revolution of the pedals turned the front wheel once, the larger the wheel, the further each revolution would propel the cycle. So, front wheels with 54-inch or even 64-inch diameters were common, while the rear wheel shrank to as little as 12 inches.

These asymmetrical vehicles, known as ordinaries or highwheelers, made cycling easier on the legs, but harder on the head. Since the rider sat high above the huge front wheel, he could not reach the ground with his feet when the vehicle began to tumble. A rider striking a stone or hole in the road could easily be thrown forward on his face. Serious injuries, even death, were not rare among avid cyclists. Still, the ordinary's popularity gained steadily. By 1878, 50,000 highwheelers were in use in England alone, not to mention thousands of tricycles for the less daring.

The American bicycle industry had been born the year before when Colonel Albert A. Pope of Boston commissioned the Weed Sewing Machine Company to make 50 "Columbia" bikes in a corner of their shop in Hartford, Connecticut. Bicycle manufacture quickly became one of America's leading mass production industries. By 1892, applications for bicycle patents had grown so numerous that the U.S. Patent Office had to establish a special department for cycles and their parts.

Salt Seller

In 1848, the company that was to become Morton Salt, the largest salt producer in the United States, was founded in Chicago. Morton now maintains salt processing plants in a number of states, and works almost every large salt field in the nation, with major deposits in New York, Pennsylvania, Ohio, West Virginia, Michigan, and the Great Salt Lake area of Utah. The Morton girl, with her umbrella and salt canister, has graced packages of the firm's salt since 1914, though she's been redesigned a number of times since then.

Salt is found on earth in three basic forms: salt water, brine deposits, and rock salt crystal. The oceans hold by far the largest supply. Each gallon of sea water contains about four ounces of salt. It's been estimated that all the seas of the world contain some 4.5 billion cubic miles of salt, an amount equal to over 14 times the bulk of Europe!

Ancient Cut-up

The Roman word for scissors, *forfex*, has given us "forficate," an adjective meaning "forked." But our word "scissors" actually came from two other Latin words. One was *cisoria*, the plural of the word for a cutting instrument. The other was *scissus*, a form of *scindere*, a verb meaning "to cut," which spawned the Latin *scissor*, "one who cuts." *Cisoria* led to the Old French *cisoires* (the modern French is *ciseaux*), and in turn to the Middle English *cysowres*, while the Latin *scissor* produced *sisours*. The latter word and *cysowres* together became the modern "scissors."

We offer this incident as perhaps the height of nervy interference. One Benjamin Webster actually tried to improve the text of the Bible. He was offended by the verse in Job which reads: *Why died I not from the womb? Why did I not give up the ghost when I came out of the belly?*"

Webster had the consummate gall to change these lines to: *Why did I not expire at the time of my birth?*"

Something Rotten in London

Medieval Londoners, like their Parisian contemporaries, traditionally directed their waste to the nearest stream or storm drain. At first, the accumulated sludge was carted off to nearby farms for use as manure. But as the city grew and the surrounding farmland moved further away, almost all waste found its way to the Thames. Medieval monks complained that the stench of the river overcame their incense and "caused the death of many brethren."

Covered public sewers connected to London mansions became common during the 18th century, but sanitation in the poorer quarters remained primitive. In 1841, the Fleet River in London, or the Fleet Sewer as it could more aptly have been termed, was replaced by a sewer main in a massive construction project that entailed, in the words of one contemporary, the "diversion of a miniature Styx ...from a bed of half-rotten bricks to an iron tunnel...without spilling one drop of Christian sewage."

By the 1850s, the Thames was sufficiently rank to prompt talk of moving Parliament—whose windows had not been opened in years—from its building on the river. Large-scale renovation and enlargement of the city's sewer system was finally inaugurated. Many of the sewers had already backed up to the houses they served, sending foul gases and rats into even the finest homes. An old clogged main in Westminster yielded 400 cartloads of sludge. Gases in some sewers were so thick that lanterns carried by workers caused explosions.

By 1870, an overhauled sanitation system, including 83 miles of new sewers, carried 420 million gallons of waste from the city each day. Equally important, the sewers were now being cleaned regularly. One of the brave band of workers who toiled in the depths preferred this job because he "didn't like the confinement or the close air in the factories." Londoners were delighted. "Nothing can be more satisfactory," one contemporary proudly wrote, "than a good water closet apparatus, properly connected with a well-ventilated sewer." The Prince of Wales himself declared that if he could not be prince, he would choose to be a plumber.

Shoes have been regarded as a sign of dignity since well before the Christian era, while going barefoot has often demonstrated humility and piety in the presence of God. Hindu documents, thousands of years old, warn worshippers to remove their footwear before entering a shrine; and Moslem tradition demands that shoes be removed before entering a place of worship. In the book of Exodus, 3:5, when God appears to Moses in the burning bush, His first command was "Put off thy shoes from thy feet, for the ground whereon thou standest is holy ground."

Precision Timing

The first electronic watch placed on the market was the Accutron, produced by the Bulova Watch Company in 1960, although electronic watches had been made as early as 1948. The Accutron's tuning fork vibrates exactly 360 times per second to provide the oscillations formerly furnished by the balance and spring. Electronic watches with a digital readout, rather than a dial and hands, were introduced in 1972. Digital watches now account for over five million watch sales in this country alone. An electronic watch—according to its manufacturers, at least—is accurate to within one minute per month or better.

Passing the Buck

Mark Twain in 1872, first referred to this expression. During card games, namely poker, in early American history a "buck" was passed from one player to another as a reminder of who had the next deal. The "buck" in this instance was usually a piece of buckskin or buckshot. Although the practice no longer exists, the meaning remains, that is, to shift responsibility on to the next one.

More than 150,000 new and different words and brand names have been added to the American language by manufacturers through their newspaper, radio and television commercial advertising.

Cheese-making

For the most part, cheese-making techniques have been developed independently in various parts of the world. Some of these techniques have been kept secret by cheesemakers since well before the Christian era began. There is good reason for this secrecy, for the making of fine cheese is an extremely delicate operation.

Minute changes in the processes or ingredients used to make cheese will produce marked differences in the final product. Cheese, like wine, is very much a product of the area in which it is made. Just as wine grapes from, say, Burgundy, which are replanted in California will never produce a wine identical to French Burgundy, a cheese made in a particular area cannot be exactly duplicated anywhere else.

Probably the greatest woman bowler of all-time, (her average for 8,090 games over one ten-year span was 201!), Floretta McCutcheon, never had a bowling ball in her hands until she was 33!

Fore!

We first find a reference to golf in Scotland in a 1457 decree ordering that the game "be utterly cryit doun and nocht usit," since it interfered with the practice of archery, a more useful sport to the defense of the realm. Another ordinance of 1471 decried the playing of "golfe and futeball;" and in 1491, yet another decree stipulated punishments for law-breaking linksmen.

This last edict was the work of King James IV, who for a time forbade golf in Scotland, declaring: "It looketh like a silly game." But within a few years of his decree, the king himself became a keen golfer, and entries appear in accounts of James's lord high treasurer, which show the purchase of balls and other golf equipment.

In 1592, the laws against golf were modified. The sport was forbidden only on the Sabbath. That law was later softened to outlaw golf only "in time of sermons."

Since the time of James IV, golf has remained a popular royal sport in Britain. Golf has long been officially known as the "royal and ancient game." James's son, James V, was a regular on the links. His daughter, Mary Stuart, was seen with clubs in hand just a few days after the murder of her husband—an indelicacy that should not surprise many of today's avid linksmen.

Measure for Measure

A tape measure is used for very long measurement, or for the measurement of a bent surface. Calipers consist of two prongs joined by a pin; they are best for measuring thickness or the distance between two surfaces.

As any draftsman can tell you, there's a world of difference between a ruler and a straight edge. No draftsman worth his T-square would use a ruler for drawing an accurate straight line, since rulers are designed chiefly for measuring, not line drawing. For a crisp, straight line, it's best to use a triangle or other device specifically designed for line drawing.

Bicycles

Curiosity bicycles appeared on the scene as European and American inventors attempted to make the bike a more utilitarian vehicle. Traveling professionals took their shops on wheels, with bicycling barbers, cigar dealers, ice cream peddlers, lawn mowers, and hurdy-gurdy men among them. In 1899, a water bike was constructed with paddles fitted to the pedals. Ice bikes appeared, fitted with skates and propelled by a spiked wheel. One enterprising inventor from Germany even constructed a bicycle that ran on dog-power, with two pooches running on treadmills fitted to the bicycle frame!

The so-called *Eiffel Tower* bicycle lofted its rider 10 feet above ground atop a metal framework that did indeed resemble the Parisian landmark. In 1897, a Boston manufacturer constructed an eight-man tricycle that weighed close to 3,000 pounds with its riders. The 17-foot-long trike was fitted with two 11-foot-diameter rear wheels and 18-inch tires! The front wheel was a mere six feet in diameter.

At the other end of the scale we find *midget* bikes, complete in every detail, that measured as little as nine inches from axle to axle. As early as 1869, P.T. Barnum had ordered a custom-built velocipede for the midget Tom Thumb. The bike is now on exhibit in the Henry Ford Museum in Dearborn, Michigan. The smallest working bicycle of all time, a two-pound vehicle with two-and-one-eighth-inch wheels, was ridden regularly by a full-grown Las Vegas showman, Charlie Charles.

"40-Love"

Because the circle, meaning nil, drawn on the scoreboard reminded them of an egg, early French tennis players used the word *l'oeuf* when calling the score. L'oeuf meant egg. This word was adopted and anglicised into the word "love" which signifies nil or no score.

Telling Time

All early clocks were weight-driven, and therefore quite large. But around 1500, the German Peter Henlein's invention of the mainspring eliminated the need for heavy clock mechanisms, and timekeepers could be made portable. Some historians maintain that Henlein himself made the world's first watch shortly after his invention of the mainspring, but recently other experts began making a case for an Italian origin for the watch.

The earliest watches were large and unwieldy, often four or five inches in diameter and up to three inches thick, certainly too large for the pocket. Some watches were worn around the waist on a belt, while the wealthy had their servants lug around their portable timekeepers.

The only beneficial effects from suntanning are psychological. Dermatologists say stay out of the sun between 11 and 2.

The jogger, burning off only about 100 calories a mile, will burn off about 10 lbs. jogging a mile a day for a year. An individual must burn off 3,500 calories before he sheds a single pound.

Poughkeepsie Pins

The father of the American pin industry was Samuel Slocum, who in 1838, founded a pin factory in Poughkeepsie, New York, capable of turning out 100,000 pins a day. Though Slocum was not the first to design a machine for manufacturing pins, his pins were the first to be mass-produced in America. Slocum's pins had solid heads, and came to be known as *Poughkeepsie pins*. Slocum was also the first to devise a machine for packaging pins in grooved paper boards.

The Court Determines the Rules

Unlike most other sports, which develop slowly and gradually attain popularity, basketball was an instant success throughout the United States. The ranks of YMCA members swelled as boys flocked to their gyms to learn the new sport. As early as 1893, one year after James Naismith published his rules, an issue of the *YMCA Review* noted that "Ministers, lawyers, bankers, editors, merchants, clerks, mechanics, boys, young men, older men, yes, everybody plays basketball now."

But various organizations, including the YMCA, soon banned the sport, claiming that a game allowing only 10 or 20 boys in a class of perhaps 50 to participate created too much ill-will among the non-players. Banishment of the game led to a huge decrease in YMCA members; many basketball players were forced to rent gyms for their games—and therefore they had to charge admission, a practice that eventually resulted in the professionalization of the sport.

As the game continued to catch on, basketball rules slowly evolved, with the rules for each game somewhat dependent upon the court it was played on. In 1896, the first basketball rules committee was formed to coordinate the various sets of regulations, and the first college basketball rules committee was founded in 1905. By 1913, there were five complete sets of rules for the game, and teams sometimes switched from one set to another at halftime. It wasn't until 1915 that the rules of the game were standardized for the first time.

In the early years, the size of the basketball court and the number of players on each team varied widely from game to game. A Cornell University class once tried a game with 50 players on each side, but the experiment failed dismally as all 100 players converged on the ball. For a time, teams consisted of either five, seven, or nine players, depending upon the size of the court, until the five-man team became the rule in 1897.

High Wheeler!

In 1934, a vaudeville performer named Walter Nilsson set an unenviable record when he pedaled from coast to coast on an eight-and-a-half-foot-high unicycle! Nilsson covered 3,306 miles in just 117 days on the single-wheeled vehicle without falling once, an achievement that earned him Robert Ripley's award for "The Most Unbelievable Feat of the Year."

Speaking of unicycles: in 1967, Steve McPeak of Tacoma, Washington, climbed atop a 32-foot-high unicycle and pedaled between two towers 100 feet apart!

At least one child every day in the U.S. dies as a result of child-beating by an adult, a practice rare with Orientals, Greeks, Jewish and Italian families.

Fresh, Smoked or Pickled

There are billions of herring in the ocean. Fishermen catch more than ten billion herring each year.

One reason herring are among the easiest fish to catch is because they group together in vast schools. Sometimes as many as three million herring can be found together in one area of the sea.

Because they are so plentiful, herring are relatively inexpensive. Thus, more herring are eaten all over the world than any other fish.

Banana Recipes

Banana oil does not come from the banana, for banana plants produce no commercial oil of any kind. Banana oil is actually a synthetic compound, so-named because its aroma was thought to resemble the banana's.

The soft, sweet fruit of the banana is usually eaten raw in the U.S., but bananas can be broiled, baked, sauteed, grilled, or even frozen. Bananas make a delicious ingredient in dips, drinks, salads, breads, pancakes, fritters, and a variety of desserts. Innumerable recipes derive their special flavor by using the banana as a major ingredient. Bananas are cheap as well as versatile, costing no more today than they cost 20 years ago.

For a quick, nutritious drink, try a banana shake: mix a cup of milk, a banana, and a teaspoon of vanilla in an electric blender, turn on the switch, and enjoy.

If you prefer a more potent banana beverage, there's always the frozen banana daiquiri. You can make a banana daiquiri in your blender, too: just fill the container with a jigger of rum, an envelope of daiquiri mix, ice cubes, and a ripe banana. Then turn on the machine, and let the blender do the rest.

For those who really love bananas, there's even a "bananawich," made with sliced bananas and peanut butter, with or without ham.

The Assyrians (in ancient times) devised the wheeled towers which years later the Romans perfected and used extensively. The towers often had battering rams for attacking city walls, as well as a platform for carrying troops.

The abacus was invented by pre-Christian Chinese but is still used today in many oriental countries. In a 1946 speed contest between an abacus operator and an electronic calculator operator, the abacus operator won addition, subtraction, division, and lost *only* in multiplication!

The French superstar "who popularized tennis more than anyone, past or present," tempestuous Suzanne Lenglen, lost only one match between 1919 and 1926! (Her famous walk-off against Mrs. Mallory).

The *nautical mile* is defined three different ways, since navigators once regarded the nautical mile as the length of one minute of the meridian at the place where they were taking the reading. The U.S. nautical mile has been identical to the international unit since 1959, measuring 6,076 feet.

Postal authorities in Texas received a telephone call from a woman who complained about the substitute mailman on her route. "The regular carrier gets along fine with our dog," she explained irately, "but whenever the substitute makes the rounds, he upsets the dog."

"Oh? Where is your dog now?" a postal official asked.

"He's out in the yard, under a tree," the woman replied.

"And where is the mail carrier?"

"He's up in the tree. He's upsetting my dog and making him bark."

Bicycle Paths

The most famous bicycle path in America was probably the Coney Island Bikeway in Brooklyn. Opened in 1895, the route stretched five miles between Prospect Park and the amusement area of Coney Island. The road, known as Coney Island Boulevard, consisted of two crushed bluestone pathways on either side of a central boulevard reserved for carriages. Each pathway took bikers in a different direction, making the bike paths perhaps the first one-way streets in the nation. The entire route was lined with trees. The road still exists, renamed Ocean Parkway, though the two bike lanes have long since become service roads for the central boulevard.

One of the oddest bikeways in the nation stretched between Pasadena and Los Angeles in Southern California. Called by some the predecessor of the modern superhighway, the Pasadena Cycleway consisted of a narrow elevated road, similar to a boardwalk, wending its way between houses and over empty fields. Lamps provided for night riding. Bike rental and repair shops stood at each end of the cycleway, and toll booths appeared sporadically along the nine-mile route.

Incidentally, the era of the bikeway is far from over. The Federal Government has already approved $120 million for bikeway facilities all across the country.

San Francisco has the highest VD rate of cities in the U.S. although California ranks 14th among states, with Alaska and Georgia ranking in first and second highest places respectively.

The quartz crystal was developed in America at the Bell Laboratories in the late 1920s, and introduced at retail by the Bulova Watch Company in 1970. The quartz crystal watch depends on the natural vibrations of a pure quartz crystal, and is considerably more accurate than earlier mechanical devices.

On My Hands

This herb is so called from the Latin *thymus* which means sacrifice. Ancient Romans burnt thyme on their altars, the fragrance of the burning plant added to the dramatic atmosphere of their pagan sacrificial rites.

The average male in the United States is 45, has a wife of 42; 2 teen-age children; and eats a ton of food a year.

A Tick in Time

It is said that when Emperor Charles V of Spain retired to the monastery of Yuste, he indulged his mechanical bent by lining up several clocks and trying to make them tick in unison. He finally gave up in despair, observing that if he could not make any two clocks run together in the same rhythm, how could he possibly have believed he was able to make thousands of men think and act alike?

However, William H. Prescott, the noted historian, refused to credit this story. In his book, *The Life of Charles the Fifth After His Abdication*, Prescott wrote: "The difficulty which he found in adjusting his clocks and watches is said to have drawn from the monarch a philosophical reflection on the absurdity of his having attempted to bring men to anything like uniformity of belief in matters of faith, when he could not make any two of his time-pieces agree with each other. But that he never reached the degree of philosophy required for such reflection is abundantly shown by more than one sentiment that fell from his pen, as well as his lips, during his residence at Yuste."

The chief companion of Charles V at his retreat was one Torriano who was reputed to be highly skilled in the manufacture of timepieces and who had made many elaborate clocks to adorn his monastic apartments.

Eyes Right

Over 100 million Americans, including two-thirds of all adults, now wear eyeglasses. Another 10 million or so regularly don contact lenses. Eyeglass wearers range from the slightly dimsighted, who slip on specs for reading or driving, to the virtually blind who would be helpless without their lenses.

Even those fortunate enough never to need glasses should be grateful for their invention. For corrective lenses rank along with printing, paper, and electric illumination as the major technological milestones along man's road to universal literacy. Today, eyeglasses are considered so vital that it's hard to imagine a world without them. Yet eyeglasses were not commonplace anywhere in the world until about 450 years ago—and precision, individualized lenses date back no further than the 18th century.

Pinned Down

In Medieval Europe, the wealthy used elaborately fashioned safety pins of ivory, brass, silver, and gold, while the poor had to make do with simple wood skewers. By the 15th century, pins were being manufactured from drawn iron wire, and a pin-making industry was well established in France.

But for centuries, metal pins remained rare and costly items reserved for the rich. You've heard the expression *pin money*, meaning a small sum allotted by a husband for his wife's use, or money for incidental items. Well, when the term originated in the 14th century, "pin money" was just that, for at that time, pins were expensive enough to be real items on the budget. By custom, a husband would present his wife on the first or second of January with enough money to buy her pins for the year. "Pin money" went by the boards in the 19th century, when mass-production made pins the inexpensive purchase they are today.

Saltcellar

Sea water close to the polar regions contains slightly less salt than water near the equator. The salt content of enclosed seas such as the Red Sea and the Mediterranean is also higher than ocean water. The most saline of all water, the Dead Sea, covers only about 350 square miles, yet contains some 11.6 billion tons of salt. The highly saline River Jordan pours six million tons of water into the Dead Sea daily, which after evaporation leaves behind about 850,000 tons of salt each year, much of it sodium chloride. The peculiar taste and smell of the salty Dead Sea water moved ancient Arab writers to call it "the stinking sea."

The desert Arab uses the urine of the camel as a hair tonic and medicine.

The tallest structure in the world is the Polish National TV Service Tower at Plock, Polland. Built of tubular steel, and completed in 1973, this tower stretches 2,100 feet into the air.

Curds Away

Cheese has been called "milk's leap to immortality." To those who consider cheese merely a colorful addition to a hamburger, the scientific expertise and tender loving care that go into the production of fine cheese may well seem extravagant. But to connoisseurs, who savor above all else a perfectly ripened piece of creamy Camembert, tangy Gorgonzola, or pungent Limburger, the world of *belle fromage* truly marks man's most ambitious effort in the pursuit of gustatory pleasure

Cheese is, prosaically enough, the consolidated curd of milk. The cow, and to a lesser extent, the goat and sheep, are by far the most common providers of milk for cheese. But the milk of the buffalo, eamel, horse, llama, yak, reindeer, ass, and zebra have also been used to make cheese in various parts of the world.

Oh! For the Good Old Days

When the first nip of winter bites, and you pull out your favorite sweater only to find it has been ravaged by moths do you ever wonder what they fed on before they had your nourishing sweaters? Would it help you to know that insects such as moths, beetles, bedbugs originally lived in caves, where, indeed, some still do. They fed on animals and animal products, such as the hide and hair of dead animals. Various species of insects attached themselves to mammals and ultimately to man living in the caves. Then, when man moved out, these insects followed him. They soon learned to live on the products man adorned himself with.

If you want proof of what America's favorite pastime is, note this: the weekly magazine with the highest circulation is *TV Guide*, which averages over 19 million copies per week.

The *Reader's Digest* circulates over 17,750,000 copies per month in the United States, and over 12 million more abroad in 15 different languages.

"My Yiddish Mama" was right—chicken soup *is* good for what ails you. Mount Sinai hospital in Miami Beach, Florida announced that chicken soup was "efficacious upper respiratory tract infection therapy." It helps to expel mucus from nasal passages, thus getting rid of germs.

The greatest number of ships and aircraft ever involved in a sea-air action was 231 ships and 1,996 aircraft in the battle of Leyte Gulf, in the Philippines, during World War II. This battle raged from October 23 to October 27, 1944, with 166 U.S. and 65 Japanese warships engaged, of which 26 Japanese and 6 U.S. ships were sunk. In addition, 1,280 U.S. and 716 Japanese aircraft were engaged.

The wristwatch was still a novelty as late as 1900, when almost all watches were carried in the pocket. The English developed the custom of carrying a watch in the vest pocket when Charles II began the fashion of wearing long vests in 1675. During the 18th century, the Englishman carried his watch in a vest pocket at the end of a chain, which was frequently ornamented with dangling seals and charms. For a time, fashion dictated the wearing of a watch and chain in both vest pockets, although one chain was usually attached to a false watch.

Quintessential Wedding Dress

What did Lady Diana Spencer wear for her fairy-book wedding that transformed her into a princess? Why, something old, something new, something borrowed, and something blue, of course. Her father provided a diamond tiara. Her dress was made by the designers, David and Elizabeth Emanuel, of ivory silk taffeta, hand-embroidered with old lace panels on the front and back of the fitted bodice, and a multi-layered tulle crinoline under the diaphanous skirt. Diamond drop earrings were borrowed from Lady Diana's mother, Frances Shand-Kydd. And a blue bow was sewn into the waistband of Lady Diana's dress.

Should you covet such elegance, you can buy an Emmanuel-designed wedding dress at Harrods in London for about $3,700.

If your name happened to be Jim Smith, you'd be privileged to join the Jim Smith Society and attend its annual gatherings. The 12th annual gathering of this society was held one weekend in July, 1981 in Boiling Springs, Pennsylvania. The highlight was a softball game in which all 45 players were named—Jim Smith, of course. The first ball was thrown out by Jimmie D. Smith, the first woman to be a member of the society. Her husband is Jim Smith, and so is her son.

Beefaloburger

What's a beefalo? Why, it's five-eighths cow and three-eighths buffalo. How do you get a beefalo? Well, it's not all that easy. The problem is that when you mate a cow and a buffalo their offspring are sterile so that's the end of the line. But it's not impossible; it just takes time. The first time a cow is inseminated with beefalo semen, the offspring are 3/16ths buffalo. The U.S. Department of Agriculture says it isn't beefalo until it's at least three-eighths buffalo. So it takes two or more generations to get this particular mix. But then you have it; this hybrid is likely to be fertile.

But why bother? Well, for one thing ground beefalo contains more protein, less fat and less cholesterol than beef, and it tastes delicious. For another, it's easier and cheaper to feed beefalo than standard cattle, and the beefalo yield more meat per pound of carcass. So who knows, it may not be long before beefaloburger stands will dot America.

Green Lake, at Spicer, Montana, claims the distinction of having the purest water of any lake in North America. The water in this lake is 98.99 per cent pure.

At the funeral of Panama's powerful leader, Brigadier General Omar Torrijos Herrera, on August 4, 1981, the procession to the Amador Cemetery was led by a riderless horse with black riding boots backward in the stirrups, and the general's cowboy-style hat in the saddle.

Why can a bird fly and man cannot? Simply because birds are structured to fly and man is not. Birds have hollow bones and other physical adaptations that lighten their skeleton. They also have a high metabolic rate and specially modified pectoral muscles to enable them to meet the extreme physiological demands of flight.

If you thought there could be lightning without thunder, or thunder without lightning, you're wrong. Thunder is simply a by-product of lightning, produced by the rapid expansion and contraction of highly heated air along the path of the lightning. However, it is possible to see lightning and not hear thunder, or to hear thunder and not see lightning. This is because lightning may occur so high in the sky it is not visible although the thunder is heard. Or, if the lightning flash takes place at a great distance from you, you may not hear the thunder as the sound waves don't travel that far.

Halley's comet makes an appearance once every 76 years, and is coming in 1985. It last appeared in 1910, when methods of study were not as sophisticated as they are today, and will then sweep out of the solar system until 2061. The European Space Agency, the Soviet Union, and Japan have separate plans to send spacecraft to the comet's vicinity for research.

Why is this comet of such scientific interest? It is believed that knowledge about a comet could shed light on the origin of our solar system, and even on the origin of life itself. It is difficult to probe the origin of planets since they evolve over billions of years, and have undergone extensive reshaping externally and internally. However, comets and planets probably formed from the same gas and dust reservoir, and since comets are the most primitive objects entering our solar system, they may yield up information more easily.

Even though the 55-mile-an-hour limit on interstate roads in the U.S. is exceeded by an estimated 80 per cent of drivers now, state safety officials report that most traffic is slower than in the past—averaging from 55 to 65 m.p.h., compared with from 65 to 75 or more in past years. Traffic engineers state that the lower speed limit has the tendency to keep most cars moving at the same speed, rather than some traveling much faster than others, and thus creating passing hazards.

To the Brim

European men wore their hair long from the earliest days of recorded history until about the fifth century B.C.; they wore their hair short until the end of the Roman Empire, about a thousand years later. Yet neither men nor women in ancient Rome and Greece regularly wore hats. A typical hat of the period was the *petasos*, a flat, circular hat of felt, fur, or leather, similar to the beret. Most of these hats had a band at their edge to keep the hat snugly on the head; bits of material that protruded from under his band eventually became the hat brim.

Jack Nicklaus, the great golfer, has been dubbed "The Golden Bear."

Ice is Nice

Ancient Indians made ice the simplest and least dependable way possible—leaving water in special outdoor receptacles overnight. The ancient Romans cooled their wine cellars with snow brought from nearby mountains. They also discovered, as did the Indians, that water could be cooled with the addition of saltpeter. The Romans sometimes chilled liquids by immersing bottles in vessles filled with water and saltpeter, and rotating the bottles rapidly.

Say Cheese!

Among the latest products of photographic simplification is the Kodak Instamatic, complete with built-in flash, fixed focus, and fixed aperture, a camera so simple and foolproof it practically takes pictures by itself—or as George Eastman boasted in 1888, "You press the button, we do the rest." Even more remarkably, some modern "instant" cameras are now on the market for less than $20, while even in the 1880s the earliest Kodak roll-film cameras sold for $25!

In the Same Vein

In blue-vein mold ripened cheeses, curing is aided by a characteristic mold culture that grows throughout the interior of the cheese. The most popular blue-veined cheeses include *Roquefort, Gorgonzola,* and *Stilton.*

Here, Kitty

There is no record of domesticated cats before 3,000 B.C., though by that time the kitty was already regarded as sacred in some Near Eastern cultures. The Egyptians tamed a species of wild African cats, *Felis lybica,* an animal about the size of the modern house cat, and put him to work protecting grain supplies from rodents. Egyptian artwork also depicts small cats killing snakes.

Rodent-hunting cats proved so valuable that the Egyptians considered them representations of the gods—a designation that conveniently helped protect the cat from ancient ailurophobes. The Egyptian cat-god *Bast,* was a symbol of the kindly powers of the sun, as opposed to *Sekmet,* the lion-god, who represented the destructive forces of nature. The cat was also worshipped or in some way connected with religious observance in Babylonia, Burma, Siam, Japan, and China, where the domesticated cat first appeared around 500 B.C.

The Egyptians went so far in their ailurophilia as to embalm cats, as they were considered members of the royal household.

If This is Tuesday

For the record, the fastest round-the-world trip by commercial airliner was not set until 1976, when a Pan Am 747 returned its 98 passengers to New York City after a flight of 46 hours, having stopped only twice for refueling.

How Dry I Am

A desert is defined as a region which is partly covered by scanty vegetation, and sometimes none. A desert can support only a limited and special animal population which has over long periods of time adapted to its surroundings. The so-called *cold deserts* are caused by extreme cold and are often covered by perpetual snow or ice. These are quite distinct from the deserts of warm regions. Cold deserts cover about one-sixth of the world's surface. Warm deserts cover about one-fifth of the surface.

Mother-of-Pearl

Mother-of-pearl, or *nacre,* is the substance that lines the interior of the shells of various mollusks, including the pearl oyster. It's similar in nature to pearl itself, for mother-of-pearl, pearl, and the material that forms the shell are all secreted by cells in the soft parts of the mollusk.

Mother-of-pearl is most often used for buttons, inlays, utensil handles, and jewelry. Its iridescence and luster are due to a phenomenon known as "interference of light," which results in shifting changes of color when light strikes the mother-of-pearl.

Long Shot

In 1946, Rhode Island was playing Bowling Green in Madison Square Garden. Rhode Island was behind two points. There were only three seconds left to play. Ernie Caverley of Rhode Island threw the ball from back court with all his might. The 55-foot shot went in, and tied the game. Rhode Island won it in the overtime by 82 to 79.

In the early decades of this century, many apartments in American cities were equipped with a bathtub in the kitchen. When European immigrants arrived here, many considered the bathtub an unnecessary luxury, and used the tub as a planter for flowers and vegetables.

Roller skates, which originally consisted of four wheels on rubber pads, were invented in about 1860.

The Paper it's Printed On

The least valuable bill in existence today is the *one-cent* Hong Kong note, worth just one-fifth of a U.S. penny.

Beast Against Man

Man has managed to subjugate a sizeable part of the animal kingdom, but there are still many species that have not come under man's sway. In fact, looking at these illustrations by noted artists, one could easily conclude that man is prey and not master.

Drawing by Harold Montiel

Life

Punch

Life

Comic Almanac

Jumbo Entertainer

Century, Vol. 3

Punch

Cautionary Catches

Competitive frisbee throwing began about twenty years ago, and the longest throw over level ground now on record is one of 285 feet by Robert F. May, of San Francisco, in July of 1971.

Immigration to the United States over the past 100 years shows that the greatest number of people have come from, in order, Germany, Italy, Ireland, Austria, Russia, Great Britain, Mexico, the West Indies, and Sweden.

Within thirty seconds after you begin reading this, another car will be stolen in the United States. The latest figures show that 3 out of 4 stolen automobiles have been left unlocked, and in over 40 per cent of them, trusting owners have gone off leaving the keys in the ignition.

The largest mint in the world is the one completed in 1969 in Philadelphia, covering an area of 11 and one-half acres and with an annual capacity of 8,000 million coins. A single stamping machine in this mint can produce coins at a rate of 10,000 per minute.

Cool It

The 1870s saw vast improvements in refrigeration techniques. A refrigerator car—really a rolling icebox—had made its earliest appearance in 1851, when several tons of butter made the journey by rail from Ogdensburg, New York, to Boston. But the first application of refrigeration technology to marine food transportation came in 1880, when the steamer *Strathleven* carried a meat cargo from Australia to England. Oddly enough, the meat was meant to be cooled, not frozen—but freezing did take place, and the excellent results led to the subsequent freezing of all meat cargoes.

The finest of all fabrics in the world is Shahtoosh, a wool from the throats of Indian goats. It is sold by some of our finer stores at costs of up to $18.50 per square foot and is both more expensive and finer than vicuna. A single hostess gown in Shahtoosh can cost up to $5,000.

The racehorse "Broker's Tip," sensational winner of the Kentucky Derby in 1933, experienced only one "day of glory" in his racing career. He had never previously won a race, and never won a race after the Derby!

Lake Superior, with an area of 31,020 square miles, is the largest freshwater lake in the world. Superior, however, is dwarfed by the largest salt-water lake, the Caspian Sea between Russia and Iran. It has an area of 143,550 square miles.

Stingy with the Stickum

Cellophane was still in its infancy when cellophane tape was born in the laboratories of the Minnesota Mining and Manufacturing Company. The first seeds for the new product were sown in 1925, when a 26-year-old lab assistant named Richard Drew invented a new kind of masking tape for painters in the auto industry. Drew perfected a rubber-based adhesive that allowed the tape to be wound on a roll without sticking to itself, and christened his creation "Scotch Brand Masking Tape"—complete with its now familiar red and yellow plaid trademark.

Why Scotch? That depends upon whom you ask. One apocryphal tale suggests we owe the name to a grumbling painter. When the masking tape was first being tested by painters, adhesive was applied to only the outer edges of the tape, leaving the center of the two-inch strip clear, and one painter complained: "Why so Scotch with the adhesive?"

The largest wine cellars in the world are near Capetown, in the center of the wine district of South Africa. They cover an area of 25 acres and have a capacity of 36 million gallons. The largest blending vats have a capacity of 54,880 gallons.

The first golf tee was invented by George F. Grant of Boston, in December of 1899—a wooden tee with a tapering base portion and a flexible tubular concave shoulder to hold the golf ball.

The "laser" in "laser beam" is an acronym (word made up from the first letters of other words) derived from the term, "light amplification by stimulated emission of radiation."

Oh for the Pony Express!

Speedy courier service was not unknown in Biblical times, as evinced by Job's comment: "My days are swifter than a post." As early as 2000 B.C., an Egyptian courier system linked the royal government with local princes and military outposts, employing foot runners and boats plying the Nile. Assyrian couriers delivered three-inch-square clay tablets, inscribed with cuneiform and enclosed in clay envelopes. By the seventh century B.C., the well-developed Assyrian system was widely imitated by nations throughout the Mideast, including Persia.

Spud Studs

Of all the foodstuffs indigenous to the Americas, none is as useful as the potato. Potatoes are easy to cultivate and can be stored for long periods of time. To give you an idea of the fecundity of the potato, in 1968, an English farmer reported that just six seed potatoes had yielded a whopping 1,190 pounds of spuds.

Whole Clawth

No matter what the dish, lobsters must be cooked alive for full flavor. If killed first and placed in boiling water later, they will be decidedly inferior in flavor and tenderness. But what about ready-boiled lobsters? There's a simple way of finding out if the ready-boiled lobster you're looking at was cooked dead or alive. Just straighten the critter's tail and release it. If the tail springs back quickly, the lobster was probably boiled alive. If it sags back—well, good luck.

If you buy your lobsters live, you can store them together in the same tank without fear they'll attack one another. But if one of the lobsters is injured—missing a claw, for instance—the healthy lobsters are likely to destroy it immediately. Which brings to mind the old joke about the diner who was served a lobster with only one claw.

"I'm sorry, sir," the chef explained to the complaining diner, "but it must have been in a fight."

"Then take it back," the diner replied, "and bring me the winner."

Curds and Whey

As long ago as 4000 B.C., cheese-making was well known to the Sumerians of Mesopotamia. Cheese molds found among the ruins of the Egyptian and Chaldean civilizations show that cheese was a common food there before 2000 B.C. The Old Testament mentions "cheese of the herd," and tells us that David was delivering cheese to Saul's camp when he encountered Goliath. The long-suffering Job complained: "Thou hast poured me out as milk and curdled me as cheese."

In 1890, a strange auction took place in Egypt. Some 180,000 mummified cats had been found near Cairo, and were auctioned off. The auctioneer used a cat as a hammer, and he knocked down the remaining cats in ton lots. Many of the cats were used as fuel.

Carre's Machines

The modern domestic refrigerator is based to a great extent on the work of the Frenchman Edmond Carre. In the 1830s, Carre perfected the first refrigerating machine to be widely adopted for individual use. Carre's machines were used in many Paris restaurants for the production of ice and ice cream products. The first household refrigerator patent in the United States was granted in 1899 to one Albert T. Marshall of Brockton, Massachusetts.

The Luckiest Flyer

Eddie Rickenbacker may have been America's most well-known ace, but a pilot named J.H. Hedley was surely the luckiest. On January 6, 1918, Captain Hedley was flying over German territory in a plane piloted by a Canadian named Makepeace, when the plane was attacked by German fighters. To evade the enemy, Makepeace took his plane in a vertical dive that pulled Hedley right out of his seat and into the ozone. Makepeace continued his descent for several hundred feet, *sans* co-pilot, then leveled off. Incredibly, the plunging Hedley landed smack dab on the tail of the airplane, then pulled himself back into his seat and landed safely!

Helmets and Shakos

In the military dress, the plumed helmet was common in many parts of the ancient world. Greek helmets often bore horsehair crests, and plumes marked the helmet of the Roman centurion and other officers. In pre-Columbian Mexico, priests and warriors wore elaborate feather headdresses. North American Indians wore feathered war bonnets, perhaps due to earlier contacts with their their southern neighbors. As late as the 18th century, military dress in Europe often featured a tall hat, perhaps ornamented with plumes, to make a soldier appear more formidable to his enemy. A familiar example is the cylindrical *shako*.

Thespianism

The first member of the famous Barrymore acting family was Maurice Barrymore, who was born in Agra, India in 1847. He was educated at Cambridge University in England, and held a law degree. He first appeared on the stage in England, but moved to America, where he married Georgina Drew, the daughter of John and Louisa Lane Drew, also actors. Their children were John, Lionel and Ethel Barrymore, who all became leading actors in their own right.

Is a Tomato a Fruit?

Is the tomato a fruit or a vegetable? The question is difficult to answer. Botanically, the tomato is a fruit, the seed-bearing berry of the *Lycopersicon esculentum*. But in the United States, the tomato is classified as a vegetable for trade purposes, since it is most often eaten *with* the meal, rather than *after* it. In short, the "fruit" is used as a "vegetable." But to further cloud the issue, a U.S. ruling dating from 1893 defines the tomato as a fruit when it is eaten out of the hand or as an appetizer. Legally, then, the tomato in the juice you sip before dinner is a fruit, and the tomato in the salad that follows is a vegetable!

Those Infernal Machines

Early pinball machines were vulnerable to sharp blows by players that could jar a ball into a desired hole, making pinball a game of brute force than finesse. When Harry Williams observed a player smacking the bottom of an *Advance* machine to jar open mechanical gates that were supposed to be opened only by a well-aimed ball, he decided to devise a mechanism to prevent such rough treatment. His first attempt was crude: nails were hammered into the underside of the machine to provide a painful surprise to players attempting to slap the board from underneath.

Soon after this, Williams devised a more gentle deterrent. Called a "stool pigeon," the device consisted of a small ball set atop a pedestal, with a metal ring underneath. When the machine was lifted or pounded too heavily, the ball fell from the pedestal to the metal ring, stopping play. A player trying out the newly equipped *Advance* game, surprised when his strong-arm tactics ended the game, exclaimed: "Look! It tilted!" And "stool pigeon" became "tilt" forevermore.

Williams was also the inventor of the electric "pendulum tilt" built into many modern machines. The device consists of a plumb bob hung by a wire, with a thin metal rod protruding from the bottom of the bob. If the machine is pushed too far in any direction, the rod makes contact with a metal ring, completing an electric circuit that stops the machine and illuminates the "tilt" light. Needless to say, this device is not overly popular among pinball fans, but it does increase the challenge of the game and limits wear and tear on the machines.

In 1933, Harry Williams broke new ground with the invention of the first electric pinball machine feature. Included in a game called *Contact*, the battery-powered device was the forerunner of the modern kick-out hole. A ball landing in a certain hole completed a circuit that triggered an electrically powered peg and ejected a ball placed in another hole. Shortly after, Williams added an electric doorbell to one of his games. Other electrical innovations followed, completely revolutionizing an industry that had heretofore been entirely mechanical.

Williams included in his first electric tilt mechanism in *Multiple*, a game produced in association with the Bally Company, founded by Chicago manufacturer Ray Moloney. Moloney had been a coin machine distributor for Gottlieb and other firms until 1931, when he built his first pinball machine, *Ballyhoo*. The game included a "Bally Hole," similar in principle to the Baffle Point. At 10 balls for a penny, *Ballyhoo* was an immediate sensation, launching Moloney on a pinball-machine making career, and laying the groundwork for the Bally Manufacturing Company, today the world's largest producer of slot machines and other electric coin game equipment.

It is believed that windmills were not known in Europe before the 12th century.

The sport of piano smashing has been a popular pastime in the British Isles for some time. In 1968, six Irishmen in Merton, England—well, smashed all previous records in their sport, by demolishing an upright piano and passing the pieces of wreckage through a circle nine inches in diameter in just two minutes, 26 seconds!

Cut Glass

A cut glass article is ornamented by grinding and polishing after it has been shaped by another glass-manufacturing process. A design is first roughed out on the article in water resistant paint. Then this design is cut into the glass by an abrasive wheel made of iron, silicon carbide, or alumina.

Intaglio is a similar process that uses smaller wheels to produce shallower depressions in the glass. In *engraving*, the even shallower depressions are produced by abrasive wheels that may be as small as a pinhead. Engraving can produce the most delicate "drawings" on glass.

Best Bed

In England, the earliest medieval bedroom, called a *bower*, was no more than a simple lean-to set against the outside wall of the house, or against a fence, with no passageway joining it to the house itself. Waking up on a winter morning was certainly a chilling experience. Perhaps that's why most people slept fully dressed, or swaddled in linen sheets. Bedtime comfort was evidently neither sought nor particularly missed, for the 10th-century English ruler Edgar banned "warm baths and soft beds" as effeminate.

In feudal days, only the lord and lady of the house were afforded the luxury of a bedroom. The servants still slept in the hall on piles of straw. Most bedrooms contained a bed, chest, chair, bench, and a clothes rack called a perch, with walls whitewashed or covered with curtains. The bed was usually made of wood fitted together with nails or pieces of iron, with a headboard or footboard decorated with crude carvings. Many beds were fitted with bolsters that raised sleepers to a nearly sitting position.

Aristocratic Europeans of the period moved frequently from one manor to another, carrying their furniture with them rather than furnishing each home. Therefore, many beds and couches were portable. The French word for furniture, *meubles*, and the German word *Möbel* are both derived from words meaning *movable*. And since a family's belongings had to be continually transported from house to house, furniture was kept at a minimum. A single chair was usually reserved for the lord of the house—from this tradition came our word chairman, to signify the predominant member of a group.

The heavy wood bedstead was left behind in the bedroom, however, while the lord carried along only his mattress, blankets and other bedding from home to home. Bedding was considered a possession valuable enough to be included in wills. Ransacking soldiers usually headed straight for the bedroom when they entered a home, claiming bedding as booty. And it was not uncommon for a man to name his bed, as he would a pet!

Never at Night

Until the second century, men and women bathed together in Rome. Then emperor Hadrian ordered segregated bathing. However, Hadrian's decree was frequently overlooked during the more decadent eras of the Empire. In most cities outside Rome, men and women used the bathing facilities at different hours, but it was always considered immoral for a woman to bathe at night.

The Roman baths were the social centers of the time, combining the modern barroom, health spa, and community center. They were open continually except for religious holidays and times of national crisis. Customarily, a Roman would bathe before the principal meal of the day, but some of the more idle—and cleaner—citizens went through the entire bathing ritual as many as six times a day.

As the Empire waned and barbarian invaders destroyed the Roman aqueduct systems, most baths were shut down. But the public bath lived on in the Eastern Empire, and was eventually adopted by the Arabs, who liked vapor baths. The Turkish bath is a direct descendant of the Roman bath, via Constantinople.

The Teutonic tribesmen who overran Europe bathed for the most part in cold rivers or streams. During the Middle Ages, among some communities, bathing was considered a sin and an act of pride. Probably, the Church's opposition to bathing stemmed from the excesses of the Roman public bath.

In November 1929 at Hayback Park of England, the longest of long shots came in first. Coole paid 3410 to 1.

The Cravat

Croatian soldiers, known as *Cravats*, were on duty guarding the frontier of Turkey and Austria. These men wore a type of linen neckcloth as part of their uniform. When a French regiment modelled their style of uniform on this neckcloth, they applied the name of the soldier to the article of clothing.

As Simple as A, B, C

If one man could be credited with the invention of the alphabet, he would probably stand as the greatest inventor in human history. For its long-reaching importance, the alphabet is the most significant of all cultural inventions. Writing would be possible without an alphabet, but hardly as accessible as it is today, and hardly as precise. The effects of widespread literacy and precise written languages have touched in some way on almost every other invention and cultural advance.

An alphabet is a code, a shorthand for human speech sounds. The alphabets of the world range from 11 letters to 72 letters, with the average in the 20s. Those letters cover the entire range of sounds in a language, yet are simple enough to be learned by a first-grader.

But the alphabet was not, of course, the invention of a single person. The alphabet was produced by a gradual evolution of written language from primitive picture drawings. Despite the invention of printing and typing, that alphabet has undergone relatively few important changes in 3,000 years.

The horseshoe crab is the only creature on earth that chews its food with its legs.

Feminists may object, but the United States issued its patent 1,180,753 for a device for catching female fish. It was a mirror attached to fish bait, which, it was deemed by the inventor, would attract female fish who would be vain enough to want to see themselves in a mirror.

In 1930, the British Board of Film Censors, in a welter of obfuscation, declared that Jean Cocteau's *The Seashell and the Clergyman* should be banned because "This film is apparently meaningless, but if it has any meaning, it is doubtless objectionable."

Cutting a Wide Swath

The manufacture of a pair of scissors or shears from raw metal may require as many as 175 individual steps. Formerly, the blades were sharpened by grinding on a natural stone, and polished with a wooden wheel. Today, the blades are die cast, then forged, trimmed, ground, heat-treated, polished, and finished. That leaves only about 165 other steps.

The Chinese custom of binding women's feet to keep them small is many centuries old. Originally, the practice owed little to pedal aesthetics—bound feet were thought to insure faithfulness, since with such deformed feet the wife would supposedly find it difficult to travel very far on her own.

The largest planet in our solar system is Jupiter; the smallest Pluto.

Jupiter has a diameter of about 88,700 miles. Its mass is about 2½ times the mass of all the other planets combined.

Estimates of Pluto's size are difficult to make since it is so very far away. Scientists guess that its diameter is about 3,600 miles.

Boats of ancient Egypt were constructed by binding together bundles of papyrus stems. It was long believed these boats were unsafe for anything but river travel. However, this theory was exploded when recently Thor Hyerdahl successfully sailed a papyrus craft across the Atlantic Ocean!

The first fingerprinting for criminal identification occurred in Argentina in 1892. Before that Alphonse Bertillon had devised a system of measuring certain bones of the body.

And before that criminals were usually identified by means of maiming, branding, or tattoing!

Clean Passage

In the smaller cities of medieval Europe, the sanitation systems were poor or non-existent. Monasteries generally boasted the best facilities. Monks frequently diverted a nearby stream so that it ran under the *rere-dorter,* or sanitary wing, as well as under the kitchen and under the infirmary. The "secret passage" that often connected a monastery and neighboring convent—to shatter some fantasies cherished by the profane—actually was a sewer connecting the two structures with the main watercourse.

All right, when it comes to cats, you can name the Siamese, Persian, Angora and Manx (calico doesn't count), but what about the other 23 recognized cat· breeds? Restrict yourself to the domestic variety please; jungle stalkers aren't included. Did you list all of these:

Abyssinian, Balinese, Birman, Bombay Burmese, Egyptian Mau, Havana Brown, Himalayan, Japanese Bobtail, Korat, Leopard Cat, Maine Coon Cat, Ocicat, Rex, Russian Blue, Scottish Fold, American Shorthair, Colorpoint Shorthair, Exotic Shorthair, Lilac Foreign Shorthair, Oriental Shorthair, Wirehair Shorthair, Sphynx.

An Eye for a Tooth

What did Pharoah do when he had a toothache—exactly what you'd do, consult a dentist. Bet you thought that the art of dentistry is a relatively modern phenomenon. Well, it's not. Egyptian writings from way back in the 18th century B.C. have prescriptions for swollen gums and toothaches. The Etruscans evidently did some very good crown and bridge work in the 7th century B.C.

Unfortunately, these skills seem to have been lost in the Middle Ages. Dentistry then, and for a long time, was practiced by barbers, or by almost anyone who wanted to set up a chair at a marketplace or fair. There are many places in Africa and Asia where this is still common practice today.

It is Pierre Fauchard, who practiced in Paris around 1715, who is credited as being the founder of modern dentistry. It is he who asserted that tooth decay was caused by lack of care and cleansing, and not by a tooth worm.

The record distance for bed pushing was achieved in 1975, by 12 young people in Greensburg, Pennsylvania, who wheeled a hospital bed a total of 1,776 miles in 17 days. A group of students attempting to match that feat once fitted a wheeled bed with a 197-cc. engine—and accumulated 52 traffic summonses during their maiden voyage.

The first railroad sleeping car in this country appeared in 1836, on the Cumberland Valley Railroad. In 1858, George Pullman introduced the sleeping car that was to make his name synonymous with railroad comfort. When introduced on the Chicago and Alton Railroad, Pullman's simple, practical vehicle cost but $1,000. By 1865, luxury Pullmans including everything *and* the kitchen sink were selling for 20 times that amount.

Victorian publications never dared show a bed in any of their advertisements. When illustrations of the bedroom were required, the bed itself was decorously hidden by curtains. At the same time, advertisers began to peddle inventions we now call alarm clocks, but which the class-conscious Victorians preferred to call "servant regulators."

Victoria herself could boast a few peculiar bedtime habits. Even after the death of her husband, Prince Albert, the queen always slept in a double bed, and had her servants lay out the deceased Prince's bedclothes each night. A picture of Albert's dead body hung continually above her bed.

Not My Cup of Tea

The rarest coffee in the world is Jamaica Blue Mountain. That particular coffee is sold in only a few stores in the United States. Only 800 bags, or 100,000 pounds, are produced each year.

Spoil the Child

Eskimos love their children and do everything they can to make the youngsters happy. They give them special food, and make sure they answer all the children's questions.

Oddly enough, however, some Alaskan Eskimo boys are allowed to smoke pipes when they are only three or four years old. Their fathers believe this makes the boys very manly.

The Eyes Have It

The most unusual of all reptiles may be the tuatara of New Zealand, the sole survivor of a large group of reptiles known to us only through their fossil remains. What is so unusual about the tuatara is that it has three eyes instead of the customary two.

On top of the tuatara's head, protected by a hard transparent scale, is a small third eye. The optic nerve of this third eye is completely developed, but the iris—the colored portion of the eye—is lacking. Just what use the tuatara makes of its third eye is not clear to us at present, but scientists are trying to solve that mystery.

At one time in the long-distant past many creatures had three eyes. Other lizards, even today, still have a third eye, but it is grown over and no longer useful. Even human beings have the remains of a third eye. Called the *pineal gland*, it is buried in the back of our heads.

The tuatara remains the only living creature that has kept its third eye virtually intact, and appears to be continuing to make use of it.

Speaking of Crosswords

Speaking of crossword court capers: recently, a West German puzzle buff became so frustrated by a particularly difficult crossword, that she woke her husband for assistance three times as she battled the poser through the night. The fourth time the puzzled frau woke her weary consort, he strangled her to death. The court acquitted the husband on the grounds of temporary insanity.

In early America, simple wood beds and straw mattresses were the rule in all but the wealthiest homes. American inns of the Revolutionary period offered little more in the way of comfort—an innkeeper would think nothing of asking a guest to share his bed with a stranger when accommodations became scarce.

A recent survey disclosed that about half of all American shoppers buy bananas at least once a week. And with good reason, for the banana is one of the most compact, inexpensive, and nutritious foods available. Bananas are high in potassium, iron, and various vitamins, and low in sodium. They are 99.8 percent fat free, and devoid of cholesterol. The fruit is so easily digestible that it's often the first solid food fed to babies. But most important, bananas are delicious. It's hard to disagree with British statesman Benjamin Disraeli who, writing from Cairo in 1831, called the banana "the most delicious thing in the world."

Come Play With Me

The male Australian bowerbird constructs a beautifully decorated, covered playground where he can woo his lady love.

He takes great pains decorating the bower, and sprinkles it with dozens of bright trinkets—such as snail shells—all of his favorite color.

The playground of one bowerbird—whose favorite color obviously was blue—had dozens of trinkets, including a blue hair ribbon, a blue railroad ticket, a string of blue glass beads, and 178 blue tags taken from a nearby laundry. One bowerbird tints the inside of its bower by using a wad of bark fiber as a paintbrush, and the juice of berries as paint! This is an exceptional example of a bird using a tool.

After the courtship, the female bowerbird goes off and builds a nest in which to raise her family.

A Matter of Life or Death

As many as 25 different versions of tables existed in medieval Europe. The modern backgammon board has existed since at least the 14th century, when the game was already quite popular in England. Chaucer mentions tables in the *Canterbury Tales*, with the line "They daucen, and they playen at ches and tables." James I of Scotland was said to have spent the night before his murder in 1437 "playing at Chess and Tables." A psalter dating from 1499, considered one of the earliest illustrated books ever printed, contains a picture of a man and a woman playing tables. Shakespeare acknowledged the game in *Love's Labour Lost*, when the character Biron says:

> This is the ape of the form, Monsieur the Nice,
> That, when he plays at tables, chides the dice
> In honourable terms.

A story is told that the Duke of Albany, the brother of James III of Scotland, used tables to win far more than cold cash. While imprisoned in Edinburgh castle in the 1480s, the Duke invited the captain of the guard into his cell one night to play tables. In the morning, the captain was found dead in the cell, and the Duke had made good his escape.

"Euzkara," the language of the Basques, colorful inhabitants of seven provinces of Spain and France, is considered one of the most difficult languages in the world to learn. No foreigner has ever learned to speak it fluently, and no one has ever mastered its eight separate dialects. Its vocabulary and syntax have puzzled linguists for centuries.

Obesity, considered a symptom underlying emotional problems of frustrated individuals, now has been called "an addictive behavior disorder," as complex as alcoholism. The obese eat, not because they are hungry, but because the food is there. 80% of all obese children grow up to be obese adults.

Cheese! Cheese! Cheese!

There are many ways to make cheese, some simple, some quite complex. Most cheese-making begins with the coagulation and separation of milk into two components, curds and whey. Untreated milk wil coagulate naturally, but the separation of the curd from the whey is uually aided by the addition of bacterial cultures or rennet, an enzyme found in the stomachs of calves.

When the milk has separated, the watery whey is removed, leaving the semisolid curd, or fresh cheese. Heat is sometimes applied to aid in the coagulation. The curd is pressed into shape, coated with wax or other wrapping, then cured and ripened in any of hundreds of different ways. About 10 volumes of milk are required to produce one volume of cheese, but cheese contains almost all of milk's fat, protein, and calcium.

The first woman state governor in the United States was Nellie Taylor Ross, who succeeded her husband, William T. Ross, as governor of Wyoming after his death in 1925, and served for two years. In 1933, Mrs. Ross also became the first woman to hold the position of Director of the United States Mint, serving in this post until 1953.

Don't Fool with a Mongoose

The agile mongoose, an animal about the size of a cat, is very quick on its feet. When it meets a snake, it usually wastes no time in tackling it. It will dance around the serpent until a chance comes to dart in and bite the snake behind the head, well out of the way of the reptile's fangs. Even if the mongoose encounters a cobra, it generally manages to avoid the serpent's desperate attack.

The battle may last but a few moments, or it may go on for a considerable time; but in the end, the mongoose usually gets in the death blow and kills the snake.

Steve Sokol was a center of attraction in the Oakridge Mall in San Jose, California on June 28, 1981. Completeing 52,003 sit-ups in 32 hours, Mr. Sokol set a new world record.

If you think setting a new record was Mr. Sokol's end in itself, you don't know this 29-year old chemical engineer. Mr. Sokol was raising money for the Red Cross—a penny for each sit-up.

I'm Forever Blowing Bubbles

Bubble gum first appeared in 1933. But it wasn't until 1947, when the Topps Chewing Gum Co. began to offer the familiar Bazooka penny piece, that bubble gum became the ubiquitous source of oral gratification it is today. Later, Topps included baseball cards with slabs of gum.

In England nearly ¾ of early syphilis is homosexually acquired.

Surely the most peculiar game of basketball ever played took place in Sweden in 1974, when a boys team defeated its rival by the incredible score of 272-0! And get this: a 13-year old named Mats Wermelin scored *all 272 points* for his team!

Who Was First?

In 1306, a Pisan monk delivered a sermon in Florence that included these comments: "It is not 20 years since there was found the art of making eyeglasses which make for good vision ... I have seen and conversed with the man who made them first." That would date the invention of eyeglasses to around 1287. But who was the man whom the monk conversed with, the man who *invented eyeglasses?*

Some historians believe that man was Alessandro di Spina, a Dominican monk who lived in Pisa. But a document recording Spina's death in 1313 claimed that Spina had seen spectacles on a man who had chosen to remain unknown. Spina merely copied the invention, and distributed it "with a cheerful and benevolent heart."

A tombstone in Florence credits Armato degli Armati, who died in 1317, as the "inventor of spectacles." But the tombstone has been found to be of relatively recent origin; the claim is a fabrication. All we know for certain is that eyeglasses first appeared in the area of Pisa late in the 1280s.

After Marco Polo visited the Orient during the 1270s, he claimed to have found an old Chinese man reading with the use of spectacles.

If this is true, then the Chinese invented eyeglasses before any European. At the time, the Chinese claimed to have learned to make lenses from Arabs two centuries earlier. But this claim is regarded as doubtful.

In any case, the appearance of spectacles in Europe caused little furor among the general populace, since at the time few people could read. For a few centuries, eyeglasses were regarded as a sign of respect, suggesting learning and importance. Contemporary paintings often depicted saints wearing spectacles. A portrait of St. Jerome, painted in 1480 by Domenico Ghirlandajo, showed a pair of spectacles dangling from the saint's desk, although Jerome had died a thousand years earlier. Thus it was that St. Jerome later became the patron saint of the spectaclesmakers' guild.

Only Three, Oswald!

A Chicago court, faced with a wife's claim that her husband was spending too much time on his crosswords at the expense of providing for his family, decreed that the husband limit himself to just three crosswords a day.

Basic Metal

Copper has been known to have been used by the human race from its earliest beginnings. Its alloy with tin makes bronze, which was the first metallic compound in common use by mankind. The employment of bronze in ancient times was so widespread that the epoch in which it was used is known as the Bronze Age.

Copper in French is culled *cuiere,* and in German is called *kupfer.* Copper takes a brilliant polish, and is highly malleable. In tenacity it falls short only of iron, exceeding in that quality both silver and gold. Copper is not affected by exposure to dry air, but in a moist atmosphere copper becomes coated with a green basic carbonate. Copper is widely distributed in nature, occurring in most soils.

The Versatile Rose

Exactly why the rose came to be a symbol of secrecy is open to speculation. Perhaps the unopened rosebud suggests beauty or truth hidden by the closed petals. In any case, medieval alchemists used the rose as a symbol of the need for secrecy in their art, and has a representation of certain highly guarded scientific principles important in their work. The secret society of the Rosicrucians—from "red cross"—used a cross with a red rose as their symbol.

In medieval England, many families employed a representation of the rose in their coat of arms: the red rose of Lancaster and the white rose of York are two well-known examples. During the 15th century, these two houses fought for control of the English crown in a struggle that came to be known as the War of the Roses.

The rose has, of course, proved useful in more ways than the symbolic. Rose water was first distilled around the time of the Crusades. When the Moslem leader Saladin retook Jerusalem from the Crusaders, he refused to enter a mosque until all the walls and the objects had been purified with rose water. Over 50 camels were required to transport the aromatic cargo from Baghdad to Jerusalem.

Rose oil, used in perfumes and lotions, likewise originated in the Near East, and did not appear in Europe until 1612. A 17th-century German book lists 33 diseases that supposedly can be cured by rose water or oil.

During the 18th century, rose petals occasionally were included in English salads, and essence of roses was used to flavor ice cream.

Don't Give It a Tumble

To ensure the success of a social evening during the eighteenth century, the drinks were served in a round-bottom glass known as a tumbler. You could not put this glass down until it was empty. Eventually, the extraordinary shape of the tumbler proved too inconvenient so the bottom was squared off giving it its present day shape.

French Christmas

The night before Christmas, the French children polish their shoes and leave them by the fireplace. Le Pere Noel or Saint Nicholas will fill them with candles, nuts and fruits. He also brings gifts in a big basket on his back. Le Pere Noel travels on a donkey. After midnight church, families gather for a very fancy supper. In many parts of France people stay up all night on Christmas Eve.

Bad Apples

The only apple we might dub truly "evil" is an apple with a worm in it. These pesky critters do not crawl inside the apple that provides their home—they're born there. Fruit flies stab holes in the skin of a ripening apple and release eggs into the fruit. The eggs hatch into white worms, which feed on the apple tissue as they grow. When the apple falls to the ground, the worms crawl out and burrow into the earth; the following summer, they emerge as fruit flies and begin searching for a likely apple for their eggs.

Another apple that might deserve the name *malus* is the crab apple—which owes its name not to a crustacean, but most likely to a Scottish word for a wild apple. Crab apples comprise a number of *Malus* species, whose high acid content and sour taste make them unsuitable for eating. Crab apple trees are often used as ornamental plants, and some of the fruits find their way into jelly or apple cider.

Clang! Clang! Clang!

Streetcar lines in general began to rapidly disappear in the 1930s, in the face of competition from cars and buses. An intermediate step in the trolley-to-bus transition was the trackless trolley, a buslike vehicle that ran without tracks but was powered by electricity from overhead lines like the trolley. The first trackless trolley began service in 1910 in Los L.A. once boasted one of the nation's finest streetcar systems. Brooklyn, New York, maintained trackless trolleys until as late as the 1950s.

London did away with its last trolley in the 50s; Paris had ripped up its streetcar tracks about 20 years earlier. Today, the streetcar is virtually extinct in America, but the trolley is still widely used in Germany, Austria, Switzerland, and Eastern Europe.

But trolley-lovers, take heart. You can still catch a glimpse of the ancient streetcar in various museums throughout the country. The museum in East Hartford, Connecticut, contains 92 trolleys, ranging from some 1880 relics to a New York model from the 1930s. In that museum, trolley buffs can ride an open-sided car—complete with bell—over a two-mile route.

Streetcars were inexpensive to construct and clean. Although dependable, they were not without disadvantages. Among these was the danger posed to idle strollers by a speeding trolley. The Brooklyn Dodgers of baseball fame were not so-named because of their agility on the playing field. Initially, the team was called the "Trolley Dodgers," in tribute to the maze of trolley lines crisscrossing Brooklyn at the height of the streetcar era.

In the days of ancient Greece, aristocratic women owned as many as 20 pairs of shoes, with a style to match every occasion. Slaves were employed solely to carry a supply of their lady's shoes when she left home, assuring that she would be appropriately shod throughout her travels.

Expensive Toys

If you're serious about your shutterbugging, you might take a look at the Nikon system, the most expensive available, which with all accessories, including 19 cameras and 62 lenses, will set you back more than $110,000. You might also take a look at the F-1 35-mm. Canon system, with 40 lenses and more than 180 available accessories.

But a newer camera, made by Canon—the electronically powered A-1, could someday make the F-1 and similar cameras obsolete. The A-1, introduced in 1978, has the capacity to automatically select either shutter speed or aperture, or both, 41 milliseconds. Its aperture range can be adjusted continuously rather than by increments, or *stops*. These and a host of other innovations make this precise, versatile camera almost as simple to use as the Instamatic. How much will a modern photographic marvel cost you? Under $350, plus lenses.

Along with Canon, the other major producers of top-of-the-line photographic equipment include the German Leica firm, whose cameras sell chiefly in the $700-$1,200 range, and the Japanese Nikon and Minolta companies—Minolta is presently the second largest-selling camera in the world, after Canon.

Oh, That Java!

No one need be told that human beings are lovers of the grape. But did you realize that the brew of the coffee bean is drunk by more people than any other beverage on earth?

Coffee is regularly consumed by about one-third of the world's population, and consumption continues to rise steadily. At the turn of the century, world imports totaled about one million tons. But by 1950, that figure had doubled. Today, the total stands at about three-and-a-half million tons—making coffee the second largest item of international commerce after petroleum!

The first apples to reach America arrived from England in 1629, along with seeds and propagating wood. Ten years later, the first apples grown in the United States were plucked from trees planted on Beacon Hill, Boston. By 1741, New England was producing apples for export, and apple cultivation was sweeping westward across America.

Cutting Ice

Ice skating has spawned a number of sports, but to purist skaters there are only two: speedskating and figure skating. Speed-skating events began in the Netherlands at least 200 years ago. English speed-skating had its formal beginnings in 1814, and was dominated by the Smarts. William "Turkey" Smart won his first championship in 1854, and remained speed-skating champion for more than a decade. In 1878, "Turkey's" nephew, George "Fish" Smart, took the title, which he held until 1889, when his brother James took over. In the United States, the Donoghue family of Newburgh, New York, held a similar grip on speed-skating superiority. At various times, each of three members of the family was considered the fastest speed skater in the world.

Sticking with Cinnamon

Cinnamon has been used in Europe longer than most other spices, since it is native to India which is closer to Europe than the East Indies, where a majority of spices originate.

Biologically, the cinnamon plant is known as *Cinnamonum zeylanicum.* The second word is derived from the Portuguese name for Ceylon. *Cinnamon* itself comes from the Greek *kinnamon,* in turn derived from the Hebrew *qinnamon.* The Germans called the spice *Ceylonzimt,* while *cannelle* is cinnamon in France.

Produced from the dried inner bark of a small, bushy evergreen tree, cinnamon is one of the few spices made from the bark of a plant rather than the leaf, root, flower, or seed. Untended cinnamon trees will grow up to 40 feet high, but to facilitate harvesting they are usually pruned to about eight feet.

At the plantation, the bark is stripped from the trees, fermented, scraped, and dried. The yellow, rolled strips of bark are then inserted one within another for shipping, forming solid rods about three-eighths of an inch in diameter and three feet long. Some of the bark is instead pounded, macerated in sea water, and distilled to produce cinnamon oil.

Ceylon, now known as Sri Lanka, still produces the world's best cinnamon. Other supplies hail from India, Indonesia, Brazil, and the West Indies.

Cinnamon and other spices cost but a fraction of their worth just a few centuries ago, but international spice trade still totals over $200 million a year. Pepper accounts for about a quarter of the total.

Caseus to You

The Latin word *caseus,* however, is the basis of our word *cheese,* as well as the German *kase* and the Spanish *queso.* The Greek word *formos,* applied to the wicker baskets used for draining cheese, became *forma* in Latin, *formaggio* in Italian, and *formage* in French before it evolved into the modern French *fromage.*

A La Mode

Human nature doesn't change, but styles do. Ever since prehistoric times men and women have been obsessed with how they might adorn themselves.

The Hebrew prophets of old constantly inveighed against the preoccupation of the women of Israel and Samaria with furbelows, gewgaws, bodices, and trappings. In the Orient, and in ancient Greece and Rome, styles remained pretty constant for centuries. Fashion, in the sense of couture, originated in Europe in the 14th century. Rose Bertin, Marie Antoinette's dressmaker, may have been the first noted designer. Today, haute couture designers from America (Norell, Blass, Trigere), England (Quant), as well as other countries (Pucci), compete with such well known Parisian designers as Worth, Chanel, and Schiaparelli.

A quick gaze through these pages will show how appearances have changed during the past hundred years. Some of the costumes illustrated here may seem weird, but certainly no weirder than those of today will appear 50 years from now.

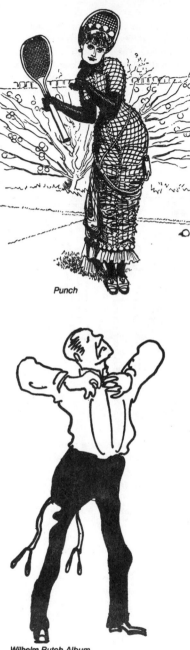

Punch

La Vie Parisienne

Wilhelm Butch Album

Punch

La Vie Parisienne

Drawing by Harold Montiel

Nana

Judge

Triviata

For Whom the Cloche Tolls

Punch

La Vie Parisienne

Punch

La Vie Parisienne

Punch

Punch

279

Wilhelm Butch Album

La Vie Parisienne

Drawing and Design

La Vie Parisienne

Punch

La Vie Parisienne

Punch

Life

Bizarre

La Vie Parisienne

For Whom the Cloche Tolls

Time to Pray

Speaking of ecclesiastical timepieces, medieval monks invented the world's first alarm clock. Monks sometimes slid a lit candle between their toes before dozing, so that the flame would rudely awaken them at the desired hour. For obvious reasons, the hot-foot alarm clock did not catch on elsewhere.

The invention of a mechanical clock has been attributed to the Chinese of the eighth century, but the first mechanical timekeeping devices appeared in Europe in the 12th or 13th centuries. Almost all of the earliest clocks were turret clocks built into church towers to help the faithful get to church on time. A bell and striker system provided the hour—there were no hands.

The world "clock" comes from the French *cloche*, bell. Originally, the word was applied only to those timekeeping devices that struck the hour with a bell or gong.

Among the most famous medieval church clocks were those of the Cathedral of Strasbourg in France, and St. Paul's Cathedral in London. The astronomic clock in Strasbourg church, called the most elaborate clock ever built, was not installed until 1842, relacing an earlier model. St. Paul's clock, built in 1286, contained mechanical figures that struck a bell on the hour.

The gong clock in the Cathedral of Notre Dame in Dijon, France, has struck the hour every hour since 1383. In 1950, an ambitious mathematician computed that by then the gong had tolled the hour 32,284,980 times.

The gorilla was almost unknown to science less than 100 years ago. The first living specimen was brought to England in 1887, where it created a sensation!

The gorillas at the Frankfurt (Germany) Zoo have had a television set installed in their cage to keep them from getting bored.

Tulips

The Turks prized the tulip, and were cultivating that flower on a large scale by the mid-16th century when the Austrian ambassador to the Turkish empire brought some tulip bulbs from Constantinople to his garden in Vienna. From Austria, the flower found its way to the Low Countries. In 1562, the first large shipment of Turkish tulips reached Antwerp, then part of the Dutch nation.

The tulip quickly became a favorite among European gardeners and the Netherlands soon took the lead in producing prized specimens.

Take a Letter

More people are trained for the operation of the typewriter than for any other machine on earth—any machine requiring specialized training, that is. The typewriter has indeed come a long way. The early models resulted in machine writing being slower than handwriting. Today's modern machines are capable of speeds faster than speech, fulfilling the prediction of the Remington Company, the typewriter's first manufacturer, that the machine would "free the world from pen slavery and complete the economic emancipation of womankind."

Pain, almost wholly mental, was not felt by many American soldiers wounded at Anzio...they were so relieved at finding themselves alive and out of combat.

Anything Including the Kitchen Sink

Biggest of all birds is the eight-foot tall, 300-pound ostrich. To keep its huge body fed, the ostrich eats just about anything. It has been known to gobble lizards, rodents, small animals, grass, and not so appetizing keys, glass bottles, beads, and stones.

Bananas of Sorts

There are over 100 varieties of banana now in cultivation. The two most common varieties are the Gros Michel and the Cavendish. The Gros Michel, grown in large quantities in Jamaica, Panama, and Costa Rica, was for many years the overwhelming favorite in this country. But the tall Gros Michel is particularly susceptible to wind storms. Winds of just 20 to 30 miles per hour can devastate an entire plantation in minutes. The shorter, sturdier Cavendish has therefore become the most popular variety on most plantations.

The *plantain*, a short, green banana is usually cooked, since its fruit is starchy rather than sweet. Many Caribbean and Central American dishes use the plantain in much the same way that we use the potato.

The weirdest of all bed sportsmen are surely those human beings who subject their tender flesh to a bed of nails. The record for nonstop endurance of such an inhospitable bower was set in 1980 in Birmingham, England when Barry Walls lay atop a bed of sharp six-inch nails for 74 hours. And unverified claims for bed-of-nails endurance by fakirs range as high as 111 days!

The secretary bird can run as fast as a horse.

With sturdy bedsteads and spring mattresses at their disposal, 19th-century Europeans began to turn their attention to the amenities of bedroom comfort. Tin hot-water bottles had been in use since the 17th century, but the rubber models were surely a vast improvement. Belly-warmers were also popular for a time, complete with a concave depression for the stomach.

Electric blankets have made such devices obsolete, although the earliest warming blankets were a dangerous proposition—electric blankets caused an estimated 2,600 fires during the first three years of their sale here.

Hot Spot

The emperor penguin has developed a special hatchery to keep eggs warm in the quick-freezing cold of the Antarctic. The penguin wiggles a single egg onto its feet. Then the penguin tucks the egg into the skin pouch over its stomach. The feather-covered pouch warms the egg, protecting it against temperatures that sometimes drop to 70 degrees below zero. And when the little chick bursts out of the egg, it keeps warm in the same cozy spot.

During the 19th century, English manufacturers began to turn out cast-iron bedsteads in quantity. Gradually, mattresses stuffed with feathers, leaves, hair, moss, wool, or seaweed gave way to the spring mattress, which had been patented in the late 18th century. The first spiral mattress—similar to the one you may sleep on—appeared first in 1826, intended for use aboard ship as an aid against seasickness. In 1857, the first box springs, one foot deep, reached the shores of America from France.

The 18th century saw the appearance of the first metal bedsteads since the days of ancient Rome. Metal beds had one large advantage over wooden beds: they were less likely to be infested with "sleep's foe, the flea, that proud insulting elf." Feather pillows became common during the era.

Banana Bonanza

"Yes, we have bananas" may not be as humorous nor as rhythmic as "Yes, we have no bananas," the well-known words to the once-popular song, but it's certainly closer to the truth. Americans do have bananas—billions of them! Our ever-growing taste for the fruit has made the United States the world's largest consumer of this yellow-skinned wonder. If Americans consume bananas at the present rate, this country may soon earn the sobriquet of "banana republic."

The banana is now America's favorite fresh fruit. More apples and oranges are consumed here than bananas, but both these fruits are frequently enjoyed in juices and other processed products. Bananas are almost always eaten fresh. Americans now devour over 12 billion bananas each year—close to 19 pounds per person. Yet, virtually no bananas are grown within this country—and the fruit was almost unknown here until just a century or so ago!

Cyrano

Toucans, a family of tropical American fruit-eating birds, have extremely large beaks. Indeed, among some members of the family, the bill is actually bigger than the bird's body! This gives the toucan an ungainly, comical appearance. However, although it is so large, the toucan's thin-walled bill is light in weight and not hard for the bird to carry.

In California, the public school enrollment in 1975 reached 4,419,571 children. This is over one million more children than were enrolled in the public schools of New York State.

Less than three percent of the population of the United States is Jewish. The concentration of Jews in the United States is in New York and in the neighboring state of New Jersey. In New York State, about one out of every 20, and in Florida, about one out of every 25 people is Jewish.

The state where the average income is the greatest is, of all places, Alaska. Here the personal income for every individual during 1977 averaged $10,586.

By far the greatest number of roller skaters live in the state of California, where there were 102 roller skating clubs in 1978.

The state with the most elderly people is Florida. Here, over 16 percent of the population is deemed to be of advanced age.

Backgammon can be played easily enough with just a pair of dice, a makeshift board drawn on a piece of cardboard, and a few checkers. But that hasn't stopped some buffs from shelling out hundreds, or even thousands, of dollars for more elaborate equipment. Stores devoted exclusively to backgammon equipment display such luxurious equipment as a pearl-and-onyx inlaid board rimmed with gold, with pieces made of jade or ivory. Backgammon fanciers have coughed up over $600 for sets that include elephant-hide boards and sterling silver doubling cubes. And one backgammon board, made from batik leather, sells for well over $2,000!

A Dangerous Game

You may have heard that the ancient Aztecs of Mexico played a game similar to basketball, and thus were the real originators of the sport. True, 16th-century Aztecs did play a team game called *tlachtli* or *ollamalitzli*, but the Indian games actually resembled soccer more than basketball. The object of the Aztec game was to propel a ball through vertical stone rings placed at each end of the court, about eight feet above the ground. The rubber ball was about the size of a cantaloupe, and the opening in the ring slightly larger. Players could use various parts of the body to strike the ball, but could not touch it with their hands, *à la* soccer. Spectators at *tlachtli* matches frequently took to their heels the moment a player scored a goal, since a goal earned the scoring player the right to collect clothing and jewelry from the crowd. The captain of the losing team was often beheaded. Talk about pressure games!

Piggyback

The grebe, mute swan, some ducks, and the loon, have a special way of caring for their youngsters.

Very often, especially at the first sign of danger, the crested grebe sinks until its back is level with the water. Its young climb onto its back. Then the parent grebe rises to its swimming position and with strong strokes carries them across the water to safety.

Bound for Glory

Until the 17th century, books were often displayed without a binding—the buyer could select his own binding when he purchased the book. And as long ago as ancient Rome, the author Seneca complained that book buyers were paying more attention to a book's cover than they were to its contents!

It is very likely that many deaths in the U.S. reported as "heart attacks from causes unknown" are due to bee stings.

People who wear tight clothing indicate feelings of anxiety and even inferiority, while people who wear loose clothes tend to be optimistic.

Free-wheeling

In the United States, where the automobile is king of the road it's easy to underestimate the importance of the bicycle. To many Americans, cycling may mean cruising around Central Park in Manhattan, or along Lake Shore Drive in Chicago, or pedaling lazily over suburban streets on a modern 10-speed. But while in America the bicycle is chiefly a sporting vehicle or a plaything for children, in much of the world, the bike remains man's primary means of transportation.

It should come as no surprise that the bicycle is the principal vehicle in the Orient, in parts of Africa, and the Near East. But even in the developed nations of Europe, the bicycle retains an importance wholly out of proportion to its use in America. The streets of Amsterdam, Brussels, and Paris teem with bicycles, and during working hours many European squares become forests of parked bicycles. Though exact figures are impossible to come by, there's little doubt around the world that bicycles vastly outnumber automobiles.

Ice Show

People evidently enjoy watching others skate as much as they do skating themselves, for ice skating has acquired a definite place in the entertainment world. The first large skating spectacle in America took place in 1862, when 12,000 costumed skaters took part in a carnival in Prospect Park, Brooklyn. The first ice show with a large cast was a 1913 extravaganza in Berlin. The 65-member troupe's show, *Flirting in St. Moritz,* was brought to the New York Hippodrome in 1915, and enjoyed a three-year run.

The year 1936 was a banner year for ice skating, marking the first appearance of Sonja Henie in a film, and the first Ice Follies spectacular, a stage show on ice. The Ice Capades have presented musicals and operettas on an ice-rink stage since 1940, when the show began in Atlantic City, New Jersey. Ice skaters have even made it to television—in 1952, an entire Arthur Godfrey show was presented on ice skates!

The longest bar with beer pumps in the world was built in 1938 in Victoria, Australia. It has a counter 287 feet in length, served by 32 pumps.

Ripening Cheese

Soft ripened cheeses are ripened by bacterial cultures that begin growing on the surface of the cheese and progress from the rind to the center. Popular cheeses in this category include *Brie, Camembert,* and *Limburger.*

Semisoft ripened cheeses such as *Bel Paese, Munster,* and *Port du Salut* ripen from the interior as well as from the surface.

Firm ripened cheeses such as *Cheddar, Emmenthaler,* and *Edam* are generally ripened for considerably longer than the softer cheeses.

Very firm ripened cheeses like *Parmesan* and *Romano* are ripened for an even longer period, and are usually used for grating. The Swiss *Saanen* is the world's hardest cheese, requiring about seven years to fully ripen.

Just about every city of importance is referred to in the American underworld by a nickname. New York is called *The City,* Chicago is called *The Village,* and Hot Springs, Arkansas, is called *Bubbles.* Richmond, Virginia, has been dubbed *Grantsville,* and the site of Sing Sing, a prison at Ossining, New York, is called *Stirville.*

Don't Bug Me

The familiar Volkswagen "beetle" was first produced in 1938. By the 1950s, Volkswagen was the largest car producer in Europe; and in 1972, the "beetle" surpassed the Model T in total sales for a single model, with over 15 million sold throughout the world.

The accuracy of clocks and watches improved steadily during the 16th and 17th centuries, but the basic mechanism of timekeeping devices remained the same. All mechanical watches link a device performing regular movements—a balance and spring, for example—to a counting mechanism capable of recording the number of those movements. The mainspring stores energy imparted by winding and transmits the energy to the balance and spring. The oscillations of the balance and spring trigger—after a few dozen intermediate steps—the movement of the hands. If it sounds fairly simple, it isn't: hundreds of years and thousands of refinements were necessary before the clock and watch could be called truly accurate.

Cocktail Time

The production of alcoholic beverages in the United States now stands at over 100 million proof gallons per year, with an estimated half-billion proof gallons in stock. Not bad for a nation in which about one-third of the population are teetotalers.

Today, about 77 percent of adult men and 60 percent of women are regular consumers of alcoholic beverages. Studies have shown that the wealthy and better educated are more likely to be numbered among the drinkers. But in France, where there are few abstainers, those who do swear off the grape are more likely to come from the well-educated, monied classes.

Burgers in Europe

Burger joints have been mushrooming all over Europe, led by a British chain known as Wimpy's. And you'll have no trouble in Paris finding a MacDonald's for *Le Cheeseburger*.

Have a Cuppa Java

Americans presently put away about one-and-a-quarter million tons of coffee each year, more than the entire world drank just 50 years ago. Coffee is, to say the least, an institution in this country, with the average American gulping down two-and-a-half cups daily. You won't have to look far to find someone who insists he couldn't live without it. And speaking of institutions, in many states, the coffee break is not only a fixture in almost all offices and factories, it's dictated by law.

Still, Americans are not the world's heaviest coffee consumers—the average Swede consumes close to 30 pounds of coffee each year! In fact, in much of Western Europe, the word for coffee, *cafe* has come to be synonymous with an eating place. Even in this country, we prefer to call our beanery a coffee shop, a coffee house, or a cafeteria—which literally means "coffee store" in American Spanish.

The first great American lexicographer was Noah Webster, who was born in 1758 and died in 1843. The first edition of his book appeared in 1783, and was known as *Webster's Spelling Book*. For years, the annual sales of this book were more than a million copies.

Webster then followed with his *Compendius Dictionary of the English Language*, which he brought out in 1806. In 1828, Webster's *An American Dictionary of the English Language* was published in two volumes.

God *Bless America* was written by Irving Berlin, who was born with the name Israel Bayline. Berlin's profits from this song were donated to the Boy and Girl Scouts of America.

Marilyn Monroe, who was born in 1926, died in 1962 by her own hand. Her real name was Norma Jean Baker. She had three husbands. The first was James Dougherty, the second was Joe Di Maggio, and the third was Arthur Miller.

Way Back Then

The people of the Netherlands have been associated with skating for so long that most of us would probably choose that canal-crossed land as the most likely birthplace of the ice skate. Roller skates? Invented by an American, you would say? Well, the Dutch did not invent the ice skate—but a Hollander did devise the first roller skate! And the roller skate's most recent incarnation, the skateboard, was invented not by a roller skating enthusiast, but by a surfer!

As you may imagine, ice skates are a good deal older than their wheeled cousins—older than the Dutch nation, in fact. The earliest written reference to ice skates comes from second-century Scandinavia, but archaeological evidence suggests that skates may be much older than that. The oldest surviving ice skate, made in Sweden sometime between the eighth and tenth centuries, consisted of a piece of cow rib fastened to the foot with leather thongs. The god Uller, of Icelandic mythology, surely must have had a fancier pair of ice skates, for he was exalted in literature for his "beauty, arrows, and skates."

Auto-Intoxication

Without doubt, the automobile ranks among the two or three most important inventions of our age. The car has determined the shape of our cities and the routine of our lives, made almost every inch of our nation easily accessible to everybody, ribboned our country with highways, cluttered the landscape with interchanges, gas stations, parking lots, drive-ins, and auto junkyards, and covered over 50,000 square miles of green with asphalt and concrete!

Considering that there is now one automobile in this county for every two persons (compared to, say, China, with over 14,500 persons per car), it's certainly easy to agree with a writer who described the American as a "creature on four wheels."

Way Way Back Then

Scissors are one of those ubiquitous everyday objects so common and useful today that it's hard to imagine a time when they weren't around. You don't have to—scissors of one kind or another have existed for almost as long as man has had something to cut!

Scissors are probably as old as the loom, but the oldest pair still in existence is a bronze tool from Egypt, dating from the third century B.C. These scissors were richly decorated with figures of metal inlay, and the blades could be detached for separate sharpening. But they probably belonged to a wealthy family, and weren't typical of the kinds customarily used by ancient people.

In 1892, Mr. E. F. Smyth Pigott, an official examiner of plays, who was questioned by a Parliamentary committee, said "We are not censors. We just tell the exhibitors what pictures they can't show."

Snakes have no ears and no larynx nor vocal chords. Yet they are able to produce hissing sounds and to detect sound vibrations of low frequency.

A Jewel of a Watch

The English finally came around to wristwatch production in 1901, and the Swiss began making watches on a large scale in 1914. That year, a wristwatch displayed at the Swiss National Exhibition at Bern was regarded by most viewers as merely a "passing fancy." Passing fancy, indeed! Today, wristwatches make up about 80 percent of all Swiss watches, and the wristwatch has become the single most popular item of jewelry in the world. An estimated half-million womens' watches are purchased annually during the Christmas season in the United States alone.

Good and Plentiful

When we eat and drink, we consume hundreds of chemicals combined in an appetizing form, and our bodies do the work of separating and distributing them. But there are two chemicals that we consume largely in their pure form, and these are two of the most important: H_2O and $NaCl$—water and salt.

Fortunately, these are also two of the most abundant chemicals on our planet. Two-thirds of the earth is covered with water, and the oceans are about three percent sodium chloride—that's the chemical term for ordinary table salt. Considering its abundance, it might seem odd that salt has been so highly valued by man throughout the ages—salt not only *costs* money, in some places it has been used *as* money.

Salt occurs in crystals of various sizes, made up of any number of individual modules, each of which contains one atom of the element sodium, and one atom of the element chlorine. In the body, salt bathes all living tissues and helps flush out wastes. Unfortunately, it will also flush out water from our cells. For if a man could drink salt water, there would be no need for many of the extensive water-carrying systems we've constructed through history to bring water to our cities. And there would be little need for a salt trade.

But salt water, instead of replenishing living cells with water, has the opposite effect: Salt water, denser than pure water, draws water out of the cells through osmosis. Thus, even a man dying of thirst dares not drink salt water, as Coleridge's Ancient Mariner bemoaned in the oft-misquoted lines:

> *Water, water, everywhere,*
> *Nor any drop to drink.*

As you might expect, the use of salt dates back to the oldest of man's civilizations, though there are still peoples of today who do not use it. Before the beginnings of agriculture, nomadic man subsisted on milk and roasted meats, which retain their natural salt, and therefore he did not need additional salt in his diet. But the rise of agricultural societies, with their vegetable and cereal diets, created the need for salt supplements.

We know that the ancient Sumerians ate salted meat and used salt to preserve food as long ago as 3500 B. C. According to a Mesopota-

mian legend, the benefits of salt were discovered when a wounded pig ran into the ocean and drowned. The pork thus soaked in brine was found to taste better than unsalted meat.

Because the habitual use of salt accompanied man's transition from nomadic to agricultural society, salt has long been esteemed as an object of religious significance and a gift of the gods. According to a Finnish myth, the god of the sky struck fire in the heavens, and the sparks fell to the ocean and turned into salt. Another ancient myth held that our salt water oceans are made up of all the tears ever cried. Early man often included salt in his sacrificial offerings to the gods, and used salt-filled pendants to ward off evil.

Each year, the world produces one automobile for every person on the earth! Recent production ran about 26.5 million cars!

Scissors vs. Shears

Have you ever wondered what the precise difference is between "scissors" and "shears?" The use of the two words is fairly arbitrary. Generally, the former is used for a pair of blades less than six inches in length, with usually two small matching finger holes in the handle. "Shears" is generally applied to a tool longer than six inches, with one small hole in the handle for the thumb and one larger hole for a finger.

The first Murphy bed appeared in 1909, manufactured by the Murphy Door Bed Company of San Francisco. Initially called "in-a-door beds," the Murphys were designed to fold back on a pivot behind a door or closet.

What's the Hurry?

Modern man is certainly time conscious. But is our preoccupation with the exact time due solely to the availability of the means to measure it? Not likely. If ancient man was without the means to closely measure time, it's also true that for the most part he simply didn't need to.

The ancient Babylonians, who used a calendar with 12 30-day months, were apparently the first to apply the number 12 to a system of telling the time of day. They were also the first to divide the day into 24 segments, a custom later adopted by the Greeks.

The earliest timekeeping devices depended upon the movement of the sun to provide an approximation of the hour. In Egypt, the sundial—the oldest scientific instrument in continuous use—told time by day; the water clock, similar in principle to the sandglass, was used at night. Lamp clocks or simple candles were later employed to count the hours. The sandglass itself was popular right up into the 16th century, when it was often used in church to measure the length of a sermon.

After X-rays were discovered in 1895, the news of their penetrating power made headlines throughout the world. Then a rumor spread about that if anyone wore X-ray spectacles he could see right through cloth. Many English women believed the rumor and were horrified. A wily merchant in a London department store cashed in on this groundless fear. He made and sold X-ray-proof underwear, and thousands of British females flocked to the store to protect their modesty.

High Jinks

Skateboarding speed records are significantly higher than those set by roller skaters, but most skateboard tracks, or skateparks, enjoy the advantage of a downhill incline. The record speed achieved in 1979 by Richard K. Brown stands at almost 72 miles per hour.

But skateboard tournaments often include competitions of finesse as well as speed. In 1979 a skateboard ace set the high jump record when he launched himself from a moving skateboard leaping five feet, two inches high and landed atop the board again. In 1977, a 19-year-old Californian set the barrel jumping record by leaping from a moving skateboard, jumped over 17 barrels, 12 inches in diameter, and landed on another skateboard. The best barrel jumping performance by an ice-skater was a 28-foot leap, in 1965, by Ken Lebel, in Liberty, New York.

As skateboarding popularity soared, auxiliary enterprises have been quick to follow. *Skateboarder* magazine is back. Manufacturing companies are doing a booming business in helmets and kneepads, and turning out exotic boards that sell for over $100. Skateboard tournaments, such as the New York Masters Contest, are flourishing from coast to coast. Skateboarding organizations proliferate and there is even an International Professional Skateboard Association. Yes, that's right: *professional* skateboarders!

Arabian Flights

When completed around 1982, the Jidda airport will sprawl over 41 square miles of desert land outside the city, which is located on the Red Sea. By contrast, Manhattan Island is 22.6 square miles in area. The airport complex will include a year-round pavilion for the Saudi ruling family and guests, a cargo terminal, an air force base, a hospital, a quarantine area, a hotel, seven mosques, a maintenance plant, housing for airport staff, and a desalination plant—with all concrete surfaces faced with marble! The three runways will be among the longest in the world.

But the most spectacular feature of the Arabian facility, which may cost as much as eight billion dollars when completed, will be an immense haj (pilgrimage) terminal. This terminal alone will cover 10 million square feet, more space than the two World Trade Center towers in New York combined. Yet the terminal will be open for only one month each year! The facility is designed exclusively to handle the three million Moslems who converge on Jidda during the holy month on their pilgrimage to Mecca, 30 miles away.

Accident-Prone

In the mid-1950s, close to three million Americans were killed or injured each year in automobile accidents—about 570 deaths for every 10 billion miles driven, compared to 14 deaths for every 10 billion airplane miles, 13 deaths for the bus, and just five for the train.

But Americans are far from the world's most reckless drivers. That honor belongs to the Austrians, who in a recent year suffered 386 auto deaths per one million population. That year, drivers in West Germany, Canada, and Australia also suffered more fatal accidents than their American counterparts, with the United States in fourth place with 272 deaths per million persons. The lowest rate among major car-using nations belonged to Mexico, with just 83 deaths per million persons.

One of the most popular Irish songs is *I'll take You Home Again, Kathleen,* but strange to say, this song is not of Gaelic origin. It was written about 1875 in Chicago by an American composer named Thomas Westendorf, and represented the composer's promise to his wife, Kathleen, that he would take her back to visit her old home in Germany.

A piano constructed during the late 19th century contained a number of special-effects keyboards, including a "bassoon" pedal that brought a piece of parchment into contact with the lower strings to produce a buzzing sound reminiscent of the reed instrument; a pedal that activated a triangle and cymbal; and another that beat a drumstick against the underside of the soundboard.

Tulip Fever

In the 1630s, a rage of tulip speculation, called tulipomania, gripped much of Holland, and farmers rich and poor began speculating in the tulip trade. Single bulbs of prized varieties sold for as much as $1,000—one particular bulb for $4,000, a small fortune at the time. Alas, the tulip rage tapered off within a few years, leaving thousands of Dutchmen penniless. The economic scars of the tulipomania were felt in Holland for decades.

Rolling Along

If you live in a warm climate, you may never have enjoyed the thrill of gliding over a glassy strip of ice, Zamboni-smoothed or otherwise. But who hasn't strapped, buckled, and clamped himself into a pair of roller skates, "skate key" dangling from belt or neck? This curious pastime actually originated during the 18th century, when an unknown Hollander strapped crude wooden wheels to his feet—perhaps hoping to keep his skating form well-honed during the iceless months. In 1760, an Englishman named Joseph Merlin placed the first skates on the market in Huy, Belgium. But for many years, roller skating remained too difficult and uncomfortable, and failed to achieve any kind of popularity.

A century later, the easily warped boxwood wheels of early skates gave way to metal wheels with wheel trucks, or frames that hold the axle and wheels. In 1863, an American named James Plimpton devised the first four-wheel skate with a cushioned truck, making roller skating a comfortable, easily-mastered pastime. Three years later, Plimpton opened the first public roller skating rink in the United States, in Newport, Rhode Island, beginning a skating craze that swept America and Europe alike during the end of the century.

The average American woman now buys about five pairs of shoes each year, and the average man, about two pairs—as a rule men's shoes last longer and remain in fashion longer than women's footwear.

Ticker-tape

There were few inventions of the late 19th century that Thomas Edison didn't at least dabble with, and the typewriter was no exception. In fact, Edison constructed the first electric typewriter, which printed letters on a moving roll of paper. Edison's device eventually became the ticker-tape machine.

Paperbacks

Though books with paper covers are age-old, the paperback boom in the United States really began in 1939, when Pocket Books offered its smaller, cheaper books at newsstands and bookstores. By 1946, when Bantam Books was founded, paperbacks still cost but a quarter. Bantam is now the number-one paperback publisher in the United States, accounting for 18 percent of the market, while Dell Books is number two.

The Cardigan

This garment was a knitted woolen jacket worn over a waistcoat and was popularized by the Seventh Earl of Cardigan, who led the famous charge of the Light Brigade at Balaclava in 1854. It was noticed that the Earl was seldom without this jacket so the fashion-conscious folk of the time decided it should bear his name.

Bring Home Mr. Bacon

The technological revolution that has produced our mobile, car-oriented society has taken place almost entirely in the last 70 or 80 years. But the idea of a self-propelled vehicle had been on man's mind for centuries before the first automobile cranked into gear. As long ago as the 13th century, Roger Bacon predicted the use of vehicles propelled by combustion.

Room for a Camera

You may have heard the expression "in camera," meaning "in secret," and chuckled over the image of a meeting or conversation held within the dark, hidden confines of your Kodak or Polaroid. Amusing, perhaps, but *camera* happens to be the Italian word for "room." Well then, how did our picture-taking devices come to be known as "rooms?" Quite simple: *camera obscura*, literally "darkened room," was the term applied to the earliest image-focusing devices of Renaissance days.

Upright and Grand

The upright piano may be smaller, cheaper, and more convenient to transport than the concert grand, but it cannot match the latter instrument in tone quality. With a concert grand, the floor underneath the horizontal strings acts as an additional sounding board, and the raised lid helps project the sound. Also, the concert grand employs gravity in part to return a hammer to place after it strikes the strings, while the hammer of an upright is returned by a spring mechanism. Thus the grand has slightly better action.

Some male spiders strum the strands of their web to attract a mate.

Peripatetic

The British seem to have a penchant for choosing unorthodox ventures. George Meegan has chosen to continue this tradition. On January 26, 1977, he launched on a walking trip across the length of the Americas. Starting from Ushuaia, a town in Tierra del Fuego, at the southernmost tip of South America, he wended his way toward his ultimate goal, the northernmost tip of the Americas in Trudeau Bay, Alaska.

People along the way were very generous in providing the 28-year-old Mr. Meegan with food, shelter and money. He was also offered rides, but turned those down, of course. That would be cheating.

Osculating Star

For out-and-out kissing, nothing will quite equal the play, *Don Juan*, which was performed at Warner's Theater, New York on August 6, 1926. John Barrymore was the star, and in the less than three hours that the play ran, Barrymore kissed various senoritas 191 different times, an average of one kiss every 53 seconds.

Rolling Along...and Along

The biggest speed-skating event in the Netherlands is the *Elfstedentocht*—"Tour of the Eleven Towns"—which has been held annually ever since the 18th century. The route stretches over 124 miles of rivers, lakes, and canals in Friesland, in the northern Netherlands, and is the longest regularly held skating race in the world. In 1954, 26-year-old Jeen van den Berg established the all-time record for the race when he completed the course in seven hours, 35 minutes, besting the previous record by more than an hour!

Speaking of shoe size, the largest pair of shoes ever sold—apart from those specially built for elephantiasis sufferers—were a colossal size 42, built for a Florida giant named Harley Davidson. (Yes, it's the name of a British motorcycle manufacturer.) Let's see—a size 42 equals 39 barleycorns plus 29 for a total length of some 22½ inches!

Bound and Determined

The mistress of French novelist Eugene Sue dictated in her will that a set of Sue's books be bound in her own skin!

Everything Nice

If the value of spices has dropped sharply over the last few centuries, so has our need for them. No longer employed on a large scale for food preservation or medicine, most spices are used today as simple flavorings. Cinnamon, with a warm, sweet flavor, is used mostly in confectionery and baked goods. Much European chocolate contains cinnamon, as do many liqueurs. Mincemeat pie, pumpkin pie, baked apples, and the coffee concoction known as *cappucino* all include cinnamon as an essential ingredient. And without cinnamon, could you hope to bake the grandmother of all American desserts, apple pie?

Methusaleh

We have no idea how old that unfortunate feline was when it lost its ninth life, but on the average, a house cat can be expected to live from eight to twelve years, with one year in a cat's life equivalent to about seven years in a man's life. However, many cats have survived for considerably longer, and life spans of over 20 years are not at all uncommon. The oldest domestic cat on record, a tabby owned by a woman in England, died on November 29, 1939, at the ripe old age of 36 years!

Steaming Ahead

Through much of the 18th century, steam-driven passenger vehicles—both with and without tracks—were in regular operation in England. The early steam engine, however, was found to be impractical on ordinary roads, for it required great engineering skills on the part of the driver. Numerous fatal accidents stiffened resistance to the new machines, and beginning in 1830, Parliament passed a number of laws greatly restricting their use. One such regulation, called the Red Flag Law, stipulated that horseless cars must be preceded by a person on foot with a red flat in hand, or a red lantern at night, to warn of the car's approach. Another law limited the speed of horseless vehicles to a blinding four miles per hour. The limit was not raised until 1896, when English motor club members celebrated with an "emancipation run" from London to Brighton, initiating what was to become an annual event.

Brilliologists are reluctant to estimate the number of umbrellas in use throughout the world, but the country with the highest per capita use of the gamp is definitely England. As late as 1954, 300,000 umbrellas were produced in the British Isles each *month!* Today, most umbrellas are imported from Hong Kong and Japan. During the 50s, the Japanese exported almost 12 million bumbershoots to us within a 12-month period.

Track Star

There are three kinds of electric streetcars. One is drawn by cable; another is powered by an electrified third rail; and the third is powered by overhead transmission lines, with the car connected to the power lines by a collapsible apparatus called the *trolley.*

Strictly speaking, then, only a streetcar powered by overhead lines can be called a "trolley."

There are two varieties of trolley system, one utilizing two overhead wires—the European preference—and the second using one wire and one electrified track to complete the electric circuit. The latter type is the overwhelming favorite of American lines.

Berlin got its first electric tramway in 1881, Budapest in 1897, and Paris in 1901. A gas-powered streetcar was placed in operation in Providence, Rhode Island in 1872, while the first commercially owned electric streetcars in this country plied their course in Baltimore in 1885. The first "soundless, shockless" tracks were laid in New Orleans in 1930.

It is ten times easier, according to statisticians and mathematicians, to shoot a hole-in-one in golf than it is to roll a perfect game of 12 consecutive strikes in bowling. The odds against the golfer are 30,000 to one; the odds against the bowler are 290,000 to one.

Snappy Products

Miniature cameras include a Japanese model called the "Petal," which is just 1.4 inches in diameter and only a half-inch thick. Various cameras used in cardiac surgery and espionage are even smaller. At the other end of the scale, we find a Rolls-Royce camera built in England in 1959, which occupies 2,470 feet and weighs about 30 tons—one of these babies will set you back a clean $240,000! The largest camera of all time, though, was constructed around the turn of the century to photograph railroad equipment, and was itself the size of a railroad boxcar!

In England, Tintern Abbey employed the rising tide of the nearby Severn River to flush out its latrines. At Redburn Abbey, a private latrine for the Abbot was constructed after monks complained that they were "ashamed when they had to go to the necessary in his presence." At the abbey at St. Albans, latrines were positioned over a 25-foot ditch that, hundreds of years later, still contained some of the buckthorn seeds the monks used as a laxative. Also found in the ditch were pieces of cloth torn from old gowns that the monks used for toilet paper.

Spuds and More Spuds

Americans consume literally billions of spuds each year—production usually hovers around 34 billion pounds—with the most well-known varieties hailing from Idaho, Maine, and Long Island.

Smooth Sailing

During the 17th and 18th centuries, skating on metal-faced runners became a very popular pastime in many countries. In France, Marie Antoinette was particularly fond of skating. Samuel Pepys, describing mid-17th-century London, wrote of "people sliding with their skates, which is a very pretty art." The skates he saw were most likely attached with straps to a base made of wood. The blades were frequently curved in front, and shorter than the shoe in back to allow for braking.

Then, during the 19th century, a host of ice skate innovations appeared, most of them designed to attach the skate to the foot more securely. In the United States alone, over 200 patents were granted for improving ice skates. Most important was the work of E.W. Bushnell. In 1850, the Philadelphian designed the first all-metal skate. By the 1870s, Everett Barney of Springfield, Massachusetts, was marketing all-metal skates attached to the shoe with screw clamps. From there, ice skates evolved into the skating boots we're most accustomed to.

Invaluable

As any schoolboy can tell you, it was the desire of Europeans to find a faster, cheaper route to the spice supplies of the Far East that spurred the great explorations of the 15th and 16th centuries. Have you ever wondered why men were eager to undertake those long, dangerous journeys in pursuit of such lightly-regarded items as pepper, ginger, and cinnamon?

The answer is simple: spices were as valuable to contemporary Europeans as the gold so avidly sought by California prospectors a century ago. A shipload of spices could make a man rich for life, and the nation that controlled the spice trade to a great extent controlled the commerce of Europe.

Spices were highly prized at the time not only because of their rarity, but because of their extreme importance in daily life, and the wide variety of uses they served. In the days before refrigeration, spices were needed to preserve food, to disguise poor-tasting, often tainted dishes, and to salvage sour wine. Herbs and spices were also used for embalming, and to make incense, perfume oils, and medicines. In fact, the earliest known treatise on medicine was a 2700 B.C. Chinese work entitled *The Classic Herbal*.

Marvellous Marva

The world's greatest typing buff must certainly be Mrs. Marva Drew of Waterloo, Iowa. Over a six-year span, Marva exercised her skills by typing the numbers one to one million on a manual typewriter—a feat requiring 2,473 pages!

Cry, Baby

Onions can be stored for longer periods of time than any other fresh vegetable. But cooks looking for shortcuts—or protecting their tear ducts—can resort to an array of even longer-lasting onion products, including dehydrated, minced or flaked onions, onion powder, and onion salt.

Private Lives

Today, bidets are prominently displayed in almost all French hotels, and in many hotels in Italy, Greece, and Spain as well, though the device is rearely seen in any but the finest English or American hotels. The Ritz Carlton Hotel in New York was originally equipped with bidets, but the hotel was forced to remove them after a flood of complaints from outraged puritanical guests.

In Kenya, Africa, there exists a strange hotel called *Treetops*. It is built 40 feet above the ground in the branches of a giant tree directly overseeing a salt lick. Every night, the animals from the jungle come to the salt lick to drink, and the guests at the hotel sit on the screened-in porch of Treetops Hotel in easy chairs and watch the proceedings. The hotel accommodates about 20 people. The rates are high, but the sight is memorable.

China a generation ago used some 22,000 tons of opium annually that involved one-quarter of all her people. Today, China is virtually drug free.

Shoe Enough

The average person has literally thousands of shoe styles to choose from today, from the modern machine-stitched leather shoe, or the rubber-soled sneaker, to such ancient favorites as the sandal, the clog, the platform shoe, and the pump. The pump is thought to owe its name to the early use of the shoe for ceremonies of "pomp." Footwear ranges in price from rubber *thongs* selling for less than a dollar to mink-lined golf shoes—with 18-carat gold ornamentation and ruby-tipped gold spikes—selling in England for some $7,000 a pair.

The U.S. Patent Office has on a file a design for boots with pockets—for use by nudists. A bit outlandish? Well, it the shoe fits, wear it!

Bahadur IV was the Maharaja of Mysore from 1895 until his death in 1940. He was an orthodox Hindu, and adhered to all the Hindu rules and laws. He would not eat with a European nor, in fact, would he eat with anyone who came from a meat-eating country. The irony was that Bahadur could not eat with his own chef, for the worthy cook was a Brahmin and therefore of a higher caste than the Maharaja, and was not permitted to engage in any social activities with one from an inferior caste.

Built to Last

The palace at Knossos, Crete, constructed around 1600 B.C., offers the finest surviving example of pre-Roman domestic drainage. Each quarter of the palace was served by a separate drainage network. The ceramic latrine drains were completely separated from water-supply and storm drains, to prevent sewer gases from entering the palace.

If the Romans were not the first to install sewers, they were surely the first to devise a well-maintained sanitation system for a large city—Imperial Rome was the largest city the world had seen up until that time. The Roman sewer system had its humble beginnings in the sixth century B.C., when Tarquinian kings ordered the construction of a ditch to drain the swampy land below the Seven Hills, which later became the Roman Forum and cattle market. The ditch, an open channel lined with masonry, followed the patch of an old stream and emptied into the Tiber.

The ditch was covered by a stone vault early in the Republic, and later enlarged and connected with smaller subsidiary drains. Marcus Agrippa, the first-century engineer and statesman responsible for many of Rome's fountains and aqueducts, personally rode a boat through the giant main to direct its renovation. Though the oldest surviving parts of the *Cloaca Maxima* ditch were constructed during the third century B.C., the sewer continued to serve as a storm drain right into the 20th century!

For the Highbrow

In 1928, Erich Maria Remarque's *All Quiet on the Western Front* became the first book from outside America or England to top the best seller list. F. Scott Fitzgerald never made it to the top of the list, but *The Private Life of Helen of Troy* was the best-seller of 1926.

A number of books have topped the best-seller list for two years in a row. Pearl Buck's *The Good Earth* was number one in 1931 and 1932, Hervey Allen's *Anthony Adverse* in 1933-1934, and Margaret Mitchell's *Gone with the Wind* in 1936-1937. *The Robe*, by Lloyd C. Douglas was number one in 1943, and number two the next year, then became the number one best-seller all over again in 1953, upon the release of a movie version.

Clubbing us to Death

By the late 1940s, the book clubs could list three million members, accounting for about 30 percent of all American book sales.

Boston ranks second in the U.S. in per capita consumption of alcohol. San Francisco is first. One out of 10 in the United States who drink is an alcoholic.

Driving Dutchmen

In 1472, a Frenchman named Robert Valturio described a vehicle combining wind power and a cogwheel system for propulsion.

If, in 1600, you happened to be walking along a Dutch canal, you might have been surprised to see a two-masted ship bearing down on you. Not in the canal—on the road! There was one such ship that was said to have reached a speed of 20 miles per hour while carrying 28 fear-stricken passengers. In his notebooks, Leonardo da Vinci had envisioned some sort of self-propelled vehicle; and some Dutchman, quite naturally, had modeled such a vehicle after a sailing vessel.

Up, Up in the Air

Noticing that smoke always floats upward, in June, 1783, the Montgolfier brothers constructed a bag 30 feet in diameter, held it over a fire until it had inflated with smoke, and watched it rise high into the air above Annonay, France.

As word spread of the Montgolfier's balloon flight, another pair of French brothers, the Roberts, set out to build their own balloon. Not knowing what gas the Montgolfiers had used to fill their balloon, the Roberts chose hydrogen, which had been isolated 17 years earlier. The Roberts' 15-foot balloon was launched into the rainy skies above Paris. It drifted 15 miles before settling down near the village of Gonesse, where frightened peasants attacked the "apparition" with scythes and pitchforks and tore it to pieces.

In September, 1783, the Montgolfiers repeated their earlier balloon success before the court of Louis XVI at Versailles. A crowd that included Benjamin Franklin watched while a sheep, a rooster, and a duck rose into the air in a basket attached to the smoke-filled balloon. When the balloon touched ground, all three creatures were in perfect health. If animals could survive flight, it was reasoned, so could man. But who would be foolhardy enough to be the first man to climb into the balloon basket?

So It Shouldn't Be A Total Loss

During the 1890s, Emporer Menelek II, monarch of Ethiopia, had heard that electric chairs were being used in the United States to execute criminals. It seemed like a good idea to the king, so he ordered three of these electric chairs. But electricity had not yet been introduced into Ethiopia, and the chairs were useless. So Menelek decided to use one of the chairs for his royal throne, and the hot seat was actually employed in this way for many years.

Smooth As Ice

In 1917, the National Hockey League was founded and hockey has been flourishing ever since, on both sides of the Atlantic. In 1948, the game was virtually unknown in the Soviet Union, but it now ranks as one of that nation's most popular sports. In the 1950s, there were but 1,500 hockey players in Sweden, and only one arena with artificial ice. Since then, the number of registered Swedish players has soared to over 160,000.

Incidentally, the Zamboni machine, the mechanical ice surfacer you may have marveled at during a hockey match or ice skating exhibition, was invented during the 1940s by a Californian named Frank J. Zamboni. The machine shaves the surface, scoops up loose snow, washes the ice, and squeezes out excess water in one fell swoop.

Double or Nothing

Incredible as it seems, cars of the Crandic Line between Cedar Rapids and Iowa City in Iowa once claimed top speeds of 110 miles per hour!

Within the city, streetcars were the first motor-driven means of public transportation. Streetcars provided the first dependable intra-city travel in the days before the bus, auto, and subway. Dependable, yes; fast, often not. The first streetcar in this country, in fact, was powered by only a few horsepower—provided by, yes, a few horses!

This horse-drawn conveyance was constructed by John Stephenson in Philadelphia, and placed in service in New York City in 1832 by the New York and Harlem Railway. Called the *John Mason* after a prominent banker who had organized the railroad company, the car seated 30 passengers in three unconnected compartments. It ran between Prince Street and 14th Street in Manhattan, with a later extension to uptown Manhattan. The fare was then a rather steep 12½ cents. No, we don't know what the conductor did for change of a penny if you didn't want a round-trip ticket.

Worth its Weight in Gold

As early as the seventh century B.C., the Assyrians of Mesopotamia were importing dozens of spices from India and Persia, including cinnamon. There are four references to cinnamon in the Bible. The ancient Egyptians used spices for embalming as well as for food flavoring and preservation. Spices were valued so highly in Egypt that many monarchs, including Cleopatra, had supplies placed in their tombs along with jewels and precious metals.

Since Biblical times, caravans laden with spices traveled from India and points east to the Mediterranean. The ancient route brought caravans through Mesopotamia to the Phoenician port of Tyre. After Alexander the Great captured Tyre in the fourth century B.C., the city of Alexandria in Egypt gradually became the center of the space trade in the Mediterranean.

The ancient Romans used a wide variety of spices and imported them in large quantities. Spices were so valuable during Imperial times that a single sack of peppers could pay a man's ransom. In the fifth century, the Visigoth chieftain Alaric accepted 3,000 pounds of peppers as part of a tribute to lift the siege of Rome.

The barbarian invasions of the Empire killed much of the spice trade in Western Europe, but some shipments from the East continued to reach Europe via Constantinople. Throughout the Middle Ages, spices were far too costly for the average person. Some spices were even worth as much as gold and silver. One pound of ginger could buy a sheep; a pound of cloves, seven sheep. Spices were often included in wills, or given as part of a marriage dowry.

King Prajadhipok was ruler of Siam from 1925 until he abdicated in 1937, but Praj was a wary fellow and he had taken out unemployment insurance policies in France and England. After he abdicated he was able to live in considerable style from the income of these policies until his death in 1941.

Positively Negative

The English scientist William Fox Talbot, often called the "real father of photography," began work in 1834 on a photographic process involving a negative and positive print. This process, patented in 1841, had the overwhelming advantage of furnishing a reproducible print, the "negative" from which any number of positive prints could be made. Talbot's *calotypy* produced fixed, reproducible images that were less sharp than Daguerreotypy, but its advantages made it the basis of most of the later experimentation that eventually led to modern photography. By the way, some of Talbot's negatives still exist, and yield excellent prints!

Wrighteous

Wilbur Wright had naively written that the airplane would make war impossible, since air observation could expose an army's movements. In 1911, the Italians demonstrated the use of aircraft equipped with bombs during the Italo-Turkish War in North Africa. Nevertheless, French commander Ferdinand Foch declared that aircraft would never be more than sporting devices. At the beginning of World War I, military aircraft were used almost exclusively for reconnaissance, with pilots carrying no more than an occasional pistol or rifle to fire on enemy reconnaissance.

Shaggy Dog Story

The story of a cat that fell from the Washington Monument and survived has been batted about for years. According to some, the facts are these: during construction of the Monument, workers came across a cat lurking in the framework near the top of the structure. The cat panicked and leaped from the scaffolding. Incredibly enough, the cat survived the 500-foot-plus fall—but, even more amazingly, the stunned creature was pounced upon and killed almost immediately by a wandering dog.

Windmill on a Wagon

About 1700, a Swiss inventor mounted a windmill on a wagon. It was hoped that as the windmill wound up a huge spring, the vehicle would lope along under its own power.

In the early 18th century, another Frenchman designed a machine run by a series of steel springs, similar to a clock movement, but the French Academy had the foresight to declare that a horseless vehicle "would never be able to travel the roads of any city."

Back in 1850

By 1850, the publishing business in the United States was centered in New York, and many of today's publishing giants were already in existence. These firms initially sold their books only at their own stores. Before World War I, however, 90 percent of American books were not sold by stores at all, but by mail order and itinerant book hawkers.

The four fastest growing consumer products in America are air conditioners, television sets, clothes dryers, and boats. During the past 15 years, production of each of these items has increased by more than 400 per cent.

The most massive clock in the world is the Astronomical Clock in Beauvais Cathedral, in France. Constructed between 1865 and 1868, this huge clock measures 40 feet high, 20 feet wide and nine feet deep, and contains 90,000 parts.

Wyoming was admitted as a State to the United States in 1890, despite a good deal of protest in Congress against its constitution, which had the then unheard-of provision which allowed women the right to vote.

It Can't Happen Here, But It Did

It was 1936, and the night was October 27th, when a play by Sinclair Lewis entitled *It Can't Happen Here* opened up simultaneously in 21 theaters spread throughout 18 cities and 14 states. This is a record for simultaneous presentation that has never been equaled.

Paying for Comfort

The latest roller skating mania has been attributed to the new boot skates now on the market, with smoother, wider urethane wheels similar to those used on skateboards. Many skates are now fitted with a rubber toe stop—a skater simply tilts the toe of his skate forward, presses the stop against the ground, and slides to a quick halt. But the new skates will cost you a lot more than the clamp-on skates of yesteryear—from $50 to over $200 for a good pair.

Time Saving Device

Believe it or not, in animated films only three fingers and a thumb are shown on each hand. No one ever notices this discrepancy in detail, but the device saves a lot of money when it is considered how many hands are drawn.

Some historians believe that the true forerunner of football was a Greek game adopted by the Romans some time before the beginning of the Christian era. We don't know much about how the game was played, but its object was probably to drive a ball beyond a line drawn behind the opposing team. Most likely, the game was not played with the foot alone, since the name of the game, *harpastum*, was derived from a Greek work meaning "handball."

Sweet Orchid

Rumor has it that Thomas Jefferson, credited with introducing spaghetti, French fries, and a number of other foods to America, was also the first to use vanilla as a flavoring agent. During the last 200 years, vanilla has become one of the most popular confectionary flavorings in the United States, and is now widely used in candies, baked goods, ice cream, carbonated beverages (cream soda is made from vanilla), sauces, and surprisingly, perfume.

The vanilla plant that the Aztecs harvested is the *Vanilla planifolia*, but another species native to Oceania is called, appropriately enough, *Vanilla tahitensis*. Vanilla is a climbing orchid that attaches itself to trees with aerial rootlets, though the plant does possess ordinary soil roots. The fruit, or pod, is long and thin, measuring from six to 10 inches in length and a half inch in diameter. The pods of the best varieties are, strangely enough, chocolate-colored, and are flecked with a crystalline substance called *givre*, or vanillin, a fragrant chemical secreted by the pod lining that gives vanilla its characteristic flavor. Vanilla is unique among the 20,000-odd species of orchid known throughout the world, for it is the only orchid that produces a commercially useful commodity.

Sight for Sore Eyes

An 11th-century Arab work, *Opticae Thesaurus*, mentioned corrective lenses, but as described, the lenses could not have been suitable for improving vision. It wasn't until the 13th century that some scientists began to deal with vision defects more seriously.

Englishman Roger Bacon was the first to suggest the use of lenses for reading, and the first to describe a practical lens, with a thickness less than its radius. In 1268, Bacon wrote that by holding part of a glass sphere over a page, with the convex side up, a reader could magnify the characters and see them more clearly. He also predicted the use of lenses for microscopes and telescopes, hypothesizing that "from an incredible distance we might read the smallest letters and number of grains of dust and sand ... So also we might cause the sun, moon, and stars in appearance to descend here below."

The next step, naturally, was to move the glass closer to the eye. Historians have been unable to determine the inventor of the first eyeglasses, or the exact date of their appearance, but we do have a number of clues. In 1289, an Italian named Sandro di Popozo wrote: "I am so debilitated by age, that without the glasses known as spectacles, I would no longer be able to read or write. These have recently been invented for the benefit of poor old people whose sight has become weak." So we can conclude that spectacles first appeared shortly before 1289.

On the Road

Surprisingly enough, the death rate per vehicle mile has actually declined here since 1941, due in large part to the proliferation of divided highways. The Interstate Highway System, the largest single construction job ever undertaken by man, will, when complete, include about 42,500 miles of divided highway, accommodating an estimated 25 percent of all United States traffic. The system was 80 percent complete in the mid-70s.

Today, the foot-measuring system used in England is one size different from the American system in both length and width. In metric countries, one size indicates a difference of about two-thirds of a centimeter.

Simple Soccer

Why is soccer so universally popular? Think of the amount of equipment and organization necessary for a simple high school football game—and think of the complex rules. A soccer game, on the other hand, requires little more than a ball, and can be played on a field of almost any size. The play is swift and continuous, involving both individual effort and teamwork—and the rules are simple enough to learn in a minute!

You'd probably guess that soccer is a good deal older than its American cousin, football. In a sense that's true; but, surprisingly, organized soccer competitions played under uniform rules are less than a decade older than football.

The first soccer organization was formed in 1863, and the first intercollegiate football game took place just six years later. (Coincidentally, both football and baseball had beginnings of sorts in the year 1869, when the Cincinnati Red Stockings became the first professional baseball team.) But the origins of football undoubtedly go back to a much older game whose evolution has produced not only soccer and American football, but rugby as well.

What's the Point?

Pointed shoes became the vogue in France, reportedly because of a Count of Anjou who wished to hide his deformed hooves. To assure that the peasantry did not ape the aristocrats, the 12th-century French King Philip Augustus decreed that the points of his subjects' *souliers* should be between six and 12 inches long, depending upon one's station.

But the rush toward outlandishly long shoes went on unabated. Fashionable shoes were soon so long that their toes had to be stuffed to prevent the wearer from constantly tripping over the ends. In the 14th century, the points of shoes grew to such monstrous lengths that some had to be fastened to the wearer's leg just below the knee. The clergy objected vehemently to the fashion, claiming that the long-pointed shoes prevented the faithful from kneeling in church. In many communities, shoe-point length was eventually limited by law to about two inches.

In the 16th century, aristocratic French women began wearing high-heeled shoes so steep that the—er, well-heeled wearer was literally standing on her toes when she wore them. Later, stiltlike wooden platform shoes became the rage in Venice. The heels eventually became so high that women could not walk in them, and servants were hired to help the ladies in and out of their gondolas. The fashion reportedly owed much to the Venetian husband's desire to make sure his wife didn't travel far while he was away—the same concern that motivated the Chinese to bind their women's feet.

Among 16th-century Venetian prostitutes, the vogue for the stiltlike shoes was carried to absurd lengths. Eventually, high heels were proscribed by law, because of the high death rate resulting from ladies of the night tripping and falling to their deaths.

The spruce tree was once used to make chewing gum. It was replaced by the South American chicle tree, which is now being replaced by "gum" made from plastics!

Women as young as six and as old as 62 have become mothers. Men as young as 13 and as old as 100 have become fathers.

The Winner!

The first auto race in America was held on Thanksgiving Day, 1895, over a snowy 55 mile course stretching from Chicago to Waukegan, Illinois. Sponsored by the *Chicago Times-Herald*, the event included about 80 entries. But only six vehicles managed to leave the starting line.

Only two finished—the victorious Duryea, and a rebuilt electric Benz that had to be pushed over a considerable part of the route. The victory of the gasoline-powered Duryea did much to establish the internal-combustion vehicle as the car of the future.

Early Typing

The earliest typewriting machines in America were crude attempts to mechanize the printing of Braille so that the blind could write as well as read. A machine called the "typographer," capable of printing ordinary letters, was patented in 1829. This type was set on a semicircular frame that had to be turned by hand, so that only one letter at a time could be shifted into position and printed. Needless to say, the machine was much slower than writing, as were most early typewriters. And many typewriting machines were as large as a piano, with keyboards resembling black and white ivories!

My Fair Lady

"Carriage pots" were often placed under the seats of carriages for those in too much of a hurry to duck into the bushes. A woman could lift the seat cushion, then sit down on the open board below, and shielded by her wide hoop skirt, relieve herself in broad daylight as her coach rattled through a crowded city street.

Time On My Hands

The first wristwatch was made in Geneva in 1790, but for the most part the "bracelet watch" was unheard of until the 1880s. According to one story, a watchmaker saw a woman suckling a child on a park bench with a watch and chain wrapped around her wrist, and was struck by the logic of wearing a timepiece on the wrist. At first, the idea of a wristwatch was scorned by the English, so the French took the lead in early production.

The hardest of all gems, and the hardest known naturally occurring substance is the diamond, which is chemically pure carbon.
The diamond is 90 times as hard as the next hardest mineral, corundum.

The number of cats extant throughout the world today is anybody's guess. The United States ranks first among ailurophilic nations. There are an estimated 20 to 25 million cats in American households today, but with the inclusion of all alley cats and other strays, the total cat population could well top the 40 million mark, which is the population figure estimated for American dogs. The popularity of cats in this country continues to grow. The cat-care business is now a multimillion-dollar industry, providing cat food and accessories, cat hospitals, kennels, and even kitty cemeteries. Pedigreed cats can sell for upwards of $200.

The precise origin of our word "cat" is uncertain, but similar words designate the feline in many unrelated languages. One Latin word for the feline was *catus*, and the Anglo-Saxons dubbed the creature *catt* or *cat*. In French, we find *chat*, in Italan *gatto*, in Spanish *gato*, and in German *katze*.

The origin of "puss" is unknown, but "kitty" comes from *chaton*, a diminutive of the French *chat*. Since at least 1450, "Tom" has been used to designate a male. A polecat, by the way, is not a cat at all—in the United States, the term designates a skunk.

The earliest occasion upon which any tennis player secured all four of the world's major titles was in 1935, when Frederick Perry, of England, won the French title, the Wimbleton, the U.S. title and the Australian title.

There is no foundation to the popular belief that when an ostrich wishes to hide it buries its head in the sand and imagines that it cannot be seen because it cannot see. The truth is that when an ostrich sticks its head into the sand, it is for the purpose of seeking water, which is frequently found beneath the sand of the desert.

Previous to the resignation of U.S. Vice President Spiro Agnew, the only other Vice President ever to resign his office was John P. Calhoun, who in 1832 gave up the position to become a U.S. Senator.

Probably the youngest pair of parents in history, so far as is known, were two Chinese children, the mother eight years old and the father nine years old, to whom a perfectly normal male child was born on January 8, 1910, in Amoy, China.

Birmingham, England, an inland city, has more miles of canals than Venice.

Scissors Mystique

Scissors managed to find their way into the mythology of the ancient world. The Three Fates of Greek myth were Lachesis, who determined the length of the thread of life; Clotho, who spun the thread; and Atropos, who used shears to snip the thread. And while we're on the subject of legend and superstition, an old belief of Northern Europeans held that the giving of cutlery as a gift would lead to the severing of a friendship—unless the receiver of the gift gave a penny to the donor.

Lobster Without Tears

Soft-hearted cooks have long bemoaned the fact that the preparation of fresh lobster demanded boiling the innocent critter alive. More than one diner has shown a reluctance to partake of a dish that just an hour or so before may have been crawling, quite alive, across the kitchen floor. Modern science and culinary art still have not devised a better method of putting the dinner-to-be to rest. But tests have shown that there is a more humane way to dispose of the lobster—and improve its taste in the bargain.

The tests compared the lobster's reactions to two different methods of cooking. In the first case, the shellfish was plunged alive into boiling water. In the second, it was submerged in cold water that was then slowly brought to a boil. The lobster plunged rudely into boiling water perished within 58 seconds, squeaking and moving about in the pot in apparent pain. But the second lobster remained quite passive as the water heated up, eventually swooning and passing on gracefully—without squeaking. The tests are of interest to the diner as well as the lobster, for lobsters boiled slowly were found to have tenderer, tastier flesh than those put to a speedy death.

Diners with a squeamish bent may refuse to partake of lobsters for another reason: the lobster and related shellfish are, in a manner of speaking, "insects of the sea." Lobsters are arthropods, a group which includes the insects, and crustaceans, a class that also includes shrimps and crabs. Crustaceans, like insects, have a horny exoskeleton, jointed appendages, and segmented bodies. In short, if a lobster a half-inch long were crawling across your wall, you'd probably swat it.

Initially, lobstermen used hooked staffs to snare their prey from the sea bottom. Later, they lowered nets to the sea bottom, raising them every so often to see if a lobster had clambered aboard for the small piece of bait inside the net. Now, lobstermen use pots, called *creels*, baited with dried herring or cod. The lobster slips through a funnel-shaped opening for the bait, but cannot escape through the opening without getting entangled in the net. The lobstermen merely pull up their creels in the morning to count their catch.

The shellfish then end up on dinner plates in a number of different guises. Lobsters may be baked, boiled, or broiled, served au gratin, devilled, creamed, scalloped, or stuffed with crab meat. Lobster meat makes excellent salads, omelets, and croquettes, as well as a creamy soup called lobster bisque. But boiled or broiled lobster served with drawn butter is by far the favorite in the U.S.

Drawn butter, by the way, is not simply melted butter. Melted butter is prepared over a flame, drawn butter melted over hot water. Drawn butter can not burn.

Mastermind

Leonardo da Vinci, in his plan for "Ten New Towns," proposed the use of the *vie sotterane*, or sewer, to carry waste, garbage, and rainwater to nearby rivers. But even in Paris and London, sewer systems as "modern" as the one Leonardo designed in the 15th century were not to appear until the 19th century!

Dollar

The word dollar comes from the German word thal, meaning dale. In the 16th century money was being coined from silver mines in Joachim's Dale in Bohemia. These coins were called Joachim's thaler, which was later shortened to thaler.

Listed in an old French dictionary was a Jacondale which was also called a daler. Today's paper dollar evolved from these coins.

Anticlimax

After Abraham Lincoln was shot by Booth in a Washington, D.C. theater, reformers who looked upon the theater as the abode of Satan launched a campaign to suppress the theater altogether. Meetings were held which demanded the closing of all playhouses in Boston, Cincinnati, Cleveland, Columbus, Pittsburgh, and New York.

Each model of a modern shoe is manufactured in some 150 sizes, with length designated by a number and width by a letter. But a size 10 shoe is not 10 inches long—so where does the number come from? Believe it or not, it stands for 10 barleycorns!

Footsore

Compared to modern footgear, the shoes of earlier centuries were, for the most part, highly uncomfortable. It wasn't until the development of woven stockings in the 17th century that footwear could be made snugfitting and shaped to the foot.

To give you an idea of the crudity of earlier shoes, it wasn't until the invention in 1818 of the left-shoe last and the right-shoe last that the left shoe was constructed differently from the right shoe. Prior to that, either shoe could be worn on either foot with equal discomfort!

Blackmail

Chicago gangsters weren't the first to practice extortion. As early as the 18th century, Scottish Border farmers were being extorted by freebooters. They were forced to pay a fee for protection and the word for tax rent or tribute was *mail*. Black mail was money paid in this manner.

In 1882, a Hungarian patented a piano that employed six keyboards, three tuned a half-tone higher than the other three. Designed to facilitate the fingering of certain chords and arpeggios, this piano enjoyed a brief vogue during the 1890s, when schools teaching the instrument's playing style were established in New York and Berlin.

What's the most popular play among small-town dramatic clubs in the United States? The answer is *Aaron Slick from Punkin Crick*. Since it was first produced in 1919, this play has been staged in more than 25,000 communities and has enjoyed an audience of over 10 million people.

Rapid Transit

Early in this century, it was possible to ride by trolley from New York all the way to Boston for less than four dollars! Of course, there were frequent changes of line.

The longest continuous streetcar route—again with frequent changes of line—ran from Freeport, Illinois to Utica, New York, a distance of over 1,000 miles!

One Colorado line climbed over a 10,000-foot peak to reach the mining boomtown of Cripple Creek.

With even the fastest modern trains rarely exceeding 60 miles per hour, it now seems hard to believe that the normal operating speed of the interurban streetcar line was *80 miles per hour.*

Salutary

The United States is the world's largest producer of salt, turning out about 45 million tons each year. Other large salt-producing nations include the U.S.S.R., China, India, France, West Germany, and the United Kingdom. Annual worldwide production stands at around 160 million tons.

That may seem like a lot of salt for the salt shakers of the world. But the fact is, less than 10 percent of the salt produced in the United States is used in food industries, and only about three percent as table salt. Salt is now produced predominantly for use in the manufacture of major chemicals and household products such as bleaches, glass, soap, cement, paints and dyes, plastics, and water softeners. On the farm, salt is fed to livestock in large blocks. And since salt lowers the melting point of snow, it's often strewn over icy roads to speed up melting.

Singularity

Haven't you ever wondered if the word "scissors" is singular or plural? The dictionary tells us that "scissor" is much less preferred than "scissors," but that the latter word may take either a plural or singular verb. To avoid the question completely, you might opt for "pair of scissors"—for what's one "scissor" without the other? As Charles Dickens wrote in *Martin Chuzzlewit*: We are the two halves of a pair of scissors, when apart, pecksniffs, but together we are something."

In the West, shoes have had a place in marriage ceremonies for many centuries. In some cultures, the bride's father threw his shoes at the newlyweds to signify the transfer of authority from father to husband. In Anglo-Saxon ceremonies, shoes were as indispensable as the wedding ring is today. Instead of exchanging rings with her betrothed, the bride customarily passed her shoes to her husband, who then tapped her on the head with a shoe.

When Time Is of the Essence

More than any other single facet of modern technology, timekeeping devices and the importance we attach to them illustrate the steadily increasing pace of civilized life. Ask anyone in the street for the time today and you're likely to receive a reading from an electronic digital watch down to the exact minute. Yet just a few centuries ago, knowledge of the exact time was thought to be so unimportant that clocks of the day were constructed without hands—the hourly striking of a bell was all the enlightenment anyone thought was necessary. And the idea of a portable clock reading the hour, minute, and second—how preposterous!

Six hundred years ago, the few existing clocks were accurate to within only about an hour per day. Until 1582, even the calendar in use was 10 days out of line with the seasons. In contrast, we now have atomic clocks—utilizing the oscillations of individual cesium atoms for time measurement—that are accurate to within one second every 60,000 years. And, as if that weren't quite sufficient, a time-measuring device installed in the U.S. Naval Research Laboratory in 1964, which utilizes hydrogen masers, is reputedly accurate to within one second per 1,700,000 years!

Over 600,000 people in Calcutta live in the streets. The sidewalks are their homes.

Waste Not, Want Not

American cities were young enough to profit from the 19th-century advances in Europe, and to build sewers continually as they grew. But not all American cities were without sanitation problems. In Chicago, waste carried directly to Lake Michigan had by 1870 sullied the lake up to four miles from shore. During the 1890s, a system of drainage canals was constructed to flush the city's sewers with lake water at the rate of up to 600,000 cubic feet per minute!

Fasten-ating

The earliest fasteners used by man were straight pins, usually simple thorns. Relics of prehistoric man 20,000 years old include bone needles with eyes, and pins with decorated heads. The art of pin making actually predates agriculture, pottery, and metalworking.

The Egyptians didn't use the safety pin or button, but they did fashion straight pins and needles from metal. Bronze pins eight inches long have been found in Egyptian tombs, many with decorated gold heads.

Every period of classical Greece and Rome had its own forms of safety pin and clasp. In fact the forms of each period were so distinctive that a safety pin can frequently be used to accurately date an entire archaeological find. During some periods, safety pin heads commonly took the form of serpents, horses, and lutes; other periods produced heads with abstract designs.

Homer tells us that a dozen safety pins were presented to Penelope, the wife of Odysseus by her suitors, suggesting that the Greeks considered pins fitting gifts, even for royalty. Presumably, almost all early Greeks used safety pins to fasten their tunics, since the button wasn't to arrive from Asia Minor until considerably later.

Athenian women used long, daggerlike pins to fasten their chitons over their shoulders. According to Herodotus, when a group of angry women used the pins to stab to death an Athenian soldier, the city forbade the wearing of all but the Ionian tunic, which did not require pins. The law was later revoked; but by then, women were using buttons as well as safety pins.

The Romans called the safety pin *fibula*, a term still used for a clasp, and also for a certain leg bone. A bust from the late Empire shows a consul wearing a tunic fastened by two safety pins as long as his head, suggesting that in Rome the size of a *fibula* may have indicated rank.

The now-extinct moa bird of New Zealand grew up to twelve feet tall and was flightless.

Pin a Rose on Me

Exactly why the rose came to be a symbol of secrecy is open to speculation. Perhaps the unopened rosebud suggests beauty of truth hidden by the closed petals. In any case, medieval alchemists used the rose as a symbol of the need for secrecy in their art, and as a representation of certain highly guarded scientific principles important in their work. The secret society of the Rosicrucians—from "red cross"—used a cross with a red rose as their symbol.

In medieval England, many families employed a representation of the rose in their coat of arms: the red rose of Lancaster and the white rose of York are two well-known examples. During the 15th century, these two houses fought for control of the English crown in a struggle that came to be known as the War of the Roses.

The rose, has, of course, proved useful in more ways than the symbolic. Rose water was first distilled around the time of the Crusades. When the Moslem leader Saladin retook Jerusalem from the Crusaders, he refused to enter a mosque until all the walls and the objects had been purified with rose water. Over 50 camels were required to transport the aromatic cargo from Baghdad to Jerusalem.

Rose oil, used in perfumes and lotions, likewise originated in the Near East, and did not appear in Europe until 1612. A 17th-century German book lists 33 diseases that supposedly can be cured by rose water or oil.

During the 18th century, rose petals occasionally were included in English salads, and essence of roses was used to flavor ice cream.

The "Kissing Disease" (mononucleosis) although discovered in the 1920's did not become well-known until the 1950's when the chief physician at West Point Military Academy, due to the high incidence of the disease after week-end leave, accurately reported that the disease was spread primarily by prolonged kissing.

Dandies and Swells

Every age has its own foppery flaunted by the dandies and swells of the day. Beau Brummell (1778-1840) may have been the most noted of these. Although he had a penchant for elaborate neckwear, his fastidious appearance actually influenced the aristocracy to appreciate the elegance of simply cut clothes. It is he who led men to abandon breeches for trousers.

On these pages there is a miniature gallery of men who have lavished attention on their personal appearance. Whether you regard these fashion plates as egomaniacs, or as men of advanced taste, there's no denying that they contributed to the vigorous color of their day.

Punch

Mark Twain's Library of Humor

Caruso

Punch

Century

Punch

Punch. 1878

Punch

Mark Twain's Library of Humor

Punch, 1878

Fifty Years of Soviet Art

Drawing by Grandville.
La Vie des Animaux

Leslie's

Harper's

Punch

311

Punch

Fliegende Blätter

Lustige Blätter

Punch

Leslie's

Leslie's

Leslie's

Life

St. Nicholas

St. Nicholas

Harper's

Leslie's

Made in America

To an American sports fan, soccer and football appear so dissimilar that it's hard to believe the games were once virtually identical. And even today, outside the United States, the names for the two sports are identical. The word *football* is used around the world to refer to the game Americans call "soccer." Only in America is the terminology confusing, because only in America is there a difference between the two games.

When it comes to football, America stands alone. Football is the only spectator sport that's played exclusively in the United States. Baseball has spread to Latin America and the Far East; basketball and hockey are played in many countries. The Irish play Gaelic football, but that game is a variation of soccer; Australian football is actually a good deal like rugby; and even Canadian football has some major differences from its American counterpart. Football remains strictly an American sport.

Soccer, relatively unknown in the United States until a decade or so ago, is now the most popular sport in the world. It's played in over 140 nations under uniform rules, and in most countries is either the only or the major professional sport. Soccer matches regularly draw the world's largest sports crowds, and soccer players are among the highest paid of all athletes.

Straitjacket

Hindu plays are subject to many conventions, which are usually strictly followed. The title of a Hindu play is generally composed by linking the name of the hero and the name of the heroine. The hero must appear in every act. The scene must be laid in India. The ending must be happy; tragic incidents are forbidden. And, to make things more difficult, no scene must ever portray eating, drinking, kissing, or sleeping.

The year 1972 was a peak year for marriages in the U.S., with a rate of 11 per thousand population. After that there was a slump for a few years, until 1975 when the rate started rising again until it reach 10.6 per thousand in 1979.

However, or maybe inevitably, the National Center for Health Statistics reports that 1979 was also a record year for divorces, with a rate of 5.4 per thousand population.

The median age of brides and bridegrooms is rising, too. It was 23.4 for brides in 1979, compared to 21.7 in 1970; and the median age for bridegrooms in 1979 was 25.8 in 1979, up from 23.6 in 1970.

Oh, My Stars!

For fidelity to detail, nothing can quite compare to the movie *Caesar and Cleopatra*, which was released in 1947. For example, in the moonlight scene which took place beside the Sphinx, the hundreds of stars in the sky in the year 45 B.C. were replicated in their exact position for this movie. Astronomers made sure of the accuracy.

Subterfuge

There are many animals whose chief defense is good acting. This is true of the opossum of America, and the dingo, a wild dog of Australia. When it is trapped, the dingo will allow its trapper to beat and maul it, and even tear away pieces of its skin. Meanwhile the dog is garnering up its strength and when the trapper lets up, the dingo will jump up and run away.

If shot at when it is hiding in a tree, the opossum will fall to the ground as though it had been hit. It then assumes its classic pose; it will lie limp with its tongue hanging out of its mouth, its eyes open, trying to convince its assailant that it is dead.

Horse Sense

Ever hear of a horse who could read? Well, back in the 1900s a vaudeville act played throughout Europe which was billed as "Hans, the Educated Horse." Promoters asserted that Hans could read. They would set out a mathematical problem on a blackboard, and Hans would tap out the answer with his forefeet. For example, if the problem was how many people do 19 men and 27 women add up to, Hans would tap four times with his left foot, and then six times with his right foot. How did the horse manage to learn mathematics? Well, actually, he didn't. But what he did do was almost as magical. He learned to read signals from his trainer. The signals were so obscure and imperceptible that the system was not discovered for years. The trainer would simply bend his fingers in an imperceptible way to disclose to Hans exactly what his response should be.

Tanned leather has been a favored material for footwear since the Arabs introduced fine leatherwork in Spain in the eighth century. The leather-making trade of the Spanish Arabs was centered around the city of Cordova—to which we owe the origin of the cordovan, a soft, fine-grained leather shoe.

Cutting a Fine Figure

Figure skating was first included in the Olympic Games in 1908. Norwegian Sonja Henie was the most noted figure skater of the period, winning the Norwegian championship at age nine and the world title at age 13. She captured gold medals at the Winter Olympics in 1928, 1932, and 1936, then went to Hollywood to star in close to a dozen movies. Among her other innovations, Sonja was the first woman skater to wear the short skating skirt. Among Americans, Richard Button was the outstanding figure skater of recent times, winning the Olympic gold medal in 1948, and again in 1952.

Step into a modern shoe store and take a look around. High-heeled and platform shoes, boots, sandals, moccasins, wooden-heeled clogs—quite a variety for today's shopper. Recent fashions? Well, not one of the footwear styles you see today is less than 400 years old!

Dragon Fly

Dragon in this case has nothing to do with the mythical, fiery monster. The name alludes to the fact that the insect has large eyes. Dragon is from drakon, a Greek word meaning to look.

Motown

Henry Ford is usually credited with introducing mass-production techniques to automobile manufacture, but Ford actually adapted innovations made earlier by Ransolm E. Olds. Olds was but 30 years old when he designed his first internal-combustion vehicle in 1897. Later, Olds was forced to seek financial help from a friend, who agreed to advance the needed capital if Olds would locate his plant in Detroit, then a city of less than 300,000 people.

By 1902, Olds was turning out 2,500 cars annually with assembly-line techniques, and the "Motor City" was born. Today, the Detroit-Flint corridor in Michigan produces about one-fourth of all American cars.

Pay the Piper

The earliest known indoor plumbing facilities in Europe were found in the palace of Knossos, Crete, which dates from about 2000 B.C. Terra cotta pipes were ingeniously constructed of tapered sections and fitted together, narrow end into wide end, to give the water a shooting motion. One latrine at Knosos with a wooden seat over an earthenware pan evidently had a reservoir and piping for flush water. With a few scattered exceptions, no such sanitary device was to appear in England until the 18th century.

Unseasoned Salt

About 45 percent of the salt mined today comes directly from sea water. But in the United States, the largest supply comes from the evaporation of natural and artificial brines. In an artificial brine, water is pumped into a salt dome and then brought back to the surface, where the water can be evaporated and the salt collected.

The brine is first placed in settling tanks to remove impurities, then fed to a vacuum pan evaporator to eliminate the water. Invented in 1886 by the American Joseph Duncan, the vacuum pan evaporator allows salt producers to turn out the uniformly-sized cubic grains of salt we're likely to see in our salt shakers. Before the vacuum pan, salt was packaged in crystals of varying shapes and sizes.

After the salt is removed from the pans, it's filtered again, dried by heat, and passed through screens to produce grains of the desired size. Chemicals such as magnesium silicate and tricalcium phosphate are then added to table salt to make it free flowing. Since 1924, potassium iodide has also been added to some table salt to assure that Americans living inland receive an adequate suply of iodine, normally supplied by fresh seafood.

Rolling Champs

How fast can a roller skater travel? Surprisingly or not, the official speed record achieved on roller skates is less than half the record speed for an ice skater. In 1963, an Italian named Giuseppe Cantarella averaged almost 26 miles per hour over a 440-yard course, setting an official world's record that may have been broken, unofficially, many times since then. An impressive record was achieved by Pat Barnett, a Londoner who at one time or another held every women's roller skating record from two miles to 201 miles. In 1962, Pat covered close to 21 miles in an hour on a London rink. Alas, Pat's record was topped by Marisa Danesi six years later in West Germany.

Sharp Bloke

The production of scissors and cutlery of all sorts has long been centered in the European cities of Thiers, France, and Solingen, Germany. In England, Sheffield was already noted for its cutlery by the time of Chaucer. All three cities are situated near mountain streams that turn waterwheels to produce the power needed for grinding and sharpening blades.

From earliest times, New England was the center of the cutlery industry in the United States. But the man who was largely responsible for the development of the American cutlery industry, Jacob Wiss, plied his trade instead in Newark, New Jersey. In 1847, Wiss emigrated to the United States from Switzerland and joined the old cutlery firm of Rachus Heinisch. A year later, Wiss founded his own company—with his power initially provided by a dog running on a treadmill!

Wiss and his descendants found a way of utilizing two metal alloys together to produce the sturdiest, longest-lasting scissors. By 1914, Jacob Wiss & Sons was the largest producer of shears in the world. Wiss's firm was also responsible for introducing pinking shears on a national scale—pinking shears have notched blades that produce a saw-toothed cut—and for popularizing scissors whose handle can double as a bottle opener.

Among mammals only men and monkeys are capable of distinguishing colors.

Pure Waste

Today, cities in America, Europe, and increasingly, in the rest of the world, employ two unconnected drainage systems to carry off their waste. Rainwater and street sweepings collected in storm drains are rarely treated, while domestic drainage usually undergoes some kind of purification before it is deposited in a body of water. The job of managing the sewerage is a big one, for 22 billion gallons of waste must be collected nationwide *each day* in the United States—about 100 gallons for each person!

Zippety-Do-Da

The 19th century was the big era for fasteners of all kinds. Buttons are thousands of years old, but it wasn't until 1863 that Louis Hannart invented the *snap*.

And 1896 saw the first patent for a "slide fastener," a device invented five years earlier by Witcomb Judson as a "clasp locker and unlocker for shoes." The term we use today, *zipper*, originally referred only to a boot equipped with a slide fastener.

Judson, a Chicago inventor, became so tired of lacing and unlacing his high boots that he set out to devise a quicker, easier way of fastening them. At first, he peddled his invention door-to-door as the *C-Curity Placket Fastener*, using the slogan "Pull and It's Done." But Judson's zipper, a series of hooks and eyes, was crude by modern standards, and tended to open or stick.

Judson eventually sold his patent rights to Lewis Walker, who, with the aid of a Swede named Gideon Sundback, developed the first modern zipper in 1906. Zippers began to appear on tobacco pouches, mailbags, and galoshes around 1920; but by and large, the garment industry regarded the zipper as a passing fad. At the time, the only garments fitted with zippers were theatrical costumes for quick-change artists.

The 1930s saw the development of an improved zipper, with the metal teeth die cast directly onto the zipper tape fabric. Die cast teeth with rounded edges made the zipper completely dependable for the first time. Soon, everyone was using zippers.

Those of you who are presently struggling with torn, toothless, or unlockable zippers might be interested to know that modern zipper manufacturers claim their products can withstand 200,000 openings and closings without showing signs of wear. Tell it to the marines!

The tallest species of tree in the world is a kind of eucalyptus, or blue-gum, in Australia. Some of these trees attain a height of almost 400 feet.

Take Me for a Ride

In 1908, there were over 500 car companies in the United States, but that year marked the beginning of General Motors' eventual domination of the automobile market. The corporation was largely the work of William Crapo Durant, the millionaire grandson of a Michigan governor. Durant gained control of his first car company, Buick, in 1004, and moved his plant to Flint, Michigan. In 1908, Durant took over the Olds Company. Durant now began to absorb a number of ailing car and accessory companies under the corporate umbrella of General Motors. The Cadillac Company—named for Antoine de la Mothe Cadillac, the founder of Detroit—joined GM in 1909. Durant even approached Ford with an offer to join General Motors, but Henry turned him down.

Reading Matter

Today, the largest publishing companies in America include McGraw-Hill of New York, and Time, Inc., whose net revenues, including publishing, are over a billion dollars annually. But the largest publisher in the world is actually the U.S. Government Printing Office in Washington, D.C., which disperses about 150 million items each year!

A Singapore film censor declared that he used the following rule of thumb to determine whether a picture should be allowed to be shown or should be banned: "If a film gives me a funny feeling, I know it is dirty; but if I feel nothing, I know it is culture."

My Hat's Off To You

The word milliner has an interesting origin. At one time, Milan, Italy governed all Europe in matters concerning taste, dress, and elegance. Hence, a Milaner was a style-setter.

Bedroom Chic

In wealthier homes, the simple bed of the early Middle Ages gradually gave way to a curtain-enclosed bed so large that it formed a room within a room. A canopy, called a *tester*, was suspended over the bed on rods or chains to form the ceiling. Beneath the canopy hung curtains, which completely enclosed the bed, holding in heat. The warm space between the bed and the wall, called the *ruelle*, was sometimes used to receive intimate guests. Bedding now included silk or leather-covered cushions, and velvet, silk, and—ouch!—pearl-studded pillows. By the end of the Middle Ages, bedrooms were roomy and well-lit, with glass windows, fireplaces, and hand-crafted beds and bedding. Gradually, the comforts worked their way down to the common man.

Teutonic Toppers

The Teutonic tribesmen who overran the Roman Empire brought with them round hats edged with fur from the colder regions of Northern Europe. But the hat was still little worn by men and women in the early Middle Ages. Men favored hooded cloaks, while women swaddled their heads in the cloth *wimple* that completely hid their head. The wimple may owe something to the custom of covering a woman's head in church. (The Christian man bares his head in a place of worship, but the Jewish man covers his.)

There are 336 impressions on a golf ball.

Iron Money

Iron money was used for a time in ancient Sparta. According to some accounts, Spartan monarchs cleverly minted coins so large they could barely be carried—to prevent the citizens from leaving the country.

Tilt!

In an age when amusement arcades offer their patrons electronic tennis, basketball, baseball, hockey, auto racing, tank, airplane, or rocket warfare, and an unlimited array of other videoscreen games, an older, simpler pastime still holds center stage in most modern arcades: the venerable pinball machine.

Despite the allure of competing video games, pinball buffs in unprecedented numbers are now feeding coins into their favorite machines for a chance to test their reflexes against a flashing, ringing device that offers neither a cash reward, prize, nor congratulatory acknowledgment. Pinball is, quite simply, man versus machine. And though the machine is almost always the winner, man has been undauntingly accepting the challenge for close to 50 years—with no sign of surrender.

Games in which round objects are propelled into holes or against pegs probably predate written history. But the most immediate precursor of pinball may be the game of *bagatelle*. Popular during the 19th century, bagatelle was played on an oblong slate or cloth-covered board, with players using a cue stick to shoot balls into nine numbered scoring cups. Obviously, bagatelle was much more like billiards than modern pinball.

In 1871, a Cincinnati man named Montague Redgrave pagented a game that might be considered the "missing link" between bagatelle and pinball. Called *Improvements in Bagatelle*, Redgrave's game employed a spring plunger rather than a cue stick to propel the balls onto the playfield, pins to alter a ball's direction, and bells to indicate a high score—all familiar elements of modern pinball. Redgrave's invention spawned many imitators, including the *Log Cabin* of the 1880s, a table-top game with pins that many people mistakenly call the first pinball game. Gradually, bagatelle-type games began to resemble pinball, but it wasn't until the 1920s that games similar to modern pinball really caught on in the United States.

The mayor of Uruguay's second largest city, Paysandu, recently opened a new jail there. Twenty-four hours later he became its first inmate when he was jailed on charges of smuggling in cars from neighboring Argentina.

Nose Cambric

The use of handkerchiefs as love tokens was well established during the Renaissance, perhaps as a continuation of the older European custom of an exchange of handkerchiefs between a betrothed couple. The handkerchief —called *fazzoletto* from the Italian word for "face"—was no mere trinket at the time, but an expensive personal item.

A handkerchief given as a love token plays a most crucial role in Shakespeare's *Othello*. The Moor gave his wife Desdemona a "handkerchief spotted with strawberries" as his "first remembrance."

> *He conjur'd her she should ever keep it,*
> *That she reserves it evermore about her*
> *To kiss and talk to.*

The treacherous Iago managed to obtain the treasured handkerchief and used it to convince Othello that his wife had been unfaithful. To Othello, this was proof positive:

> *To lose't or give't away were such perdition*
> *As nothing else could match.*

The French Monarch Louis XVI can be credited for the uniform shape of today's handkerchiefs. At one time, handkerchiefs came in almost any size and shape—round, square, oval, or whatever. According to one tale, Queen Marie Antoinette told the king she was tired of seeing hankies in all kinds of extravagant shapes. The king quickly decreed that "the length of the handkerchief shall equal the width throughout the kingdom." Since French hanky makers dominated the industry for centuries, Louis's dictum became unwritten law throughout Europe.

The word *corn* is applied to the leading cereal crop of any major region. What we call corn is *maize*. In England, corn means *wheat*; in Scotland and Ireland, it means *oats*.

Whiz Kid!

A record was set on February 28, 1975, when an amateur basketball player named Ted St. Martin sank 1,704 free throws without a miss.

The world's longest bicycle is the bicycle built-for-twenty in England. It measures over thirty-five feet and weighs two tons.

Silly Game

The early 1970s marked a major milestone in golf history: the opening of the 10,000th golf course in the United States. Figuring conservatively at 6,000 yards per course, we can estimate that some 34,100 miles of this country are regularly traversed by some 10 million golfers.

Assuming a figure of eighty yards as the average fairway width, we can conclude than an area of about 1,550 square miles is now devoted solely to swatting a small ball into a four-and-a-quarter-inch hole—a total area larger than the state of Rhode Island!

The oldest musical wind instrument is generally conceded to be the fife. The oldest string instrument is the lyre, or harp. And the oldest percussion instrument is the drum.

Of every 100 Americans today, 63 now claim membership in some church—which is a substantial increase over a century ago, when only about 20 of every 100 Americans were members of a church.

The name "penknife" is a holdover from the days when pens were made of quills. The original penknife was a small knife carried in the pocket for the purpose of making and mending quill pens. It was once customary for each person to cut his own pens as he needed them.

The first woman to become a member of the U.S. Congress was Miss Jeannette Rankin, of Missoula, Montana. In 1916 she was elected representative-at-large from that state to serve in the Sixty-fifth Congress (1917-1919). She was a Republican and served one term.

There are 30 times as many people buried in the earth as there are people now living.

Weight-Worthy

The average household kitty weighs from eight to twelve pounds, but the largest puss on record, a tom from Connecticut, weighed in at a hefty 43 pounds. And the most valuable cat on record is, depending on how you look at it, either a tabby inappropriately named "Mickey" who killed more than 22,000 mice during a 23-year career with an English firm, or a pair of house cats which, in 1963, inherited the entire estate of their ailurophilic owner, a California doctor. The estate was valued at $415,000!

Brrrr!!

The coldest inhabited spot in the world is Oymyakon in Siberia, where the temperature has been known to drop to 95 degrees (F) below zero.

An angry llama will spit in its antagonist's face.

Good Old Times

Imagine a vast network of streetcar lines connecting America's cities, with trolley cars whisking passengers between neighboring towns at speeds of seventy or eighty miles an hour. A prospect for the distant future? No, a fairly accurate description of American interurban travel around the turn of this century. Yes, that's right, we said *trolley cars!*

Today, most people would think of the streetcar as a creature of the big city. True, most American cities have operated trolley systems at one time or another. But before the country was laced with freeways and interstate highways, streetcar travel was the best means of transportation to and from the city, as well as within its boundaries. Trolley lines took salesmen to small towns to peddle their wares, and trolleys brought farmers and housewives into town to shop or deliver goods, and trolleys carried city dwellers to nearby beaches and resorts.

Over a Billion

The McDonald burger has now spread from coast to coast, and through much of Europe and Japan. As of January 9, 1978, there were 4,612 McDonald's stands throughout the world. And, yes, there's a McDonald's in Hamburg!

In the Middle Ages

In the Middle Ages, besides aristocrats, only monks, who used spices to make medicines, could afford them in any quantity. Most commoners who wanted to use spices had to content themselves with onions. Oddly enough, saffron, one of the few affordable spices in medieval times, is now the most expensive spice in the world.

Palettable Camera

The history of photography begins with the camera obscura, a darkened "room"—actually, a darkened box—with a small hole that projected an image of the scene outside onto a sheet of white paper. The earliest attempts at producing a picture-taking device were aimed at aiding the portraitist or landscape painter rather than driving him out of business. For the camera obscura was used chiefly by artists, who sketched the outlines of the projected image and later painted in the colors.

The invention of the camera obscura is usually ascribed to one Giovanni Battista della Porta in 1553, although other men had written of similar devices some 400 years earlier, and Leonardo da Vinci described and sketched a camera obscura early in 1500s. In 1568, Danielo Barbaro fitted a convex lens to the camera obscura aperture for greater sharpness in the projected image, and an Italian named Danti further refined the process by fitting a mirror behind the lens to correct the reversed image. By the beginning of the 18th century, the portable camera obscura was widely used by artists to sketch scenes from nature.

The horse and its cousins, the donkey, the wild ass, and the zebra—have only one toe on each foot—the one corresponding to our middle finger or toe. The side toes are represented only by small split bones.

No fish can live in Great Salt Lake, in Utah. With the exception of the larvae of certain flies, the only living animal found in the lake is a small brine shrimp.

More than 50 per cent of Americans suffer from headaches, with women suffering more than men. Youngsters evidently have more headaches than adults, with 78 per cent of those under the age of 20 suffering from them, while only 28 per cent of those over 60 seem to be afflicted.

James Shields is the only man in American history who has had the distinction of serving as U.S. Senator from three different states. He was born in Ireland in 1806, and emigrated to the United States at an early age. He represented Illinois in the U.S. Senate in 1849-55. He moved to Minnesota in 1855 and represented that state in the Senate from 1858 to 1859. After living for a time in California, he settled in Missouri and served in the Senate from that state in 1879.

The English language contains about 490,000 words, plus another 300,000 technical terms, the most of any language in the world. It is doubtful if any individual uses more than 60,000 words.

More people emigrate from the United Kingdom than from any other country in the world. The country which regularly receives the most immigrants is the United States.

The heaviest brain of all animals today is that of the sperm whale. The brain of one 49 foot long bull, captured in 1949, weighed about 20.24 pounds.

The first transcontinental telephone line in the United States was opened between New York City and San Francisco on January 25, 1915, spanning a distance of 3,400 miles and supported by 130,000 poles.

William "Buffalo Bill" Cody, famous U.S. western pioneer, is credited with having originated the term "Wild West"—applying this to his traveling show of Indians, top marksmen and untamed horses. The term "dude ranch" was also coined by him—and he called himself a "rough rider," the name later applied to Theodore Roosevelt and his cavalry in the Spanish American War.

Frozen Image

The earliest Kodak cameras were preloaded at the factory with film for 100 pictures—each *round* in shape and just two-and-a-half inches in diameter. After the film was completely exposed, the camera itself was returned to the factory, where the film was developed and a new roll inserted in the camera for return to the photographer.

Professionally, the camera was first used for portraiture. While previously only the wealthy could afford a painted portrait, now everyone could, and did, have a good portrait taken by Daguerreotypy or later processes. The long exposure time necessary for an adequate shot in the earliest portrait studies required the photographer to attach a head clamp to the sitter to prevent movement and a blurred image. This clamp did much to produce the rigid, artificial facial expressions typical of most early photo portraiture.

The hottest town in the world is Dallol, Ethiopia, with an average mean temperature of 94 degrees Fahrenheit.

On January 22, 1981 the venerable Académie Française took an unprecedented step. It welcomed the first female Immortal into its august company. The recipient of this momentous honor was Marguerite Yourcenar, author of such works as *Memoirs of Hadrian*.

Carriage Trade

The long distances spices had to be transported to reach Europe during the Middle Ages only partly explains their great expense at the time. Until the 13th century, Arab merchants owned a virtual monopoly on the spice trade, and closely guarded the secrets of where they were obtained.

To justify their high prices, the Arabs maintained that they had brought back their wares from "paradise," or from barbarous lands fraught with danger. Cinnamon, they claimed, grew only in deep glens infested with poisonous snakes. Since few Europeans had visited the Far East, the general public was ready to believe anything.

The "secrets" of the Arab spice trade were exposed when the Crusaders seized the ports used for spice export. The cost of spices fell quickly in Europe, and the demand increased. Gradually, merchants from Genoa, Pisa, and especially Venice, took control of the Mediterranean trade.

At the time, spice supplies were still brought overland by caravan from the East. The main route followed the Euphrates River and ended in Constantinople or the Levant. High custom duties imposed by kingdoms along the route forced many caravans to cross Arabia and the Red Sea and trek through Ethiopia and Italian ports. From there, spices were shipped over the Alps or up the Rhone River to Northern France and Flanders, then on to England.

Wasps are the paper makers of the insect world. They build their nests of wasp paper, which is a mixture of old wood and tough fibers, which the wasps chew to a pulp, using their saliva. Then they form it into masses like felt, a very real paper. It is said that the Chinese invented paper after watching wasps make it.

The unaided human eye, under the best possible viewing conditions, comparing large areas of color in good illumination, and using both eyes, can distinguish 100 million different color shades.

The candidate who ran the greatest number of times for the Presidency of the United States was Norman Thomas, who was the well-known Socialist leader. He made six unsuccessful bids—in 1928, 1932, 1936, 1940, 1944, and 1948.

The loneliest tree in the world is believed to be the one at an oasis in the Tenere Desert, in the Niger Republic, in Northwest Africa. There are no other trees within thirty miles of this tree.

Penguins have been timed to swim under water as fast as 22 miles an hour, which is a respectable flying speed for some birds.

The most children ever born to a human mother, so far as is known, was 69 by the wife of a Russian peasant, Fydor Vassilet, during the last century. In 27 confinements, this woman gave birth to 16 pairs of twins, 7 sets of triplets, and four sets of quadruplets. Most of the children attained their majority. Mrs. Vassilet became so famous that she was presented at the court of the Czar.

The brightest, steady artificial light sources known to man are laser beams, with a luminosity exceeding the sun's 1,500,000 candles per square inch by a factor of well in excess of 1000.

Only two persons in history have received two Nobel Prizes. One was Marie Curie, discoverer of radium—for physics in 1903 and for chemistry in 1911. The other was Dr. Linus Pauling, chemistry winner in 1954 and peace winner in 1962 for his fight against nuclear testing.

The area drained by the Amazon River in South America is so extensive it would cover three-fourths of the United States.

The oldest bridegroom in history, so far as is known, was Ralph Cambridge, who was 105 years old when he married Mrs. Adriana Kapp, age 70, in South Africa in September of 1971.

Cats—Loved and Feared

The domesticated African cat spread from Egypt to Europe, where it interbred with a European wild cat known as *Felis silvestris*, literally "forest cat." The Greeks kept few cats which they used as household mousers. Phoenician traders brought the domesticated cat to Italy long before the days of the Roman Empire, and cats were not uncommon as household pets among aristocratic Romans.

The first record of domesticated cats in Britain dates from around the year 936, when a law was enacted in Wales for their protection. Throughout the Middle Ages, in most countries, cats—especially black cats—were suspected of sorcery, perhaps due to their stealth, independence, and nocturnal habits.

Jeepers! Peepers!

Sunglasses became all the rage in 1939, and again after 1947, when *Business Week* called them a "definite style item," reporting that "Hollywood turned them into a fad." The latest word in sunglasses is a lens that darkens or lightens by itself according to the amount of light available.

As anyone who has ever visited a modern optician's shop knows, eyeglasses now come in an almost infinite variety of shapes, utilizing a wide range of materials. Checked or leopard-spotted frames are on the market, as are glasses with one-way lenses—the wearer can see through them, but to anyone else the lenses are mirrors. Glasses have been designed with peekhole-shaped frames, and equipped with roll-down awnings. Fishermen can now purchase goggles that enable them to see through reflections on water, and music lovers can buy glasses fitted with a tiny transistor radio. And grapefruit eaters will be happy to learn that they can purchase a pair of spectacles fitted with miniature, battery-powered windshield wipers!

Many people believe that eyeglasses, exotic or plain, are made fore the eyes. This, as we all know, is untrue. As Dr. Pangloss points out in Voltaire's *Candide*: "Noses are made for spectacles; therefore we have spectacles."

The foam rubber mattress is the most familiar slumbertime development of the 20th century, but the water bed is probably the most controversial. Some people now maintain that the water bed is unequaled for a slumber par excellence, while others warn that the watery bower leads only to seasickness, cold feet, and the threat of a bedroom deluge.

Can diamonds be made artificially? Yes. Since many gems are composed of common materials, it is only necessary to duplicate the conditions under which nature caused them to be made.

This means duplicating extreme pressure, temperature, and long germinating periods. Diamonds, sapphires, zircons, rubies and emeralds have all been "grown" by subjecting carbonaceous material to pressures of $1^1/_2$ million pounds per square inch, and temperatures over 5,000 degrees.

If people on earth were able to land on and colonize Mars, travel time to reach that planet would be less than one year.

However, the nearest star beyond our solar system, in "outer" space, is Proxima Centauri, more than four light years away. Traveling at a rate of 25,000 m.p.h. it would take a spaceship 75,000 years to reach that destination!

Mandrake is a plant used in ancient times as a medicinal herb. In large doses it supposedly acts as an anaesthetic, and in weaker doses as an aphrodisiac.

Ja, We Like to Read

West Germany, with a population a quarter as large as the United States, has a bookstore for every 10,000 persons, and publishes more books annually than the United States!

How Cool Are You?

True or false: (1) Ice cream will cool you off on a hot summer day; (2) Americans invented the dessert; (3) Since mechanical refrigeration techniques were not developed until late in the 19th century, ice cream is obviously a recent arrival to man's dessert table.

Three answers of TRUE would place you among the majority of Americans, who are ice-cold when it comes to the finer points of ice cream lore. If you answered false to all three of the above statements, you've proved you really have the scoop on man's favorite frosty confection.

First, ice cream is not a cooler. Oh, it may cool your taste buds momentarily, and its psychological effect may convince you that you're cooling off. But ice cream is chock-full of calories, the unit of measurement of heat. So the ultimate effect of a bowlful of ice cream is to make you warmer, not cooler!

Second and third, the frozen dessert goes back to 15th or 16th century Italy and England, and is not a product of Yankee ingenuity.

Slim Comfort

Of all common objects, there is none you're more likely to use on a day to day basis, or take more for granted, than the bed. You might drive your automobile for an hour or two a day; you might watch television for as many as four or five hours daily; but you probably spend about one-third of your life stretched out on a mattress of some kind. Yet we devote a woefully small part of our budget to bedtime comfort. A recent poll disclosed that the average American spends 120 times more money each year on tobacco products than on beds and bedding!

Eight hours of sleep daily may be considered the average, but side by side with the proverb "Early to bed, early to rise, makes a man healthy, wealthy, and wise," we must mention: "Six hours of sleep for a man, seven for a woman, and eight for a fool." Naturally, some people spend a good deal more time in bed than others—for sleeping as well as for sundry pastimes. Noted authors who often worked in bed include Cicero, Horace, Milton, Voltaire, Jonathan Swift, Alexander Pope, Mark Twain, and Marcel Proust. And speaking of bona fide lovers, British writer Max Beerbohm once declared that his ideal of happiness was "a four-poster in a field of poppies."

Considering the length of time man has spent sleeping, the bed, as we know it, is a rather recent development. The first bed in history was a patch of earth where a tired caveman laid himself down to rest. We know little of the sleeping gear of primitive man, since all wooden objects from prehistoric times have vanished—not to mention piles of leaves, grass, moss, or feathers. The simple stone slab beds that do remain cannot be regarded as proof that all primitive peoples slept on stone. The bed as an item of furniture is primarily a Western predilection. Our ancient ancestors probably slept much the way people in India, Africa, and other places still do today, which is to say on a mat, cloth, paper, or, if they're lucky, a rug, on the ground.

Dining

It was Lucretius first, and Beaumont and Fletcher later who observed wisely and symbolically that one man's meat may be another man's poison. Certainly, human beings enjoy preparing and eating a vast variety of foods in an almost unlimited number of cooking styles. What is taboo in one country may be a delicacy in another, and while a gourmet is considered an epicure and a gourmand a glutton, eating is a favorite hobby for both.

Public eateries seem to have been abundant as far back as the early 17th century, when meals were served in taverns, coffee houses, cookshops and chophouses. But the first restaurant as such, called the Champ d'Oiseau, was opened, appropriately, in Paris in 1765.

Dining in or out is an activity enjoyed by people all over the world, and in some societies it is elevated to a cherished rite. Eating at home can be a pleasure, and eating at restaurants can be a wonderful diversion. From time immemorial, artists have drawn people in the act of enjoying food. Some of these artistic efforts are presented on the pages which follow.

Judge

Lustige Blätter

Drawing by Grandville. *Petites Misères*

Judge

Wilhelm Butch Album

Punch

Comic Almanac

Harper's

Bizarre

Drawing by Grandville. *Jérome Paturot*

Bizarre

She-Shanties

Punch

Punch

Triviata

Life

Art of the Book

Punch

Bab Ballads

Ruthless Rhymes

Felicitous Felines

Domesticated house cats fall into two broad groups: short-haired and long-haired. The long-haired variety developed in Persia and Afghanistan, and the two prevalent types of long-haired cats are now called the Persian and the Angora. As a pet, the Persian has replaced the Angora in most Western countries.

The Abyssinian, a beautiful short-haired feline, developed entirely from the African wild cat.

The tailless Manx cat is common in the Far East, where few long-tailed cats are found. The name comes from the Isle of Man, off England, though it is unknown whether the cat was brought there or developed there by mutation.

The Siamese cat, a much favored pet, first reached the United States in 1895 and has flourished ever since. Incidentally, almost all Siamese cats are cross-eyed.

The most expensive of all ordinary fruits to produce and market are bananas, and were it not for large-scale production methods, a banana's cost to the consumer would be prohibitive.

The largest museum in the world is the American Museum of Natural History in New York City. Founded in 1874, it comprises 19 inter-connected buildings with 23 acres of floor space.

The languaged used in more places in the world is English, with an estimated 340 million speakers at latest count. English is spoken by 10 per cent or more of the population in 29 sovereign countries.

The highest surface wind speed recorded in history was 231 miles per hour, recorded in 1934, at Mt. Washington, New Hampshire.

The generally accepted birthstones are the garnet for January, the amethyst for February, the aquamarine for March, the diamond for April, the emerald for May, the pearl for June, the ruby for July, the sardonyx for August, the sapphire for September, the opal for October, the topaz for November and the turquoise for December.

The tallest totem pole in the world is the one in McKinleyville, California. It is 160 feet tall and weighs 57,000 pounds, and was carved from a 500-year-old tree. It was erected in May of 1962.

More than 10,000 marriages in the United States in a year, according to one recent estimate, are now directly traceable to the business-world coffee break...romances which blossom quickly when secretaries meet junior executives around the coffee urn.

A Clear Picture

The 1920s saw the introduction of *miniature* cameras, the light, compact cameras most amateurs and professionals use today to shoot 35-mm. film. Almost all still photography and motion-picture cameras now employ film of the same 35-mm. width, for the miniature camera was originally designed to test 35-mm. motion-picture film. The term *miniature* is now applied only to a camera utilizing film less than 35-mm. wide.

The first successful commercial model of the lightweight modern camera was the Leica, marketed by the German Leitz optical firm. The flash bulb popped onto the photographic scene in 1925—before that, the photographer used burning magnesium or flash powder for added illumination. In the later 1930s, reversal color film became generally available. Improvements in photographic techniques have continued without interruption since then, toward simplification as well as precision.

Pablo Picasso was the most prolific painter of all time. In a career that lasted more than seventy-eight years, he produced about 13,500 paintings or designs, 100,000 prints or engravings, 39,000 book illustrations, and 300 sculptures or ceramics.

More than 50 per cent of all American women who are employed today are married.

Tasteful Pursuits

It was largely the demand for spices—and the great profits that could be made by selling them—that triggered the great discoveries of the 15th-16th centuries. The Portuguese explorer Vasco da Gama was searching for a cheaper, all-water route to the East when he rounded the Cape of Good Hope and sailed to India. In 1503, he returned to Portugal laden with supplies of cinnamon, nutmeg, ginger, pepper, and other spices from ports on the Malabar Coast. And it was Columbus' attempt to find a faster western route to the Far East that led to his discovery of America.

Without cargo ships suitable for ocean travel, the Venetians quickly lost their spice trade. Portuguese merchants soon owned a monopoly on much of Europe's Eastern imports. Then the Dutch, and later the English, began to roam the Eastern seas, seizing many of the lands where the Portuguese had carried on their trade. By the beginning of the 17th century, Portugal had a monopoly on only one spice: cinnamon.

At the time, cinnamon thrived along the Malabar Coast of India, which was still in the hands of the Portuguese. But in the mid-17th century, the Dutch deviously took control of cinnamon commerce, buying the right from Malabar kings to destroy all cinnamon plantations in the area in order to enhance the value of the new Dutch plantations on the island of Ceylon. Thus, when the English seized Ceylon in 1795, they inherited the Dutch monopoly.

The Columbia River, which flows through the State of Washington and British Columbia, Canada, contains a third of the potential water power in America. The largest dam on this river is Grand Coulee Dam, the greatest power-producer in the world.

The record attendance in history for any fair was achieved by Expo '70 in Osaka, Japan, in 1970. More than 65 million people attended this fair.

There really is no concrete proof that shaving causes body hair, on the face or elsewhere, to grow faster, as many people think. It is possible that the skin irritation caused by the shaving creates an increased flow of nourishment to the hair follicles and makes the beard grow stiffer and heavier, but it is doubtful. Shaved beards and cut hair may seem to be coarser because cutting blunts the naturally tapered ends of the hairs.

The Mouse Trap was a play written by Agatha Christie. It was originally titled Three Blind Mice. The Mouse Trap holds the world's record for the longest running play. It made its debut in 1952.

The words of the first Ten Amendments to the U.S. Constitution, known as the Bill of Rights, came from the pen of President James Madison. The Bill of Rights is generally acknowledged to be the finest expression of simple human freedom in the history of the world.

Home, Jeeves

The Rolls-Royce Corporation was founded in 1904 by two Englishmen named—you guessed it, Rolls and Royce.

Apple-Pie Order

When knights were being dressed and equipped for battle, their squires would not rest until their lords were satisfied that they were in "cap-a-pie" order. This was Old French for head to foot and the phrase referred to the fact that they were completely and correctly dressed from head to foot.

Apple pie order is a corruption of this term and describes the state of things when they are correct and in place.

High blood pressure persists in one out of 10 adults and is considered the most common cause of death from heart disease in the U.S. today. Medical men to not know what causes it; nor does it present symptoms. Some 60,000 deaths a year occur from it; many are avoidable. Hypertension, for reasons unknown, is more prevalent among blacks than among other groups.

Know Your Onions

The onion family consists of two main branches, the *dried onion* and the *green onion*. We eat the bulb of the former, and the green top and unformed bulb of the latter. But there are hundreds of individual varieties, for onions grow in the widest range of types among all vegetables.

Waves, during a storm at sea, rarely reach a height of more than 50 feet, although you might not think so if you're on a ship on the open sea. The highest wave ever reported reached 86 feet.

Lightening the Burden

Officer William C. Potts of the Detroit Police Department became tired of the constant traffic tangles experienced in that city and reasoned that if the intersection could be controlled by lights it would give police officers a chance to do more important duties. Traffic lights were introduced in Detroit in 1920. However, the first electric traffic lights in America had been installed in Cleveland, Ohio on August 5, 1914.

Arrowroot

North American Indians were known to use an herb to cleanse wounds incurred in savage inter-tribal wars. A poultice made from the root of this herb had great drawing powers and could lift the poison left in the flesh from arrow heads. Thus, the herb came to be called arrowroot.

In Print

There are now over 4,000 publishers "making many books" in the United States, and some 80,000 stores that sell books of some kind. A list of books currently in print might contain more than 400,000 titles, and in an average month about 3,000 new titles join the list. Some works are printed in editions of a few hundred, others in many thousands—and each year about 40 books will be printed in a million or more copies!

Please Don't Squeeze

The first toilet paper manufactured in the United States, incidentally, was unbleached pearl-colored manilla hemp paper made in 1857 by a New Yorker named Joseph Gayetty. Gayetty's name was watermarked on each sheet. The paper, which sold for 50¢ per 500 sheets, was called "Gayetty's Medicated Paper," and billed as a "perfectly pure article for the toilet and for the prevention of piles."

In the Swim

When Mark Spitz arrived in Munich, West Germany for the 1972 Olympic Games, the whole world was watching him. This dark, handsome, powerfully built young man had already established himself as the most outstanding swimmer of modern times. He had been swimming since early childhood, and set his first U.S. record in 1960 in a 50-yard butterfly competition for nine- and ten-year olds.

Spitz, who lives in Carmichael, California, had won two gold medals at the 1968 Olympic Games in Mexico City, and at various times had broken 28 world freestyle and butterfly records. In 1971 alone, he had won four national and two collegiate championships in the United States, and had set seven world and two U.S. records.

All the spectators at Munich's 9,000-seat Schwimhalle were aware of this record-shattering possibility as Spitz leapt into the pool for his first test, the 200-meter butterfly, on the afternoon of August 28, 1972. Spitz reached the finish line first, beating the world record which he himself had set several weeks before at the U.S. Olympic Trials in Chicago.

A few hours later, as a member of the winning U.S. team in the 400-meter freestyle relay, Spitz won his second gold medal. The next evening, finishing first in the 200-meter freestyle, he won his third.

Spitz won two more medals on September 1:

the 100-meter butterfly, in which he set a new world record, and the 800-meter freestyle relay, in which he anchored the winning U.S. team. On September 3, by winning the 100-meter freestyle, Spitz became the first Olympic athlete ever to garner so many gold medals at one Olympiad.

Finally, on September 4, swimming the butterfly leg for the U.S. team in the 400-meter medley relay, the 22-year old Spitz won his seventh gold medal.

As the winner of 11 medals, Mark Spitz holds the record for the most Olympic medals won. He won two gold medals, a silver and a bronze medal in the 1968 Olympics, and nine gold medals in the 1972 Olympics.

The invention of the alphabet, which is the basis of modern writing, is ascribed to the ancient Phoenicians, who are thought to have taken some of the signs used in hieroglyphics of Egypt and made them into characters which represent the sounds of the voice as we now find them in our alphabet.

A mere seven languages are spoken by half of the human race.

I'll Race Ya

The first automobile race ever held was won by a car that was powered by a steam engine. On June 22, 1894, Paris was bubbling with excitement as 20 horseless carriages lined up for the 80 mile race from Paris to Rouen and back again to the big town. Could these newfangled things run at all? And if they did, would they prove as fleet and durable as a few changes of horses?

Less than five hours later, a De Dion Bouton lumbered down the boulevards of gay Paree. The steamer had covered the distance at the daredevil rate of 17 miles per hour.

Americans undoubtedly consume more carbonated soft drinks than any other people in the world, averaging 30 gallons per person per year at latest count.

Only one former U.S. President has ever become Chief Justice of the Supreme Court. This was William Howard Taft, who was appointed to that post in 1921 by President Warren G. Harding. He resigned in 1930, a few weeks before his death.

The ten most common American surnames are Smith, Johnson, Williams, Brown, Jones, Miller, Davis, Martin, Anderson, and Wilson.

The twelve major languages in the world, (those with the greatest number of speakers) are, in order, Chinese, English, Russian, Spanish, Hindi, Bengali, Arabic, Japanese, German, Portuguese, French, and Italian.

The first solo trans-Atlantic airplane flight was achieved by Charles A. Lindbergh, in May of 1927. His flight of 3,610 miles from New York to Paris lasted 33 hours, and 29 and one-half minutes. The present New York-Paris trans-Atlantic record is 3 hours 19 minutes—established in 1961.

Holstein cattle, the black-and-white dairy cattle, originated in Friesland in the Netherlands. They have been bred for over 2,000 years, which makes them one of the oldest existing breeds.

The highest body temperature a human being is known to have survived is 115.7 degrees Fahrenheit.

The United States takes first place in the average number of letters each person mails during one year. The figure was 445 letters per person in 1978.

The word "Bible" is the Anglicized form of the Greek word, "book." The word "Bible" does not occur in the text of the Holy Scriptures.

Handball is sometimes called the "granddaddy of all ball games." It originated in Ireland during the 10th century and finally found its way to the United States in the late 19th century.

Probably the most prolific classical composer of all time was Wolfgang Mozart (1756-91), of Austria. He wrote 600 operas, operettas, symphonies, pieces of chamber music, masses and litanies, of which only 70 were published before he died at the age of 35. Some of his most famous compositions were written in as few as 18 days.

From Tool to Toy

Amateur photographers were responsible for most of the advances in camera design and photographic processes during the mid-19th century. But in the 1880s, experimental work was largely taken up by photographic equipment companies. In 1884, George Eastman and an associate literally developed the first roll film, greatly simplifying photography for amateur shutterbugs. Four years later, Eastman's company, Eastman Kodak, marketed the first portable roll-film camera, with fixed focus and aperture. Photography was now accessible to everyone, with or without technical expertise—or a darkroom— and amateur photography quickly became a popular pastime in Europe and the United States.

Possibly the first person in American history to sound off about the population explosion was Benjamin Franklin, who observed back in the 1760's that the way the world population was headed, under normal conditions, it was going to double every 25 to 35 years.

According to law, the owner of land on which buried treasure is found has no right to it. It belongs to the finder. Of course, this applies only to coins and valuables, buried or hidden on the land, and not to ore or other natural deposits.

The largest marching band in history was one composed of 1,976 musicians and 54 drill majors, flag bearers and directors who marched two miles down Pennsylvania Avenue, Washington, D.C., in former President Nixon's second Inaugural Parade on January 20, 1973.

Of countries of over 1,000 square miles, one of the most densely populated is the Netherlands, with a population (at latest count) of over 14 million people on 14,103 square miles of land, giving a density of 988.4 people per square mile.

A Cat's an Asset

Even today you find an occasional individual who's convinced the cat has some supernatural powers. As Sir Walter Scott wrote, "Cats are a mysterious kind of folk. There is more passing in their minds than we are aware of."

Today, some ailurophiles entertain the idea that mass cat slaughter during the Middle Ages led directly to the spread of the Black Death, because of the consequent rise in the rat population. Actually, considering the unsanitary conditions of the day, rats, fleas, and the plague would have flourished with or without the intervention of the feline.

The largest prairie area in the world are the Pampas of Argentina, Uruguay, and Paraguay, in South America. Second largest is the Great Prairie in the United States which begins in Central Ohio and extends west some 800 miles.

In his lifetime, John D. Rockefeller (1839-1937) gave away sums totaling $750 million.

Human muscles develop their greatest horsepower between the ages of 20 and 25. After 25, the muscular powers diminish so gradually at first that one is scarcely aware of becoming less strong.

The largest field for any team ball game is that used for playing polo. The average field for this game covers 12.4 acres, or a maximum length of 300 yards and a width of about 200 yards.

Chesapeake Bay produces more sea food—oysters, crabs, clams, and fin-fish—than any other comparable body of water in the world.

The greatest major league baseball hitter of all time was Ty Cobb, of the Detroit Tigers. He had the highest lifetime batting average (.367), made the most base hits (4,191), and scored the most runs (2,244), as well as stealing the most bases (892).

The youngest person ever to accumulate an estate of a million dollars was the child movie actress, Shirley Temple (now Mrs. Charles Black.) She accumulated wealth in excess of a million dollars before she was ten years old.

Pedal Mania

The growth of the American bicycle industry played a large part in the development of both the automobile and the airplane. Almost every mechanical improvement in the early automobile can be traced to the bicycle, including ball bearings, the pneumatic tire, speed transmission, shaft drive, and brakes. Automotive pioneers Charles Duryea, Elwood Haynes, and Alexander Winton were all involved in the bicycle business before turning their sights to the horseless carriage. Wilbur and Orville Wright were bike repairmen in Dayton, Ohio before they made their historic flight at Kitty Hawk.

It wasn't until around 1880, with the introduction of the safety bike, that the two-wheeler began to resemble the modern bicycle in general outline. Invented by Englishman H.J. Lawson, the safety bike reduced the size of the front wheel and set the seat lower over the bar so that the rider could stop his bicycle with his feet when a fall was imminent.

Then, in 1879, came another major development: the chain-driven *Flying Dutchman*. Now the pedals, instead of turning the front wheel, moved a rope that turned a grooved pulley on the rear axle. The *Rover*, an early safety bicycle built by J.K. Starley of England, included chain drive, direct steering, brakes, cushion tires, and a diamond-shaped frame, all features of the modern bicycle. The year 1887 saw the introduction of the curiously named *Psycho*, with a lamp and a bell fitted to the frame. Other bikes with less than inviting names included the *Broncho* and the *Kangaroo*. By 1893, the highwheeler had gone the way of the hobby horse and the velocipede.

The ensuing bicycle craze of the 1890s reached unbelievable heights in both England and the United States. Bicycles of the time were not the utilitarian vehicles they are in many parts of the world today, but sheer playthings. Everyone had to own one.

By 1895, English and American bicycle manufacturers could scarcely keep up with the demand as bike riding became *the* warm-weather pastime. Streets and roads were filled with sporting bikes driven by both sexes. Bicycle cops appeared, on the lookout for "scorchers" who dared to race their bikes on public thoroughfares at speeds of up to 20 miles per hour. "Wolves awheel" jockeyed for position behind female riders for a glimpse of their seated derrieres. Bicycle paths began sprouting up in many cities.

Cy Young, baseball's immortal pitcher, won 511 games in a 21-year career.

On April 6, 1935 the Amateur Athletic Union held a contest in Madison Square Garden. In the foul shooting contest, Harold Levitt started heaving foul shots into the basket at seven o'clock. By midnight, he had dunked 499 consecutive free throws.

Variety Is the Spice of Life

If it is convenient and agreeable to all concerned, Eskimo men in north Greenland and in the Canadian Arctic often trade wives, and Eskimo women trade husbands. This complicates but apparently does not harm their family life.

The trade may last for days, weeks, months, even for years—and sometimes for life. The wife takes all her children to the new home.

Thus, fathers get new families, and mothers and children get new homes. Fortunately, these trades usually work without a hitch and the children get just as much love from their new fathers.

High Hoops

With early baskets, balls that were thrown past the goal often ended up in the stands, where a fan could throw the ball in bounds to the favored team. So, beginning in 1895, a screen was usually placed behind the basket to serve as a rudimentary backboard. Glass was first used as a backboard in 1908, and the now popular fan-shaped backboard was legalized in 1940. Since 1946, most good courts have been fitted with transparent rectangular backboards.

The basket itself has changed a great deal since the early days. Naismith's peach baskets were quickly discarded. Lew Allen of Hartford, Connecticut developed a cylindrical basket of heavy woven wire in 1892, and the following year, the Narragansett Machinery Company of Providence, Rhode Island, marketed the first iron hoop basket. But it seems odd today that early players and basket makers were so slow to see the advantages of a basket with a hole at the bottom. Even the first hoop and basket sets sold by the Narragansett Company were closed-bottomed, and a ladder had to be used to retrieve the ball after each basket. Later, a small hole was cut in the bottom of the basket—not for the ball, but for a pole the referee used to dislodge the ball. Incredibly enough, it wasn't until 1912—20 years after Naismith's rulebook—that open-bottomed baskets were placed into official service on the court.

At first, Naismith had consdered using both the oval rugby ball and the soccer ball before deciding on a round ball. In 1894, the Overman Wheel Company of Chicopee Falls, Massachusetts, a bike manufacturer, marketed the first "basketball," four inches larger in circumference than the soccer ball. In 1948, the circumference of the ball was reduced to 30 inches, and the laceless ball was declared official.

Even the players' dress varied greatly in the early days. Players on one court might opt for knee length football trousers, other players for jersey tights like those worn by wrestlers, still others for short padded pants and knee guards. The latter uniform evolved into modern basketball dress.

The rules of the sport were changed many times during this century to combat early basketball's biggest drawback: the slow pace of the game. Even after the introduction of the open-bottomed basket—and the farewell to the ladder—basketball games were for the most part dragged-out affairs, with the winner rarely scoring over 30 points, and stalling was the major weapon of the team with the lead. The pace was speeded up somewhat in 1932, when a rule was passed allowing a team only 10 seconds to advance the ball past midcourt, and again in 1936, when the three-second rule was put into effect. The following year, the time-consuming jump ball after every basket was eliminated. The 24-second clock was put into use in professional basketball beginning with the 1954-55 season.

The entry of the "big man" in basketball has also necessitated a number of rules changes. Goaltending—interference with the ball on its final arch toward the basket—was declared illegal in 1944. The appearance in 1967 of seven-foot, two-inch Lew Alcindor—later Kareem Abdul-Jabbar—forced the NCAA to outlaw the dunk shot.

The jumping mouse, or kangaroo mouse, which is only slightly larger than the common mouse, can leap distances of up to 12 feet.

West Germany has the highest reported per capita beer consumption, with 47.88 gallons per person in 1978.

Ball vs. Blip

The names of modern pinball machines are no less imaginative than their earlier counterparts. Old machines bore name such as *Wang Poo, Who's Goofy, Stop and Sock, Jiggilo,* and *Hell's Bells.* Newer games include *Cue Tease, Op-Pop-Pop, Rawhide, Hula-Hula,* and *Love Bug.* A list of all machine names, old and new, would include well over 1,500 entries, so only the most dedicated pinballer can claim to have played even half the games now in existence.

Now that most anti-pinball legislation has been removed from the books, the future of pinball looks bright, indeed. A small home pinball machine recently sold 50,000 models in its first week on the market. Manufacturers are now experimenting with games that can be played by two persons at once, games with multi-level playfields, and machines with video back screens.

Speaking of video screens, the first all-electronic video pinball machine was *Spirit of '76,* constructed in 1976 by Micro Games. A pinballer can now battle wits with video pinball machines whose playfields change design every half-minute or so, or after a certain score has been attained. Video pinball games use blips instead of balls, and an entirely different range of sound effects. It's too early to tell whether pinball buffs will take kindly to these games. But the keenest players will likely remain loyal to the older electric games, for body English (twisting one's body to exert slight pressure against the machine in a particular direction), one of the most important elements in a good game of pinball, is completely useless against a video machine.

There is one trend in the pinball industry that is indeed disheartening to players of any ilk. Pinball machines must now compete in many arcades with a complete range of video games, most of which have a shorter playing time than their pinball neighbors. To discourage arcade managers from removing pinball machines in favor of the shorter-playing and therefore more lucrative video games, pinball manufacturers are now turning increasingly to games that offer just three balls per play, rather than the customary five.

Experienced players will undoubtedly cry "tilt!"

Tam-O'-Shanter

The colorful *tam-o'-shanter* with its center tassel became popular in Scotland during the 19th century, and was named after a character in a poem by Robert Burns. It's actually a form of an old Celtic hat. The Scottish *glengarry*, creased lengthwise and ornamented with ribbons in the back, was named after a valley in Scotland. The expression "hold on to your hat" may also have originated in Scotland. In the 18th century, Scottish soldiers were exhorted to keep their hats on in battle so that they would recognize one another.

Thermos Be a Reason

The first "refrigerator" in the United States was invented in 1803 by Thomas Moore of Baltimore, but Moore's machine was really a "thermos" device—two boxes, one inside the other, with insulating material in between. Food stored with ice in the inner box would remain cool for a long time, but not cool enough to inhibit bacterial growth for very long.

The giant step toward successful refrigeration came in 1834, when Jacob Perkins, an American living in England, developed an ice-making machine functioning on the compression principle. Gases subjected to high pressures will remain in the liquid state at temperatures beyond their normal boiling point. Perkins showed that when these compressed liquids were used as refrigerants, they would absorb a great deal of heat before changing to the gaseous state.

Jerry Lewis, the American comedian, actor and director, was born Joseph Levitch. Since 1951 he has raised 100 million dollars for muscular dystrophy.

Dracula has been one of the most intriguing subjects in movie history. These movies were all based on Bram Stoker's 1897 novel called *Dracula*. In this regard the following movies are notable:

Dracula, 1931
Dracula's Daughter, 1936
Son of Dracula, 1943
Return of the Vampire, 1944
House of Dracula, 1945
The House of Frankenstein, 1945
Abbott and Costello Meet Frankenstein, 1948
Blood of Dracula, 1957
The Horror of Dracula, 1957
The Return of Dracula, 1958
The Curse of Dracula, 1959
Brides of Dracula, 1960
Kiss of the Vampire, 1963
Billy the Kid Meets Dracula, 1965
Dracula, Prince of Darkness, 1965
Dracula Has Risen from the Grave, 1968
Taste the Blood of Dracula, 1969
Count Dracula, 1970
Countess Dracula, 1970
Dracula Must Be Destroyed, 1970
Scars of Dracula, 1970
Dracula A.D. 1972, 1971
Dracula is Dead and Well and Living in London, 1972
Blacula, 1972
The Satanic Rites of Dracula, 1973
Dracula Has Risen from the Dead, 1974
Dracula, 1973 (for TV)

Beethoven's Third Symphony was called *The Eroica*. It has been recorded numerous times on discs.

George Gipp, Notre Dame's immortal football player, died at age 25. Knute Rockne, one of the greatest football coaches of all time, is said to have rallied his teams by telling them that the Gipper said "sometime when the boys are up against it and the pressure is really on Notre Dame, tell them to win one for the Gipper."

My *Fair Lady* is a musical adaptation of George Bernard Shaw's play, *Pygmalion*, which was written in 1912. The role of Eliza Doolittle in *My Fair Lady* was played by Julie Andrews. The play was a great hit, and has been revived in 1981.

A curlew can fly non-stop for more than 2000 miles. Most of the flight is over water and the curlew cannot swim.

Renoir, one of the great masters of the Impressionist school of painting was partly disabled by arthritis and gout during the later years of his life, yet never ceased painting. He often could not hold his brushes; they were strapped to his wrist.

Greek and Roman women at times wrapped broad bands of cloth around their bodies in order to make their figures more shapely. During the Middle Ages a short close-fitting lace bodice was worn around the waist, and by the 16th century the bodice was usually made of leather stiffened with whale bone or wooden splints. Fashion in those days demanded the slenderest possible waist. Today, the girdle has replaced the corset, but the objective remains the same.

The Mailman's Oath

"In snow or rain or sleet, the mail must go through," is an expression sometimes heard, in various forms, in compliment to the men and women whose task it is to deliver the mails. Is this a slogan coined recently in homage to the sure, speedy postal service of our modern world? Well, the Greek historian Herodotus used much the same words to describe a contemporary postal system, close to 2,000 years ago!

Herodotus was describing the mounted courier system of the Persians, a network of road stations, each a day's ride from the next. "These men will not be hindered from accomplishing at their best speeds the distance which they have to go," the historian wrote of the couriers, "either by snow or rain, or heat, or by darkness of night." Herodotus' words have been incorporated into the oath taken by a mail carrier in a number of countries, and stand chiseled in stone across the front of the General Post Office building in New York City.

Little Things Mean a Lot

Without nitrogen-fixing bacteria in soil, plant life would be impossible. Bacteria and other microorganisms aid in the digestive processes of most animals, including man, and play a vital part in the manufacture of cheese, the leavening of dough for baking, and the production of alcohol. Bacteria are also responsible for one of man's oldest and most useful culinary substances: vinegar.

The song "Dixie" was composed by Daniel Decatur Emmett in 1859 in a single afternoon for use in a minstrel show on the following day.

The American is not the greatest meat-eater in the world. New Zealand leads all countries with a per capita annual consumption of 224 pounds, followed by Uruguay, Australia, Argentina, and the United States.

All that Goes Up

You may think that at least the fold-up or transparent umbrella is a recent invention. Not true! An enterprising gentleman by the name of Gosselin of Amiens constructed a fold-up "pocket" model with four interjoined steel tubes in 1785! In fact, the construction of the umbrella hasn't changed very much since 1760, when most bumbershoots were already built with eight ribs, a sliding brace, and a curved handle.

The world's oldest gloves, discovered in King Tut's tomb, are over 3,300 years old.

Privy Life

By 1815, water closets were in general use in fashionable English homes. But the poor still had to content themselves with public privies, which were sorely lacking in both quality and quantity—many blocks had but one privy. At night, most people had to make use of the chamber pot, called *jerry pot* in England. The jerry was descended from the medieval *orignal*, a wide-mouthed vase usually kept at the foot of the bed so that those in need might relieve themselves without surrendering the warmth of their blankets.

Nineteenth-century jerries often bore humorous drawings or poems, both inside and outside. Popular thunder-mug ditties included this gem:

Use me well and keep me clean,
and I'll not tell what I have seen.

Spirited Flavors

Tequila is distilled from the sap of an agave plant indigenous to Mexico, not from the mescal cactus, as so many people believe. Flavored spirits like gin, aquavit, and absinthe are produced by redistilling alcohol with a flavoring agent. Juniper is used to flavor gin; caraway seeds to flavor aquavit.

Round, Red and Delicious

Oddly enough, even while the tomato was being widely cultivated and eaten in southern Euorpe, many people in England and northern Europe considered the raw fruit poisonous until the early 19th century, and cultivated the tomato chiefly as a decorative plant. Though the tomato is a New World native, most Americans shied away from the presumably poisonous plant until Robert Gibbon Johnson stood on the steps of the Salem, New Jersey courthouse in 1830, and dared to eat a raw red tomato. Onlookers were horrified, and fully expected Johnson to die before the next morning!

Johnson did not, of course, suffer death by tomato; and by 1860, the plant was accepted by most Americans as versatile, delicious—and safe. By 1900, the tomato was a major farm crop in the United States. Today, tomato production tops the 40-million bushel mark each year. But that's not enough for the American appetite—another three or four million bushels are imported each year from Mexico and Europe.

Snips

The production of scissors and cutlery of all sorts has long been centered in the European cities of Thiers, France, and Stolingen, Germany. In England, Sheffield was already noted for its cutlery by the time of Chaucer. All three cities are situated near mountain streams that turn waterwheels to produce the power needed for grinding and sharpening blades.

A Spud in Time

In the late 17th century, the German monarch Frederick William decided that the potato could solve his nation's food shortage, and he decreed that all peasants should plant spuds. Those who refused, would have their noses and ears cut off. It's unknown how many farmers lost their features because of the bog apple, but Frederick's decree may help explain why potatoes have become so popular in Germany.

Funny Types

There's a musical notation typewriter capable of printing 50 different notes and symbols. And a shorthand typewriter—invented in 1910—that can record up to 200 words per minute. Modern versions of the latter are used today by court stenographers.

And let's not forget the cows. Each year, the females of the *Bos* genus donate some 200 billion quarts of their milk to the world's food supply. We should be thankful indeed that, in the words of Ogden Nash:

The cow is of the bovine ilk;
One end is moo, the other milk.

Concert Grands

The standard concert grand piano is now almost nine feet long, with a compass of seven octaves plus a minor third, although some European pianos have a compass of eight full octaves. Ebony has long been used for the black keys—according to some, it was originally adopted to better show off feminine white hands—but many pianos now use black plastic instead. Concert grands still employ ivory as a covering for their white keys, but most upright pianos substitute a clear plastic. The modern piano, incredibly intricate in construction, contains close to 12,000 individual parts.

A Truer Word...

"Of making many books,
there is no end."

Are those the sentiments of a browser in a modern bookstore? Or a worker at the U.S. Copyright Office, besieged by thousands of new books and manuscripts each year? A librarian? A printer?

No, those words were written thousands of years ago, by the author of the Old Testament Book of Ecclesiastes!

Astronomy has been defined as that branch of science which studies the motions and nature of celestial bodies. Anthropologists claim that astronomy is the oldest of the pure sciences. In many primitive societies the regularity of celestial motions was recognized, and an attempt was made to keep records and predict future events.

As early as the 13th century B.C., the Chinese had a working calendar. The Babylonians, Syrians, and Egyptians were also very active in the field of astronomy. Thales, a Greek philosopher of the 6th century is credited with introducing geometrical ideas into astronomy. About one hundred years later, Pythagoras imaged the universe as a series of concentric spheres. Aristotle, who flourished roughly about 360 B.C., became the absolute authority about astronomy and remained so until late in the Middle Ages. His belief that the earth does not move, but that the sun revolves around the earth was to have a retarding effect on scientific progress. However, Aristotle gave the correct explanation of lunar eclipses, and he also presented a sound argument for the spherical shape of the earth.

Galileo, who lived in the latter part of the 16th century and the beginning of the 17th, made fundamental discoveries in astronomy, and he can be accounted as the single man responsible for the founding of modern scientific astronomy.

Keyboards

There are two basic ways to produce musical tones: with wind or with vibrating strings. Wind was first employed by a keyboard instrument as early as the third century B.C., Ctesibius of Alexandria built a hydraulic pipe organ activated by a keyboard. A keyboard may have been applied to a stringed instrument as early as the 10th century, but the keyboard instruments that led to the invention of the piano did not appear in Europe until four centuries later.

Vive the Potato!

France was the last European nation to accept the potato. A soldier who had spent considerable time in Germany returned to his homeland to convince fellow Frenchmen that the potato was both edible and delicious, despite medical advice that the vegetable was "toxic and the cause of many illnesses."

For the most part, canned foods suffer no loss of nutritive value. Despite popular belief to the contrary, most vitamins are unaffected by long-term presevation. The notion that food should not be stored in open cans in the refrigerator is simply an old wives' tale. Food will spoil no faster in an open can than it will in any other kind of open container, and the occasional discoloration of the can after opening does not affect the food.

Beef is now the third most popular food item in the United States—the average American consumes 89 pounds per year. Among the top dozen most popular home-cooked dishes in the United States, five are beef dishes: roast beef, beef stew, meat loaf, pot roast, and swiss steak. The ground beef patty known as the hamburger is far and away the most popular eating-out dish—the McDonald's Corporation alone sells over four billion hamburgers a year!

The Onion Crop

New York and Texas are the primary suppliers of the American onion crop, which usually stands somewhere around the three-billion-pound mark annually. Europe produces about twice that amount each year. Even without taking into account the mammoth onion production of the Soviet Union, the worldwide figure is usually over 20 billion pounds a year!

Smokers

Despite the Surgeon General's warning—repeated on every pack of American cigarettes—the United States still leads the world in per capita cigarette smoking. In 1973, the average American 15 years of age or older smoked 3,812 cigarettes—that's about a half pack daily for each person, and well over a pack for each smoker. Japan is close behind with 3,270 cigarettes per capita annually, the United Kingdom third with 3,190, and Italy fourth with 2,774. West Germany, Denmark, and Sweden round out the top seven.

Vatican City, the smallest country in the world, has an area of only 0.17 square miles.

The greatest auction ever held was that on September 11, 1969, for some tracts of land in Alaska. The highest single bid was one of $72,777,133 by an American oil company.

Plating Silver

Around 1742, a Sheffield cutler named Thomas Boulsover accidentally discovered the method of plating copper with silver by a process called *fusion*. While repairing a knife, Boulsover noticed that a piece of silver and the copper it was attached to, when heated, fused and could be worked as one metal.

In the manufacture of silver plate by fusion, a metalsmith used ingots of copper alloy and sheets of silver about an eighth of an inch thick. The silver was cut to the size of the ingot's face. Then the two metals were bound together with wire and placed in a furnace until the silver melted slightly, adhering to the copper.

By 1765, silver plate made by the fusion process was virtually indistinguishable from silver. But a century later, the fusion process had been completely replaced by electroplating—the process of coating copper alloys with silver by means of an electric current and a fluid bath.

One, Two, Three

The abacus is an extremely ancient device still widely used in China, Japan, and parts of the Middle East. The most common form today is the Chinese *suan-pan*, or "reckoning board," with seven beads in each column. The columns are divided by a crossbar, with two beads above the bar on each column and five beads below. A bead above the crossbar has the value of five beads below the bar on the same column. Numbers are "entered" on the abacus by sliding them against the crossbar.

The far-right column is the "units" column. Each bead below the crossbar represents one, each bead above the bar represents five. The next column is the "tens." Each bead below the bar represents ten, each bead above the bar represents fifty. The next column is the "hundreds," the next is the "thousands," and so on.

The abacus is basically an adding and subtracting machine. A skilled operator can calculate with an abacus as quickly as an electric adding machine.

Bed and Broad

Elizabethans attach great ceremony to the marriage bed. Often, an entire wedding party accompanied the bride and groom to their bedroom for music, games, and the official blessing of the bed by a cleric. When the bride began to remove her wedding dress, she customarily tossed one of her stockings to the revelers, and the person who caught the garment was supposed to be the next in the room to marry—thus our wedding custom of "tossing the garter."

Speaking of the nuptial bower, the marriage bed of Philip, Duke of Burgundy, and Princess Isabella of Portugal was probably the largest bed of all time, measuring 19 feet by 12½ feet. Constructed in 1430, in Bruges, Belgium, the bed has long since been dismantled. The largest bed still in existence is the Great Bed of Ware, built around 1580 for the Crow Inn in Ware, England. Now on exhibit at the Victoria and Albert Museum in London, this ponderous bed measured about 11 feet square and close to nine feet tall. Compare that with the largest bed now on the market, the nine-by-nine foot Super Size Diplomat, which sells for well over $2,000.

All About Handkerchiefs

The handkerchief displays a split personality: as an ornamental accessory, it may waft the scent of perfume from a lady's hand or purse. As a utilitarian object, it carries less savory connotations. As you might expect, purely functional usage preceded the handerkerchief's entry into the realm of *haute couture*. Yet, among all but the aristocracy, the association of the nose and the hankerchief is a relatively recent development. It took a long time for the handkerchief to become an object of common usage.

The word *kerchief* comes to us from the French *couvrir*, "to cover," and *chef*, "head," since at one time the hanky was used chiefly to cover the head—a use not unknown today. Later, the prefix "hand-" was added, to differentiate the kerchief carried in the hand or pocket from the neckerchief usually worn around the throat.

Primitive man wore woven grass mats over his head for protection from the sun and rain. The mat doubled as a handkerchief to wipe sweat from the face. The head kerchief apparently made its first appearance in China, with silk tissue and paper as the favored materials.

The ancient Greeks and Romans wore simple squares of flax tucked into folds in their robe-like garments. The Romans called their hanky a *sudorium*, from the word *sudor*, "sweat," which leaves little doubt as to its main usage. During the first century B.C., when linen from Egypt was very expensive, the *sudorium* was considered a fashionable luxury. But increases in flax imports lowered the cost of handkerchiefs until they were affordable by all citizens during the later Empire.

The fourth century saw the appearance of the *muscinium*—from the Latin word for "mucous"—whose usage should also be quite evident. During the later years of the Roman Empire, spectators at the gladiatorial arena waved their *sudaria* or *muscinia* to indicate to the Emperor whether they wanted to see a vanquished gladiator spared or slain.

Churchmen were the first to use the handkerchief widely in medieval Europe. Clerical handkerchiefs became part of various Christian rituals. For a time, carrying a hanky was considered a privilege reserved for the clergy.

The handkerchief remained relatively rare right up into the 16th century. We know, for instance, that the 15th-century wife of French king Louix XI had but three handkerchiefs. In those days, hankies were considered valuable enough to be included in wills!

Money is a Five-Letter Word

The English *guinea* comes from the African area where gold for the coin was originally mined. *Franc* is an abbreviated *Francorum Rex*, "King of the Franks." And the word *money* itself is the legacy of the Roman goddess Juno Moneta.

There is an uncirculated Lincoln Penny stamped with a profile reproduction of John F. Kennedy looking at Lincoln. There are many coincidences relating to these two men. Some coincidences are:

Lincoln and Kennedy each have 7 letters in their last names.

Both were slain in the presence of wives.

Both were concerned with civil rights.

Lincoln's secretary Kennedy warned him not to go to the theater.

Kennedy's secretary Lincoln warned him not to go to Dallas.

Both of their successors were named Johnson. Andrew Johnson and Lyndon Johnson—each had 13 letters in their names.

John Wilkes Booth shot Lincoln at the theater and hid in a warehouse.

Lee Harvey Oswald shot Kennedy from a warehouse and hid in a theater.

Lee Harvey Oswald and John Wilkes Booth each have 15 letters in their names

Oswald and Booth were both murdered before trials could be arranged.

On warm days, bees air-condition their hives by fanning the air with their wings.

Hats and Hats

In the 14th century the hat truly became part of fashion. Men of the time wore hats shaped like the fez, or brimmed hats remarkably similar to the top hat. The beaver hat first appeared in Flanders, and spread around Europe. Women's headgear took on fantastic shapes—the tall, conical hat with attached veil, or the "butterfly" headdress with folds of gauze raised above the head on long pins.

In the 16th century, women's hats grew lower, and men's hats regularly took on a brim. But the hat had surely lost some of its association with status; in England, there was a short-lived attempt to force all apprentices to wear wool caps, and in France, an equally abortive effort to force bankrupt merchants to wear a green hat as a warning to prospective customers.

A computer has been defined as a device capable of performing a series of calculations or logical operations without human intervention. Although such devices as the abacus and the desk calculating machine have limited calculating capabilities, the computer is recognized by the number and complexity of operations it can perform, and its ability to store, retrieve, and process data. In the 19th century, British mathematician Charles Babbage designed a mechanical digital device capable of processing information as a modern computer does. In 1930, Vannever Bush built a mechanically operated device called a *Definition Analyzer*. In 1944, Howard Aiken, an American engineer, built an electro-mechanical device. Using thousands of electron tubes, it was the first digital computer.

Ulysses S. Grant's saddle horse was called Egypt.

Doctors

The science—or art—of medicine has existed ever since man existed. True that the earliest doctors were more like witch doctors using incantations and black magic, but more rational scientific approaches were used very early. Surprisingly advanced surgical procedures were used by the ancient Chinese, Hindus, and South American Indians.

The Hippocratic Oath is attributed to Hippocrates, the Greek physician who lived from about 460 to 370 B.C., and who is regarded as the father of medicine. Many modern universities still administer this oath to their medical graduates: "You do solemnly swear, each man by whatever he holds most sacred, that you will be loyal to the profession of medicine and just and generous to its members, that you will lead your lives and practice your art in uprightness and honor; that into whatsoever house you shall enter, it shall be for the good of the sick to the utmost of your power, you holding yourselves far aloof from wrong, from corruption, from the tempting of others to vice; that you will exercise your art solely for the cure of your patients and will give no drug, perform no operation, for a criminal purpose, even if solicited, far less suggest it; that whatsoever you shall see or hear of the lives of men which is not fitting to be spoken, you will keep inviolably secret. These things do you swear. Let each man bow the head in sign of acquiescence. And now, if you will be true to this, your oath, may prosperity and good repute be ever yours; the opposite, if you shall prove yourselves forsworn."

Female Approach

Female Approach

Punch

Drawing by Harold Montiel

Mark Twain's Library of Humor

Lustige Blätter

The High Cost of Clean Living

To say that all Romans enjoyed the benefits of a modern water-supply and drainage system would be far from the truth. While the wealthy brought water through sewer mains to their homes, the poor often had to make do with an inadequate supply of public latrines flushed by waste water from the public baths. For many people, an open window was far more convenient, and the only thing available. Water-supply pipes rarely reached above the ground floor of the poor Romans' *insulae,* or tenements, and most poorer folk had to rely on public fountains. The privileged few, meanwhile, paid fees or bribes to connect their homes with public water mains.

At its peak, the aqueduct system of Rome brought 300 million gallons of fresh water daily to the capital. Compare this figure with that of modern New York. With a population close to eight times that of ancient Rome, New York City brings only five times the amount of water in each day—one-and-a-half billion gallons.

King Size

Henry VIII initiated the vogue for wide-toed shoes in England, presumably to hide his gout-swollen feet. Shoes soon grew to such widths that Parliament passed a law limiting the width of a shoe to six inches.

That European lawmakers have historically taken such an oppressive interest in their subjects' footwear can be partly explained by the way in which fashion was dictated in earlier centuries. To a great extent, the king himself was often the trend-setter; the aristocracy was expected to follow suit; and the peasantry was forbidden to emulate their betters.

Many monarchs opted for shoes that would best veil their physical shortcomings. If the fashion didn't catch on naturally, well, laws could guarantee its implementation. For instance, the custom among men of wearing high-heeled shoes at the court of Louis XIV grew out of the Sun King's desire to mask his diminutive stature

Salt-Free

Once one of the most highly prized materials on earth, salt is now one of the cheapest products available in the supermarket—it costs only about 15¢ per pound. In fact, salt is so cheap and plentiful that the overuse of salt has become a bigger health problem than salt deficiency. The sodium in salt can contribute to high blood pressure and other ailments. Nutritionists have begun to petition the food industry to remove some of the salt now added to almost all prepared foods.

But convincing Americans to forsake salt may be a difficult task. After all, salt cellars will be found on the tables of every restaurant, diner, and coffee shop in the nation. Salt is still one of the very few things that you can get for free!

More than 90,000 vehicles travel some 30 million miles *each week* to deliver U.S. daily newspapers to their readers.

"Bojangles" was the nickname of Luther Bill Robinson, a black tap dancer who was popular in the 1920s and 1930s.

Roller Disco

In 1937, after Fred Astaire and Ginger Rogers danced around on roller skates in the film *Shall We Dance,* roller skating briefly became a fad in the United States. Now, roller skating is again reaching the level of a craze—and so is roller dancing!

Americans are increasingly donning skates for a spin through the park or a trip to the store, and some devotees are even rolling to work. Roller skate dancing, or roller disco, is really taking off. In some cities, rinks are converted into discotheques complete with flashing lights and quadraphonic sound systems. Roller disco clubs have alreay sprung up in New York, with such picturesque names as the Roller Rockers and the Jigaboo Jammers.

Timeservers

Today, about 80 million watches and an equal number of clocks are produced annually throughout the world. The Swiss account for about half of the watch production. The United States, Japan, and the Soviet Union each produce about 35 million clocks and watches a year, with the American figure consisting mostly of clocks, the Japanese mostly of watches.

No one has to be told of the tremendous variety of watches available on the market today—electric, electronic, digital, jeweled, illuminated, waterproof, shockproof, self-winding—you name it. When did they originate? A self-winding watch was made in London as long ago as 1780, but a patent was not secured until 1924. The first hermetically sealed, or waterproof watch was produced by the Rolex Company in 1926—although a completely airtight watch still does not exist. For the clock-watching executive, or the occasional cat-napper, the first watch successfully fitted with an alarm was brought out in France in 1947. Other novelty watches include a device with a braille face and gong for the blind, and complex astrological models that calculate the rising and setting of the sun and moon and the position of the stars.

Tut! Tut! Tut!

From a letter to Mr. Herbert Farjeon from the Lord Chamberlain's office: "It is agreed that mention of the distressing complaint of constipation is hardly one which would affect the morals of the public...Yet it is a very unpleasant thing and calls up very unattractive pictures and, as such, is likely to cause embarrassment to a proportion of the average audience. As the word is, in its context, and spoken by Miss Baddeley, it would give as little offence as it could possibly do, but to allow it once would open the gate to its future use by lesser playwrights, actors and actresses."

The first shoe manufactured in the United States was the handiwork of one Thomas Beard, a *Mayflower* pilgrim, who nailed together the first pair of American shoes in 1628. At that time, the colonists also learned how to make animal-hide moccasins from the Indians, and the moccasins became so popular in the mother country that the colonies began exporting moccasins to England as early as 1650. America's first factory for mechanized shoe production was established in Lynn, Massachusetts in 1760.

Rough Hewn

Most early Egyptian and Greek scissors resembled the Roman *forfex*, which consisted of two blades connected by a curved bowspring handle. There was no pivot screw, and the tool was forged usually from one piece of iron. The scissors were worked by finger pressure against the handle or the blades themselves. A pair of *forfices* from Pompeii with crude iron blades and a bronze spring, along with comments by contemporary authors, suggest that a trip to the Roman *tonsor* for a haircut or shave could indeed be an uncomfortable experience.

Used for clipping wool, trimming plants, and a host of other tasks, as well as for cutting hair and thread, scissors of the Roman type remained in widespread use into the Middle Ages. These primitive shears were still being made as late as the 16th century—and in the Far East, the 19th century.

But pivoted shears, with a pivot pin of some kind connecting the blades, were in occasional use as early as the first century, and perhaps earlier. Most of these ancient shears looked more like a pair of modern pliers than the scissors we're familiar with today. By the fifth century, shears with pivot pins were in common use by the tailors of Seville—and yes, by the barbers too. Steel blades were already replacing iron blades before the end of the Roman Empire, due in part to the metalsmiths of Damascus and their work with hard "Damascus" steel.

An impressive endurance record was established in 1967, when 67-year-old Heinz Arntz played piano continually—except for two hours of sleep daily—for 1,056 hours. Beginning his stint in Germany, Arntz was carried in a van to a seaport, traveled by steamship to the United States, and finished his performance at Roosevelt, Long Island, 44 tuneful days later!

The potato is one of the most versatile vegetables. You can do almost anything to the spud and still it insists on remaining edible. Potatoes can be *home-fried, French-fried, deep-fried, mashed, hash-browned, baked, boiled, oven-roasted,* or *made into chips, sticks, salad,* or *pancakes.* They can be coal-roasted as *mickies,* or powdered into *instant potatoes*—well, you get the idea.

Versatile Vegetable

The French enjoy a dish which they intriguingly named *Ratatouille.* It is usually baked in a casserole, and consists of eggplant, tomatoes, peppers, onions and zucchini.

Today, in many Greek restaurants, one of the leading offerings is a dish called *Mousaka,* made from eggplant, lamb, onions, and spices, prepared with an egg sauce. This venerable dish is reputed to have developed in the early Middle Ages.

Trans Atlantic

The term *crapper,* little used in England, was introduced to the American idiom by GI's returning from World War I who found Thomas Crapper's name emblazoned on many English toilets. To those who remain skeptical, we might point out that the firm of "Thomas Crapper & Co., Merchants of Sanitary Equipment," has achieved four royal warrants and operates "By Appointment to Her Majesty the Queen."

Sterling Silver

Sterling silver is an alloy containing at least 92.5 percent silver, along with 7.5 percent other metals, usually copper. The addition of copper makes the resulting alloy harder and more fusible than pure silver.

The sterling was the name of the English silver penny during the late medieval period. Originally, sterling silver was silver with the same degree of purity as the silver penny. The "pound of sterlings," or 240 silver pennies, was the origin of the English "pound."

The average sterling silver teaspoon contains one ounce of silver.

"Bojangles" was the nickname of Luther Bill Robinson, a black tap dancer who was popular in the 1920s and 1930s.

Faenza Ceramics

Faenza is a city in Italy about 30 miles southeast of Bologna. The pottery made there during the early Renaissance period was considered the highest achievement of the potter's craft in Europe.

Most Faenza pottery was *majolica,* earthenware coated with an opaque tin glaze or enamel as a recipient for painted decoration. The name was first used for pottery imported aboard Majorcan trading ships. Faenza became so predominant in the majolica craft that the name Faenza was adopted in Europe for enamelled earthenware in general, becoming *faience* in France.

The majolica technique was used mostly for wall panels, vases, and large decorative dishes.

Rum is Fermented Cane Sugar

Rum is obtained from fermented sugar cane or molasses, and produced primarily in the Caribbean.

Keyboard Whiz

The longest nonstop typing stint was 162 hours, one minute, set by California high school teacher Robin Heil in 1976. A blind English office worker named Mike Howell holds the duration record for a manual machine: 120¼ hours.

No Sam Necessary

The *player piano* is probably the only musical instrument in history that replaced the musician altogether. Patented in the United States in 1897, after an earlier English model, the player piano employs a spinning roll of perforated paper; the pattern of perforations governs the passage of air acting on a valve, which in turn sets the keys in motion. All the proud owner of a player piano has to do is preset the tempo for a particular piece of music. Some player pianos were self-contained units, while others were attached to a regular piano for automated playing. Though player pianos enjoyed a brief resurgence during the 1960s, they have, by and large, disappeared in the wake of radio and phonographic records.

Limoges China

Limoges owes its dominance in French ceramics production in part to the rich deposits of *kaolin* or china clay found near the city.

Early in the 18th century, a German named Johann Bottger, a suspected alchemist, was imprisoned by the King of Saxony and forced to work on the production of alchemic gold. Instead, Bottger found a way to use kaolin in the manufacture of glazed white porcelain, or "true" porcelain, a Chinese craft that was almost entirely unknown in Europe at the time.

Limoges was renowned for its fine enamel work during the Renaissance period. After the discovery of kaolin deposits in the vicinity early in the 19th century, the manufacture of fine porcelain became the city's chief industry.Today, most major French china makers are located in Limoges.

Salad Dressing

Vinegar can be manufactured from any saccharine, or sugar-containing, substance capable of converting to alcohol. Fruit juices that produce wine can also be used to produce vinegar, as can grains that are used to make beer and whiskey.

Bos Helps Man

The dog may be man's best friend, but from a strictly utilitarian point of view, the most important of man's allies in the animal kingdom is without doubt a group of large, docile creatures known collectively as cattle. The single genus to which these animals belong, *Bos*, provides man with his number-one draught animal, supplies half his meat, 95 percent of his milk, and 80 percent of his leather. Civilization as we know it today might not exist without domesticated bovines.

Canning

ODE ON AN EMPTY TIN CAN

> *Consider this dismal tin can:*
> *Once contained a mess of good fare,*
> *It may have held prunes, or soup, or fried loons;*
> *But now its insides are bare.*

This bathetic lament could serve as a paen to one of the more ubiquitous products of technology—the tin can. There is now scarcely a person on earth who has not eaten canned food at one time or another. Despite the advent of frozen foods, there is litle chance that the use of canned foods will decrease in the future.

The explanation should be obvious. Frozen foods require continual refrigeration. Canned foods require no upkeep, and unlike frozen foods, will remain edible almost indefinitely. Incredibly, a recently discovered tin of rations dating from the Civil War was fed to a dog, and the pooch found the century-old victuals quite delicious!

The newest island in the world is Surtsea, belonging to and southwest of Iceland, which arose from the sea on November 15, 1963, and is now 590 feet high and almost a square mile in area.

The loudest voices in the animal kingdom, according to the consensus, are possessed, in order of volume, by the lion, the elk, the sea lion, the wolf and the elephant.

The Great Pyramid at Gizeh, Egypt, embodies extraordinary architectural skills. So accurately were the facing stones cut and fitted, for example, that a sheet of paper can scarcely be inserted in the joints between. The southeast corner stands only a half inch higher than the northwest corner, and the difference between the longest and shortest side is less than eight inches, a discrepancy of less than 0.09 per cent.

The most extensive and oldest underground railway system in the world is that of London, England, with 257 miles of track. This subway was opened in January of 1863.

The zebra has at one time or another been broken to harness as a stunt or for show purposes, but it does not have the stamina or temperament of a good draft animal like the horse.

What Price Flavor?

Spanish saffron is presently the world's most expensive spice, selling in England for as much as $780 per pound. About 32,000 saffron flowers are required to produce just one pound of the powder.

At the other end of the scale, Portuguese rosemary and Canadian mustard are the cheapest spices available today, selling for as little as seven or eight cents a pound in the United States.

Fast Flash

While the earliest Daguerreotypes required exposure times of close to an hour, exposure times of a mere 1/25th or 1/250th of a second are now the most common. The Imacon 600, a camera made in England for use in physics research, can take 600 pictures per second. Movie cameras have reached speeds of 11 million pictures per second. If such a camera were used to photograph a bullet traveling at the speed of 1,900 miles per hour, three minutes of normal-speed projection would be required to show just one foot of the bullet's travel.

The nickname "Limey" was applied to a British sailor some 200 years ago, and sprang from the fact that at that time the Admiralty ordered a regular ration of lime juice to prevent outbursts of scurvy.

Streetcar Chic

Interurban streetcar lines operated with heavy, individually powered cars, quite unlike the lighter, locomotive-drawn railroad cars. Trolleys ran more frequently than mainline trains, and they usually served areas inaccessible by railroad. It was common, too, for a streetcar company to construct an amusement park in an otherwise inaccessible suburban area along its trolley line in order to increase weekend and night travel on the line.

The first interurban streetcar line in the United States connected the cities of Granville and Newark, Ohio, beginning in 1889, and the first high-speed interurban trolleys ran between Cleveland and Akron in 1895. Within a few decades, many of America's cities, large and small, were linked by streetcar lines, especially in Ohio, Indiana, Illinois, and Michigan. No burgeoning town was considered major league until it was connected by a streetcar line with at least one neighboring city.

The pharmaceutical field claims to have seen the most rapid rate of product obsolescence. During the past fifteen years or so, a new drug product has been brought out on the average of one a day, but most of these new product discoveries have had the effect only of making an old product obsolete.

The first woman member of a U.S. Presidential Cabinet was Frances Perkins, who was appointed Secretary of Labor by President Franklin D. Roosevelt in 1933.

The largest known pearl, "The Hope Pearl," weighs three ounces and is about two inches long and four inches in circumference.

Sausage trees in Florida resemble outdoor delicatessens, with long sausage-like fruits hanging from the branches.

Cats of Yore

Dogs and cats are far and away the most popular pets in the world today. But the dog has been a friend of man for much longer than the cat, having been domesticated some 50,000 years ago. On the other hand, the cat was not tamed to any extent until just 5,000 years ago. Yet the dog, as we know it today, is in evolutionary terms a rather recent development. The cat family, on the other hand, evolved into its present form some seven million years ago, long before most surviving mammals. During the intervening ages, it has undergone little changes.

Over the ages, the feline species spread to all parts of the earth, with the exception of Australia and a few islands. The original ancestors of the cat evolved into two general families. One family, called the *Hoplophoneus*, included the Smiladon, or saber-toothed tiger, and other extinct animals. The second group, the *Dinictis*, produced all our modern cats.

Triple Base Hit

How would you like to go into the delivery room expecting to give birth to twins and end up with triplets? Apparently this is not so rare an occurrence. Donald Keith, the executive director of the Center for the Study of Multiple Birth at Northwestern University Medical School, reports that in about 50 percent of the cases multiple births are not diagnosed until about two weeks before delivery, and in some cases not until the woman is actually giving birth.

The National Organization of Mothers of Twins Clubs estimates that one of 90 American births produces twins, and one in 9,300 produces triplets.

The expression, "baker's dozen," originated with King Henry VII, of England. He ordered bakers who sold underweight loaves to be beheaded and so, in order to save their necks, bakers began the practice of adding an extra loaf to each order of twelve loaves, just to be sure.

The most common minimum legal marrying age in the U.S. is 21 years for men and 18 for women—or 18 and 16 with parental approval. However, the bride can be as young as 12 in one state and 14 in four states, while the bridegroom can be as young as 14 in one state and 15 in one state, and 16 in ten states.

Very few people are able to speak articulately at a sustained speed of above 300 words per minute. Generally conceded to have been the fastest broadcaster was Jerry Wilmot, the Canadian ice-hockey commentator in the post-World War II period. A broadcaster for the British Broadcasting Corporation, Raymond Glendenning, once spoke 176 words in 30 seconds while commenting on a greyhound race.

Chinese Mail

By 1000 B.C., the Chinese had established an imperial postal system that included the use of homing pigeons. Confucius, like Job, used the post as a symbol for speed, declaring that "the influence of righteousness travels faster than royal orders by stage and couriers." After his journey to the East in the 13th cntury, Marco Polo declared the Chinese postal system superior to any in Europe, describing a network of 10,000 courier stations and a force of 300,000 post horses.

The Venetian traveler claimed that Chinese foot couriers running between stations three miles apart carried most of the mail. Urgent messages were carried by men on horseback, traveling up to 250 miles a day. Chinese foot couriers ran with bell-studded belts so that couriers waiting at the next station would be warned of their approach. At night, they carried torches. In return for their services, the couriers were exempted from taxation, and were presented with a badge that allowed them to requisition any horse needed for mail delivery. In China as well as Japan, the postal system was restricted to government use for many centuries, with private companies serving the public until the postal systems of both nations were modernized around the beginning of this century.

The 1500-pound leatherback turtle carries a shell as big as a king-sized bed.

Shears or Scissors?

Have you ever wondered what the precise difference is between "scissors" and "shears"? The use of the two words is fairly arbitrary. Generally, the former is used for a pair of blades less than six inches in length, with usually two small matching finger holes in the handle. "Shears" is generally applied to a tool longer than six inches, with one small hol in the handle for the thumb and one larger hole for a finger.

All Kinds of Cocktails

The names of certain popular cocktails are obvious; others, lost in history. The *Rickey*, for example, is said to be named after a certain Colonel Rickey. The word *Julep* comes from the Arabic *julab*. The *Black Russian* is named for its primary ingredient, vodka. (It's not black, but it's certainly Russian.) The *Grasshopper*, consisting of green creme de menthe, with creme de cacao, and cream, owes its name to its green color. The *Martini*, *Tom Collins*, and *Alexander* are named after individuals. The origins of the *Fizz*, *Sour*, and *Stinger* shouldn't be hard to imagine. As for the *Zombie*, you won't need three guesses—the talk is that three Zombies will turn you into one.

But the names of modern cocktails are certainly not lacking in color. Witness the *Red Devil*, *Sitz Mark*, *Bourbon Fog*, *Hurricane*, *Barbed Wire Fence*, *Rhett Butler*, *Cable Car*, *Sombrero*, *Tequila Sunrise*, *Pink Lady*, *Pink Elephant*, *Godfather*, *Harvey Wallbanger*, and a warm wine-and-brandy concoction billed as the *Instant Cold Cure*.

Among the less exotic—and more popular—cocktails we find the *Old Fashioned*, a mixture of whiskey, sugar, bitters, and club soda. The *Screwdriver* combines vodka and orange juice; the *Bloody Mary*, vodka and tomato juice. A *Daquiri* includes rum, lime juice, and sugar. A *Mint Julep* usually includes bourbon, mint leaves, sugar, and water. A *Margarita* combines tequila, salt, lime juice, and Triple Sec. A *Manhattan* is made with whiskey, vermouth, and bitters. And the ever popular *Martini* includes gin, a dash of vermouth, and an olive.

French Fries

More than one American tourist has been known to ask his confused French waiter for *French fries*. The French actually call them *pommes frites*—and the French word for potato is *pomme de terre*, literally "earth apple."

No Privacy

By the fourth century, many private homes in Rome were equipped with flush toilets. Stone reservoirs stored flush water, and drains connected the latrines to outdoor sewers. Some homes found in ruined Pompeii were equipped with as many as 30 water taps. But most of the less fortunate Romans had to contend themselves with public latrines, of which there were never more than 144 in the presumably odoriferous capital.

Fast Typing

What's the fastest typing speed ever recorded? The top speed ever achieved by a typist, 216 words per minute, stands as the record, set by one Stella Pajunas in 1946 on an IBM electric. To give you an idea of her accomplishment, 60 words per minute is considered good professional speed. The record for top speed for over an hour of nonstop typing is 149 words per minute, also set on an IBM machine.

Young, growing spiders can regenerate missing legs and parts of legs.

Domesticated house cats fall into two broad groups: short-haired and long-haired. The long-haired variety developed in Persia and Afghanistan, and the two prevalent types of long-haired cat are now called the Persian and the Angora. As a pet, the Persian has replaced the Angora in most Western countries.

The Abyssinian, a beautiful short-haired feline, developed entirely from the African wild cat.

The tailless Manx cat is common in the Far East, where few long-tailed cats are found. The name comes from the Isle of Man off England, though it is unknown whether the cat was brought there or developed there by mutation.

The Siamese cat, a much favored pet, first reached the United States in 1895 and has flourished ever since. Incidentally, almost all Siamese cats are cross-eyed.

The Book Club

The book club—a German idea—first appeared in America in 1926, with the Book-of-the-Month Club and the Literary Guild. By the way, the first work offered by the Book-of-the-Month Club was *Lolly Willowes, or the Loving Huntsman*, by Sylvia Townsend Warner. By the late 1940s, the book clubs of America could list three million members, accounting for about 30 percent of all American book sales.

The English Umbrella

The man usually credited with popularizing the umbrella in London was one John Hanway, a 17th-century traveler who brought the brolly to England from Portugal. Hanway created quite a stir by strolling through London under the strange contraption. He perambulated about in all kinds of weather, and was often greeted by jokes from passersby. He was likely to suffer abuse from coachmen, who feared the popularity of such a device would cut into their trade.

A sneeze is an involuntary, violent expiration of air through the nose and mouth. It results from stimulation of the nervous system in the nose, causing sudden contraction of the muscles of expiration. Sneezing can be caused by an inflammation of the nose tissues, or by irritating substances such as snuff and dust.

Take it or Leave it

When you're given Hobson's choice it means you really have no options at all—you take what you offered, or nothing at all.

Here's how it came about: Thomas Hobson, who lived from 1544 to 1631, was the proud owner of livery stables in Cambridge, England. He took great care of his animals and was determined that each horse should be used in turn. Thus, anyone wanting to hire a horse was obliged to take the next in line—or none at all.

The most popular beef breeds in the world are the *Shorthorn* and the *Hereford*. Both were originally developed in the British Isles, and are favored for their hardiness and rapid maturation. Henry Clay is credited with introducing the first Herefords to the United States, in 1817. The Hereford is generally the heaviest of all breeds: a cow may weigh up to 1,700 pounds, and a bull may weigh a ton. The largest bull on record, in fact, was an American-raised Hereford-Shorthorn that tipped the scales at a prodigious 4,720 pounds!

The mixed drink is a recent invention. In the past, not only wine and beer, but hard liquor, too, was usually drunk straight, or at most, diluted with water. As for tomato juice, tonic water, ginger ale, club soda, orange juice, and other mixers, few of these had yet made the trip from the grocery store to the barroom as recently as 200 years ago.

Alcohol itself, of course, has been with us since well before recorded history began. Alcohol still ranks as the oldest and most widely used drug on earth. Primitive man probably discovered the first alcoholic drinks by accident, since any sugar-containing mish-mash left exposed to warm air will eventually ferment. Alcohol was used by prehistoric man primarily in conjunction with war, religious worship, and various rites of passage—baths, marriages, funerals, and feasts.

Recently, the art of walking, and even running, have been extolled as healthful activities. But man never really thought much of his own two legs as a primary means of locomotion. The slogan "Don't walk if you can ride" has an old history.

The ancient Sumerians fashioned simple wagons using two stone discs as wheels as far back as 3000 B.C. The Egyptians and Greeks kept improving on these carts and created magnificent chariots. After the 12th century four-wheeled carriages came into use and were the chief means of transportation until railroads were built in the 19th century.

Today, given a choice of car, train, or plane, you might still enjoy a nostalgic look at some of the vehicles of old depicted here.

In a Pickle

Oddly enough, vinegar is both a product of bacterial life, and an inhibitor of bacterial growth. The specific bacteria that play a role in the production of vinegar are called *acetobacters*. In the presence of oxygen, these microorganisms convert alcohol into acetic acid, which can kill or limit the growth of other bacteria. When the strength of an acetic acid solution reaches a certain level, no bacteria, including the acetobacters themselves, can grow. Foods kept in an acetic acid solution will remain free of bacterial contamination for as long as the acid solution remains potent.

Bidet Ever So Humble

The *bidet*, that peculiarly Gallic instrument for feminine hygiene, made its first appearance during the early 18th century. The device, first mentioned in 1710, must have been unfamiliar to many Frenchmen in 1739, when a dealer offered a bidet as a "porcelain violincase with four legs." By 1750, portable metal bidets with removable legs were commonly secreted inside pieces of furniture.

Angostura bitters, the most popular variety, have been with us since 1824, when a German doctor living in Venezuela prepared them as a tonic for his ailing wife. He reportedly learned the recipe from sailors, who frequently added bitters to rum as a cure for seasickness. When angostura bitters became part of the Manhattan cocktail, their place behind the bar was established forevermore.

The Babylonian Code of Hammurabi, dating around 1750 B.C., set down regulations for drinking houses. Egyptian doctors frequently prescribed alcohol as a medicine. By studying the remains of the Egyptian and Babylonian cultures, we can conclude that alcoholism has been a problem for well over 4,000 years.

The Chinese have been distilling an alcoholic beverage from rice since at least 800 B.C., and the Arabs have swilled alcohol from palm sap for many, many centuries. The earliest alcoholic beverage in the West was wine, brewed either from grapes or honey. Mead, a sweet wine made from honey, was widely enjoyed in Poland as recently as the 19th century.

The first pencil with an attached eraser was patented in 1858.

Out of the Rain

What is brilliology? Why, it's the study of the brolly, of course—the gamp, the parasol, the parapluie, the bumbershoot, the bumbersoll—to you, the umbrella.

If you think the ribbed, collapsible umbrella was the invention of some clever 18th- or 19th-century Englishman determined to fight back against the soggy weather of London town—you're all wet. The fact is, the umbrella is one of the oldest artifacts in man's history, already a familiar item in many cultures by the time man began to write.

In 1957 the Ford Motor Company put out the Edsel. Some 110,000 of these cars were produced in one year and they sold for from $2,500 to about $3,850. But the market wasn't going for them. People were becoming economy-minded and wanted smaller cars, not the luxury Edsel. So the Edsel went out of production. But some of the original owners are still very attached to their Edsels, and there is even an Edsel Owners Club. Shelley Cleaver, for example, of Jacksonville, Texas, is the proud owner of 14 Edsels. But then again, Mr. Cleaver is an automobile mechanic and is prepared for any emergency.

The monster who is supposed by some people to inhabit Loch Ness in Scotland may or may not exist, but his fame is indubitable. But do you know about Champ, the monster that is thought to inhabit Lake Champlain? In July, 1977 Sandra Mansi of Winchester, New Hampshire, photographed this being, and ever since scientists have been trying to account for it. The consensus of opinion seems to be that if it exists, the creature is likely to be a primitive whale or reptile.

The longest stairway in the world is reputedly at the Mar Power Station in Western Norway. Built in 1952, this stairway is 4,100 feet long, and contains 3,875 steps at an angle of 41 degrees.

National Drink

As a rule, tipplers in most countries prefer a beverage produced from a native product—in effect, the "national drink" of that nation. For instance, vodka, an unaged spirit obtained from potatoes or grain and filtered through vegetable charcoal, is the overwhelming favorite in Poland and the Soviet Union, where the raw materials are plentiful. Vodka, by the way, has recently replaced bourbon as the most popular liquor in America.

Fading Images

In the 1720s, J.H. Schulze of Germany proved that the blackening of silver salts was caused by light. (All photography is based on this simple principle, and all photographic films contain silver.) Schulze's discovery led Thomas Wedgwood—son of the great potter Josiah Wedgwood—to find a "method of copying paintings on glass and of making profiles by the agency of light upon nitrate of silver." Even at that date, then, photography was seen chiefly as an aid to the painter, rather than as potential competition.

Sir Humphrey Davy experimented with Wedgwood's findings, discovering that silver chloride was more sensitive to light than silver nitrate. But all photographic processes of this era failed to produce a fixed image. The pattern of light and dark recorded on plates coated with silver compound was obliterated upon exposure to light.

The largest known grass in the world is the bamboo which grows in the tropics and sometimes attains a height of 120 feet and a diameter of eight to twelve inches.

One of the first statutes of limitations in history can be found in the Old Testament of the Bible, which relates to an old Hebrew law which forced a creditor to release a debtor from his obligation after seven years.

Without a Bank Roll, You Eat Bland

In the 15th century, a pound of pepper cost an Englishman about six times the average daily wage of a laborer. As late as the 17th century, a load of spices imported from the East for 3,000 English pounds could be resold in England for as much as six times that amount.

Silver is harder than gold, but softer than copper. It can be hammered into sheets so thin that it would take 100,000 of them to make a stack one-inch high. These sheets are so thin that light shines through them. Silver can also be drawn out into wires finer than human hair. And it is the best conductor of electricity among metals.

The largest single-issue of a newspaper was *The New York Times* of Sunday, October 10, 1971. This massive issue included 15 sections with a total of 972 pages, and each copy weighed more than seven pounds.

The state of Michigan sprawling along four of the five Great Lakes, has a shoreline 3,100 miles long, which is longer than the entire Eastern seaboard from Maine to the tip of Florida. And the state boasts of more than 11,000 inland lakes and 36,000 miles of rivers and streams.

Uphill in Frisco

The famed San Francisco cable cars were the world's first cable-drawn cars. The Bay City's cable car was invented by Andrew Hallidie, and introduced in 1873 on Sacramento and Clay Streets.

Cable cars were drawn by an endless cable that runs in a slot between the rails. Cable cars are best suited for steeply inclined streets—thus, their early popularity in San Francisco and Seattle. But a cable car can run only at a constant speed, and a cable jam can stop every car on the line.

By the turn of the century, most cable car lines had been replaced by electric trackage, although Seattle retained its system until the 1930s.

The San Francisco cable car lines still operating today are maintained chiefly as tourist attractions, with most lines long since replaced by buses or trolley bus systems.

Fixed Image

During the early 1800s, Frenchman Joseph Niepce was experimenting with various materials for use in lithography. Since Niepce could not draw, his son Isaac provided the artwork for Niepce's experiments. When Isaac was drafted by the army, his father was spurred to invent a way of producing images by photographic process.

At first, Niepce experimented with coated metal plates in a camera made from a cigar box and a lens from a solar microscope. In 1822, he obtained a fixed photography image on glass. Four years later, he captured the courtyard of his country home on a pewter plate after an exposure of about eight hours. Either picture, or *heliograph*, may be considered the first permanent photograph on record.

In 1829, Niepce formed a partnership with Louis J.M. Daguerre, a painter who had been carrying out his own photographic research. Daguerre discovered that an image could be recorded on an iodized silver plate fumed with mercury vapor. The discovery came about by accident. The artist had left an exposed photographic plate in a cupboard overnight, and in the morning found that the plate bore a visible image. Daguerre traced the fortuitous accident to a quantity of mercury stored in the cupboard, whose vapor had condensed on the plate.

The first pictures produced with Daguerre's techniques, called *Daguerreotypes*, were not reproducible, and could be viewed only by tilting the picture a certain way. Furthermore, early Daguerreotypes required exposures of an hour or more, ruling out the shooting of scenes with moving objects. Yet the entire world applauded Daguerre's work—with the exception of a few portrait artists who could read the writing on the wall. In 1839, Daguerre sold the rights to his invention to the French government for a lifetime annuity, and his photographic process, called *Daguerreotypy*, flourished until replaced by better processes developed in the early 1850s.

No Middle Ground

Are you an ailurophile or an ailurophobe? In plain English: Do you love or hate cats? Either way, you're in large company.

Ever since the domestication of the feline, the cat has been variously regarded as a representation of the gods or as an embodiment of the devil. Even today, there seems to be no middle ground. People's reactions to dogs range across a wide spectrum but when it comes to cats, well it's either for or against.

The oldest letter in our alphabet is the letter "O," which has been unchanged in shape since its adoption from the Phoenician alphabet in about 1300 B.C. The newest letters in our alphabet are "J" and "V," which have been in use only since about 1630.

The longest artificial seaway in the world is the St. Lawrence Seaway, which is 189 miles long, along the New York State-Ontario border.

Lombard Street in London, England takes its name from the Lombard merchants and moneylenders from Italy who settled there in the 13th century.

Classy Influence

Giacomo Meyerbeer's opera, *Le Prophète*, contained a skating scene which became famous—and promoted the growing interest in roller skates. Jackson Haines, of ice-skating renown, also contributed to the roller skate's rise to popularity by demonstrating his balletic skating style during an 1860s European tour. The ballet master had little idea that his graceful turns would help put drive-in waitresses on roller skates a century later!

Do You Know Why Birds Sing?

Nature equips her creatures with very purposeful instincts. It is thought that the bird sings in order to protect its territory against other birds of the same species. It's just a lovely way of calling out, "Stay clear, I got here first."

The mockingbird has a syrinx (or larynx) that is different from other birds'. True to its name, the mockingbird can imitate the calls of many other birds. This probably gives the mockingbird a lot of elbow room, since it gives other birds the impression that the area has already been possessed by the various birds the mockingbird imitates.

On May 14, 1948, the new state of Israel was proclaimed in Tel Aviv. The new Foreign Ministry attempted to send out cables informing foreign governments that a new state had come into existence and requesting official recognition. However, the clerk in the Tel Aviv telegraph office refused to transmit the cables. This would be, he claimed, in violation of his standing instructions to send cables only for those paying cash, or for those with established credit accounts. The new Foreign Ministry had neither, but managed to scurry around and find the one person in Tel Aviv who the telegraph clerk said would be empowered to authorize the cables.

Deservedly renowned for his often self-deprecating wit, Abraham Lincoln is supposed to have made this pointed riposte to Stephen A. Douglas' calling him two-faced: "I leave it to my audience. If I had another face, do you think I would wear this one?"

The quickest-acting poison known is the barbiturate, thiopentone, which if given as a large intracardiac injection, will cause permanent cessation of respiration within one to two seconds.

Telling the Boys From the Girls

Each human being has a total of 46 chromosomes, the chemical determinants of heredity. Each of these chromosomes has been identified by number, except for the sex chromosomes. The female person has two X chromosomes, and the male person has one X and one Y chromosome.

John McEnroe may be as famous for his temperamental behavior as for his superb tennis skill. His temper tantrums have earned him a bad press in England where decorum matters, and he has gathered up some very colorful nicknames, such as Super Brat, the Incredible Sulk, and McTantrum. After he won the U.S. Open Tennis Championship in Flushing Meadow Park, which is in his home borough of Queens, in New York City, he won a new title in the English press: King of Queens.

Doing It Up Brown

An advertisement in the New York Times read, "You are about to spend more money for a theater ticket than you ever thought possible." Well, some people did. Opening on Broadway on October 3, 1981, *Nicholas Nickleby* was selling seats for a uniform $100 each.

This production by the Royal Shakespeare Company runs for an astounding eight and a half hours, and is presented in two parts, with a 45-minute break in between for a quick dinner. There are 43 actors in the cast, and they double and triple up to enact some 150 roles. They perform not only on the stage, but scurry up and down ramps through the orchestra and the mezzanine. It's a novel experience, all right. Wonder what Charles Dickens would make of it all.

One out of every four human beings living in the world today is Chinese.

There's a Chinese typewriter called the Hoang with 5,850 characters on a keyboard two feet long and 17 inches wide. Top speed on the Hoang is about 10 words per minute.

Have you ever heard of a condition called polydactylism? Well, that's a condition where a person has more than the usual number of fingers on a hand or more than the usual number of toes on a foot.

There was a family in Georgia named Johnson that seemed to hold the record for having the largest number of extra fingers and toes in one family. The mother transmitted this condition to seven of her 10 children. The Johnson family could claim 18 additional normal digits. Among these were: one boy who had an extra toe, two sons who had two extra toes, and one daughter who had three extra fingers.

In this world there are approximately 2,000 midgets. These are people who are perfectly formed, but who are simply much smaller than the rest of us. They are not to be confused with some 60,000 dwarfs. A dwarf has a normal-sized head and a normal-sized body, but he is stunted in growth because his legs are abnormally short.

Wishing Won't Make It So

False pregnancy is a strange delusion that is not as rare as you'd suppose. Probably the most famous case in history is that of Mary I, Queen of England, who twice experienced this delusion. Psychologists would tell you that the reason for Mary's strange quirk was that she had an intense yearning to have an heir to the throne. A year after her marriage, she and her household were so certain that she was going to be confined for childbirth that public announcements were made and services were held in the churches of London. But it was a false alarm, as was the second time Mary thought she was pregnant.

Happy Hour

The cocktail party is thought to have originated as an outgrowth of the aperitif hour before dinner. As the "hour" gradually lengthened, a buffet of some kind became necessary to allay the appetites of the imbibers. Psychologists attribute the popularity of the cocktail party, and the before-dinner cocktail itself, to their function as a separation between the working day and the evening relaxation. In recent years, many other countries have followed the American example and have adoped both the cocktail hour and the cocktail party.

Gliders

German inventor Otto Lilienthal carried out aviation research that was to heavily influence the work of the Wright Brothers. Concentrating on the sheer dynamics of flight rather than the problems of self-propelled aircraft, Lilenthal constructed the world's earliest gliders. By 1896, when he perished in a crash, Lilienthal had experienced over 2,000 successful glider flights—including one of 1,000 feet.

According to some accounts, the expression "to fight like Kilkenny cats" dates back to a somewhat ailurophobic custom among Hessian soldiers stationed in Ireland: tying two cats together by the tails and hanging them over a fence or clothesline. One day, the story goes, an officer approached a group of soldiers thus occupied. To hide their deed, one soldier cut off the tails of both tormented animals. The officer was then told that the cats had fought so hard that they'd devoured each other, leaving only the tails.

The notion that a cat can fall from a great height and survive is not an old wives' tale, and many have contributed to the idea that a cat has nine lives. One cat fell from the 20th floor of a Montreal apartment building in 1973 and suffered only a pelvic fracture.

Clowns and Jesters

No one knows for sure whether a clown is funny or sad, or whether a jester is foolish or wise. Perhaps this is why the clown and the jester have always been of interest, to kids and adults alike, throughout the centuries. Or maybe it's because the best way to expose the truth is by clothing it in farce. At any rate, jesters have been attached to courts far and wide—in the Far East, as well as in ancient Greece and Rome, in the court of Montezuma, and in the courts of England and Europe.

Some of Shakespeare's most endearing characters are jesters. Till Eulenspiegel was immortalized in chapbooks of the 15th century. And Robin Goodfellow, or Puck, was a favorite in old English tales.

On these two pages you will find some of the best illustrations of all kinds of clowns and jesters.

Drawing by Harold Montiel

Punch

Fliegende Blätter

364

Art of the Book

Life

Catchpenny Prints

Caruso

365

On the Ice

The Dutch may not have invented ice skating, but today they are probably the world's best skaters. Of 13 million Netherlanders, an estimated 25 percent are speed-skaters—and rural women skaters are confident enough to carry egg baskets on their heads!

In ancient Egypt, the sandal demonstrated a person's rank in society. Slaves either went barefoot or wore crude sandals made from palm leaves. Common citizens wore sandals of woven papyrus, consisting of a flat sole tied to the foot by a thong between the toes. But sandals with pointed toes were reserved only for the higher stations of society, and the colors red and yellow were taboo for anyone below the aristocratic rank.

The Spice of Life

Understandably, many of the herbs and spices shipped to Europe found their way into the hands of the wealthy. One 15th-century German monarch insisted that his women bathe in tubfuls of expensive aromatic oils. French noblemen at the court of Louis XIV often enjoyed perfumed foods, such as meats sprinkled with rose water, eggs flavored with musk, or cream mixed with ambergris.

Take Your Picture?

Though Japanese firms now dominate camera production, most of the world still relies on film produced at Kodak Park, in Rochester, New York, and at other Kodak plants, making the United States the world's largest producer of photographic goods. In one recent year alone, the estimated 2,500 film laboratories in America boasted a film-processing business of some $850 million! About 90 percent of that figure was spent on color film. And about 40 percent of all film materials are purchased by amateurs!

Not included in these film-processing figures are the photos taken with the Polaroid camera, which are developed in the camera, rather than at the lab. Polaroid cameras utilize a process called diffusion-transfer to produce positive prints within a minute after the picture is taken. Invented in 1939 in Europe for use in office copying machines, the diffusion-transfer process was first adopted for use in a camera in 1947, by American inventor Edward Land, who went on to found the Polaroid Corporation.

Black-and-white Polaroid film consists of two sheets, a positive and a negative. The positive carries pods of jellied processing solution. After the image is recorded on the negative sheet, the negative and positive sheets pass between rollers, and the pressure ruptures the jelly pods and spreads the processing solution over the positive sheet. Ten seconds later, the negative sheet is peeled away, leaving a completely developed positive print. Polaroid color film, available since 1963; works on a more complicated process, utilizing six layers of active chemicals.

Until the introduction of mass-produced footwear in the 19th century, shoes were usually handmade in the cobbler's shops, with nails or pegs used to bind the sole to the upper. As mechanization set in, machines were devised for sewing shoes together. By 1900, most footwear was being made, at least in part, by machine.

The Irish were the first Europeans to recognize the potato as a table food product. That is how it acquired the misnomer, "Irish potato." The potato apparently originated in Peru, South America.

The fragrance of flowers is due to special essences or oils which the plants produce. These oils are complicated compounds of only two elements—carbon and hydrogen—and are known as volatile oils, since they escape readily into the air.

Cocktails for Two

Just as nations have their favored beverage, most have a favored toast as well. The term originated in the custom of dunking a slice of toast in a glass of wine, for reasons unknown. Englishmen like to toast with *Cheerio, Cheers,* or *Down the hatch.* Scandinavians say *Skoal. Prosit* is a German favorite, though the word is Latin. Italians clink glasss to the tune of *Cin cin.* The Spanish favor *Salud,* and the French *Culs secs.* Americans have coined the likes of *Bottoms up,* and *Here's looking at you*—as well as some more indelicate expressions from the frontier West.

Clang Went the Trolley

The earliest electric trolleys were powered by storage batteries, which proved expensive and inefficient. The first electrified streetcar tracks, too, often short-circuited in the rain.

One of the world's first electric lines was constructed in London in 1860 by the American G.F. Train—that's right, Train—with two more tramlines following shortly after in that city. But it was the invention of the electric generator that led to the application of transmitted power to streetcar lines and fostered the proliferation of tramlines throughout Europe and the United States.

Jungle Cats

There are many ways of classifying the members of the cat family, but the most commonly accepted divides the felines into three genera. The *Panthera* genus includes the great cats, such as the lion, tiger, leopard, and jaguar. The lion is the only gregarious member of the cat family. Its nickname—"king of the jungle"—is something of a misnomer. The tiger is generally larger and stronger than his unstriped cousin. Fortunately, the two creatures rarely meet—there are no tigers in Africa, and few lions anywhere else.

"Ligers and Tigons" may sound like a classic spoonerism, but these animals actually exist. They are the hybrid offspring of the lion and tiger, and there are about a dozen of these creatures in captivity today. When the father is a lion, the cub is called a liger; when the sire is a tiger, the cub is a tigon. And if a liger and tigon mate—well, you figure it out.

The *Acinonyx* genus includes only, since ancient times, the cheetah, a sleek spotted cat that has been domesticated and used in hunting in Egypt, India, and other Asian lands. The cheetah has been called the fastest animal on earth, and can race along at speeds of 60 miles per hour—though some claim to have clocked this quick-footed cat at close to 75 miles per hour!

The third genus, *Felis,* includes the puma, ocelot, bobcat, serval, lynx, and of course, the common house cat, known rather plausibly in zoological circles as *Felis catus.*

Detroit on the Skids

American dominance of the automobile market has slipped somewhat in recent years, yet the United States still ranks first in total production, with 6.7 million passenger cars turned out in 1975. Japan ranked second that year with 4.5 million cars, followed by West Germany and France with just under three million each, Great Britain and Italy with about 1.4 million each, Canada with one million, and the Soviet Union with 670,000.

Death Be Not Proud

Terry Fox was one of the best athletes in the local high school he attended in Vancouver, British Columbia. He entered Simon Fraser University in 1977. Shortly afterwards, it was discovered that he had bone cancer in his right leg, and it had to be amputated.

Terry decided the best thing he could do was to raise money for cancer research. He launched on a marathon run across Canada. He started out on April 12, 1981, dipping his artificial limb in the Atlantic Ocean at St. John's, Newfoundland. In four and a half months he covered over 3,000 miles, stopping in towns along the way for fund-raising rallies. More than 20 million dollars was donated to the Canadian Cancer Society as a result of his campaign.

On September 1, 1981, he had to stop while he was halfway to his final destination point in Vancouver. He was hospitalized in Thunder Bay, Ontario, where it was discovered that the cancer had spread to his lungs. He was brought back to Vancouver, and was given the Order of Canada, the country's highest civilian honor. Among other honors this young hero received was a commemorative stamp carrying his name.

On June 28, 1981, Terry Fox died in Vancouver hospital. He was 22 years old.

Although the U.S. is the world's biggest producer of cheese, the most active cheese eaters in the world are the people of France, with an annual average of 29.98 pounds per person.

Cocktails, Oriental Style

In the Orient, millet and rice are most commonly used for distilling spirits. *Ng ka py* is how you order a shot in Peking. It's made from millet, with various aromatics added. Sake, a beverage made from rice, is the favorite in Japan.

Not all Slavic languages use the Cyrillic alphabet. Missionaries who worked among the Poles and Czechs introduced the Roman alphabet instead of the Greek. In Yugoslavia today, we find two alphabets in use to transcribe the same language: the Serbians use a Cyrillic alphabet for Serbo-Croatian, while the Croatians use a Roman alphabet.

The largest private house in the world is the 250-room Biltmore House in Asheville, North Carolina. This house was built between 1890 and 1895 by George W. Vanderbilt II (1862-1914) at a cost of $4,100,000.

The best caviar is sold by weight, is slightly salted, and extremely nourishing. Malossol caviar contains up to 30 percent protein. Due to its salt content, caviar will remain fresh for a long time. But never place it in a freezer or you'll end up with a worthless lumpy broth!

The practice of climbing to elevated places for sport or pleasure is a very old pastime, but it has recently received a great impetus because intrepid adventurers have conceived of mountain climbing as one of the grandest of sports, and they are looking for new peaks to scale.

In 1865, Edward Whymper scaled the Matterhorn. In 1889, Albert F. Mummery conquered Kilimanjaro. In the 1950s Edmund Hillary ascended Mt. Everest.

Asparagus Purée

Botanically, asparagus is a genus of the lily family, comprising some 120 species growing widely in the temperate zones of Europe and America. *Asperagus officinalis*, the popular edible variety, is a native of the temperate zones of the Old World, and grows naturally in southern England and the Russian steppes. Though the plant produces a flower and a small whitish berry, we eat only the stem, or shoot, of the plant.

Asparagus has been cultivated around the Mediterranean for many centuries, and there is evidence of the vegetable in Egypt as long ago as 3000 B.C. The Greeks and Romans were both fond of asparagus, and by the second century B.C. the green shoots were already considered a luxury food. The Romans cultivated asparagus in trenches, vying for the biggest shoots, and served it often in puréed form at banquets. We know that Cleopatra entertained Marc Antony with asparagus at such a feast. The Roman expression "You can do it in less time than it takes to cook asparagus" was the Latin equivalent of "two shakes of a lamb's tail."

Decoy

A cage in Old Dutch was known as a kooi. A duck-kooi was a trap set for ducks, usually baited with an imitation duck carved in wood and painted. From this we have the word *decoy*, which is applied to animals or humans that are used as a bait to ensnare others.

The most common albino animal is the Siamese cat.

No Potatoes

The English did not become large-scale potato eaters until the latter half of the 18th century. The Scots, meanwhile, continued to resist the spud, with some Presbyterian clergymen declaring that since the vegetable was not mentioned in the Bible, it could not be fit for human consumption.

In the Chips

In 1969, Australian Paul Tully set a record for potato chip devouring by consuming 30 two-ounce bags in 24½ minutes—without a drink. And while we're on the subject, the record for potato gobbling is three pounds in one minute and 45 seconds, set in Worcestershire, England in 1976. We have no idea if the spuds were peeled or unpeeled—or served with or without Worcestershire sauce.

No Strawberry

When the Spanish explorer Cortes arrived at the court of the Aztec king Montezuma in 1519, the Aztecs offered their guests bowls of a frothy black liquid chilled with snow. Chocolate, which Cortes had already heard of, was the primary ingredient of the beverage; but Cortes learned through court gossip that the Aztecs sweetened their drink with a secret ingredient, an extract from a wild orchid called *thixochitl*. The Spaniards dubbed the white bean of the orchid with a diminutive of the word *vaina—vainilla*—or "little pod."

When cocoa from the New World reached Spain, vanilla came with it, for the two beans do have one important difference: chocolate in its unadulterated form is bitter tasting; vanilla is sweet. Wealthy Spaniards began enjoying a chocolate beverage sweetened with vanilla decades before coffee and tea became popular in Europe. The Spaniards guarded the secrets of their preparation for years, and it was almost a century before the two beans were widely enjoyed elsewhere in Europe.

Vanilla and chocolate reached France in 1660, when Maria Theresa of Spain arrived at the French court, with her maids and cooks, to become the bride of Louis XIV. The new queen enjoyed a vanilla-flavored chocolate beverage prepared by a maid each morning, and other members of the court were soon clamoring for vanilla. The clergy then decried the beverage as "provocative of immorality"—it was rumored that vanilla, like chocolate, was an aphrodisiac.

In a Pickle

Vinegar is used today as a food flavoring and a household cleaner, but by far its most important historical role lies in its use as a food preservative. Before refrigeration and chemical preservatives were developed, man had to rely on salting, drying, and pickling to keep food edible for any length of time. The most important pickling solution has always been vinegar.

Care About Caries

Americans presently consume over one billion tubes of toothpaste each year, each tube a product of the very latest refinements in modern dental science. Yet caries, or tooth decay, is by far the most common disease in the United States today, afflicting about 90 percent of all people. Ancient peoples had neither effective toothbrushes nor toothpastes of any seeming worth, but we have no proof that they suffered from tooth decay any more than people do today!

Twenty-one million Americans—about one of every 10—now play the piano, more than the number who play all other musical instruments combined.

Caviar's the Thing

The roe of various fish have been enjoyed as a delicacy by the rich for thousands of years. "Red caviar," however, is a cheap imitation made from salmon roe.

The French have been connoisseurs of caviar from medieval times on. Rabelais speaks of the delicacy in *Pantagruel*, calling it *caviat*. In Shakespeare's day, caviar was recognized as a food for the more discerning, as Hamlet suggested when he said: "The play, I remember, pleas'd not the million; 't was caviare to the general." In other words, the play, like caviar, was pleasant only to a trained palate.

Ballet

The first ballet was presented in France at the court of Catherine de Medici in 1581. In the 1600's, ballet was chiefly a court entertainment. King Louis XIV performed in ballets presented at his own court for nearly 50 years. For many years all the dancers were male, with boys taking female roles, using wigs and masks to make themselves resemble women. The first ballet in which trained women dancers appeared was *The Triumph of Love*, presented in 1681. The women's ballet costumes which we think of as traditional first appeared in the 1800's. The calf-length, filmy skirt was first worn in 1832 by Maria Taglioni, in La Sylphide. The *tutu*, the short ballet skirt, appeared nearer the end of the century, along with ballet slippers with a blocked toe which permitted women to dance on the points of their toes.

Versatile Vegetable

There are four basic varieties of asparagus in widespread cultivation today. The French *Argenteuil* has a thick stem and a purple head. The English *Green* is, not surprisingly, green, smaller, thinner, and more flavorful than the Argenteuil. The Genoa variety—called *asperge violette* in France—is, as you might have guessed, purple. Mildly flavored white asparagus is also grown in Europe, chiefly for canning. The most popular edible variety is the *Lauris*, a French hybrid developed from the English Green and now grown extensively in southern France. And other species—mainly African climbing varieties—are used as decorative plants.

The asparagus spears we eat are actually shoots growing out of the soil from submerged roots, and if not picked before maturity, would eventually blossom into flowers and fruits. Each plant formerly produced less than a dozen shoots, but with modern cultivation techniques one plant can now furnish as many as 70. They're in season, by the way, from January through September—don't expect anything but canned spears at most other times.

When Julia was first born, her mother, Kay, showed no interest in her. So Louisa Gillespie took Julia home to live with her. Julia took over the bedroom that Louisa's daughters had used some 26 years ago.

Every day, Mrs. Gillespie took Julia to the Bronx Zoo for a two-hour visit. Julia loved it. Why wouldn't she—Julia's a gorilla. On her first birthday, Julia had a party at the zoo, with a cake and all. Julia loves oranges and lemons, and that's what she had—a lemon cake with orange icing.

North Carolina is the nation's largest furniture, tobacco, brick and textile producer. It holds second place in the southeast in population, and first place in the value of its industrial and agricultural production.

The largest fair hall in the world is in Hanover, West Germany. Completed in 1970, this hall has dimensions of 1,180 feet by 885 feet, and a floor area of 877,500 square feet.

Speaking of cheap accommodations, Parisian flophouses of the 19th century offered their more indigent guests a place at the "two-penny leanover," a long bench with a rope stretched in front of it, which the sleeper could lean over during his sit-up slumber. In the morning, an inappropriately named "valet" rudely awoke the guests by cutting the rope.

Sweet Bean

Queen Elizabeth of England, the owner of a notorious sweet tooth, was wont to fill her pockets with candies; she would nibble on the sweets throughout the day. Many of the candies were made from chocolate or from vanilla, or from a mixture of both. English confectioners vied to create new specialties to delight the queen, and one apothecary struck on the idea of using the juice of the vanilla bean as a flavoring for *marchpane*, almond paste. The occasion marked the first time that vanilla was used to flavor anything but chocolate, and Elizabeth loved the results.

By the late 17th century, chocolate was popular as a beverage throughout much of Europe, and chocolate houses—the forerunners of coffee houses—were common in many cities. But sugar gradually replaced vanilla as a sweetener for chocolate, and vanilla struck out on its own as a flavoring.

It wasn't until 1836, however, that scientists found a way of growing vanilla outside Mexico. Charles Morren, a Belgian botanist, discovered that the vanilla plant was pollinated by the Melipone bee, a tiny insect that lives only in Mexico. Thus, the plant could not be naturally pollinated in other countries. Morren found a method for artificially pollinating the plant, and vanilla plantations soon began appearing in many of France's colonial possessions.

Ranking Rinks

There are now an estimated 20 million ice skaters in the United States, and the U.S. Figure Skating Association can boast over 30,000 members. In 1950, there were but 120 indoor ice rinks in this country. Today, American ice skating rinks number over a thousand, logging about 20 million admissions annually. The best known ice skating rink in the United States is in Rockefeller Center, New York City, a small outdoor rink that has been opened to the public every winter since 1936.

But the largest artificial ice skating rink in North America can be found in Burnaby, British Columbia. The quadruple rink, completed in 1972, covers 68,000 square feet of ice surface. (Coincidentally, the largest roller skating rink in history, the Grand Hall in London, measured precisely 68,000 square feet— but it closed in 1912.) The largest outdoor ice skating rink now stands, surprisingly, in Japan. Completed in 1967, the colossal 165,750-square-foot ice palace cost close to a million dollars to construct.

Watches always make great gifts, so if you're shopping for a present you might take a look at the *Swiss Grande Complication*. The most expensive watch in the world without a jeweled case (excluding antiques), this plain-looking timepiece will set you back a mere $60,000! You prefer something in a jeweled case? How about a Piaget men's model, the world's costliest at $67,500! After all, what's more important than the correct time?

Tit for Tat

When Menachem Begin was reelected Prime Minister of Israel in 1981, he appointed retired general Ariel Sharon as his Defense Minister. Mr. Sharon's grandfather and Prime Minister Begin's father were Zionist friends in Poland, and Mr. Sharon's grandmother was the midwife at the birth of Mr. Begin.

Seeing It Through

"Scotch" masking tape was a multimillion-dollar seller by 1935, and led to the development of over a hundred other products— including cellophane tape. At the time the masking tape was introduced, cellophane was just coming into widespread use as a food wrap. But cellophane wrapping presented a problem—how to seal the cellophane wrapping itself with an equallyu transparent tape.

In 1929, Richard Drew, the inventor of masking tape, was presented with another problem: a St. Paul, Minnesota firm manufacturing insulation for refrigerator cars asked the 3M (Minnesota Mining and Manufacturing) Company for a tape to seal the wrappings of their insulating material, which had to remain waterproof against refrigerator moisture. At the same time, one of Drew's assistants proposed that 3M use cellophane to package their Scotch masking tape. On June 18, 1929, Drew had a brainstorm: why not coat cellophane itself with an adhesive and use it as a tape for cellophane wrapping? After all, it's transparent and waterproof!

Drew ordered 100 yards of cellophane from DuPont and began experimenting with various rubber-based adhesives. At first Drew found that his adhesives turned the cellophane a "dirty amber" color. Experimentation continued, but the product was far from perfect—it curled near heat, split easily, and failed to adhere evenly, and was amber-colored to boot.

Success came in 1930, when Drew found a stronger, more transparent adhesive. The first roll of the new product was sent to the Shellmar Products Corporation to seal cellophane-wrapped bakery goods. The tape was an instant success—it was adhesive, cohesive, elastic, and proved reliable at great temperature extremes. And it was—well, *almost*—transparent, a pale amber color.

Approximately 50 per cent of the world's fresh water supply is contained in the five Great Lakes of North America.

Daring Dames

While Jane Suzanne Mellor, 20 years old, of Yorkshire, England, and Lori Love, 31, of Wichita, Kansas, were attending the United States National Parachute Championship in Muskogee, Oklahoma, they cooked up a daring scheme. Fifty miles away, in Wagoner, Oklahoma, there was a television tower that soared 1,909 feet into the air, almost 500 feet higher than the Sears Tower in Chicago, the world's tallest building. The two girls decided to climb the television station tower and parachute off its peak. And, on August 19, 1981 that's exactly what they did. It took five hours to climb the tower, but only a short time to float gracefully down. When they landed a quarter of a mile from the tower's base, Deputy Sheriff Tom Powell was waiting for them in his pickup truck.

Whiskey

Whiskey is usually distilled from the fermented mash of grain—usually oats, barley, rye, or corn. Whiskey is produced primarily in Scotland, Ireland, Canada, and the United States.

Tin Lizzie

Preparation for the Model T's production brought Ford so close to bankruptcy that he had to borrow $100 from a colleague's sister to pay for the car's launch. That $100, by the way, was eventually worth $260,000 to the generous donor. The first "Lizzie" rolled off the line in 1908, with a four-cylinder, 20-horsepower engine capable of speeds of 40 miles per hour. It carried a price tag of $850.

Mass-production innovations continued to lower the price of the Lizzie. In 1916, a new Model T sold for just $360! Each vehicle finished its turn around the assembly line in just 980 minutes, compared to the earlier day-and-a-half assembly-line run.

Stop, Thief

As you might imagine, thievery is a common problem in truffle-growing areas. A clever truffle-snatcher can become rich virtually overnight, since most varieties will sell for well above $100 a pound. The white truffle of the Piedmont district of Italy presently sells for over $200 a pound, making it the most expensive food in the world. On the streets of Milan, truffle vendors hawk this delicacy at the price of 5,000 lire (approximately $5.88) per truffle.

Mayan and Yours

Libraries have not fared well anywhere in the world. In the 1560s, the Spanish Bishop of Yucatan, in Mexico, burned the entire native literature of the Mayan Indians, claiming that the writing contained only "superstition and lies of the devil."

Sparrow-Grass

Asparagus cultivation lapsed for centuries, then reappeared in the 16th and 17th centuries in France and England. French monarch Louis XIV took great pride in serving his guests forced-grown asparagus in January.

"Asparagus" is a second-century Latin word based on the Greek word for "sprout" or "shoot." In 18th-century England the vegetable was known as "sparagus," "sparage," or "sparagrass," and later—somewhat tongue in cheek, perhaps—as "sparrow-grass."

Thomas Jefferson was one of the first farmers to cultivate asparagus in the United States, growing the vegetable in his greenhouse with seeds imported from Europe. Cultivation on a large scale began here in the 1850s. Today asparagus is grown in 15 states from Maine to Virginia; from California, well over 120,000 tons reach the market each year. In some places the plant has escaped cultivation and can be found growing naturally in salt marshes and along roadsides.

The King Ranch is popularly regarded as the largest cattle ranch of all time. Actually, the largest cattle range in the world today is in Australia, covering some 6,500 square miles. Another Australian ranch, now partitioned into smaller units, once covered 35,000 square miles—about the size of the state of Indiana!

Play Me a Tune

About 180,000 new pianos are sold in the United States each year, close to double the annual total for the 1930s. We have no idea how many of those pianos are played regularly, and how many merely occupy space in a living room. But there's no question that the piano, though less than 300 years old, is the most popular instrument throughout the Western world. If the present trend continues, the piano may someday be No. 1 in the Orient as well!

The earliest known city planner is Hippodamus, a Greek architect who lived and worked in the 5th century B.C. He was the designer of Piraeus, the port city of Athens, and of the city of Rhodes, among others. His geometrical layouts were imitated by other cities of the ancient world.

The Girl Scouts were founded on March 12, 1912, by Juliette Lowe.

The Confederacy was composed of 11 southern states. The first to secede from the Union was South Carolina, who at the end of 1860 broke its ties with the United States of America. This state was followed by a wave of secessions, starting January 9, 1861, by Mississippi. The last state to secede was North Carolina, who on May 20, 1861, broke its affiliation with the Union.

By 1870, all of the 11 states had been readmitted.

Typing Record

Perhaps the most remarkable typing record is held by Albert Tangora, who during a 1923 business show in New York, ran off a total of 8,840 correctly spelled words in one hour of nonstop typing, a rate of 147 words per minute. Incredibly, Tangora achieved his record on a cumbersome old *manual* typewriter that would seem crude in comparison with modern models. Judges estimated that Tangora executed an average of 12½ strokes per second!

Fire-eater

Christopher Columbus observed the Indians of the Caribbean smoking tobacco, writing of "men with half-burnt wood in their hands." According to one story, the first European to smoke was Rodrigo de Jerez, one of Columbus's crew members, who sampled tobacco in the West Indies and brought a pinch home with him to Spain. Jerez's wife, so the tale goes, later denounced him to the Inquisition as a man who "swallows fire, exhales smoke, and is surely possessed by the devil."

Note About Bacteria

In many minds, the word "bacteria" suggests the scourge of disease, the threat of sinister microorganisms lying in wait for us and the plants and animals we rely on. But only a small percentage of all bacteria are in any way harmful to man. A great number are not only useful, but essential.

Note About Onions

If you've been finding your onions a bit too lachrymal for comfort, try chilling them before you begin cutting. You can remove onion odors from your hands by rubbing them with lemon juice before washing. If onion aroma clings to your knife, just run the blade through a raw potato.

The Adulterated Hamburger

Burgers were first popularized in the United States by German immigrants settling around Cincinnati. But the first burger wasn't laid between the halves of a bun until early in this century. Officially, the first *hamburger sandwich* appeared at the 1904 Louisiana Purchase Exposition in St. Louis, Missouri.

As for the modern hamburger, the last decade has seen a huge increase in burger corruption, with soy protein a common culprit. And other scientists with tainted tastebuds have proposed a burger made from cotton.

Result of a Misspent Youth

Games such as croquet, archery, and lawn bowling are usually considered pastimes of the upper classes, while many gambling and team games find their most avid players at the other end of the social scale. Billiards has historically been one of the few games to find its greatest popularity at *both* ends of the social spectrum.

The first professional billiards championships were played by English gentlemen dressed in black tie and tails. Even today, the game is sometimes referred to as the "aristocrt of sports." Yet for many years, the pool hall was considered a house of ill fame, the hangout of juvenile delinquents, hustlers, and petty criminals. Politicians and clergymen decried the game, blaming the pool hall for everything from truancy to alcoholism.

Today, billiards and pool seem to find their fans closer to the middle of the social spectrum. Experts predicted that the advent of television would spell the doom of billiards in this country, but middle-class Americans are now taking up the game in increasing numbers. An estimated 20 million Americans play pool each year. Over a half-million homes in North America are now equipped with a billiard table of some kind. The game is booming in many other countries, too. During the 1960s, close to 9,000 new billiard parlors were built in Japan each year!

Umbrellas are for Losing!

Modern umbrella makers contend that today's models are so well constructed that the average person needn't go through more than two in his lifetime. But they make no mention of the phenomenon of the lost umbrella, which more often than not is the reason for a new purchase. To suggest the scope of this problem, it may help to know that close to 75,000 umbrellas are lost each year on the bus and subway systems of London alone!

It is strange that the role of the Chinese detective, Charlie Chan, created by Earl Derr Biggers, was never played in movies by a Chinese. The best known actor who assayed this part was Warner Oland. The Charlie Chan episodes were serialized in 1925 in the *Saturday Evening Post*. All were based on the following novels:

The House Without a Key (1925)
The Chinese Parrot (1926)
Behind That Curtain (1928)
The Black Camel (1929)
Charlie Chan Carries On (1930)

Some kinds of honey are poisonous, for example, the honey made from Rhododendron flowers.

Money is so Precious

During the early Middle Ages, the coinage of the Eastern Empire at Byzantium, and later, the coinage of the Arabs, became the most important species in the eastern Mediterranean. In Western Europe, in the late eighth century, Charlemagne sanctioned the abandonment of the gold standard and established a monetary system based on silver. A silver penny, or *denarius*, was the basic unit, with 240 pennies to a pound of silver. The words *livre*, *lira*, and *pound* as used in British currency, date from this era. The Pound Sterling was originally 240 sterlings, or silver pennies, and literally weighed one pound.

Pipeline

The Romans were the first to construct water-supply and drainage systems on a large scale. Thirteen aqueducts brought water to the Imperial City from nearby mountains, though contrary to general belief, most of these aqueducts were underground. Of the 220-mile total length of Rome's eight main aqueducts, only 30 miles were constructed above ground. At its peak, the water-supply system of ancient Rome provided about 300 gallons of water per person daily. Today the London water system provides only about 50 gallons per person each day.

When President Lincoln received news of General Lee's surrender on April 10, 1865, he asked his band to play *Dixie*.

The Unmakable Model

There is one model everyone would like to see that simply cannot be made. It would be a representation of our galaxy. In it, the earth would be a ball but one inch in diameter, but the nearest star, *Alpha Centauri*, would have to be placed nearly 51,000 miles away.

Hic!

France is the nation with the highest per capita consumption of alcohol: 22.66 liters of pure juice per year, more than twice the American figure. Italians are the highest per capita consumers of wine, downing on the average 153 liters to the American's mere eight. West Germans are the number one swillers of hard spirits—barely beating out the Americans in that category. The Germans are also far and away the leading drinkers of beer and ale, with the average German consuming 182 liters of brew per year. There is a claim, however, that the residents of Australia's Northern Territory far outpace the Germans.

But He Wound Up In Jail

One of the most incredible swindles ever pulled is the old con game of selling the Brooklyn Bridge. Yet that hoax has been tried again and again, and there are some people who fell for it.

George C. Parker, who died in Sing Sing in 1937 at the age of 76, was one of the greatest swindlers who ever lived. He sold unsuspecting visitors to New York City Grant's Tomb, the Statue of Liberty, the Metropolitan Museum of Art, and of course, the Brooklyn Bridge. It may be hard to believe that Parker sold the Brooklyn Bridge on an average of twice a week. When the yokel was intrigued by the bridge and really wanted to buy it but did not have enough money to pay for it, Parker would accept a down payment and take the balance in installments.

Body Contract

A man who lived in Stockholm in 1890 was dead broke. After much cogitation he thought of a way to get some money. He sold the ownership of his body after his death to the Royal Swedish Institute, which bought the prospective cadaver for dissection.

But fate has its surprises, and 20 years later the man inherited a fortune. He then approached the Royal Swedish Institue and asked them to sell him back the contract he had made. The Institute refused. When the matter was brought to the courts, the Institute successfully defended its case.

Furthermore, the Institute claimed that the body had been mutilated without its consent. The man had had two teeth extracted, and the Institute was awarded damages for the impairment of the prospective corpse.

Approximately 90 percent of all thoroughbred horses are descended from Eclipse, an Arabian stallion who was brought to England in the early 1700s.

Hors de Combat

Only one American city has attempted to legalize prostitution. In 1857, the New Orleans City Council passed an ordinance in which it would issue licenses for $100 to any would-be prostitute, and a license for $250 to a brothel keeper.

The United States Supreme Court has held that the Great Lakes may be considered the high seas because these lakes have the general characteristics of seas, and are navigable by large vessels for international trade between Canada and the United States.

That's Justice

In 1900, some Buddhist idols fell off a temple shelf and killed a man. The family of the deceased insisted on bringing the statues to justice, and brought suit in Foochow, China. The statues were found guilty by the court, and were sentenced to death. Accordingly, in a public execution, 15 wood statues were beheaded.

Hello, Ronald!

McDonald's is a story in itself. A chain known as the White Castle was the first to serve cheap, mass-produced hamburgers. Since then, hamburger joints have proliferated. Today McDonald's is definitely the leader of the pack. Beginning with a stand in Des Plaines, Illinois, which raised its now-famous yellow arches on April 15, 1955, McDonald's has grown into a huge corporation with well over several billion dollars in annual sales. McDonald's sales average a billion hamburgers every three months!

To date, McDonald's has sold 25 billion hamburgers—stack them up and you'd have 20 piles the size of the tallest building in the world, the Sears Tower in Chicago.

The largest number of artists ever to work on a single picture amounted to 130 individuals. They all joined in to help paint the *Pantheon de la Guerre*. This famous painting was made in France between 1914 and 1918, and represents a gigantic panorama of World War I. The painting itself was 402 feet long, 45 feet high. It depicted battlefields, flags, monuments, symbolic figures, and no less than 6,000 war heroes and leaders of 15 countries.

Can You Spare a Thong?

Leather money was used in Russia right until the 17th century, as was tea money in China. Hundreds of other items have served for a time as legal tender, including slaves, tobacco, gunpowder, pig jawbones, and glass beads. Manhattan Island, you recall, was bartered for 24 dollars worth of glass trinkets. Salt once passed for specie in Ethiopia, and skulls were hard cash in Borneo.

Card playing is of ancient origin. It has been recorded that cards were played in Egypt during the days of Joseph, and that their use extended as far east as Hindustan and China at a period long before their introduction into Europe.

The fact that a dog's nose is dry is not an indication that he is in poor health, as some people suppose. A dog can have a dry, warm nose and be perfectly all right. If, however, the nose is cracked or crusted as well as dry, then it is quite likely that the canine is sick.

The Virgin Islands were discovered by Christopher Columbus during his second voyage to the New World in 1493. He named them Las Virgines, in honor of St. Ursula and her 11,000 martyr companions who, according to legend, perished on the banks of the Rhine.

In the Country

Philip Morris's "Marlboro" remains the most popular cigarette on earth, the 136 billion sold annually making the entire world "Marlboro Country."

In 1924, two neophyte publishers named Dick Simon and Lincoln Schuster were looking for their newly-formed company's first manuscript when they realized that no book of crossword puzzles had yet appeared in this country. They contacted Margaret Petheridge, who agreed to compile a crossword book along with two of her *World* co-editors. Simon and Schuster presented Ms. Petheridge with a $25 advance, then began searching for a printer who would work for deferred payment. They found one—a crossword addict.

In April of that year, Simon and Schuster brought out *The Crossword Puzzle Book*, an anthology of 50 puzzles from the *World*. On the advice of friends who could see only disaster ahead in the crossword book game, Simon and Schuster omitted their firm's name from the book, opting instead for the Plaza Publishing Company. The book sold for the then rather high price of $1.35, but each copy came complete with a neatly sharpened pencil—provided free by the Venus Pencil Company as an advertising gimmick.

The success of the book was immediate—within three months, 40,000 copies of *The Crossword Puzzle Book* had been sold. A later 25-cent edition was so popular that one distributor placed an order for a quarter-million copies, the largest book order of the time. Volume Two followed later that year, bearing the name of Simon and Schuster, although Plaza Publishing Company was to remain on the firm's crossword collections until their 50th volume. Within a year, the firm had sold 400,000 crossword books, and they were to follow with two crossword collections per year for decades after. Today, Simon & Schuster is one of the largest publishing houses in the world—and it all began with the crossword!

Capulet

The straw hat was first produced in America in 1798, by a 12-year-old girl in Rhode Island. The first hat factory in the United States, opened in Connecticut late in the 18th century, produced crude fur caps. One kind of hat that is distinctly American is the broad-brimmed ten-gallon hat still popular in the Southwest. A ten-gallon hat, in case you've wondered, can hold about three quarts.

It's Now or Never

As the Roman Empire perished, so did plumbing in Europe. Monasteries could boast the best plumbing facilities of the later Middle Ages. Most monasteries included a sanitary wing, known as the *rere-dorter*, that contained all of the monastery's latrines. The schedule of the monk was so tightly regulated that most members of the monastery were required to use the latrine at the same time. Therefore, the reredorter was usually quite large—145 feet long at Canterbury.

An Honest Man

Lew Worsham leaned over his putter on the 18th green of the Jacksonville Country Club. He needed to sink the ball in 2 to win the 1948 Jacksonville Open Championship, a $10,000 feature. He moved his putter carefully behind the ball. Suddenly, he straightened, dropped his club, and went to the side of the green.

"I touched the ball," he told the tournament official. "Call a penalty stroke."

Worsham then returned to take the 2 putts that now gave him only a tie.

The next day, Lew lost the playoff to Clayton Haefner on the 21st green. But even in defeat Worsham was marked as a great champion—a champion in sportsmanship. Not even his victory in the 1947 National Open earned him the respect he won by calling against himself a penalty nobody else had seen.

Watch Me Wash

Traditionally, in Japan, the bath was a large wooden vat placed outside in the garden and filled with very hot water. The entire family bathed together at the same time. In Japanese baths, both public and private, there is rarely an attempt to achieve privacy. Public baths often have large unprotected openings through which people passing in the street can observe bathers. But nowadays, bathing in Japan—especially in the cities—is becoming westernized.

According to the Nielsen ratings, the average American spends 29 hours a week in front of the TV set. The people who are at the upper end of the viewing scale are women over the age of 55. At the lowest end of the scale are men between the ages of 18 and 24; they spend a mere 20^1/$_2$ hours weekly. Believe it or not, children between the ages of two and five use the TV as a baby sitter for as much as nearly 27 hours a week!

Good News and Bad News

There are 120 million people in Brazil, making it the most populous nation in Latin America. It is by far the largest country in South America. With 3.3 million square miles of territory, it is the fifth largest nation in the world. It has more land under cultivation than all of Europe.

Brazil raises almost twice as many cattle as Argentina, more sugar than Cuba, and this year will build more ships than any other country in the world except Japan. Sad to say, over 20 million people in Brazil live in absolute poverty.

Here's a real whiz of a quiz for you. If you started out the month earning just one penny for the first day and if every day after that you earned twice the amount of your previous day's earnings, would you have earned very much by the end of the month? Well, not *very* much—just $5,368,709.12, for a 30-day month.

The first pay telephone was installed in Hartford, Connecticut, in 1889. The charge for a call was 10¢.

Doing What Comes Naturally

In Europe, the medicinal spring bath has been popular for centuries. During the 18th century, the English city of Bath—so named after an ancient Roman spa built there—became the most fashionable resort in all Europe, thanks chiefly to the restorative work of Beau Nash. Such luminaries as Pitt, Nelson, Gainsborough, Garrick, Gay, Pope, Steele, and Fielding came to enjoy the social life and the hot, restorative waters of the natural spring. Like earlier baths, however, the resort at Bath eventually became associated with debauchery, and with the spread of disease.

What, No Crackers?

There are an estimated four to five hundred different names for the cheese produced around the world, but many of these names are merely different terms for one cheese commonly produced in the area. *Limburger* cheese, for examle, may be called *Algau, Lanark, Marianhof, Morin, Tanzenberg, Briol,* or *Lindenhof* when produced in the town bearing those names. Actually, there are but 18 or 19 distinct varieties of cheese. Furthermore, all cheeses fall into one of six general categories.

Unripened cheese, such as cottage cheese, cream cheese, *ricotta*, and *mozzarella* is eaten fresh, without curing or ripening.

In Your Easter Bonnet

Where did you get that hat?
Where did you get that tile?
Where did you get that hat?
Is that the latest style?

It should come as no surprise that the ditty above is the product of another age—the 1890s, in fact. If there is a "latest style" of hat in contemporary America, it's no hat at all. For the first time in centuries, the hat has lost its place in the well-dressed man *and* woman's wardrobe.

The skunk is a favorite food of the Canadian Indians.

Savory Flavor

Like the mushroom, also a fungus, the truffle has almost no nutritive value. But its taste, aroma, and ability to heavily flavor anything it comes in contact with have made it a prized edible since classical times. The Roman writers Juvenal and Plutarch both expressed the opinion that truffles were formed by lightning bolts that heated water and minerals in the ground where they struck.

Ouch!

To the ancient Egyptians, Greeks, and Romans, vinegar was the only acid substance known. In the fourth century B.C., the Greek philosopher Theophrastus gave directions for the preparation of pigments from vinegar and lead, while the physician Hippocrates prescribed vinegar as a medicine. In the Roman Petronius's *Satyricon*, a character who scratches his legs for vinegar the way we might reach for a bottle of iodine.

Some Stuffing

The chicken of today, rooster, hen, pullet, springer, and capon alike, is the product of many centuries of domestication. The wonderful fowl that now graces so many of our dinner plates is believed descended from *gallus gallus*, a jungle bird of India and Southeast Asia. The chicken may not have been domesticated on any large scale until as recently as 1500 B.C., in contrast to the cow and sheep, which were domesticated well before recorded history began.

But the chicken was a common fowl in Europe by the time of the Roman Empire. The Romans may have been the first to raise chickens in batteries, roosts in which large numbers of birds can be raised together cheaply. To improve the flavor of the meat, the Romans sometimes treated their chickens to a diet of barley and milk; to improve their chicken dishes, they often stuffed the birds with sausages, eggs, peas, and other delights.

Arrowroot

North American Indians were known to use an herb to cleanse wounds incurred in savage inter-tribal wars. A poultice made from the root of this herb had great drawing powers and could lift the poison left in the flesh from arrowheads. Thus, the herb came to be called arrowroot.

Queen Elizabeth I of England reportedly bathed once a month, "whether she needed it or not."

Dribble and Pass

The game of basketball, as played today, is actually less than a hundred years old, the brainchild of Canadian-born James A. Naismith. In 1891, while working as a physical education instructor at the International YMCA training school in Springfield, Massachusetts, Naismith sought to invent a new indoor game to relieve the boredom of contemporary gym classes, which were usually limited to less-than-thrilling calisthenics, marching, and apparatus work. After much trial and error, Naismith borrowed and modified elements from football, soccer, hockey, and other sports to produce his new ball game.

Of all the western gunfighters, with the exception of the James brothers, probably the most notorious was Wyatt Earp. He is said to have been born in 1848 and to have died in 1929. At least eight movies are based on this character. They are:

Law and Order, 1932
Frontier Marshall, 1939
My Darling Clementine, 1946
Wichita, 1955
Gunfight at the OK Corral, 1957
Cheyenne Autumn, 1964
Duel at Rio Bravo, 1965
Hour of the Gun, 1967

X-Rays

X-rays have proved useful beyond medicine, too. Engineers use X-rays to examine the internal structure of building materials and to search for possible weaknesses in existing structures. For instance, an X-ray inspection of St. Peter's Cathedral in York, England, revealed damage to the roof beams from insect borings, and the beams were replaced before they could break. X-rays are also used to sterilize medical supplies that cannot be boiled, to inspect luggage at airports and customs entry points, and to distinguish diamonds from imitation gems.

The city of Paris, France, is over 2,000 years old.

Arabian Arabica

Arab legend maintains that the coffee bean was actually discovered by goats. According to the tale, a goatherd named Kaldi, living around the year 850, was puzzled one day by the queer antics of his flock. After watching them cavort around the fields on their hind legs, the goatherd discovered that the animals had been nibbling on the berries of a wild shrub, and decided to sample the fruit himself. The snack produced a delightful sense of exhilaration, and Kaldi went on to loudly proclaim his find.

According to some historians, the *arabica* shrub was taken to Southern Arabia for cultivation sometime before the year 600, though the Arabs didn't learn how to brew the hot beverage until the 10th or 11th century. The word *coffee*, by the way, comes to us either from the Arabic *qahwah*, or from Kaffa, a province in Ethiopia that is reputedly the birthplace of the *arabica* plant.

Once the Arabs had learned to brew a hot beverage from the fruit, coffee became very popular on the Arabian peninsula, especially in connection with long Moslem religious services. Orthodox priests soon pronounced the beverage intoxicating and banned its use, but still the dark brew spread throughout the Near East.

Rev. George Clements may be the first Father ever to become a father. Father Clements, a black Roman Catholic priest in Chicago, signed papers officially adopting Joey, a 13-year old. Although the archdiocese did not bestow formal approval on Father Clement's move, neither did it oppose it. Apparently a priest's celibacy vows do not preclude adoption.

Who Invented the Auto?

No single man can be termed the inventor of the automobile. Rather, advances on motor cars were made by many men working in various countries around the same time. But credit for the first mechanically propelled vehicle is generally given to the French engineer Nicholas Cugnot, who, in 1769, built a three-wheeled steam-propelled tractor to transport military cannons. Cugnot's machine could travel at speeds of up to two-and-a-half miles per hour, but had to stop every hundred feet or so to make steam.

Four movie actors have played the role of secret agent James Bond in the Ian Fleming series:

Sean Connery: *Dr. No*, 1963; *From Russia with Love*, 1964; *Goldfinger*, 1965; *Thunderball*, 1965; *You Only Live Twice*, 1967; *Diamonds are Forever*, 1971.

David Niven: *Casino Royale*, 1967.

George Lazenby: *On Her Majesty's Secret Service*, 1970.

Roger Moore: *The Man with the Golden Gun*, 1974.

The earliest bathtubs in America were simple wooden tubs lined with metal, and the water was poured in by hand. The first public bath was opened here in 1852. An 1895 law ordered all municipalities in new York State to provide free public baths for their citizens, many of whom had no other means of washing.

"Shears" to You

Haven't you ever wondered if the word "scissors" is singular or plural? The dictionary tells us that "scissor" is much less preferred than "scissors," but that the latter word may take either a plural or singular verb. To avoid the question completely, you might opt for "pair of scissors"—for what's one "scissor" without the other? As Charles Dickens wrote in *Martin Chuzzlewit*: "We are but the two halves of a pair of scissors, when apart . . . but together we are something."

Sweet Potato vs. Yam

To settle an oft-heard dispute: no, the sweet potato and the yam are *not* the same vegetable. The yam is in fact almost never seen in this country—no matter what food packagers claim to the contrary!

The *Mouse Trap* was a play written by Agatha Christie. It was originally titled *Three Blind Mice*. The *Mouse Trap* holds the world's record for the longest running play. It made its debut in 1952.

So Much Manure!

Around 1800, American cities were certainly in desperate need of horseless carriages—and horseless streets. Around the turn of the century, New York City's equine helpmates were depositing some two-and-a-half million pounds of manure and 60,000 gallons of urine on the streets each day!

Go Proof It!

Most liquor bottlers identify the alcoholic content of their product by "proof." The term dates back to the earliest days of liquor distilling—when dealers would test the strength of an alcoholic product by soaking gunpowder in the beverage, and then igniting it. Spirits with enough alcohol to permit the ignition of gunpowder were considered to be 100 proof—the idea being that the gunpowder test was "proof" that the juice was strong. In England, 100 proof was established as eleven parts of alcohol by volume to 10 parts of water. In the United States, the proof figure was set as double the alcoholic percentage. Thus 86 proof whiskey is 43 percent alcohol, and pure alcohol is 200 proof.

Although President George Washington chose the site of the White House, the cornerstone of which was laid in October of 1792, he never lived there. President John Adams entered the White House in November of 1800, and Mrs. Adams hung her washing in the uncompleted East Room.

There have been four U.S. Vice Presidents up to now who have succeeded to the Presidency and filled unexpired terms and then were elected on their own to serve second terms. These were Theodore Roosevelt, Calvin Coolidge, Harry S. Truman and Lyndon B. Johnson.

An average horse performing average work produces only two-thirds of one horsepower. This is because James Watt, the Scottish inventor of the first practical steam engine, deliberately understated power of his engine when he first devised the term "horsepower" in relation to machines and horses in the 1780's.

The Celtics Had That Thing!

The first widely-known professional basketball team was the Original Celtics, begun in 1915 by a group of New York City youngsters. During the 1920s, older, more skilled players were gradually added to the team, and by 1928, when the squad disbanded, they were considered invincible. The team was regrouped in the '30s as the New York Celtics, before permanently disbanding in 1936. At the height of their popularity, the Celtics played a game every night, two on Sunday, and were almost continually on the road—yet during the 1922-23 season the Celtics amassed a whopping 204 wins against just 11 defeats!

Toilets

Among the many names now applied to the toilet, *pissoir* and *crapper* are probably considered two of the more vulgar. Actually, *pissoir* is the accepted term for the enclosed public urinals that still appear on the sidewalks of Paris and other French cities. And the term *crapper* is derived, in the most curiously coincidental linking of an inventor with his invention, from Thomas Crapper, a 19th-century English sanitary engineer.

Making a Spectacle

During the 14th and 15th centuries, glass spectacles gradually came into use. By the 1360s, we can already find references to "spectacles makers." The increased availability of reading matter that followed Gutenberg's printing press gave the industry a major boost. By 1507, a spectacles-makers' guild was firmly established, with Venice and Nuremburg the centers of eyeglass manufacture. Spectacles were now cheap enough that everyone could afford them.

Physicians by and large remained skeptical of eyeglasses, clinging to the older medicinal remedies for poor vision. As late as 1583, Dr. Georg Bartisch of Dresden, one of the most famous oculists of the 16th century, advised patients to do without spectacles. "A person sees and recognizes something better when he has nothing in front of his eyes than when he has something there," the doctor reasoned. "It is much better that one should preserve his two eyes than that he should have four."

The All-Time Champs

Without question, the best-selling book of all time is the Bible. No one know for sure how many copies of the Good Book have been printed through history, but a good guess would be around three billion. Trailing far behind in second place is *Quotations from the Works of Mao Tse-tung*, with some 800 million copies in print. Sales of *The American Spelling Book* by Noah Webster may approach 100 million, and Dr. Spock's *The Common Book of Baby and Child Care* has sold about 24 million copies. Other books that have topped the 20-million mark include the works of Marx, Lenin, Stalin, *The World Almanac*, and *The Guinness Book of Records*.

The cross hairs in certain optical instruments are made of spider silk.

Fine wool fiber will stretch one third its length.

Spirited Spirits

Spirits differ greatly in alcoholic content. Most wines contain from 8 to 12 percent alcohol, with certain aperitif and dessert wines, like vermouth and sherry, as high as 18 percent. The strength of beer ranges from a weak 2 percent brew, produced in Scandinavia, to about 8 percent. Four or 5 percent is the average in the United States. Most hard liquors contain from 40 to 50 percent alcohol, with cognac as high as 70 percent. Cordials and liqueurs contain from 25 to 40 percent alcohol.

Most snakes travel only a few miles from the place where they were born.

Don't Spear Me

Our word *garlic* is Anglo-Saxon in origin, a combination of the words *gar* ("spear") and *leac* ("leek"), due to its spearlike leaves. But garlic was by and large spurned in England for centuries, and thus it had little place in the cuisine of early America. The later arrival of large numbers of immigrants from Southern Europe made garlic an American staple—try to find a Mediterranean dish that doesn't include garlic!

Today, about 20 million pounds of garlic are produced in the United States each year, principally in Texas, California, and Louisiana. Argentina is now the world's largest producer, while other nations that cultivate it on a larger scale include China, India, Iran, Italy, Spain, and the U.S.S.R. Indeed, garlic is one of the few food items that have long been used in cuisines as diverse as Chinese, Indian, and European.

Oh! That Polish Vodka!

The strongest spirits that can be produced are raw rum and certain vodkas which contain up to 97 percent alcohol. Polish White Spirit Vodka is the strongest liquor sold commercially, packing a wallop of 80 percent alcohol.

The kindergarten originated in Germany in 1837. It was founded by Felix Froebel, an educational theorist. The word "kindergarten" means "garden of children" in German.

The House That Robby Built

The neighbors complained to the county inspectors that the house that Robby Van Pelt had built in Richmond, Virginia, violated the building code because it was close to neighboring property.

So the inspectors and lawyers came to have a look-see. They decided that with some modifications Robert's house might be able to remain. Robby, a 13 year-old, started building himself a playhouse and got caught up in it and went on and on. He ended up with a three level house, complete with electricity, furniture, and wall-to-wall carpeting.

In 1938, plastic contact lenses began to replace glass contacts. But until 1950, contact lenses were made to fit over almost the entire eye, with a fluid applied underneath the lens to aid against eye irritation. Today's contact lenses fit over the cornea only, floating on a layer of tears and moving with the eye. Contacts can now be worn by any person who wears eyeglasses, and by some for whom eyeglasses would be useless. The biggest problem contacts wearers now face is finding their lenses, for the average contact is under 10 millimeters in diameter, and usually less than a half-millimeter thick. Incidentally, at present, 65 percent of all contact lens wearers are women.

Augustus Was Smart

In Rome, the Emperor Augustus instituted the imperial post office, or *cursus publicus*, during the first century. The Roman system was initially restricted to government and military officials, but a bribe in the right place could avail a private citizen of the service. A pass called a *diploma* was issued to authorized users of the government service. Private mail and parcel companies also flourished. Imperial couriers transported the mails between stations from five to 12 miles apart, with local communities responsible for providing horse and food for the mailmen.

Scissors are one of those ubiquitous everyday objects so common and useful today that it's hard to imagine a time when they weren't around. You don't have to—scissors of one kind or another have existed for almost as long as man has had something to cut!

Caviar to the Czar

The Czar Alexander I is often credited with introducing caviar to the social elite of paris. The word "caviar," however, is not Russian in origin (the Russians call it *ikra*), but comes from the Italian *caviola*, derived from the Turkish word *khavyah*.

Flipped Out

In 1941, the police commissioner of New York City took a stand against pinball, declaring that "children and minors who play these machines and frequent the establishments where they are located sometimes commit petty larceny in order to obtain funds, form bad associations, and are often led into juvenile delinquency and, eventually, into serious crime." In 1941, Mayor Fiorello La Guardia went on the campaign trail with a sledgehammer in hand, personally smashing pinball machines for the benefit of newspaper photographers. In December of 1941, pinball was declared illegal in New York.

As pinball machine factories were converted to other uses for the war effort, it appeared for a time that pinball was dead in the United States. But, after the war, those pinball manufacturers who survived began campaigning for a relaxation of the laws against machines without pay-outs, claiming that pinball was a game of skill rather than chance. In 1947, the Gottlieb Company brought out *Humpty Dumpty*, the first machine equipped with flippers. Flippers are the short arms near the bottom of the board activated by control buttons on the side of the game. By manipulating the flippers, a player can return a ball to play when it is about to drop through the outhold. Pinball makers could now claim that flipper pinball was completely a game of skill, and as such should not be outlawed along with gambling games of chance.

In 1956, a Federal court decision made a distinction between gambling devices and flipper games without a pay-out. Soon all pinball machines were fitted with flippers, and the pay-out pinball machine disappeared almost completely. To make the game more rewarding, manufacturers substituted free games or "add-a-ball" bonuses in place of cash pay-outs. Even today, pinball machines intended for use in different parts of the nation are manufacturered differently to comply with local standards, since add-a-ball, free games, and automatic plungers are still illegal in some places.

Most anti-pinball legislation was erased from the books during the late 1960s. In 1972, pinball addicts could again exercise their reflexes legally in Los Angeles. In 1976, pinball again became legal in Chicago, the city of its birth. And the same year, the New York City Council voted to allow pinball machines in the Big Apple—though thousands of illegal machines were already in use there at the time. Pinball was once again respectable.

Today, few people think of pinball as anything but a harmless, fun game for players of all ages. Pinball machines are turning up in shopping malls, department stores, airports, college dormitories, and restaurants, as well as in the video game center, the modern version of the penny arcade. The success of the movie *Tommy*, which featured a "pinball wizard," did much to spur a new interest in the game. In 1975, after the release of the movie, Bally's *Wizard* became the fastest-selling pinball machine in the United States.

An Army Lives on its Smoke

Tobacco cultivation was important in the American colonies from their earliest history. In fact, before the Revolution, tobacco was legal tender in several Southern colonies with large plantations. Virginia enacted a law ordaining that taxes be paid in tobacco. George Washington, you'll remember, was reported to have written from Valley Forge: "If you can't send men, send tobacco."

The house mouse is found throughout the world. It usually measures about six inches long and weighs under one ounce. It has grey to brown fur, large rounded ears, a pointed muzzle, and a naked, scaley tail. An omniverous feeder, it causes great destruction and contamination of food. It may carry human diseases, such as typhoid and spotted fever. Females produce litters of four to eight young after a gestation period of three weeks. Under favorable conditions, mice breed throughout the year. The young mature in two months.

Mill's Machine

The first recorded attempt to invent a typewriter took place in 1714, when an Englishman named Henry Mill filed a patent for what he rather long-windedly described as "An Artificial Machine or Method for the Impressing or Transcribing of Letters, Singly or Progressively one after another, as in Writing, whereby all Writing whatsoever may be Engrossed in Paper or Parchment so Neat and Exact as not to be distinguished from Print." If Mr. Mill was as verbose as this description suggests, it's no wonder he saw the advantages of a typewriting machine. In any case, Mill's typewriter was apparently never constructed, and no drawings of his project were ever found.

America easily leads the world today in bathtubs per capita. Many American homes are equipped with two or three or even four tubs. The shower has recently replaced the tub as the preferred washing ritual. A shower, by the way, uses up only about half as much water as a tub bath.

Hats

The expression "a feather in your cap" was first recorded in the 17th century, but feathers in the cap were a sign of nobility more than 500 years earlier. The phrase may be related to the custom of sticking feathers in a soldier's cap to indicate the number of enemy slain.

Thomas Crapper contributed a major innovation to toilet improvement with the invention of a mechanism that shut off the flow of clean water when the reservoir was filled. Previously, the supply of clean water had to be turned on and off by the user, and many fastidious Victorians preferred to leave the water running continually to assure cleanliness.

In Crapper's W.C., the user pulled the chain to raise a plate inside the reservoir that propelled water up a tube and into the pipe leading to the bowl. As the water level in the reservoir went down, a float sank until it opened the attached intake valve. The same float closed the valve when the reservoir was filled again. Since the clean water valve could not open unless the chain was pulled, the saving of water with Crapper's W.C. was considerable.

The ingenious sanitary engineer advertised his product as "Crapper's Valveless Waste Preventer—Certain Flush with Easy Pull," although individual models later took on such names as Deluge, Cascade, and Niagara. In the 1880s, Crapper's firm installed the sanitary facilities in Queen Victoria's Sandringham House—including 30 toilets and a bathroom with side-by-side sinks labelled *Head, Face, Hands,* and *Teeth.* Expensive cedar wood was used for the toilet seats, since the wood, in the words of a Crapper official, "has the advantage of being warm . . . and subtly aromatic."

During the Zulu War, fought in Africa during 1880-81, the field correspondent of the London Morning Post was a 23-year-old girl named Lady Florence Caroline Douglas Dixie, the daughter of an English nobleman.

Modern hats are made from all kinds of materials, in all kinds of styles, from all around the world—but no single style predominates. Most of the hat styles of today are from another land or another age.

For instance, you wear a bit of history when you don a fedora, a bowler hat, or a derby. The soft felt, creased *fedora* owes its name to an 1882 production of French playright Sardou's *Fedora*, in which a Russian princess wore such a hat. The *bowler* owes nothing to the kegler. It was named after William Bowler, the English hatter who, around 1850, introduced it as a hard-shelled headgear for horsemen. In the United States, the hat came to be known as the *derby*, after a famous horse race held in Derby, England.

The *shapka*, the Russian fur hat, originated in the Coṣsacks' sheepskin hat. Early in the 16th century, it was introduced in England by a Russian ambassador. The felt *Homburg* owes its name not to Hamburg, but to a German town called Homburg where it was first made. The *Panama* hat, made from the leaves of the jijippa plant, have never been made in Panama. Most are manufactured in Ecuador, Colombia, or Peru, but the hat originally reached America through distributors in Panama.

Siberia is over 5,000,000 square miles in area.

The Bible Mentions Vinegar

Alcohol was the first pure organic compound made by man, and acetic acid produced by the natural souring of wine was man's first acid. The origin of vinegar's use is remote, but pickled meats and vegetables were important items in the diets of many ancient civilizations. Vinegar was mentioned in the Bible, and widely used among early people as a food, a preservative, and a medicine.

The first tooth-cleaning device was undoubtedly the toothpick. Gold toothpicks dating from around 3500 B.C. have been found among ancient ruins in Mesopotamia, many of them encased in skillfully decorated gold boxes.

The only presidential pair of father and son in the history of the United States were President John Adams and his son, President John Quincy Adams.

Scissors are probably as old as the loom, but the oldest pair still in existence is a bronze tool from Egypt, dating from the third century B.C. These scissors were richly decorated with figures of metal inlay, and the blades could be detached for separate sharpening.

Meat and potatoes are the foundation of most American cooking, and of many European cuisines as well. The spud is so rooted in Western cooking that it's hard to believe the vegetable was totally unknown in Europe just a few hundred years ago.

In the mid-16th century, Spanish conquistadores in South Amerca discovered that the Incas ate a white tuber they called "papa." (Perhaps it was the "father" of their diet.) The Incas used the plum-sized vegetables in hundreds of ways, baking them in hot ash, eating them raw or dried, and even pounding them into a flour.

All A-Glow

On November 5, 1895, Wilhelm Konrad Roentgen, professor of physics at the University of Wurzburg, was carrying out some experiments with cathode rays. These rays are beams of electons, produced by a high voltage current traveling between two electrodes within a closed glass tube. Roentgen covered the tube with black paper so that none of the light generated by the current could escape. But then something happened that was totally unexpected: when the current was turned on in the cathode-ray tube, a fluorescent screen lying nearby began to glow as if it were receiving light.

When the scientist turned off the current in the cathode-ray rube, the screen stopped glowing. Sinc the glass tube was completely covered, Roentgen knew that the cathode rays were emitting some invisible form of radiation capable of activating the fluorescnt coating of the screen. He named the mysterious radiation *X-rays*, since X was the usual mathematical symbol for an unknown.

Because of the medieval aristocracy's aversion to bathing, many of the more famous places surviving today are completely without sanitation facilities.

Oliver Wendell Holmes, Associate Justice of the United States Supreme Court from 1902 to 1935, was the son of a famous essayist and poet, also named Oliver Wendell Holmes.

Today, the most valuable truffle fields, or *truffieres*, are located in the Perigord district of France, near Bordeaux, and in the Vaucluse area north of Marseilles. The Perigord variety have been prized as the best since the 15th century. Truffles can be found in other areas, including North America, but are extremely rare outside of southern France.

In the Bible it is recorded:
It rained for 40 days and 40 nights.
Moses was on the mount 40 days and 40 nights.
Israel spent 40 years in the wilderness.
Elijah spent 40 days and 40 nights in the wilderness.
Joah gave Nineveh 40 days to repent.
Christ's sojourn in the wilderness was 40 days.
(Lent is also 40 days long)

There were no toilets of any kind in either the Louvre or in the palace at Versailles. Members of the court were expected to relieve themselves before they entered the palace; the rows of statues that lined the garden promenades provided convenient niches for an undisturbed tinkle.

The Teutonic tribesmen who overran Europe bathed for the most part in cold rivers or streams. During the Middle Ages, among some communities, bathing was considered a sin and an act of pride. Probably, the Church's opposition to bathing stemmed from the excesses of the Roman public bath.

Women's Basketball

Women's basketball has been around since the 1890s, when Clara Baer introduced the game at a New Orleans college using Naismith's published rules (although another claim traces the first women's basketball to Smith College in 1892). But Clara misinterpreted some of Naismith's diagrams, assuming that certain dotted lines Naismith had drawn to indicate the best area for team play were actually restraining lines to be drawn on the court. Thus, for many years, women's basketball was played under different rules than the men's game, with each player limited to movement only within certain parts of the court. Today, women's games are played under men's rules, and the old game is now called "rover" or "netball."

Cheese Tax

Many of the cheese-making advances of the Middle Ages were the work of cloistered monks who were among the few people of the era with the time to experiment and the literacy required to write down and evaluate results. Outside the monasteries, cheese-making remained basiclly a family industry until the 15th and 16th centuries, when cheese-makers began joining together to form cooperatives. Road taxes actually played a part in the change to community cheese-making. At the time, carts were assessed a tax for using a highway according to the number of cheeses they carried, rather than the total weight of the cheese. Thus cheese-makers who joined together to produce large cheeses could transport their product much more cheaply.

The four Horsemen of the Apocalypse were Conquest, Famine, Pestilence, and Death.

Fungus Among Us

Hunting the truffle is a difficult, delicate operation. Since the fungus grows underground, it's virtually impossible to tell where a crop of the delicacies might be found, but French farmers have developed a number of tricks. Some farmers with a nose for the truffle claim they can locate their catch by examining the ground around oak trees. Others maintain that columns of small yellow flies hovering over truffle patches lead them to the buried treasure.

Most truffle hunting, however, is carried out with the aid of specially trained pigs or "rooting hogs." The pigs are better at scenting out the truffles, but they present the farmer with an additional problem. Once a pig locates a truffle, he's likely to gobble it right up before the farmer can chase him off. The pig's palate, it seems, is as partial to the truffle as man's. Farmers can train pigs to search for truffles in a matter of days—but it may take two or three years to teach them not to eat their find!

A Billion on Chewing Gum

There are gum-chewers galore in this country, male and female, young and old, from every stratum of society. No one knows for sure how many people chew gum, but some 35 *billion* sticks will find their way into American mouths this year. That's about five billion packets, or 25 packets for each man, woman and child in the United States. At, say, 20 cents a throw, Americans will spend about a billion dollars on gum this year. And you thought gum-chewing was on the wane?

Tricorn

The three-cornered hat, or tricorn, was the universal men's hat in Europe for most of the 18th century. But after the French Revolution, the tricorn was abolished in France in favor of the smaller, round hats. These new hats were considered so subversive in the rest of Europe that Russian Czar Paul I gave their wearers a paid vacation in Siberia.

The National Sport

The first organized baseball team, the Knickerbocker Baseball Club, was formed in New York City in 1845. The first baseball rule book was written in 1858 by Henry Chadwick. In that same year, the first governing body of baseball, the National Association of Baseball Players, was formed.

Chickens Are Nourishing

Pound for pound, chicken is a more economical, nourishing meat than either beef or pork. A hundred grams of chicken meat (about three-and-a-half ounces) contains from 150 to 200 calories, while a like quantity of beef contains 273 calories and pork about 450. Chicken is twice as rich in protein as an equal portion of pork, and contains only a fraction of the fat (from seven to 12 grams per 100) in either beef (22 grams) or pork (45 grams).

The earliest Kodak cameras were preloaded at the factory with film for 100 pictures—each round in shape and just two-and-a-half inches in diameter.

Cider Vinegar

The flavor of the vinegar produced by any process is determined by the kind of fermented materials used. In the United States, cider vinegar made from apples and apple cider is the favorite, while in France wine vinegar made from grapes remains the most popular. Vinegar has also been made from fruits such as oranges and pineapples, and—believe it or not—from honey.

Toothpaste and Tooth Decay

Isn't it puzzling that so many people who never put a brush to their teeth go through life without a single cavity, while others who brush regularly spend considerable time in the dentist's chair. Diet certainly has an effect on dental health, for people sharing certain cuisines are conspicuously free from tooth decay. But the precise nature of tooth decay—and the way to prevent it—remain largely a mystery.

Did you ever wonder why most canned foods are packed in water or syrup? In 1927, American Can Company researchers found that preserved foods surrounded by liquid rather than air were less likely to spoil or lose their vitamins. Foods that could not be packed in liquid were henceforth vacuum-packed—sealed in cans from which all air has been excluded. Food canning is now considered virtually foolproof.

Coffee Has Caffeine

Caffeine is an alkaloid that mildly stimulates cerebral and cardiac activity—in short, it's a pick-me-up. Try to image the difference in American offices and factories if the drug were suddenly to disappear, for caffeine is often the oil that makes the American brain run smoothly. And not without its price; caffeine causes gastric acidity and nervousness as well as heightened cardiac action. But coffee-swillers, take heart. Though theoretically the drug can be fatal in large doses, there is no case on record of a caffeine overdose.

Oddly enough, though coffee is today a fixture from Titicaca to Timbuktu, the beverage was virtually unknown in most of the world just a few centuries ago. For years on end, the tribesmen of Ethiopia and Central Africa crushed coffee berries and mixed them with animal fat to form balls which they devoured before their war parties. The Africans also made a wine from the coffee fruit, though they never brewed a hot coffee beverage.

Will She Kiss You Again?

The proportions of sugar and water in onions determine the taste of particular varieties. But the way in which an onion is cut or cooked will also influence its taste. A finely-cut onion will more easily lose its oils in cooking, resulting in a milder flavor. Onions cooked in liquid quickly lose water, increasing the proportion of sugar and resulting in a sweeter-tasting, less odorous onion. As Jonathan Swift noted:

But lest your kissing be spoil'd
Your onions must be thoroughly boil'd.

"Strength" is the only eight-letter word in the English language with just one vowel.

Tulip Tree

The tulip tree is not related to the tulip. It owes its name to its tulip-like green-yellow flowers. This tree is also known as the canary whitewood in England and the yellow poplar in the United States. Tulipwood, a white or yellow wood prized by cabinet makers, is, as you might expect, not a product of the tulip, but rather of the tulip tree.

The hot dog was invented in 1852 by members of a butchers' guild in Frankfurt, Germany—hence its nicknames "frank" and "frankfurter." The hot dog first appeared in the United States in 1883. One year's consumption of hot dogs in the U.S. would, if linked together, stretch from earth to the moon—and back.

No known wild sheep are wool-bearing.

The longest continuous tunnel in the world is the Delaware Aqueduct, which provides part of the water supply of New York City. It is 85 miles long.

On the Throne

French monarch Louis XIV made use of a comfortable, highly decorated close stool euphemistically known as a *chaise percée* (open chair), *chaise d'affaires,* or *chaise necessaire.* His palace at Versailles at one time included 264 stools, but Louis' favorite was a black laquered box with inlaid mother-of-pearl borders, a red lacquered interior, and a padded seat of green velour. The monarch's *chaise percée* sometimes served as a throne, and it was considered a high honor to be granted an audience with His Majesty while he was heeding the call of nature that all men, rich and poor, are similarly obliged to answer.

Don't Rib Me

The English didn't invent the umbrella, but they did develop the first *practical* waterproof bumbershoot. This happened in the late 17th century. By 1700, umbrellas were in regular commercial production, with whalebone the favored material for the ribs.

Sun Shield

The first headgear used by primitive man was probably a simple band worn around the head to keep hair from falling in front of the eyes. Ancient people in the Mediterranean area wore plaited straw or rushes on their heads to shield them from the sun and rain. In Egypt, ordinary workers wore caps or kerchiefs against the sun, while the wealthy often donned wigs, or curled or braided their hair with beeswax, and wore helmets ornamented with symbols of their rank.

The art of ancient Mesopotamia depicts gods and rulers with tall headdresses, and ordinary men wearing simple caps or no hats at all. By the way, the *beret,* so popular in many countries today, was actually worn in Mesopotamia thousands of years ago. Ninth-century Frankish ruler Charlemagne owned some 500 berets!

Did you know that it is against the law in Pueblo, Colorado, to raise or permit a dandelion to grow within the city limits?

The circus presumably originated with the horse and chariot races of ancient Rome. The structure known as the *Roman Circus* was a round or an oval structure with tiers of seats for spectators. This building enclosed a space in which the races, games and gladitorial combats took place.

The modern circus originated with performances by equestrian specialists. The ring, strewn with sawdust, was a familiar sight during the closing years of the 18th century.

Today the circus is a nomadic tent show, with trained animals, acrobats, and clowns. The main tent is known as the *Big Top*.

Circuses were common in the United States and in England after 1830. In 1869, two additional rings were placed in the main tent, and audiences were introduced to the three-ring circus. The most celebrated circus in America was that of P.T. Barnum, who modestly called his presentation "The Greatest Show on Earth."

Thump and Gunch

Each European country has developed a pinball lingo all its own, but we don't have to delve into any foreign languages to find a colorful array of terms pertaining to America's most popular coin game. *Gunching*, for instance, is body English applied to the machine. *Kickers* are targets made with stretched rubber that send a ball rebounding quickly in the opposite direction, while *kickout holes* are holes in the playfield that electrically propel a captured ball back onto the playfield. *Drop-targets* may be struck only once by each ball, falling below the playfield after contact.

Thumper-bumpers are the large circular targets, usually equipped with a bell and a light, that send a ball careening off rapidly after each score. Motion is imparted to the ball by a spring system that spins the thumper-bumper when a ball makes contact with it. Most thumper-bumpers bear the words "100 Points When Lit," or some such legend to explain the scoring provided by the target. A *free game* mechanism is just that—a player attaining a certain score, or hitting a certain target, moves a numbered drum inside the machine that allows him to push a button for a replay without inserting another coin.

Roll 'Em

In the early days of cigarette manufacture, a factory worker could hand-roll about 18,000 cigarettes per week. Crude machines for cigarette-rolling began to appear in the mid-1870s. In the following decade, the machines replaced hand-rollers almost completely, with one machine doing the job of 50 workers. A modern machine can turn out about 1,500 cigarettes per minute, or 36,000 packs in an eight-hour day.

Erathosthenes estimated the circumference of the earth within one percent—about 200 years B.C.

Fred Had Ideas

If medieval man rarely carried a handkerchief, what did he use to wipe his nose? The finger and the sleeve—customs not altogether unknown today. In the Middle Ages, when there were no forks, and food was eaten with the hands, etiquette demanded that the cultured individual touch his food only with the right hand, and his nose only with the left. The medieval English *Boke of Curtasye* advised that it was proper to blow one's nose with a finger, as long as the finger was then wiped on the sleeve or skirt.

In the 16th century, when the upper classes were beginning to use handkerchiefs to dab their noses, the peasant still had to make do with his finger or sleeve. The Dutch scholar Erasmus felt compelled to point out that "to wipe your nose on your cap or your sleeve is boorish," though he conceded that it "may be all right for pastry-cooks." A riddle of the era asked: "What is it that the king puts in his pocket but the peasant throws away?"

Incidentally, we can blame Frederick the Great of Prussia for the vestigial buttons still found on men's jacket sleeves. It seems that the monarch was so displeased with the slovenly appearance of his troops, due in large part to their use of the cuffs of their uniforms for nose and sweat wiping, that to discourage this habit, he ordered a row of buttons sewn on the top side of all uniform sleeves. Thereafter, the unmindful soldier would receive a nasty scratch on his face whenever he used his sleeve as a towel. The buttons still survive on men's jackets, though they've been moved from the top of the sleeve to the side.

The ornamental use of handkerchiefs was far more prevalent than its practical use. Embroidered and fringed silk handkerchiefs began to appear in Europe during the 16th century, and quickly became *de rigueur* for all fashionable ladies. In the 17th century, the French developed hanky craftsmanship to a fine art, turning out elegant handwrought laces with delicate threadwork and embroidery. They even ornamented some of their masterpieces with precious gems!

The commonest disease in the world is dental caries, or tooth decay, known to afflict over 53 per cent of the U.S. population. During their lifetime, few people completely escape the effects of this particular disease.

Income Tax

While it is true that incomes were occasionally taxed in medieval Italian cities, the income tax is chiefly a modern institution. The first important income tax was instituted in Great Britain. It was levied from 1799 to 1816, in order to pay for the wars against Napoleon. Imagine how happy the British taxpayer was when Napoleon was defeated at Waterloo! The United States had a temporary income tax from 1864 to 1872, in order to pay for the Civil War. As we all know, the income tax is no longer a temporary measure. In England the permanent income tax was adopted in 1874. In the United States, there was a brief reprieve when the income tax law of 1894 was declared unconstitutional. But in 1913, with the passage of the 16th Amendment, the income tax became legal in the United States. Paid at first by only a small minority of the population, it is now a major source of revenue for the national government, in some years providing as much as 85 per cent of all its revenues.

The Truffle is No Trifle

The truffle is a fungus of the class *ascomycetes*, found mainly in the temperature zones. There are about 70 species of truffles, of which only seven are edible. Truffles are usually black with warty surfaces, ranging in size from a pea to an orange, with the average truffle about the size of a golf ball. Most truffles grow close to the roots of trees, from one to three feet below the surface, and seem especially partial to the roots of the oak.

Vinegar Has Plenty Bacteria

In earlier times, most vinegar was produced from wine. The English word "vinegar," in fact, is derived from the French words *vin*, "wine," and *agire*, "sour." France has long been noted for its fine vinegars, which have been exported since at least the 16th century. Frenchman Louis Pasteur used vinegar to a great extent in demonstrating the existence of bacteria.

The island of Sicily has been invaded and settled in turn by the Pheonicians, the Greeks, the Carthaginians, the Romans, the Vandals, the Saracens and the Norman French. It became part of Italy in 1127.

Dandy

In 1764, a group of dapper English gentlemen formed the Macaroni club, in tribute to the Italian fashions they considered the finest in Europe. The word "macaroni" became associated with English fops in their powdered wigs and fancy hats, and found its way into that familiar American ditty, *Yankee Doodle.*

> *Yankee Doodle came to town*
> *Riding on a pony*
> *Stuck a feather in his cap*
> *And called it macaroni.*

It Was a Clavichord

The immediate precursor of the first stringed instrument with a keyboard was the *monochord*. This instrument consisted of a wooden sounding box with a single string and a movable bridge. The bridge could be shifted at fixed intervals to determine the length of the string, and hence, its tone. The ancient Greek philosopher Pythagoras used the monochord to investigate the nature of musical sound. In later centuries, an unknown inventor devised a stringed instrument in which the length of the strings was fixed by hammers activated by a keyboard. This was the clavichord.
was fixed by hammers activated by a keyboard. This was the clavichord.

The first atomic aircraft carrier was the U.S.S. Enterprise, commissioned in 1961.

The first hoop and basket sets sold by the Narragansett Company were closed-bottomed, and a ladder had to be used to retrieve the ball after each basket.

Bathing in Fashion

The word "spa" comes to us from the Belgian town of Spa. A mineral spring discovered in 1326 helped make the town a very fashionable resort during the 18th century. Today, the most famous spas in the world are at Baden-Baden in Germany (*bad* means "bath" in German), Carlsbad in Czechoslovakia, Vichy in France, and Hot Springs in Arkansas.

Marengo

Napoleon was an avid chicken fancier. While campaigning, he had his cooks prepare a fresh chicken every half-hour so that one would always be ready when he decided to eat. Napoleon's chef is credited with the invention of one of the most familiar and delicious of all chicken dishes. During the battle of Marengo in Italy, the Little Corporal's chef found himself without butter, so he obtained some native olive oil in which to fry his chicken. To mask the flavor of the oil, he added tomatoes, mushrooms, wine, and herbs. Napoleon loved the dish, and *Chicken Marengo* entered the world of chicken cookery.

Bamboo Brim

The most common hat in the world today is the so-called "coolies hat" of China, which is worn by one-third of the people on earth. The wide-brimmed hat is made from bamboo, with leaves as padding. The oldest hat in the world may well be the familiar "chef's" hat, which was worn in ancient Assyria as a badge of office in the kitchen. And the most expensive headdress in the world is a hat worn by Napoleon, which recently sold at auction for a handsome $30,000.

Bowled Over

It was late in the 18th century that the water closet, or W.C., began to appear in Europe. Developed mainly by Englishmen Alexander Cummings and Joseph Bramah, the earliest W.C.'s consisted of a stool with an attached handle. When the handle was pulled, water from a reservoir mounted above the stool was channeled into the bowl, while a plug was opened to drain the latrine. Oddly enough, the English patent office had been opened for 158 years before it received its first application for a water closet patent, that of Cummings in 1775—almost 300 years after an unnamed genius built the first London W.C.

If the Nicotine Fits

Spanish explorers in Mexico found the Aztecs smoking crushed tobacco leaves in corn husks. Tobacco reached the European continent at least as early as 1558, when a Spanish physician named Francisco Fernandes, sent to the New World by King Philip II to report on its products, brought back some plants and seeds. The following year, Jean Nicot, the French ambassador to Portugal, sent tobacco seeds to the French court of Catherine de Medici. The queen reported that tobacco cured her of crippling headaches, and she immortalized Nicot by proclaiming the new plant *Nicotiana*, a name recognizable in our word for tobacco's most baleful element, nicotine.

The tarpon fish has scales that are almost four-inches wide.

Amo, Amas . . .

Did you know that an *ani* is a South American bird, but an *ana* is a collection of anecdotes? How about *anil*? It's an indigo dye. *Ara*? That's a genus of birds. And if someone asked you for a "diva's forte," would you respond immediately with *aria*? Well, if you were an addict of that ubiquitous indoor sport known as the crossword puzzle, these words would be as familiar to you as *emu, gnu, ort,* and *ait.*

You'd be in rather large company, too. A 1959 Gallup Poll found that matching wits with crossword compilers is the number one indoor game in this country, surpassing such favorites as checkers, bingo, and poker! An estimated 30 million Americans regularly wrack their brains for the name of "an East Indian shrub" or "an African antelope," and in England, an even larger percentage of the population regularly accepts the crossword challenge. In fact, the crossword puzzle is a familiar sight to speakers of every language that uses the Roman alphabet. And speaking of the Roman alphabet, some stuffy crossword buffs have gone so far as to construct their puzzles in Latin!

Premiums

Thirty-year-old William Wrigley, Jr. moved to Chicago in 1891 and set up the Wrigley Company with just $32 of his own money and a $5,000 loan. The firm initially sold soap, then branched out into baking powder. In 1892, Wrigley ordered some chewing gum from the Zeno Manufacturing Company to offer jobbers as an inducement to buy his baking powder. Wrigley's salesmen dispensed two packs of gum with each 10-cent package of baking powder, and the jobbers soon reported that they found it much easier to sell the gum than peddle the powder. It didn't take Wrigley long to see the possibilities.

By the turn of the century, Wrigley's gum was being sold, coast to coast, in stores and vending machines. Chewing gum factories were soon springing up in a number of foreign countries, including Canada, England, Germany, Australia, and New Zealand. By the end of World War II, the taste for Wrigley's product in America, Europe, and Asia was so great that his factories could barely keep pace with the demand.

Noble Discovery

The "cheese of kings" is not to be confused with the "king of cheeses," *Roquefort*, by far the most popular sheep's milk cheese in the Western world. According to a legend, this blue-veined mold ripened cheese was discovered many centuries ago by a shepherd boy who left a bunch of bread and sheep's milk cheese in a cave. Returning weeks later, he found that his cheese had been miraculously transformed into the marbled delicacy so popular today.

The U.S. record for rope-skipping was established in December of 1933, by Tommy Thompson of Pueblo, Colorado, who made 20,010 skips in one hour and 53 minutes without missing.

Celery is a close relative of the herbs dill and caraway and of the vegetables parsnip and carrot.

Nero Wolfe, the corpulent detective created by Rex Stout, raised orchids as a hobby. In the movies, Nero Wolfe owned over 10,000 orchids, weighed about 278 lbs., stood 5 feet, 8 inches tall, and declared that his favorite color was yellow. He was played by Edward Arnold, and also by Walter Connolly.

The language spoken by the people of Brittany, in France is closely related to the language spoken by the people of Cornwall, in England. Both are old Celtic languages, much older than either English or French. The other Celtic languages are Manx, Welsh, and the Gaelic of Ireland and Scotland.

John Wesley was born at the beginning of the 18th century in England, and became famous as the founder of Methodism. He is said to have preached 40,000 sermons, and to have travelled 250,000 miles in his religious efforts.

The English Discover Coffee

Coffee became widely popular in London during the 17th century. The first coffee house opened its doors in 1652. Soon coffee houses became the centers of political, social, literary, and business life in the city. In America, the first popular coffee houses opened as early as the 1680s—and the *Mayflower* listed among its cargo a mortar and pestle to be used for grinding coffee beans.

At that time, almost all European coffee was imported from Yemen and Arabia, since the Arabs had jealously guarded their coffee monopoly by forbidding the export of fertile seeds on pain of death. But around 1700, Dutch traders managed to smuggle some coffee shrubs out of Arabia, sending the embezzled botanica to the island of Java, then a Dutch possession. The growth of coffee plants in Java soon became so prolific that the island's name became synonymous with the brew.

The French, too, managed to get their hands on the coveted shrub, and established coffee plantations in many of their colonies.

Bovines were without a doubt one of the first animals to be domesticated. Early man found that the cow produces milk far in excess of that needed for its offspring, and that the male can be made docile enough for work as a draught animal. Also, the digestive system of these creatures enables them to subsist on roughage and other plant parts that might otherwise be useless to man. For thousands of years, cattle were employed as work animals and raised for their milk; raising cattle for meat is a relatively recent development. There are still parts of the world, like India, in which beef is never eaten, despite an abundance of cattle.

The Kentucky Derby is held every year at Churchill Downs, Louisville, Kentucky on the first Saturday in May. It has been running since 1876.

Head Coverings

In the East, the *turban* has been the customary headgear for many centuries. The color and shape of a turban has historically indicated rank or occupation. The longest turbans may contain more than 20 feet of material. Some Hindu turbans also contained a circular metal blade that could be hurled at an enemy.

Among Arabs, the common headdress is the *kaffiyeh*, a piece of cloth folded in a triangular shape and secured to the head with a round cord. Another hat from the Near East, the *fez*, was popular as long ago as the 11th century. Most fezes are made from red felt. In a 1920s attempt to westernize Turkey, the fez was abolished as part of that country's national dress; tradition-conscious Turks who insisted on wearing the hat changed their minds after a few fez wearers were led to the gallows.

Remember Hoover

"A chicken in every pot" is no longer a dream or an idle campaign slogan: it's a reality. The chicken, the most abundant of all domesticated creatures, now numbers over four billion, or one for every person on earth. And the expression "an egg on every plate" might be equally apt, for each year the world's chickens produce some 390 billion eggs—enough to provide every human being with a hundred eggs a year!

Gum and Baseball Cards

The Topps Company estimates that there are now more than 100,000 serious baseball card collectors in the United States. Enthusiasts will pay surprisingly high sums for a valuable specimen. The largest collection of baseball cards in the world—200,000 cards—belongs to the Metropolitan Museum of Art in New York, and the most prized Topps card in existence is the 1952 Mickey Mantle, valued as high as $100.

Pinball Machines

The back glass—the upright portion of the modern pinball machine—made its first appearance during the late 1930s. Originally intended to hold various electric features such as the point totalizers, the back glass was soon sporting the comic artwork so much a part of the modern pinball machine. Artwork quickly began to appear on the playfield itself. Attracted by the colorful illustrations, the electric buzzers and bells, and the continuing innovations of Williams, Gottlieb, Moloney, and others, gamesters began swarming around pinball machines in unprecedented numbers.

But at the same time that pinball manufacturers were turning out new electric games to challenge the growing number of players, pinball came under increased opposition from political and church groups opposed to gambling. During the early 1930s, slot machines and other pay-out games were still legal in many parts of the country. Since pinball was a novelty game played for fun only, many players began to turn their attention to games that offered cash as well as self-satisfaction for a skillfully played, or lucky, game. In 1933, Bally introduced *Rocket*, the first automatic pay-out pinball machine. Now a player reaching a certain score, or hitting a special target, received an immediate cash pay-out from the machine —a highly attractive feature to Americans of the Depression era.

Until then, pinball had suffered little from legal restraints. But once Bally, Williams, and other manufacturers began to produce pay-out games, opponents of gambling cast a suspicious eye toward pinball. Newspapers carried stories incorrectly linking pinball operators with organized crime. Politicians accused pinball makers of teaching and encouraging gambling among teenagers. In 1939, the city of Atlanta passed a bill stipulating a fine of $20 and imprisonment of up to 30 days for operating a pinball machine in the city. Other cities and states rushed onto the anti-pinball bandwagon, banning not only the pay-out games, but all novelty pinball games as well.

One of the first entrepreneurs to move into the pinball industry was David Gottlieb, a Chicago-based film distributor and arcade machine manufacturer. In 1931, Gottlieb produced a counter top game called *Baffle Ball*, the first widely successful horizontal pinball game. *Baffle Ball* was a simple game by modern standards: for one penny, players attempted to shoot seven balls into four circular scoring areas, or into lower-scoring slots at the bottom of the playfield. A ball shot into a cup called the "Baffle Point" doubled the score of the entire table, provided it was not knocked off by a subsequent ball. The added challenge of the Baffle Point struck the fancy of pinball players from coast to coast. Within a year, Gottlieb was producing 400 *Baffle Ball* machines a day.

One of Gottlieb's West Coast jobbers was Harry Williams, considered by many the true father of the modern pinball industry. At a 1929 convention, Williams was intrigued by a coin-operated game called *Jai Alai*, in which players attempted to flip balls into scoring hoops mounted on an upright playfield. Williams immediately took out a franchise for *Jai Alai*; then founded a manufacturing company in Los Angeles and began turning out his own coin-operated games.

At first Williams bought and modernized old bagatelle-type machines, designing new playfields and installing them in the old bagatelle cabinets. Later, he began to invent entirely new games, devising many of the features still common to pinball machines around the world. His first invention was called *Advance*, a 10-ball game whose intricate design demanded more skill of players than any previous game. More importantly, *Advance* was the game that spawned the familiar "tilt" mechanism so detested by avid pinballers.

During World War II, the phrase "Kilroy was here" was the most ubiquitous graffito. Supposedly, Kilroy was an Inspector Sergeant, who, after checking anything, wrote on it "Kilroy was here."

Delight

The chicken is such a common creature today that we have more than a half-dozen words for the bird, and the terminology might be confusing to anyone who didn't grow up on a poultry farm. *Chicken* itself usually refers to any member of the *gallus domesticus* species, male or female. The word comes from the Old English *cycen*, which was in turn derived from *kukin*, "little cock."

A *cock* is a male chicken, or a *rooster*. The word *hen* which designates a female chicken, usually one of egg-laying age, is also derived from an Old English word for rooster, *hana*. A *pullet*, meanwhile, is a hen less than a year old. The term comes from the French word for hen, *poule*, from which our *poultry* is derived. A *capon* is a castrated male chicken, and a *springer* is a female chicken a few months old.

Join the Club

The first golf club in England, The Royal Blackheath, was founded around 1787, when there were already six clubs in Scotland. The most famous Scottish course, the Royal and Ancient Golf Club of St. Andrews, was founded in 1754, and remains the supreme authority in the sport, framing and revising rules for clubs throughout the world—except for clubs in the United States, which has its own governing body. There are now some 1,800 golf courses dotting the island of Great Britain.

All Aboard

There is no skateboard hockey, derby, or dancing just yet, but judging from the way the sport of skateboarding is catching on around this country, those pastimes won't be long in coming. Skateboarding did not reach the public eye until 1962, when the proprietors of the Val Surf Shop in North Hollywood, California, contracted with the Chicago Roller Skate Company to produce roller skate trucks for skateboards. The new skateboards sold quickly to surfers, who used the boards for equilibrium exercises to improve their surfing.

By 1965, many companies were manufacturing aluminum, wood, and fiberglass skateboards. But trouble was just around the bend. Skateboards were objected to as being noisy and dangerous. When the California

Medical Association released a report announcing that the skateboard had replaced the bicycle as the chief source of childhood injuries, cities all across the country began to outlaw skateboards on public streets. The skateboard fad died, along with dozens of manufacturing companies and *Skateboarder* magazine.

Then, in 1973, a California surfer named Frank Nasworthy devised the first skateboard with urethane wheels, which provided more traction and a quieter ride than the earlier wheels. New fiberglass boards increased board control. Skateboarding became safe and acceptable, and the sport took off again.

Skateboards are now a familiar sight in almost every American city, and are gradually working their way into everyday American life—welcome or not. In 1975, Emery Air Freight announced that deliverymen in some cities had taken to the skateboard to shorten delivery time. And, in Sepulveda, California, two men held up a doughnut shop, making off with $125 aboard this unusual get-away vehicle.

Shell Out

Lobsters live on the rocky bottom of shallow sea waters. They can usually be found at a depth of about 120 feet, but lobsters have been found at depths up to 1,350 feet. For the most part, they are sedentary creatures, swimming only in an emergency or at night, when they seek the small shellfish that form their diet. A hardy specimen can live as long as 50 years— but thanks to hungry diners, few ever get the chance.

Lobsters are so small at birth that hundreds can fit in the palm of a hand. As the creature grows, it must continually shed its shell and replace it with a new one to fit the enlarging body. Young male lobsters molt twice a year, young females once every two years, while a mature specimen will shed its shell once every three or four years. After molting, the lobster will remain unprotected for months until its new shell has formed, during which time the defenseless lobster must, indeed, "lay low."

After about eight years, the lobster reaches full adulthood, usually measuring from 12 to 14 inches in length and rarely weighing more than 10 pounds. The largest lobster on record measured three feet from mouth to tail, and tipped the scales at 42 pounds! The giant crustacean is now on exhibit at the Museum of Science in Boston. There have also been unverified claims of lobsters four feet long caught off the coast of New Jersey, and of a 48-pounder and a 60-pounder caught off New England.

Before your mouth begins watering, we might point out that large lobstrs are not very palatable, for their flesh grows quite tough as they age.

Like their insect cousins, crustaceans are well equipped with legs. The lobster has five pairs of legs, the first three equipped with pincers. Each of the lobster's pairs of legs serves a different function. One grasps food, another crushes it, another passes it to the mouth, another flaps to provide a current to aid in respiration.

"As red as a lobster" may be a cliche, but uncooked lobsters are actually dark blue or green in color. The shell turns red or orange only when boiled, as English writer Samuel Butler noted:

And like a lobster boiled, the morn
From black to red began to turn.

What's at Steak

When the hamburger arrived in America, it was eaten quite raw—the way the French, for instance, still prefer their meat.

The English and Irish were the first to cook their beef patties well-done. The English called the burger *Salisbury Steak* after Dr. James H. Salisbury, who, in the 1880s, recommended to his patients that they eat well-done beef patties three times daily, with hot water before and after, to relieve colitis, anemia, asthma, and other ailments.

Whew!

The Chevrolet plant in Lordstown, Ohio, the nation's most modern, can produce over 100 vehicles an hour.

Chewsy

Pioneers settling the American West found the Osage Indians chewing a chicle-based gum made from the hardened sap of the sapodilla tree. The Osage, who'd been chewing chicle for many hundreds of years, had apparently obtained their first chews from Indian tribes living south of the Mexican border, where the sapodilla grows.

The Mexican General Antonio Lopez de Santa Anna—yes, the same Santa Anna of Alamo notoriety—thought that chicle could be used in the manufacture of rubber. So in 1839, he brought some sapodilla sap to the American inventor Thomas Adams. Attempts to manufacture rubber from the tree sap failed, but by the 1870s, Adams' company was marketing the nation's first commercial chicle-based chewing gums.

Apples originated in the land between the Black and Caspian Seas, now part of Russia. Peaches and oranges came from China, where they were cultivated 4,000 years ago. The Near and Middle East gave us lettuce, carrots, peas, and spinach. The Irish potato came from South America.

The oldest subway system in the world is London's. It went into service in 1863.

Paint Job

The use of body paint for ornamental and religious purposes has been common since prehistoric times. The use has been recorded in Egypt, whose ancient tombs have yielded cosmetic jars and cosmetic applicators. The Egyptians used *kohl* to darken their eyes. Kohl was a crude paint. Greek women used charcoal pencils and rouge sticks, and coated their faces with powder. Roman ladies used chalk.

In the United States, cosmetics intended for interstate commerce are controlled under the Federal Food, Drug, and Cosmetic Act of 1938.

An increasing number of surgeons today are using staplers to close incisions instead of suturing with needle and gut. In 1980 more than 300,000 Americans were stapled in surgery, and more than half of the nation's medical schools are now teaching the technique. According to authorities, there is less handling of, and injury to, the tissues with stapling. This reduces operating time and makes surgery of the lungs and intestines easier. Staple-suturing reduces anesthesia time and blood loss, and leads to shorter (thus cheaper) hospital stays.

The longest natural bridge in the world is the Landscape Arch, near Moab, Utah. This natural sandstone arch stands 291 feet and is about 100 feet above the canyon floor.

Royal Roe

The taste for caviar flourished in the Middle Ages, when sturgeon roe was prepared as a feast for kings. The Cossacks of Russia organized massive caviar-hunting expeditions twice each year, with every member of the community taking part in the two-week campaigns. Among other things, the Cossacks used cannons to stun the fish in the water!

Today, the gathering of roe is somewhat more specific. The fish live in the salt water of the Caspian and Black Seas but spawn in fresh water, depositing their roe at the bottom of river beds. The fish are caught as they prepare to spawn: the roe, at that time, is barely edible.

The captured fish are placed in submerged floating cages, where due to the lack of food, they are forced to use up the reserve nourishment stored in their roe. When the roe is fit for consumption, the fish are killed and the eggs extracted.

The roe is then pressed through a sieve to remove membranes from the eggs, and then steeped in a brine solution. The production of caviar requires only 15 minutes, but must be carried out with great skill.

The World War II phrase, "Praise the Lord and pass the ammunition," is credited to Howell M. Forgy, a Navy chaplain aboard the cruiser "New Orleans." The ship was at Pearl Harbor at the time of the Japanese attack, and the chaplain encouraged the men who were manning the guns against the attack with his famous saying. The phrase was later made into a popular song, written by Frank Loesser.

The greatest flow of any river in the world is that of the Amazon River, of South America, which discharges an average of 4,200,000 cubic feet of water per second into the Atlantic Ocean. The lowest 900 miles of the Amazon average 300 feet in depth.

Write It Right

By the eighth century, a "perfect minuscule" alphabet had been developed in Western Europe. This script, called the Carolingian, later became the model for the modern lower case alphabet. At the time of Gutenberg, around 1450, the Gothic or black letter script was the most common in Europe. Black letter remained in use through much of Europe until the 17th century—and in Germany into the 20th century.

Early in the Renaissance period, scribes in Florence developed a script, based on the earlier Carolingian minuscule, that was more sloping and cursive than black letter. This writing gradually became the modern Italian script you undoubtedly use today, as well as the modern *italic* type.

Our alphabet hasn't necessarily seen its last change, either. Many people are eager to see a reform of English orthography, or spelling, that would bring the written language more into line with the spoken language. In some modern tongues—Spanish, Italian, and German, for instance—the spoken language is fairly accurately transcribed by the written language. But in English, due to the retention of archaic forms, there is often no correlation between the way a word is spelled and the way it is pronounced—which makes the spelling bee a distinctly English or American activity.

The English words *cite*, *site*, and *sight*, are all pronounced the same, but spelled differently. And the letter combination *ough* has a different pronunciation in each of the following words: *through*, *bough*, *cough*, *rough*, *brought*, *hiccough*, and *dough*. It's not that far-fetched to think that, a few centuries from now, those words might be spelled *thru*, *bow*, *cawf*, *ruff*, *brawt*, *hikup*, and *doe*—or perhaps with letters that aren't even in our alphabet today.

George Bernard Shaw, for one, proposed an alphabet of 40 symbols, in which each sound in our language would be represented by one letter. As Shaw pointed out, according to contemporary orthography, the word *fish* might be spelled *ghoti*—taking the *gh* from *enough*, the *o* from *women*, and the *ti* from words such as *nation*.

Our spelling is not, after all, as simple as *abc*.

The longest-lived animal is generally conceded to be the Galapagos Island tortoise. While figures on the longevity of animals are not very accurate, it is estimated that these giant tortoises live to be as old as 200.

The names and faces of famous Americans keep popping up on postage stamps all over the world. More than 300 U.S. citizens have appeared on stamps issued by scores of other governments. High on the list are U.S. Presidents—John F. Kennedy, Franklin D. Roosevelt, Abraham Lincoln, Dwight D. Eisenhower, and George Washington, but the glossary also includes astronauts and athletes, poets and physicists, missionaries and ministers, actors and actresses.

The most expensive land in the world at the present time is that in the City of London, England. The price on small prime sites in 1974 reached $4,875 per square foot.

Detectable Delectable

Through most of the 19th century, garlic was so little known to most Americans that a cookbook of the era could recommend that "garlics are better adapted to medicine than cooking."

While there are still many who believe garlic has medicinal, even magical powers, the pungent vegetable has by now found its way into most kitchens in the United States, as Americans discover what their European ancestors have long known: garlic is a useful, flavorful addition to almost any dish.

Garlic is a member of the lily family, and specifically of the *Allium* genus, which also includes the onion, leek, shallot, and chive. We eat only the bulb of this perennial plant. A bulb contains about a dozen cloves, or smaller bulbs, each wrapped in an onionskin-like shell that makes garlic both convenient to use and long-lasting.

Garlic probably first grew in southern Siberia, and it is now found growing naturally in Central Asia and the Mediterranean. Man has eaten the bulb since earliest times, principally as a flavoring. The Israelites of Biblical times cultivated garlic, and during their exile in Egypt longed for a return to the Promised Land with its bounteous flavorful produce.

The ancient Egyptians also cultivated garlic, though among priests it was considered unclean—no one was permitted to enter an Egyptian temple with garlic on his breath. The workers who toiled on the construction of the Pyramids probably ate garlic and onions in large amounts. The Romans fed garlic to their soldiers in the belief that it promoted strength and courage, but the Senate forbade a Roman to enter the Temple of Sybil after eating the aromatic vegetable. In India, too, garlic was condemned by the priestly class while being enjoyed by the masses.

The points of highest and lowest elevation in the 48 contiguous states of the United States are only 85 miles apart. Mt. Whitney, in California, towers 14,494 feet above sea level, while less than two hours drive away, Death Valley reaches a low of 282 feet below sea level.

It seems that we're all looking to get more fun out of life. Yet there are some individuals who psychiatrists claim are *cherophobiacs*—people who fear having fun. It reminds me of the statement made about the Puritans who were opposed to bear-baiting, not because it gave pain to the bear, but because it gave pleasure to the spectators.

The largest attendance at any classical musical concert took place when 90,000 people came to listen to a presentation by the New York Philharmonic Orchestra, conducted by Leonard Bernstein at Sheep Meadow, in Central Park, New York City, on August 1, 1966.

New York is America's largest city, its richest port, and its leader in business, manufacturing, service, industry, communications, fashion, art, music, and literature, as well as the world's chief financial center, and as host to the United Nations, the "Capital of the World."

The biggest alcohol drinkers in the world are the white people of South Africa, with 2.05 gallons of proof alcohol per person per year, and the most abstemious are the people of Belgium with 1/8 of a gallon per person per year.

When the City of Houston, Texas, was founded in 1836, property there sold for less than $1.50 an acre. Today property in downtown Houston sells for about $2,000 a front inch.

Slick Lick

In 1921, the *Eskimo pie* was introduced in Des Moines, Iowa, by the same Russell Stover who was to go on to fame and fortune in the candy trade. The *Good Humor*, meanwhile was the handiwork of one Harry Burt, an ice cream parlor owner from Youngstown, Ohio. Before starting out in the ice cream business, Burt had sold a lollypop he called the *Good Humor Sucker*. The bright idea to mount a chocolate-covered Eskimo pie on a lollypop stick led to ice-cream-on-a-stick, and the familiar white wagons that still ply our streets with their tinkling bells. Good Humor bars are now sold in most supermarkets as well.

Today, the manufacture of ice cream is, of course, mechanized. Factories first produce a liquid product made of 80 percent cream or butterfat, milk, and nonfat milk solids, and about 15 percent sweeteners. Next they pasteurize, homogenize, whip, and partially freeze the mixture. Then flavoring is added, and they freeze the product in its containers at temperatures of about 240 degrees below zero. The finished product is frequently as rich in vitamins as an equivalent amount of milk.

Frozen mousse is a cold dessert made from sweetened whipped cream, flavoring, and gelatin. *Sherbet* consists of milk, sweeteners, and fruit flavoring, while *Italian Ices* is made from fruit juices, water, and sweeteners. *French ice cream* is definitely different from other varieties; in the U.S., only ice cream made with eggs can legally be sold as "French."

The chameleon, the familiar lizard of the southwestern United States, has the ability to change its color rapidly to match its surroundings. The chameleon can also roll either eye independently. Because of this ability, the chameleon can keep one eye on its food and the other on the surrounding scenery.

Although in children the brain is larger than the liver, by the time adulthood has been reached, the liver weighs from three to four pounds and has taken first place in size among the organs of the body.

The tallest block of apartments in the world is the Lake Point Towers, in Chicago, Illinois. These apartments are 640 feet high and comprise 70 floors.

The largest volcano crater in the world is that of Mt. Aso, in Japan. It measures 17 miles north to south, ten miles east to west, and 71 miles in circumference.

Catastrophe

According to some accounts, the expression "to fight like Kilkenny cats" dates back to a somewhat ailurophobic custom among Hessian soldiers stationed in Ireland, who tied two cats together by the tails and hung them over a fence or clothesline. One day, the story goes, an officer approached a group of soldiers thus occupied. To hide their deed, one soldier cut off the tails of both tormented animals. The officer was then told that the cats had fought so hard that they'd devoured each other, leaving only the tails.

The notion that a cat can fall from a great height and survive is not an old wives' tale, and may have contributed to the idea that a cat has nine lives. One cat fell from the 20th floor of a Montreal apartment building in 1973 and suffered only a pelvic fracture.

Bring on the Ham

A single farmer can care for as many as 50,000 chickens at one time, and can bring his flock from egg to market in only three months. In the largest chicken farm in the world, the so-called "Egg City" of Moorpark, California, four-and-a-half million chickens are housed on a mere 600 acres, and turn out over two million eggs each day!

No Cross Words, Please

A mathematician once computed the number of permutations possible with a standard 11 x 11-square crossword puzzle; that is, given 121 squares and a 26-letter alphabet, how many different puzzles could be constructed? The answer was found to be a number that would blow the lid off any pocket calculator: 24,873 plus 222 zeroes. That's higher than the number of seconds that have elapsed since the beginning of the universe!

Where did crosswords begin? No, the ancient Greeks and Romans did *not* test their wits against the familiar black and white squares. But the crossword does owe a large debt to two other word games, the acrostic and the word square, both of which date back to classical times.

An *acrostic* is a composition—a verse or a series of words, for instance—in which letters of each line or word, usually the initial letters themselves, form a word or words when arranged in order. For example, the first-letter acrostic of "this heavy elephant" is *the*. The ancient Greeks dabbled with this kind of puzzle, and 12 poems in the Old Testament form acrostics. In Psalm 119, for instance, the first letters of each line form the Hebrew alphabet.

The Dick Tracy comic strip by Chester Gould was created in 1931.

The deepest lake in the world is Lake Baykal in the Soviet Union. At some points it is more than a mile deep.

It's a Lulu

The urge to masticate seems to be quite strong in the human animal, for gum-chewing has been popular in many cultures over the last 2,000 years. The ancient Greeks chewed a gum obtained from the resin of the mastic tree. Our words "mastic" and "masticate" are both derived from the Greek word for "chew."

Over a thousand years ago, the Mayans and other American Indians chewed chicle-based gums. But the first gums American colonists encountered were spruce gums introduced to the Pilgrims by the Wampanoog Indians in the early 17th century. Made from wads of resin the Indians found stuck to the bark of spruce trees, spruce gums were waxy and tough, more cordial to the teeth than to the taste buds.

Yet spruce gums were to remain the only chews available in the United States for close to 200 years, until the introduction, in the 19th century, of paraffin gums. The first spruce chewing gum to be commercially manufactured in this country was the "State of Maine Pure Spruce Gum," brought out in 1848 by a Bangor, Maine, entrepreneur named John Curtis. Curtis later sold spruce gums under such names as "American Flag" and "200 Lump Spruce." He also sold paraffin gums dubbed "Licorice Lulu," "Sugar Cream," and "Biggest and Best."

Jupiter, the largest planet in the solar system, has the shortest day of all the planets. Jupiter completes a rotation on its axis in less than 10 earth hours.

Let's Talk About Legs

Insects have six, a spider has eight, an octopus also has eight, and a squid has ten.

Leningrad was founded by Peter the Great in 1703. It was known as St. Petersburg from that date until 1914, and as Petrograd from 1914 through 1924.

Busy, Busy

On the basis of airplane traffic, some lesser-known airports come to the fore. Chicago's O'Hare remains America's busiest airport, handling close to 700,000 takeoffs and landings each year. But the second busiest of America's 7,000-plus airports is located in Santa Ana, California. Van Nuys Airport is third, followed by Long Beach Municipal. Much of the operational volume at these three airports —all located in the Los Angeles area— is accounted for by private planes or test vehicles flown by nearby airplane manufacturers. Surprisingly, John F. Kennedy airport in New York ranks 16th in the nation in takeoffs and landings; although at peak hours, the facility can handle more than 80 planes an hour.

The Davis Cup was named after Dwight Davis, a former Secretary of War, and General Governor of the Philippines. This trophy, signifying world tennis supremacy, was first awarded in 1900.

The earth is revolving at the speed of 1000 miles per hour, and orbits the sun at 66,700 miles per hour.

A sea creature only one foot long called the urchin fish is capable of killing a 20 foot shark. After being swallowed by the shark, the urchin fish blows up its prickly body like an inflated balloon, rips apart the shark's belly and swims away.

The Australian walking fish occasionally leaves the water and climbs a tree to enjoy a snack of insects.

The crown of thorns starfish derives its name from prominent poisonous spines that cover the upper portion of its body. The starfish has 16 to 17 arms which grow up to 20' in diameter. They have been found in concentrations of up to 3,000,000 per square mile.

Make Mine Espresso

Cappuccino is a combination of coffee and frothy milk with nutmeg or cinnamon added. Turkish coffee is a heady, usually bitter decoction made from a strong, aromatic bean. Viennese coffee is usually served with a large dollop of whipped cream. And Irish coffee, a mixture of coffee, whiskey, and whipped cream, can be good to the very last drop—even if you don't like coffee.

Beans and Brew

Americans and Europeans may be avid consumers of the brew, but it's likely that most Western coffee addicts go through their lives without once laying eyes on a coffee bush. The reason: coffee simply won't grow in the climate of Europe or the United States. The coffee plant is a tropical evergreen shrub indigenous to the Eastern Hemisphere; 25 species grow wild in Africa, Asia, and the Near East. Oh, there is some coffee grown in the United States—but only in Hawaii.

Most coffee shrubs flourish best in year-round temperatures of from 77 to 88 degrees; a temperature dip to around 32 degrees will kill most coffee plants. And many species require more than 60 inches of rain each year.

Two species of the coffee plant are far and away the most common. *Coffea arabica*, the oldest known variety, hails originally from Arabia or Ethiopia, and is now grown extensively in South America. *Coffea robusta* originated in East and Central Africa and is still the major coffee plant of that continent. *Robusta* is not—well, "robuster" than *arabica*. Actually, it's milder in taste and aroma, and is less favored by Westerners; but in recent years, Africa has become increasingly important as a coffee exporter.

The average coffee shrub grows to a height of about 30 feet, with white flowers and red, fleshy fruits. Each fruit contains pulp and two seeds, and it is the seeds—not "beans"—that are used to make the brew. Why? Caffeine, of course.

There are now more than 20,000 high school basketball teams from coast to coast in the United States. Attendance at these games is something like 125 million people each season.

Between 1600 and 1612, four different pretenders to the Russian throne claimed to be either Dimitri, the murdered son of Tsar Ivan the Terrible, or Dimitri's son. All four of them took the name of Dimitri. All four died violent deaths.

In 1970, Oil City in Pennsylvania had a population of 15,000 people. The city was founded after Edwin L. Drake struck oil in 1959. Today, Oil City is a major refining and shipping center for the state's oil industry. Oil City today is a financial and banking center for northwest Pennsylvania.

The largest bowling establishment in the world is the Tokyo World Lanes Bowling Center, in Tokyo, Japan, which includes 504 lanes.

It's Greek to Me

We know that the Greek alphabet was derived from one or more of the Semitic alphabets, for the Greek and Semitic alphabets employed similar names for the letters, and listed the letters of their alphabets in basically the same order. Also, the names of the Semitic letters had some meaning in the Semitic tongues—*aleph*, the first letter, meant "ox," while *beth*, the second letter, meant "house"; the Greek names for those two letters, *alpha* and *beta*, had no meaning in Greek. Our word *alphabet* is formed from the names of the first two letters of the Greek alphabet, though it was the Romans who coined the word, not the Greeks.

But the exact origins of the Greek alphabet are still open to question. According to one theory, simplified Egyptian hieroglyphics evolved into an alphabet used in the Sinai Peninsula around 1,500 B.C., which later evolved into the various Semitic alphabets that fathered the Greek. Another theory holds that these Semitic alphabets developed independently of the Egyptian writing system somewhere in the Near East. Two alphabets in this area during the first millenium B.C. were those of the Phoenician language and those of the Aramaic, the region's most common language of the time. The Greek alphabet probably evolved from one or both of these scripts.

It's possible that the Greeks first came in contact with a form of the Aramaic alphabet that was used by Semitic peoples in Asia Minor before 1,000 B.C. A second borrowing of a Semitic alphabet may have come through Phoenician traders who roamed the Mediterranean in the earliest days of Greece. The Phoenician writing system was used in ancient Carthage, and formed the basis of the modern Berber alphabet. By the fourth century B.C., a number of Greek scripts had merged into a uniform Greek alphabet.

A Rash of Nashes

The Studebaker and Packard, both introduced before 1902, eventually merged, and the Nash Company—founded by Charles Nash, who had replaced Durant at General Motors—joined the Hudson Company in the 1950s to form the American Motors Corporation. As early as 1914, 75 percent of all American cars were manufactured by the 10 largest companies.

Some American Indians once printed paper money. The Chocktaws issued a 75-cent note in 1862. The Arapahoes issued a $5 bill in 1850, and the Cherokees issued a $1 bill in 1862. Both of these bills are on view in New York City in the collection of Moneys of the World, owned by the Chase National Bank.

The Top Hat

In the 19th century, the shiny black top hat became *de regueur* for the well-dressed gentleman.

Women's hats grew large and showy, with jewels and flowers for occasional ornament. King George III of England helped things along by decreeing that all hats must bear on their linings the name of their maker. By 1850, a writer could confidently declare that the hat had reached its "ultimate degree of excellenc."

Arabian Goat Cheese

The earliest cheeses made by man were probably unripened cheeses, similar to modern yogurt or cream cheese. One such cheese, the Arabian goat cheese called *kishk*, is the oldest cheese still made today. Ripened cheeses such as *Parmesan* and *Brie* were developed during the Middle Ages, while many semisoft cheeses appeared much later. Most of the cheeses produced today were developed only within the last few centuries.

Buenos Aires, Argentina, is the largest city south of the equator.

Caviar is the prepared roe, or eggs, of the *acipenser*, a fish found in the Caspian and Black Seas, and the Girond River in France. At one time, the *acipenser* could be found in many European rivers, and even in some North American lakes; but since the onset of the industrial age, that fish's habitat has been reduced to portions of Russia, Iran, and Rumania. Today, virtually all caviar is produced in those three countries.

There are three kinds of *acipenser* that most graciously donate their eggs for the benefit of man's palate, and thus there are three kinds of "true" caviar. The Beluga is the largest fish of the three, growing up to twelve feet in length and weighing up to a ton! One Beluga can produce up to 130 pounds of caviar.

Another species, the Sevruga, is much smaller; four feet long and weighing 60 pounds, the Sevruga can produce only about eight pounds of caviar.

The Ocietrova, or sturgeon, may weigh up to 400 pounds and will produce about 40 pounds of caviar. The term "sturgeon" is often applied to all three kinds of caviar-producing fish, but the Ocietrova is, in fact, the only true sturgeon.

Stick-'ems

The 1927 invention of moistureproof cellophane by two American chemists soon made the product the premier protective wrap for food. By 1950, America was producing about 250 million pounds annually, or half the world's supply, with over 50 varieties of the wrap on the market. Cellophane is widely used today for food and cosmetic wrapping—it's strong, attractive, moistureproof, odor-proof, grease-proof, gas impermeable, and transparent.

The word *cellophane* is still considered a brand name in England, France, and many other nations, where the term is traced legally to the La Cellophane firm. But a court decision declared cellophane a generic term in the United States, the name of the substance rather than a particular product.

Root of All Evil

In Western cultures, cattle became a favored standard of exchange at a very early date, since cattle, to a great extent, already formed the basis of wealth. Cattle were generally owned by rich and poor alike; land, only by the aristocracy. Our words *capital* and *chattel* come from "cattle," or rather from "head of cattle," based on the Latin *caput*, "head."

The original one-way street was created in 1791 in New York, near the John Street Theater, to clear up horse-drawn traffic congestion.

Flights of Fancy

In 1909, the Frenchman Louis Bleriot became the first man to fly across the English Channel. A year later, Jorge Chavez became the first man to fly across the Alps, though a prize offered by the Italian Aviation Society remained uncollected when Chavez was killed on landing.

Crusty Crustacean

Lobster Newburgh is definitely an American invention. During the mid-19th century, a regular diner at the famous New York restaurant, Delmonico's, told the proprietor of a dish made with lobster and cream that he'd enjoyed in South America. The next night, the diner was presented with a lobster cooked in a chafing dish with sherry, thick cream, and egg yolks. The invention was promptly installed on Delmonico's menu, christened Lobster Wenburg—after the diner, a shipping magnate.

But fame is indeed short-lived. Lobster Wenburg remained on Delmonico's menu until the night its namesake became embroiled in a drunken brawl that ravaged the restaurant. Wenburg was ejected from the restaurant, and from the menu as well—Lobster Wenburg became Lobster Newburgh forevermore.

Famous impresario, David Belasco, had a reputation for injecting realism into his stage productions. One of his most successful plays was *Hearts of Oak*, which opened at Hamlin's Theater in Chicago in 1879. Each night as the curtain rose, the stage showed a living room, and a cat would crawl from under an armchair and stretch itself before the log fire which faced the audience. How did Belasco come to manage such perfect timing?

Months later, it came to be known that an hour before curtain time, the feline was squeezed into a small box which was concealed under the chair. The box would be opened by the pull of a cord off stage, and the cat would emerge at once, and, of course, would stretch its cramped muscles.

Noise, if loud enough, can kill you. At 105 decibels (dbs), the sound of planes roaring off aircraft carriers is the most painful and the loudest that man is forced to endure. Damage to hearing appears at 85 dbs; the lethal level is 140 dbs. Concerned personnel aboard carriers must wear noise suppressors.

Asparagus presents a problem in cooking, since the tender tips will cook much sooner than the fibrous stem bottoms. Chefs recommend that you cook the spears upright in a pan, with water reaching slightly more than half-way up the spears, so that the submerged bottoms are boiled, and the tips merely steamed. They also suggest that undercooked asparagus is preferable to overcooked spears, and warn against using strongly flavored sauces or win with asparagus, since the vegetable contains high amounts of sulfur that can ruin a wine.

Wordmakers

There are now about 65 alphabets in use around the world. The alphabet with the most letters is Cambodian, which has 72. Naturally, the logographic Chinese system has many more characters than there are letters in any alphabet; one Chinese dictionary listed almost 50,000 signs, including 92 for a single sound! And the most complex Chinese character has 52 individual strokes!

The alphabet with the least letters is Rotokas, a South Pacific tongue, which has 11 letters and only six consonants. Two Caucasian alphabets include just two vowels, while another Caucasian tongue, Ubyx, has 80 consonant sounds, the most of any language on earth. A Vietnamese language called Sedang can claim the most vowel sounds, 55.

Eggplants

Most American eggplants come from Florida, Texas, and New Jersey. We produce about a milion-and-a-half bushels of the purple fruit each year, and smaller quantities are imported from Mexico. But by and large, the average American isn't very fond of eggplant, and the national consumption comes to about four ounces per year. A pity, because the versatile eggplant has unusual properties, and can be fashioned into a multitude of forms and dishes.

Oh That Bugatti!

The largest car ever produced for regular road use was the 1927 "Golden Bugatti," which measured 22 feet from bumper to bumper. Only six of these cars were made, and some of these survive in excellent condition.

The Great Experiment

Religious proscription has done little to thin the ranks of the dipsomaniacs. The Koran forbids alcohol use. Devout Buddhists and Hindu Brahmins also spurn the grape. And many Christian sects have forbidden drinking—with mixed results.

As for legal prohibition, the longest on record is a wee 26 years, in Iceland, from 1908 to 1934. Russia tried to illegalize the grape early in this century, but the attempt lasted a mere 10 years. Our own "noble experiment" lasted only 13 years—much too long in the minds of many people.

Cutting Remarks

Modern scissors are plain, utilitarian tools, but in past centuries shears sporting fanciful shapes and designs abounded. During the 18th century, scissors with shanks in the shape of women's legs—called *Jambes des Princesses*—were the rage in France. The 19th century saw scissors in the shape of castles, butterflies, and birds, with the blades forming a bird's bill. Today, there are scores of specialized shears, scissors, nippers, and snips, from barbers' to bankers', surgical to cuticle, ranging in size from tiny scissors fitted to pocketknives to huge tailors' shears up to 16 inches in length.

Let's Have a Chat

The number of cats extant throughout the world today is anybody's guess. The United States ranks first among ailurophilic nations. There are an estimated 20 to 25 million cats in American households today, but with the inclusion of all alley cats and other strays, the total cat population could well top the 40 million mark, which is the population figure estimated for American dogs. The popularity of cats in this country continues to grow. The cat-care business is now a multimillion-dollar industry, providing cat food and accessories, cat hospitals, kennels, and even kitty cemeteries. Pedigreed cats sell for upwards of $200.

The precise origin of our word "cat" is uncertain, but similar words designate the feline in many unrelated languages. One Latin word for the feline was *catus,* and the Anglo-Saxons dubbed the creature *catt* or *cat.* In French, we find *chat,* in Italian *gatto,* in Spanish *gato,* and in German *Katze.*

The origin of "puss" is unknown, but "kitty" comes from *chaton,* a diminutive of the French *chat.* Since at least 1450, "Tom" has been used to designate a male. A polecat, by the way, is not a cat at all—in the United States, the term designates a skunk.

King Lear's father, Bladud, was cured of leprosy in 863 B.C. by hot mud brought from the springs at Bath.

About 4,000 people a day queued up at St. James Palace from August 5th to October 4th, 1981, to pay $2.80 to see a display of some 1,200 wedding presents, selected from all the gifts recived by Prince Charles and Princess Diana. They gawked at the enormous varity of items, ranging from tape recorders to fabulous jewels. The women's favorite item seemed to be Diana's wedding dress, and the men's (who constituted a minority of the viewers) was a radio-controlled model yacht.

Angels Have Wings

Twenty miles was about the farthest a primitive man could hope to travel in a day, using the only means of transportation he had available—his feet. When recorded history began, a good day's journey by horse might cover as much as 80 miles. A few thousand years passed before the railroad lengthened the distance a man could travel in eight hours to about 150 miles. By 1925, the automobile had doubled that distance.

Then, about 25 years later, the distance that could be traveled in eight hours skyrocketed to over 4,500 miles. By today, it has doubled again. Man can now travel literally halfway around the earth in the time it took his primitive ancestors to trek just 20 miles. The entire world is within reach of a day's journey. How did this come about? Man left the earth and took to the air!

Flying has been man's dream ever since he first watched birds soaring through the air. But for a long time man relegated flight to the realm of the gods, who in the Egyptian, Minoan, and other ancient cultures were often depicted in birdlike form. Greek and Roman gods were thought capable of flight, though only the winged Mercury bore any visible means of support. The angels of Hebrew and Christian lore, on the other hand, were always depicted with wings. In order to strengthen their claims to divinity, kings in Persia, China, and other lands sometimes had their magicians and historians create legends suggesting the monarchs were capable of flight. But myths such as the Greek story of Icarus show what would happen to a mortal who dared imitate his divine superiors.

With a population of eight million people, Moscow, the Soviet capital, has fewer than 400,000 passenger cars. About 80,000 of these are Communist Party and Government cars, all of which are black. The Russians favor large cars. The $130,000 Z.1 seats eight; the Chaika is only slightly less grand; and the Volga is for smaller fry.

The commonest surname in the world is the Chinese name, Chang. There are at least 75 million Changs—more than the entire population of all but seven of the 145 other sovereign countries of the world.

Love Apple

"Apple of Love." Yes, that's what the tomato was called for hundreds of years after its introduction in Europe. The origin of the term is uncertain, but one doubtful tale suggests that Sir Walter Raleigh dubbed it thus when he presented a tomato plant to Queen Elizabeth and affectionately told her his gift was an "apple of love." Another story has it that love apple, or *pomme d'amour* in French, is derived from the Italian *pomo di mori*—"apple of the Moors," since Italians at the time called the Spanish *Mori*. And claims have been heard for the erstwhile belief that tomatoes, along with vanilla, cocoa, and many other New World novelties, were aphrodisiacs.

Happy Hour

Walk into any American bar today and you'll find dozens of different kinds of spirits lining the shelves. You'll also notice that very few of the patrons are imbibing their favored spirit straight from the bottle. To Americans, the mixed drink may seem quite a time-worn tradition, and the fact is that the cocktail is an American invention—a fairly recent one at that.

The ancient Greeks had a cocktail hour in the late afternoon or evening, complete with hors d'oeuvres. An Athenian gentleman would drop by a neighbor's house during the "happy hour" with a goatskin of wine, and expect to be treated to an outlay of appetizers—the Greeks called them "provocatives to drinking"—that might include caviar, oysters, nuts, olives, shrimp, and paté. Compare that spread to today's bar fare of peanuts, cheese, and crackers and you'll have to agree that in some ways we haven't come very far in the last 2,500 years.

Apple-pie Order

How much of the American apple harvest is currently used for good old-fashioned American apple pie is unknown. Also unknown is the origin of the phrase "apple pie order," for there's nothing particularly orderly about the apples in an apple pie. Some etymologists have suggested the phrase may have originated in the French *cap-à-pied*— "head to foot"—or *nappes-pliées*—"folded linen."

Other popular apple phrases include "apple polisher," a person who curries favor with gifts—like a student who brings his teacher an apple. "To upset the apple cart" requires no explanation.

Then there's "an apple a day keeps the doctor away"—it might also keep the dentist at bay—and of course, the "Big Apple," one of the more kindly epithets for America's largest city, New York.

But the most profound comment on *Malus pumila* can be credited to William Shakespeare. "There's small choice," the bard wrote, "in rotten apples."

Line 'Em Up

The United States has been the leader in automobile production for many years. Over a million cars were produced here in 1916, and over three million in 1924, when there were some 15 million cars registered in America. In 1952, about four million American passenger cars rolled off the line, 10 times the number produced by the second-ranking nation, Great Britain. At the time, there was a car on the road here for every 3.5 persons alive, compared to, for example, one car per 564 persons in Japan. The second-ranking nation in car use was, surprisingly, New Zealand, with six persons for each car.

And in Reverse!

Surely, the most incredible automobile record ever achieved belongs to Charles Creighton and James Hargis who, in 1930, drove a Ford Model A roadster from New York City to Los Angeles *without stopping the engine once.* The two men then promptly drove back to New York, completing the 7,180-mile round-trip in 42 days.

Oh, one more thing: on both coast-to-coast journeys, the car was driven exclusively *in reverse!*

Up, Up in the Sky!

Initially, it was proposed that condemned criminals be used as guinea pigs in the first manned balloon flight. Then Jean-Francois Pilatre, arguing that the honor of man's first flight should not be squandered on criminals, stepped forward to volunteer. Together with the Marquis d'Arlandes, Francois Laurent, Pilatre climbed into the basket of a Montgolfier hot-air balloon in the Bois de Boulogne, Paris on November 21, 1783. The first manned balloon climbed 3,000 feet into the air while its two occupants fueled a fire on board to keep the balloon filled with hot air. After a 23-minute flight, the two pioneers touched down 10 miles away. The world was abuzz with the sensational news.

About Libraries

In 1747, the first public library was opened in Warsaw, Poland. America's first public library was opened in 1895, in New York City. The New York Library, now the world's largest public library, presently contains over eight million volumes, plus millions of manuscripts. But the largest library of any kind in the world is the Library of Congress in Washington, D.C., which houses over 75 million volumes and manuscripts—including a copy of every book ever copyrighted in the United States!

The Beefsteak Club was one of the most well-known London social clubs of the 18th and 19th centuries, including among its members such luminaries of the art and theater worlds as William Hogarth, John Wilkes, and David Garrick, plus the Prince of Wales. The club reportedly was so named because its original members met to enjoy a steak dinner. Members were later called "Steaks," and the club the "Sublime Society of Steaks."

I Can See Clearly Now

"Held together with Scotch tape" is hardly a complimentary description of any item, but our use of the cliche does suggest the extent to which Scotch tape itself has become part of the American household. You might forget from time to time that "Scotch" is merely a brand name, and owes nothing at all to Scotland—but did you realize that the word *cellophane,* too, is regarded as a brand name in most of the world?

What is cellophane? Despite common belief, neither the product nor its name originated in the United States, and both are a good deal older than you might imagine.

Cellophane is a thin film made from cellulose, the chief constituent of a plant's cell walls. In 1892, three British chemists discovered viscose, a solution of cellulose; and six years later another Englishman was granted a patent for producing films from viscose. But the cellophane industry was launched in 1911, when a Swiss chemist, named J.E. Brandenburger, invented a machine for the mass production of a strong, transparent viscose film. He named the new product *cellophane,* combining the French words *cellulose* and *diaphane,* "transparent."

The French firm La Cellophane began making the product in 1920; and three years later, sold the U.S. manufacturing rights to E.I. Du Pont de Nemours & Company. DuPont built the first American cellophane plant in Buffalo, New York, in 1924, selling the transparent wrapping at $2.65 a pound.

Tattoo

Tattoo is from the Tahitian word 'tatua' which means mark. This form of adornment where pigments are rubbed into punctures of the skin was first observed by Capt. James Cook during 1769 and was subsequently introduced by him into the western world.

In 1903, the Steinway Company presented its 100,000th piano to the White House, where it resided until 1938, when it was replaced by the firm's 300,000th model. Today, the Steinway remains for most pianists the last word in fine American pianos, but in sheer numbers the largest piano producers in this country are Aeolian, Baldwin, Kimball, and Wurlitzer.

The Greeks made their wine from grapes, but usually drank it diluted with water. Thus, the wine Athenians quaffed during their cocktail hour was probably less than 8 percent alcohol, a weak beverage by modern standards. In fact, most of the wine the Greeks and Romans enjoyed would probably taste rather crude to the modern palate. After all, we live in an age where an avid oenologist paid over $14,000 for a single bottle of 1806 Chateau Lafite-Rothschild!

Red and Round

The tomato is now such an integral part of many southern European cuisines, especially Italian and Spanish, that you'd surely surmise that the plant is a native of Mediterranean parts. But spaghetti sauce and Spanish omelettes notwithstanding, the tomato was unknown in Europe until the 16th century—the fruit is actually indigenous to South and Central America.

Salt of the Earth

Synonymous with opulence is that salty, lumpy marine delicacy known as caviar. The word is rich with princely connotations for almost everyone—including those with no idea what caviar actually is. For it has been said that those who respect caviar's place in the elite of epicurean treats far outnumber those who have actually tasted it. Many who do have a chance to sample the delicacy can only wonder why it is so prized. But as any connoisseur can testify, caviar is an acquired taste that—for reasons of the pocketbook—is best not acquired.

Juicy Fruit

Apples were cultivated largely in monasteries until the 16th century, and thereafter in small private orchards. Over 100 varieties of apple were known in medieval Europe. The fruit continued to spread, to North America, to South America, to Australia, even to the Orient; Japan is currently one of the top apple-producing nations! And the apple in all its varieties is now the most widely cultivated tree fruit of the temperate climes.

The first apples to reach America arrived from England in 1629, along with seeds and propagating wood. Ten years later, the first apples grown in the United States were plucked from trees planted on Beacon Hill, Boston. By 1741, New England was producing apples for export, and apple cultivation was sweeping westward across America.

The earliest known library was a collection of clay tablets. This library existed in Babylonia in the 21st century B.C. Through the Greek writers we know about Egyptian libraries which certainly existed as far back as 1200 B.C. Assurbanipad, the monarch of Nineveh, who dates around 600 B.C., had an extensively cataloged library in his capital city, and the Temple of the Jews in Jerusalem contained a sacred library of dimension.

The first public library in Greece was established in 330 B.C. The early Christian libraries were to be found in monasteries. The Benedictines amassed a fine collection of books at Monte Cassino in Italy.

The tropical catfish "synodontis" swims upside down while eating.

It's been said that the Pyramids owe their existence to the onion, since the workers who constructed them subsisted largely on the vegetable. The Roman historian Herodotus claimed to have seen an inscription on the Great Pyramid at Giza that listed the amounts of onions, garlic, and radishes eaten by the workers who built the monument. For some reason, Herodotus also maintained that the onion was good for sight, but bad for the body. Many a tearful cook might disagree.

Gargantuan Aircraft

The Concorde, has opened up a new frontier in commercial aviation: supersonic flight. Jets faster than the speed of sound (660 miles per hour) have been a reality, officially, since 1955. But the French- and English-built Concorde is the first jet to offer travel at supersonic speeds to commercial passengers. In 1977, the Concorde began regular flights from Paris and London across the Atlantic and to the Middle East. London to New York trips that once took seven hours can now be made in half that time. In the Concorde, passengers can ride at altitudes of up to 60,000 feet, high enough to view the curvature of the earth!

The Concorde is not the fastest jet in the world, however. That honor goes to the Lockheed SR-71, a reconnaissance aircraft capable of speeds up to 2,200 miles per hour. Nor is the Concorde the fastest commercial aircraft in the world, for the Russian Tupolev TU-144 can reach speeds up to 1,520 miles per hour. Despite a crash in 1973, the Russian jet is already in service on selected domestic routes.

In 1920, Sinclair Lewis wrote *Main Street*, which depicted the small-town narrowness of Gopher Prairie in Minnesota.

Pressed Glass

Pressed glass is a kind of molded glass often used in the production of identical vessels with precise dimensions. Molten glass is poured into a mold, which may consist of one or more sections depending on the shape of the article to be made. A lever and crank are then used to bring a plunger down into the mold. The plunger or piston compresses the warm glass plate into the shape defined by the mold.

Pressed glass was first made in Boston around 1827. By the middle of the century, it was widely produced throughout America. Lacy designs in imitation of cut glass or cut crystal were especially popular.

Ketchup is Great!

There is no standard formula for ketchup, but most are made from various combinations of tomato pulp, sugar, salt, vinegar, spices, and sometimes, mustard. The U.S. Food and Drug Administration merely stipulates what optional ingredients may be added, and the maximum amounts of sugar and preservatives allowed.

How Old Are Lenses?

What did man do before the invention of eyeglasses? In ancient times, aging scholars often had to give up reading altogether. The more fortunate could afford to pay others to read to them. The Roman dramatist Seneca claimed to have read with the use of a water-filled glass sphere that magnified characters when held just above the page.

Lenses existed even in Seneca's time, but no one seems to have put them to use as vision aids. A rock crystal lens found in the ruins of the ancient Assyrian city of Nineveh was probably used as a burning glass. In *The Clouds*, Greek playright Aristophanes mentioned the use of lenses to burn parchment and to erase writing from wax tablets. Roman historian Pliny wrote that burning lenses were sometimes used to cauterize wounds—though the "emerald" that he claimed the Emperor Nero used to view the gladiatorial games was probably just a curved mirror.

Parchment

The ancients wrote on scrolls of papyrus, made from the papyrus reed, or *biblos,* that grew in the Nile Delta. In the second century B.C., the craftsmen of Pergamum, in Asia Minor, learned how to produce parchment from the skins of calves, goats, sheep, and other animals. Parchment did not crack when folded, and could accept writing on both sides. While a papyrus manuscript was constructed of overlapping squares of papyrus pasted together, then rolled up, a parchment manuscript could be arranged in folded leaves.

So the introduction of parchment led to the *codex,* or parchment-leaf book, which was already in use during the Roman Empire. Apparently the codex was first adopted for law books, since the pages of a codex could be added or deleted easily as laws changed.

Not a single scroll or codex from the golden ages of Greece or Rome has survived. The oldest Latin work we possess dates from the fourth century. Libraries were established in the ancient world to preserve written works, but these libraries were plundered or destroyed centuries ago. Among the largest ancient libraries were those in Pergamum and Ephesus in Asia Minor, and in Alexandria, Egypt. At its height, the Alexandria library contained some 750,000 scrolls—all of which were destroyed by various invaders.

A housefly beats its wings about 20,000 times a minute.

O. Henry was the pseudonym of William Sydney Porter, who was born in 1862 and died in 1910. O. Henry was a short story writer who achieved great success in his chosen profession. His forte was to incorporate an unexpected twist into each one of his stories.

The black side of the picture is that O. Henry served three years in the Federal Penitentiary in Ohio for embezzlement of bank funds.

Gout

Cartoonists may joke about this complaint but those who suffer it do not. Gout gets its name from the French *gouette* which means a drop. The very early diagnosis of gout was that it was caused by "a drop of acrid matter in the joints."

Clavichord

The word *clavichord*—formed from the combination of the Latin *clavis*, "key," and *chorda* "string"—was first mentioned in 1404, but the instrument probably appeared during the preceding century in England, France, or Spain. By the 15th century, the clavichord was well known by musicians throughout Europe. In some ways, the clavichord was closer in function to the piano than the harpsichord and other later keyboard instruments.

The center of the United States is located near Castle Rock, South Dakota.

The four Horsemen of the famous Notre Dame football backfield of 1922 were Harry Stuhldreher, quarterback; Don Miller, halfback; Jim Crowley, halfback; and Elmer Layden, fullback.

Mr. Wiss Was a Sharp One

Wiss and his descendants found a way of utilizing two metal alloys together to produce the sturdiest, longest-lasting scissors. By 1914, Jacob Wiss & Sons was the largest producer of fine shears in the world. Wiss's firm was also responsible for introducing pinking shears on a national scale—pinking shears have notched blades that produce a saw-toothed cut—and for popularizing scissors whose handle can double as a bottle opener.

Columbus Started It!

From ancient times through much of the Middle Ages, cattle and wealth were virtually synonymous. Our words "capital" and "chattel" are both derived from the word for cattle—or rather, from the Latin *caput*, "head," from "head of cattle." In the language of the Aryans who invided India centuries before the Christian era, the word for war literally meant "desire for more cattle." In Europe cattle were used as the standards of exchange as late as the eighth century.

Cattle came to the New World almost as soon as the Europeans themselves, for Christopher Columbus brought a few head to the Americas on his second voyage. As early as 1611, English settlers at Jamestown were raising cattle; by 1624, the colony could claim 20,000 head. By the mid-18th century, America was already beginning to export its cattle.

Ferdinand Was a High Flyer

In 1900, Ferdinand von Zeppelin, the German who gave his name to the rigid-framed airship, launched his first hydrogen-filled craft above Lake Constance. By 1914, the Zeppelin Company was offering the first regularly scheduled air flights between German cities. Despite the dangerously volatile nature of hydrogen, Zeppelin's airships achieved a remarkably safety record on their commercial flights. By 1936, airships were carrying as many as 117 people on transatlantic flights.

Ketchup

The ubiquitous red condiment, catsup, reportedly was based on an Oriental invention, called "kaychup" in Malay, and was enjoyed in England for some 100 years before becoming popular in the United States. Some dictionaries, incidentally, will accept not only "catsup" and "ketchup," but "catchup" as well. The H.J. Heinz Company of Pittsburgh, packers of pickles and horseradish, began marketing their catsup in 1876. The Heinz name soon became virtually synonymous with the condiment.

The Romans Loved Onions

The ancient Greeks and Romans cultivated onions extensively, as do the people of Greece and Italy today. The Romans fed onions to their soldiers, believing the vegetable would make them brave. The Emperor Nero favored the leek, a member of the onion family eaten in the Mediterranean area since Biblical times, because he thought it would improve his singing voice.

In return for grass and grain, each head of cattle rewards the rancher with about 450 pounds of beef suitable for the retail market, along with 150 pounds of by-products and 150 pounds of low-value salvage. By-products include the hide (for leather), hair (felt, brushes), suet (margarine), and inedible fats (soap), along with the bones used for glue and gelatin, and the blood that in a dried form is used as animal feed.

Over the years, there were probably scattered incidents of man mixing hard liquor with a sweet beverage, but the cocktail did not become a popular drink until early in the 19th century. The origin of the word *cocktail* is uncertain. One claim maintains that it comes from a French drink served in New Orleans in the 1800s, called a *coquetier*, named for the tiny egg-cup in which the drink was usually served to women.

First Auto Accident

The first traffic accident in the United States was recorded in 1896, when a Duryea Motor Wagon collided with a bicycle in New York City, sending the cyclist to the hospital and the driver to jail. Three years later, a 68-year-old real estate broker named Henry Bliss became the first American to die as a result of an auto accident, when he was run over while stepping from a New York streetcar. By the early 1920s, traffic fatalities were already topping the 20,000 mark annually—not to mention an estimated 700,000 auto injuries each year.

Among the medieval landed classes, the lack of a need to bathe was considered a sign of wealth and leisure. Many an aristocrat bragged of never having taken a bath.

Modern fruit and vegetable canneries are located as close as possible to the farm. Some foods are canned just three or four hours after picking. Basically, the canning process works like this: the fruits or vegetables are first cleaned with water or blasts of air. Then the food is trimmed, husked, sectioned, sliced, diced, peeled, cored, or pitted, to prepare it for packaging. Some products are then blanched in hot water to drive out gasses and shrink the food to its desired size.

All About Apples

In the United States, we use the word *cider* for both the fermented and the unfermented juice of the apple. But in France, *cidre* always packs a punch of at least 3.2 percent alcohol. More than three-quarters of all French apples are used for cider—France produces over 40 million gallons a year! Most cider comes from Normandy and Brittany, from apples that would make poor eating fruits.

Some 900 million bushels of apples are currently harvested around the world each year, and more than a quarter of them find their way into cider. Worldwide apple production has almost doubled in the last 40 years. The largest apple growers are France and the United States, both of who harvest more than 100 million bushels a year. Apples are grown in quantity in all of Western Europe, and in Japan, Australia, Argentina, and Canada.

In America, apples are grown from coast to coast, but the Pacific Northwest accounts for about 35 percent of the annual apple harvest, and the Northeast about 25 percent. Washington is the number-one apple growing state. New York, Virginia, Michigan, Pennsylvania, Oregon, and California are also large producers. Perhaps some of those Pennsylvania apples are relatives of the trees Johnny Appleseed planted!

The first potato to reach the shores of North America arrived around 1622, imported by Virginia colonists as a food. The first potato cultivation didn't begin in America until 1719, when Irish immigrants planted spud fields in New Hampshire. Thomas Jefferson, by the way, was the first American to serve french fries with beefsteak, a combination now as institutionalized in America as the Declaration of Independence. And it was the German immigrants you can either thank or blame for potato salad.

The musical instrument which the Bible calls the psaltery is actually the ancestor of today's harp.

Spuds to You

The French contributed *pommes soufflées*, or soufflé potatoes, to our gastronomic repertoire. The delicacy was reportedly created by the personal chef of Louis XIV. In this case, necessity was definitely the mother of invention. One afternoon, the king left the palace to inspect his army, then engaged in warfare with the Dutch. On the return voyage to the palace, the Sun King's coach was delayed by a downpour that made the roads impassable. When his master did not appear at the expected hour, the Royal Chef began to panic. The Great Monarch was a most fastidious diner, who insisted that his repasts be served the instant he arrived at the royal dinner table. The cook had prepared a huge batch of the king's beloved *pommes frites*, but as the hours passed and still Louis failed to appear, the fries began to frazzle and turn cold and soggy.

Suddenly, a herald announced the entrance of the king. The agitated chef, in dismay, grabbed the deep-fat fryer and submerged the wilted French fries in sizzling oil, shaking the fryer madly from side to side. Et voila!—a dish fit for a king was born. The potatoes emerged from this second bath in deep hot oil all puffed up—golden brown and heavenly delicious.

To make *pommes soufflées* is a culinary feat. The heat of the oils must be perfect. Consult a good cookbook and try it. You, too, might achieve gastronomic immortality.

Typewriters by IBM

The IBM Corporation broke new ground in 1959 with the development of the Executive Electric, the first typewriter capable of line justification (the printing of lines flush with one another on the right sides as well as the left) and differential spacing. In machines without differntial spacing, letters as narow as an "i" nd as wide as an "m" are alloted the same amount of space on the page. With differential spacing, letters are allotted space in accordance with their width, making possible line justification and a much neater, printlike page.

INDEX

A

Abacus, 345
Abertondo, Antonio, 148
Abortion
  In U.S., 162
Academy Award
  Multiple winners, 27
Accordion, 57
Acupuncture, 221
Adding machine, 109
Advertising
  Taboo words, 239
  New words, 271
Age
  Median, U.S., 83
Aircraft, 363
Airline
  Freelandia, 43
  Hostess, 49
Airplane
  Early records, 410
  Fastest around-the-world trip, 259
  Landing on carrier, 119
  Lindbergh, Charles, 336
  Military use, 299
  Speed, 128
  Trans-Atlantic flights, 336
Airport
  Largest, 13
  Most dangerous, 41
  Jidda, 291
Ackeley, Carl, 38
Alaska
  Average income, 284
  Gonorrhea, 163
  Price, 50
  Size, 162
  Temperature, 50
Albino
  Cats, 369
Alcohol
  American consumption, 160, 287, 297

Ancient use, 359
Content in wine & spirits, 384
Famous alcoholics, 13
Forbidding use of, 45, 411
Freezing temperature, 98
Highest consumers, 376, 405
Lowest consumers, 405
Oldest, 192, 358
Proof, 383
Alexander the Great, 86
Alger, Horatio, 101
Alligator
  Age, 135
  Body processes, 93
  Eating habits, 108, 194
  Eating of, 75
  Endangered, 169
  Hatching eggs, 133
  Hibernation, 179
  Hide, 112
  Malayan, 29
  U.S., 36
  Wallows, 132
  Young, 35
Alphabet
  Alphabetic, 170
  Arabic, 225
  Carolingian, 403
  Cyrillic, 225, 368
  English orthography, 403
  Evolution, 192
  Fewest letters, 411
  Gothic, 403
  Greek, 237, 241
  Hawaiian, 111
  Italic, 403
  Logographic, 170
  Most letters, 411
  Newest letters, 361
  Number of, 411
  Oldest letter, 361
  Phoenician, 335
  Syllabic, 170
  Uncials, 173

Amazon River
  Area drained, 323
  Breadth, 92
  Flow, 403
  Length, 145
  Location, 92
Ambergris, 9
Ambulance, 136
American Museum of Natural History, 38
American Revolution
  Black soldiers, 76
Amoeba, 250
Amphibians, 78
Anableps, 134, 198
Andretti, Mario, 36
Anemone
  Host to clam fish, 111
  Prey to shrimp, 12
Angel Falls, 138
Anne, Queen, 109
Ant, 175
Antelope
  Dik-dik, 146
  Eland, 146
  Pygmy, 28
  Royal, 146
Anthem, national
  American, 110
  Longest, 170
  Shortest, 170
  Wordless, 170
Anthropomorphism, 102
Appendectomy, 179
Appert, Nicolas, 52
Apple
  Bad, 273
  Britain, 240
  Consumption, U.S., 219
  Johnny Appleseed, 206
  Names and phrases, 413
  Of discord, 151
  Origin, 224
  Rome, 240
  Varieties, 219
  Water content, 113
Appliances, 299
Archer fish, 93
Arctic
  Aurora borealis, 168

  Fish, 139
  Ground, 27
  Ice melting, 40
  Insects, 61
  Night and day, 25
  Pink show, 24
  Preserved animals, 109
  Snow, 186
  Sound, 14, 28
  Summer, 25
  Wolverine, 98
Argonaut, 20
Arlington National Cemetery, 70
Army
  Dutch, 100
  Large, 94
  Nations without, 94
Art
  Anachronisms, 28, 49, 120
  Forgery, 49
  Le Bateau, 101
  Sistine Chapel, 21
  Tableaux, 154
Ascension Island, 37
Asia
  Area, 116
  Extremes, 93
Asparagus
  Cooking, 411
  Cultivation, 369
  History, 369
  Varieties, 43
Asphaltum, 36
Aspirin, 136
Asthma, 211
Astronomy
  Earliest Science, 344
Atlantic Ocean
  Sediment, 95
  Solo yacht crossing, 90
Attila the Hun, 86
Auctions
  Alaskan land, 345
  Mummified cats, 407
Audubon, John James, 15
Aurora borealis, 168
Australia, 146
Automobiles
  Aston Martin Lagonda, 53

Bugatti, 411
Dog-powered, 186
Driving speed, 257, 294
Edsel, 359
First American company, 224
General Motors, origin of, 317
Idea, 292
Importance in U.S., 288
In reverse, 414
In Russia, 412
Largest, 411
Mercedes, 46
Most expensive, 46
Most popular U.S., 234
Packard, 60
Pre-engine-powered, 297, 299
Production, 234, 245, 289, 315, 367, 401, 413
Races, 302, 335
Rolls-Royce, 333, 373
Safety, 225, 291, 301
Steam-driven, 294
Theft, 175, 406
Aviation, *see* AIRPLANE
Awards
Academie Francaise, 322
Golden Fleece, 131
MacArthur Foundation, 83
Nobel, 323
Aweto, 119
Azores, 37

B

Baby
Animals, 118
Bach, Richard, 87
Backgammon
Boards, 284
History, 159, 194, 215, 220
Rules, 209
Spread of, 163, 212, 270
Tournaments, 163
Bacteria
To produce vinegar, 342

Bagpipe, 42
Bahadur IV, 296
Balloon
Gas-filled, 297
First flight, 414
Bamboo, 360
Banana
Antiquity, 195
Consumption, U.S., 287
Cultivation, 165, 332
Daiquiri, 253
First recipe, 212
First, U.S., 162, 221
Nutritive value, 270
Oil, 253
Ripening, 212
Sandwich, 253
Shake, 253
Split, 239
Varieties, 283
Baptist, 175
Barnacles, 169
Barry, Dr. James, 11
Barrymore, John, 293
Barthold, Frederick Augustus, 137
Baseball
Brown, Mordechai, 186
Cobb, Ty, 339
Curve, 112
Invented, 27
Longest throw, 15
Ruth, Babe, 189
Basketball
Associations, 158
Awards, 52
Aztecs, 284
Chamberlain, Wilt, 129, 208
College, 47, 164, 195, 208
Courts, 161
Early courts, 161
Fixed, 164
Free-throw record, 319
Harlem Globetrotters, 222
High School, 195
Highlights, 208, 213, 271
Hoop, 339
International, 214
Long shot, 259
Most valuable player award, 52

Origin, 238, 339
Original Celtics, 383
Popularity, 163, 252
Professional, 158
Rules, 252, 339
Women's, 239
Bat, 35
Bath
English town, 379, 412
Mineral, 379
Japanese, 379
Bathtub
First in U.S., 42
Hoax, 187
In America, 387
In Kitchen, 259
Public, 171, 189, 191
Ritual, 141, 189
Roman, 189, 266
Sharing, 117
Singing, 101
Trapped in, 79
Battle of Leyte Gulf, 256
Battleship
Vasa, 40
Bay of Fundy, 54
Beans
British consumption, 27
Rent, 177
Beard
Amish, 20
Lady, 34
Longest, 34
Rate of growth, 12
Beatles
First album, 13
Beau Brummel, 308
Beaver, 53
Bed
Box springs, 283
Camp, 199
Canopy, 186
Cardinal Richelieu's, 118
Chinese, 197
Comfort, 325
Contests, 152
Early American, 269
Egyptian, 197
French Kings', 222

Greek, 206
Howard Hughes', 218
Indian, 197
Japanese, 197
Largest, 186
Louis XIV, 196
Mattresses, 283, 324
Medieval, 266
Metal, 283
Middle Ages, 318
Murphy, 290
Nuptial, 186
Of nails, 283
Pushing, 268
Richard III's, 186
Roman, 193
Seventeenth century, 171
Time spent, 325
Trundle, 199
Victorian, 269
Warming, 283
Water, 153, 324
Beefsteak Club, 414
Beefalo, 257
Beer
Consumption, Greenland, 235
Greatest consumers, 339
Beetle, 151
Begin, Menachem, 372
Beheading, 171
Beidler, George C., 82
Belasco, David, 410
Belfast, 12
Bell
Largest, 120
Belladonna, 172
Belmont Stakes, 70
Beverages
Carbonated, consumption, U.S., 336
Bible
Best-seller, 101
Creation, 90
Debtors, 360
Guttenberg, 144
Name, 336
Number 40, 97
Bicycle
Amsterdam, 22
Army, 214

Around the world, 208, 285
Cross-country, 213, 252
Giant, 251
History, 210, 338
Hobby horse, 210
Paths, 254
Popularity, 338
Racing, 243
Related to auto, 338
Riding backwards, 193
Sales, U.S., 175
Six-day race, 213
Tandem, 217
Tour de France, 213
Unicycling, 252
Unusual, 251
Bidet
  Early, 358
  In hotels, 296
Big Ben, 56
Bill of Rights, 333
Billiards
  In Shakespeare, 287
Binet, Alfred, 106
Biofog, 61
Bird
  Adapted for flight, 257
  Bowerbird, 270
  Caring for young, 285
  Cowbird, 235
  Eating habits, 111, 145, 150
  Egret, 238
  Eskimos, 38
  Hearing, 86
  House wren, 165
  Hummingbird, 40, 108, 239
  Life span, 86
  Man-of-war, 212
  Of paradise, 220
  Oxpecker, 238
  Plover, 88
  Screamer, 145
  Secretary, 283
  Song, 362
  Smallest, 40
  Tailorbird, 24
Birow, Lasalo, 28
Birth
  Multiple, 355

Oldest mother, 81, 302
Rate in Africa, 94
U.S., 61
Birthstones, 332
Bites
  Cat, 108
  Dog, 108
  Human, 108
  Rat, 108
Blood
  Harvey, William, 112
  Loss, 116
  Pressure, 89, 223, 334
  Thickness, 20
  Types, 51, 225
Boat
  Papyrus, 268
Bogardus, A.H., 51
Bogart, Humphrey, 117
Boleyn, Anne, 166
Bond, James, 67
Bones
  Number, 48
Books
  Best novels, 153
  Best sellers, 101, 113, 189, 297, 384
  Binding, 285, 293
  Censored, 141
  Clubs, 297
  Paperbacks, 292
  Published 1978, 81
  Publishing companies, 317
  Selling, 299, 324, 334
Bowling
  Dickinson, Lyman, 167
  Marathon record, 219
  McCutcheon, Floretta, 250
  Perfect game, 21
Boxing
  Double knockout, 192
  Gully, John, 123
  Mitu, Gogea, 221
Brain
  Child's, 405
  Heaviest, animal, 322
Brasilia, 143
Brazil, 379
Breeding
  Elephant, 22

Opossum, 22
Russian mother, 22
Termite, 22
Toad, 22
Brezhnev, Leonid, 206
Bridge
    Combinations of players, 153
    Most common hand, 79
    Rarest hand, 79
Bridges
    Brooklyn, 68, 74
    Longest, 11
    Longest natural, 402
    San Luis Rey, 74
    Y-shaped, 171
Bright, Timothy, 143
British Museum, 147
Bronte sisters, 15
Bronze Age, 272
Brooklyn Bridge
    Construction, 68
    Selling, 376
Brush
    Camel hair, 22
Bryan, William Jennings, 90
Buddha, 98
Buddhist idol, 377
Budding, Edwin, 48
Buenos Aires, 144
Bugle call, 101
Bullfighting ring, 113
Burglary, 7
Burma Shave, 41
Burton, Chris, 130
Business school, 166
Butter, 171
Butterflies, 7
Button, Richard, 315
Byron, Lord, 216

C

Cable messages, 362
Cactus
    Hedgehog, 191

Cajun, 158
Calcutta
    Black hole, 87
    Homeless, 87, 306
California
    Desert, 185
    Rollerskaters, 284
Calories
    Apple pie, 140
    Avocado, 140
    Snacking, 140
Camel
    Bactrian, 195
    Durability, 138, 179
    Urine, 255
    Water drinking, 184
Camera
    Biggest, 294
    Cost, 274
    Daguerreotype, 361
    First permanent photograph,
        361
    Flash bulb, 332
    Instamatic, 258
    Invention, 321
    Kodak, 322
    Miniature, 332
    Name, 292
    Negative, 299
    Portraiture, 322
    Roll film, 336
    Silver nitrate, 360
    Smallest, 294
    Speed, 354
    Thirty-five millimeter, 332
Canada
    Area, 75
    Province capitals, 87
    Waterways, 14
Canal, 303
Cancer
    Breast, in men, 241
Candidate
    Origin, 71
Candy
    Most consumed, 219
Canned food, 344
Canning, 52, 353
Cans, 73

Canyon
  Grand, 57
  Underwater, 57
Capistrano, 60
Car
  See AUTOMOBILE
Card-playing, 377
Cardigan, 172
Carpet
  Ardebil, Persia, 234
Cash register, 107
Castle of St. Suzanne, 11
Catfish, 139
Catgut, 186
Cathedral of Cologne, 177
Catholic
  In U.S., 162
Cats
  Albinos, 369
  Ancient, 258
  Buried alive, 106
  Falling, 299, 363
  First domesticated, 323, 355
  Hater, 41
  Hairiest, 320
  Kilkenny, 363
  Long-haired, 332
  Mummified, 40
  Oldest, 294
  Origin of word, 412
  Popularity, U.S., 303
  Population, U.S., 412
  Powers, 337
  Richest, 320
  Short-haired, 332
  Species, 367
Cattle
  Most popular, 358
  Necessity of, 353
Caviar
  Connotation, 415
  Nutritive value, 368
  Production, 402
Celery, 397
Cellophane, 410, 414
Cellophane tape
  Scotch brand, 406 414
Censorship
  Cocteau films, 267

Constipation, 351
  Film, 317
  Plays, 288
  Song, 243
Census
  Single households, 132
Centipede, 137
Cereal
  Shredded wheat, 72
Cézanne, Paul, 40
Chamberlain, Wilt, 129, 208
Chameleon
  Changing color, 93, 405
  Eyes, 405
  Movement, 38
  Pets, 152
  Toes, 38
  Tongue, 152
Champagne
  Bottles, 72
Chapman, Jonathan, 206
Charlie Chan, 41
Cheese
  Biggest consumer, 368
  Biggest producer, 368
  Blue-veined, 258
  French, 207
  How made, 234
  Liederkranz, 234
  Making, 250, 407
  Origin of name, 275
  Ripeness, 286
  Rome, 235
  Roquefort, 397
  Source, 255
Cheetah, 56, 142
Cherophobiacs, 404
Cherry trees, 65
Chess
  Steinitz, Wilhelm, 121
Chewing
  Food, 7
  Gum, 132, 302, 401
  Gumdrops, 235
  Wrigley's gum, 397
Chicken
  Napoleon's fondness for,
    390
  Number, U.S., 211

Soup, 256
    Words for, 400
Chihuahua, 111
Child abuse, 252
Chimus
    Capital city, 141
    Irrigation, 53
    Tunics, 75
Chinese Americans, 77
Choking
    Heimlich technique, 223
Christmas
    England, 244
    France, 273
    Iceland, 161
    Ireland, 165
Chromosomes, 302
Chuckwalla, 147
Church
    Salisbury, 73
    Trinity, 73
Church, Ellen, 49
Cigarettes
    Early manufacture, 393
    France, 12
    Production, 145
    Teenage smokers, 114
Circus, 393
Cities
    Brasilia, 143
    Buenos Aires, 144
    Houston real estate, 405
    Oldest, 136
    New York, 404
Civil War
    Deaths, 221
    Draft dodging, 119
Clam
    Eaten by starfish, 107
    Giant, 112
Clay, Henry, 6
Cleopatra
    And Marc Antony, 10
    Forebears, 220
Climbing
    Bean stalk, 108
    Hops, 108
    Mountain, 80
    Scaling buildings, 80

Clock
    Babylonia, 290
    Biggest, 299
    Broken, 122
    Charles V, 254
    Church, 282, 290
    Dial, 212
    Egypt, 290
    First pendulum, 77
    Mainspring, 186, 251
    Mechanisms, 286
    Minute hand, 214
    Precision, 306
    Watchmaking, 211
    See also WATCHES
Clown fish, 11
Coat checking, 167
Cobb, Ty, 337
Cobra
    Attack, 119
    Size, 150
Cocktail hour, 413
Cocktails, 363
Coconuts, 153
Codfish, 121
Cody, William "Buffalo Bill", 322
Coelacanth, 78
Coffee
    Consumption, 271, 287
    Instant, 48
    Rarest, 269
Coffin theft, 75
Colds
    Medication, 48
Cologne, eau de, 196
Color
    Blindness, 41
    Perception, 43, 316, 323
Confucius, 194
Conquerors, 86
Conventions, 82
Copper, 272
Corundum, 111
Cotton
    500 A.D., 34
Count of Monte Cristo, 236
Counties
    U.S., 29
Court Cases, 377

Courtship
  East Java, 73
Cow, 343
Crab
  Claws, 108
  Decorator, 99
  Horseshoe, 267
Creation, 90
Creole, 158
Crime
  Highest rate, U.S., 163
  Identifying criminals, 268
  Incidence, U.S., 139
  Murders, U.S., 165
Crocodile
  Malayan, 29
  Plover host, 88
  Pygmies, 75
  U.S., 36
  Weight, 82
  Young, 35, 219
Cromwell, Oliver, 57
Crops
  Indian, 34
Crossword puzzles
  Fanaticism, 269, 273
  First, 49
  First book, 378
  Odd words, 396
Crows
  And owls, 178
  Pranks, 26
Cryogenics
  Del Mar, Annetta, 69
  Fish, 186
Cures
  King Lear's father, 412
Curie, Marie, 323
Cyrus the Great, 86

D

Daddy long legs, 171
Daguerre, Louis, 361
Dancing, 30

Dandies, 308–313
Darrow, Clarence, 90
Davidson, John, 116
Da Vinci, Leonardo
  Mona Lisa, 9
Davis, Bette
  Refused role, 68
Davis, Jefferson, 143
Day
  Naming, 50
  Sidereal, 90
  Solar, 90
Deaths
  Bee stings, 285
  Notables, 1980, 76
Deer
  Shopping mall, 72
Del Mar, Annetta, 69
De Mai, Giuseppe, 20
Demera, Ferdinand Waldo, 129
Democratic Party
  Symbol, 99
Dentist
  Antiquity, 268
  Caries, 402
  Forensic, 152
  Founder, 268
  Orthodonture, 216
Desert
  Cold, 259
  Definition, 259
Diamond
  Artificial, 324
  Compared to corundum, 111
  Hardness, 303
Dice
  Odds, 90
Dickens, Charles
  Great Expectations, 153
Dientzhofer, Georg, 73
Dining
  Portraits, 326
Dingo, 314
Dinoflagellates, 34
Dinosaur
  Extinction, 28
  Trachodon, 217
Disease
  Commonest contagious, 89

429

Commonest non-contagious, 89, 402
Contagious, 128
Hypertension, 334
Infectious, 128
Malaria, 56
Mononucleosis, 307
Orchids, 57
Schistosomiasis, 210
Sexual, 163, 254, 271
Divorce
    Grounds, 96
    Rates, U.S., 71, 167
Dixie, 342
Doctor fish, 113
Doctors
    Portraits, 348
Dog
    Chocolate story, 184
    Domestication, 55
    Fastest, 37
    Friendly, 95
    Heaviest, 222
    Husky, 60
    Largest litter, 189
    Mothering, 7
    Nose and health, 377
    Number of breeds, 109
    Odd couple, 184
    Oldest, 107
    Poodle story, 43
    Racing, 14
    Smallest, 111
    Sniffing drugs, 184
    Soccer cup retriever, 66
    Swallowing marbles, 184
    Tallest, 222
    Unfriendly, 95, 253
    Well story, 185
Domestication
    Dogs and cats, 355
    First, 200
Doubleday, Abner, 27
Dove
    Pigeon, 112
Driving
    Blind, 106
Drone, 142
Drought, 66

Duck
    Flight, 145
Duel, 113
Durian, 213

E

Eagle, 169
Ear, 120
Earth
    Circumference, 393
    Facts, 81
    Motion, 43
    Orbit, 243
Earthquake
    Mount Vesuvius, 134
    Underwater, 86
Echo
    Villa Simonetta, 140
Edison, Thomas A.
    Patents, 42
    Relations, 116
Eel, 117
Eggplant
    Imam Bayeldi, 196
    In America, 411
    Recipes, 368
Eggs
    Color, 67
    Raw or cooked, 110
Eiffel Tower, 235
Eisenhower, General
    Cat hater, 41
Electric
    Chair, 297
    Ray, 208
Elements
    Hydrogen, 144
    Table, 138
Elephant
    Purse devouring, 131
    Smelling, 172
    Swimming, 120
Elevation
    La Paz, 40

Lhasa, 40
Elizabeth, Queen, 166
Emperor Menelek II, 46
Empire State Building
  Height, 76
  Rental, 97
  Stair racing, 76
  Windows, 117
Emu, 187
Equinox, 65
Eratosthenes, 74
Ericcson, Leif, 92
Ermine, 25
Erosion, 95
Eskimo
  Bird catching, 38
  Biting power, 91
  Boats, 97
  Children, 269
  Dogs, 60
  Husband and wife swapping, 338
  Igloos, 61
Ethelred, 25
Ethiopia, 46
Evans, Donald, 81
Evolution, 90
Exodus, 150
Exxon, 66
Eyeglasses
  And physicians, 384
  Astigmatism, 233
  Bifocals, 198
  Concave lenses, 244
  Convex lenses, 244
  Early, 301, 384
  Early remedies, 197, 233
  Hyperopia, 233
  In portraits, 244, 272
  Inventor, 272
  Manufacture, U.S., 217, 255
  Oculist, 227
  Ophthalmologist, 227
  Optician, 227
  Optometrist, 227
  Patron saint, 272
  Pince nez, 160
  Style, 324
  Sunglasses, 324
  Temple, 198, 207

  Tinted, 198
  Wearers, U.S., 217, 255
Eyes, 45

F

Faces, 16–18
Faenza ceramics, 352
Fair
  Highest attendance, 333
  Largest hall, 371
False pregnancy, 363
Fantasy
  Animals, 103, 200, 260
Farms
  Number, 10
  Size, 10
Fashion
  Portraits, 276
  Tight clothing, 285
Fasting
  Bobby Sands, 61
Feet
  Binding, 267
Fencing, 8
Fertility
  Animals, 22
  Human, 22, 323
Figuero Street, 38
Films
  Animated, 300
  Caesar and Cleopatra, 314
  Casablanca, 40
  Gone With the Wind, 41
  Star Wars, 41
  Superman II, 41
  Waves Off Dover, 48
Fingerprinting, 268
Finland
  Size, 21
Fire engine
  First, 100
Fish
  Anableps, 134
  Archer, 93

Blind, 83
Catfish, 139
Chesapeake Bay, 337
Cod, 121
Coelacanth, 78
Doctor, 113
Eel, 117
Eggs, 20
Electric ray, 208
Fastest, 128
Flying, 97
Frogfish, 136
Goby, 61
Goldfish, 120
Hassar, 145
Hearing, 142
Herring, 252
Illnesses, 83
Largest caught, 10
Life spans, 110
Lumpfish, 34
Mackerel, 6
Mirror, 267
Mudskipper, 145
Nests, 20
Paddlefish, 43
Perch, 145
Piranha, 211
Puffin, 109
Smell, 142
Suffocating, 8
Sunfish, 99
Swordfish, 113
Uses, 78
Wahoo, 35
Walking, 97
Fisher, 136
Flag
  Largest, 153
  Ross, Betsy, 123
  Stars and Bars, 142
Flea
  Jumping, 68
Fleming, Alexander, 121
Fletcher, Horace, 7
Flight
  Airline hostess, 49
  Ducks, 145
  Geese, 48, 145

Homing pigeon, 39
Flowers
  Calendula, 232
  Goldenrod, 98
  Lavender, 232
  Magnolia, 232
  Odor, 69
  Rafflesia, 128
  Tulips, 282, 291
Fly
  Fairy, 223
  Number of, 223
Flying, 412
Flying fish, 97
Fog, 28
Fools, 228
Football
  Banned, 236
  Bowl games, 68
  Compared with soccer, 301
  First professional game, 99
  Leather, 50
  Origin, 232, 300
Ford
  Model T, 51
Fortress of Purandhar, 94
Fox, 146
Fox, Terry, 368
France
  Size, compared to Canada, 235
Franklin, Benjamin
  And Population, 337
  Postmaster, 40
Fraternity
  First, U.S., 142
Freelandia Airline, 43
French, Daniel Chester, 21
Frisbee, 406
Frogfish, 136

G

Galaxy
  Model of, 376
Galvanized iron, 27

Garbage, 7
Gardner, John, 67
Garlic
  Antiquity, 404
  Beliefs about, 404
  Description, 404
  Production, 384
  Use in America, 384
Gatling, Richard Jordan, 145
Gecko
  Flying, 22
  Head, 95
  Singing, 135
Geese
  Height, 48
  Speed, 145
Genghis Khan, 86
Geography
  Center of N. America, 117
George I, 40
Gerbils
  Research, 67
Geysers, 101
Giraffe, 184
Glaciers
  In Glacier Park, 178
  Melting, 52
Glass
  Egypt, 35
  Snake, 55
Glider, 100
Globetrotters, 214
Glockenspiel, 60
Gloves
  Oldest, 342
Glowworm Grotto, 222
Gnu, 77
Gobi Desert, 87
Goby, 61
Goedicke, Hans, 150
Goethe, 37
Gold
  Amount, 6, 160
  Attributes, 160
  Foundation, 94
  In sea water, 82, 164
  Use, 227
Golden Temple, 141

Goldenrod, 98
Goldfish, 120
Golf
  Clubs, 400
  Courses, 319
  History, 250, 407
  Hole-in-one, odds of, 294
  Worsham, Lew, 378
Gone With the Wind, 68
Goodwin, Daniel, 80
Gorilla
  First specimen, 282
  Julia of Bronx Zoo, 371
Governor
  First woman, 271
Graham, Sylvester, 78
Grand Coulee Dam, 333
Grant, Ulysses S., 100
Grasshopper
  Glacier Park, 178
  Jump, 143
Gravitational pull, 80
Great Lakes, 377
Great Salt Lake, 321
Green, Hetty, 56
Greenland
  Beer consumption, 235
  Largest island, 122
  Name, 59
Greenwood, John, 12
Greyhound, 57
Grog, 207
Groundhog Day, 150
Guiness Book of World Records, 101
Gully, John, 123
Guns
  Colt .45 Peacemaker, 194

Hail
  Heavy, 190
Haines, Jackson, 238, 361

Halley's comet, 257
Hamburgers
    Growth in popularity, 224, 287
    McDonald's, 321, 377
    Most eaten, 144
    Salisbury steak, 401
Hand
    Famous southpaws, 106
    Greeting, 217
    Preference, 115
    Source of infection, 217
Handball, 336
Handel, George, 178,
Handkerchief
    As love token, 319
    In *Othello*, 319
Hankins, Leonard, 24
Hare
    Arctic, 167
    Differs from rabbit, 20
    Differs from rodents, 179
    Snowshoe, 167
Harrison, William Henry, 144
Harvey, William, 112
Hats
    Berets, 392
    Coolies, 396
    Early, 258, 392
    Middle Ages, 318
    Oldest, 396
Hawaiian Islands
    Underwater mountain, 37
Hayden, Franz Joseph, 41
Headache, 321
Hearing aid
    First, 68
    For dog, 79
Heart
    Action, 89, 184
    Double, 20
    Length, 185
Hebrew, 130
Height
    American boy, 211
    Egyptian, 195
    Tallest living woman, 138
    Teng Hsiao-Ping, 172
    Twelve-year-old boy, 35

    Warriors, 116
Henie, Sonja, 315
Hermit crab, 9
Heroes of Teenagers, 10
Herring, 253
Hiccups, 153
Hippocratic Oath, 348
Hippopotamus
    Skin, 56
    Weight, 144
Hock, 196
Hockey
    First organized game, 233
    Holland, 233
    National Hockey League, 298
    Rules, 233
    Zambini ice machine, 298
Hog
    Snakes, 12
Homosexual
    Famous people, 176
    Syphilis, 271
Horned toad, 52
Horse
    Eating, 144
    Performer, 315
    Toe, 321
    Weight, 82
Horsepower, 383
Horseracing
    Belmont Stakes, 70
    Best win-loss record, 96
    Odds, 48, 191
    Triple Crown, 70
Horseshoe, 43
Hot dogs, 392
Hotels
    First bathrooms, 66
    First bridal suite, 66
    First elevator, 66
    Parisian flophouses, 431
    Treetops, in Kenya, 296
Housing
    Largest apartment block, 405
    Largest private, 368
    Oldest U.S., 193
Hubbard, Elbert, 101
Hue and cry, 11

Hughes, Howard, 218
Hugo, Victor
  Les Miserables, 68
Human Body
  Chromosomes, 362
  Extra fingers and toes, 363
  Eyes, 45
  Midgets, 363
  Selling of, 376
Hummingbird
  Cuban, 40
  Eggs, 108
Hunger, 244
Hunting
  Women, 61
Hydrogen, 144

I

Iceberg
  Color, 138
  Explosion, 57
  Largest, 99
Ice cream
  Banana split, 239
  Cone, 113, 188
  Consumption, 226
  Eskimo pie, 405
  Flavors, 22, 191, 226
  Good Humor, 405
  History, 174, 199
  Largest popsicle, 226
  Largest sundae, 226
  Manufacture, 405
  Misconceptions, 325
  Parlor, 188
  Quality, 226
  Sculpture, 179
  Soda, 199
  Sundae, 188, 199
Iceland
  Radiators, 189
  Temperature, 135, 193
Iguana
  Falling, 134

Green, 59
Land, 28
Marine, 110
I'll Take You Home Again, Kathleen, 291
Illegitimacy
  Famous people, 52
Immigration
  Ethnic groups, U.S., 21, 321, 406
  United Kingdom, 321
Imposter
  Demera, Ferdinand Waldo, 129
Imprecations, 143
Inca
  Bridges, 74
  Conquests, 53
  Courier system, 54
  Doctors, 136
  Marriage, 148
  Quipu, 133
  Roads, 8
  Wearing, 75
Income tax, 37
Indian
  Basketball, 285
  Chimus, 53, 75, 141
  Inca courier system, 54
  Inca roads, 8
  Language, 178
  Literature, 178
  Oklahoma, in, 218
  Tiahuanaco, 42
  U.S. population, 12
Indianapolis 500, 36
Inflation
  In Chile, 45
Insurance, 45
Intelligence
  Animal, 116
  Testing, 106
Irish
  Bobby Sands, 61
Islam
  Black stone, 51
  Kaaba, 51
  Mecca, 51
Island
  Newest, 354
Israel, 362

J

Jackson, Andrew, 11
Jade, 212
Jakubowski, Steve, 70
James, Henry, 91
Jeans, 111
Jefferson, Thomas
  Church, 151
  Declaration of Independence, 109
Jehovah's Witnesses, 101
Jelly Bean, 101
Jellyfish
  Largest, 219
  Stings, 135
Ji, Maharaj, 146
Jigsaw puzzle, 140
Jim Smith Society, 256
Joan of Arc, 150
Job hunting, 26
Jogging
  Burning calories, 251
  Distances, 128
Johnson, Andrew, 143
Johnson, Howard, 188
Johnson, Lyndon, 118
Jonathan Livingston Seagull, 86
Judo, 115
Judson, Witcomb, 317
Juke box, 43
Jujitsu, 115
Jumping Mouse, 339
Jumping viper, 82
Jupiter
  Year, 27
Justice
  Miscarriage of, 24

K

Kangaroo
  Names, 69
  Newborn, 113
Kapok, 130

Karate, 115
Kelp, 122
Kennedy, John F.
  Rate of speech, 142
  Women, 116
Keyboards
  First, 344
Kingston, Jamaica, 82
Kirin, 86
Klipspringer, 28
Koala bear, 245
Krill, 147

L

Lake
  Superior, 122, 406
Lamarr, Hedy
  Casablanca, 40
Langseth, Hans N., 34
Language(s)
  Aramaic, 207
  Celtic, 379
  English, 321, 332
  Euzkara, 270
  French in U.S., 158
  German in U.S., 159
  Hebrew, 130
  Italian in U.S., 158
  Most spoken, 132, 135
  Number of, 108
  Over a million speakers, 176
  Speakers, 108, 336
  Wu, 148
  Yiddish, 130
La Paz, 40
Larrey, Baron Dominic Jean, 136
Lasers, 407
Launderette
  First, 43
Law of the Sea, 377
Lawn mower, 48
Laws, strange
  Buried treasure, 337
  Dandelions, 393

Mistress, 151
Shaving, 175
Shoes, 350
Lawyers
In Washington, D.C., 175
Lennon, John, 93
Leprosy, 211
Lhasa, 40
Library
British Museum, 147
Early public, 414
Of Congress, 177
Life
First, 53
Life Expectancy
Africa, 42
Crow, 9
Elephant, 9
Horse, 9
Human, 15
Lion, 9
Mouse, 15
Ostrich, 9
Scandinavia, 42
Sheep, 9
Life span
Definition, 15
Light
Fluorescent, 100
Laser beam, 323
Neon, 121
Traffic, 334
Lightning
And thunder, 257
Fires, 171
Injuries, 108
Speed, 171
Volts, 171
Limoges China, 353
Lincoln, Abraham
Anecdotes, 362
Height, 109
Lincoln Memorial, 21
Lindbergh, Charles A.
First solo flight, 336
Linen, 12
Linnaeus, Carolus
Marijuana, 69
Linoleum, 210

Liquor
American consumption, 160
Bitters, 359
China, 368
Discovery, 358
Flavoring, 342
Grog, 207
Mixed drinks, 358
National drink, 359
Sake, 368
Liver
Size, 405
Lizard
Anolesp, 178
Basilisk, 93
Chameleon, 38, 93
Differ from snakes, 29
Eggs, 133, 176
Flying, 179
Frilled, 93
Fringe-footed, 22
Gecko, 22
Glass snake, 29, 55
Horned toad, 52
Iguana, 28, 59, 110
Preserved, 243
Skinks, 178
Speed, 179
Tegu, 48
Water, 93
Worm, 29
Llama, 320
Lobefins, 78
Lobster
Claws, 407
Consumption, U.S., 218
Cooking, 304, 407
French, 218
Growth, 401
Largest, 401
Newburgh, 410
Shell, 10
Tails, 218
Loch Ness Monster, 359
Log cabin, 193
Lombard Street, 361
London
Population, 81
Price of land, 404

London, Jack, 80
Longevity
  Africa, 42
  Famous oldsters, 37, 41
  Favorable regions, 146
  Galapagos tortoise, 403
  Oldest man, 175
  Russia vs. U.S., 213
  Scandinavia, 42
Longfellow, Henry Wadsworth, 8
Lope de Vega Carpio, Felix, 14
Lottery, 89
Ludwig II, 217
Luminescence, 147
Lumpfish, 34
Lung, 213
Lustiger, Jean-Marie, 27

M

Macao, 148
Macaroni sculpture, 81
MacCready, Paul, 123
Machine gun, 145
Macy's Department Store, 106
Madeira-Mamore Railway, 68
Madison, Dolley, 11
Madison, James, 149
Magazine
  First, U.S., 144
  Reader's Digest, 256
  TV Guide, 256
Mail
  Delayed, 80
  Most valuable, 336
  U.S. Postal Service, 218
Mailer, Norman
  The Naked and the Dead, 153
Maine, 69
Malaria, 56
Mammoth Cave, Kentucky, 83
Mandrake, 324
Mao Tse-Tung, 101
Marble Dry Goods Palace, 137
Marc Antony, 10

Marijuana
  People who grew it, 69
Marriage
  Age, U.S., 314, 355
  Business, 91
  Coffee break, 332
  Contest, 115
  Lady Diana's wedding dress, 256
  Long life, 109
  Nevada, 167
  Oldest bridegroom, 323
  Rate, U.S., 314
  Twice married U.S. presidents, 13
Match
  Book, 100
  First, 100
Matisse, Henri, 101
Maturation, 23
Mead, 19
Measurement
  Atto-meter, 215
  Nautical mile, 253
Meat
  Beef, popularity of
  Consumption, 225, 342
Medici, Catherine de 132
Medicine
  Doctors portraits, 348
  First school, U.S., 185
  Hippocratic Oath, 348
  Staple suturing, 402
Melville, Herman
  Moby Dick, 153
Mencken, H.L., 187
Mendelssohn, Felix, 77
Mengele, Joef, 25
Mental disorder
  in hatters, 196
Meteor
  Longest, 86
Meteorite, 222
Methodists
  In U.S., 166
Meyerbeer, Giacomo
  Le Prophete, 361
Michelangelo
  Longevity, 37
  Sistine Chapel, 21
Michigan, 360

Mick the Miller, 14
Midgets, 363
Mineral baths, 379
Miss U.S.A. Pageant, 78
Mistakes
  Dog, 43
  Funeral, 80
  Job, 130
Mona Lisa, 9
Monatsschloss Castle, 98
Money
  American Indian paper, 46
  Cattle, 410
  Different kinds, 377
  Hong Kong one-cent note, 259
  Largest mint, 406
  Lincoln penny, 225
  Play, 14
  Recovered, 70
  Spending, 110
  U.S., early, 58
  Youngest millionaire, 337
Money quiz, 379
Mongoose, 271
Monopoly, 14
Mont-Saint-Michel, 7?
Moon
  Distance from earth, 6?
  Visibility, 116
Morgan, William G., 69
Mormon, 162
Morton, George Thomas, 179
Moscow, 412
Mosquito
  Cure for bites, 68
  Varieties, 49
Motel
  First, 100
Mother-of-pearl, 259
Moths
  And butterflies, 7
  Prehistoric, 256
Motorcycles
  Kansas, 161
Mountain
  Highest, 140, 224
Mountain sheep, 69
Mouse
  Common, 386

Movie theater
  Drive-in, 59
  First, 48
  Largest, 48
  Muhrecke, August Gary, 76
Mummies, 150
Murphy, Audie, 122
Murre, 60
Murrow, Edward R., 69
Muscles, 337
Museum
  Largest, 332
Mushroom, 149
Music
  Highest attended concert, 404
  Largest marching band, 337
  Mohammedan religion, 118
  Mozart, 336
  Oldest instruments, 320
  Players, U.S., 139
Musk ox, 97

N

Nails
  Fingers, 100
  Toes, 100
Naismith, James A., 238, 339
Names
  Animal young, 118
  Days, 50
  Graham cracker, 78
  Monks, 50
  Most common, 116, 338, 413
  Nicknames of cities, 286
  Pseudonyms, 39
Narcolepsy, 162
Narrow escape, 22
Narwhal, 42
Nast, Thomas, 99
National Parks
  Largest, 225
Nautilus, 40
Nautilus, chambered, 144

Neill, A.S., 143
Neon, 121
Nest
  Fish, 20
  Tailorbird, 24
  Termite, 48
New Guinea, 122
Newspaper
  Delivery, 350
  First daily, U.S., 145
  Largest single issue, 360
  Pravda, 210
Niepce, Joseph, 361
Nixon, Pat, 81
Nixon, Richard, 179
No theater, 232
Nobel prizes, 323
Noise, 410
North Carolina, 371
North Pole
  Ice melting, 40
  Winter and summer, 25
Norway, 120
Novel
  First, 80
Nuclear power, 59
Numbers
  Combinations, 89
  Forty, 97
  Million, 88
  Trillion, 45
Nursery rhymes, 241

O

Obesity, 270
Oblonsky, Prince Alexis, 163
Ocean
  Depth, 99
  Pacific, 95, 99, 149
  Sediment, 95
  Trenches, 75, 151
Octopus
  Changes color, 23

Jet propulsion, 87
Odds
  Dice, 90
  Horse racing, 48
  Poker, 29
Ohio
  Education, 218
Oil
  U.S. Consumption, 107
Olympics
  Basketball, 214
  Bicycle racing, 243
  Figure skating, 315
  History, 6
  Longest participator, 8
Onion
  Crying, 55
  Production, 345
  Products, 295
  Taste, 392
  Types, 334
  Use, 47
Ono, Yoko, 93
Ophites, 121
Opium
  China, 296
Opossum
  Birth weight, 151
  Playing dead, 314
Oratory, 47
Orchid
  Symbol, 57
  Vanilla, 300
Organ, 146
Osgood, Samuel, 40
Osiier, Ivan, 8
Ostrich
  Eating habits, 282
  Egg, 61
  Head burying, 303
  Stride, 61
Owens, Jesse, 215
Owl
  And crow, 178
  Hearing, 86
Oxford English Dictionary, 43
Oxymoron, 91
Oyster
  Mouse trap, 114

Pearl, 122
On trees, 112

P

Pacific Ocean
Depth, 99
Sediment, 95
Size, 89, 149
Packard, 60
Paddlefish, 23
Page, Sir Francis, 57
Pain, 282
Paintril, 377
Panda
Eating, 172
Weight, 172
Paper
Invented, 29
Wasp, 323
Paper nautilus, 20
Paradise fish, 20
Parents
Oldest father, 302
Oldest mother, 302
Youngest father, 303
Youngest mother, 302
Pasteur, Louis, 167
Patterson brothers, 79
Pauling, Linus, 323
Peanut butter, 235
Pearl
Largest, 355
Oyster, 122
Pedagogues, 84
Pen
Ballpoint, 28
Pencil
Eraser, 359
Lead, 109
Penguin
Protecting egg, 283
Riding on ice, 158
Speed, 323
Penicillin, 121

Penny
Savings, 41
Minting, 79
Pentagon
Telephones, 82
Per capita income, 96
Perch, 145
Periwinkle, 144
Perkey, Henry D., 72
Pharmaceutical products, 355
Phi Beta Kappa, 142
Phobias, 45
Photocopier
First, 82
Photography
See CAMERA
Piano
Concert grand, 343
Endurance record, 352
First, 9
Grand, 293
Player, 353
Steinway, 415
Upright, 292
Picasso, Pablo
Longevity, 37
Productivity, 333
Pig
Intelligence, 116
Sleeping, 83
Pigeon
Dove, 112
Speed, 94
Vision, 94
Pin
Ancient, 307
Manufacture, 251
Money, 255
Patent, 209
Pinball machine
First, 318
Legislation against, 386
Lingo, 393
Manufacture, 47
Planets
Earth, 81
Jupiter, 27
Largest, 267
Order, 90

Reaching Mars, 324
  Smallest, 267
  Venus, 75. 113
Plankton, 74
Plath, Sylvia, 80
Plover, 88
Plow, 69
Poison, 362
  Antidote, 15
Poker
  Odds, 29, 139
Poland
  World War II casualties, 219
Polar bear, 98
Polecat, 303
Police, 62, 63
Polo
  Field, 337
Polyandry, 55
Polygamy, 55
Pompeii, 134
Pope Bonitace VIII, 38
Pope John XII, 38
Population
  Chinese, 362
  Dead vs. living, 320
  Density, 148, 337
  Elderly, U.S., 284
  Figures, 117
  First census, 15
  Jewish, U.S., 284
  Rate of growth, 13, 337
  U.S. cities, 219
Porcupine, 224
  Quills, 224
Porpoise, 112
Postal systems
  Balloons, 58
  Early, 407
  In Greece, 342
  Pigeons, 58
Postmaster General, 40
Potato(es)
  American consumption, 294
  Chips, 142, 369
  Cultivation, 407
  English consumption, 369
  French acceptance, 344
  Indian, 34

  In Germany, 343
  Scots, 55
Prairie, 337
Prajadhipok, King, 298
Prayer
  Cromwell, 57
Prejudice, 67
Presidents, U.S.
  Harrison, William Henry, 144
  Madison, James, 333
  Taft, William Howard, 336
Prince Charles, 46, 412
Prison
  Fetus inmate, 110
  Kharkov, 82
  Russian, 37
  Sing Sing, 81
  Tree trunk, 82
Procaccino, Mario, 15
Prohibition, 45
Prostitution, 377
Protein
  Requirement, 70
Protocol
  Birthday, 168
  French, 77
Proust, Marcel, 53
Proxmire, William, 131
Proxy marriage, 50
Prune, 145
Public bath, 42
Public exhibits
  Wedding gifts, 412
Puffin fish, 109
Pulse, 89
Pure Food and Drugs, 108
Pyramids
  Architecture, 354
  Size, 222
Python, 159

R

Rabbit
  Differs from hare, 20
  Differs from rodents, 179

Racehorse
  Broker's Tip, 406
  Raft, George, 117
Railroad
  Barn story, 185
  Sleeper, 268
Rain
  Amount of water, 101
  Australia, 146
  Fish, 195
  Frogs, 152
  Wettest cities, U.S. 191
Raleigh, Sir Walter, 172
Rape, 210
Ratatouille, 352
Reading, 216
Recording
  Highest sales, 71
Red tide, 74
Redheads, 37
Refrigeration
  Ancient methods, 258
  As a cause of change, 58
  Modern methods, 406
Religion
  American church members, 32[
  Baptist, 175
  Catholic, 162
  Methodist, 166
  Mormon, 162
Reno, 49
Republican Party
  Symbol, 99
Restaurants
  Coat checking, 167
  First, 326
  Michelin ratings, 245
  New York, 160
Revolving door, 26
Ribs, 177
Richelieu, Cardinal, 118
River
  Longest, 117
  Water power, 333
Roads, 8
Robbery
  Ring, 131
Rockefeller, John D, 337
Rodeo, 214

Rope-skipping, 397
Rose
  Empress Josephine, 227
  Fragrance, 227
  In poetry, 244
  Myths, 161, 173
  Symbol, 161, 245, 273, 307
  Thorns, 173
  Universality, 161
  Uses, 173, 227, 273, 307
  Varieties, 244
  War of Roses, 273
Ross, Betsy, 123
Roxy Theater, 48
Rubik's cube, 168
Rugby, 232
Rulers
  Accuracy, 209, 250
  End standard, 209
  Line standard, 209
  Types of, 250
Rum
  Source, 352
Running
  Jesse Owens, 215
  Speed, 56, 142
  With handicap, 35
Ruth, Babe, 189
Rx, 119

S

Safety pins, 251
Saffron, 78
Sahara Desert, 50
Salisbury Cathedral, 73
Salmon
  Downstream swimming, 117
  Leaping, 176
Salp, 12
Salt
  Antiquity, 289
  As currency, 243
  Brine, 316
  Cathedral, 13, 239

Cost, 350
Customs, 240
Expressions, 240
In seas, 255
Manufacture, 316
Producers, 306
Uses, 306
Value, 289
Saluki, 37
Salvation Army, 118
Sands, Bobby, 61
Sandwich
  Biggest, 99
Sanitation
  See SEWERS
Sardine, 27
Sargasso Sea, 177
Scarecrows
  African, 77
School
  Enrollment, 284
Scissors
  And shears, 190
  Antiquity, 288
  Construction, 240, 251
  Grammar, 306
  Manufacture, 267, 316, 343
  Myths, 303
  Name, 246
  Pinking, 316
  Pivot pins, 351
  Shapes, 411
  Types, 411
  Uses, 351
Scopes, John T., 90
Screamer, 145
Sea hare, 113
Seahorse, 20
Seal
  Abstinence, 193
  Migration, 24
Sears Tower
  Height, 76
  Scaled, 80
Seasons
  Explanation, 65
Segovia, Andrés, 172
Sermon
  Longest, 235

Sesquipedalianism, 107
Seven Wonders of the World, 87
Sewers
  Ancient, 242
  Chicago, 306
  Da Vinci, Leonardo, 304
  Drainage, 316
  London, 242
  Ministery, 268
  Paris, 223, 239
  Quantity, U.S., 316
  Roman, 242, 296, 350
Sex
  Hormones, 207
  Peak age, 238
Shackleton, Ernest, 217
Shakespeare
  Longest roles, 111
Shaving, 333
Shaw, George Bernard, 37, 403
Sheep, 6
Sherry, Louis, 188
Shields, James, 321
Ship
  Largest, 111
  Longest, 123
Shivering, 216
Shoes
  Comfort, 305
  Cordovan, 315
  Customs, 306
  Fashion, 242, 274, 296, 315, 350
  First, U.S., 351
  High-heeled, 302, 350
  Largest, 293
  Loafers, 236
  Men, 292
  Moccasins, 351
  Pointed, 302
  Sizes, 237, 301, 305
Shorthand, 143
Shredded Wheat, 72
Shrimp, 12
Siamese twins
  Chang and Eng, 71
  Operation separating, 67
Silver
  Characteristics, 360
  Plate, 345

Sterling, 352
Sing Sing, 81
Singer, Isaac Bashevis, 130
Sistine Chapel, 21
Sit-ups, 271
Skating
  Endurance record, 234
  Figure, 238
  Hockey, 233
  Ice shows, 286
  Metal, 295
  Netherlands, 366
  Origin, 288, 295
  Rinks, 372
  Roller, 234, 259, 284, 292, 300, 316, 350,
    361
  Roller derby, 234
  Skateboards, 400
  Speed, 275, 293, 316
Skiing
  With handicaps, 197
Skin
  Human, 39
Skink, 178
Skywriting, 109
Smokey Bear, 88
Smoking
  Portraits, 180
  Teenagers, 114
Snail
  Mating, 185
  Speed, 56
Snake
  Antisocial, 26
  Cobra, 119, 150
  Courtship, 64
  Differ from lizards, 29, 164
  Eyes, 164
  Female, 233
  Glass, 55
  Hog, 12
  Jumping viper, 82
  No ears, 288
  Python, 159
  Rattlesnake, 120
  Teeth, 9
  Travel, 384
  Two-headed, 184
Snake Pagoda, 73

Snow
  Area without, 128
  City with most, U.S., 160
  Largest snowflake, 45
  N.Y. vs. Arctic, 186
  Sahara, 191
  Virginia, 59
  Water content, 129
Soccer
  Compared with football, 301, 314
  Origin, 232
Social scene, 124
Socrates, 113
Sothebys, 23
Sound
  Arctic and Antarctic, 14, 28
Soy bean, 196
Spa
  Bath, 379
  Famous, 191
  Name, 191
Spacecraft
  Soyuz T4, 115
Speed
  Animals, 56, 142
  Fish, 35
  Human, 142
Sphinx, 96
Spices
  Cheapest, 254
  Cinnamon, 275, 293, 333
  Middle Ages, 321, 322, 333
  Most expensive, 354
  Pepper, 360
  Promoted exploration, 333
  Routes, 322
  Saffron, 78, 354
  Uses, 295, 298, 366
  Value, 298
Spider silk, 384
Spider web, 222
Spock, Benjamin, 101
Sponge, 139
Spoonerism, 111
Squid
  Food for whale, 23
  Luminescence, 147
  Sepia sac, 21
Stainless steel, 109

445

Stairway
  Longest, 359
Stamps
  Foreign, featuring Americans, 404
  Imaginary, 81
  Portrait, 185
Star
  Nearest, 324
Star Spangled Banner, 110
Starfish
  Clam eaters, 107
  Luidia, 140
  Oyster eaters, 96
State
  Biggest, 118
  Commonwealths, 150
  Four-state boundary, 87
  New York workers, 214
  Smallest, 118
  Tri-States Rock, 192
  University of New York, 223
  Where actors live, 163
  Wyoming, 297
  Also see individual states
Stationery, 122
Statue of Liberty
  History, 137
  Size, 72, 137
Stealing
  Fieldstones, 89
St. Evdokia's Day, 150
St. Helena, 37
St. Lawrence Seaway, 235
St. Peter's, 121
Steinitz, Wilhelm, 121
Stock Exchange, 227
Stomach, 120
Stork, 56
Stowe, Harriet Beecher, 113
Streetcar
  Cable cars, 360
  Connecting U.S. cities, 320, 354
  Earliest electric, 367
  Longest route, 305
  New York City, 298
  Rise and decline, 274
  Types, 294
Streets
  Longest, 38

Most popular names, 25
Numbered, 24
One-way, 410
Studebaker, 78
Stylites, Simeon, 26
Submarine
  Atomic, 40
Sugar, 175
Suicide
  Famous people, 80
  Highest rate, 115
  Lowest rate, 115
  Mass, 45
  Of Hindu wives, 45
Summerhill, 143
Sun
  Facts about, 65
  Power for plane, 123
  Tan, 251
Sunfish, 99
Swimming
  English channel, 148
  Portraits, 248
  Spitz, Mark, 335
Swordfish, 113
Syphilis, 221

T

Tableaux, 154
Taft, William Howard, 113
Tailorbird, 24
Talbot, William Fox, 299
Tale of Genji, 80
Talking
  Arctic, 28
  Speed, 142, 355
  Woman, 6
Tamerlane, 86
Tape
  Cellophane, 402
  Scotch Brand, 372, 402
Tarpon fish, 396
Taxicab
  First, 142

Taxidermy
  Carl Akeley, 38
  Fees, 61
  Northeastern School, 15
Teachers, 84
Texas, 199
Teenagers
  Easy boss vs. higher pay, 131
  Leisure activity, 61
Teeth
  Fairy, 6
  George Washington, 241
  Snake, 9
  Also see DENTIST
Tegu, 48
Telephone
  A.T.&T. employees, 187
  City with most, 128
  First pay, 379
  First transcontinental U.S., 322
  Pentagon, 82
  Police emergency, 131
Television
  Brenner, Dave, 116
  Murrow, Edward, 69
  Viewing, 379
Temperature
  Biofog, 61
  Celsius, 88
  Coldest cities, U.S., 244
  Coldest spot, 320
  Earth, 59
  Fahrenheit, 88
  Highest survived, 338
  Hottest cities, U.S., 174
  Hottest spot, 135
  Lowest, 159
  Wind-chill, 65
  See also WEATHER
Tennis
  Lenglen, Suzanne, 253
  Love, 259
  McEnroe, John, 362
  Perry, Frederick, 303
  Players, U.S., 162
Termites, 48
Texas
  Counties, 109
Thales, 69

Theater
  Amateur, 305
  First drive-in, 59
  Hindu, 314
  It Can't Happen Here, 300
  Nicholas Nickleby, 362
  No, 232
  Realism, 236
  Suppression, 303
  Ten Nights in a Barroom, 237
  Ticket prices, 302
  Uncle Tom's Cabin, 232
Thomas, Norman, 323
Thrones, 46
Thyroid, 112
Tiahuanaco Indians, 42
Tides
  Analyzing, 115
  Bay of Fundy, 54
Tilefish, 72
Timbuktu, 135
Time
  Daylight saving, 12
  Mean solar day, 36, 90
TNT, 188
Toasts, 366
Tobacco
  As legal tender, 386
  From New World, 396
  Marlboro brand, 378
  Nicotine, 390
  World wide consumption, 345
Toilets
  Bidet, 358
  Crapper, Thomas, 352, 387
  Early, 295, 302, 315
  Louis XIV's, 392
  Names for, 383
  Old English, 295
  Paper, 334
  Public, 342
  W.C., 396
Tolstoy, Leo
  Life, 163
Tomato
  Arrival in Europe, 58
  Considered poisonous, 343
  Largest, 192
  Names, 413

Native to South America, 415
Tongue Twisters, 235
Toothbrush
    First, 110
Torrijos Herrera, General Omar, 257
Totem pole, 332
Toucan, 284
Tower
    Assyrian, 253
    Roman, 253
Track
    Jesse Owens, 315
    Mile run, 35
Traffic lights, 58
Transportation
    Bicycle, 285
    Speed of, 412
    Taxi, 115
    Train, 151
    Underground, 354
    See also AUTOMOBILE, RAILROAD,
        STREETCAR
Trapshooting, 51
Travel
    American, 174
    Speed of, 412
Tree
    Carbon storage, 64
    Loneliest, 343
    Sausage, 355
    Spruce, 302
    Tallest, 317
Trichinosis, 150
Triplets, 10
Trolley, See STREETCAR
Ts'ai Lun, 29
Tuatara, 269
Tulip tree, 392
Tunnel, 392
Tutankhamen, 239
Twirling, 166
Tyler, John
    Children, 69
    Wives, 106
Typewriter
    Chinese, 17, 363
    Early, 302, 387
    Edison's, 292
    Feats, 295

First, 142
Musical notation, 343
Operation of, 282

U

Ulcer
    Prevalence in men, 185
Umbrella
    Brilliology, 359
    English invention, 392
    Folding, 342
    Production, 294
Umiak, 97
Uncle Tom's Cabin, 232
Underwater mountains, 37
United States
    Average male, 254
    Elevation, 404
    Highest inhabited point, 98
    Highest uninhabited point, 98
    Lowest inhabited point, 98
    Lowest uninhabited point, 98
    Most popular products, 299
Uranium, 14
Usher, Bobby, 36

V

Vacuum cleaner, 118
Van Meegern, Hans, 49
Vanilla
    And chocolate, 191, 369, 371
    And cocoa, 369
    Discovery, 369
    How grown, 187, 300, 371
    In France, 369
    In Mexico and Spain, 369
    Orchid plant, 57, 300
    Where grown, 187, 300, 371
Vasa, 40

Vatican City, 345
Vegetation
  Origins, 402
Vehicles
  Ancient, 358
Venezuela, 138
Venus
  Distance from Earth, 113
  Rotation, 75
Verdi, Giuseppe, 27
Vice President, 303
  Filling unexpired term, 383
Victoria, Queen
  Bed, 29
Vikings, 92
Vinegar
  For preservation, 358
  Source, 353
Violin, 24
Virgin Islands, 377
Vision
  Color discrimination, 323
  One eye, 108
Vocabulary
  English, 321
  Ine words, 22
Voice
  Loudest animal, 354
Volcano
  Active, 69, 235
  Ash, 82
  Eruptions, 235
  Largest crater, 405
  Mauna Kea, 150
  Mount St. Helens, 119
Volleyball, 69
Voltaire
  Coffee drinking, 95
  Longevity, 37
Von Kannel, Theophilus, 86

Walking
  Across America, 293
  Dan O'Leary, 186
  Men vs. Women, 185
Warren, Robert Penn, 83
Warts, 211
Washington, D.C.
  Cherry trees, 65
Washington, George
  Monument, 235
  Teeth, 12, 241
Wasp, 323
Watch
  English, 211, 216
  First American, 234
  First electric, 233
  Most expensive, 372
  Novelty, 351
  Pocket, 256
  Production, 351
  Quartz crystal, 254
  Swiss, 211, 216, 288, 351
  Varieties, 351
  Wristwatch, 288, 302, 351
  See also CLOCKS
Water
  Birds, 122
  Body weight, 83
  Fresh, 14
  Fresh, source, 372
  Ocean waves, 66
  One inch of rain, 101
  Purest, Lake, 257
  Purity, 66
  Red tide, 34
  Salt, 289
  Sea, 14
  Snow and rain, 129
  Strider, 208
Water supply, 376
Watermelon, 101
Watteau, Antoine, 39
Waves
  Height, 334
  Internal, 134
  Predicting, 66
  Underwater earthquakes, 86
Weather
  Drought, 66

W

Wahoo, 128
Walker, Madame, 79

Seasons, 65
Temperature, 376
Wind-chill, 65
Wind speed, 332
See also TEMPERATURE
Weaver bird, 168
Weight, body
Gain, 209
Gravity, 80
Obesity, 270
Water, 83
Weiner, Norbert, 216
Wesley, John, 397
Westminster Abbey
Longfellow, H.W. 8
Whale
Ambergris, 9
Blubber, 94
Blue, 9, 23, 114, 120, 147
Eskimo use, 67
Humpback, 325
Killer, 57
Legs, 60
Mammal, 114
Norwhal, 42
Playful, 94
Sonar, 100
Sperm, 23, 72, 322
Spouting, 114
Wharton, Edith, 91
Wharton, Joseph, 166
White Christmas, 71
White Cliffs of Dover, 95
White House
First occupations, 383
Rooms, 79
Williams, Kit, 54
Willig, George, 80
Wind-chill factor, 65
Wine
Healthful, 217
In Greece, 415
Largest cellars, 407
Winte, 115
Wiss, Jacob, 316
Witchcraft
Leek, Dame Sybil, 194
Wolfram, Stephen, 83
Wolverine, 98

Women
First Cabinet member, 355
First member of Congress, 320
Voting, 299
Wood
Fuel, 137
Tulip tree, 392
Wool, 384, 392, 406
Word oddities, 392
Word origins
Advertising, 250
Amen, 109
Apple, 413
Apple of discord, 151
Apple of the eye, 224
Apple-pie order, 334
Arrowroot, 334
Baker's dozen, 355
Berserk, 207
Between Scylla and Charybdis, 169
Bible, 336
Bistro, 212
Blackmail, 305
Bonanza, 194
Bonfire, 192
Boycott, 241
Burglar, 206
By hook or by crook, 241
Calendula, 232
Candidate, 71
Cat, 303, 412
Clock, 282
Cobweb, 237
Coconut, 233
Cravat, 266
Curfew, 172
Decoy, 369
Dollar, 305
Dragonfly, 315
Dude ranch, 322
Eavesdropper, 172
Fathom, 216
Feather in one's cap, 387
Fine kettle of fish, 195
Foolscap, 215
Fortnight, 116
Garlic, 384
Gathering nuts in May, 232
Haversack, 198

Hobson's choice, 358
Honeymoon, 186
Hue and cry 1
Humble pie 224
Ice cream, 188
Kindergarten, 241
Knot, 216
Knuckle down, 210
Lavender, 233
Limey, 354
Long, 107
Loafers, 236
Magnolia, 232
Milliner, 317
Mother Goose, 241
Pass the ammunition, 403
Pass the buck, 250
Penknife, 320
Pin money, 255
Pinafore, 173
Porpoise, 236
Related to animals, 22
Rosary, 173
Rough rider, 322
Salt, 240
Sub rosa, 245
Tabby, 236
Tattoo, 415
Tennis' love, 251
Terrier, 217
Thyme, 254
Tomato, 58, 413
Umpire, 211
Wild West, 322
World Trade Center
  Height, 76
  Scaled, 80
Worm
  Racing, 64

Wren 16t
Wu 148
Wynne, Artnur 49

X

X-rays, 290

Y

Yak, 209
Yellowstone National Park, 101
Yiddish, 130
Young, Noah, 35
Yourcenar, Marguerite, 322

Z

Zebra, 354
Zipper
  Evolution, 317
  Fly, 107
Zoo
  First in U.S., 34
Zulu War, 387